THE
CUISINES
OF
ASIA

❦ THE CUISINES ❦

China : India

Indonesia : Japan

Korea : Malaysia

The Philippines

Thailand : Vietnam

❦ THE TECHNIQUES ❦

Steaming : Stir-Frying

Deep-Frying : Currying

Simmering : Barbecuing

and More

THE CUISINES OF ASIA

❧❧❧

JENNIFER BRENNAN

Macdonald

Excerpts from the introduction to the chapter on Curries appeared in different form in the Los Angeles *Herald Examiner*, "Learning to Favor Curries," August 5, 1981.

Excerpts from the introduction to the chapter on Steaming appeared in different form in the Los Angeles *Herald Examiner*, "Steam Cooking: There's More to It Than Hot Air," October 3, 1979.

Excerpts from the segment on China appeared in slightly different form in the Los Angeles *Herald Examiner*, "Chinese Regional Cuisines and How to Recognize Them," May 14, 1980.

Excerpts from the introduction to the chapter on Charbecuing appeared in different form in the Los Angeles *Herald Examiner*, "Roasts with the Most," July 22, 1982.

Excerpts from the introduction to the chapter on Breads appeared in slightly different form in the Los Angeles *Herald Examiner*, "Breads of India" (approximate title; no date).

Excerpts from the segment on India appeared in different form in the Los Angeles *Herald Examiner*, "Tandoori Cooking" (approximate title; no date).

Excerpts from the chapter on Kitchen Equipment (mortars and pestles) appeared in *Cuisine* magazine, "Mortar and Pestle," September 1982.

Excerpts from the segment on Thailand appeared in different form in *Diversion* magazine, "The Thais Have It." July 1981.

Translation on page 165, the story on Chinese soup, is from *Food in Chinese Culture*, edited by K. C. Chang, Yale University Press, 1977.

A Macdonald BOOK

© Jennifer Brennan 1984

First published in Great Britain in 1984
by Macdonald & Co (Publishers) Ltd
London & Sydney

A member of BPCC plc

First published in the United States in 1984 by St. Martin's Press

Brennan, Jennifer
   The cuisines of Asia.
   1. Cookery, Oriental
   I. Title
   641.595   TX724.5.A1

ISBN 0-356-10350-1

Filmset by Haddon Craftsmen. Printed and bound in the United States by R. R. Donnelly

Macdonald & Co (Publishers) Ltd
Maxwell House
74 Worship Street
London EC2A 2EN

TO MY SON, ADAM,
who loves to experience life and
suffered most of our culinary
experiments with patience, equanimity
and, occasionally, genuine affection.

CONTENTS

❧ ❧ ❧

PREFACE

❧ ❧ ❧

THIS BOOK began as an attempt to share my memories of and delights in the wonderful food of Asia: to introduce people to a whole new style of cooking and eating.

Any effort to share an adventure with another who has not actually experienced it can be a challenge and, sometimes, rather frustrating. How do you depict the alluring and exotic sights, smells and flavors that assail you at every turn in the marketplaces and food shops of a strange continent? How do you spin a one-dimensional web of words and instructions that will transport someone else into a three-dimensional world of culinary fascination and continual, mouth-watering enchantments and surprises?

It soon became evident that merely to describe was not enough. If description were sufficient, then any practiced cook could lift the printed words off a cookbook page and transform them into a gastronomic symphony without a dress rehearsal.

In order to re-create an experience for another person or, more properly, to instruct others to create it afresh for themselves, that experience must be translated into terms of reference that are familiar and common coinage. The reliving of my Asian gastronomic adventures in terms of foods and cooking must be transmitted to you in your frame of reference and your kitchen.

For you to cook and eat and enjoy the great cuisines of the Orient as I have been lucky enough to do, you must first picture the magic and seduction of the food, understand something of the backgrounds and cultures of the peoples, and then read about and master the techniques and sensible rules and philosophies that govern Asian cooking and lead to a perfect reconstruction of the dishes.

EXPLANATORY NOTE

The measurements that appear in italics within parentheses and follow the standard American measurements are British Imperial measurements. British terms such as *courgette* for the American zucchini are also set in italics within parentheses.

THE
CUISINES
OF
ASIA

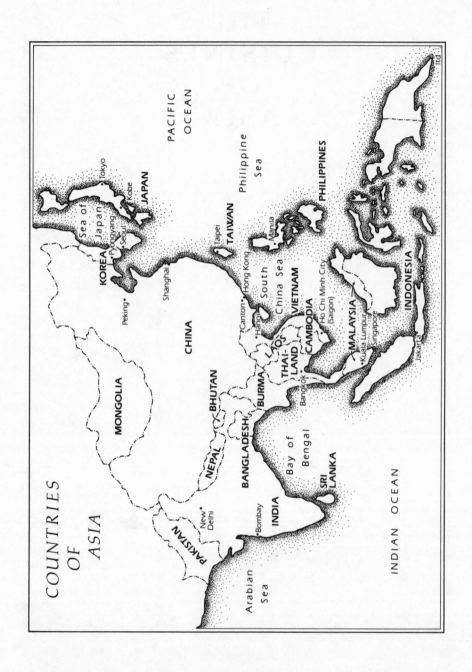

COUNTRIES
OF
ASIA

PACIFIC
OCEAN

Sea of Japan

Tokyo
Kobe
JAPAN
Pyongyang
Seoul
KOREA
Peking

Shanghai

CHINA

MONGOLIA

Taipei
TAIWAN

Philippine
Sea

PHILIPPINES

Manila

Hong Kong
Canton

South
China Sea

Hanoi

BHUTAN

NEPAL

BANGLADESH

BURMA

LAOS

THAI-
LAND

VIETNAM

Bangkok

CAMBODIA

Ho Chi Minh City
(Saigon)

MALAYSIA

Kuala Lumpur
Singapore

INDONESIA

Jakarta

PAKISTAN

New
Delhi

Bombay

INDIA

SRI
LANKA

Bay of
Bengal

Arabian
Sea

INDIAN OCEAN

ltd

INTRODUCTION

⊗ ⊗ ⊗

THE EAST COMES TO THE WEST

Over the last one hundred years, human waves of Orientals have washed against the shores of the Occident, spreading out and settling in like the lacy foam of breakers on the beach. As the tides of world events advanced and receded, so successive floods of immigrants from one Asian nation after another have sought their fortunes in our land.

It has not been a one-way arrangement. We, in turn, have been enriched immensely by the influx of new cultures, bolstered by the legendary Oriental capacity for hard work, and stimulated by the novelty of their cuisines.

As years passed, Chinese, Indian and Japanese restaurants opened in our towns and cities: initially, to provide the food from home for the immigrants, but later, to introduce us to the delights of Asian food. The Koreans followed and, just over a decade later, the Southeast Asians: the Vietnamese, the Thais, the Indonesians, Cambodians, Laotions, Filipinos and Malays, bringing with them additional intriguing cuisines to widen our food horizons.

Chow mein, chop suey and curry have been familiar names to the West since the previous century. Tempura, teriyaki and Mongolian barbecue soon became almost as commonplace. Today the enterprising diner can choose from Tandoori Chicken, Mee Krob Crisp-Fried Noodles, Vietnamese Spring Rolls and all manner of satays and other Asian gastronomical delights.

In our larger cities, Asian grocery stores *(shops)* have opened wherever there is a supportive immigrant population, and strange herbs and exotic spices and sauces have begun to appear in the Oriental sections of the larger super-markets, alongside the rice, noodles and soy sauces.

Asian implements and utensils such as the wok, cleaver and steamer are now fairly commonplace in the rapidly expanding cookware areas of depart-ment stores. Food writers and nutritionists extol the virtues of Asian food for its lightness, economy and healthful qualities—in fact, as a new way of eating to Westerners accustomed to punishing their bodies with vast quantities of cholesterol-laden dairy products and red meat, sugar-burdened, rich cakes and heavy desserts, and, of course, all manner of strange-sounding food additives lurking in convenience foods and packaged preparations.

So, if we are already enjoying Asian food in restaurants, why aren't we cooking it at home?

Because there is a gap stemming from intimidation. The dishes appear complex and difficult to prepare. The spicing and ingredients look unfamiliar, and most people assume that Asian food needs four or five Asian cooks—that preparing it at home is far beyond their expertise and time frame. (Immedi-ately, I can chase away the illusion that Orientals are the only experts in the preparation of their food. In one of my favorite expatriate Thai restaurants, the owner employs only Mexican cooks, whom he has trained personally. The food is some of the finest and most authentic to be found outside Thailand.) Shortly we'll take a look at the belief that an Oriental meal demands a battalion of cooks. As to intimidation, this book is going to help you dispel that gap.

COOKING THE BEST CHOW MEIN IN TOWN
Asian food is extremely simple to prepare. The secret lies in understand-ing the cooking techniques. There are few, and they are easy to learn. Once the techniques are mastered, you can swing happily from one Asian cuisine to another with the ease of an expert merely by substituting ingredients.

Most dishes require very little time and effort expended in the actual cooking. The preparation, which traditionally has been time-consuming, can now be handed over to our genies of the kitchen: blenders, food processors, spice grinders and the rest of the legion of magical electric appliances that take the sting out of kitchen drudgery and reduce hours of work to minutes of pleasure.

But what about all those unfamiliar ingredients? You don't want to plan an Oriental dinner and then have to search all over the city for spices and foods that are unobtainable in your neighborhood. That obstacle has also deterred many people from plunging into the delights of Asian cooking.

We are going to take a look at easy and imaginative substitutes for the rare and exotic. A visit to your supermarket should yield almost all the ingredients you will need to cook a wide and wonderful range of exciting Oriental meals.

THE "NUTS AND BOLTS" OF ASIAN COOKING

A very important section of this book is devoted to basic techniques and formulas. The techniques of basic preparation will show you such things as: the Asian methods of cooking perfect rice; how to cut, chop and slice like an Oriental chef; quick ways of preparing clarified butter for Indian recipes and coconut-milk substitutes for Southeast Asian dishes; easy-to-follow instructions for garnishes that will look as if you had spent months at an *haute cuisine* cooking school; and the inside information on many impressive Asian culinary tricks and shortcuts, as well as the reasons why they are used. The techniques, under which the recipes are grouped, are at the beginning of each relevant chapter.

The formulas, or basic recipes, are the foundations of Asian cooking. You will find easy spice pastes to make ahead, which will create superb curries and stir-fried dishes; new blends of the commonplace powdered herbs and spices, producing fresh taste sensations for barbecued and grilled meats, fish and rice dishes; sauces and marinades which will lift the ordinary into the exotic, and all manner of instructions for making your own substitutes for commercially made, imported ingredients that are unavailable in most supermarkets.

RECIPES FOR SUCCESS

In the part of the book devoted to the recipes, these are gathered under specific cooking techniques rather than under meal course, main ingredient or country. The foreword to each chapter gives a detailed description of the featured cooking technique, the reasons why it is used and how it works. After the explanation of each technique, all the recipes from the various Asian countries in the grouping will illustrate that cooking procedure. For instance, after learning the basic how-to's of barbecuing and grilling, you can move on to Chinese Barbecued Ribs, and after preparing that succulent dish, you will then be able to cook Malaysian or Thai Barbecued Spareribs, or Indian Oven-Barbecued Chicken, merely by repeating the basic technique with a few local variations and using different combinations of ingredients to give each local dish its character and personality.

The recipes indicate preparation and cooking times so that you can plan your day accordingly, and they suggest substitute ingredients so that you can pick the freshest and finest seasonal food in your market. They also warn you of any tricky points to watch for, and, for the busy cook, let you know how much you can do ahead, what you can freeze and what shortcuts you can use.

SIMPLICITY AND NECESSITY

When you find out how utilitarian an Asian kitchen is, you will realize that you need very little in the way of special equipment to become adept at Asian cuisines. As you decide to enlarge your existing collection with a few additional pieces of equipment, this section will show you what to purchase, and why. You will find out how to get the best value for your money and how to take care of your Asian utensils when you get them home so they will give you a lifetime of honest service.

SHOWING OFF YOUR SKILLS

An important part of the fun of cooking and eating an Asian meal is in presenting it. This does not mean that you are going to invite your guests to sit on the floor, use gold or silver dishes, or even dine off banana leaves. However, after you have spent time and expertise in turning out a great meal, it is nice to know how that meal would be served in its country of origin.

Asian styles of dining vary considerably. In Thailand they eat with a spoon and fork, not with chopsticks. Laotions use little bundles of sticky rice as an implement to scoop up food. The northern Indians use unleavened bread for the same purpose. A circular tray, called a *thali,* is the meal server in southern India: small mounds of each of the foods composing the meal are decoratively arranged around a central portion of rice. The Koreans also use trays of different sizes, according to the number of people. Presentation is extremely important to the Japanese. They favor elegant simplicity, and slices of food are laid out on trays or platters like a carefully balanced painting. Throughout the Orient, small cloths dipped in perfumed water are presented to each diner before and after the meal, so that they may wipe their face and hands and refresh themselves. These are often heated at the outset of the meal, and at the conclusion, iced towels are offered.

All these meal presentations and customs are in the sections on the various countries of Asia. In each, the foods, culture and background of the cuisine are also described. Menu suggestions for formal and informal occasions are also given.

ASIAN INGREDIENTS

Throughout this book, substitutes for the more esoteric spices, herbs and general ingredients have been utilized in the recipes so that you may shop and cook from foods available in most good supermarkets. At the end of the book there is a full glossary of authentic Asian ingredients, with a description of each. Each, where possible, also indicates a substitute that is commonly available, to make your shopping easier.

After living, journeying, adventuring and eating throughout Asia, from the snows of Kashmir to the tropical gardens of Mysore State; from the teeming streets of Hong Kong to the night food markets of Singapore; from the food stalls of Vietnam to the food boats of the canals of Bangkok; and from the country inns of Japan and Okinawa to the luxury hotels of Manila, I have become enchanted with and addicted to the exciting food of the Far East. I hope that you will duplicate those culinary experiences in your kitchen and re-create some of the magic.

KITCHEN EQUIPMENT

❀ ❀ ❀

Its Selection and Care

No matter whether you are in a small house in Delhi, a hut in Bali or a high-rise block of resettlement apartments *(council housing flats)* in Hong Kong, when you visit the kitchen, you will find it clean, sparsely furnished and very simply equipped. Asian cooking does not require the battery of specialized utensils and implements that one expects to find in an American or French kitchen. In many parts of Asia electricity is still a luxury, so food preparation is undertaken by hand and with the minimum of gadgets.

The stove dominates the kitchen. It may be a hollow brick cube with holes in the top to serve as burners, or a tough earthenware firepot. Whatever its shape or size, it will have a hole in the front through which the fuel is placed and the spent ashes shoveled out. Firewood, charcoal or dried cow dung are common fuels. In some areas, simple kerosine stoves are used. Ovens are rare: there is very little baking in the cuisines of Asia. In large cities where there is electricity, the wealthy will invest in electric stoves complete with ovens, but even these are a spartan relative of our gleaming monsters and do not possess the luxury of automatic timers or thermostats. Where gas is available, it is generally bottled.

In Bangkok, some years ago, there was talk about supplying piped gas to the city. People threw up their hands in horror. There were already many fires caused by coals falling from the stoves. Imagine what would happen if gas lines ran to every house! Whole blocks of the city would surely blow up, as the population would never be able to grasp the idea that a gas tap had to be turned off after use. Right or wrong, Bangkok never got its piped gas, and does not have that facility to this day.

All this merely underlines the point that, to cook Asian, you will need only the minimum of equipment in your kitchen. Your modern stove already puts you ahead of millions of Asians. Any electrical appliances that you possess will reduce preparation time.

While you can happily use your existing pots, pans and casseroles to cook most of the recipes in this book, there is one basic utensil in the Oriental kitchen which is very useful to have: a wok. Few people need to be introduced to it. Curved like a shallow bowl and made of metal, either with a looped handle at opposite sides or with a single long handle, like a frying pan, woks come in many sizes and varieties of material. While Oriental restaurants may use woks up to four feet across, the most useful, all-purpose size for an average family is a wok of about 14 inches in diameter. Stainless steel, copper and a variety of other materials are rapidly coming into vogue, but I still prefer the original cast-iron wok. I find it holds the heat better and, when well seasoned, is very easy to cook with and keep clean. It is also inexpensive.

A wok has numerous advantages over a frying pan or saucepan. Its convex form makes it easy to toss, turn and scrape ingredients, which is so necessary when stir-frying. The shape also allows very little oil to be used, not only in stir-frying but also in deep-frying. When placed on its base, or collar, the wok may be tilted as necessary or even rotated to allow access to the ingredients. The absence of angles makes for easy cleaning, as there are no awkward corners in which food can get stuck. Above all, the continuous curve of a wok convects heat up the sides with the maximum of efficiency—an essential role in conserving fuel and energy.

If you have decided to purchase a cast-iron wok, look for a heavy one with no rim. Some manufacturers design them with rolled edges, hiding the fact that the wok may be rather thin, or the metal inferior. At the same time that you buy your wok, unless you have a gas stove with a wide ring into which its base will fit, you will need to purchase a collar for it. This is a circle or crown of metal with angled sides and holes to allow for heat convection. The collar will sit over your burner or electric ring and support the curved bottom of the wok.

WOK SET

You will also need to buy a long-handled metal spatula or wok-stirrer. The blade should have a curved edge to follow the curve of the wok and the handle should be made of some material, generally wood, that will insulate your hand from the heat. This is the utensil with which you execute all stir-frying and quick-frying. You may also want to get a frying strainer—a shallow wire-mesh basket with a long handle for straining and lifting solids from the oil when deep-frying. A steaming trivet is also useful. When this perforated metal tray is placed inside your wok and water poured into the space underneath, it converts the wok into a steamer. Finally, you should buy a metal cover—a raised lid that sits snugly inside the rim of the wok. Sometimes you will find all these accessories in a boxed set, together with the wok.

When you have brought your cast-iron wok home, you will need to season it. This process is exactly the same one used for frying pans and saucepans made from similar metals. Wash and dry the wok thoroughly to remove any protective film. Then rub a little cooking oil over the entire surface, inside and out. Heat your oven, place the wok inside and allow it to become really hot. Let it cool, and then repeat the process several times. This will put a nonstick coating on the wok and make it easy to clean.

A little soap and water is all you need to clean a wok. If food has become stuck on the surface, soak the wok, then gently remove the residue with a nylon-mesh pad. Never scrub it and never use steel wool. This will remove the protective coating that you have applied. In the Orient, a black wok is a thing of beauty. It proudly shows the amount of use to which it has been put and boasts of the marvelous dishes it has helped to create.

After washing your wok, dry it immediately to prevent any rust from forming. Should you find that your wok has rusted, you will, despite the injunction in the above paragraph, have to scour it thoroughly with steel wool and reseason it. To prevent this from happening, wipe it over with a paper towel, moistened with a little cooking oil, to protect it before putting it away.

I always hang my wok on a hook in the kitchen so that I have it immediately at hand when I want to cook. Besides, it takes up a great deal of room in a cupboard. After you become familiar with it, you may want to use your wok for other kinds of cooking besides Asian. It can be used for just about any stove-top cooking, and you will be amazed by its versatility.

The next, and almost indispensable, article of equipment in most Asian kitchens is a cleaver. Although well-sharpened chef's knives will perform most of a cleaver's functions, the cleaver itself is a great boon to the cook. Most Westerners regard it with suspicion tinged with horror—in short, they are scared of it. When measured against the fined-down gentility of French and

THREE CLEAVERS

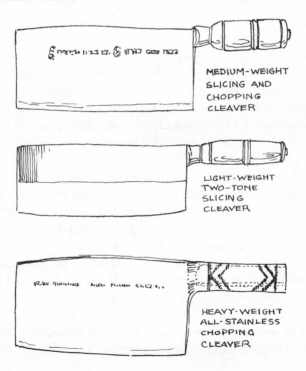

MEDIUM-WEIGHT
SLICING AND
CHOPPING
CLEAVER

LIGHT-WEIGHT
TWO-TONE
SLICING
CLEAVER

HEAVY-WEIGHT
ALL-STAINLESS
CHOPPING
CLEAVER

German knives, the cleaver appears, at first glance, to be a brutal, clumsy, dangerous hunk of metal. In fact, nothing could be further from the truth. The very heft and weight of a cleaver is protection against careless cuts and slips.

Cleavers are the perfect tools for cutting, chopping, slicing, crushing, mincing and scooping food. They are available in various weights and sizes. Lighter, small cleavers are for slicing and mincing; heavier and larger ones are for chopping through bone, such as that in chicken parts, spareribs and chops.

Mastering the technique of using a cleaver takes a little practice. The tool feels unusually heavy and unwieldy when first handled, but the basic techniques are easy to learn. In the section Basic Cuts in Food Preparation (page 82), there are step-by-step instructions on becoming proficient with a cleaver, as well as all the different cuts employed when preparing food.

The secret of efficient and speedy use of a cleaver is that the blade *must* be razor-sharp—a fact that should apply to all your kitchen knives. Use a good whetstone and sharpen the cleaver before each cutting session. It takes quite a while to put a good, deep cutting edge on a cleaver. The blade is far thicker than that of a Western knife, so the angle of the cutting edge is wider. It will blunt quickly after use until accumulated hours of sharpening have deepened and narrowed it. Persevere and acquire the habit of regular sharpening, and before too long, your cleaver will have a cutting edge that would win the approval of any Oriental chef.

Most cleavers are made of carbon steel, but some stainless-steel cleavers are also available. Both types have their advantages and drawbacks. Carbon-steel cleavers hold a sharper edge. They are also less expensive. However, they do need more care. When purchased, they are coated with a rust-resistant finish, which, as in the case of the wok, must be removed by washing and scrubbing before use. They should always be dried promptly after washing and then lightly oiled (use a paper towel dipped in a little cooking oil).

A final word about the different weights and sizes of cleavers. For a first purchase, I would suggest a medium-weight, all-purpose cleaver. A light-weight slicing cleaver, perhaps with a curved blade for rocking cuts, should be your next acquisition. Later, a heavy-duty chopping cleaver should be added. If you do not already have a heavy chopping board that will withstand the blows of a cleaver, now is the time to get one.

I would also suggest you purchase a mortar and pestle—a staple of every Oriental kitchen. Since the dawn of time, these have been used for grinding grains, spices, mashing pastes, concocting sauces and bringing back the elusive fragrance to dried herbs.

But why use a mortar and pestle? Haven't blenders, food processors and electric spice grinders superseded this primitive piece of equipment? For some tasks, such as the fine cutting and mixing of herbs and raw or cooked vegetables together with oils and liquids, yes, they have. But all these electrical appliances rely on the rotating action of cutting blades to perform the work: a mortar and pestle act by pulverizing hard ingredients into tiny fragments. There is no substitute in efficiency for coaxing the valuable fragrant oils from such hard spices as peppercorns, cinnamon bark, cardamom, coriander and cumin seeds. The resultant powders have a pungency and efficacy which is vastly superior to the ready-ground, bottled spices that may have been standing too long on the supermarket shelves.

The ideal mortar should be manufactured from a material that does not retain the odors and oils from pungent ingredients. Suitable materials include nonporous, acid-proof porcelain, basalt, brass and stone. A tough earthenware mortar also does a workmanlike job. Wood mortars are fine for occasional use, but must be confined to the same range of ingredients, as wood has a long memory.

Pestles are made from any material that will withstand the jarring shocks of repeated blows. Brass, stone or hard woods are the most common favorites. The shapes of mortars and pestles vary considerably from country to country and generally follow traditionally evolved designs. The most practical mortars are from about 4 to 6 inches in height, with a mouth of between 5 to 7 inches in diameter. They should have a heavy base so that they do not "walk" or tip

MORTARS AND PESTLES

under the blows of the pestle. The inside of the mortar should be slightly rough. The grinding action of a pestle within a mortar is facilitated by the friction between the surfaces.

A pestle should have a correspondingly rough striking or pounding base and should fit fairly snugly inside the mortar, but with enough maneuverability so that a scraping motion for pastes can be used, as well as the classic pounding technique. Also, it is advisable to search for a mortar with a fairly narrow well at the bottom. This ensures that small amounts of herbs and spices can be as efficiently pulverized as the larger quantities of ingredients needed for pastes and sauces.

The final item of kitchen equipment that you may wish to purchase after a while is a steamer. Although the steaming trivet in your wok, will perform a very utilitarian job, as indeed will any arrangement of homemade trivet inside a tightly lidded saucepan, a multi-tiered Oriental steamer does enable you to cook large amounts of a food at one time, or to prepare several dishes at once, thus conserving energy. Turn to the section on the techniques of steaming (page 246) for further details on steamers and their use.

MULTI-TIERED STEAMERS

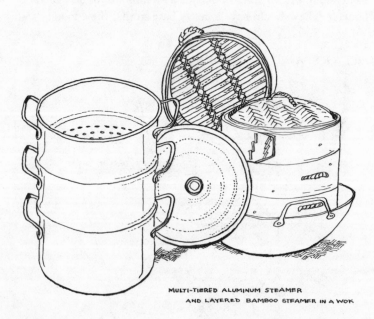

MULTI-TIERED ALUMINUM STEAMER
AND LAYERED BAMBOO STEAMER IN A WOK

BACKGROUNDS ON THE COUNTRIES AND THEIR CUISINES

❧ ❧ ❧

CHINA

Chinese food is the sum of its regional cuisines, which have been refined over centuries of practice, yielding some of the world's finest and most varied eating. It is said that if you ate a different Chinese dish every day for twenty years, you would not exhaust the repertoire.

Geography and climate contribute toward the wide range of styles in cooking, as does the conglomeration of races which have made China their home over thousands of years. When you compare the size of China with the whole of Europe, and think of the multiple variations of terrain, climate, cultures and food in the latter, you can appreciate how so many styles of cooking and eating can have developed in a single country.

The climatic zones of China range from the subarctic in the north to the subtropical in the south and encompass deserts, lakes, rivers, fertile plains and rugged mountainous regions, as well as thousands of miles of seacoast, each with its own, indigenous vegetation and animal life.

Several other factors have determined the characteristics of Chinese food. Because of the rigors of the weather, which has, in turn, brought floods, drought and, sometimes, famine to the country, and because of the frugality and ingenuity of the peasants and farmers who have learned to stretch a little food a long way, the cuisine is hallmarked by its economy in the use of both materials and fuel. Meat and fish are used in small quantities, eked out with vegetables and eaten with rice or wheat products. No part of an animal is wasted: hoofs, innards and head are all turned into delicious dishes, and the trimmings, scraps and bones are simmered for stock. Fruits, fish, fungi and roots are dried, smoked and preserved in the spring and summer, to be used in the long and frequently harsh winters.

To utilize precious fuels, the Chinese have evolved cooking methods such as stir-frying—the quick cooking of small pieces of food in a little oil over fierce heat—and slow-simmering, which tenderizes tough, inferior cuts of meat, stewing them in liquid, together with root vegetables, over the dying embers of the fire for several hours.

The ancient Chinese philosophy of food has always emphasized the harmonious blending of flavors, textures and colors. The Five Flavors—salt, sweet, sour, bitter and hot—must all be paid the proper attention so that they are skillfully combined, with no one accent dominating a meal. Rich foods must be counterbalanced by bland, brightly colored by pale, the smooth texture by the crunchy, and the hot dish by the cold.

Chinese cuisine falls into two basic agricultural divisions. In the north, the people eat wheat and other grain products; in the south, rice is the basis of every meal. But, for a more accurate description of the foods, China can be divided into four main regions, each comprised of the principal provinces contributing the most to the character of that area's cuisine: the northern region (Hopei province, including the capital city of Peking, Shantung and Honan provinces), the southern (Kwantung province, including the city of Canton), the eastern (mainly Fukien, but also Kiangsu, including the city of Shanghai) and the western (Szechwan, Yünnan, Hunan and Kweichow provinces).

The first Chinese to emigrate to the West in any large number came from the overcrowded city of Canton. Finding work within many of the major cities of the world, they settled in tightly knit groups and formed the Chinatowns. Restaurants were opened, serving Westernized versions of Chinese foods because only local ingredients were available. Gradually, authentic Chinese foods were imported, adding variety to the menus, but by then Occidentals were familiar with the ersatz versions of Chinese dishes and seldom requested any of the more authentic fare from the Kwantung province.

Over the years, Chinese from other provinces migrated to different parts of Asia, Europe and America, but, although other regional restaurants were opened, for a long time Cantonese cuisine dominated the dishes offered. As Western palates became more familiar with Chinese food, so our tastes became gradually more sophisticated. The "chop suey" style of bastardized Chinese cuisine was no longer sufficient. Nowadays we are fortunate to be able to sample the cuisines of almost any region of China within our larger cities. However, it is still rare to find a restaurant that specializes exclusively in one cuisine alone, and seldom do the menus inform us of the area or city in which a dish originated. So it is useful, in both cooking and eating Chinese food, to be able to identify the main characteristics of the cuisines of the four regions. Because of the general unfamiliarity with Chinese pronounciation, I have chosen the traditional Wade-Giles transcription system for romanizing the language. While the *pinyin zimu* or northern Mandarin was adopted in 1958 and is the official form of transliteration—Peking becomes Beijjin—I feel there is enough confusion; I want everyone to enjoy and experience the food and not get lost in a language primer.

THE NORTH

The cuisines of the northern provinces of Shantung, Hopei and Honan are often grouped together and referred to as the "northern" school of cooking. The food is light, elegant and mildly seasoned, although there is liberal use of garlic, chives and green *(spring)* onions.

Peking, in Hopei province, as the home of the Imperial Palace and a cultural and intellectual center of civilization, exerted great influence on the region. Until the seventeenth century it was the gourmet capital of China. The best chefs were attracted to the Imperial City and the banquets and feasts they produced were legendary. However, because it was the focus of all China, Peking became a melting pot of the best dishes from the rest of the country and therefore is not totally representative of the area's cuisine. Shantung province is really the major source of the indigenous cooking of northern China. Other influences on the northern style of cooking came from Mongolia, whose people, the Mongols, conquered China and supplied several successions of emperors. From the vast northern wastes of both Manchuria and Mongolia came the Chinese Muslim cuisine of the nomadic tribes, including barbecued and roasted mutton and lamb dishes, despised by the southerners as "barbarian food." Muslim enclaves still exist in China today.

Wheat, millet and barley are the staple crops of the north, and noodles, steamed buns and dumplings take the place of rice in the cuisine. Apart from the use of the onion family for flavoring, dark soy sauce, rice wine and fermented soybean paste provide dominant seasoning accents.

The northern school of cooking originated the world-famous Peking Duck, that succulent roast fowl with honey-basted, crisp skin which is eaten rolled in delicate pancakes spread with sweet bean paste and stuffed with green *(spring)* onions. Spring rolls, soft-fried foods, roasts and wine-cooked meats are all characteristic of the area.

Honan province is famous for its Yellow River carp and sweet-and-sour dishes. Mu shu pork, a mixture of sautéed pork and crisp, diced vegetables, wrapped in small, steamed pancakes which are then dipped in sauce, is a country dish eaten widely throughout the north.

Just to clear up one confusing point: the term "mandarin" actually means a Chinese official. The name was used by foreigners to refer to a certain high class of Chinese and loosely came to mean an aristocrat. With a little transference, it was gradually used in reference to elegant foods, supposedly eaten by "mandarins," suggesting that the food was high-class.

THE SOUTH

Kwantung is the southernmost province of China. It has a tropical climate and the longest seacoast of all the provinces, and has given birth to a cuisine of tremendous versatility with an abundance of ingredients and many seafood dishes.

Canton, a large port city on the Si Kiang, or West River, attracted a tremendous amount of foreign trade. In the fourth century, Arab traders, having learned the secrets of sailing with the prevailing monsoon winds, found their way into the port. In the fifteenth century the Portuguese arrived, followed shortly by the other Europeans.

Through centuries of foreign trading, the merchants of Canton became very prosperous and this was reflected in their consumption of the finest foods. Their chefs specialized in rich and extravagant dishes containing rare ingredients, and they strove to bring out the individual flavors rather than masking them with heavily seasoned sauces. The fame of the Cantonese chefs spread throughout China, even to the Imperial Court, two thousand miles to the north, and the royal household frequently traveled to Canton in an early forerunner of the gastronomic tour.

Because of this diversity of ingredients, history and influences, it is difficult to single out dishes that are characteristic of the area. They have, however, certain features in common. Dishes are often sauced with thick but delicate sauces having cornstarch *(cornflour)* as the thickening agent. Vegetables are used in quantity, but meat, sparsely. Rice is eaten rather than the wheat products of northern China. Fermented bean curd, oyster sauce (a viscous, dark-brown condiment fermented from oysters and soy sauce), salted black beans, rice-wine vinegar and ginger are the usual seasonings. Exotic ingredients, such as shark's fin, bird's nest and lobster (the latter little known outside Canton) are common. Sweet-and-sour dishes are said to have originated in answer to the demanding tastes of the foreigners.

In general, the cuisine of the south is subtle. Color, texture and harmony of ingredients are all-important. Stir-fried, roasted and steamed dishes are prevalent and the use of cooking oil is kept to a minimum. *Dim sum* dishes are popular daytime fare.

Lobster Cantonese, barbecued lacquered duck, lemon chicken and steamed fish in ginger sauce are all Cantonese delicacies, as are the famous shark's fin and bird's nest soups.

THE EAST

In the east of China the climate is also mostly subtropical and the four provinces (Fukien, Kiangsu, Anhwei and Kiangsi) provide the rice for most of the country. But in the northern part of the region, around Shanghai, the winters can be severe, and wheat and barley are grown. This is the region through which the famous Yangtze River flows, and the delta irrigates vast areas in which all kinds of fruit and vegetables flourish.

The foothills of the southern mountains in Fukien provide a hospitable environment for tea plantations, and some of China's finest teas, including the world-renowned Dragon Well green tea and the Iron Goddess of Mercy black tea, grow in this province. Fukien is also known for its soy sauce.

With so many miles of coastline, both Fukien and Kiangsu provinces enjoy a remarkable variety of seafood, and the Yangtze River, the lakes and canals provide many freshwater species, including the Shanghai hairy crab. Wildfowl are also prolific.

For centuries the city of Shanghai was one of the world's cosmopolitan centers of commerce, and it boasted a large and wealthy foreign population. Over the years, both Nanking and Hangchow served as centers for Imperial courts-in-exile, which, naturally, refined and raised the standards of the cuisine of the area.

Eastern cuisine is characterized by the use of sugar to sweeten dishes and to balance the use of salt. Rice wine, produced in Shaohsing, gives a pungency to many sauces, and the vinegars from Chekiang were combined with sugar to provide a range of sweet-and-sour inventions. The famous Chinese delicacy pressed duck was invented in Nanking during the sojourn of the royal household, and Hangchow was renowned for its freshwater fish dishes.

The cooks of Shanghai, having access to wheat and barley, baked breads and provided dumplings and noodles in the winter months. Preserved foods, including mushrooms, fish and the famous "hundred-year-old" buried eggs, were said to originate in the neighborhood of the city.

Fukien is renowned for its "red-cooked" dishes, in which ingredients are simmered slowly in soy sauce until the liquid evaporates, leaving a reddish tinge to the food. Congee, or rice gruel, the "crystal-cooking" method of stir-frying and the distinctively flavored *hung chiao,* a paste sauce made from the lees of red wine, are all associated with the province.

THE WEST

Other than Cantonese food, the cuisine of Szechwan is fast becoming the most popular with the Western world. Hot, spicy and distinctively seasoned, it is also common to the three other provinces of western China, Yünnan, Hunan and Kweichow. This land, ringed by mountains, was traditionally separate from the rest of China and developed its own culture and foods. Influenced by the incendiary spicing of Indian cooking, which was brought to the area by Indian Buddhist missionaries traveling the famous overland "Silk Route" to China, the cuisine was further enlivened by spices and herbs introduced by traders following the footsteps of the missionaries. The cuisine has many similarities with the foods of Thailand and Burma—partly because the T'ai tribes, which originated in the western provinces, later migrated south into both those countries. During World War II the American presence in Chungking caused the cuisine to become known to the West.

Szechwan pepper, a dried brown flower bud with a cologne-like flavor and unrelated to black pepper, was the indigenous spicing of the area until Europeans introduced chilli peppers from the New World to Asia in the sixteenth century. They were quickly adopted by the cooks of Szechwan and grew well in the hot and humid climate, induced by the four rivers enclosed by the mountain ranges. Szechwan food is not uniformly hot, however; the spicy heat is judiciously applied and essentially complements the other ingredients. Chilli peppers do not appear in most banquet dishes.

Other flavors of the region include the aforementioned Szechwan peppercorn, an essential ingredient of five-spice powder (also employed in regional dishes), garlic and green *(spring)* onions, fennel, ginger and dried tangerine peel. Rice, maize and millet, sugar, potatoes and all manner of vegetables are grown in the fertile basin. Deer and other game are hunted in the bamboo forests in the north of the region. Ducks, chickens and pigs are raised, the latter providing the famous Yünnan hams. Freshwater fish, particularly carp, figure largely in the cuisine, often sauced with a pungent black-bean puree.

The Chinese hot-and-sour soup originated in Szechwan. This soup is echoed by a similar dish in Thailand, probably a direct offshoot of its ancestor. Sauces are uncommon in the regional cuisine, but texture plays an important

part in the dishes. Nuts, such as cashews and walnuts, are often combined with
softer ingredients like chicken, mushrooms or bean curd. Beef is frequently
cooked until dry and then shredded, rather like a tender jerky. An unusual
flavor sensation is achieved by smoking poultry over tea leaves and camphor
wood.

Two of the other provinces are notable for a few unusual aspects of
Chinese cookery. The cuisine of Hunan is even hotter than that of Szechwan.
Smoked venison and hams are regional favorites, as is the dish named Kung
Pao chicken, after an exiled mandarin. In this dish, cubes of chicken are
stir-fried with enough fiery-hot chilli peppers and bean sauce to wake up the
most jaded palate. Yünnan, lying between Szechwan and the Thai and Burmese borders, has a cuisine largely unknown outside China. Its food was
influenced by thousands of Moslem officials, brought in by the Emperor Kublai
Khan to colonize the area. Some of the Yünnanese dishes can be found in the
northern parts of Laos, Thailand and Burma, including a spiced steak tartare,
which Marco Polo wrote about in his journals when he visited the province.

Cooking and eating in China have always been serious business. For
centuries, philosophers have written about food, and poets have composed
numerous odes to its qualities. Good cooks are much valued and have been
lured away from their establishments by all manner of inducement. But the
craft of cooking has not been confined to chefs and housewives. Nobles,
scholars and eminent men of letters have indulged in it; it has been regarded
as an art. Nowhere in the world, except perhaps in France, has cooking
reached such heights of perfection.

The Chinese eat a morning meal and an evening meal. The northerners
will also eat a lunch, as such, but in the south, people tend to snack during
the day—mid-morning, mid-afternoon, or both. Breakfast usually consists of
a bowl of rice gruel or congee, together with a assortment of salt fish, vegetables, minced pork and eggs. Lunch can be a choice of *dim sum*—dough-
wrapped, steamed dumplings filled with pork, vegetables or fish—slices of
roast meat and pickled vegetables, or bowls of noodles topped with slices of
meat and vegetables. The whole repast is accompanied by countless pourings
of fragrant tea. Dinner will consist of meat and fish dishes, vegetables, soup
and, of course, rice. As a rule there is no dessert, but sometimes fruit may be
served. Puddings and such are reserved for special occasions and banquets.

The number of courses in a Chinese meal depends on the number of
diners; generally one course to each diner. Dishes appear on the table in no
special order: they are served as they are cooked, but soup will arrive somewhere in the middle or toward the end of the meal, as its function is to wash
down the rice. Dishes are communal and diners help themselves to portions
of everything. There is seldom any order of precedence in seating arrange-

ments, except at a banquet, where the host and honored guest must sit in prescribed places. Because of this, and the necessity that the dishes be within reach of all, round tables are used with rotating centers so that no one need stretch for a dish.

Seasoning and cutting belong in the chef's domain, and a cook would be insulted by the addition of soy sauce at the table. Because all ingredients are presliced, knives and forks are not used, and chopsticks are the only utensils needed. (The accompanying illustrations show you how to use them.) Porcelain spoons are provided for rice or soup. Diners place rice in their bowls and then eat a few morsels of the other foods at a time from the top of the rice. The diner is expected to consume every last grain of rice in the bowl. Failure to do so is considered wasteful and an insult. In China, tea is normally served at the conclusion of the repast, except at *dim sum* lunches in the south, when it is served during the meal.

At a Chinese banquet, however, the etiquette and serving style is different. Preserved and crystallized fruits and nuts are served as hors d'oeuvre before the guests are seated. Hot towels are brought to the diners before the feast com-

HOW TO USE CHOPSTICKS

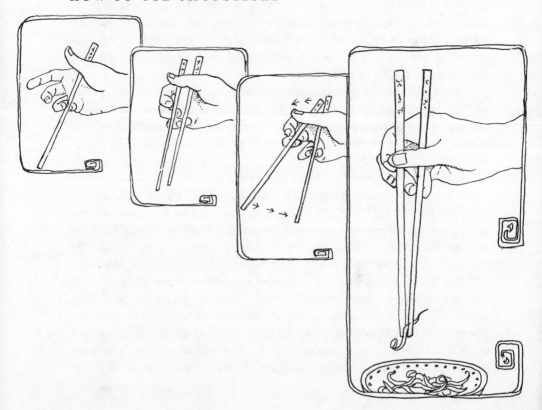

mences. Dishes are served in courses, the cold dishes first, followed by the hot foods. Chinese wine is served with the meal, and toasts are frequent throughout. Following the hot dishes, a thick soup is served, and then come the "main dishes," such as a whole roast pig, Peking Duck or braised ham. These are followed by a light, clear soup to cleanse the palate. A dessert such as Eight Precious Pudding (rice studded with crystallized fruit) may appear halfway through the meal. The end of the repast is signaled by the arrival of a whole fish set on the table with its head pointing toward the guest of honor. Rice, which is seldom served during a formal banquet, will make its appearance at the end of the meal as a token gesture. The guests are not expected to eat it because it merely signifies the superabundance of food provided by the host, who must, in the name of hospitality, provide more food than the guests can eat.

MENUS

For two:

(1) Spinach and Bamboo Soup
   Spicy Szechwan Chicken with
      Cashew Nuts
   Crab Toasts
   Plain Rice

(2) Steamed Shrimp Dumplings
   Szechwan Stir-Fried Cabbage with
      Hot Peppers
   Roast Pork
   Mixed Pickles
   Plain Rice

For four:

   Egg Rolls
   Radish-and-Carrot-Curl Salad
   Egg and Shrimp Savory Custards

   Beef Braised in Soy Sauce
   Chinese Almond Cookies
   Plain Rice

For eight:

   Hot and Sour Meat Soup
   Crispy Chicken Noodle Salad
   Whole Steamed Fish with Spiced
      Ginger Sauce
   Stir-Fried Squid with Vegetables

   Barbecued Spareribs
   Plum Sauce
   Eight Precious Treasure Rice
      Pudding
   Plain Rice

Chinese Dim Sum Buffet:

   Fried Dumplings
   Steamed Quail Egg Dumplings
   Crab Toasts
   Pork and Shrimp Rice Noodles in
      Broth
   Steamed Buns with Curry Filling

   Steamed Buns with Sweet Red
      Bean Paste Filling
   Roast Pork
   Pickled Ginger
   Chinese Sesame Cookies *(biscuits)*

INDIA

I belong to a small and rapidly disappearing group of people: those who grew up in India as offspring of the ruling or colonizing British, a group now romanticized in the novels of John Masters and M. M. Kaye. But that world *was* romantic. India is colorful, warm, exciting, hospitable and unforgettable.

When I went home to England, to the obligatory boarding school designed to give me the proper education, I returned to a country I hardly knew as a pale, skinny girl, aged nine, who was dreadfully homesick for her real homeland. The sights, sounds, smells and wonderful food of India were my real life, and the gray, rainy skies of England and the bland school diet seemed to be part of a dreamlike prison sentence.

It was to be eighteen years before I saw that beloved subcontinent again, and when I stepped off the plane in Karachi, even in the airport the old familiar sights and smells assailed my senses, and I started to cry. I had come home.

What is it about the cuisines of this land that binds people with ties of affection, and even addiction? It is because we have been lucky enough to experience and cook real, authentic Indian food—not the pallid but stinging stews which bear the label "Indian" and are full of semicooked curry powder, those stews thickened with cornstarch and burying their inadequacies under a multitude of picky little side dishes of peanuts, hard-cooked (boiled) egg, raisins and the everlasting sweet mango chutney. Do not misunderstand me —I have nothing against side dishes of freshly prepared condiments and accompaniments; I just crusade against the indiscriminate use of commercial curry powder.

To understand a little about the glorious cuisines of India and to rid ourselves of misconceptions and prejudices born out of ignorance, let's take a look at this vast and ancient land and its kaleidoscopic peoples and cultures.

India, cradled by the everlasting snow walls of the Himalayas to the north, girdled by tropical seas in the south and shaped by monsoon winds and rains, is more than a country—it is a subcontinent of deserts and barren plains; of swift-flowing, mud-laden rivers, lush jungles and rolling grasslands; of high, alpinelike valleys and fertile rice paddies. It carries enough geographic diversity to embody a little piece of almost every country in the world.

A seat of civilization dating back to two and a half thousand years before the birth of Christ, India has seen the invasions of the Greeks and the Scythians, the birth of Buddhism, the conquests of the Persian and Mongol hordes, the inroads of the spice-hungry Arab traders and, finally, the martial reds and golds of the relentless British. Bearing the buccaneering qualities of the merchantmen of the British East India Company (to whom my ancestors belonged,) the self-righteous invincibility of empire builders, and wearing the ubiquitous solar *topee* or pith helmet, beloved badge of the civil servants and administrators ("Yes, we do dress for dinner!"), the British sought to create order and unity out of the maelstrom of Indian castes and religions and to leave a legacy of sound government and, "Thank God, old chap!", at least, good roads.

But the British were but a brief chapter in the historic and cultural panorama of the seventh largest country in the world, with the second largest population. There are fifteen official languages recognized by the government, and two hundred and twenty-five dialects. This explains why the names of foods will change, depending on which part of the country you are in, and so will the names of many dishes. However, in most restaurants outside India, the menus feature the names in Hindustani (the simplified form of Hindi and Urdu).

Geographically, India is divided into three main regions: the mountainous north, descending from the snowfields and glaciers of the Himalayas in a series of high, lush valleys and rocky plateaus to the fertile center, rich, alluvial plains of the three great river basins: the Indus, the Ganges and the Brahmaputra. To the south, as the bulk of India diminishes into the apex of an inverted triangle, lies the Deccan plateau, an area of ancient rock separated from the wide plains by a line of mountains. The largest density of population is in the central fertile area of the great rivers.

The monsoon climate roughly divides the year into three seasons: the cold season, corresponding to our winter; the hot season, which lasts through our spring and early summer; and the hot wet season, which runs from June to around the end of October. Because of the geographic differences and the sharply contrasting seasons, you can eat apples, pears and walnuts in Kashmir and northern India, where sheep and cows are raised and mutton and milk products are universal, and a day later, by courtesy of the airways, feast on tropical fruits, coconuts and seafood in the south.

It was always the British colonial custom to move to the "hills" in the hot weather, and the business and local government offices moved as well. I remember, as a child, leaving the hot and dusty plains and the mango season of Bangalore in Mysore State, and traveling on the romantically named Blue Mountain Express up to Ootacamund, in the Nilgiri Hills, where we feasted on strawberries and where the ditches beside the mountain roads were filled with regal wild arum lilies.

This diversity of produce gives wide variety to the cuisines of India—a variety which is further enhanced by the meat, game and fish available. Deer, goats, wild boar and pig, wild ducks and geese, pheasants, snipe, partridge, grouse, quail and pigeons are all to be found in the northern and central areas, as well as domesticated sheep, cattle, pigs, chickens and ducks. Trout and salmon are plentiful in the northern rivers and streams; catfish and edible carp are widespread, as well as pomfret and herring and a plentiful variety of seafood off the southern coasts of Coromandel and Malabar.

The most marked division in Indian cuisine is the prevalence of wheat and wheat products to the north and the large rice culture of the central river basins and the southern area. This division is further fragmented by cultural and religious differences. The three great civilizations and religions of India—Hindu, Buddhist and Muslim—together with other cultural and religious divisions, such as Brahmin, Parsee, Sikh, Jain, Catholic Christian, Tamil and Dravida, dictate the style and form of cooking and eating as well as the content.

The dominant religion is Hinduism, which, although embodying the divisive caste system, has also been the greatest unifying force in India. Although in olden times the religious tenets of Hinduism were less strict with dietary laws, the cow is now a sacred animal to Hindus, who will eat no beef and in many cases consume no milk products. In fact, the rigid current strictures of the Hindu scriptures, aimed at purity of mind and spirit, demand that meat, fish, fowl and even eggs are all dietary taboos. There are exceptions: some coastal Hindus are given a dispensation to eat fish, which they call "the fruit of the sea." In Kashmir, the priest caste of Brahmins eat lamb, but not chickens.

This tendency toward vegetarianism is further strengthened by the Buddhists, who believe in the theory of reincarnation: how could one eat a chicken today when to be a chicken might be one's fate in the next life?

The Muslims, followers of the Prophet Muhammad, and a fairly recent influence on Indian culture, hold fast to the dietary laws set down in the Koran, which are very similar to the dietary strictures of Judaism. They may eat beef, but eat no pork nor shellfish because these are considered unclean foods.

Even vegetables are not immune from all these taboos. In some places, garlic and onions are considered unsafe to eat "because they inflame the passions and heat the blood!" Similarly, tomatoes and beets are forbidden to a few because of their bloodlike color.

The result of such restrictions has been the development of a vegetarian cuisine of amazing diversity and imagination. Grains and legumes are extensively used, together with all manner of vegetables and herbs and spices. As a rule, the finest vegetarian dishes come from the southern areas of India, although vegetarians are to be found in every part of the country.

The Indians have an immense enjoyment of life which is reflected in their lusty sense of humor and their sensual approach to all facets of living, including eating. They appreciate food deeply and are preoccupied with everything to do with its production and preparation. This is easy to understand in a country which, although amply endowed with natural resources, is subject to enormous vagaries of weather, and the term "feast or famine" was never more appropriate than when applied to Indian harvests.

Food also plays an important part in the fabric of Indian lives. It plays a starring role during public festivals and more personal celebrations such as births, marriages, graduation from school, reunions and such. What is to be prepared and served and in what manner is a topic of conversation, an important consideration and a measure of position in class and society. Catering is unknown. It is the mark of a good housewife and head of the household that a woman be an excellent cook and an able manager. Indian hospitality is legendary. From the poorest to the most wealthy, a welcome is extended to any stranger or visitor. Food and drink are always pressed upon the guest and cannot be refused. Entertaining is always done at home. It would be an insult to one's wife and to the guest to eat in a restaurant, and few Indians eat out. Because of this, the finest food in India is always found in individual homes.

An Indian kitchen is simple by our standards, like most other kitchens in Asia. The stove, or *chula,* is built of brick or cement, or, in the houses of the poor, of dried earth. It is a simple rectangular shape with holes at the top for burners and another aperture at the front near the floor for the solid fuel, such as charcoal, wood or dried cow dung. The large pans, or *dekshis,* sit over the holes. They have flat, indented lids, because there are no ovens, and in order to apply heat from all sides when required, further burning coals are heaped on the lids. Beside the deep pans, a curved wok-like vessel, called a *karhi,* is also used. It is for frying and braising, and some people say that this is where the term "curry" comes from. For the cooking of the flat, unleavened breads, a *tava* is necessary. This is somewhat like a skillet with a long handle, but the surface is slightly curved and there are no sides.

In the south, steamers are used. They look like the basic *dekshi,* but with a perforated disc or trivet fitted halfway to the bottom. A coconut scraper is also mandatory in the southern kitchen for the daily task of preparing coconut milk. Kitchens of north and south both will have mortars and pestles for the all-important preparation of spice pastes, and the northern kitchen will also have a stone grain mill called a *chakki* for the grinding of flour.

To prepare Indian food in a Western kitchen, we need virtually no special equipment. Our saucepans and heavy frying pans will substitute beautifully. Spice grinders and food processors and blenders will perform the more arduous work more quickly and thoroughly than it can be done in the traditional Indian kitchen.

Apart from food prepared at home, there is one category of food that is eaten outside the house—snacks. The Indians, like so many other Asians, are inveterate snackers—with good reason. The markets and bazaars are full of food stalls that prepare all kinds of tantalizing and seductive delicacies: flaky pastry turnovers, filled with spiced potato and vegetables or meat fillings, called *samosas;* deep-fried crisp balls of lentils, onions and spices, which are known as *vadas; pakoras,* which are a more substantial version of the Japanese *tempura* (see page 312), although they predate that delicacy by hundreds of years; *sev,* which is like a deep-fried, crunchy noodle, spiced with turmeric and cayenne, and *chiura.* The nearest way that I can describe the last snack is to tell you that it is the Indian equivalent of a highly nutritious "trail mix," being composed of a mixture of peanuts, lentils, vermicelli of chick-pea flour, puffed rice and, possibly, raisins, each ingredient fried until crisp, and seasoned with salt, sugar, a dash of lime and Cayenne pepper. There are at least two hundred more savory snacks, not to mention the incredible array of Indian sweetmeats and candies. It is small wonder that to be plump in India is to be wealthy and beautiful, and no surprise that the bulk of food eaten during the day is in the form of snacks.

To understand the basic structure of the cuisines of India and to grasp the diversity of the food, it is necessary to learn a little about the history of the country and some of the dominant influences which have shaped and refined it. Two of the most important have been the abundance of spices that grow in India and the advent of the Moghuls, whose empire fostered one of the most lavish and refined cuisines in the world, a cuisine which easily rivaled French cuisine during the heyday of Carême.

The wealth of spices and herbs that grow in India and adjacent areas of Asia and Asia Minor has basically affected the course of history of the entire subcontinent. Ancient Sanskrit writings from about three thousand years ago outline the medicinal uses of such spices as turmeric, cloves, cinnamon, ginger, pepper and coriander. These spices have also been used to preserve food—the latter an important reason for their use in a country where the temperature can rise to 110°F. and more in summer, and where the humidity in the south approaches steam-bath proportions.

Fennel, caraway, dark and light cumin seeds, white and green podded cardamoms, poppy seeds, black and yellow mustard seeds and many other more esoteric spices all play their part in the all-important spice pastes of Indian cuisine, as do saffron and chilli peppers, garlic and onions. Seasonings enrich simple vegetable dishes and disguise a sometimes paucity of ingredients in a country where the great majority of the population lives for a year on considerably less than we spend in a week. Spices increase the longevity of cooked foods for people to whom refrigeration would be an unheard-of luxury.

This natural wealth of spices, along with other much sought-after commodities such as ivory, gold, sandalwood and gemstones, made the subcontinent a focus for traders, merchants, adventurers and conquerors, many of whom left an indelible imprint on the customs, culture and food of India.

Aryans, Greeks, Mongols, Parthians, Huns, Arabs, Turks, Moghuls, Afghans and Europeans all invaded parts of the subcontinent. The path of these invasions lay from Asia Minor, across Afghanistan, what is now Pakistan, and into northern India, creating a tapestry of legends and history.

That rich tapestry has an area of gleaming gold threads corresponding to the establishment of the mighty Moghul Empire, a period during which India's culture and cuisine rose to unparalleled heights.

The conquering Turks originally brought Islam to India in about 1000 A.D. and the religion became further established with the Arab incursions. On several occasions, under the Turkish-Mongol leader Timur (the fabled Tamerlane), they burst into the Punjab and even reached Delhi before being repulsed. By this time a large proportion of India was already Muslim and many local kings dreamed of ruling over a united empire of both Muslim and Hindu.

By the twelfth and thirteenth centuries, the Mongol Empire under Genghis Khan stretched across North China and Central Asia, including Persia. The Persians named the Mongols "Mughals," and by the time that India was also occupied the name became Indianized into Moghul.

A subsequent conqueror of India, Babir, established the Moghul dynasty in India. This dynasty existed in splendor for more than two hundred years and reached its cultural flowering under Babir's grandson, Akbar the Great, and his grandson, Shah Jehan, who built the famous Taj Mahal. By the mid-sixteenth century, Persia was regarded as a kind of Paris of Asia Minor, and the new Moghul courts in India adopted Persian customs, language, art, architecture and, of course, cuisine.

Babir was the first to introduce many central Asian fruits and vegetables to India, including pomegranates, peaches, almonds and pistachios. Persian fruit-based drinks, cooled with snow, were introduced to the court, some of which were made with rosewater and almonds. These drinks, which the Indians called *sharbats,* were the forerunners of our sherbets, or fruit ices.

Simple Indian dishes of rice or lentils and vegetables were adopted by the

Persian chefs of the palaces and turned into intricate masterpieces. *Pulao,* or *pilau,* a Persian dish of rice cooked with meats and spices, was transformed into a lavish Moghul presentation, and has since given rise to a whole category of rice-based dishes. These include *biryanis* roasted or fried lamb and chicken, cooked with rice, saffron, pistachios, almonds and raisins) and intricate vegetarian *pilaus* such as *Navrattan pilau,* a triple-layered dish of rice cooked with vegetables, nuts, curd cheese and fruit, each layer tinted a different color and flavored with different spices and ingredients. *Navrattan* means "nine gems," and the dish was dedicated to the Emperor Akbar's nine favored courtiers.

Each chef at the palace had his own speciality, and the food became increasingly elaborate as the cooks competed for the emperor's favor. In the time of Akbar, one hundred dishes could be prepared at one hour's notice, such was the number, skill and efficiency of the cooks. Toward the end of the Moghul period, as during the decline of the Roman Empire, the cuisine of the courts became lavish to a legendary degree, and chefs were paid phenomenal salaries. One chef created a dish of rice in which each grain was coated with a combination of real gold and silver leaf pulverized into an edible paint with the yolk of an egg. The grains of rice were then stuffed into the neck of a chicken and heated until the coating fused and they resembled pearls. These precious edible grains were then incorporated in a *pilau* with meats and poultry! Even today, when an Indian wishes to honor a guest on a special occasion, the rice dishes and sweetmeats will be decorated with thin sheets of silver leaf or, if he is wealthy, gold leaf.

The vegetarians reclaimed and adapted many of the Persian rice dishes and Hindu and Muslim alike became partial to many of the lavish sweets that originated in Asia Minor such as *halva; burfi,* an Indian milk sweet with almonds and pistachios; *gulab jamuns,* solid balls of reduced cream, floating in a rosewater syrup—*gulab* means rose, and the quality of the dish is judged by the rose syrup that seeps inside, leaving the exterior quite firm like a protecting shell. Although these sweetmeats are all delicious, my favorites are *jalebis,* spirals of a crisp, delicate fried batter, leavened with yeast or baking powder. When bitten into, they release, as if by magic, a fragrant rose-flavored syrup. Reserved for special occasions, *jalebis* are thought to be difficult to make, and they must be served fresh or they become soft after an hour. However, I have found them fun to prepare, and relatively easy, after a few simple rules have been followed. All these sweets, and many more, are a legacy of the Moghul era; food for emperors, ambrosia for dessert eaters and a superb ending to any Indian banquet.

Apart from the rich foods of the Moghuls, the majority of Indian food is light and flavorful with its artful combinations of spices and herbs, and, when properly cooked, it provides a delicious balance of ingredients, textures and aromatics. It falls into categories that are dictated by the style and technique employed in creating the dishes.

Curries, or *turrkarhis* as they are also called, are merely dishes made aromatic with spice powder or paste mixes and then slow-simmered or stewed with a generous amount of water or other cooking liquids. (See the chapter "Currying Favor" for details of these and similar dishes.)

Kormas are often included in the curry category as "dry" curries. The word *korma* is synonymous with braising, and these dishes use only a small quantity of stock or yogurt, even cream, which is absorbed into the meat or solid ingredients, coating them with its residue. The liquid is added in small amounts at various times during the cooking and evaporated between each introduction. The spices may be added at the beginning, as in a curry, or introduced in various combinations halfway through and toward the end. *Korma* dishes are most frequently made with lamb, chicken or fish, with or without vegetables. The meat *kormas* originate in the north and were adapted by the southerners to include only vegetables. The southern dish is called a *sukke.* The Indians tend to regard *kormas* as *haute cuisine* dishes suitable for entertaining, and curries as everyday dishes, somewhat humble, simpler in construction and appropriate for simple family meals.

The word *dum* refers to steaming, and when it is found in the title of a dish it means that somewhere in the preparation the dish has been steamed. This does not necessarily infer that a steamer has been used, although sometimes rice *pilaus* and vegetables may be cooked in a pan with a trivet. A dish may be *dum*med by adding a small amount of liquid, placing a tightly fitting lid on top and steaming the contents in a low oven. This is the wet, or direct method of steaming referred to in the section on steaming techniques, page 247. Indian dishes often use this technique in conjunction with other cooking methods. For example: ingredients may be sautéed lightly with spices in a wok or frying pan, then transferred to a casserole, a little liquid added; the casserole is then covered and *dum*med in a low oven. In India, traditionally this would all take place on the range top in the same deep pan or *dekshi.* To *dum* it, liquid is added, the lid placed on top and coals heaped on the lid. The weight of the coals closes the lid tightly and the top heat creates a form of low-pressure cooking.

Tandoori cooking means oven roasting or baking and deserves an full explanation because it is rapidly becoming well known and popular in the West. The technique originated in the Punjab, the northwest corner of former India, now Pakistan. A *tandoor* is a clay oven shaped like a large Ali Baba jar or water pot. Traditionally the oven is sunk up to the neck in the ground, but if it is free-standing, then a thick layer of plaster is added to the walls for extra insulation. Burning charcoal is placed in the bottom of the *tandoor* and the foods to be cooked are placed on long spits after marination in spices. The spits are positioned vertically inside the oven.

Tandoor meats are first marinated to flavor and tenderize them; many of the marinades containing the red coloring agent that is a frequent hallmark of *tandoori* food. This marinade is allowed to dry on the meats before they are cooked. The foods are never larded before or during cooking, but the spits are greased or oiled beforehand. Characteristically, *tandoor*-cooked meats should be crisp and hard on the outside, moist and tender within. First the meats are seared with high heat, then repeated applications of the marinade are allowed to dry on the surface, leaving a residue that forms a crust and seals in the internal juices.

Since a *tandoor* oven is expensive to construct, substitutes may be devised for cooking *tandoori* style, in your own kitchen. (Small portable metal *tandoor* are available, complete with hooks and spits, but they are not insulated and they do heat up the kitchen. They also tend to smoke a lot.) Charcoal barbecuing is the best substitute if you have a back yard. If you do not, the rotisserie

TRADITIONAL TANDOOR OVEN

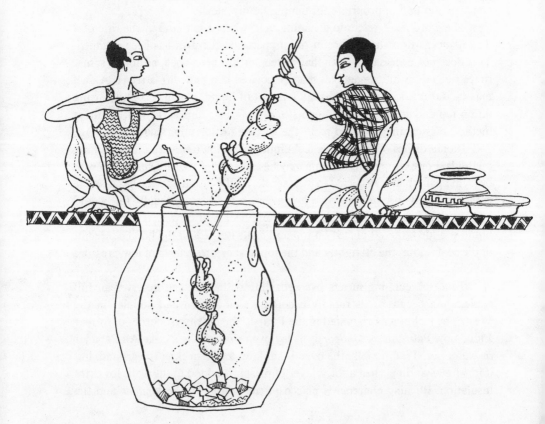

spit of your oven, or even the broiler *(grill)*, will produce good results. Place the meat on a spit or rack over a pan so that the marinade is retained to be reused for basting, and raise and lower the racks to control the searing process. *Tandoor* breads such as *naan* can also be cooked in your own oven.

Both shallow-frying *(bhoona)* and deep-frying *(talawa)* have an important place in Indian cuisine. Shallow-frying generally means sauteeing, the cooking of ingredients in very hot fat (generally clarified butter) with spices and herbs, after which it may be finished off by a *dum* or a *korma* or curry. Deep-frying is often carried out in a *karhi,* the Indian utensil shaped like a wok, but deeper and narrower (a wok is a good substitute). Many Indian snacks are deep-fried after being dipped in batter. These include *pakhora* (vegetable fritters), *koftas* (deep-fried balls of ground meats, vegetables or fish), *samosas,* which are really curry puffs, and *vadas,* balls or patties generally made from ground lentils, spices and herbs.

The Indian rice dishes also deserve a category of their own. Besides the *pilaus,* mentioned earlier, there are also the grand *biryanis,* where the meat is cooked together with the rice and spices, and also the humbler *kitchdis,* or combinations of rice and lentils, sometimes together with vegetables. These last dishes have been Anglicized into kedgerees, those dishes with rice, cooked fish (often smoked) and hard-cooked eggs beloved of the English for hearty breakfasts or light suppers.

Indian meals are rounded out with fresh *chatnis* (chutneys), *raitas,* salad-like combinations of fresh vegetables and fruits in yogurt, and the enormous array of Indian unleavened breads such as *chapattis, parathas, puris, naan* and *luchi.* These breads are described in detail in the chapter "Baker's Dozen," page 430.

This is, by necessity, a brief description of Indian foods and there are literally hundreds of other dishes. An Indian meal, whether from the north or the south, will be a carefully balanced presentation of dishes, with much thought given to flavor, texture, spice heat and principal ingredients. The main meal in India is eaten in the middle of the day; only banquets are given at night. All the dishes are brought in at one time except at banquets, when they are served in courses. In many areas of India the diners sit on the floor and the individual portions of dishes are arranged on a tray, on a low table or on the floor. The tray is called a *thali* and the foods are placed in small bowls or pots around a central mound of rice. (In the south, large banana leaves are often utilized as trays, and the dishes placed in little heaps around the leaf.) When properly laid out, the left-hand side of the *thali* will contain the accompaniments, chutneys, *raitas* and pickles, and the right-hand side, the main dishes. Depending on which area of India the dining is taking place, these might consist of a meat dish, two vegetable dishes (one gravied and one dry) and a

LAYOUT OF A THALI

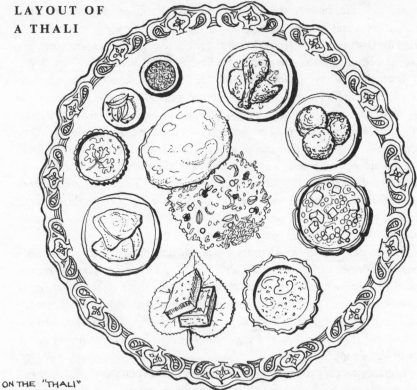

ON THE "THALI"

CLOCKWISE:

CHICKEN CURRY
CURRIED MEATBALLS
GREEN PEA AND CURD CHEESE CURRY
FAMILY SPICED LENTILS

MILK FUDGE SWEETMEATS
STUFFED PASTRY ENVELOPES
YOGHURT SALAD
MANGO PICKLES
FRESH CORIANDER CHUTNEY

CENTER:
FLAKY, BUTTERY UNLEAVENED BREAD
RAISIN RICE WITH PEAS

lentil dish. A southern vegetarian dinner would offer a greater variety of vegetable dishes and no meat.

Indians traditionally eat with their hands; the right hand is always used as the left hand is considered unclean. Nowadays spoons and forks signal a more Western approach to eating. It is considered a sign of a bad host if a guest is allowed to get up from the table any less than overstuffed, and the host will press the guests to eat at least one more bite. Those on a diet should be prepared to leave it behind when traveling in India! Bowls of perfumed water scattered with rose petals are brought at the conclusion of the meal for guests to wash their hands, and a tray of *paan* (assorted digestive ingredients which also act as breath fresheners) is passed around. And that will be the end of one of the most delicious meals you have ever eaten.

MENUS

For two

(1) Meatball Curry from Madras
    Fresh Tomato Chutney
    Family Spiced Lentils
    Plain Rice

(2) Curry Soup (Mulligatawny)
    Vegetable and Shrimp Fritters
    Fresh Coriander Chutney

For four:

    Pork Curry
    Banana and Coconut Salad
    Lentil or Split-Pea Ball Curry

    Indian Sweet Lime Chutney
    Unleavened Whole-Wheat Bread
    Plain Rice

A Moghul meal for six to eight:

    Meat-Wrapped Eggs Variation
    Whole Chicken with Spices,
      Moghul Style
    Vegetarian Raisin Rice with Peas
    Yogurt Salad

    Mint and Fruit Chutney
    Flaky, Buttery Unleavened Bread
    Potato-Filled Bread
    Carrot Fudge Pudding

An Indian buffet:

    Stuffed Pastry Envelopes
    Lady MacFarquhar's Tomato
      Chutney
    Beef Curry from Madras
    Shrimp Ball Curry
    Vegetable Fritters

    Fresh Coriander Chutney
    Oven-Barbecued Chicken
    Indian Oven Bread
    Rice of the Emperor's Nine Gems
    Fried Batter Spirals in Syrup

INDONESIA

If it had not been for the lure of the fabled Spice Islands of Indonesia, the Americas would probably have remained largely unknown to the rest of the world until far later than the fifteenth century. This tropical archipelago, the world's largest island chain, has drawn traders and merchants to it like a magnet since the beginnings of recorded history.

It is inevitable that Indonesia is referred to in terms of statistics and superlatives. The numbers by which it can be measured are mind-boggling and they emphasize the kaleidoscope of contrasts that represent the country. Indonesia covers an area of almost 783,000 square miles, the scattered beads of a broken necklace of emergent mountaintops which links the Indian and Pacific oceans with Australia and the Indo-Chinese peninsula. There are nearly 13,700 islands, containing more than 400 volcanos. The principal and largest islands are Sumatra, Java, Borneo (now called Kalimantan) and the octopus-shaped Celebes (Sulawesi). These islands contain the world's fifth largest population—over 135,000,000 people, comprised of some 300 ethnic groups speaking more than 250 dialects. It is a monument to human persistence that a country and a nation have been forged from such incredible fragmentation—and the national motto, "Unity in Diversity," says it all.

The warm, hospitable climate, fertile land and monsoon winds have nurtured the human race on the islands for about half a million years. Today's Indonesians are descendents of the waves of immigrants from the Asiatic mainland and the Pacific who came to Indonesia between 10,000 and 500 B.C.

The history of Indonesia is founded on trade. As early as the first century A.D., Indonesian outriggers were trading off the coast of Africa and Indian merchants may have found their way to the Spice Islands several hundred years earlier. The Malacca Straits, between the Malay peninsula and Sumatra, were an essential segment of the sea route between India and China, and the earliest trading posts were set up on Sumatra, Java and Borneo. Here ships could wait until the north-blowing monsoon winds would propel them to China. These posts became Indianized city-states, ruled by local chiefs who protected the interests of the Indian merchants.

By the fifth and sixth centuries, Indian culture had a firm foothold on the Islands, propagated by Hindu and Buddhist priests and monks who, together with settlers, quickly followed the seafarers and traders.

By the eleventh century, the Arabs had largely taken over the Indians' trade and the Islamic religion supplanted Buddhism and Hinduism. Marco Polo was the first recorded Westerner to visit the "Spice Islands," and, it is said, he gave them that nickname. He listed the spices he found on the islands, including pepper, nutmeg and cloves, and seems to have enjoyed the local food and drink. He remarked that the coconut contained "an edible substance that is sweet and pleasant to the taste, and white as milk," and observed that the natives raised "no wheat, but live on rice." He also appears to have enjoyed the local toddy, saying that the palm produced "an excellent beverage," and he wrote down a recipe for palm wine. It is recorded that Marco Polo landed in Sumatra in 1292; he was followed, in quick succession, by the Portuguese, Spaniards, English and Dutch.

The Western nations further expanded the trade in valuable spices, and they vied with each other for control over the islands. In 1511 the Portuguese gained a stronghold in Malacca, on the west coast of the Malay Peninsula. For one hundred years following, the Spice Islands became a battleground for supremacy between the Portuguese and the Dutch. In 1596, the Dutch East India Company established control of the islands, naming them the Netherlands East Indies, and the Dutch held them until the Japanese occupation in 1942.

Just before and following World War II, emerging Indonesian nationalism sought independence from the Dutch. Sukarno proclaimed the Republic of Indonesia on August 17, 1945, in Jakarta, but sovereignty was not granted until 1949, and then only after intervention by the United Nations.

What of the islands themselves? Lands of breathtaking beauty and extreme violence of nature: cruel, jagged volcanic mountains, rolling mats of green jungles, white-sand beaches and pounding surf—a country that witnessed one of the largest volcanic eruptions in the history of the world when Krakatoa, on Pulau Island, between Sumatra and Java, blew up on August 27, 1883. The explosions were heard in Australia, over 2,000 miles away, and five cubic miles of rock and ash were hurled fifty miles into the air. A resultant tidal wave, 120 feet high, drowned 36,000 people in the coastal areas of both Java and Sumatra.

Sumatra is the northernmost island of Indonesia and the fifth largest in the world. In the south of the island, slow-moving rivers curl through inpenetrable jungles that resemble the Matto Grosso of Brazil. To the north, rolling highland plateaus are carpeted with tea and coffee bushes, flanked by geometric rows of sugar, sago and oil palms. Teak and other valuable timber forests provide sizable revenues, as do rubber, cotton and tobacco plantations. Lake Toba, 3,000 feet above sea level, fills a gigantic extinct volcano crater 50 miles long, and itself boasts a large island which, in turn, hosts yet another, smaller lake—a natural Indonesian puzzle box of land and water. Ninety volcanoes stud a 1,000-mile long mountain chain that runs down the length of the island.

Java, the next island to the southeast, is the site of Jakarta, the jangling modern capital of Indonesia. Two-thirds of Indonesia's population live on the island, which is the center of the world-famous batik cloth industry.

The fabled island of Bali lies east of Java. It is a panorama of volcanic slopes terraced with frozen waves of rice paddies; small picture-book villages; sandy shores that tempt one to take up residence as a beachcomber; and ten thousand temples. Orderly and tranquil, Bali is the cultural center of the nation, home of thousands of craftsmen and the land of endless festivals.

These larger land masses tail off into thousands of islands that stud the seas all the way to Iran Jaya, or West New Guinea. Above and to the northeast of the archipelago looms the enormous bulk of Kalimantan (Borneo). The third largest island in the world, Kalimantan is the size of Cambodia, Laos, southern Vietnam and a goodly portion of Thailand put together. A portion of the island is hewn into the independent kingdom of Brunei. This island still remains completely primitive in its densely forested hinterland. Monkeys and orchids, rhinoceros and rhododendrons coexist in primeval jungles.

Beyond Kalimantan, the tentacles of the mountainous Sulawesi (Celebes) stretch out to the Spice Islands of the Moluccas and, beyond them, prehistoric New Guinea. This southeastern book end of Indonesia is Australasian rather than Asian. The peoples are dark-skinned Negritos, Papuans and Melanesians with South Pacific roots and the animal and plant life share a heritage more antipodean than Indonesian.

The history and development of Indonesia is inextricably linked with the spice trade. Pepper, cinnamon, cassia, nutmeg and mace, cloves, ginger and turmeric are all native to the islands, although there is a theory that pepper was introduced very early on from India. Cassia and cinnamon were used by the ancient Egyptians as part of the embalming process. It is thought that they were taken from Indonesia to Madagascar in primitive outrigger canoes and then transported northward to the Nile valley, this as early as the second century B.C. It is also possible that the cassia is Chinese in origin and was brought to Indonesia by early traders, chiefly Indians. Nutmeg and cloves from the Moluccas were introduced to China as early as the third century B.C. and it is reported that noblemen at the Imperial court of China were required to sweeten their breath with cloves before addressing the emperor. Through trade with the Indians and the Arabs, nutmeg and mace reached Europe around 600 A.D. The Arabs and Indians had learned the secrets of the seasonal monsoon winds, using them to sail to and from the Spice Islands and, in the case of the Arabs, across the Indian Ocean to the Middle East. For years these sailing secrets were jealously guarded, for they held the key to the spice trade and therefore to great wealth. But, in time the secret was discovered and the Arabs lost the spice monopoly, causing the astronomical prices of spices to fall.

The decline and fall of the Roman Empire led to the opening up of the Eastern world to Arab domination and to the spread of Islam, and the Arab traders were largely responsible for the present-day domination of the Islamic religion and, to a lesser degree, the cultures of Indonesia.

The Arabs, besides exporting the indigenous spices, also introduced spices from the Middle East and India to Indonesia. Coriander, cumin, caraway, dill and fennel are all used in present-day Indonesian cuisine. Cloves, however, are the dominant spice of the islands in a very tangible sense. The Indonesians grind cloves and mix them with tobacco for cigarettes, and the sweet smell of burning cloves hangs like a pall over most Indonesian towns and villages.

There is really no *haute cuisine* in Indonesia. The food is primarily peasant food; the nobility, although immensely cultured and refined, reserved their creativity for literature and the arts and seemed to take eating for granted.

The preparation of food is a communal craft, although the matriarch of the family will be head of the kitchen. Both male and female members of the family are involved in the chores, the men gathering the firewood and shouldering the rice sacks, the women marketing and chopping and slicing the raw ingredients.

The kitchens are simple, like those of the rest of Southeast Asia. A wok, here called a *wajan,* is used, as are a *cobek* and *ulek-ulek* (mortar and pestle). The cuisine is primarily stove-top, with charcoal or wood providing the fuel.

The eating patterns, too, are similar to those of the rest of Southeast Asia. A nation of rice-eaters, the Indonesians eat rice three times a day. The first meal may consist of rice, together with a fried egg or fried plantains. During the day, the street vendors ply their delicacies up and down the houses, selling satay (or *sate*), the ubiquitous tidbits of barbecued meat skewered on thin bamboo sticks and then dipped into sauces. Satay originated in Java, but has spread throughout Indonesia to Malaysia and up to Thailand. It may well have originated with the Arab and Indian traders as a more delicate form of kebab. Sticky rice cakes and all kinds of snacks wrapped in banana leaves are also purveyed, as well as glasses of hot tea sweetened with cane or palm sugar. Work generally finishes about one o'clock and the families gather for a late lunch. This will consist of rice, accompanied by two or three dishes of meat and vegetables, the latter sometimes cooked and dressed in a sauce of coconut milk thickened with ground peanuts.

The main meal of the day is eaten in the evening, generally at dusk. It may consist of four or five cooked dishes: a hot and spiced curry, one or two vegetable dishes, a fish dish, and, perhaps, fritters as a contrast to the sauced items. Fruit generally serves as dessert.

Because of the numerous festivals celebrated throughout the islands, feasts are common. They are not merely occasions for overeating or showing off one's cooking prowess; they are expressions of religious significance as well —food for the spirit as well as for the body. The Indonesians have a word for these feasts—*selamatan*—which, although untranslatable into English, roughly corresponds with thanksgiving and the bestowing of grace upon the participants. The feasts are communal and ritualistic. The centerpiece will often be a dish of festival rice, tinted yellow with turmeric and this will be accompanied by as many dishes as the community can provide.

The cuisines of Indonesia, quite naturally, vary from region to region and island to island. Sumatran food has strong Indian and Arab influences. It is more substantial than many of the other cuisines. Lamb is often used in currylike dishes, beef is cooked in gravies, spiced with coriander, cumin, lemon grass and fiery chilli peppers. It is then simmered until the gravy has evaporated, leaving a delicious, strongly flavored dish of meat, which, being so heavily spiced, keeps quite well without refrigeration. Pilau-type rice dishes, with meats cooked together with the rice, are also eaten.

The food of Java is more subtle, often a combination of sweet, sour and hot flavors. The Javanese have a decided sweet tooth and specialize in a variety of sweetmeats, cakes and candies. Coffee is drunk, and indeed the name "Java" has become a sobriquet for the beverage. In West Java, however, the cuisine undergoes a decided transformation. The food is more simply cooked, less highly flavored, and meats and fish are often wrapped in banana leaves and grilled or steamed. Salads of raw vegetables appear frequently.

Balinese food has subtle Hindu influences. The population, unlike that of the other islands, is mainly Hindu, and pork is eaten, with beef relegated to a very minor role. The spicing is lively and the flavors in the dishes are distinct and immediately recognizable.

Naturally, the foods of the other islands, including Kalamantan and Iran Jaya, are rather primitive. The Malay influence is strong in the former, while the food of the latter bears a slight resemblance to the Polynesian.

No account of Indonesian food would be complete without mentioning the *rijsttafel*. The origins of the meal are unclear, and at first, to those who are acquainted with Southeast Asian food, the translation "rice table" seems a bow to the obvious, for in most Asian meals rice takes the central role at the table, the other dishes playing a subsidiary role. It may be explained by the banquets of the colonial Dutch, in which their wealth was displayed by ostentatious processions of dishes; sometimes as many as 60 or 70. Each dish would be brought from the kitchen by a servant or "boy" and arranged around the central mountain of rice. The gargantuan meals would be referred to as "sixty- or seventy-boy *rijsttafels.*" The overweight colonialists would proceed to loosen the belts around their rotund bellies and exult in the opulent extravaganza of food.

Needless to say, upon the advent of independence and the nationalistic pride that accompanied the defeat of colonialism, the *rijsttafel,* as a symbol associated with foreign domination, fell from favor. It lives on in restaurants in Holland and in buffets in Indonesian luxury hotels aimed at tourists.

When cooking Indonesian, remember to balance the dishes in your menu. Spiced foods should be offset by bland; wet by dry; soft by crisp. Color, texture and flavor are all equally important. Quick stir-fries, which are last-minute preparations, should be programmed together with make-ahead dishes so that you are able to relax and enjoy the meal with your guests. The Indonesians eat with their fingers, but you may want to provide forks and spoons. Decorate the table with vivid flowers and heap any tropical fruit you can find onto a large platter.

Salamat makan! (Bon appetit!)

MENUS

For four:

(1) Lamb Curry from Sumatra
    Spiced Cabbage with Coconut Milk
    Peanut Fritters
    Sweet and Hot Chilli Sauce
    Fried Noodles
    Plain Rice

(2) Cooked, Mixed Vegetables in Thick
    Dressing
    Beef Curry (Dry)
    Fish Relish
    Spinach and Corn Soup
    Plain Rice

An Indonesian Rijsttafel *(Rice Table) (Between eight and twelve):*
    Mixed Vegetable and Seafood Salad with Thin Dressing
    Balinese Coconut Pork
    Twice-Fried Spicy Peanut Fritters
    Lamb Curry from Sumatra
    Beef Satay
    Satay Sauce
    Green Pepper Relish
    Peanut and Coconut Sambal
    Shrimp Fritters
    Steamed Nut Cake
    Plain Rice (lots of it)

JAPAN

Japanese cuisine is world-renowned for its meticulous preparation and extreme refinement in presentation. The food is served in small, carefully arranged portions, with emphasis on visual appeal—the interplay of colors, textures, shapes and overall design.

Because the islands that comprise the Japanese archipelago are mainly mountainous, very little land is available for agriculture, and even with the most modern technology, harvests are frugal. The Japanese have traditionally learned to husband their food resources and to appreciate quality over quantity.

They have also developed a sensitivity to the individual foods as they are processed for eating. Unlike the Chinese and other Asians, who blend herbs, spices and main ingredients into a bouquet of flavors, the Japanese prize the particular properties of each ingredient and emphasize the equal importance of their individual flavors and textures.

The historic insularity and xenophobia of the Japanese has perpetuated a style of cooking relying on the indigenous ingredients of the country. With a comparatively limited assortment of foodstuffs from which to draw, a culinary tradition developed that emphasizes variety in methods of preparation.

To show off this versatility in treatment and to compensate for the small range and amount of food being served, presentation becomes all-important, much in the same way that the *nouvelle cuisine,* while reducing the richness and quantity of the food and the complexity of the sauces, now emphasizes its visual appeal. Japanese food arranged on a plate becomes a carefully composed painting.

Theme is another dimension. A dish will convey a message or mood— a oneness with nature. Seasonal foods are presented with a quiet flourish, a subtle indication to the eater of the spirit and content of that season. The hint is embodied in the composition, arrangement and garnish. Each presentation is unique and is not repeated. That is the pride and skill of the cook.

Like the culinary habits of all nations, those of Japan reflect the geography, history, climate, ethnic inheritance and culture of the people. The earliest inhabitants of the islands were probably immigrants from the barren lands of Siberia and the peninsula which later became Korea. They found a country infinitely more hospitable than their homelands. The islands were covered with vegetation, the climate was benevolent and the seas stocked with an abundance of fish. They developed a deep appreciation for all forms of nature, which grew into a cult of worship for the fertility of the land and the spirits of the countryside. Later migrations of invaders from South China, using the Bonin island chain and the Ryukyus, merged their clan worship with the nature worship of the earlier peoples to produce Shintoism. Shintoism, for so long the principal religion of Japan, is a direct outgrowth from and formalization of this nature worship (animism). Although it has been supplanted largely by later forms of religion, it can still be traced in the many festivals of Japan devoted to celebrations of the harvest and various aspects of nature, and to the reverence with which the Japanese regard forms of plant life and their incorporation into their foods.

The diet of the early Japanese was simple: fish, vegetables, fruits, seaweed. Occasionally, when it was available, meat or game was added. Unlike the Asian nations of the mainland, whose cultures and food styles became intermingled with those of their neighbors, this simple regime descended down through the centuries virtually unchanged.

Because the Japanese are an island people whose land lies farther away from the contiguous countries of the Asian mainland than those of Great Britain from the mass of Europe, they were, until fairly recently, somewhat insular in accepting influences and imports from the rest of the world. Throughout its long history, Japan did open its shores to foreigners and alien ideas from time to time, only to change its policies and shut them off again.

During periods of receptiveness, both soybeans and tea were introduced from China, and indeed it is from Chinese cuisine that Japan has derived most of its major culinary influences.

Between the sixth and ninth centuries A.D., when China was enjoying the full flowering of the T'ang Dynasty, Japan opened up to the full range of Chinese cultural and religious influences, including Buddhism. In the middle of the ninth century, when the T'ang Dynasty disintegrated, Japan again closed its doors to outside influence, refining the ideas, customs and foods which it had adopted. One hundred and fifty years before that embargo, the golden age of Japanese culture had already begun. From 794 A.D. until 1200 A.D., the Heian era (named after the capital of the Imperial court at Heian-kyo, now Kyoto), marked a blossoming in all the arts, the development of an elaborate code of etiquette and a defining of style.

While the Heian age, unlike the opulence of the Chinese dynasties, did not affect the basic simplicity of the Japanese cuisine, and the diet of noble and commoner alike remained frugal, this period inspired the nobility to develop and refine the presentation of food—a standard which remains intact today.

A long feudal period followed the collapse of the Heian era, during which the samurai, or members of the warrior class, rose to eminence and power. Through the Samurai, the culinary practices of the nobility filtered down to the lower classes.

Tea, which was imported from China in 800 A.D. but only drunk by the nobility or used as a medicine by the masses, became a widespread beverage in the fifteenth century, partially through the Japanese court's adoption of the Buddhist tea ceremony. This ceremony has now become formalized and stylized into a cornerstone of Japanese culinary culture.

By the middle of the sixteenth century, the Portugese, then the world's foremost sailors and navigators, had already infiltrated a large part of Asia. They arrived in Japan and began trading. Although the Japanese despised them for their barbaric appearance—their beards, clothes, lack of bodily cleanliness—they nonetheless were willing to foster the relationship with the strange Europeans and gradually absorbed some of their practices. This is when the technique of dipping fish and other foods in batter and frying them originated. This technique, called *tempura* by the Japanese, stems from the Latin word *tempora,* referring to the Ember Days, or *Quattuor Tempora.* During these days, the Roman Catholic Europeans were forbidden by their religion to eat meat and so substituted seafood, which they fried in batter.

As is the historical pattern, the traders were followed by the priests—in this case, the Jesuits, who began to interfere with the internal affairs of the Japanese. Xenophobia, understandably, came to the fore once more, and the Japanese banned all foreigners from the country for several hundred years. Again, during that period of isolation, the Japanese refined that which they had adopted. After they changed both the batter and the frying oil to produce the feather-light concoction we now recognise as tempura, that culinary master-piece became one of the principal joys of Japanese food.

After another long period of isolation, in the 1850s the Japanese were forced to recognize the outside world. Word spread of the incredible advances in technology and industrialization made by the Western nations, and some Japanese wanted to share in that growth. At the same time that they began to industrialize, they also borrowed from the Western diet. The Shinto tenets of vegetarianism were gradually abandoned and beef, pork and poultry began to make an appearance in Japanese dishes.

Carefully studying Western methods of raising livestock, the Japanese began to rear the world's finest beef, again improving on and refining existing techniques. Their success is demonstrated by the internationally renowned Kobe beef and the scarcer Matsuzaka.

To expand a little on Kobe beef. Before I ever visited Japan, I sampled what passed for "Kobe" beef in many restaurants in Southeast Asia. In fact, judging from the quantity of eating houses offering what they boasted was the genuine article, it is surprising that Japan had any beef left for home consump-tion. I was not impressed, but laid it at the door of my European-bred aversion to large slabs of meat.

It was not until some years later, when the California-bound freighter on which we were romantically traveling stopped at Kobe, that I found enlighten-ment. Some of the ship's crew invited our family to their favorite restaurant in Kobe where, they swore, the beef was "the real thing." Merchant seamen are rather like truckers or (in Europe) lorry drivers. They have an unerring instinct as to where the best food may be found, so we accepted the invitation with alacrity. We were not disappointed. Sitting up at a counter, in a small, warm, but unpretentious restaurant, we were served several dishes of the most outstandingly flavored and finely textured beef that my palate has ever encoun-tered.

By comparison, I realized that the "Kobe" beef I had eaten prior to this experience was probably buffalo meat that had been cradled in papaya leaves to achieve respectability.

It still remains a personal goal of mine to sample Matsuzaka beef but, with Oriental patience, I am working on it.

While the Japanese were absorbing some of the foods and dietary styles of the West, there was little reciprocation. Japanese food and cooking did not begin to catch on until the middle of this century, when the American presence in Japan during the Korean war really brought it into focus. From then on, Japanese restaurants opened in many countries, and Westerners gradually began to appreciate the simplicity and beauty of Japanese food.

Fish, soybean products, seaweed, vegetables, rice and fruit are still the pillars upon which Japanese cuisine is built, the first two staples providing the main sources of protein in their diet.

To understand Japanese cuisine, one must grasp the important role that seafood plays. Fish or other seafood is eaten at every meal, and it is unthinkable to prepare a Japanese meal without any of these. The coastal waters around Japan have always supported a rich marine life, which has more than compensated for the paucity of agriculture in the mountainous islands above them. Every conceivable variety of bony fish, crustacean and mollusk is available, and the Japanese have taken full advantage of that bounty. They are, undoubtedly, the world's experts in seafood preparation, having a deep appreciation and understanding of every type of marine life.

To eat fish in Japan is a completely different experience for a Westerner and will convert even those who have previously disliked it. To begin with, the fish tastes different—richer in flavor, more tender in texture and as fresh as the ocean from which it was so recently taken.

There are no seafood restaurants in Japan as we understand the term. Fish is naturally part of the fare served at every meal. Apart from the general restaurants, there are food houses that specialize in one type of fish only, or in one style of preparation. Such dedication to fish is quite awesome.

One of the biggest stumbling blocks to the Westerner is the Japanese predilection for raw fish. The idea initially strikes the novice as repugnant. But to blind-test it is to bite into something with the texture of the finest and most tender beef filet, with no hint of "fishiness" in either odor nor flavor. Only the freshest fish and the finest cuts are used, and the presentation, whether in *sushi* or *sashimi,* is a culinary masterpiece. *Sushi* and *sashimi* are the names for the two styles of serving uncooked fish. In the West, we are now becoming more familiar with these categories because of the recent proliferation of *sushi* bars which have opened in our major cities.

Briefly, *sushi* is the presentation of fish in combinations of lightly vinegared rice garnished with either raw or cooked fish and seafood, strips of seaweed, vegetables and egg. Each *sushi* is a delight to the eye; the shapes and combinations of colors and textures are almost endless. *Sashimi* consists of cuts of the finest raw fish and seafood garnished with crisp shavings of *daikon* (a long, white radish) and dipped into soy sauce and the hot, green, creamy Japanese horseradish called *wasabi*.

Seawater fish, freshly caught and chilled, but not frozen, are prepared for *sushi* and *sashimi*. Freshwater fish are rarely served because of the danger of parasites. Frozen fish may also be used, but they lose some of their flavor in defrosting.

In *sashimi,* various cuts are utilized, each relevant to the texture of a particular fish. Fragile-fleshed fish are cut in rectangles the size of dominos; firm-fleshed fish, such as halibut or bass, are cut in thin, almost translucent, slices; a threadlike ribbon cut is used for the more densely textured flesh, such as that of squid. The thicker slices are generally served with regular soy sauce. A more delicately flavored citrus-accented soy sauce is served with the thinner cuts.

Bluefin or yellowfin tuna *(maguro)* are the fish most readily available in Western *sushi* bars and are used for both *sashimi* and *sushi*. Tuna is recognizable by the deep red hue of the flesh. The highly prized portion of the bluefin tuna is the delicate and soft underbelly, *(toro),* which has no fishy flavor and tastes of rich butter—an unbelievable experience. Albacore *(shiro)* is a soft-fleshed fish, making it difficult to handle. It is well worth trying, although you may need to request it specially.

Other fish and seafood commonly used for *sashimi* and *sushi* and largely available in Japan and the West are imported young yellowtail *(hamachi),* bonito or skipjack tuna *(katsuo),* mackerel *(saba),* salmon *(sake),* halibut *(hirame),* sea bass *(suzuki),* porgy and red snapper (both called *tai*), marine eel *(anago),* freshwater eel *(unagi),* squid *(ika)* and octopus *(tako),* horseneck clams or geoduck *(mirugai)* and abalone *(awabi).*

There are some excellent books on the market that deal with both *sashimi* and *sushi* at length, including *Japanese Cooking, A Simple Art,* by Shizuo Tsuji, and published by Kodansha International Limited, and *Sushi,* by Mia Detrick, published by Chronicle Books of the Headland Press.

The three main soybean products—*miso, tofu* and *shoyu*—are the second-largest source of protein for the Japanese. *Miso* is a savory paste made from fermented soybeans and, in its many varieties, provides a distinctive flavor to hundreds of dishes. It is used in soups, as a marinade ingredient, as a topping to savory snacks and in a wide range of sautéed dishes. *Tofu,* otherwise known as bean curd, is a white, custardlike curd made from soybean milk. It can be incorporated in dishes either in its original state or pressed and compacted to extract more moisture. The firmer bean curd can then be deep-fried to a crisp golden brown and used in many stir-fried dishes. The Japanese sauté, broil, scramble and fry *tofu,* as well as using it to garnish soups. A richer source of protein than most meats, bean curd is rapidly becoming a meat substitute in the diets of poorer nations and has been adopted widely by vegetarians. *Shoyu* (soy sauce), an extract of soybeans, wheat, barley, salt, malt and water, is used to flavor Japanese food, as well as the dishes of most of the other nations of Asia.

In addition to fish and soybeans, seaweed is commonly eaten by the Japanese—as a wrapper for fish and other foods, as a garnish and in a variety of snack foods, including the tiny, crisp cocktail rice crackers. Six edible types of seaweed are harvested off the coasts of Japan. The two principal ones are *nori* (laver), which is rich in vitamins A, D and B12, and *kombu* (kelp), a vital ingredient in the Japanese soup stock called *dashi,* and a source of vitamin C and iodine.

The main starch in the Japanese diet is rice, but wheat noodles *(udon),* and buckwheat noodles *(soba),* are also liked, not only in soups but also hot or cold with a variety of accompaniments and dressings.

Besides soy sauce, other flavoring agents—used sparingly to preserve the distinct character of the main ingredients—give Japanese food its individualistic quality. These include the Japanese sweet rice wine called *mirin,* the more potent *sake* (another rice wine, which is familiar to Westerners who eat in Japanese restaurants) and sesame oil. Ginger, both pickled and raw, members of the onion family and dried mushrooms are all frequently used, as are the condiments familiar to the Western table such as salt, pepper, sugar and mustard.

The easiest way to grasp the wide range of Japanese food is to take a brief overview of the styles of preparation. All foods fall into orderly categories. In each category, substitutes are freely made. A fried dish that uses beef can be cooked with chicken, fish or vegetables alone without losing its essential character.

Timing is the most important factor in Japanese cooking. Foods are cooked to the exact point of perfection—not a second more or less. The Japanese, like other Asians, rarely bake or roast, so most cooking takes place on the stove or range top. As in Chinese cuisine, the ingredients are cut into small pieces and are fried, broiled, steamed, boiled or grilled.

Dashi and *owanrui* are stocks and soups. *Dashi,* a stock made from dried bonito shavings, called *katsuobushi,* and *kombu,* or kelp, is the foundation of all soups and many sauced dishes. It can be considered the Japanese equivalent of chicken or beef stock. Japanese soups fall into three categories, similar to those of China: thin, clear soup, generally served at the start of a meal; a thicker soup, often flavored with *miso,* which is eaten toward the end of a meal; and a substantial soup with various solid ingredients. Closer to a stew, the last variety of soup is generally eaten as a meal by itself.

Aemono and *sunomono* correspond to salad courses in a Western meal.

Aemono actually means "mixed ingredients." Foods such as vegetables, fish and poultry are cut into fine pieces and served raw or (in the case of the last) lightly cooked, tossed in a sauce or dressing. *Sunomono* refers to ingredients which are vinegared. These can be fish or vegetables. Again, these correspond roughly to our small salads.

Sushi and *sashimi,* as we have already seen, are dishes that primarily incorporate raw fish. It is considered impolite to serve *sashimi* in odd numbered groups and the varieties of fish slices are generally served in pairs.

Gohan means a meal or cooked rice and refers to a wide range of rice dishes as well as plain, steamed rice. The Japanese have also adopted the Chinese custom of serving a bowl of plain rice at the end of a long dinner to ensure that the guests have had enough to eat.

Menrui refers to the other starch in Japanese meals—noodles. In the hot summers of the south of Japan, noodles are served iced to refresh and cool the palate of the diner.

Yakimono is the term for broiled *(grilled)* foods. The Japanese use the same techniques that we do, the variations being in the combinations of ingredients and in the marinades. Among those that are relatively well known are *teriyaki* dishes (in which the ingredients are first marinated in soy sauce and *mirin,* the sweet rice wine), *yakitori* (marinated, skewered chicken), *shioyaki* (in which the fish is rubbed with salt to seal in the fat under the skin before broiling, producing a wonderfully moist texture) and *teppan-yaki* (food cooked on a tabletop grill in front of the diner). *Teppan-yaki* restaurants are now opening up in the West, as this style of cooking appeals to Occidentals.

Agemono is the term for deep-fried foods and includes batter-coated foods or *tempura.* The lightness of the batter, for which the Japanese are famed, is produced by the inclusion of baking soda and ice-cold water.

Nimono and *nabemono* are foods simmered or boiled in flavored liquids, and one-pot dishes. The former are often served in small amounts as side dishes. *Nabemono,* the latter category, includes the famous *Sukiyaki,* a mixture of beef and vegetables sautéed and then simmered in soy sauce, sugar and *sake,* and *Shabu Shabu,* in which meat and an assortment of vegetables are individually cooked in broth by the diners and then dipped into sauce. This dish probably originated in Mongolia as it is similar to the Mongolian hot pot.

Mushimono refers to steamed foods and includes delicate, savory egg custards as well as steamed shrimp and chicken. *Bento* are picnic or snack foods, generally artistically arranged in modular lunch boxes *(obento).* *Zensai* are hors d'oeuvres or appetizers. Many of the recipes can be interchanged, but the best way to differentiate between the two groups of "little things" is to understand that *bento* are served at room temperature as rather elegant picnic foods and are neither sauced nor dressed, while *zensai* are often served hot, with or without a dressing, to start off a meal.

The Japanese, like most other Asians, do not serve in courses but set all the dishes on the table at the start of the meal. It is useful to plan a Japanese menu around a main course and then add side dishes. If you are serving a large dinner, the dishes can be brought out two at a time. The food is mostly served at room temperature, which makes advance preparation very easy. Exceptions to this, of course, are some of the *yaki* dishes and *tempura.* Featuring these as the star attraction will dictate that you make up the rest of the menu with cold arrangements that are prepared ahead of time.

Sake or tea are the usual beverages that accompany a meal. *Sake* is the brewed rice wine which is heated and served warm. It is served from small porcelain carafes and drunk not in a glass but in a little decorative china cup. Green tea, *nihon-cha,* is the tea drunk daily in Japan, before, after and during any meal. It is different from black tea in that the young leaves are picked green and are not processed any further. This is not the tea drunk at the famous Tea Ceremony. That classic ritual demands special leaves and has even dictated a whole category of food called *kaiseki* which accompanies the ceremony.

The Japanese select their tableware very carefully. The dishes may be round or rectangular and are made of pottery, porcelain or decorated lacquer. The food to be served dictates the size, shape and material of a dish, tray or platter, and, like everything else to do with Japanese food, a great deal of thought is given to the finished appearance. Food is eaten with chopsticks. Japanese chopsticks differ from the Chinese chopsticks in that they have slender, tapered ends rather than square. They are generally made of lacquer and are beautifully decorated with flowers or other designs from nature.

The table will be graced with a perfectly balanced flower arrangement, hinting at the season during which the food is being served. Less is more. One carefully trimmed branch will set off an exquisite single blossom at its base. The container will also have been chosen to complement the arrangement in size, shape, color and material.

Finally, the food arrangement and presentation are all-important. Again, less is more. One delicately carved radish flower sets off a simple arrangement of two pieces of shrimp. Dishes are garnished with a single chrysanthemum leaf or a spray of pine needles—the season or message dictates the garnish. Study all the pictures of Japanese food that you can, watch the artistic arrangements in Japanese restaurants and then have a lot of fun experimenting in your own home.

MENUS

For four:

(1) Smoked Fish Sushi
   Chicken Soup
   Turnip Chrysanthemum and Carrot
     Salad
   Quick Teriyaki Chicken
   Plain Rice

(2) Spinach Soup with Eggs
   Barbecued Meats
   Ginger Sauce for Grilled Meats
   Cabbage Pickle
   Plain Rice

For six to eight:

   Cooked Shrimp Sushi
   Omelet Sushi
   Beef and Vegetable Fondue

   Dipping Sauce for Meat Fondue
   Variation Number One
   Plain Rice

KOREA

Korea, about which most of us know very little, except as the scene of a bitter war in modern times and the background for the popular television series "M*A*S*H*," is a country with a long history, a rich culture, an ancient court and an elaborate system of etiquette. As for Korean food, it is hearty, boldly flavored, delicious and extremely nutritious.

It is hard to talk of the country as a whole without referring to political divisions, but the land does, in fact, divide fairly clearly into two regions. To the north, it is a land of high mountains, pine, fir, spruce and cedar forests, and deep valleys. While the earth of the high plateaus is rather thin and poor, the rich soil of the western river plains supports a wide variety of crops including rice, maize, millet, barley, wheat. Vegetables such as soybeans and sweet potatoes are prolific and there are large fruit orchards. Even in the north, although the winter temperature plunges to somewhere between −8°F. and 21°F., in the summer the thermometer will rise to the mid-seventies.

Korea is still subject to the monsoon-influenced climate of the rest of Asia and the monsoon winds bring heavy rains in the summer, while the winters are relatively dry. The south of the country, which juts out into the ocean equidistant between Honshu, Japan, and the Shantung peninsula of China, divides the waters into the Yellow Sea to the west and the Sea of Japan to the east. The southern summers are long and humid with temperatures somewhere in the high seventies or eighties.

The Koreans like to say that they are descended from a single, ancient race, and, indeed, they are primarily Mongolian, slightly more stocky than the northern Chinese, but taller than the Japanese. Around the time of Christ, there were three kingdoms in ancient Korea, Koguryo to the north, Paekche and Silla in the south. These kingdoms were culturally advanced and boasted royal courts, nobility, class systems and centralized governments. It was around this time also that Buddhism was introduced to the area, becoming the preserve of royalty, while Confucianism flourished among the minor aristocracy. With the aid of the Chinese, Silla conquered first Paekche and then Koguryo and established a unified country with elaborate palaces, imposing monuments, temples, tombs, an advanced civil service and five provincial capitals.

In the tenth century the Koryo dynasty was founded, lasting until 1392, and accepting and coexisting with the Mongols, whose invasion the Koreans at first withstood. Despite emnity with China, who regarded Korea as a threat to its northern borders, and, later, hostility from Japan, the Koreans maintained autonomy, establishing one of the longest dynasties in history, the Yi dynasty, with a succession of twenty-six kings.

During the seventeenth and eighteenth centuries, Korea made great strides into the future. Social, cultural and agricultural changes occurred in every sector. New systems of irrigation and farming techniques brought new crops, such as rice, ginseng and tobacco, and the farmers and merchants became wealthy. A middle class developed and culture became the property and right of the commoner as well as the nobility.

The Europeans also began to arrive in the mid-seventeenth century, bringing with them Catholicism; it was incompatible with Confucianism, and Catholics became subject to systematic persecution during the early nineteenth century, as the religion became widespread. The Koreans tried to preserve their autonomy, repulsing both friendly and hostile overtures by the Westerners and the Japanese. But finally, in 1876, the Japanese concluded a trade treaty with Korea, to the alarm of the Chinese. Gradually, treaties were signed with the United States and the European powers, and Korea opened its gates to foreign influence. However, as the Yi dynasty grew more feeble, the Japanese ascendancy grew stronger. The Russo-Japanese war created an excuse for the Japanese to use much of Korea as an operating base against the Russians. It was the thin end of the wedge. In 1910, Japan annexed Korea, ruling over the country until the end of World War II.

Essential to the formation of a distinctive cuisine are the structure of a social system, to provide special occasions for the development of special foods; a long and prosperous court life (or the equivalent), to evolve refinements in the cuisine; and the establishment of a solid religion, to provide rituals and occasions for festivals and feasts. Korea has had all these. Its cuisine developed into two distinct types of cooking: the home cooking of the common people, developed within the traditional family and as the province of the housewife, and the complex and elegant cuisine of the royal courts, using a wider variety of seasonings and spices, more intricate cooking methods and elegant presentation of food.

Throughout Korea, the main meal of the day is still breakfast, which evolved to fortify the men before a hard day's work. Lunch, even in the royal courts, was, and still is, a light meal: noodles or rice, mixed with red beans, nuts and seeds for protein. Dinner in the courts and homes of the wealthy families was an elaborate affair of nine to twelve dishes accompanying a central bowl of rice. Every day, dinner in the home usually consists of between three and seven dishes, depending on the size of the family. Special occasions, such as the celebration of a wedding or a sixty-first birthday (any birthday after sixty is considered as a victory over death), or a birth or memorial anniversary, will all have their appropriate foods and table arrangements.

Koreans have always believed that good health is maintained by sensible eating and a good nutritional balance. They also follow the Oriental rule of Five Flavors: salt, sweet, sour, hot, bitter. Salt, soy sauce and salty bean paste provide the first; beet sugar, honey and sweet potatoes are used to sweeten food; chilli peppers and mustard provide heat; vinegars are used as souring agents, and ginger is regarded as a bitter flavor. In addition to the Five Flavors, the Koreans also try to follow an arrangement of five traditional colors: red, green, yellow, white, black. The last does not easily occur in nature, but such foodstuffs as dried cloud-ear mushrooms provide a semblance. Seaweed is not widely used in the cuisine, as it is in Japan.

The predominant elements characteristic of the cuisine are garlic, green *(spring)* onions, sesame seeds (toasted and used whole or ground), ginger, dried red chilli peppers. Ground cinnamon, hot mustard and black pepper are also included. Meats and other foods are often marinated in mixtures of green onions, sesame seeds and oil, vinegar and soy sauce before being cooked. Dips and combinations of condiments for sauces, such as hot bean paste, vinegar and soy accompany such dishes as barbecued or broiled *(grilled)* meats, deep-fried vegetables, etc. Dishes are often garnished with eggs, cooked into a thin omelet and then rolled, before being sliced into strips.

Beef is the most commonly used meat, in soups, barbecues and hot pots. Variety meats, such as tongue, heart, liver and tripe, are also included in many dishes such as soups and stews. *Kim-chee,* or pickled vegetables, accompany most meals. These pickles compensate for the scarcity of fresh vegetables during the long winters, but summer pickles are also popular.

Korean meals are eaten from bowls. Rice and soup demand spoons. Chopsticks are used only to take portions from the serving dishes. The meals are presented on dinner trays, rather in the manner of the Indians or the Thai. Small trays are used for one or two people; a large, round tray, called a *Kae-ryang Sang,* is used for a crowd. A compartmented lacquer dish is proper for such dishes as the Beef and Vegetable Rolls, with many components. Firepots, the bronze or brass utensils with a bowl surrounding a central chimney that houses charcoal to cook the food or keep it warm, are used for special dishes and for some soups. The Mongolian barbecue, where various ingredients are diced into small pieces and then stir-fried on a convex iron griddle shaped rather like a Mongolian helmet, is rather a hybrid and, because of its association with an ancient enemy, is not a common item in Korea, although many Korean restaurants outside the country do feature it.

MENUS

For four:

(1) Stir-Fried Chicken Breasts with
    Vegetables
    Barbecued Beef Short Ribs
    Dipping Sauce II
    Cabbage Pickle
    Plain Rice

(2) Pear Salad
    Beef and Egg Savory Custards
    Roast Pork
    Dipping Sauce II
    Plain Rice

For six to eight:

(1) Chicken Soup
    Beef and Vegetable Rolls
    Whole Steamed Fish in Vegetable
    Sauce
    Cabbage Pickle
    Rice Pudding with Fruit, Nuts and
    Honey

(2) Hot and Sour Soup
    Beef and Vegetable Fondue
    Dipping Sauce I
    Pear Salad
    Cabbage Pickle
    Plain Rice

MALAYSIA AND SINGAPORE

Malaysia is white sand beaches, rain forests and rugged mountains; cool, highland plateaus, which look curiously British, with temperate climate, English cottages, and log fires in the timber-beamed fireplaces, European gardens and impenetrable, steamy jungles where tigers stalk and sluggish rivers wind past the wooden stilts of the longhouses of headhunting tribes.

Malaysia is orderly rows of rubber trees and glamorous hilltop gambling casinos; quiet, sleepy towns, stamped with their colonial ancestry, and gleaming spires and domes of Islamic mosques.

The entire area is ethnically and culturally mixed and the cuisines reflect this. There are three separate and different geographic and political entities: the familiar shape of the peninsula of Malaya (known as West Malaysia), stretching southward from the mainland of Southeast Asia; the states of Sarawak and Sabah (known as East Malaysia), perched on the northwest corner of the enormous island of Borneo, shared with Indonesia; and the island city/pocket republic of Singapore, poised between the southern tip of Malaya and the equator. The peoples of the area are Malays, Chinese and a mixture of Indian, Dyak, Arab and other minorities, with the Malay strain concentrated on Borneo and in areas of the peninsula.

Back in the mists of history, Malaya and Indonesia were one: parts of the kingdom of Srivijaya, and their culture and customs intermingled because the peoples traded and traveled freely between the land masses of Malaya, Sumatra and Java. To this day the ethnic Malay cuisine is very close to that of Indonesia, and many of the dishes bear the same names. Satay belongs as much to Malaysia as it does to Indonesia; so do a variety of curried dishes.

After the time of Srivijaya, the Malay peninsula came under the influence of a Hindu-Javanese empire, and the remnants of that culture are still to be found in many Malay customs. In the fifteenth century, Malacca, overlooking the strategic straits between Sumatra and Malaya, became a powerful state, and it embraced Islam. As in Indonesia, this gradually became the dominant religion of the people, affecting the culture, customs and, of course, the style of food for most of Malaya. Today it is the official religion of Malaysia and the source of many festivals throughout the year.

For two hundred years after the establishment of Malacca, the key area of the southern tip of Malaya and the Straits became a hotbed of piracy, local wars between petty rulers and a base for European adventurers and traders, all seeking their fortunes in spices. The Portuguese conquered Malacca, losing it in turn to the Dutch. Finally, the British, who had established small settlements on the peninsula, gained control over the area and separated the Malayan peninsula from Dutch-held Indonesia.

Tin and rubber became cornerstones of the new, prospering, colonial country, and in the nineteenth century tin mining became a magnet for large influxes of Chinese immigrants. At one point certain districts of Malaya held more Chinese than Malays. These Chinese were laborers, single men who arrived without families, and many of them took Malay wives. They became known as Straits Chinese and their womenfolk, bringing their own native cuisine to the kitchen, developed a blend of Malay and Chinese dishes which, to this day, is referred to as *Nonya* cooking.

The rubber plantations, on the other hand, attracted Indian labor, mostly Tamils from southern India and from Ceylon. Indian civil servants, well trained by the British Raj in India, also arrived in numbers and settled in to administrate under the somewhat benevolent British colonialists.

The pre-World War II patterns for Malaya became set. The British colonialists led easy and luxurious lives, immortalized by Somerset Maugham. The sultans, protected by the British, did virtually nothing and yet amassed large fortunes. The hardworking Chinese also became prosperous. The Indians, the eternal middlemen, settled and traded and supplied services to the many different communities. The life of the easygoing Malays remained essentially unchanged, rooted in the villages, but with very little share of the new-found prosperity. No ethnic community mingled with any other.

The war fractured these patterns irrevocably. Tens of thousands of British, Chinese and Indians were imprisoned, massacred or made to work as slave labor on the infamous "Death Railway," the ambitious Japanese transportation project designed to link Malaya with Thailand and Burma, and provide the pipeline for material with which to invade India.

After the war, the two major racial groups, Chinese and Malay, were completely at odds. With the threatened withdrawal of the British presence, the Malays became aware that the threads of financial power would be securely in the hands of the upstart intruders, the Chinese. In addition, Chinese guerrilla fighters, trained in insurgency by the British during the war, had now become Communist-influenced, and they turned their skills against their former leaders, instituting a reign of terrorism throughout Malaya. That was finally quelled but, worn out by jungle fighting, tired of the balancing act between the races, and impoverished by the heavy load of a major war, the British finally withdrew their presence, and in 1963 present-day Malaysia was born, with the two Malay states of Sarawak and Sabah as a counterweight against the heavy Chinese population.

Singapore, while sharing some of the history of the peninsula, has its own colorful origins. Stamford Raffles, an ambitious young merchant of the British East India Company, founded a small trading post on the island in 1819. His vision was of a prosperous staging port for the ships of the world on the heavily traveled China run, and he turned his talents and energies toward the realization of his dream. As the port became steadily more affluent, it attracted immigrants from China and India, who, together with the native Malays and some Javanese laborers, became ancestors of today's teeming and prosperous millions. The British controlled Singapore until World War II, losing it to the

Japanese with its mirror island, Hong Kong. After the war, Singapore and Hong Kong again came under British control, but unlike Hong Kong, Singapore remained only briefly under the British. A young, Cambridge-educated Chinese, Lee Kuan Yew, returning to Singapore from Europe in 1950, determined that the island should be free from foreign influence. In 1959, he came into power, and he worked steadily to clean up the city, literally and politically. Even the ejection of the island from the Federation of Malaysia did not halt the progress of Singapore, and its prosperity is still increasing.

Today, in the "roads," the waterways that stretch as far as the eye can see, ships from every country unload and load merchandise and tourists. Oil refineries mar some of the beauty of the satellite islets. High-rise luxury hotels stretch all the way along Orchard Road from the city center out to the garden suburbs. Singapore is the cleanest, most orderly and modern city in Asia and an international center of banking and finance. It is also a fascinating culinary melting pot of cuisines.

Apart from the history of Malaysia and Singapore, other factors contribute to the development of their cuisines, mainly the warm, balmy monsoon climate and the varied terrains of the area. Tropical fruits and vegetables are plentiful; the seas are rich in fish, including mullet, snapper, tuna, king and Pacific mackerel, a variety of pike, perch and a close relative of whiting. Coconuts grow everywhere. Imported spices and exotic foodstuffs arrive daily on the many ships, and all kinds of livestock are raised for food.

It seems that everything goes in threes: three geographic areas; three factors that contribute to the development of the food—history, climate and terrain; and, finally, three major cuisines that are characteristic of Malaysia and Singapore: Malay, Straits Chinese or *Nonya,* and Indian (mainly southern Indian or Tamil). All three cuisines coexist separately, as did the original communities that developed them. In Singapore and in the major cities of Malaysia you can walk into street markets and find food stalls side by side serving specialities from each cuisine.

During the short time that I lived in Singapore, I would often take my sons down to the Orchard Road Car Park, opposite the Cold Storage Department Store, for a meal. The name Cold Storage is an odd one for a department store—it derives from the original storage facilities for food there—and a car park sounds like a bizarre location for eating. But the fantastic is often normal in the East. In the daytime, the car park functions normally for shoppers at the store and for surrounding offices. As dusk takes over, the cars leave the car park and the vendors arrive. Hawkers set up stalls; cooks light stoves and the junior helpers string electric lights. By nightfall, the car park is transformed into one large eating emporium. Rickety chairs and rusted, metal tables accommodate diners. You pick the food and cuisine you desire and sit at a nearby table. The children of the vendors take your order and bring you bowls or dishes of food. And what delicious fare! Charcoal-barbecued fish basted with coconut milk and chilli peppers, onions and garlic; Chinese noodles, enlivened with bits of pork, shrimp and a variety of vegetables; pockets of Indian whole-wheat bread crammed with curried meats or vegetables; Chinese omelets, stuffed with chopped oysters and piquant with sauce; crisp, deep-fried egg rolls, accompanied by little saucers of tangy-sweet dipping sauce. The menu is dictated only by your appetite and your pocketbook, and the former can be sated without seriously depleting the latter. Sadly, I hear a report that the market has now been banished from its location in the interests of modernization or zoning or whatever it is that devours local color in the name of progress. However, there are still similar markets in Singapore that will satisfy your appetite and cater to your desires.

Although this smorgasbord of food is a wonderful introduction to the local cuisines, it can be very confusing. Each cuisine should really be appreciated separately. The finest and most authentic Indian food that I have eaten outside India was not in the glossy Indian restaurants, but in the little, open-fronted food shops of the Indian area. And although I ate heartily and well in some of the large Chinese restaurants (one that I remember, had a full-fledged band and evening-gowned singers at lunchtime!), I had a memorable Chinese meal in the upstairs room of a little restaurant fronting on the infamous Bugis Street, very late one night.

Set the table with chopsticks if you are serving a meal of Chinese origins; otherwise, have spoons and forks for your guests. For six or eight guests, you would present between four to six dishes, together with rice, bringing the dishes to the table at the same time. Soup is generally served along with the meal and is sipped to clear the palate between different dishes.

Malay food lends itself well to picnics and barbecues. A barbecue of satays and spareribs might be accompanied by a peanut-dressed salad. Finger foods, such as curry puffs or spring rolls, could start the meal. Experiment with serving local style—lettuce or cabbage leaves for plates and finger bowls for rinsing after eating with your hands.

MENUS

For two:

Pork and Shrimp Rice Noodles in Broth
Curried Deep-Fried Crab
Plain Rice
Southeast Asian Sweet and Hot Chilli Sauce

For four:

(1) Spiced Chicken Soup
   Straits Chinese Cooked, Mixed
      Vegetables in Thick Dressing
   Whole Steamed Fish in Chilli Sauce
   Pickled Ginger
   Plain Rice

(2) Straits Chinese Chicken Packets
   Pork Curry
   Fried Noodles
   Plain Rice

Malaysian Barbecue Party (For eight to ten):

   Curry Puffs
   Straits Chinese Spring Rolls
   Mixed Vegetable and Seafood Salad
      (*See* Indonesia)
   Thick Coconut Salad Dressing

   Fried Noodles (Singapore)
   Barbecued Spareribs
   Pork Satay
   Southeast Asian Peanut Sauce for
   Satay

THE PHILIPPINES

The 7,000 islands of the Philippines stretch in a direct line south of Taiwan to just east of Borneo (Kalimantan). At once the most Westernized and Christian of all the Asian countries, the Philippines are indelibly marked by 400 years of Spanish domination, followed by half a century of rather more benign American occupation. The majority of the fragmented small islands are sandwiched between the northern land mass of Luzon Island and the counter-weight of Mindanao in the south. This geographic balance is echoed in the religious division of Spanish-implanted Catholicism, centered in Luzon, and Malay Islam, introduced by Arab traders to the south around the second half of the fifteenth century.

Discovered in 1521 by Ferdinand Magellan, who called them San Lázaro, the Islands got their permanent name twenty-one years later, when Ruy López de Villalobos named them in honor of Prince Philip, heir to the Spanish throne of Emperor Charles V.

The Spanish were delighted with the mild climate, fertile volcanic soil and white sand beaches of their new possession and fired with a zeal to covert the friendly peoples to Catholicism. However, they were less than enchanted when they discovered that their conquered territories possessed neither silver nor gold nor any indigenous spices whatsoever. To compensate, the Spanish transformed Manila into a trading capital between the Latin Americas, Spain and China, Japan, Siam (Thailand), Cambodia and the Spice Islands.

At the same time, as rice production improved on Luzon, it attracted large numbers of Chinese immigrants, drawn to the Philippines by tales brought back to China by the traders. Intermarriage with the Filipinos produced descendants of mixed Chinese-Malay ancestry. By 1793, an enterprising Spanish governor had augmented the rice crop by introducing cinnamon, sugar, pepper, tea and coffee. These crops flourished, together with cotton, silk, hemp and tobacco.

By the latter half of the nineteenth century, a prosperous middle class of Filipinos, many with mixed Chinese or Spanish blood, had established itself, leavening the imbalance of Spanish overlords and peasant workers. It was this class that gave weight and impetus to the eventual struggle for Philippine independence—a struggle that was further exacerbated by the Muslim Moro rebels in the south. Although the ruling Spanish were also bedeviled by the Dutch, who fought to reduce Spanish influence in the area and extend their territory of the Spice Islands, the Spanish held the Islands until 1898, when the Philippines was surrendered to the United States as part of a larger settlement after the wars.

American control lasted until 1946, broken only by the Japanese occupation in 1942. When it ended, a nation was created out of Asians stamped with Latin culture, customs and religious structure—educated first by the Catholic church, then by the school systems of the United States, and drawing from the civilizations of the Old World and the New.

These varied influences manifest themselves in the cuisine of the Philippines. The wealth of seafood around the islands is indicated by innumerable fish dishes. The warm climate and tropical vegetation encourages the use of coconut milk, tamarind and garlic as well as the tropical fruits and vegetables.

The Malay origins and geographic closeness to Southeast Asia are evident in the use of Southeast Asian fish sauce *(patis)*, the fish or shrimp paste, called *bagoong*, the dried fish favored by the peasants, and the custom of eating with the hands. The Chinese influence shows itself in the rice and noodle dishes and the ubiquitous egg roll (called *lumpia* in the Philippines).

The Spanish contributed many dishes: the sautéing of foods in lard and in olive oil (a definite break in Asian cooking practices); the Iberian *paella;* mixed stews of beef, chicken and vegetables called *pucheros;* and a browned whole chicken stuffed with eggs, sausage and pork, called chicken *relleno*— the last, a cousin to our roasted, stuffed birds. From the Spanish colonialists also came the custom of *merienda,* an afternoon tea break that ends the siesta. This provides a welcome opportunity to feature a whole range of snacks, cakes and sweet pastries, many of which are direct descendants of their Spanish forebears. This Filipino predilection for sweets also shows itself in the custom of desserts to end meals. One food where the stamp of the Spanish is unmistakable is cheese made from *caribao,* or buffalo, milk. The use of chocolate in the Philippines is a direct legacy of the Spanish galleon trade with Mexico.

The American influence, relatively recent, is apparent in the moving forward of the evening meal from the late Spanish hours; in the availability of supermarkets and fast food chains; and in the consumption of Coca-Cola. But these facets of Americana manifest themselves throughout most of Asia and are products of modernization and economic domination rather than political conquest.

The dishes of Manila and most of Luzon reflect the Spanish heritage, being substantial and somewhat bland, with few spices. In the Muslim and tropical south, pork is not eaten and the spicing is closer to the Indonesian, including the use of hot peppers.

Rounding out the culinary picture are the adoption of the traditional whole roasted pig of the Pacific, the raw fish, marinated in lime juice and coconut milk, and the use of souring agents such as lemon juice and vinegar, all of which are a common heritage with parts of Polynesia, Micronesia and Melanesia.

This souring is evident in dishes such as *sinigang,* a dish of fish or beef with an assortment of vegetables, soured with tamarind, salted with fish sauce and garnished with tomatoes, beans or slices of *calamansi,* a small Philippine lemon. It is also triumphantly apparent in the dish which typifies the cuisine of the Philippines to me: *adobo.* Chicken, beef or pork are marinated in palm vinegar, lots of garlic and spices before being simmered in the marinade, together with soy sauce. When the liquid is considerably reduced, the meat is removed and fried to a rich brown. It is then served with the remaining liquid, which forms a concentrated, flavorful sauce.

Another dish that typifies Philippine cooking is *kari-karing.* This stewlike dish is colored with annato seeds *(achuete, achiote)* to a bright orange and flavored with peanuts. The meat may be calf's leg, oxtail or tripe and the stew is thickened with onions and garlic. It is a delicious country dish, and I have found a counterpart in Guam, where the Philippine influence is strong because of geographic proximity.

To sum up: Philippine food is typified by the use of sour flavors, such as lemon and vinegar; by salty tastes, produced by fish sauce and shrimp paste; by the use of garlic and onions; by the predilection for sweets, pastries and desserts, and for the medleys of several meats and vegetables together in dishes. Of all the cuisines of Asia, it is the hybrid that comes closest to the Western palate and taste and is therefore an excellent introduction to Oriental food. It is generally served in Western style and in Western meal form, and requires no fundamental changes in kitchen equipment for its preparation.

MENUS

For four:

(1) Hearty Chicken Soup
    Mixed Vegetable and Seafood Salad
    Deep-Fried Stuffed Crab
    Southeast Asian Sweet and Hot
       Chilli Sauce

(2) Stuffed Squid
    Braised Beef with Vegetables
    Coconut and Cheese Cakes

For a Philippine fiesta party:

Fried Meat Turnovers
Whole Boned Stuffed Chicken
Whole Steamed Fish with Tomato
   and Green Pepper Sauce
Chicken and Pineapple Adobo

Braised Stuffed Rolled Steak
Egg Noodles with Meats and
   Vegetables
Rice (try coloring it with annato
   seed liquid)

THAILAND

The food of Thailand is unique among the cuisines of Southeast Asia. It has an intrinsic blend of ingredients and an unmistakable bouquet of flavors that proclaim its identity far more clearly than that of neighboring cuisines. This is partly due to the geographic location of the country, right in the center of Southeast Asia, and partly due to the fact that Thailand, unlike the other countries of the region—Burma, Kampuchea (Cambodia), Laos, Vietnam, Malaysia and Indonesia—has never been colonized.

The genesis and the principal culinary influence on the food of Thailand is Chinese, and this shows in the cooking techniques. Thai food is stir-fried, steamed, or grilled over charcoal. The wok dominates the kitchen, and the cooking is done on the top of the stove.

The culture of India has also affected Thai food, manifesting itself in the spice pastes used to make curries and similar stewed dishes. However, the Thai cuisine has neither the cornstarch thickenings and complicated sauces of the Chinese nor the use of dairy products and the heaviness and richness of Indian food. It is a totally identifiable cuisine in its own right, largely due to the ability of the Thai to absorb outside influences and transform them into something uniquely their own.

The cuisine was born in the mountainous valleys of southwestern China, which was the original homeland of the T'ai tribes. Between the sixth and thirteenth centuries they emigrated southward into the land that is now Thailand. The cuisine they brought with them was nourished and augmented by the wealth of tropical plants, game, fish, herbs and spices that awaited them at the end of their long migration. It then reached a pinnacle of perfection in the palace kitchens of the Thai kings, whose devotion to good living equaled that of the European monarchs in the seventeenth and eighteenth centuries.

The Thai, while fighting for their existence as a nation with the Mon (Burmese) to the west and north and the Khmers (Cambodians) to the east, founded two successive kingdoms: Sukhothai, in the center of northern Thailand, and the kingdom of Ayuthia, which was established a short distance north of the present-day capital of Bangkok. During the early 1500s, Ayuthia was a prosperous city of over one million inhabitants—a size which surpassed London under Henry VIII during the same period.

The Thai cuisine, which had begun to blossom and establish itself during the benevolent reign of the kings of Sukothai, now developed a sophisticated and elegant tradition of cooking, nurtured by the wealth of the royal court and the talents of the palace cooks. This tradition was enhanced by the Muslim and Arab influences—traders and officials who flocked to the river ports and courts of the flourishing kingdom.

After the rape and destruction of Ayuthia by the Burmese in 1767, the Thai fled south and established a new capital at Dhonburi, across the Chao Phya River from present-day Bangkok. The general Chakri, who finally drove the Burmese back out of the country, became Rama I, the founder of the present royal dynasty. He rebuilt a fine capital city in the mold of Ayuthia, calling it Krung Thep, the Thai name for Bangkok. The city and nation (then named Siam) flourished. Despite the rapacious overtures of the Europeans and marauding attacks of the now powerful Vietnamese, the Thai managed to keep both their sovereignty and culture intact.

As their culture refined and developed, so did their cuisine. The original, somewhat spartan diet of short-grain rice, freshwater fish, vegetables and occasional meat and game of the inland empire of Sukhothai was now augmented by the wealth of seafood from the fecund Gulf of Siam, and the more tropical vegetables and fruits of the fertile south. Long-grain rice was grown and sugar cane cultivated by fresh waves of Chinese immigrants. The indigenous spices of black pepper, garlic and the various edible gingers were supplemented by coriander and cumin, brought by the traders from the Middle East and India, and hot chilli peppers, introduced by the Portuguese.

The kings of the Chakri dynasty were devoted to good food. One monarch reputedly held cooking contests among the ladies of the palace. Another, an excellent cook himself, devised new dishes as a pastime. During such a period of prosperity, the cuisine of the nobility filtered down through the classes of

Bangkok society, although today there are special forms of regional and rural cooking that bear no resemblance to those of the court.

There is historical reference to a palace feast in honor of King Rama I in the early nineteenth century at which an Indian curry was served. It is thought that the Muslim harbor officials of the port of Bangkok either brought it to the court or instructed the palace cooks in the art of its preparation. This dish survives to the present day in two forms, both as Thai curry: *gaeng Mussaman,* a curry containing aromatic spices such as cinnamon and nutmeg (spices not otherwise favored by the Thai), and *gaeng karee,* a yellow-sauced curry of either chicken or beef. The latter dish is tinted with turmeric and often contains cumin, ground coriander seeds and dried, ground red chillies—spices that are found in Indian curries.

A bewildered but much traveled gourmet, when pressed by friends to describe Thai food, says that it has the quality and consistency of Chinese food, the spiciness of Mexican, the lusciousness of Polynesian and the exact flavors of none of the above.

The distinguishing feature of Thai food is the predominance of six ingredients: fresh coriander, chillies, coconut, garlic, fish sauce and flavoring, and citrus flavorings, which are derived from lemon grass, lime rind and citrus leaves. Another earmark of the cuisine is the Thai skill in combining flavors, which stems from the Chinese discipline of the Five Flavors: sweet, sour, salt, bitter, hot. This balance is noticeable in the Thai sweet-sour-hot soups; in snacks, which can be at once both sweet and savory; and in their partiality to both palm sugar and salt in desserts and fruit drinks.

The Thai have a fondness for coriander (also called Chinese parsley or cilantro). They use the leaves and stems to flavor and garnish food, and incorporate the roots and seeds in spice pastes.

Prior to the introduction of chilli peppers to Thailand, black peppercorns were used to provide a more modified tingling heat to dishes. This fiery quality is a hallmark of the cuisine, although amounts of heat vary from dish to dish; some are almost unspiced. The Thai chilli peppers correspond closely to the Mexican varieties and, indeed, the Mexican Serrano chile is now being grown and marketed in Thailand.

The use of the coconut and its milk in cooking is a feature that the Thai have in common with other Southeast Asian and Pacific countries. The milk is extracted by pulverizing the flesh of the coconut, steeping it in water and then squeezing out the liquid. Coconut milk has the quality of blending together and mellowing the flavors of the dishes in which it is used. Used as the liquid medium in meat and fish curries, it offsets the pungency of many of the stronger ingredients.

Garlic is used in enormous quantities in Thai food. Almost no savory dish is prepared without the initial frying of many cloves of garlic, or without a spice paste in which they are a principal ingredient. However, when fried slowly until it becomes a buttery yellow, garlic mellows and loses much of its pungency. The inclusion of a bouquet of herbs and spices into the dish further reduces the pervasive flavor of the garlic.

Fish sauce, or *nam pla,* as it is called in Thai, is used in the same way that the Chinese and Japanese use soy sauce. However, it blends far more comfortably into stir-fried dishes and stews than the latter and mingles happily with both fish and meat. Despite its name, and the fact that it is extracted from dried fish, it has no noticeably fishy flavor. Fish sauce also provides large amounts of protein and B vitamins.

The last dominant feature of the cuisine is a wonderful, tangy and perfumed citrus flavor provided by the rind and leaves of limes and by lemon grass, the fibrous root stem of a grasslike plant.

In addition to the "big six" above, three edible varieties of ginger are used to flavor Thai food. One is the ginger that we are familiar with; the other two are local varieties indigenous to Thailand with a somewhat similar taste. A small red onion, something like a shallot, is also minced and fried, along with the garlic. Mint and several varieties of basil provide fresh green accents.

Thailand is now regarded as the rice bowl of Asia, and the average Thai will consume almost a pound of rice a day. The rice most favored is the long-grain variety, although in the northeast the short-grain glutinous rice, which the T'ai tribes brought with them from China, is still cultivated and eaten. A normal Thai meal revolves around a central dish of rice, and rice is the constant background to the intricate combinations of meats, vegetables and hot and cold dishes. It dilutes the fiery qualities of curries and soups and acts as an extender to the small portions of highly flavored stir-fried dishes.

Breakfast is usually a bowl of rice soup—a chicken or pork-flavored broth with rice and seasonings such as crisp-fried garlic, a sprinkling of dried red-pepper flakes, a dash of fish sauce and an optional pinch of crumbled peanuts. The Thai eat little at a time and often. During the morning, vendors parade the streets offering delicacies such as green mango served in thin slices with a dusting of sugar, salt and pepper flakes, or roasted chickens hanging in a glass case on their carts, from which slices of meat are served, together with a small spoonful of spicy sauce.

Midday brings the noodle vendors. Noodle soup in all its various forms is the universal lunch. Rice, wheat and egg noodles are widely eaten throughout Thailand, either stir-fried with combinations of meats and vegetables, or in an endless variety of soups. All these are one-meal dishes, and noodles are seldom included in formal dinners.

The main meal of the day is eaten in the evening when the heat of the day abates and work in the fields or factories is over. Thai food is brought to the table as soon as it is cooked, and there is no particular order or structure of courses, but a meal is planned carefully so that textures, flavors and foods balance each other. A crisp salad, or *yam,* will cool the palate after a hot beef curry. A stir-fried dish of chicken nuggets with ginger and mint will be balanced by a creamy corn soup. Bland steamed cucumbers stuffed with ground pork may be followed by a dish of crisp-fried catfish with a sharp sauce. A meal will generally finish with a bowl of fresh fruit. Desserts are seldom eaten except at a formal banquet, although sweets and sweet cakes are purchased ready-made in the markets for snacks.

Spoons and forks are the order of the day. The Thai do not use chopsticks unless they are dining in a Chinese restaurant. Small hand towels wrung out in perfumed water and chilled are brought at the conclusion of a meal to wipe the hands and faces of the diners.

The two principal cooking methods in Thailand are stir-frying and steaming. Thai food is long on preparation but short on cooking time. Like Chinese cuisine, the food is chopped and cut into small pieces in advance and knives are not used at the table. When the food is all prepared and set out in orderly piles, the actual cooking is a matter of mere minutes. Food can be prepared in advance and many dishes made ahead of time. Thai food is generally served at room temperature, and there are few dishes in the cuisine that must be cooked at the last minute.

Like the Japanese, the Thai place great emphasis on presentation. Fruit and vegetable carving is an art in Thailand and manifests itself in beautifully fashioned garnishes. Scarlet chillies become lilies, onions blossom into chrysanthemums, and cucumber skin is carved into leaves to be cooked in, and to ornament, soups. Some salads are presented as a bouquet of flowers: each blossom is a carved vegetable. The finished masterpiece is dismantled by the diners, who then dip the fresh vegetables into a rich and spicy sauce. Ginger and root vegetables are carved into flowers, fishes and birds and butterflies. During the early years that I spent in Thailand, I found a small shop in the section of Bangkok near the Pramane Ground and the Temple of the Emerald Buddha where jars of finely carved, pickled ginger, looking like an emperor's ransom of precious, pink jade, were sold. The edible cameos testified to such superb craftsmanship that it was a real wrench to eat them; somewhat akin to defiling or defacing a work of art in a museum. Unfortunately, the little store has since closed and such exquisite carving is becoming rare, although the dedication to patient and time-consuming food sculpture remains. The edible fantasy shows the Thai love of beauty and the joy with which they celebrate life and food.

MENUS

For four:

(1) Stuffed Baby Squid in Soup
    Garlic Pork
    Meatball Curry
    Plain Rice

(2) Mixed Vegetable and Seafood Salad
    Thin Salad Dressing
    Pork and Egg Savory Custards
    Whole Spiced Chicken in Coconut
      Milk
    Plain Rice

A light Thai lunch for four:

    Pork and Shrimp Rice Noodles in
      Broth
    Spicy Stir-Fried Chicken with
      Peanuts

    Curried Crab Cakes
    Sweet and Sour Fresh Cucumber
      Salad

A dinner for eight:

    Hot and Sour Seafood Soup
    Crispy Noodle Chicken Salad
    Muslim Beef Curry
    Crisp-Fried Catfish
    Chilli and Garlic Fish Sauce

    Pickled Ginger
    Thai Pork Curry, Country Style
    Plain Rice
    Coconut Bananas in Batter

VIETNAM

Few Americans who were in Vietnam during the war had the time, opportunity or desire to sample the Vietnamese culture and food, and indeed, the acquaintance of most Americans with the Vietnamese cuisine was limited to a bowl of *pho,* or beef-and-rice-noodle soup to go *(takeaway).* It is a great pity, because the cuisine of Vietnam is delicate, complex and sophisticated, combining the techniques of Chinese cooking with the indigenous ingredients, the light accents of French finesse and, in the south, some of the herbs and spices of India.

Wrapping itself around the east side of the Southeast Asian mainland, Vietnam is a little longer than California and has a land area of approximately the same size as Malaysia. Starting inland of the Red River delta area and running right down the length of the country to just above the Mekong River delta is a chain of mountains that forms a natural barrier between Vietnam and Laos and Cambodia to the west. Culturally and geographically, the country divides into three areas: the fertile Red River delta to the north; the long, mountainous and rather barren highlands; and the lush Mekong River delta to the south. This tripartite division has also applied to the regional cuisines, with Hanoi, Hue and Saigon (Ho Chi Minh City) being the culinary capitals.

This same division, for so long considered political, is, in fact, historical. The Vietnamese are believed to have originated around the Red River delta, although ethnically they are racially kin to the ancient Mons and Khmers, being a mixture of Melanesian, Indonesian, Negrito and T'ai. They were known to the Chinese as *Lo-yueh* and they established a strong local culture long before their conquest by China, in 208 B.C., when this area was incorporated into the kingdom of Nam Viet (Nan Yueh in Chinese). It is from this that the Vietnamese people obtained their name. This kingdom lasted for almost one hundred years until it was conquered, in turn, by the Chinese in 111 B.C. This conquest started one thousand years of Chinese rule and domination over Vietnam.

Before and during this period the southern portion of, what is now present-day Vietnam had come under Indian influence. This was not by martial domination but by the burgeoning Indian trade with China. Traders, merchants, seafarers and priests had traditionally put in at stopping places along the southern Vietnamese coast during their long voyages from India, through Indonesia, to China. Gradually the villages became small towns which were Indianized in culture and religion. The peoples of the extreme south, around the Mekong delta, were absorbed into an Indianized state called Funan, founded in the first century A.D., which stretched into much of present-day Cambodia. During a period of weakness in Chinese colonial rule, a second state in the south, called Champa, was founded in 192 A.D. This state extended from north of the Mekong delta to the 18th parallel. Funan was eventually conquered, in the sixth century A.D. by Mon-Khmers from the northwest, and it became part of the Khmer (or Cambodian) Empire. Champa, however, became strong and existed as a neighbor of Vietnam after its eventual independence from China.

Thus the area of present-day Vietnam was already divided into the three regions: Nam Viet in the north, Champa in the center and Funan in the south.

The Chinese domination of Vietnam lasted until 939 A.D., when the decline of the T'ang dynasty helped the Vietnamese to throw off the colonial yoke. The Vietnamese retained the cooking techniques and eating methods of the Chinese. (They still eat with chopsticks—the only Southeast Asian nation to do so.)

At the time of Vietnamese independence, the Chinese cultural characteristics only applied to the people of the north, Nam Viet. The people of the center, the fierce Chams, were mountain people, and lacking agricultural land

and river deltas they became pirates, attacking trading ships for their subsistence and waging war on their neighbors and even on China.

During the Le dynasty in the 1600s, the Chams were eventually conquered. Finally, Saigon was wrested from the weakened Khmers in the last years of the same century. Vietnam reached its present size by 1757. During and after this period, Vietnam was already divided into north and south, but was finally reunited under Gia Long in 1802.

Following the pattern of the rest of Asia, the Westerners started to establish spheres of influence in Vietnam, starting as early as 1516, when the Portuguese arrived in the country. Later, French Catholic missionary centers were established and the French, while making rather unsuccessful attempts to found a trading empire because of the anti-Western stance of the Vietnamese rulers, finally became convinced that they needed a base for colonial expansion and determined to set it up in Vietnam by martial means. After eight years of war, the French became masters of Cochinchina (their name for the south of Vietnam). At this time, the West referred to the north of Vietnam as Tongking. The center was known as Annam. By 1883, Vietnam was a French protectorate, a state that lasted until after World War II.

Although periodically decimated by periods of war, the wildlife remained abundant. The forests supported tigers, elephants, wild boar, oxen and deer, as well as a variety of wildfowl. Domesticated animals included buffalo, goats, pigs, ducks and chickens. Coconut palms, jackfruit, mango, orange, lime and rubber trees, as well as coffee bushes, were cultivated. The paddy fields of the south were so prolific that the country was known as the "Rice Bowl of Asia." All kinds of fruits, including melons, and such vegetables and herbs as ginger, sesame, peanuts, mint and basil, were plentiful. The Chinese and French influences ensured that the finest and freshest of the livestock, game and produce were incorporated in the cuisine.

During the period that I lived in Vietnam, although the country was ravaged by war, nonetheless I was immensely impressed by the Vietnamese capacity to improvise a superb meal from very little: a capacity they share with, and may have inherited from, the Chinese. Some of the finest food that I have enjoyed in Southeast Asia I have eaten in Vietnam. Their finely tuned use of gentle seasonings, their aptitude for balancing crisp, raw vegetables and aromatic herbs with meats, fish and soups, contribute to a cuisine appealing to the senses and subtle in its refinement. The large, pearly sheets of translucent Vietnamese rice paper, when softened, wrapped around a simple blend of filling ingredients and then deep-fried, make spring rolls which are feather light and, to my taste, infinitely superior to those of China.

The influence of China is seen in the Vietnamese stir-fried dishes, although the local vegetables and spicings make them subtly different from those of the country of their origin. The use of fish sauce (which, in Vietnam, is known as *nuoc mam*) produces a lighter accent in simmered dishes and soups than the soy sauce of China. The Vietnamese habit of wrapping meats and snack mixtures in lettuce leaves and including fresh herbs in the little bundles is a vestige of the original civilizations that existed before the centuries of Chinese influence.

The cuisine of the northern part of Vietnam more accurately resembles that of China. Black pepper is used for spicing, as well as ginger. Stir-fried dishes are prevalent. Reflecting the climatic conditions, there is not the great variety of foods that one finds in the south.

In the center of the country, the cuisine is more refined. Spicier dishes are in evidence and the use of chilli peppers (introduced by the Portuguese) is widespread. Thick, fermented fish sauce is incorporated in dishes as a seasoning, and game from the highlands is often included in the meals of the more affluent.

To the south, the cuisine is varied. Traces of Indian and French influence are seen in the Vietnamese curries, in the inclusion of potatoes and asparagus, and in the Vietnamese talent for making exquisite pâtés from both meat and fish. Sugar cane is grown and is used in both sweet and savory snacks. One of the latter is a delicious combination of shrimp and pork paste which is molded around lengths of sugar cane, before being baked or fried.

One of our delights in Saigon was to visit a Bo Bai Mon restaurant. These eating places specialize in the dinner of beef, prepared in seven different ways. Dishes come in courses, including a soup of rich broth, in which the beef from an earlier course has been cooked. We always ended up the meal with *flan,* the creamy, caramelized baked custard which is a legacy of European domination in Asia.

One such festive meal was chosen by my younger son to celebrate his fourth birthday. I had bought him a French sailor suit for his birthday, oblivious to the fact that he apparently disliked it intensely. We arrived at the Bo Bai Mon restaurant after a monsoon shower of rain and took a table under an awning in the earth-floored courtyard. My son fidgeted through four or five courses after his appetite was satisfied and finally asked if he could walk about. I agreed to his request, stipulating that he should not bother the other diners but stay close to the table. My concentration on the deliciously flavored beef in front of me was broken by gasps from Vietnamese diners surrounding us. I looked up in time to see my small son take a running jump into the middle of an enormous and very muddy puddle at the front entrance, whereupon he sat down with a splash and a beautific grin spread over his face. The blue-and-white sailor suit was totally obscured with brown mud. As it was his birthday, there was no punishment. My chocolate-colored, dripping son sat next to me and consumed quantities of flan while the Vietnamese women brought towels and, clucking in consternation, dabbed ineffectively at his suit and the young Vietnamese men stood by and grinned broadly.

Another delight of Vietnam was the legacy of excellent coffee and crusty French bread and croissants, which the Vietnamese of the south enjoyed as much as the French. The many coffee houses of what was then Saigon were crammed with Vietnamese enjoying a *petit dejeuner,* reading newspapers and arguing about politics in Gallic style. I also remember the delectable yogurt which was delivered to restaurants and houses in little earthenware pots. Its creamy texture and thick crust bore no resemblance to the thin curds that we buy in the supermarkets.

When setting a table for a Vietnamese meal, arrange the fresh salad greens and accompanying herbs on platters. Make a pile of dough wrappers as thin as you can, and include small bowls of dipping sauces for the guests. Do not forget to put chopsticks on the table—if your guests can handle them.

MENUS

For four:

(1) Chicken and Squash Soup
    Carrot Salad
    Roast Pork
    Dipping and Table Sauce
    Stuffed Baby Squid
    Plain Rice

(2) Vegetable and Seafood Salad
    Thin Salad Dressing
    Stir-Fried Chicken with Vinegar
    Pork and Shrimp Rice Noodles in
      Broth
    Plain Rice

Dinner for six to eight:

    Spring Rolls
    Southeast Asian Sweet and Hot Chilli Sauce
    Dipping and Table Sauce
    Whole Steamed Fish with Fennel Sauce
    Beef Stew
    Crispy Chicken Noodle Salad
    Plain Rice
    Fried Fish Toasts

BASICS

❧ ❧ ❧

Techniques, Ingredients,
and Basic Recipes

SKINNING A CHICKEN
OR A DUCK

Our Western fowls are much plumper than the skinny Oriental birds. Unfortunately a great amount of fat lies in pillows under the skins. This is principally due to the modern methods of raising the birds; they sit like fat eunuchs with no exercise except to extend their necks and gobble up their ample daily food ration.

Because so many of us are restricting the amount of animal fat we consume, it is necessary to remove this fat, either before cooking a bird, by drawing it off with a bulb baster when it has liquefied into oil, or by refrigerat-

ing the finished dish, if it is a liquid one like stew, and then scraping the
congealed fat from the top.

The most efficient way to remove the fat is to skin the bird, and this is
surprisingly simple to do. When you have removed the skin, instead of discarding it, you may want to render the fat in a slow oven until the skin is crisp,
then cut the skin into squares, sprinkle it with a little salt and serve it,
accompanied by a sweet-and-sour dipping sauce, for an appetizer.

To remove the skin you will need a pair of kitchen scissors and possibly
a sharp, thin-bladed boning knife.

1. Place the bird in front of you, breast uppermost. With your thumb
inside the neck cavity, firmly grasp the bird and, with the other hand, grip the
flap of skin at the top, breast side of the bird. With a strong, steady pull, lift
the skin from the flesh and peel it downward toward the tail end. You will find
that the skin adheres in places to the underlying flesh and bone—and this is
where you will need the kitchen scissors or the knife to snip or cut between
the skin and the flesh, releasing it.

2. As you reach the level of the wings, you will find that you can pull them
through the stretched neck opening, rather like getting a child out of a tight
sweater. Wiggle them through, elbow joint first. Don't worry if a little piece
of skin stays attached to the wing tips. You are going to chop them off later.

3. Having peeled the skin at the front down about two to three inches,
you will realize that you can go no farther until you have freed it from the back.
Turn the bird over. The skin at the back is attached firmly to the spine. This
is also where there are large cushions of fat, so you will want to remove those
as well. In the same way as you did at the front, grasp the bird firmly and begin
to pull the skin up and away from the back. At the first point that it is caught,
nick or snip it away from the spine. If you are using a blade, don't be afraid
to cut too deeply: you will merely remove more fat. Keep on pulling and
cutting or snipping until you have pulled the skin all the way down to the
thighs.

4. The legs can be pulled through the skin somewhat the way the wings
were—this time, rather like removing legs from stockings. Insert your index
finger inside the top of the "stocking," underneath the leg, and push it down
and around the underside. There is a small amount of fat there, but by keeping
your finger close to the flesh, you can hook it right underneath. Now insert
your thumb in the top and push it around the top of the thigh until your thumb
and finger virtually encircle the leg. Grip the leg firmly, and with the other
hand, lift and peel the skin downward toward the end of the leg. It will pull
inside out, just like a stocking, and, as there is no foot, it can be drawn right
off the end. Repeat with the other leg.

SKINNING A CHICKEN

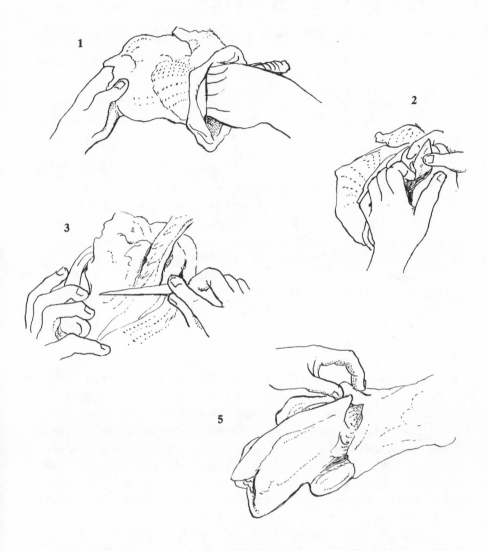

5. Now pull the skin off the remaining few inches of the carcass. The skin will break and remain on the tail, but you can either chop off the tail later or leave it, skin and all.

6. When you have completely skinned the fowl, you will have a very naked and comical-looking bird in front of you. You will also see that it looks considerably thinner. Use your scissors or knife to cut away any remaining pieces of yellow fat and discard these. The bird is now ready to be cut into pieces for stir-fried dishes, stews or curries.

BONING A WHOLE CHICKEN
FOR STUFFING

The idea of this technique is to remove the bones from the chicken, leaving the skin and flesh intact, so that it may be stuffed and coaxed back into shape, presenting a wholly edible chicken. This technique is used for such dishes as Philippine Boned Stuffed Chicken.

1. Remove the pockets of fat on either side of the tail opening. Remove the two sacs on either side of the neck opening, if they have not already been removed. Pull the neck open and locate the wishbone. Use your thumb and finger to pinch either side of it so that you can see how it lies, then, using a sharp boning knife, carefully cut it free and discard it.

2. Using the point of the knife, locate the joints where the wings are attached to the main carcass (the shoulders) and cut the tendons, then nick at the joints until you have severed them through.

3. Find the keel bone or breastbone of the chicken (the central, sharp ridge on the breast side) and, sitting the chicken up on end, insert the knife under the skin and scrape downward to detach the breast flesh from the bone. You may also do this quite well by digging in your thumbnails and prying the flesh away from the bone. Do not attempt to pry the flesh and skin away from the central ridge at this time, but work either side of it. When you have pushed away most of the flesh, carefully insert the point of the knife under the skin, between the breast ridge and the skin and, with a series of tiny nicks, carefully separate the skin along the ridge. By stretching the skin carefully, you should be able to work halfway down the chicken and free the carcass to that point. (After that, you must work on the back so that the skin does not tear with too much stretching.)

4. Turn the chicken around and begin to work on the back in the same manner. By studying the bird and pulling at the skin, you will discover that it is attached at intervals to the bone and separated in places by a very thin layer of compacted fat. With the knife blade parallel to the chicken, slide it under the skin and gently nick the back skin loose. As you pull back the skin, the carcass will gradually come into view. Work on the front and back alternately, until you have the skin completely detached to just about halfway down the bird. When you reach the rather sharp, elongated shoulder blades, lying along the back, carefully pull them up from under the skin and then break

BONING A CHICKEN

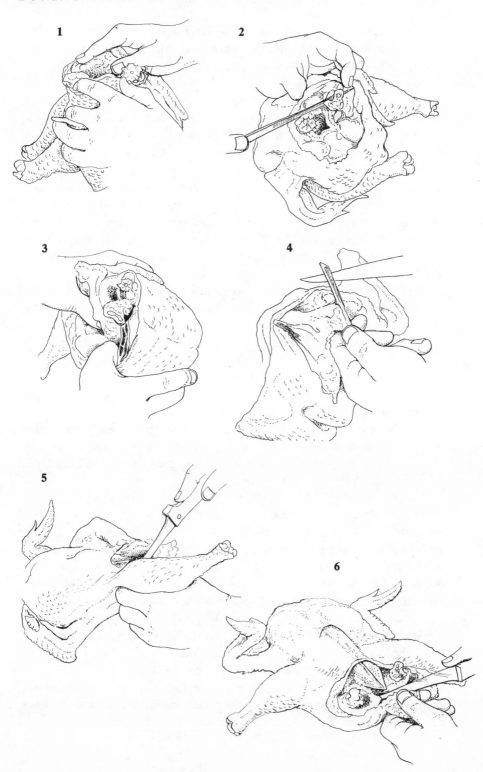

them off. (If they are left attached to the carcass, they may pierce the skin.)

5. Hold the bird and, with the other hand, wiggle the leg joints so you can feel where and how they are attached at the hip. (The hip joints are surprisingly high up along the back of the chicken.) Insert your hand down the chicken, between the skin and the carcass, and feel for the configuration of the joint. You will find a large cushion of thigh flesh which is somewhat in the way, and you may have to cut the tendon which attaches it to the joint before you proceed further. Insert a finger and feel for a tendon, then slide the knife down to the same point and sever the tendon. You are working blind, so take care not to cut the skin nor your fingers. Every now and again, take your hand out and move the leg joint backward and forward to aid you in locating all the tendons. When you think that you have it nearly freed, grasp the leg joint firmly around the thigh and move it sharply against its normal motion, which will dislocate the joint. It can now be completely severed from the body carcass. Repeat with the other leg.

6. The carcass is now shorn of wings and legs and attached only toward the tail end. Working alternatively from the tail opening and the neck opening, continue to pry and scrape the flesh away from the remainder of the carcass. When you get to the tail, study it to see how it is attached and then cut it through the vertebrae so that it remains attached to the skin on either side and not to the carcass. Try to do this with the point of the knife to minimize the size of the hole which you will leave in the skin at the tail end. Sever the tendons on either side of it.

7. Check the entire length and circumference of the carcass to ensure that it is not attached at any point to the flesh and skin, then carefully pull it up through the neck opening. You will now have a rather shapeless body form, with the wings and legs still attached.

8. Now grasp a thigh and, pulling open the neck aperture with your other hand, push the hip end of the thigh up into the interior of the chicken. When the end is visible, work with the knife point, severing the tendons where the flesh is attached and snipping off any large pieces of tendon. Push the meat down the thigh toward the top of the drumstick, corresponding to a knee joint. When the joint becomes visible, cut the tendons and then sever the thigh bone from the drumstick. Pull out the thigh bone and discard it.

9. Continue with the drumstick, pushing and scraping the flesh down, at the same time pulling the bone up and into the cavity of the bird. When you reach the end of the drumstick, pull it up and into the cavity of the bird, pulling the skin inside out and over the end of the bone. If it does not completely come free, but remains over the end (like a glove peeled back over a hand but not completely off), cut it evenly, close to the drumstick end. Repeat with the other leg and then push them back, right side out.

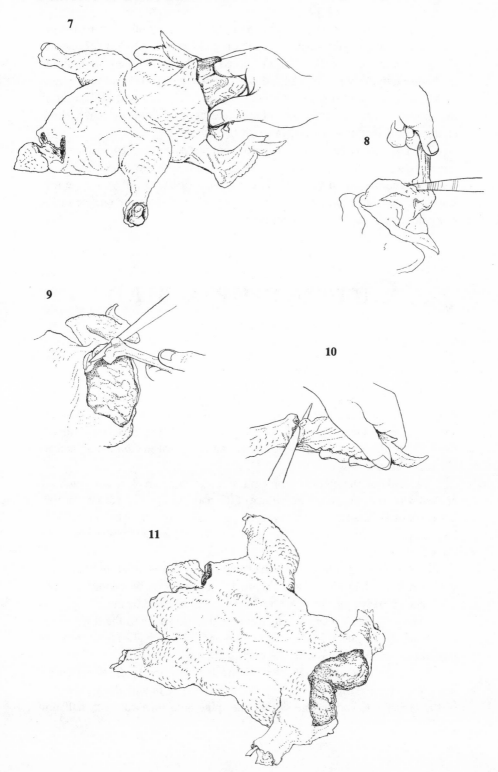

10. Now turn your attention to the wings. First, cut off the wing tip and the first joint and use for stock. You will only have the upper "arm" bone left. Using the same method that you have used for the legs, force it up and into the body cavity. Peel the flesh back down and, when you have reached the end, pull it inside out and through the wing aperture. The skin will peel easily off the end. Now turn the little tube of skin and flesh, which is all that remains of the wing, right side out, repeat with the other wing.

11. You now have a rather shapeless, but undeniably boned, chicken. Use the carcass and discarded bones for stock. Do not stuff the chicken until just before you are ready to cook it; there is danger of bacteria if you leave it in a stuffed, uncooked state for too long. Stuff according to the cuisine of the relevant country and accept compliments.

CUTTING UP A BIRD, BONE IN

As well as being more flavorful, a bird cooked with the bone in is a more economical dish than one with the carcass discarded. The Asians, who are frugal and economical in their kitchens, generally eat their fowls bone in. The exception to this is the use of boned breast and leg meat in Chinese-influenced stir-fried dishes.

Throughout the countries of Asia, birds such as chicken and duck are cooked whole or in parts about the size of the packaged parts on our supermarket trays or in bite-sized or curry-sized pieces, all bone in. The skin may be left on as many Asians do, or removed, together with any fat, before chopping up a bird.

It is more elegant to remove the backbone; it can be used for soup. You will then have eight pieces (two thighs, two drumsticks, two wings and two half-breasts). However, if you wish to copy the Asians and be more frugal you will include the back portion, which will add more flavor to the dish. If you are chopping the pieces further, you could end up with eight pieces from the legs alone—useful if you wish the dish to feed a large number of people.

There are several schools of thought on disjointing birds. Some cooks, after removing the thighs and wings, split the chicken in half along the center of the breastbone and to one side of the spine, and then cut each half into

CUTTING UP A BIRD

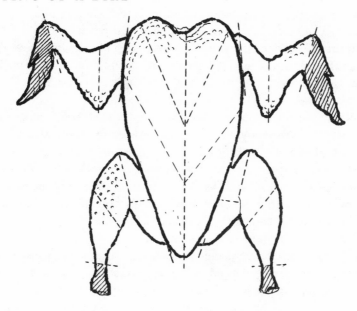

Cutting Legs

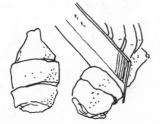

smaller pieces. Others prefer to split the carcass into two pieces, breast portion and back portion, before proceeding further. I really do not think it matters which way you tackle it as long as the job is neatly done.

To cut a bird bone in, you will need either a long, heavy and very sharp chef's knife or a heavy, sharp meat cleaver and a boning knife or pair of kitchen scissors.

1. Place the chicken before you, breast uppermost. Bend one of the legs down, away from the body, until the skin between the two is stretched taut. Nick the skin with the blade or scissors and continue to cut a slit, parallel to the body so that the leg is released to lie down flat on the table. Repeat with the other leg. Now, bend each leg backward until the end of the thigh bone pops upward and becomes visible. Cut carefully around the thigh joint and, finally, between the bones at the joint, and the leg will cut loose. Remove the other leg in a similar fashion.

2. Cut the skin between the thigh and the drumstick. When the joint connecting them is exposed, bend the leg back and forth until you have located the exact position of the joint. Cut between the bones and through the flesh and skin, so that the leg separates into thigh and drumstick. Now take the large, heavy knife or cleaver and chop off the bulbous bone end of the drumstick. Discard it or save it for soup. When you have dealt with both legs, you will now have four pieces cut off. If you want to cut to bite-sized pieces, you must now use the knife or cleaver and further chop each section in half again.

2. Now turn your attention to the wings. Locate the shoulder joint, where the wing is attached to the body, and make an incision in the skin in the same manner as for the legs. Expose the joint and cut each wing from the body. Cut off the wing tips and reserve them for soup stock. If you want smaller pieces, cut each wing in two at the joint, following the instructions for the legs. If you merely want chicken parts, then allow one whole wing as a part.

3. Stand the chicken carcass up on its neck. If you study it, you will see that the front, or breast portion, is attached to the back only by the ribs. Follow the rib line and cut right through in a curve between the breast and the back, leaving the flesh on the breast side. Repeat on the other side and, with the hands, pull the front section away from the back.

4. Lay the breast, outer side down, on the table and cut it in half lengthwise with the large knife or cleaver. If you wish the pieces to be smaller, chop each half-portion of breast into three, cutting across the breast.

5. Chop the back portion into three pieces or into five or six pieces, if you wish smaller sections. Pull out any bone fragments that are loose and discard them.

How to clean squid

Most recipes for this mollusk (yes, it is), start off, "First, clean your squid," but they seldom tell you how to proceed. I once read an amusing article by a writer who complained that cookbook experts assumed that you knew what the terms for the various parts meant, airily referring to: the "pen" and the "mantle" and the "ink." He wrote that his mental pictures were completely different from theirs, in that he immediately thought of writing equipment and articles of clothing. So let us take a look at the creature as you would, when you have bought some and are standing at the sink gazing at one with awe—and some repugnance.

A squid looks like a slippery rubber bag with a bundle of tentacles and a pair of eyes protruding from it. The bag is the body mantle, or covering, and, together with the tentacles, is the edible part. The top of the mantle has two fins sticking out in either direction. (This is one way to tell squid and cuttlefish from octopus. The first two have fins but the octopus doesn't.) The bag or mantle is speckled. This coloration is only skin-deep, and when the skin, or thin membrane, is peeled off, the mantle underneath is nice and clean and unmarked.

The squid is very much a two-part creature—the mantle portion and the head and tentacles portion and the two detach from each other quite easily. Now look at the head. The squid has ten tentacles: eight long ones and two short—again, unlike the octopus, which only has eight. Crowded near the tentacles are the eyes, and the bulge behind those is the head, which contains a central nervous system. All this is attached to the innards, which are a delicate mass of wispy matter tucked away inside the mantle. One other thing about the head—very close to the eyes is where the ink sac is located. This is literally a bag of an inklike fluid, which the squid shoots out into the water like a liquid smokescreen, when it feels threatened. In many Mediterranean countries the squid is cooked in a sauce, to which the "ink" is added to color and flavor it.

There is one other portion of the squid to note and that is the "pen." If you look again at the creature, you will notice that in the middle of the back the rim of the mantle comes to a peak, rather like a widow's peak. This is where the top of the pen is located. It is a long, transparent sheath—the vestige of a shell, which sometime in the evolutionary process the creature once had. All that is left is this long blade of chitin (the same substance from which your fingernails are made).

Having examined the squid, you are now going to separate it and clean it—a very quick and easy process.

1. Grasp the squid gently but firmly with both hands. One hand should encircle and hold the body, the other should hold the head, with the thumb and first finger encircling it behind the eyes and bulge of the ink sac and brain, as close to the body opening as you can get. When you have it securely, pull the body away from the head. The head will detach, complete with a trail of innards. Lay it down on one side and concentrate on the mantle.

2. First, pull off that thin, speckled skin—it peels off quite easily—and discard it. Now run your fingers around the edge of the mantle and, at that peak, you can feel the tip of the pen. It lies inside the mantle, flat and parallel to it, down the body. The tip is attached at that point and you can detach it by using your thumb and fingernail to nip it at the mantle point. When you have detached it, hold the hard point and pull it out from the mantle. It is an amazingly beautiful and delicate object—a long, completely transparent feather shape. (I have always thought that one might make Christmas ornaments from these, but I am not sure how.) Discard the pen.

3. Turn on the cold-water tap and hold the baglike mantle under the stream. It will fill up with water and you can use your fingers to scrape around inside to detach any remaining pieces of innards. This can be done without using running water from the tap, but I find that the tap water washes away any lingering squeamishness I may have, together with the innards. Now rub the mantle between your fingers. It should feel like the finger of a heavy-duty rubber glove, and there should be nothing left inside. If you think that there is some matter remaining, you can carefully turn it inside-out (like the glove) and detach any remaining membranes or pieces. Turn it right side again and lay it down. If you are going to stuff the squid, this is the only part of it that you will need, and you are ready. If you are going to sauté it in small pieces, then take a knife and slit it open along the length, so that it lies flat. Now cut it into strips or diamonds or any other shapes you fancy.

4. If you intend to cook the tentacles as well, turn your attention to the head. The aim is to cut the tentacles off so that they are attached to a small ring of flesh. In this way, if you put them, tips first, into boiling liquid, they will curl up and the whole configuration will look like a curly-petaled daisy. The trick is to get enough flesh attached to them without rupturing the ink sac (a messy business, when this occurs). Lay the tentacles parallel, so that they stream away from the head and, with the knife, cut behind the tentacles and in front of the eyes, leaving as much flesh attached to the tentacles as you dare. Discard the rest of the head and innards and wash the tentacles under

running water. In the center of the ring of tentacles you will feel a knob of
rather hard material. This is part of the "beak." Using the tip of your finger,
poke it out from the center of the ring. Lay the ring of tentacles down next
to the cleaned mantle. Congratulations! You have now cleaned and prepared
your squid.

CLEANING SQUID

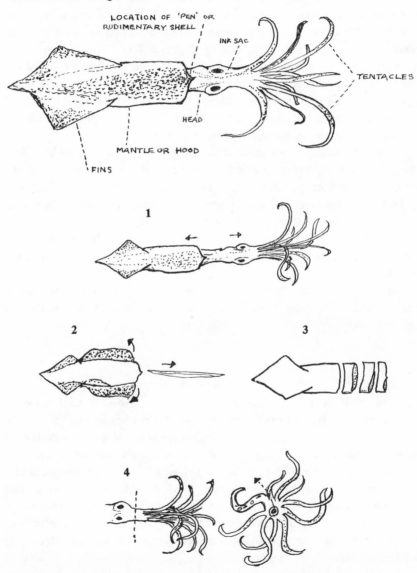

Basic cuts in food
Preparation

Throughout the book you will notice reference to "bite-sized" pieces. All over Asia, it is common practice to cut food before incorporating it in dishes, so that knives need not be used at the table. The second reason is for ease and speed in cooking, which, in turn, means economy of fuel. Vegetables and other foods are cut into small pieces, each in a way that cooks them most quickly. The sense behind this is most apparent in the technique of stir-frying, where vegetables are cut into shapes according to their texture and density and are introduced in order of cooking time, in fast succession, the whole dish is prepared in a matter of minutes—even seconds.

Cooking techniques for most of the Asian cuisines originated in China. The Chinese tendency is to cook both meat and vegetables together in one dish and at the same time, and this means that the sizes and shapes of both should be similar in appearance and should demand the same length of cooking time, and this rule applies to nearly every cuisine discussed. If a dish calls for shredded pork, whatever vegetables are included in the dish will also be cut into shreds, or at least into pieces of similar size, even though the shapes may be different.

Whether you use a cleaver or a knife, the basic cuts will still apply. Practice makes for good knife control and speed comes with practice and repetition.

THE SLICE

This is the most basic cut and is nearly always carried out by cutting across the grain of the food, whether it is vegetable, fish or meat. The reason is that cutting across the direction in which the fibers run ensures that the slice will stay intact during cooking. If an ingredient is cut along the direction of the fibers, then these will often separate during the cooking process.

There are two types of slice: the straight, which is executed perpendicular to the ingredient, and the diagonal, or slant slice, which is generally carried out at a 45-degree angle. Pieces cut on the diagonal have a larger surface than those cut on the straight. This larger surface exposes more of the interior of the food to the heat during cooking and ensures that it cooks through quickly and thoroughly.

Foods may be cut into thick or thin slices, depending on the type of

BASIC CUTS IN FOOD PREPARATION

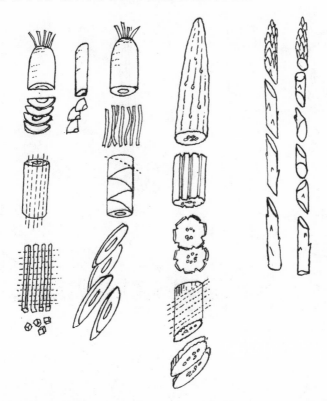

cooking they will undergo and the length of cooking time desired. The slice is also the first step toward the next cut—the shred, or sliver.

THE SHRED, OR SLIVER

This is carried out after you have executed a thin or thick slice, diagonal or straight. It is one of the most common cuts in stir-frying and is used for both meat and vegetables. If you cut a thin slice, and then cut it again along the length or width in a series of close cuts, you will have shreds, or thin slivers. If you cut the slice slightly thicker, and cut it across in exactly the same thickness, you will have what is known as julienne strips. The quickest way to execute these is to cut a series of thinnish slices and then stack them back on top of each other (like precut slices of processed cheese). You will then cut down across the whole stack, making a number of julienne strips with each slice. These are also sometimes referred to as "matchsticks." Thick slices may be cut across again to exactly the same thickness, producing rectangles. They may also be cut across thinly, producing ribbons, or long, thin slabs.

BASIC CUTS IN FOOD PREPARATION

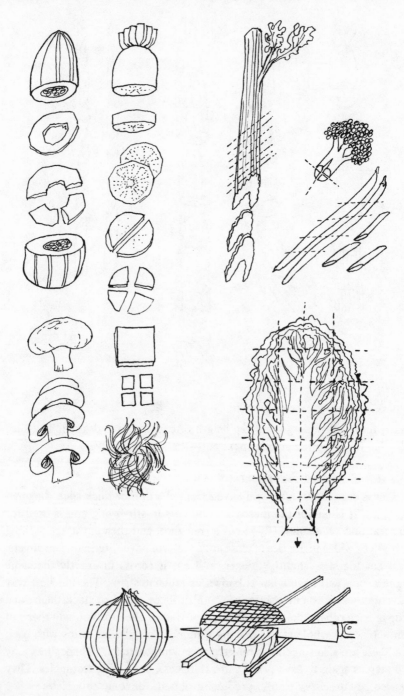

The next logical cut in this progression of making an ingredient smaller, is the dice.

THE DICE

This is carried out by stacking the shreds or strips from the previous cut into a bundle, with the ends level and equal, and then by cutting across once more at exactly the same thickness, thus producing small cubes. The size of the cubes will depend on the width of the two preceding cuts. If you have a large, dense object like a turnip, a quick way to cut it into dice is by incising it, but leaving it whole until the last cut, in the following manner: Cut the turnip in half along the "equator." Hold it by the top or the root end, exposing the flat, cut surface to the knife. Now make a series of parallel cuts, about 1 inch in depth, across the entire surface. The size of the finished dice will be dictated by the closeness of the cuts to each other. Turn the vegetable 90 degrees in the direction of the cuts, and make another series across the surface, perpendicular to and cross-hatching the first series. Now turn the vegetable with the cut surface sideways, facing you, so you are looking along it in profile and, at the depth of the cuts, cut a slice off. As the slice is cut, it will release the dice you have created. (Hopefully, you have sliced it at the exact place where the cuts finish.) In precise terminology: if the pieces you create are around ½ inch in size, then they are referred to as *cubes*. If they are approximately ¼ inch in size, then they are *dice*. Creating pieces smaller than that is referred to as *mincing*. Use this "three-cut" technique to mince onions; it seems to avoid a great deal of the eye-watering normally associated with mincing.

THE ROLL CUT

This is a variation of diagonal slicing and is employed on fibrous elongated root vegetables such as carrots, parsnips and long turnips. The aim is to expose as much of the inner surface as possible to the heat, thus cutting down the cooking time. Roll-cutting also breaks up the strings of fiber more efficiently than any other cut. It is accomplished in the following way: Hold the vegetable with one hand and make a 45-degree diagonal cut. Now rotate the vegetable a quarter turn and make another diagonal cut. Rotate another quarter turn and cut again. Continue in this manner. You will end up with a series of pieces with very odd-looking angled surfaces that expose a large percentage of their interior.

THE SEGMENT, OR WEDGE

This cut is used for medium-sized or small round vegetables, such as tomatoes and onions, and for hard-cooked eggs. Medium-sized vegetables are cut in half lengthwise. The cut half is then placed face down. Each half is then cut into 4 or 6 wedges. If the object is small, it may be stood on end (either stem or top) and cut directly into wedges or segments.

THE CYLINDER, OR ROLL

This is another cut for long vegetables and may be refined into further shapes that lend themselves to decorative cutting. Take a carrot, for instance. Make a series of parallel straight cuts crosswise down its length. Common sense dictates that where the vegetable is slender and tapered toward the tip, the cuts should be farther apart, and that they should be closer together where the root is thickest. These cuts will create cylinders or rolls, like a packet of roll candies *(roll of hard-boiled sweets)*. The edges of these cylinders may be beveled off for neatness and to ensure they do not fray during cooking.

Decorative Cuts

All these cuts involve cutting a long root vegetable into a series of cylinders, about 2 inches to 3 inches in length. The cylinder is then carved along the length into a shape which, when viewed and sliced in cross-section, creates a whole series of identical, decorative shapes. These shapes are generally simmered in clear soups, becoming at once ingredient and garnish.

FLOWER-SHAPED ROLLS

Take a long root vegetable and cut it into 3-inch cylinders. Take one of the cylinders and pare it down the length in one long cut, creating a long, flat plane. Rotate the cylinder slightly and repeat, making another plane adjoining the first. Continue around the surface until you have turned the cylindrical surface into a five-sided polygon. Now select a plane and make a V-shaped long trenchlike incision in the middle, down the length of the plane. Execute this in 2 cuts, angling the second cut to meet the first. Remove the long, sliverlike wedge and discard. Repeat the V-shaped cuts down the middle of each plane. Now, using the tip of the knife blade, round off the sharp angle where one plane joins another. Repeat until you have rounded off all the ridges. Examine the cross-section of the shape. You will see that you have created a flower shape, with the base of each petal starting from the bottom of each V, the apex of each being the ridge you have just rounded into a petal shape. Slice the cylinder into a series of flowers. These may be sliced thin or thick, depending on the length of time required to cook them.

ARROWHEADS

Cut a long, cylindrical root vegetable into 3-inch cylindrical segments.

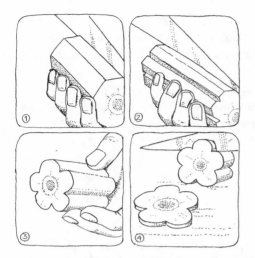

DECORATIVE CUTS

Carrot Flowers

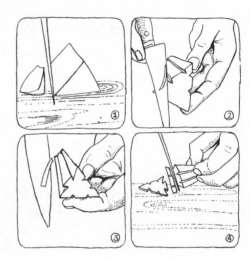

Arrow Heads

Cut each segment into a long, triangular shape by paring the sides into three planes. The triangle should have two long equidistant sides and one short one. Turn one of the wider planes toward you and cut two V-shaped trenches along the length equidistant from each other. Repeat on the other wide plane. Now turn the shape so that the narrow plane is facing you. Eyeball an imaginary center line and make two straight cuts, one at either side of the imaginary center line, but fairly close together. Now, farther out, make a long, diagonal cut, angling in to meet the first straight cut. (This still creates a V-shaped trench, but it has one straight, short side and one that is longer and at a diagonal.) Repeat with another diagonal cut, angling in toward the other straight cut, creating a second V-shaped trench. You will now have created a "stem," as you will see when you look at the cross-section of the shape. It will look rather like a rudimentary arrowhead. Slice the long shape into a series of thin arrowheads.

You will now see that by working on a cylinder lengthwise you may be able to carve a whole series of shapes which, when sliced, will turn into various decorative objects. Some shapes, such as leaves or fish, may be created by cutting the cylinder in half lengthwise before you start to carve. As you work, keep looking at the object in cross-section so that you can visualize the shape of the finished object.

FRUIT AND VEGETABLE CARVING FOR GARNISHES

The main differences between the techniques discussed in this section and those decorative cuts just discussed, are that these cutting or carving techniques create garnishes that are not cooked, but decorate the finished dish. These garnishes will be grouped under the heading of the vegetables or fruits used for their creation, rather than under the cutting techniques.

The chief requirements for creating these are a very sharp, acutely pointed knife (a razor-bladed angled knife, such as an X-acto, is fine). A well-sharpened thin-bladed pocket knife will work very well, as will wood or linoleum-block, cutting instruments. You also need a steady hand, a sharp eye, and a good deal of patience. The knife you can acquire; the rest will come with time and practice.

Tomato Garnishes

THE PEELED WEDGE

Slice off the stem end of a firm, medium-to-large tomato so that the tomato will stand up flat. (a) Cut the tomato into 8 separate wedges. Taking up one wedge, use the point of the knife to peel away the skin and a thin layer of the underlying flesh, starting from the pointed end of the segment. Peel it down to two-thirds of the way, curling it back. Repeat with all the wedges, or (b), cut the tomato into 6 wedges—these will be thicker. Carefully slide the knife point under the skin and begin to peel it back again attached to a thin, even layer of the flesh. When you have peeled it back to two-thirds of the way down, bisect the curled petal into 2 narrower petals, both attached to the same wedge. Arrange these wedges in pairs facing each other, curling petals outward, for each garnish.

THE TOMATO LOTUS FLOWER

This garnish utilizes the above technique, but takes it further. Stand a medium-sized tomato on its stem end. Do not cut off the stem slice. Using the

**FRUIT AND
VEGETABLE CARVING**

The Peeled Wedge

Tomato Lotus Flower

point of the knife, make a shallow cut, as if you were cutting the tomato in half, but do not cut it right through; stop the cut about ½ inch up from the stem. Make 2 more incisions at right angles to the first. You have now marked the fruit into quarters. You should have cut through the skin and a little of the underlying flesh, but you will not have cut all the way through, nor will you have completed the cuts all the way down to the bottom of the tomato. Still using the same fairly shallow cuts, bisect each quarter again, so that you have marked 8 segments.

Now take the point of the knife and gently and carefully insert it at the junction of the segments in the center, prying each one free. This will necessitate turning the blade of the knife under the skin, and parallel to it, and cutting back down ¼ inch toward the base of each segment. Stop the process right there. You will continue it after you have created a second petal. Study the tomato. You will see that each large segment creates a closed petal shape. About ½ inch down toward the center of a petal and directly under the apex of the point, puncture the skin with the knife point and cut a second, smaller petal within the first, paralleling the cut shape. Do not take it as far down the tomato as you did the first, larger petal. Now, go back to the center and, as you did in the previous garnish, cut and peel back both skin and a thin layer of flesh of each segment, cutting under and parallel to the surface, until you have freed a petal, complete with its inner, small petal. Continue around all the segments until you have freed all the petals. Now, with your fingers, push the inner petals in toward the center, so that they point inward and curve around the core of the tomato. At the same time, coax the larger petals to curl outward and away from the center. You will have created a formalized lotus-shaped flower.

GREEN (SPRING) ONION BRUSHES OR TASSELS

For this garnish you will need a very sharp, narrow, pointed knife. Although many people use only the white bulb end of the green/spring onion, I use both ends and make both white and green tassels or brushes. First, slice off any remains of the root at the white end of the bulb. Then cut off a 3-inch length of the white area. Trim the green ends of the onion so they are even, and then cut off the green end at least 1½ inches below where the leaves are joined to the stalk. You now have the material for a white brush, or tassel, and a green one. First work on the white. Holding the greenish stalk end in one hand, lay the section down on the table and, using the point of the knife, insert the point into the stalk, about 1 inch from where you are holding it and draw it through the layers, bisecting them lengthwise, all the way up to the white tip. Rotate the onion a quarter turn, and repeat the cut. The released slivers will spring apart into a brush shape. Now, depending on the thickness of the stalk, you may cut it further into eighths. If you find this difficult, hold the stalk upright and, inserting the knife point where the slivers start to divide, bisect any group with the knife blade uppermost, drawing it up along the length of the sliver to the top. The more you are able to repeat this, and the thinner the slivers, the more they will curl. Place the finished brush in ice water for an hour to help it curl. (Slivers that do not want to curl may be drawn between the knife blade and the thumb, in the same way that you curl ribbons.) Repeat this bisecting technique with the green end. You will find that the bases of the leaves all seem to face the same way, and you will be splitting a series of green tubes. Try to split each tube into at least 4 slivers. Again, the thinner they are, the more they will curl.

Green Onion Brushes

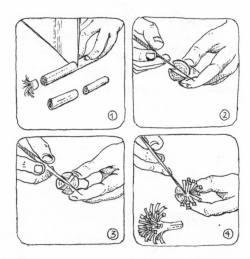

Cucumber Garnishes

FOLDED CUCUMBER GARNISH

Cut ⅓ of a cucumber lengthwise, so that you have a long slice containing mostly flesh and very little of the core and seeds. Place it cut side down. Cut the tip off, using a long diagonal cut, not a straight, right-angled one. Now, using the tip of the knife, make 7 parallel cuts or slices, on the same diagonal. Do not cut right through to the other side of the width, but stop each cut ½ inch from it. They will be all joined together at one side. The seventh cut should slice right through, so that you have detached a length of 7 thin diagonal slices, all joined together at one end. The curved top side of the slices will be dark green from the cucumber skin. The straight, underneath side will be pale green. Holding the sheaf of slices in one hand, part an end slice slightly. Take the next slice to it and bend it sideways into a loop, inserting the end back on itself and wedging it into place. Leave the next slice straight, and take the next along and, again, bend it back on itself into a loop, wedging it down into place. Proceed with alternating slices, leaving the slice at the other end straight. You will now have a small fan of alternating loops and straight slices. The thinner you manage to cut the slices, the more easily they will bend into loops. With practice, you can cut slices so thin that you may increase the number of slices to 9, 11, 13 or more, and make a more extravagant fan. The number of slices should always be odd so that you have a straight slice at either end.

STRIPED CUCUMBER FAN

Cut a diagonal section in exactly the same way as the last garnish, but do not slice it yet. First use the point of the blade to make 5 V-shaped cuts across the curved skin, running at right angles to the sliced diagonal edge. Remove the wedges of skin, revealing a dark and pale green series of stripes. Now place the segment down and, as in the last garnish, cut a series of thin parallel slices almost through to the other end. When you have completed them, take the flat of a cleaver and press down firmly on the segment, pushing it sharply sideways as you do, to fan out the slices. When you remove the cleaver, the slices should have splayed out into a striped fan.

Pepper Garnishes

CHILLI FLOWERS

For this garnish, you will need small red or yellow long chilli peppers. Hold a pepper by its stalk and cut off about ¼ inch of the tip. Using a knife or scissors, cut the long "bud" into strandlike petals, cutting them almost down to the bottom. You may wish to trim the ends into points. Make at least 8 to 10 petals to each flower. Place the flower in ice water for at least an hour, or until the petals open up. You may remove the seeds or not as you please. Some people leave them, together with the membranes, in a central core to resemble the center of a flower.

SWEET PEPPER TIGER LILIES

You may make this garnish with either red or green sweet peppers. It is even more effective when it is made with peppers that are just turning and are

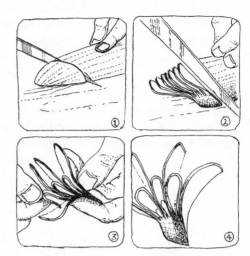

Folded Cucumber Garnish

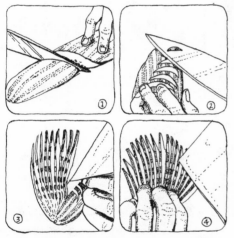

Striped Cucumber Fan

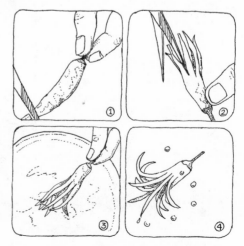

Chilli Flower

a mixture of green and orange. Hold the pepper by the stalk and study it. You will see that the flesh is divided into segments. Using the lines of the joins between the segments for a guide, cut the segments open, leaving them joined at the stem. Scoop out the seeds and carefully snip away the membranes on the inside of the flesh. Now, taking scissors, snip deep Vs in each segment, dividing it into at least 2 petals. It does not matter if the edges are irregular —it will look even more like a natural flower. The finished petals should be sharply pointed and there should be between 5 and 8 of them, depending on the formation of the original pepper. Leave it in ice water until you are ready to use it.

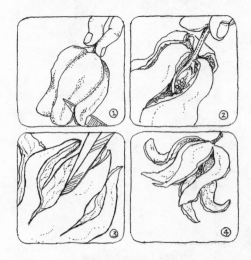

Bell Pepper Tiger Lilies

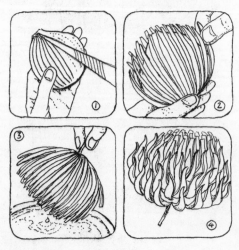

Onion Crysanthemum

ONION CHRYSANTHEMUM

Peel a large globe-shaped onion and cut off the tip end. Place the onion so that it stands on its root end and make a series of perpendicular cuts about ⅛ inch apart, all around the first layer of skin. The cuts should run from the top down to about ¼ inch from the root end. Now continue to make more cuts through the inner layers in exactly the same way. As you make more and more cuts, separating the skin into long slivers joined at the bottom, the onion will look increasingly like a white chrysanthemum. Use the long, pointed tip of the knife to reach the inmost layers and the core. Place a few drops of red or yellow food coloring in a shallow bowl or saucer. Dilute with a little water and, holding the onion upside down by the root end, dip it into the diluted coloring. The petals will immediately take on the tint. You may like to mix the colors from orange to deep red, to make the flowers more lifelike. They can be placed on a dish and garnished with coriander leaves for greenery, or you may impale each chrysanthemum on a wooden satay stick to make a bouquet for a centerpiece. Alternate with the tiger lily peppers from the previous garnish, which may also be impaled upon sticks.

OILS AND FATS

Concerning the choice of cooking oils for frying and deep-frying, there is some confusion over the terms "saturated" and "polyunsaturated." Let's take a brief look at the structure of fat in order to grasp what the terms mean.

Animal and vegetable fats are composed of glycerol molecules, each of which is joined to three molecules of fatty acids. To look further under the microscope, each fatty acid has an acid group (hydrogen, carbon and oxygen) and a long chain of carbon atoms, to which hydrogen atoms are attached. We are concerned with that long chain. Picture a carbon atom as a little ball with four hands. Two of the hands join with the carbon atoms on either side but the remaining two each hold on to a hydrogen atom. When they are linked up like this, they are in their natural state, which is called "saturated." If some of the hydrogen atoms are taken away, then the hands must join up with something. They link across with the next carbon atom that has a spare hand. Now we have an oil with less than the proper and usual amount of hydrogen atoms: this is called "polyunsaturated."

Doctors believe that saturated fats tend to increase the blood's cholesterol level and that polyunsaturated fats lower it. Animal fats are predominantly saturated and vegetable fats are mostly polyunsaturated. The thicker the fat, generally, the more saturated it is.

Here is a list of vegetable oils with the lowest degree of saturates first:

Safflower oil	Corn oil	Peanut oil	Vegetable shortening
Soybean oil	Sesame oil	Olive oil	Coconut oil

Sometimes oil is hydrogenated to make it last longer on the supermarket shelves. The hydrogenation process re-supplies the missing hydrogen atoms, and the oil then loses its capacity to lower cholesterol levels. This also occurs when oil is used repeatedly.

Below is an explanation of some of the other terms you will see on the labels.

Cold-pressed. This means that the oil is removed from the solid material by pressure only and not by the use of solvents. These oils are more nutritious than oils produced by other methods.

Refined. These oils are often processed with antioxidents, preservatives and stabilizers to purify and lighten them. Because of this, they can hold a higher temperature than virgin oils before smoking or burning, but of course they are not so healthful.

Virgin. Sometimes also called "crude" oils, these oils are not treated any further after pressing. They last longer than refined oils because the vitamin E that they retain acts as a preservative. The first pressing of olive oil is also referred to as "virgin."

Here are some additional facts about the oils and fats most commonly used in Asian cooking.

Peanut oil. The Oriental peanut oil has a stronger flavor than the Western variety. It has a high smoking point and therefore makes a good oil for deep-frying. It is widely used in Indonesia and China.

Sesame oil. This oil, which is nutritious and has a pronounced flavor, is used at the end of the cooking time to flavor dishes, or as part of a salad dressing or marinade. It is not used for frying as it is expensive to produce and has a low smoking point. The imported, Oriental varieties are stronger in flavor than health food sesame oil.

Soybean oil. Traditionally, this is the oil used in Chinese cooking for all types of frying. It is low in saturates and has a high smoking point. It also is very high in nutrition.

Coconut oil. Sometimes used in Southeast Asian and Indian cooking, it is highly saturated, as is coconut cream. However, it is believed that the large quantities of garlic (with its cholesterol-reduction properties) consumed in Southeast Asian diets tend to offset this drawback.

Vegetable shortening.   This solid fat is inexpensive, has a long shelf life and can be kept without refrigeration. Used widely throughout Asia, it is suitable for baking as well as all types of frying. However, it is highly saturated.

Clarified butter (ghee).   Used throughout India for frying and cooking, ghee is double-clarified and very pure. Because all the milk solids have been removed, it has a long shelf life and keeps without refrigeration. It also has a far higher smoking point than regular butter, which is why it can be used for frying. It gives a marvelous buttery flavor to Indian food but is rich and saturated.

Soybeans

Since the beginning of recorded history in the Orient, an unpretentious, unlovely, knobbly little bean has been grown in the carefully tilled fields of China. The lumpy pods ripen to reveal seeds of yellow, green, brown or black. Some varieties of these seeds are even camouflaged in patches of earth tones as if to escape the ravages of predatory insects and animals attracted to their succulent texture and taste. This plant is the lowly soybean *(Glycine max),* prized by the East and, until recently, despised by the West and relegated to the role of animal fodder.

The amazing bean has a high (43 percent) proportion of protein, which is very close in the structure of its fourteen amino acids to the protein we get from animal foods. This is only one part of its amazing nutritive value. It is a veritable treasure chest of vitamins and minerals, among them Vitamin A, B1, B2, B complex, iron, zinc, potassium, phosphorus, calcium and magnesium. It is relatively low in starch; it contains over 19 percent of noncholesterol oil and under 8 percent of sucrose—and we feed it to our cattle!

The Chinese, with centuries of accrued wisdom and philosophy about food, called it one of the classic Five Staples or Five Grains. They discovered very early that the soybean produces more protein per acre and per pound than any other common edible crop, whether plant or animal.

However, it is not an easy plant to transform into edible food. Because of its natural attraction for predators, the plant has gradually developed strains of protective poisons and unpleasant chemicals that are present in its uncooked or unprocessed states. Even when the beans are boiled or roasted they are indigestible.

First the Chinese, then the Koreans and Japanese, gradually evolved processes for fermenting the beans, grinding them to flour, treating them with enzymes, or combinations of all of these.

By milling the beans and mixing the flour with water, the Chinese discovered that it was possible to produce a soybean milk. Further processing created bean curd, bean cheese, bean paste and many kinds of dried bean-curd wrappers, sticks and fermented preparations, all of which, because of the fermentation or enzyme action, are even richer than the original bean in proteins and vitamins.

Throughout the Far East and Southeast Asia, soybean products supplant dairy preparations, as they are far more economical to produce, while providing similar nutrition. The cow, which to us is a four-legged dairy or a source of steaks, to the Asian is a much-prized work animal. Even today there are far more cattle to do the plowing than there are tractors on the little farms of Asia.

Soybean milk, a watery extract obtained by cooking the beans at a high temperature, is produced and used fresh in China, and as a condensed milk in Japan and Southeast Asia. The Japanese, using a standard yogurt starter, *Lactobacillus bulgaricus,* have recently manufactured a nondairy soy yogurt which is said to taste as delicious as the original, while containing far more protein.

One of the most important products of the soybean is bean curd—the white, custardlike blocks floating in liquid that we see in the refrigeration cases of our supermarkets. It has a very bland taste, but when combined with meats, vegetables and sauces, it can be deep-fried, stir-fried, simmered, sauced and turned into myriad delicious dishes. Once you understand a little more about it, you may well be tempted to add it to your shopping list. There are few better buys in nutrition and value.

The basic bean curd is called *tau-fu* in Cantonese, *tau-hu* in Hokkien and *tofu* in Japanese. There are many varieties which differ in texture, appearance and flavor.

The original curd is made by grinding the beans with water to a cream which is cooked, then strained and coagulated with gypsum or a similar substance (much in the same way as milk is coagulated with rennet or lemon juice). Any excess liquid is drained off and the resultant soft mass is then pressed into a block. This rather watery rectangle, which the Chinese call "meat without bones," is the common curd so widely available in our stores.

Firmer bean curd is achieved by pressing the liquid out. At home, you can effect this by placing the squares on a plate between paper towels, covering them with a second plate, and then placing an increasingly heavy series of weights on top in gradual progression, ending with something as massive as an iron. (Do not start off with maximum pressure or the bean curd will split.)

Bean curd is also dried in the sun to form more compact cakes. These are sometimes processed further by deep-frying and can be purchased in this form.

During the basic process of making bean curd, at the stage where the bean-and-water mixture is boiled, a skin of residue forms on the top. This skin is skimmed off and dried. It is commercially available in sheets, which must be soaked to soften before using as wrappers for foods, and in the form of sticks that bear the picturesque name of "second bamboo" in Chinese, meaning that they are the second residue from the curd. (Turn to the listing of the soybean products on page 101, together with their Chinese and/or Japanese names for descriptions and further uses.)

Probably the soybean product with which we are all most familiar is soy sauce. Called *shoyu* by the Japanese and *shih yu* in Mandarin or *si yau* in Cantonese, it is a salty-tasting brown liquid, widely used throughout Asia for salt, color and flavor in cooking.

To make the sauce, soybean flour is mixed with coarsely ground wheat, barley or rice and fermented by using a "starter" such as *Aspergillus oryzae* and/or *A. soyae* (fungi), or whatever similar microorganisms are present in that particular starter. Salt is added and then the mix is refermented with *Lactobacillus* (the bacteria that sours sourdough bread, yogurt and some sausages) and yeasts. Traditionally, this fermentation and aging procedure used to take between one and three years. Nowadays modern production methods use higher temperatures to speed up the process; however, the finest soy sauces are still those made by natural fermentation and aging.

There are three main varieties of soy sauce: light soy, made as previously described, is pale in color, delicate in flavor and often used as a table condiment or in light, clear soups and dishes where the color should not be altered; dark or medium soy, which has added caramel, is thicker and is used for the Chinese "red-cooked" dishes; and heavy or dark, sweet soy, which is treacly with molasses and used for color more than flavor in rich, dark sauces, spareribs and marinades. Incidentally, it is considered bad form in China to add soy sauce at the table. The seasoning skill of the cook is considered and respected.

As well as soy sauce, a whole variety of pastes and cheeselike substances are made by cooking the beans and then fermenting them with *Aspergillus,* yeasts, *Rhizopus* and bacteria. These products include the Japanese *miso,* which is mostly available in three types: sweet, white *miso* from the Kyoto area; a mellow, yellow-colored *miso* from Kyushu, and a red, salty paste made in the north of Japan. The white and red *miso* are the varieties most commonly specified in Japanese cookbooks.

Fermentation techniques were unknown in ancient Japan, and the processes filtered in from China by way of Korea, becoming widespread and popular by the sixteenth century. Seventy percent of the Japanese *miso* is made from soybeans and rice, steamed and crushed; about 20 percent from a mixture of soybeans and wheat; and only about 10 percent from pure soybeans.

The Chinese originated yellow and red soybean pastes, fermented black-bean mixtures, called *tou shih,* and pickled bean curd, which is dryish and fermented with fungi such as *Mucor* and *Actinomucor.* Fermented curd *(doufu-ru)* is often pickled with Chinese rice wine and brine, red peppers or even with rose essence. These more pungent and highly flavored products include the Chinese red and white cheeses, which are also made from fermented bean curd and are somewhat similar in flavor and texture to Brie or Camembert.

The techniques of soybean fermentation spread south as well as east via Chinese immigrants and traders. In Java, Indonesia, bean curd is called *tahu;* and, by enzyme fermentation of yeasts or molds, known as *ragi,* hard bean cakes called *tempe* are made. Some *tempe* manufacturers mix coconut residue left over from the production of coconut milk as an extender to the beans, but this inferior *tempe* is prone to airborne bacteria and should be avoided. *Tempe murni* or pure *tempe* is the quality to look for in Indonesian cooking.

As well as all this culinary innovation, the Chinese learned to process soybeans into all manner of meat substitutes. This technique could well have originated with the Mahayana Buddhists who, being vegetarians, developed a wide range of meat imitations which tasted good, although they were not too close in form to the originals. These imitations are still used in Chinese vegetarian cookery.

Today, 75 percent of the world's soybean crop is grown in the United States and about 17 percent in China, including Manchuria. The Asians utilize about half of the crop for human food and less than one third for oil production.

In the West, a very small percent has been utilized for anything other than animal feed, but of that minute proportion, the miracle bean has been heavily used in the commercial food industry. Soybean derivatives are incorporated into bread, confectionery, pastas, biscuits, ice cream, chocolate, sausages, sauces, lemon curd, mayonnaise, meat and fish pastes, infant and invalid foods, and in certain diabetic preparations—just read the labels on the cans, jars and packets in your supermarket.

Soybean Products

Description	Chinese	Japanese	Comments

Bean Curd

Description	Chinese	Japanese	Comments
Silky, watery white bean curd	tau fu fa	kinugoshi tofu	Sold fresh and must be refrigerated with water changed daily. Generally available in 10-ounce squares.
Dense, white bean curd	tau fu	momen tofu	As above.
Heavier, grilled bean curd		yaki tofu	A smaller square. The outside is brown and firm from grilling.
Freeze-dried bean curd		koya tofu or kori tofu	Koya is the place where it is manufactured: kori means ice.
Deep-fried bean curd	tau fu pok	abura age	Thin, flat rectangles. Store by wrapping in foil and refrigerating. Keeps for 3 days, refrigerated. Freezes well.
Dried bean curd rolls or sheets	fu chu	yuba	Made from the skin removed from the top of the bean curd liquid and dried in sheets or rolls. Must be softened with water before use. Keeps indefinitely.
Bean curd sticks	fu joke		Long, dried, cream-colored, striated hanks, ½ inch wide by 20 inches long. Sold bent in half. Must be soaked for 2 hours before use. Chewy, nutlike flavor. Used in soups or with steamed fish or braised or stir-fried, etc.
Sweet bean curd sticks	tim joke		Darker skin from natural concentration of sucroses during the boiling process. Sometimes made with the addition of cane sugar. Cut into 2-inch lengths and boil for 20 minutes until soft, or soak as above.
Spiced bean curd	tau fu kon		Thin, flat cakes, spiced with anise.

Description	Chinese	Japanese	Comments

Soy Sauce

Description	Chinese	Japanese	Comments
Light	*chan ch'an* or *sang chau*	*usu kuchi shoyu*	Made from soybean extract, flour, salt and sugar. Light-colored soy with a delicate flavor. Used in pale-toned dishes and soups.
Dark, medium	*see yu chan yan*	*shoyu*	Made in the same manner as light soy but with the addition of caramel. The Chinese use it for "red-cooked" dishes. The Japanese have now manufactured low-sodium versions, reducing the normal 14% of salt to 8% or even 6%.
Dark, heavy, sweet	*chu yan*		Also used in Indonesia and there called *ketjap manis.* This treacly, dark-brown soy has molasses among its ingredients. Used for coloring in barbecued meats, rich sauces and marinades.

Fermented Soybean Pastes and Cheeses

Description	Chinese	Japanese	Comments
Black bean paste	*dau see tau ch'ih*		Made from a variety of black soybean, salted and fermented. Pungent and salty; available in cans and jars. Also the basis of black bean sauce *(dau see jap),* together with garlic, scallions and ginger.
Sweet, white bean paste		*shiro miso*	Available in vacuum-sealed plastic bags. Manufactured in the Kyoto area of Japan.
White soy cheese	*Pai doufu-ru foo yee* (or *yu*)		Pressed, buff-colored cubes of bean curd, 1½" square. Fermented in rice wine and salt. Somewhat similar in texture and flavor to Brie or Camembert. Available in jars.

Description	Chinese	Japanese	Comments
Red soybean paste		*aka miso*	Red, salty paste from the north of Japan. Used in soups, fish and sea-food dishes. Do not confuse with the red azuki-bean paste used in desserts.
Red soy cheese or spiced red bean curd	*Hung doufu-ru nom yee* or *nam yu*		Pressed bean curd, fermented in a similar fashion to the white, but with the addition of spices and red rice to achieve the brick-red color. Pungent. Gives an "aged" taste to pork and poultry dishes. Available in cans. Cubes are mashed before use.

Miscellaneous Soybean Preparations

Description	Chinese	Japanese	Comments
Soy jam	*yun shi jeung*		Another term for classic soybean paste; the sediment from soy sauce production. Similar to molasses in color and texture. Used for flavor in cooking.
Whole, fermented soybeans		*nato*	Eaten in Japan as a garnish with rice.
Red bean sauce	*saang see jeung*		Made in China from mashed red soybeans. Used in poultry and meat dishes. Do not confuse with sweet red bean paste. Available in jars and cans.
Soybeans and malted rice		*moromi miso*	Eaten in Japan in vegetable dishes.
Hoisin sauce	*hoisin*		A sweet and spicy mixture of soy-beans, spices, garlic and hot red pepper. Used in cooking duck, seafood and spareribs; also as a table condiment. Available in cans and jars.

In addition to foods, soybean derivatives are used in a multiplicity of industrial applications—even in fire-fighting foam!

The biggest breakthrough is an outgrowth of the Oriental Buddhist processes. We have learned to isolate the soybean proteins and use them as emulsifiers and binders, and now, as textured vegetable protein (TVP). This process is still being refined but it is now possible to simulate texturally meat, fish and shellfish.

It sounds like science fiction, but the isolated proteins are concentrated into stiff doughs which are then extruded, sliced and dried or otherwise transformed into simulations of ground meat when rehydrated. With flavor and color added, they can become perfectly acceptable, if not perfect, meat substitutes to be used in stews and casseroles.

The most expensive process dissolves the soy protein into a glutinous mass which is then spun into filaments. Fats, flavors, coloring, extra nutrients and egg albumen, which is used as a binder, are added, and the fibers are then fabricated into any cut of meat that can be imagined.

While these products tend to make the chef and food lover shudder, they may be the salvation for a world in which a large percentage of the population is undernourished and meatless—a world which is looking at a very real tomorrow of mass starvation unless technology comes to the rescue, and a world that may lift off into regular space travel before the close of the century. It looks as if the humble little soybean has still a long way to travel, both in time and space.

BASIC RECIPES

❀ Long-Grain Rice

Snowy mounds of glistening, elongated grains, fluffy and cooked to perfection, the centerpiece of the dining table and the hub around which all the dishes revolve —that is long-grain rice, the most common of all the Asian varieties—and there are thousands.

In India, it is known as Patna rice, after the district in which it is mainly grown. There is also another, superior quality called Basmati. Also long-grained, with a deliciously nutlike and delicate flavor, the latter rice is tempting enough to eat by itself. Basmati rice, much prized by connoisseurs, is used in *pilaus,* those dishes of rice cooked with spices and meats in which rice, nevertheless, is the star.

It is a little-known fact that the world's finest long-grain rice comes from Iran, but, a sad casualty of the current situation, it is no longer available outside that country. Even when it was, the price per pound rivaled that of steak.

American home-grown, long-grain rice generally comes from Carolina or Texas. In Europe, the varieties available are from India. When you are buying this rice, wherever it comes from, look for a hard, long and somewhat pearly grain. Try to choose it packaged in transparent plastic, so you can inspect it first. Pick the rice with the minimum of broken grains or rice-powder residue and check it for foreign bodies, such as small stones, that have crept through the sorting and cleaning process.

This variety of rice produces the best separation of grains after cooking. The inferior shorter-grained varieties are best used for puddings and desserts, as they tend to become mushy and sticky after cooking. Except for instant rice, all varieties should be washed well before cooking. It is not enough to place rice in a sieve and run cold water through it. Put the rice in a large bowl or saucepan, cover it with cold water and agitate the grains violently with your open fingers. The water will turn milky with rice powder and stray husks will float to the surface. Pour the water off and repeat the process 5 or 6 times, or until the water remains clear. Always use cold water. Apart from ensuring a good separation of the grains after cooking, this washing process is advisable because some inferior varieties of imported rice have been known to be powdered with talcum to enhance the whiteness.

An Oriental will swear that there are as many methods of cooking rice as there are countries and areas that eat it. That is undoubtedly true, and if you want to break the ice at any gathering of Asians, just ask for the best way to produce perfectly cooked rice. The ensuing discussion can only be compared to asking members of the Hadassah for the perfect way to prepare chicken soup or chopped liver.

Those of you who already own electric rice cookers will have no problems producing perfectly cooked rice; it happens every time if the directions are followed correctly. For those who don't, here are several techniques for preparing rice, including the Indian *pilau* method, where the grains are sautéed in clarified butter or oil until they become totally opaque; then the water or stock is added. This technique produces perfect separation of the grains because each is coated with its own undetectable film of oil.

There is no particular order of preference to the numbering of these techniques, so pick the one that appeals to you the most.

Remember that one cup of raw rice more than doubles its volume when cooked. Allow ⅓ to ½ cup *(2 to 3 ounces)* of raw rice to a person.

Method 1

Preparation time: 3 minutes   Serves 4 to 6
Cooking time: 25 minutes

INGREDIENTS   PREPARATION
2 cups *(15½ ounces)* of long-grain   Washed well
   rice
Cold water

METHOD

1. In a bowl, soak the washed rice for 3 minutes in enough water to cover it, then drain.

2. Pour the rice into a saucepan and add sufficient water to cover it to a depth of approximately 1½ inches above the grains.

3. Place the pan over a high setting and bring to a boil. Reduce the heat to medium and cook for 20 minutes, stirring often.

4. When the water is completely absorbed, remove the pan from the heat and immediately pour in a cup or more of cold water to stop any further cooking.

5. Drain off the water, cover the pan with a towel to absorb the steam and place the pan in a barely warm oven. Or transfer the rice to a serving platter, cover with the towel and place the platter in the oven.

Method 2

Preparation time: 3 minutes   Serving portions as above
Cooking time: 20 minutes

INGREDIENTS   PREPARATION
As above   As above

METHOD

1. Pour water, 6 times the volume of the rice, into a saucepan and bring to a rolling boil over high heat.

2. Add the rice and cook for 10 minutes.

3. Place a colander over a bowl and pour the rice into it, returning the liquid from the bowl back into the saucepan and back to a boil.

4. Run cold water over the rice in the colander. Shake the colander to remove residual water and then return the rice to the boiling liquid, bringing it back to a boil. Cook for 3 minutes.

5. Remove and drain the rice. Transfer it to a heatproof serving dish and place it in a warm oven, first fluffing the grains with a chopstick or fork, and cover with a damp towel. (The damp towel is a good way to preserve the moistness of the rice and to prevent the top grains from drying out while keeping the rice warm, no matter which cooking technique is used.)

Method 3

Preparation time: 2 minutes   Serving portions as above
Cooking time: 30 minutes

INGREDIENTS   PREPARATION
As above   As above

METHOD

1. Pour water, 6 times the volume of the rice, into a saucepan and bring to a rolling boil over high heat.

2. Add the rice and cook for 10 minutes.

3. Reduce the heat to a simmer and loosely cover the saucepan with a lid, allowing space for the steam to escape, and continue to cook for 15 minutes more.

4. Drain any residual water, empty the rice onto a platter and fluff the grains. Keep warm as in the method above.

Method 4

Preparation time: 5 minutes   Serving portions as above
Cooking time: 25 minutes

INGREDIENTS   PREPARATION
As above   As above

METHOD

1. Place a trivet inside a large saucepan and, measuring the rice into a small saucepan, set it on the trivet inside the larger vessel. (There should be 1½ to 2 inches of space between the inside of the larger pan and the circumference of the smaller.)

2. Pour boiling water into the large saucepan to just above the bottom of the smaller pan. Fill the small saucepan with boiling water to twice the volume of rice. Place lids on both saucepans and turn the heat to high.

3. When water has reached a bubbling boil, reduce the heat to low, so that you can just hear the water simmering in the pan. Simmer for 15 minutes.

4. Turn off the heat and leave the pans *covered* for a further 10 minutes. Uncover, stir the rice with a fork or chopstick, cover again and keep the pans undisturbed until you are ready to transfer the rice to a serving dish. (The rice will keep warm for at least another 15 minutes. If a longer wait is expected, merely turn on the heat to low and let the pans sit over it for a further 10 minutes.) You may want to stir in a tablespoon of butter before serving.

Method 5

This technique of first frying the rice before adding the liquid is that used for *pilau-*style rice dishes. If you wish to turn it into a simple *pilau,* you may substitute an equal quantity of chicken stock for the water, add a little salt and some spices, such as 3 cloves, a 1-inch piece of cinnamon, ½ teaspoon of ground cumin and a bay leaf. The whole spices will be stranded on the surface of the rice after cooking and can be removed easily.

Preparation time: 3 minutes   Serving portions as above
Cooking time: 30 minutes

I N G R E D I E N T S   P R E P A R A T I O N
1½ tablespoons *(¾ ounce)* of
    clarified butter (page 139)
2 cups *(15½ ounces)* of rice   Washed well and drained until just
                                              damp

4 cups *(32 fluid ounces)* of boiling
    water

M E T H O D
1. Place a saucepan over medium heat and heat the clarified butter until a haze forms.

2. Place the rice in the saucepan and fry, stirring, until the grains turn opaque.

3. Have the boiling water ready and, when the rice is sufficiently fried, pour in the measured amount of boiling water. Stir once (this is where you would add the salt and spices) and place a lid on tightly. The contents of the saucepan will be boiling vigorously at this moment. Immediately reduce the heat to the lowest possible setting.

4. Keep the pan on the heat for 30 minutes. Remove the lid and stir the rice to let the steam escape. The water should be completely absorbed. Pinch a grain of rice between your finger and thumb. It should squash with firm pressure—not too easily, or it is overcooked. If there is a little core of hardness, then the rice needs further cooking. Pour in ¼ cup *(2 fluid ounces)* of water, cover the pan and set it back on medium-low heat for 5 to 10 minutes more, then test a grain again.

5. Transfer the rice to a serving platter and keep warm until ready to serve.

A D V A N C E   P R E P A R A T I O N   A N D
S T O R A G E   N O T E S
Cooked rice refrigerates and freezes beautifully. If you are making fried

rice, always used cooked rice that has been previously refrigerated. When rice cools, the grains dry out and it loses much of the moisture which makes it sticky when fried immediately after being boiled. Refrigerate rice in sealed plastic bags or containers. Frozen rice will keep up to 6 months. Freeze it in freezer-weight, sealed plastic bags or in special freezer containers. Thaw it at room temperature or in a microwave oven. Both refrigerated and frozen, thawed rice can be brought back to their original state of moistness and fluffiness by placing the rice in a dish on a steamer tray and steaming for 5 minutes.

Rice that has been overcooked can be rescued by placing it on a platter in a warm oven, drizzling a little melted butter over the top and fluffing and stirring the grains with a chopstick or fork from time to time. It can also be refrigerated until dry and then rewarmed.

There are 3 reasons why rice is sticky:

1. It has been cooked for too long.

2. Too much water was used (in recipes where all the water is supposed to be absorbed).

3. The rice was not washed sufficiently before cooking. The stickiness is then caused by a residue of rice starch remaining on the grains.

❀ Japanese Short Grain Rice

The Japanese prefer their rice to be slightly sticky—of a consistency that holds the grains together in a cohesive bundle so they can easily be picked up with chopsticks. Long-grain rice with its grain-separation qualities is not suitable; short-grain rice is the proper choice for Japanese meals.

In the United States this rice is grown in mostly California; is widely available nationwide in supermarkets under a variety of labels including Calrose.

An electric rice cooker is the most useful tool for preparing Japanese rice, and indeed, most rice cookers are Japanese-manufactured. For those who do not own one, here are two methods for preparing Japanese rice: one for the plain boiled rice served hot at most meals, the other for the cold, vinegared rice that forms the base of the Japanese hors d'oeuvres called *sushi*.

❀ Plain Boiled Rice

Preparation time: 15 minutes
Cooking time: 30 minutes

Serves 4 to 6

SHOPPING AND TECHNIQUE TIPS

Short-grain rice does not swell as much as the long grain and less water is used in the cooking. As a general rule, use equal quantities of rice and water plus a little more. For example, 1½ cups *(11½ ounces)* of raw rice needs 1¾ cups *(14 fluid ounces)* of water.

INGREDIENTS

2 cups *(15½ ounces)* of raw rice

2½ cups *(1 pint)* of cold water

PREPARATION

Washed well in several changes of water

METHOD

1. After washing the rice until the water runs clear, let it drain in a sieve or colander for 10 minutes.

2. Place the rice in a saucepan and pour in the measured quantity of water. Cover, bring to a boil over high heat (standing by to watch that it does not boil over), reduce the heat to low and let the rice simmer for 15 minutes.

3. Remove the saucepan from the heat and let it stand, still covered, for 10 minutes to allow the rice to cook in the residual steam.

4. Uncover and fluff and stir the grains with a fork or chopsticks. If rice is to be left longer before serving, place a towel over the saucepan to absorb any extra moisture, and then replace the lid.

ADVANCE PREPARATION AND
STORAGE NOTES

This rice is chilled if it is to be used for fried rice; otherwise the rice is freshly prepared for each meal.

❀ Vinegar-Dressed Rice

Preparation time: 1 hour and 10
   minutes
Cooking time: 30 minutes

2 cups *(8¾ ounces)* of cooked rice provides the base for appetizers for about 8

SHOPPING AND TECHNIQUE TIPS

Oriental rice vinegar is the correct seasoning to use for this rice as it is milder and sweeter than our white vinegar. It is available in the Oriental sections of supermarkets. If you cannot locate it, you will have to dilute the white vinegar with water and slightly increase the amount of sugar. The authentic way to prepare this rice is also to bury a small square of dried kelp seaweed in the rice for the time it takes to come to a boil. This imparts a delicate flavor of the sea to the rice; however, if this dried seaweed is not available, it can be omitted. The *sushi* rice is traditionally somewhat chewier than the hot rice and therefore is prepared with a little less water than the latter.

INGREDIENTS

2 cups *(15½ ounces)* of raw rice

2 cups *(16 fluid ounces)* of cold
   water
¼ cup *(2 fluid ounces)* of rice
   vinegar, or 2 *(1⅔)* tablespoons
   of white vinegar diluted with 2
   (1⅔) tablespoons of water
1 *(¾)* tablespoon of granulated sugar
   (plus an additional ½ *(⅓)*
   teaspoon if white vinegar is
   used)
2 *(1⅔)* teaspoons of salt

PREPARATION

Washed well in several changes of
   water

METHOD

1. After washing the rice well, place it in a sieve and drain for 1 hour.

2. Place it in a saucepan, together with the water. Cover and bring to a boil over high heat, taking care not to let it boil over. Reduce the heat to medium and boil for 5 minutes. Reduce the heat to low and cook for 15 minutes. Do not uncover.

3. Remove the pan from the heat and let it stand, still covered, for 10 minutes.

4. Meanwhile, place the vinegar, sugar and salt in a small pan and heat over medium heat, stirring, until the sugar has dissolved. Set aside to cool.

5. Empty the cooked rice into a wooden bowl and add the vinegar dressing, a little at a time, cutting it through horizontally with a wooden spatula (horizontal cutting motions prevent the grains from breaking up). While you are stirring the rice, fan it with a paper fan or an electric fan (even a piece of cardboard will do) to put a gloss on the grains. This entire process should take about 10 minutes. After this, the rice is ready to form into shapes for *sushi.*

ADVANCE PREPARATION AND
STORAGE NOTES

The rice can be prepared several hours ahead of use, but it should be covered with a damp cloth and left at room temperature until you are ready to mold it. Do not refrigerate. When molding, moisten the fingers with a mixture of two-thirds water to one-third vinegar so the rice will not stick to them.

& Glutinous Rice (SWEET RICE, STICKY RICE)

This rice, much beloved of the Laotians, southwestern Chinese and Thai, is short-grained, opaque and pearly in appearance. It is sold in supermarkets in paper bags under the name "sweet rice," although I always call it "sticky rice," because that's exactly what it is. It requires a lot of water for soaking, washing and cooking (a 2-to-1 ratio) and has a high percentage of rice starch. You may well remark that short-grain rice could be used instead. Well, it can, if the sticky rice is unavailable, but this rice has far more tenacious sticking power.

In early times, pressed into a lump with the fingers and used to scoop up food, it took the place of eating utensils. It is still used in this way in the more remote areas. However, it is used by both Chinese and Southeast Asians as a stuffing component for poultry, in sweet-rice soups, pastries, puddings and desserts, and to make the marvelous pearly rice coating for the meatballs that look like white porcupines after steaming. For Southeast Asian desserts it is boiled in coconut milk; for the other dishes, unless otherwise indicated, the recipe below will cook it to perfection.

Preparation time: 1 hour   Yields 4 cups *(about 1 ¼ pounds)* of
Cooking time: 35 minutes   cooked rice

SHOPPING AND TECHNIQUE TIPS
Whereas other varieties of rice do not need a preliminary soaking, glutinous rice must be soaked for at least 30 minutes before using. Some experts call for an hour's steeping, but half an hour will suffice.

INGREDIENTS
2 cups *(15 ½ ounces)* of glutinous
    rice
4 cups *(32 fluid ounces)* of cold
    water

METHOD
1. Place the rice in a saucepan and pour in enough water to cover. Let it soak for 30 minutes or longer.

2. Pour off the soaking water and continue to wash, agitating the grains, in several changes of water until the last washing runs clear. Pour away the water, using the lid to help it drain, and pour the 4 cups of water into the rice. Let it stand for 10 more minutes.

3. Cover the pan and place it over high heat. Bring to a boil and immediately reduce the heat to low. Simmer the rice for 30 minutes, or until all the water is absorbed. Do not lift the lid while the rice is cooking, but remove it

at the end of the cooking time to check if the water is absorbed. If it is not, cover again and let it simmer for a few minutes longer. The rice is now ready to use.

ADVANCE PREPARATION AND STORAGE NOTES

The rice can be made several hours ahead of using, but do not refrigerate it. Merely cover with a damp cloth and leave it at room temperature. If refrigerated, it gets extremely glutinous and sets rather like a firm custard pudding. For sweets, of course, this is desirable, and many confections using glutinous rice are refrigerated to firm them.

ॐ Coconut Milk

This is the dairy-product substitute of Southeast Asia. It is used for custards and desserts and as the liquid cooking medium in stewlike dishes and curries and is an indispensable ingredient of all the cuisines in the area. It is not the clear liquid that runs out of a mature coconut when pierced; that is known as coconut "water" and is drunk as a beverage or used as a medium in which to steep the grated flesh of the coconut. Coconut milk is the liquid obtained by steeping the grated white flesh of the mature coconut in water, coconut water, or even cow's milk, and then sqeezing it.

Coconut milk is available commercially in the West in cans or frozen in packages. Unfortunately it is rarely to be found outside the Asian food stores. However, with a little time to spend, you can make it in your own kitchen. There are many methods. The most traditional, and also the most time-consuming, is to take a whole coconut, crack it open, dig out the flesh and then pare off the inner brown rind. The flesh is then grated; or it can be broken into chunks and reduced further in a food processor or blender, together with a liquid—water, coconut water or cow's milk. The resultant liquid mash is then strained and squeezed to produce the coconut milk.

Apart from this traditional method, I have found it quicker and just as satisfactory to buy the dried, unsweetened flaked coconut that is available in the health-food sections of supermarkets or in health-food stores and steep it in cow's milk. I then pour the resultant mash into a sieve lined with a muslin cloth and, gathering up the cloth into a bundle, squeeze until the last vestige of milk is extracted.

A short time ago, while visiting friends in northern Nevada, they asked if I would prepare a Thai curry for them. I was able to get the ingredients for the curry paste, but the coconut milk eluded me. I could not even find any dried unsweetened coconut. Finally, in desperation, I bought some of the sweetened baking coconut and, taking it back to the house, washed it thoroughly to remove as much of the sugar as I could. I then soaked it in milk and squeezed it to extract the coconut milk. The resultant liquid was somewhat sweet, but I added additional fish sauce and salt to the dish, which counterbalanced the sweetness and produced a passable curry.

Desperation aside, I have now been experimenting with cow's milk and the coconut extract that is found alongside all the other sweet flavorings in the spice sections of supermarkets. It behaves very well. The flavor is a little like piña colada flavoring, but that artificial quality disappears when the milk is combined with the spices and herbs of Southeast Asian dishes. In fact, when we have conducted taste testings in cooking class, most people have not been able to detect which dish was made with the substitute and which with real coconut milk.

For your convenience, I give you both techniques: the recipe that produces coconut milk from dried coconut meat (you *can* substitute the sweetened variety in a pinch, but I really can't recommend it except as a last resort) and the easy version that uses cow's milk for the liquid.

Coconut Milk I

Preparation time: 45 minutes
Yields about 4 cups *(32 fluid ounces)*
 of thick coconut milk and 4 cups *(32 fluid ounces)* of thin (almost a cup *(8 fluid ounces)* of fluid is lost during the heating and squeezing).

SHOPPING AND TECHNIQUE TIPS
Whole milk produces a rich, thick coconut milk; water produces a thinner liquid. In Asia, they use an economical two-step process, whereby they repeat the steps, using the same coconut each time. The first squeezing produces thick coconut milk, and the second squeezing of the same coconut shreds with fresh liquid produces thin coconut milk. You may use milk for both pressings, or water if you do not wish to use dairy products; or you may use milk the first time and water the second.

INGREDIENTS
2 cups *(4½ ounces)* of dried,
   unsweetened, flaked coconut
5 cups *(40 fluid ounces)* of milk
5 cups *(40 fluid ounces)* of water

METHOD
1. Place the dried coconut and the milk in a saucepan and bring to just under a boil over medium-high heat, stirring with a spoon to blend in the coconut.

2. Turn off the heat and let it cool to a lukewarm temperature.

3. (This step is optional, but it ensures that the maximum flavor is extracted from the the coconut.) Pour the mixture in 2 batches into a blender (there may be too much volume for a 1-step operation) and blend for 1 minute.

4. Set a sieve over a bowl or pitcher and, dampening a tea towel, use it to line the sieve. Pour in the coconut and liquid and let it drain for 5 minutes, then gather up the four corners of the cloth and begin to twist them so that the coconut is caught up in a bundle. Squeeze and twist until you have extracted as much fluid as possible.

5. Pour the coconut milk in 2-cup measures into freezer bags or plastic containers and seal.

6. Empty the used coconut (sometimes known as "trash") back into the saucepan and rinse out the cloth, repositioning it in the sieve and setting the sieve over the bowl again.

7. Pour the measured water into the pan and bring to just under the boil. Repeat the whole process, steps 1 through 5, measuring out the thinner liquid into similar containers. Discard the coconut.

ADVANCE PREPARATION AND
STORAGE NOTES

Coconut milk freezes beautifully. You may prepare the milk whenever you have some free time, doubling the quantities if you wish to stock up. Label the freezer bags or containers with the quality of milk (thick or thin) and the amount, and freeze. The plastic bags will freeze flat and can then be stacked upright to save freezer space. When you wish to use the milk, thaw at room temperature or hasten the process by placing the sealed bag in hot water or in a microwave oven. Coconut milk behaves in much the same way as ordinary milk and will keep in the refrigerator for the same length of time.

Coconut Milk II

Preparation time: 2 minutes   Yields 4 cups *(32 fluid ounces)*

SHOPPING AND TECHNIQUE TIPS

You must use cow's milk for this method. Unfortunately the coconut extract is generally imitation, which gives a slightly artificial flavor to the liquid. The extract can be bought in small bottles; the flavoring range includes vanilla, orange, cherry, and others.

INGREDIENTS

4 cups *(32 fluid ounces)* of cow's
    milk
1 *(¾)* teaspoon of coconut extract
    (use approximately ¼ *(a pinch)*
    teaspoon to a cup *(8 fluid*
    ounces) of milk, but decrease the
    amount for quantities over 4
    cups *(32 fluid ounces)* otherwise
    the flavor cumulatively becomes
    too concentrated)

METHOD

Measure the milk into a bowl and stir in the extract.

ADVANCE PREPARATION AND
STORAGE NOTES

Because this is so quick and simple to make, there is no need to make it
ahead of time.

❧ Indian Curry Spice Mix

This mixture will provide you with your own individual blend of curry powder
with which to prepare Indian curried dishes. As you become more familiar with
the individual flavors of the spices you may want to vary the amounts to suit your
own taste. Remember that the Spice Mix (and therefore the curry) can be made
less hot by reducing the amount of dried red chilli pepper or Cayenne powder in
the mixture.

Preparation time: 15 minutes (20 to   Yield: 1¼ cups *(approximately 5*
   25 if you use a mortar and pestle)   *ounces)*

SHOPPING AND TECHNIQUE TIPS

The whole seeds can be found in the better spice ranges. If you do not see them,
perhaps the store manager will order them from a supplier. If you live in a city
where a segment of the population is Latin American, neighborhood supermarkets will carry many of these spices.

INGREDIENTS

½ cup *(1¾ ounces)* of coriander
    seeds or ½ cup *(2 ounces)* of
    ground coriander

¼ cup *(1¼ ounces)* of cumin seeds
    or ¼ cup *(1 ounce)* of ground
    cumin

6 to 8 dried, red chilli peppers, or 1
    ½ tablespoons *(1)* of Cayenne

1 *(¾)* tablespoon of whole black
    peppercorns, or 1 *(¾)* tablespoon
    of ground black pepper

1 *(¾)* tablespoon of mustard seeds
    (preferably black)

2 *(1⅔)* tablespoons of ground
    turmeric

2 *(1⅔)* tablespoons of ground
    fenugreek (found in the better
    spice ranges)

METHOD

1. If you use a baking tray and the oven, preheat the oven to 300°F.
(165°C.). Line the baking tray with aluminum foil and place all the *whole*
spices in separate heaps on the tray (this is so that you can easily remove the
smaller spices as they get done). Place the baking tray on the top shelf for up
to 10 minutes, or until the spices become aromatic and slightly brown. Do not
over-roast. If you use a frying pan (a heavy cast-iron pan is preferred), set it
over low heat and separately dry-roast the whole spices, stirring them and
shaking the pan constantly until the aroma is released and they begin to brown.
(When roasting the chillies, keep your face averted as they give off a pungent,
eye-watering smoke.) Do not let the spices burn.

If you are using ground spices, warm them gently on a baking tray in the
oven until they begin to give off an aroma, taking care not to burn them; this
is a quick process.

2. Feed the roasted whole spices into a spice grinder, blender or mortar
and grind or pound into a fine powder. (This will have to be done in batches.)
Accumulate the powder in a bowl or pour it into a storage jar. Add the
preground spices and stir or shake the mixture until all the spices are
thoroughly blended. Cover the bowl or cap the storage jar tightly.

ADVANCE PREPARATION AND
STORAGE NOTES

The Indian Curry Spice Mix can be prepared well ahead of time and will
keep in fresh condition for up to 3 months if stored in a dark, dry cupboard.
Use 1 to 2 tablespoons for each curry and mix it to a paste with 4 tablespoons
of white vinegar or half-and-half vinegar and water.

❧ Indian Sweet Spice Mix

This is not the curry powder that is used to cook with; it is a mixture of ground
aromatic spices added to a dish toward the end of the cooking time, or sprinkled
on top just before serving. The spices are "sweet" as opposed to bitter, and
therefore do not need a long period of cooking to mellow their flavors.

The Sweet Spice Mix, called *garam masala* in Hindustani, softens and adds
new aromatic dimensions to the rather harsh flavor combinations that signal the
better-known Indian curries. If you have had to "pinch hit" a curry, using the
storebought curry powder, the addition of this mix toward the end of the cooking
time will transform the dish into a special homemade creation.

Preparation time: 5 minutes (10 if   Yield: 6 *(4¾)* tablespoons
   you use a mortar and pestle)

SHOPPING AND TECHNIQUE TIPS

Haunt the spice departments in your supermarket and try to get as many whole
spices as possible: they are much more aromatic when freshly ground. Save time
by using an electric grinder or a good blender. A coffee grinder works perfectly
but the melody lingers on, and you may need to buy a separate grinder for the
next batch of coffee beans. A good, high-speed blender produces a fairly fine grind,
but not a smooth powder. Make up small amounts of the mix at a time (doubling
the quantities given is all right) and store in a tightly capped jar in a cool, dark
cupboard. Spices lose their flavor fairly quickly after grinding.

INGREDIENTS   PREPARATION

2 *(1⅔)* tablespoons of coriander
   seeds

3-inch or 1 *(¾)* teaspoon cinnamon   Broken into small pieces
   stick

1 *(¾)* tablespoon of cumin *(comino)*
   seeds

1 *(¾)* teaspoon of whole cloves

INGREDIENTS

1 (¾) teaspoon of the small black
    seeds from cardamom pods
    (white or green) (you may
    substitute an equal amount of
    ground cardamom)
1 (¾) tablespoon of mace (the lacy,
    outer wrapping of nutmeg)
1 (¾) tablespoon of black
    peppercorns

PREPARATION

Seed the pods and discard the husks

METHOD

In batches, grind or pound all the spices to as fine a powder as possible.
Immediately place in a jar and cap tightly.

ADVANCE PREPARATION AND
STORAGE NOTES

The Sweet Spice Mix can be prepared well in advance. It can be kept for
up to 3 months, but is stronger and more aromatic if used within days.

❧ Chinese Five-Plus-One Spice Mix

The original Chinese Five-Spice Powder, a pungent, slightly medicinal-tasting
mixture of five spices, is difficult to obtain outside Oriental specialty food shops,
although it is now being bottled commercially in the West. The mixture commonly consists of three everyday spices—fennel, cloves and cinnamon—and two
more exotic spices: Szechwan peppercorns (a crumpled, lighter and more aromatic peppercorn than the familiar black) and star anise (similar in flavor to anise
seed, this is star-shaped pod with a seed in each point). Both of these spices are
rarely found in supermarkets.

The powder is an important flavoring agent in Chinese marinades and on
barbecued pork, duck and other meats and cannot be omitted if Chinese food is
to taste authentic. So I have been tinkering with various combinations of spices
in order to produce a substitute that can be easily made from commonly available
spices. Finally the mixture below was achieved and it passed the taste test of my
friends.

Preparation time: 5 minutes   Yield: 6⅔ (5⅓) teaspoons

SHOPPING AND TECHNIQUE TIPS

Again, try to buy whole spices rather than ground. Try to ensure that the spices
are as new and fresh as possible.

INGREDIENTS

2 *(1⅔)* teaspoons of whole anise

1 *(¾)* teaspoon of fennel seed

2-inch stick cinnamon or ⅔ *(½)* teaspoon

1 *(¾)* teaspoon of whole cloves

1 *(¾)* teaspoon of black peppercorns

1 *(¾)* teaspoon of powdered ginger

PREPARATION

Broken into small pieces

METHOD

1. Grind the spices in 2 batches in a spice grinder or blender or place them all together into a large mortar and pound until you have reduced them to a fine powder.

2. Store in a tightly capped jar in a dark, dry cupboard.

❧ Chinese Salt and Pepper Dip

Where we normally use a liquid or creamy sauce for a dip, the Chinese dip their snacks into a mixture of salt and Szechwan pepper for added flavor. Black pepper and anise, in equal quantities, make a good substitute for this hard-to-find pepper.

Preparation time: 2 minutes   Yield: 5 *(4)* tablespoons

INGREDIENTS

1 ½ *(1¼)* teaspoons of black peppercorns

1½ *(1¼)* teaspoons of whole anise seeds

4 *(3¼)* tablespoons of salt

METHOD

1. Place the peppercorns and anise in a grinder or mortar and grind or pound to a powder.

2. Empty the powder into a jar and add the salt. Shake well to blend together.

ADVANCE PREPARATION AND STORAGE NOTES

Store alongside your spices. When you are serving Chinese snacks, pour about 2 tablespoons into a small dish to accompany them.

Spice Variation

To make a more emphatically flavored dip, use 1 teaspoon of Chinese Five-Plus-One Spice Mix (page 119) to 4 tablespoons of salt.

✿ Indian Sharp Spice Paste

This paste, known in India as a *vindaloo* paste, is sharp and sour because of its strong spices and the vinegar they are mixed with. It is normally used in the south of India with rich, fat meats, such as pork, duck and goose, as its acidity and astringency counteract their heaviness. Because of the quantities of oil and vinegar and the preservative qualities of the spices, this paste keeps well, as do the dishes with which it is made. You may adjust the amount of Cayenne to suit your heat tolerance.

You will find that *vindaloos,* the dishes made with this paste, are a welcome contrast to the softer, more mellow dishes of north India.

Preparation time: 15 minutes
Yield: just over 1 cup *(just under ½ pint)*

SHOPPING AND TECHNIQUE TIPS
This paste may be made with ready-ground spices, provided that they are fresh when they are bought. It is usually mixed with mustard oil (extracted from mustard seeds), which is difficult to find outside of Indian grocery shops, so I have compensated by increasing the quantities of mustard and oil.

INGREDIENTS
2 *(1⅔)* tablespoons of ground red
    chilli powder (Cayenne)
4 *(3¼)* tablespoons of ground cumin
2 *(1⅔)* teaspoons of ground ginger
2 *(1⅔)* tablespoons of ground turmeric
2 *(1⅔)* tablespoons of ground
    coriander
1 *(¾)* teaspoon of ground cinnamon
2 *(1⅔)* tablespoons of ground black
    pepper
2 *(1⅔)* tablespoons of ground hot
    mustard powder
2 *(1⅔)* tablespoons of salt
¾ cup *(6 fluid ounces)* of white vinegar
½ cup *(4 fluid ounces)* of vegetable oil

M E T H O D

1. Place all the spices and the salt in a mixing bowl and stir in the vinegar. Keep blending with a spoon until a paste is formed.

2. Heat the oil in a saucepan over medium-high heat and add the paste. Reduce the heat immediately to low and stir steadily and vigorously, scraping the bottom of the saucepan to make sure the spices do not stick or burn. (Don't put your face over the pan, as the pungent vapors from the spices will make your eyes water.)

3. Stir constantly for about 8 minutes, or until the spices have cooked and mellowed and the oil is exuded from the mixture to the edges of the pan. Set aside to cool.

4. When the mixture has cooled, spoon it into a jar, complete with any oil, and cap tightly.

A D V A N C E   P R E P A R A T I O N   A N D
S T O R A G E   N O T E S

The paste will keep indefinitely in the refrigerator and, if the jar has been sterilized, will keep for at least 6 months on the shelf. Use 1 (¾) tablespoon to every 1½ pounds of meat (more, if you prefer a more strongly flavored dish).

☙ Indian Green Herb and Spice Paste

This lovely concoction of herbs and spices is used in the same manner as the Indian Sweet Spice Mix on page 118—not to cook with, but to enhance a dish. A little, stirred in toward the end of the cooking time, will transform the humdrum to the extraordinary.

Its uses remind me of the Italian *pesto,* but I do not recommend that you toss your pasta in it! However, you may wish to experiment by adding small amounts of the paste to a variety of non-Indian dishes. It provides an undefinable but delicious flavor accent.

Preparation time: 25 minutes
Yield: approximately 3 cups *(approximately 1 ¼ pints)*

S H O P P I N G   A N D   T E C H N I Q U E   T I P S

This paste is obviously better made in the summer, when there are abundant quantities of fresh herbs in the produce departments. Of course, if you have a garden or a box or tub of herbs, you are already ahead of the game. As I said before, fresh coriander, which is so necessary to most Asian cuisines, is very easily grown from seed; even by an apartment dweller.

INGREDIENTS	PREPARATION
2 fresh, green hot chillies (Serrano or Jalapeño)	Seeded and minced
6 cloves of garlic	Peeled and minced
2-inch piece of fresh ginger root	Peeled and minced
1 cup *(3 ⅓ ounces)* of fresh coriander (*cilantro* or Chinese parsley) leaves	Washed, drained and chopped
1 cup *(3 ½ ounces)* of mint leaves	Washed, drained and chopped
2 *(1 ⅔)* teaspoons of salt	
2 *(1 ⅔)* tablespoons of sesame seeds	
½ cup *(4 fluid ounces)* of white vinegar	
1 *(¾)* teaspoon of ground fenugreek	
1 *(¾)* teaspoon of ground cardamom seeds	
1 *(¾)* teaspoon of ground coriander seeds	
¾ cup *(6 fluid ounces)* of vegetable oil (not olive oil), or a little extra, if needed	

METHOD

1. Place the chillies, garlic, ginger, coriander leaves, mint leaves, salt, sesame seeds and vinegar in a blender and blend to a fine puree, stopping the motor from time to time and scraping down the sides of the jar with a spatula. Add the spices and salt and give the blades a few more turns.

2. Heat the oil over medium-high heat and add the puree from the blender. Stir it rapidly for 2 minutes, taking care that the mixture does not stick to the bottom of the pan. Turn off the heat and let the mixture cool.

3. Fill a sterilized jar with the paste. The oil should cover the top of the mixture. If it does not, spoon in 2 more tablespoons. Cap tightly.

ADVANCE PREPARATION AND
STORAGE NOTES

This paste will keep for about 3 months in the refrigerator. The green color may darken after a while, which will not affect the flavor, but of course it looks far more appealing if the color is still bright. Use between 1 teaspoon and 1 tablespoon per dish. You may wish to use smaller amounts in dishes that are not of an Indian origin.

❧ Thai Curry Spice Paste

Although I have made many substitutions for hard-to-find ingredients, this curry paste still carries the true flavor of Thailand. Use it in all your Thai curries unless otherwise specified. A little added to stir-fried dishes or rubbed into chicken as a marinade before barbecuing or grilling will add a real Thai accent. A teaspoon added to a meatloaf mixture or to meat balls, transforms them into something rather exotic and, when combined with peanut butter and coconut milk, it makes a tangy and aromatic sauce for Thai-style satays.

Preparation time: 20 minutes   Yield: approximately 1 cup
                                                             (approximately 8 fluid ounces)

SHOPPING AND TECHNIQUE TIPS
Try to find the whole spices whenever possible. Anchovy fillets may be substituted for anchovy paste. Shallots are preferable to onions, as they have a different flavor and are less juicy, but if you are unable to locate them, use an equal quantity of a portion of a red onion. Fresh coriander (*cilantro,* or Chinese parsley) is available in the produce sections of most supermarkets, alongside the mint and parsley. If you cannot locate any, you can grow your own from coriander seeds in a window box, a flowerpot or in your garden. It grows in much the same way as parsley.

INGREDIENTS	PREPARATION
5 small dried red chillies, with their seeds, or 1 (¾) teaspoon of ground red chilli powder (Cayenne)	Broken into pieces
1 (¾) teaspoon of whole black peppercorns, or 1 (¾) teaspoon of ground black pepper	
1 (¾) tablespoon of whole coriander seeds, or 1 (¾) tablespoon of ground coriander	
1 (¾) teaspoon of whole caraway seeds, or 1 (¾) teaspoon of ground caraway	
The outer, yellow peel (*zest*) of ½ lemon	Minced
The outer, green peel (*zest*) of 1 lime	Minced
2-inch piece of fresh ginger root	Peeled and minced
8 cloves of garlic	Peeled and minced
4 shallots	Peeled and minced
1 (¾) teaspoon of anchovy paste	

INGREDIENTS

6 sprigs of coriander (*cilantro* or
    Chinese parsley) leaves with
    stems
1 *(¾)* teaspoon of salt
3 *(2⅓)* tablespoons of vegetable oil

PREPARATION

Finely chopped

METHOD

1. In an electric spice grinder or mortar, grind together the first 4 (whole) spices (chillies, peppercorns, coriander and caraway). Omit this step if you are using only ground spices.

2. Empty the powder into a blender or food processor and add the remaining ingredients, using 2 *(1⅔)* tablespoons of oil to assist the blades to turn smoothly. (The paste will necessarily be a little coarse in texture, but grind it as finely as you can.)

3. Using a spatula, transfer the paste to a jar, pour over the last tablespoon of oil and cap tightly. Refrigerate until needed.

ADVANCE PREPARATION AND
STORAGE NOTES

Under refrigeration, the paste will keep for up to 2 months. If you plan to cook lots of Thai dishes, double the quantities of ingredients.

❀ Thai Muslim Curry Spice Paste

It may seem a little strange to include a paste of such mixed ancestry, but the curry which is prepared from this mixture is delicious and widely eaten. It is a perfect blend of Indian and Thai ingredients and shows its historical origin as a dish that was brought to Thailand by the Muslims who settled there.

Preparation time: 20 minutes

Yield: 7 *(5⅔)* tablespoons (sufficient for 1 recipe to which it will be added)

SHOPPING AND TECHNIQUE TIPS

I have made this paste using both ready-ground and whole spices. This is one instance where I find the ready-ground spices to be satisfactory as long as they are new and fresh. They certainly save time. However, if you are doubling the quantities in order to have some extra paste, try to use whole spices, as the paste will keep its aroma and flavor longer.

INGREDIENTS	PREPARATION
1 (¾) teaspoon of vegetable oil
7 cloves of garlic	Peeled and minced
7 shallots	Peeled and minced
5 small dried red chillies, with their seeds, or 1 (¾) teaspoon of ground red chilli powder (Cayenne)	Broken into pieces
3 whole cloves, or ¼ (just under) teaspoon of ground cloves
½-inch piece of cinnamon stick, or ⅙ (very small pinch) teaspoon ground cinnamon	Broken into fragments
½ (⅓) teaspoon of black cardamom seeds, or ½ (⅓) teaspoon of ground cardamom	Pods seeded and husks discarded
¼ of a whole nutmeg, or ¼ (just under) teaspoon of ground nutmeg	Grated
The outer, green peel (zest) of 1 lime	Minced
½ (⅓) teaspoon of ground ginger
½ (⅓) teaspoon of anchovy paste, or 1 anchovy fillet	Mashed
2 (1⅔) tablespoons of vegetable oil

METHOD

1. Heat 1 (¾) teaspoon of vegetable oil in a frying pan over medium heat, and fry the garlic and shallots, stirring constantly, until they are brown. Empty them into a blender.

2. In an electric spice grinder or mortar, grind or pound together the whole spices (chillies, cloves, cinnamon, cardamom and nutmeg). Omit this step if you are using only ground spices.

3. Empty the powder into the blender and add the remaining ingredients, including the 2 (1⅔) tablespoons of oil. (The paste will be a little coarse, but try to grind it as fine as you can, using a rubber spatula to scrape the mixture down the sides of the jar as needed (turn motor off before you do this).

4. Transfer the paste to a jar, cap tightly and refrigerate until needed.

ADVANCE PREPARATION AND
STORAGE NOTES

Under refrigeration, this paste will keep up to 2 months, so it can be made well ahead of the dish (or dishes) in which you plan to use it.

❦ Indonesian Curry Spice Paste

This paste features many of the spices to be found in the Spice Islands and typically includes coconut, which acts as a thickener for the curry gravy as well as contributing extra flavor. Because the Indonesian archipelago covers thousands of square miles, the flavors of the curries change from island to island and mirror each ethnic group. However, this paste captures the authentic essence of Indonesian curries.

Preparation time: 25 minutes

Yield: Approximately 2 cups *(less than 1 pint)*

SHOPPING AND TECHNIQUE TIPS

Dried, unsweetened flaked coconut can be found in the health-food sections of supermarkets. If you do not see it, suggest that the supermarket manager order it. Peanut oil is typically used in Indonesian cuisine. Try to buy as many whole spices as you can; they are much more aromatic when freshly ground. Use an electric spice grinder but if you do not have one and use a mortar and pestle to grind the spices, you can use it all the way through this process, which obviates the necessity for transferring ingredients from one appliance to another. Be prepared to use a lot of energy, however—and it does take longer.

INGREDIENTS	PREPARATION
¼ cup *(½ ounce)* of dried, flaked unsweetened coconut	
4 *(3 ¼)* tablespoons of peanut oil	
1 small onion	Peeled and minced
2 cloves of garlic	Peeled and minced
2 *(1 ⅔)* teaspoons of whole caraway seeds, or 2 *(1 ⅔)* teaspoons of ground caraway	
5 small dried red chillies, with their seeds, or 1 *(¾)* teaspoon of ground red chilli powder (Cayenne)	Broken into pieces
1 *(¾)* teaspoon of poppy seeds	
⅓ of a whole nutmeg, or ⅓ *(¼)* teaspoon of ground nutmeg	Grated
6 whole cloves, or ½ *(⅓)* teaspoon of ground cloves	
2 *(1 ⅔)* teaspoons of ground turmeric	
1 *(¾)* teaspoon of ground ginger	
2 *(1 ⅔)* teaspoons of anchovy paste, or 4 anchovy fillets	Mashed

INGREDIENTS

The outer, yellow peel *(zest)* of 1
    lemon
1-inch piece of fresh ginger root
5 macadamia nuts
1 *(¾)* teaspoon of salt
2 *(1⅔)* or more extra tablespoons of
    peanut oil

PREPARATION

Minced

Peeled and minced
Coarsely pounded or chopped

METHOD

1. Set a frying pan over medium heat and pour in the dried coconut. Shake
the pan and stir the coconut continuously until it turns light brown. Remove
the pan from the heat immediately (the coconut will continue to brown in the
residual heat) and empty the coconut into a spice grinder. Grind it to a powder
(this may take 2 or 3 separate steps). Empty the powder into a blender.

2. Wipe out the pan and return it to the stove. Pour in 4 tablespoons of
peanut oil and heat it over a medium setting. Add the onion and garlic and
fry, stirring, until they become light brown. Empty them into the blender.

3. Grind the whole spices (caraway, chillies, poppy seeds, nutmeg and
cloves) to a fine powder in the spice grinder. (This will also need to be done
in several batches.) Omit this step if using only ground spices. Empty the spice
powder into the blender.

4. Add the rest of the ingredients to the blender and as much oil as it takes
to move the blades efficiently and smoothly. Blend everything to as fine a paste
as possible.

5. Transfer the paste to a jar, cap tightly and refrigerate until needed.

ADVANCE PREPARATION AND
STORAGE NOTES

The paste will keep for up to 1 month under refrigeration. Use in the
quantities indicated in the recipes (3 to 4 tablespoons to a recipe).

❧ Indonesian Hot Pepper Paste

The Indonesian name for this fiery-hot condiment is *sambal ulek*. It is used both
in cooking and (for those who like the flavor of Hades on their tongue) as a relish
to fire up the blander dishes in the cuisine. Many Indonesian recipes call for the
inclusion of hot peppers. Substituting this sauce (½ *(just under)* teaspoonful equal-

ling 2 peppers) saves one the picky task of stemming, coring, seeding and other time-consuming chores.

Preparation time: 15 minutes
Yield: About ½ cup *(less than ¼ pint)*

SHOPPING AND TECHNIQUE TIPS
I have made this *sambal* with the dried red pepper flakes that one finds in jars or small packages in the supermarkets, and the flakes quicken the preparation time considerably. However, many of the jars contain more seeds than flesh, which makes for an incendiary paste. If you have the time, it is worth buying the dried red chilli peppers, stemming them (removing the seeds if you want a comparatively mild *sambal*) and soaking them before using.

INGREDIENTS	PREPARATION
30 dried red chilli peppers	Stemmed (remove seeds if you wish a milder preparation)

Hot water (sufficient to just cover the peppers)
White vinegar (sufficient to make a paste)
2 *(1⅔)* teaspoons of salt

METHOD
1. Place the chilli peppers in a small bowl and cover with hot water. Let them soak for 10 minutes.

2. Remove and drain, then place them, together with 4 tablespoons of the vinegar, in a blender. Blend them to a rough paste, adding as much vinegar as necessary to achieve a pastelike consistency and to permit the blades to turn easily.

3. Add the salt and give the blades a few final turns. Transfer the mixture to a previously sterilized jar and cap tightly. Sterilize the jar again if you wish to keep the paste unrefrigerated.

ADVANCE PREPARATION AND STORAGE NOTES
This paste keeps very well, so you may make it in advance of use. Plan to add ¼ to ½ teaspoon per recipe (more, if the seeds have been removed) depending on how hot you want the dish to be.

& Malaysian Curry Spice Paste

This will create a Malay curry paste of authentic flavor, which contrasts with many other Malaysian mixtures that show a Chinese or Indian ancestry. Local, indigenous nuts, called candlenuts, are often included in Malaysian spice pastes. I have found macadamia nuts to be a close substitute, with Brazil nuts as a second choice.

Preparation time: 20 minutes   Yield: 1 ½ cups *(12 fluid ounces)*

SHOPPING AND TECHNIQUE TIPS
Try to use whole spices wherever indicated, if available, and grind them fresh.

INGREDIENTS	PREPARATION
2 *(1⅔)* tablespoons of whole coriander seeds, or 2 *(1⅔)* tablespoons of ground coriander	
1 *(¾)* tablespoon of whole fennel seeds, or 1 *(¾)* tablespoon of ground fennel	
1 *(¾)* tablespoon of whole cumin seeds, or 1 *(¾)* tablespoon of ground cumin	
1-inch piece of cinnamon stick, or 1½ *(1¼)* teaspoons of ground cinnamon	Broken into fragments
5 dried red chillies, with their seeds, or 1 *(¾)* teaspoon of ground red chilli powder (cayenne)	Broken into pieces
1½ *(1¼)* teaspoons of black peppercorns, or 1½ *(1¼)* teaspoons of ground black pepper	
1-inch piece of fresh ginger root	Peeled and minced
The outer, yellow peel *(zest)* of 1 lemon	Minced
6 macadamia nuts	Chopped or coarsely pounded
1 small onion	Peeled and minced
1 *(¾)* teaspoon of salt	
4 cloves of garlic	Peeled and minced
1 *(¾)* teaspoon of powdered turmeric	
4 to 6 tablespoons *(2 to 3 fluid ounces)* of water, or equal parts of white vinegar and water	

METHOD

1. In an electric spice grinder or mortar, grind or pound together the whole spices (coriander, fennel, cumin, cinnamon, chillies and peppercorns). If you are using a spice grinder, then this must be done in several batches. Omit this step if you are using only ground spices.

2. Empty the resultant powder into a blender and add all the remaining ingredients. Blend everything to a fine paste, using as much water (or water and vinegar) as you need to allow the blades to work smoothly. Stop the motor from time to time and scrape the mixture down the sides of the jar with a spatula.

3. Transfer the paste to a jar, cap tightly and refrigerate until needed.

ADVANCE PREPARATION AND
STORAGE NOTES

A tablespoon of oil poured on top of the paste will help keep it from spoiling. The paste will keep for up to 2 months under refrigeration. Use between 2 to 3 tablespoons to a Malaysian recipe, unless otherwise indicated.

❧ Japanese Soybean Paste Substitute

Miso, a fermented soybean-and-grain paste, is a savory seasoning with the consistency of peanut butter. More than just a flavoring, it performs a variety of culinary feats. Miso can color, enrich and thicken vegetarian stews, soups and stir-fried dishes; be used as a dip or as a component of a barbecue marinade; act as the spread in a sandwich; or help to create marvelously flavored sauces and gravies.

Originating in China, where it is called chiang or jang, the soybean paste was then adopted by Japan and Korea, so it can now be found in slightly different forms throughout the cuisines of North Asia.

Although it is gaining acceptance in the West, especially with vegetarians, it is not yet widely available. Occasionally it can be found in supermarkets that cater to Orientals, but it has yet to become a regular, everyday item.

In order to create Japanese dishes that cannot be cooked without it, I have formulated a rough approximation of the paste, an easy-to-make substitute with somewhat the same flavor, consistency and qualities of performance. Although it is not perfect, I find it works quite well when I cannot find miso. In color and flavor, it comes somewhere between the white, sweet shiro miso and the red, salty aka miso. The combination of ingredients is odd, even slightly bizarre, and has given rise to some humor, but it works, tastes good and is nutritious.

Preparation time: 2 minutes   Yield: almost ¾ cup (almost ⅓ pint)

INGREDIENTS

½ cup of refried beans *(4 ½ ounces or 4 rounded tablespoons of any cooked and mashed, dried beans)*

2 *(1 ⅔)* tablespoons of honey

1½ *(1 ¼)* tablespoons of vegetable yeast extract (such as Marmite, Vegemite, etc.)

1 *(¾)* tablespoon of beer (any ordinary brand)

METHOD

1. Place all the ingredients in a blender and blend at high speed for approximately 2 minutes, stopping the machine from time to time to scrape the sides of the jar with a spatula.

2. When everything is blended into a uniform, smooth paste, transfer the contents of the blender to a shallow, plastic container with a tight fitting lid and refrigerate until needed.

STORAGE AND PREPARATION NOTES

Use in recipes exactly the same as *miso*. Refrigerate but do not store for more than a week.

❀ Chinese Sweet Red Bean Paste

This paste with the consistency of soft marzipan, is one of the few sweet fillings that are popularly used by the Chinese, who are not much given to eating cakes, cookies and confections. It is the traditional filling for moon cakes, the delicacies that look like raised pies with an embossed design on the crust. These cakes are eaten in large quantities during the Moon Festival. Tasting like a paste made from dates, though not as sweet, Red Bean Paste is also used as a filling for other pastries and sweet bun snacks and is a component of the Chinese rice pudding with candied fruits and preserves known as Eight Treasure.

The Sweet Red Bean Paste is available in cans in Oriental food stores, but for those who are unable to locate it easily, here is a recipe.

Preparation time: 2 minutes

Cooking time: 2 hours (less if using a pressure cooker)

Yields: 2 cups *(20 fluid ounces)*

SHOPPING AND TECHNIQUE TIPS
You will find the dried red beans in the dried bean area of your supermarket. They take a long time to cook, so this is a recipe in which it is an advantage to have a pressure cooker.

INGREDIENTS	PREPARATION
1½ cups *(9¼ ounces)* of red beans	Washed well
4 cups of water *(32 fluid ounces)* (if using a pressure cooker, 8 cups *(64 fluid ounces)*)	
½ cup *(3½ ounces)* of vegetable shortening (Crisco)	
1 cup *(7¾ ounces)* of granulated sugar	

METHOD
1. Place the beans and 4 cups of water in a saucepan, cover and bring to a boil over medium-high heat. Reduce the heat to medium-low and cook for 1½ hours or until beans are very soft. If using a pressure cooker, place the beans and 8 cups of water in the cooker and, following the directions, cook for about 25 minutes.

2. Strain the water from the beans (reserve as an addition to soups). Place the beans in a blender or processor and blend into a puree.

3. Press the puree through a sieve, discarding the skins which will be left in the sieve, using the back of a wooden spoon to push the puree through.

4. Place the puree in several layers of cheesecloth and squeeze gently to remove the moisture.

5. Place the thickened puree back in the saucepan, together with the sugar and lard and heat over low heat, stirring until the mixture becomes a thick paste. (Stir and scrape vigorously to make sure that it does not stick to the bottom.)

6. Remove from the heat and let the paste cool before placing it in a container with a tightly fitting lid.

ADVANCE PREPARATION AND
STORAGE NOTES
The Red Bean Paste will keep well, covered tightly, in the refrigerator. It can also be frozen until needed. Besides using it for Chinese cakes and steamed buns, it makes an interesting and nutritious filling for cookies and bar cookies.

&Indian Barbecue Marinade
(TANDOORI)

One of the reasons that the Indian *tandoori* barbecued meat or chicken is so popular in the West is the tantalizing flavor, achieved by a combination of the marinade and the smoke that envelops the meat when the juices fall on the coals. The marinade is simplicity itself; the secret lies in the length of time that the meat remains in the spices—the longer, the better.

Here is the marinade recipe—one that will enhance any meat except beef.

Preparation time: 10 minutes   Yield: 2 cups *(16 fluid ounces)* of
                                                              marinade

SHOPPING AND TECHNIQUE TIPS

The Indians sometimes use beet juice to produce the characteristic pink-orange color of *tandoor-*baked meats. I have indicated food coloring because it is readily available; however, you may use whatever you are happiest with, bearing in mind that the beet juice will cause the marinade to be more liquid.

INGREDIENTS	PREPARATION
1 small onion	Peeled and finely chopped
2-inch piece of fresh ginger root	Peeled and minced
3 cloves of garlic	Peeled and chopped
3 fresh, hot green chilli peppers (Serrano or Jalapeno)	Stemmed and chopped (seeds may be discarded if less heat is wanted)
1 cup *(8 fluid ounces)* of plain yogurt	
4 *(3)* tablespoons of Clarified Butter (page 139)	
1 *(¾)* tablespoon of Indian Sweet Spice Mix (page 118)	
1 *(¾)* teaspoon of ground cumin	
½ *(⅓)* teaspoon of paprika	
1 *(¾)* teaspoon of salt	
A few drops each of red and yellow food coloring	

METHOD

1. In the bowl of a processor, combine the onion, ginger, garlic and chilli peppers and process to a rough paste.

2. Add the yogurt, clarified butter, spices and salt and continue to process for a few more seconds until everything is well blended.

3. Gradually add the red and yellow food coloring alternately, a drop at

a time, while the machine is still turning, until the mixture becomes a bright orange-pink. (Don't worry if the color appears too concentrated and garish; it tones down considerably during cooking.)

ADVANCE PREPARATION AND STORAGE NOTES AND PREPARATION

The marinade can be made up to 12 hours before you are ready to barbecue, but it must be poured over the meat or poultry shortly after it is made. It will not keep too long because of the mixture of fresh ingredients.

❀ Chinese Barbecue Marinade

I always love the dark, rich color, spicebox flavor and shiny surface that this marinade produces on barbecued meats and poultry. It is a made-in-heaven mate for pork and beef ribs, duck and chicken, and the aroma of the barbecuing meat will bring everyone rushing from the pool, garden or from whatever activities they were pursuing.

Preparation time: 5 minutes   Yield: 1¼ cups *(10 fluid ounces)*

SHOPPING AND TECHNIQUE TIPS

Look for sesame oil in the imported foods section of your supermarket. Or you may like to try making the sesame oil from the recipe on page 139.

INGREDIENTS	PREPARATION
½ *(⅓)* teaspoon of Chinese Five-Plus-One Spice Mix (see page 119)	
2 *(1½)* tablespoons of molasses *(treacle)*	
2 *(1½)* tablespoons of honey	
1 *(¾)* tablespoon of smooth plum jam	
1 *(¾)* tablespoon of sesame oil	
1-inch piece of fresh ginger root	Peeled and finely minced
2 cloves of garlic	Peeled and finely minced
½ *(⅓)* teaspoon of Tabasco or any hot pepper sauce	
½ cup *(4 fluid ounces)* of soy sauce	
¼ cup *(2 fluid ounces)* of dry sherry	

METHOD
1. Measure the spice mix into a bowl and stir in the molasses *(treacle)*, honey, plum jam and sesame oil. Blend until the powdered spices have been dissolved.

2. Add the ginger, garlic and Tabasco and, still stirring, gradually pour in the soy sauce and sherry. Stir until all the ingredients are well blended.

ADVANCE PREPARATION AND
STORAGE NOTES
You may like to make this marinade ahead of time and store it in a tightly capped jar in the refrigerator, where it will keep for about 2 weeks. If you are baking the meat in the oven on a rack, with a tray underneath to catch the drippings and marinade, you will have a marvelous-tasting sauce to serve with the meat. You can place any leftover sauce in a jar in the refrigerator to use as the beginning of a Chinese master sauce. (See page 356.)

❧ Japanese Marinade for Grilled Meats

Some of the Japanese marinades are extremely simple, relying merely on a mixture of soy sauce and *sake* (dry rice wine) or *mirin* (very sweet rice cooking wine) to produce a subtle flavor to the meat. The marinade below is a little more hearty and, in the authentic version, would include *miso,* the Japanese fermented bean paste. Instead of *miso,* you can use the substitute mentioned on page 131. If you are marinating some of the more delicate meats, you may wish to omit the *miso* altogether.

Preparation time: 2 minutes
Yield: 9 tablespoons *(4½ fluid ounces)*

SHOPPING AND TECHNIQUE TIPS
Look in the imported food and Oriental food sections of the better supermarkets for *sake* or *mirin,* sesame oil and *miso.* If you cannot find them, then prepare and use the substitutes from the recipes in this chapter.

INGREDIENTS

3 *(2⅓)* tablespoons of soy sauce
4 *(3¼)* tablespoons of sweet sherry
   (or use *mirin*)
1 *(¾)* tablespoon of Japanese
   Soybean Paste Substitute (page
   131)
1 *(¾)* tablespoon of sesame oil,
   bought or homemade (page 139)
1 *(¾)* tablespoon of white vinegar
1 *(¾)* tablespoon of granulated sugar

METHOD

In a mixing bowl, blend together all the ingredients, stirring until the sugar has dissolved and a smooth sauce is formed.

ADVANCE PREPARATION AND
STORAGE NOTES

You may make this marinade up to 2 weeks ahead of time and then refrigerate in a tightly capped jar.

❷ Tamarind Substitute

The tamarind used in Asian recipes is the fibrous, sticky, dark-brown pulp of the tamarind tree that protects the seeds inside the leathery brown pods. It is sweet-sour in flavor and is used as a souring agent in many fresh and cooked dishes instead of lime or lemon juice.

In one of the many houses we occupied in Thailand, there was a feathery tamarind tree by the front gate. My son Adam, introduced to tamarind by the maids and fast developing a "sour" tooth, used to shake the branches until the pods dropped and then break them open and devour the tangy pulp.

Later, both he and I became addicted to the tamarind confections, sold in the markets and at the snack counters in the cinemas. These were often packaged in a long strip of cellophane that was twisted between each sweet/sour/salt tamarind ball, and then fastened into a ring.

Years before, when my elder son, Jonathan, was seven, and Adam a small baby, I had returned to Thailand from Hong Kong and, just before Christmas, was feeling rather rootless and resembling a somewhat penniless expatriate. No Christmas tree (it was the tropics), no Christmas decorations (their imported resplendence was well beyond our budget), and a strong case of homesickness for the traditions of Christmas in England.

In pioneer tradition, we made the best of it. Cutting down a rather skinny branch of a casuarina tree (the nearest thing to a pine in the climate), we stuck it into a pot. We went marketing and bought a great big bag of tamarind rings and hung them, glistening in their wrappings, from all the twigs. Blossoms from the garden completed the decoration. From the expressions on my sons' faces, you would have thought it to be the best Christmas tree in the world. And, as a bonus, we ate the tamarind while we unwrapped our gifts!

Outside Asia, tamarind is available in Indian and Asian specialty food shops, either in packets of pulp, seeds and fiber (which need to be soaked in water and then strained to produce the necessary liquid) or, in the Indian stores, in jars of tamarind concentrate, looking rather like yeast extract. The concentrate still needs to be diluted and dissolved in water. Because it is so widely used in Indian and Southeast Asian cooking, and because it shows no signs of becoming readily available in supermarkets, I have devised a substitute—molasses *(treacle)* and lime juice—that gives a reasonable approximation, both in appearance and flavor.

Preparation time: 2 minutes   Yield: 3 *(2⅓)* tablespoons

SHOPPING AND TECHNIQUE TIPS
Try to use the freshly squeezed lime juice whenever possible, but, at a pinch, you may use the bottled lime juice (I don't mean Roses Lime Cordial.)

INGREDIENTS
1 *(¾)* tablespoon of molasses
    (treacle)
3 *(2⅓)* tablespoons of fresh lime
    juice

METHOD
Measure the molasses *(treacle)* into a bowl and gradually pour in the lime juice, stirring continually until it becomes a somewhat thick, smooth fluid.

ADVANCE PREPARATION AND STORAGE NOTES
The mixture has the keeping qualities of fresh lime juice—which is no more than a day or two. If you must prepare it ahead, refrigerate it until ready to use, or freeze it. It freezes well.

❧ Sesame Oil

This rich, nut-flavored oil is used in Asian cooking as a flavoring agent rather than as a cooking oil. It is added at the end in cooked dishes and is often included in dressings and marinades.

Preparation time: 2¼ hours   Yield: 1⅓ cups *(10½ fluid ounces)*

SHOPPING AND TECHNIQUE TIPS
I find this recipe works very well using sunflower seed oil.

INGREDIENTS
¼ cup *(2 ounces)* of sesame seeds
1 cup *(8 fluid ounces)* of sunflower
    seed oil or any mild vegetable
    oil

METHOD
1. Place a frying pan over medium heat and dry-fry the sesame seeds, shaking the pan and scooping them with a spatula until they are an even medium brown.
2. Pour in the oil and allow the seeds and oil to heat for 2 minutes.
3. Pour into a blender and blend on high for just under 1 minute. Allow the mixture to stand for 2 hours to develop flavor.
4. Arrange a sieve over a large jug or bowl and line it with muslin or a handkerchief. Pour the mixture through it and squeeze the cloth to get all the oil from the seed residue. Pour into a jar or bottle and store in a cool dark cupboard.

ADVANCE PREPARATION AND
STORAGE NOTES
This oil can be prepared at any time when you wish to spend an hour or two in the kitchen.

❧ Indian Clarified Butter (GHEE)

Except for the cooking restrictions of a handful of religious sects, the *haute cuisine* of North and Central India has always demanded clarified butter for cooking fat. Clarification removes the milk solids and moisture from butter, leaving only the pure oil. This has a higher smoke point than olive or mustard oils and imparts a delicious flavor to any dish in which it is used. Most important, as far as the hot climate of India is concerned, *ghee* needs no refrigeration and will last as long as a year without turning rancid, if stored in a cool, dark place.

Because of the relative expense of *ghee,* many Indian families use 75 percent vegetable shortening or clarified margarine to 25 percent butter in their cooking, producing a less rich dish which still retains some of the flavor.

Preparation and cooking time: Yield: 1¾ pounds
   2 hours

SHOPPING AND TECHNIQUE TIPS
Always use *unsalted* butter for clarification; if you use salted, the result will be inedible. Ensure that it is heated over a *low* heat so that there is no danger of burning. The double clarification method, shown below, ensures a higher purity of butter oil than is achieved by the usual Western clarification methods. For those who cannot eat butter, margarine may be clarified in the same way; again, specify unsalted.

INGREDIENTS
2 pounds of unsalted (sweet) butter

METHOD
1. Place a pan over medium-low to low heat and add the butter. Melt it and bring it to just below the simmering point. Adjust your heat setting, if necessary, to keep it at that temperature.

2. As the foam gathers on top, keep stirring it back into the oil. Leave the butter oil over the heat for 45 minutes. At the end of that time, the moisture will have evaporated and the milk solids will have formed a layer of sediment on the bottom of the pan.

3. Remove the pan from the heat and let the contents cool to lukewarm.

4. Place a sieve, lined with 2 or 3 layers of paper towels, over the top of a pitcher or bowl and slowly pour the clear butter oil through it, keeping as much of the sediment as you can in the pan.

5. Discard the sediment, wash and dry the pan and set it back on the same heat setting. Pour in the oil and bring it up to under a simmer. Hold it at that temperature for 5 minutes and then remove from the heat.

6. Line the sieve with fresh paper towels and strain the oil through once more. It should now be crystal clear.

7. Pour into a wide-mouthed jar, cap tightly and store in a cool place, or refrigerate. You will notice that you will have lost about ¼ pound of the butter by removing the moisture and the sediment.

Make the clarified butter whenever you have the time to spare. If you decide to double the recipe, increase the cooking time by one-half. If the *ghee* is stored unrefrigerated, it will solidify during cold weather and liquefy when the temperature rises. This in no way affects the quality or flavor.

𝕊 Indian Curd Cheese

This is one of two milk cheeses made in Asia (the other is made in the Philippines), although the preparations made from soybean milk (bean curd) are similar. Because of the hot climate of India, this "raw" or soft cheese is freshly made when needed for cooking.

This cheese known in India as *panir,* is not eaten by itself, but is used as a source of protein in the preparation of vegetarian dishes and also in sweets. When first made, it has the appearance and consistency of bean curd and must be kneaded or pressed under weights to firm and compress it. The finished cheese has the consistency of the Greek *feta* cheese and is rather crumbly.

Preparation time: 24 hours   Yield: ⅔ cup *(3 ½ fluid ounces)*

SHOPPING AND TECHNIQUE TIPS
Whole unpasteurized milk should be used for curd cheese (obtainable from small dairies or from some supermarkets). Some people use lemon juice alone to sour and separate it, but I prefer the combination of lemon juice and yogurt or, for a richer cheese, sour cream.

INGREDIENTS
½ cup *(4 fluid ounces)* of plain
    yogurt or sour cream
Juice of 1 lemon
1 quart *(32 fluid ounces)* of
    unpasteurized milk (whole, not
    skimmed)

METHOD
1. In a small mixing bowl, thoroughly stir the lemon juice into the yogurt or sour cream.

2. Heat the milk in a large saucepan until it just rises to a boil. When the milk begins to foam, quickly remove it from the heat and stir in the yogurt-

lemon juice mixture. As you stir, the milk should immediately begin to separate into curds and a thin, watery whey. Let it cool.

3. Set a sieve, lined with a towel or cheesecloth, over a bowl and strain the cooled curds and whey through it. Gather up the corners of the towel and, twisting it into a bundle, squeeze it over the bowl to remove the excess liquid.

4. The whey can be saved, refrigerated and used in soups or as the cooking liquid for lentils, etc.

5. Tie a 12-inch length of twine around the top of the bundle and make a loop. Suspend the bundle over your sink to drip and firm up for at least 4 to 6 hours, preferably, overnight.

6. When the curds are completely drained and dry, empty them onto a board, gather them into a ball and knead the resultant curd cheese until it becomes firm and is compressed. (Alternately, you may pat it into a flat circle, place it between 2 plates and set a heavy weight, such as an iron or a pan of water, on the top plate to press it for a further 4 hours.)

7. When the curd cheese is compressed and as firm as *feta* cheese, it can be cut into cubes for cooking, or left uncut and refrigerated, covered, until it is to be used.

ADVANCE PREPARATION AND
STORAGE NOTES

This cheese can be refrigerated for up to 3 days. It is generally cubed and fried in clarified butter, to be mixed with vegetables. Use a nonstick pan for frying, if you have one, as the cubes have a tendency to stick.

❧ Indonesian Dark Sweet Soy Sauce

Our tomato ketchup, or catsup, gets its name, but not its ingredients, from the Malay *kechop* and from this Indonesian Dark Sweet Soy Sauce known as *ketjap manis*. This is very much a basic ingredient, being used to flavor soups, stews, *sambals* and stir-fried dishes. It is much sweeter than the everyday soy sauce, with a rich, mellow flavor. You may also like to try it as an ingredient in barbecue marinades and sauces.

Preparation time: 2 minutes   Yield: about 5 cups *(40 fluid ounces)*
Cooking time: 10 minutes

SHOPPING AND TECHNIQUE TIPS
The original sauce is made with palm sugar, the mellow, less sweet sugar from the Palmyra palm, and with ground, dried *laos* (galingale). I have substituted brown sugar and powdered ginger. The result is not quite as aromatic, but just as good.

INGREDIENTS
2 cups *(5⅔ ounces)* of dark-brown sugar
2¼ *(18 fluid ounces)* cups of water
1½ cups *(12 fluid ounces)* of soy sauce
¾ cup *(6 fluid ounces)* of molasses *(treacle)*
½ *(⅓)* teaspoon of ground ginger
½ *(⅓)* teaspoon of ground coriander seeds
½ *(⅓)* teaspoon of freshly ground black pepper

METHOD
1. Combine the sugar and water in a saucepan and bring to a boil over moderate heat, stirring until the sugar dissolves.

2. Increase the heat to high, position a candy thermometer inside the saucepan and boil for about 5 minutes, or until the temperature reaches 200°F. *(93.3°C.)*.

3. Reduce the heat to low, stir in the soy sauce, molasses, ginger, coriander and pepper and simmer for 3 minutes.

4. Line a sieve with a dampened paper towel and pour the mixture through into a sterilized storage bottle or jar.

5. Cap tightly and store in a dark cool place, or refrigerate.

ADVANCE PREPARATION AND
STORAGE NOTES
This sauce will keep for about 3 months on the shelf and up to 6 months in the refrigerator. Unless otherwise indicated, use about 1 tablespoon to a recipe.

❧ Quick All-Purpose Indian Curry Sauce

While I do not like using commercially prepared curry powders and I advocate the use of separate spice pastes to complement the individual curries, there are times when we are rushed and need to prepare a meal at short notice. This curry sauce will provide a shortcut to some delicious and quickly prepared dishes.

You may like to heat chunks of lobster or crab in it; to combine it with cooked, leftover meats; or even as a sauce for sautéed vegetables.

Preparation time: 25 minutes   Yield: 8 cups *(64 fluid ounces)*

SHOPPING AND TECHNIQUE TIPS

Before starting to prepare this, refresh your memory by reading the introduction (pages 326–30) to the chapter "Currying Favor." Remember that the secret of a successful curry or curry gravy is the slow cooking of the spices so that they lose their raw, bitter flavor and mellow to a rich bouquet. You may use either a homemade stock or the canned varieties. Thick coconut milk may be substituted for the yogurt.

INGREDIENTS	PREPARATION
2 *(1⅔)* tablespoons of ground coriander seeds	
1 *(¾)* tablespoon of ground cumin seeds	
1 *(¾)* tablespoon of ground turmeric	
1 *(¾)* teaspoon of ground red chilli powder (Cayenne)	
1½ *(1¼)* tablespoons of curry powder (any brand)	
⅓ cup *(2⅔ fluid ounces)* of white vinegar	
3 medium onions	Peeled and coarsely chopped
4 cloves of garlic	Peeled and chopped
2-inch piece of fresh ginger root	Peeled and minced
8 *(6⅔)* tablespoons of Indian Clarified Butter (page 139)	
6 cups *(48 fluid ounces)* of stock (chicken or beef)	
1 cup *(8 fluid ounces)* of plain yogurt	
1¼ teaspoons *(just under a teaspoon)* of Indian Sweet Spice Mix (page 118)	
1 *(⅔)* teaspoon of salt or to taste	

METHOD

1. In a small mixing bowl, combine the dried, powdered spices with the vinegar into a paste. Set aside.

2. In a food processor or blender, grind the onions, garlic and fresh ginger to a rough puree.

3. Heat the clarified butter in a large saucepan over medium-high heat. Remove puree from processor and fry until the sharp odor mellows, stirring constantly.

4. Add the spice paste and cook, stirring for at least 5 minutes, until the bitter smell of the spices disappears and the mixture darkens.

5. Pour in the stock and let it come to a boil, stirring occasionally. Reduce the heat to medium-low and stir for 10 minutes.

6. Increase the heat and stir in the yogurt, blending it until it disappears and the sauce thickens. Sprinkle in the Indian Sweet Spice Mix and add salt to your taste. Stir again, set aside and let it cool.

ADVANCE PREPARATION AND STORAGE NOTES

Measure the sauce in 2-cup amounts into freezer bags or containers and seal. If using bags, freeze them flat, and then, when they are solidly frozen, you can stack them upright in the freezer. When you wish to use the sauce, take the desired number of bags out and defrost them at room temperature. Pour into a saucepan and heat gradually, stirring over a low flame. You may wish to add a little additional yogurt to increase the creaminess of the sauce.

❀ Chinese All-Purpose Sauce

This sauce can be used instead of hoisin sauce if the latter is unobtainable in your area. Hoisin, made from soybeans, sugar, vinegar, garlic, flour and spices, is a dark brown-black, thick, slightly sweet spiced sauce which is a component of Chinese marinades for ribs, shellfish and duck and is also used as a table or dipping sauce.

This sauce is milder, but will give a definite "Chinese" flavor to marinades or to food which is dipped in it.

Preparation time: 12 minutes   Yield: 1½ cups *(12 fluid ounces)*

SHOPPING AND TECHNIQUE TIPS

All the ingredients should be readily available from a good supermarket. The yeast extract is found in the gourmet or imported foods section. Another local variety can be found in the health-foods section.

INGREDIENTS

¾ cup of canned *(tinned)* dark-red
   kidney beans
¼ cup *(2 fluid ounces)* of the bean
   liquid
3 *(2⅓)* tablespoons of molasses
   (treacle)
3 *(2⅓)* tablespoons of teriyaki sauce
2 tablespoons *(1 fluid ounce)* of red
   wine vinegar
1 *(¾)* tablespoon of garlic powder
2 *(1½)* teaspoons of Five-Plus-One
   Spice Powder (see page 119)
2 *(1½)* teaspoons of yeast extract
   (Marmite, Vegamite, etc.)

PREPARATION

Drained and liquid reserved

METHOD

1. Place all the ingredients in a blender or food processor and blend into
a puree, stopping the machine from time to time to scrape down the bowl with
a spatula.

2. Pour the mixture from the blender into a sieve over a mixing bowl, and
press it through using the back of a wooden spoon. Discard the broken bean
skins left in the sieve.

3. Pour the sauce into a tightly lidded jar and refrigerate.

ADVANCE PREPARATION AND
STORAGE NOTES

The sauce will keep in the refrigerator for at least a week. As it is
uncooked, I would not risk too long a storage period.

❀ Chinese Oyster Sauce

A dark brown sauce made from oysters and soy sauce used as a seasoning. It is
available in bottles or in cans *(tins)*. If you cannot find it, here is a recipe so that
you can make your own.

Preparation time: 15 minutes
Cooking time: 45 minutes

Yield: approximately 4 cups *(32 fluid
   ounces)*

SHOPPING AND TECHNIQUE TIPS

You are going to have to wait until oysters are in season before making this sauce. For oyster lovers, it will be a tug-of-war about whether to make the sauce or eat the oysters. For those of you who do not like oysters, you will enjoy the sauce anyway, so go ahead and make it.

INGREDIENTS	PREPARATION
2 cups *(13 ounces)* of fresh oyster meat	Washed and drained
3 cups *(24 fluid ounces)* of water	
1 cup *(8 ounces)* of bottled clam juice	
1 *(¾)* teaspoon of salt	
1 clove of garlic	Peeled and crushed
1 green *(spring)* onion (white portion only)	
1 slice of fresh ginger root, ⅛-inch thick	
¼ cup *(2 fluid ounces)* of soy sauce	
1 *(¾)* teaspoon of granulated sugar	
2 *(1⅔)* teaspoons of cornstarch *(cornflour)*	
3 *(2⅓)* tablespoons of water	

METHOD

1. Place the oyster meat, the 3 cups of water, clam juice, salt, garlic, green *(spring)* onion and ginger in a saucepan and bring to a boil over medium-high heat. Reduce the heat to low, cover and simmer for 30 minutes.

2. While the oysters are cooking, mix together the soy sauce, sugar, cornstarch *(cornflour)* and the 3 *(2⅓)* tablespoons of water in a small bowl.

3. At the end of the cooking time, uncover the saucepan and gradually pour in the cornstarch *(cornflour)* mixture, stirring. Continue to simmer the mixture for 10 more minutes, stirring as it thickens slightly.

4. Set a sieve over a large bowl and pour the oyster mixture through it, retaining the liquid and discarding the solids, including the oysters (all the goodness is cooked out of them.)

5. Pour into a jar or bottle, cap tightly and refrigerate.

ADVANCE PREPARATION AND STORAGE NOTES

This sauce will keep for several months in the refrigerator. The sauce is used to season stir-fried dishes and also as a table sauce with meats.

✣ Large Egg Roll Wrappers

This recipe makes large wrappers for spring or egg rolls. They are soft, thin and pancake-like, and instead of being rolled out, they are made by spreading the thinnest layer of batter possible over the surface of a frying pan and letting it cook till it sets. See page 154 for instructions on how to form Egg Rolls.

Preparation time: 10 minutes   Makes 12 wrappers, 10 inches in
Cooking time: 30 minutes   diameter

SHOPPING AND TECHNIQUE TIPS

The skill in making these comes with practice. The secret lies in tilting and rotating the frying pan rapidly the moment the batter is poured in to spread a layer evenly over the entire surface before it starts to set. Until you get the hang of it, do not worry if the first few are rather uneven in thickness. By the time you have rolled the wrappers around the filling and deep-fried them, no one will notice.

INGREDIENTS	PREPARATION
4 eggs	Separated
1 cup (6 ounces) of cornstarch (cornflour)	
2½ cups (1 pint) of water	
6 (4¾) tablespoons of peanut oil	

METHOD

1. In a medium mixing bowl, whisk the egg whites until they form a small-bubbled foam, but not as far as the soft-peak state.

2. Fold in the yolks with a wooden spoon and mix gently.

3. In a small mixing bowl, blend the cornstarch (cornflour) and water together. Stir to prevent the cornstarch (cornflour) from settling and pour it gradually into the eggs. Stir the batter lightly.

4. Pour the oil into a teacup and paint the surface of a frying pan lightly but completely with a thin film of oil. Set a frying pan over medium-low heat.

5. When the oil has a haze over it, pour in 2 tablespoons of the batter and, lifting the pan from the heat, rotate it immediately until the pan is covered with a thin, even layer of batter.

6. Set the pan back on the heat until the wrapper is set and solid. Do not turn it.

7. In one quick motion, invert the pan over a plate, flipping the pancake on to it. Cover the pancake with a square of waxed (greaseproof) paper.

8. Return the pan to the heat and brush with another thin film of oil. Repeat steps 5 to 7 until all the batter is used and 12 wrappers are stacked, each separated by a square of waxed paper. If using them at once, keep them warm in a low oven until you are ready to roll them up over the filling.

ADVANCE PREPARATION AND STORAGE NOTES

The wrappers can be made ahead of time and refrigerated in a sealed plastic bag. Alternatively, they can be placed in a freezer bag and frozen. After defrosting, they may need to be steamed for a couple of minutes to make them pliable again.

❧ Pastry for Turnovers

This pastry, with its unusual spiral layering of butter, makes an interestingly textured crust for the Philippine *empanadas,* the deep-fried meat turnovers, and also for *samosas,* the Indian meat or vegetable turnovers which we refer to as curry puffs.

Preparation time: 45 minutes   Makes about 20 turnovers

SHOPPING AND TECHNIQUE TIPS

This technique calls for a lot of rolling out. Make sure that your rolling surface is low enough so that you can bear down on it. If your kitchen counters are not so designed, then stand on a stool; it's less tiring. The construction of the pastry is similar to that of a jelly or Swiss roll. Each slice of roll is placed, cut side uppermost, and then rolled into the finished, individual pastry rounds.

INGREDIENTS	PREPARATION
2 egg yolks	Beaten
1 cup *(8 fluid ounces)* of cold water (a little more may be added if necessary)	
¼ cup *(2 ounces)* of granulated sugar	
1 *(¾)* teaspoon of salt	
4 cups *(1 ½ pounds)* of all-purpose *(plain)* flour	
Cornstarch *(cornflour)*	
4 tablespoons of butter (½ stick) *(⅛ pound),* or Indian Clarified Butter (page 139)	Melted

METHOD

1. In a small bowl, mix together the first 4 ingredients, stirring until the sugar and salt dissolve. Sift the flour into a large bowl and stir in the egg mixture. Mix to a stiff dough and knead until the texture becomes soft and silky to the touch and the dough is pliable and elastic.

2. Cut the ball of dough into 2 equal portions. Set one aside, covered with a damp cloth. Roll out the other portion on a floured board into a large, paper-thin circle, powdering with cornstarch and stretching the dough as you roll.

3. Brush the entire surface of the circle with half the melted butter and then roll it up as tightly as you can into a "jelly roll." To start off the roll, bend up the edge nearest you and roll it backward and forward, as if you were playing with modeling clay. As you roll, move the palms of your hands evenly along the tube, pressing it down and away from you so that there are no air spaces left in the interior. The finished roll should not be more than 1 inch in diameter.

PASTRY FOR TURNOVERS

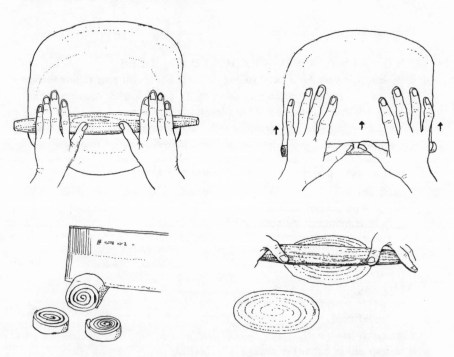

4. Cut the roll into 1-inch segments and lay them down, cut side upper-most. The end segments will have a hole in the middle; squash them slightly so that the dough fills up the hole.

5. Roll out each segment into a circle, about 3½ to 4 inches in diameter and about ⅛-inch thick. Set them on one side and repeat steps 2 through 5 with the other half of the dough. Do not refrigerate the dough, but use it directly. If you refrigerate either the rolls or the cut segments, the butter will become too firm and the spirals will not adhere to each other when baked.

A D V A N C E   P R E P A R A T I O N   A N D   S T O R A G E   N O T E S

Once the turnovers are filled, they can be refrigerated or frozen before deep-frying. Alternatively, the turnovers can be made and fried, then frozen in large freezer bags, to be revitalized in a warm oven before serving.

❧ Soft, White Wheat-Flour Noodles

Preparation time: 20 minutes
Cooking time: 1 hour, 20 minutes

Makes enough noodles for 6 to 8 servings (approximately 10 to 12 noodle sheets)

S H O P P I N G   A N D   T E C H N I Q U E   T I P S

You will need to buy the superfine cake flour—not the ordinary variety—and sift it to free the mixture of lumps. The batter must be completely smooth and should have no air bubbles, so let it sit for about 10 minutes after making it. Use two 7-inch (inside measurement) square baking pans and alternate them so that there is always a pan on the steamer. If you have 4 of these pans and a double-tiered steamer, you can halve the noodle preparation time. The pans must be washed, dried and re-oiled or sprayed between each use.

I N G R E D I E N T S

2 cups (¾ pound) of superfine cake flour (best quality, finely ground plain flour)

¼ cup (2 ounces) of cornstarch (cornflour)

¾ (½) teaspoon of salt (optional)

⅓ cup (2⅔ fluid ounces) vegetable oil, plus extra oil for the trays (or nonstick spray coating)

2⅔ cups (33 fluid ounces) of cold water

P R E P A R A T I O N

Sifted

Sifted

METHOD

1. Sift the flour and cornstarch into a mixing bowl and stir in the salt. Add the oil, a little at a time, mixing thoroughly.

2. Pour in the water gradually, mixing smoothly (not beating), until you have a smooth batter with no lumps or bubbles. Use a rubber spatula to scrape the bottom of the bowl to make sure that there is no unmixed flour. Let the batter sit for 10 minutes.

3. While the batter is sitting, pour water into a steamer and bring it to a boil over high heat. Grease or spray a square baking pan, making sure you have covered the bottom evenly.

4. When the steamer is up to full heat, pour a thin, even layer of batter (about ⅛-inch thick) in the bottom of the pan and carefully set it on a steamer tray. Cover the pan with a towel, arranging the ends inside the tray and making sure that the towel does not dip down in the center and touch the batter. (This is to absorb the condensation so that moisture does not fall on the batter.)

5. Set the tray on the steamer, cover and steam for 5 minutes, or until the noodle sheet is set and firm. Remove the tray, turn it upside down to release the noodle sheet and let the sheet cool. Wash, dry and re-oil the pan.

6. Fill the pan again and set it back on the steamer. Meanwhile, when the noodle sheet is cool, roll it up and then slice along the roll. The width of the cuts will be the width of the finished noodles. I suggest you cut them ¼-inch to ½-inch wide.

7. Repeat the process until you have used all the batter and cut all the noodles.

ADVANCE PREPARATION AND
STORAGE NOTES

You can make these noodles a day in advance. Do not refrigerate them but put the noodle sheets (uncut) in a cool place, interleaved with squares of waxed (greaseproof) paper. Cover with a dampened towel. Cut before using.

✿ Egg Noodle or Wonton Dough

Preparation time: 40 minutes   Yield: 2 pounds of egg noodles or
                                             wontons

SHOPPING AND TECHNIQUE TIPS

I have given an approximate amount of water. You may use more or less according to the variables of temperature and humidity. This dough needs a lot of kneading and should be very pliable when you have finished. If you have a noodle machine, it will cut down on the rolling and preparation time considerably. If you have a pasta machine, follow the instructions for the Italian egg-noodle dough. For wonton wrappers run the dough through the last, or thinnest, setting.

INGREDIENTS	PREPARATION
4 large eggs	At room temperature
¼ cup *(2 fluid ounces)* of cold water (plus a little extra)	
4 cups *(1 ½ pounds)* of all-purpose *(plain)* flour	
½ *(⅓)* teaspoon of salt	

METHOD

1. Break the eggs into a bowl and add the ¼ cup *(2 fluid ounces)* of water. Beat together until they are thoroughly mixed.

2. Begin to add the flour, a little at a time, together with the salt. Mix with a spoon until the dough becomes firm enough for you to use your hands. Continue to mix and add the flour until you have a very stiff dough, with all the pieces sticking together. (You may need to add a little extra water to achieve this, but do not add any until you have worked the dough thoroughly enough to be sure you'll need it.) Keep on kneading and pressing in a bowl until you have a lump of very firm dough. Transfer it to a board.

3. Knead firmly and thoroughly, bearing down with the palms of your hands and pressing away from you. Fold the dough back on itself and keep repeating the process. Knead for 10 to 15 minutes, or until the dough becomes elastic, smooth and pliable. Do not add any extra flour.

4. Let the dough rest for 5 minutes, covered with a damp cloth, then separate it into 2 equal pieces. Leaving one covered, roll out the other as thinly and evenly as you possibly can. Turn the dough sheet as you roll. When you have finished, trim it into a rectangle and set it aside.

5. Repeat with the other half of the dough.

6. If you are making noodles, roll a dough sheet up into a jelly roll and slice it into strips, ¼-inch width. If you are making wontons, cut it into 3-inch squares. Sift a little cornstarch *(cornflour)* over the sheet before cutting and smooth it over the surface. Stack the squares. (The cornstarch *(cornflour)* will ensure that they do not stick together.) Alternately, you might like to slip a little square of waxed *(greaseproof)* paper between each square as you stack them.

EGG ROLL	PACKET	TURNOVER	PANCAKE

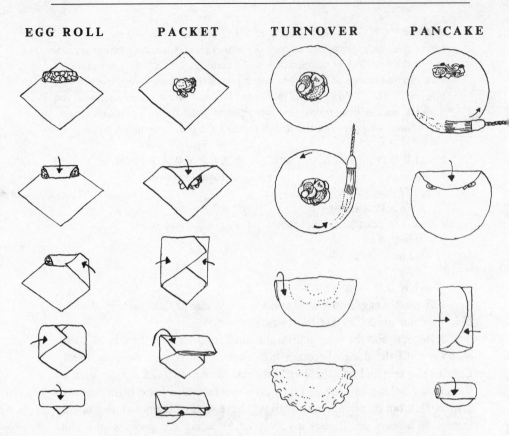

7. If you have made noodles, you may either leave them out to air-dry before storing them or use them right away.

ADVANCE PREPARATION AND STORAGE NOTES

You may wrap the wontons with freezer-weight wrap and freeze them. Thaw at room temperature before using. The noodles may be dried completely and then placed in an airtight container, or wrapped and thoroughly sealed. Use in the same manner as commercial egg noodles.

❧ Mandarin Pancakes

Preparation time: 2 hours   Makes 24 pancakes
Cooking time: 30 minutes

SHOPPING AND TECHNIQUE TIPS

These paper-thin, delicate pancakes are always rolled out and cooked in pairs as they are too fragile to be handled singly. Some cooks like to roll out a pair and cook them before making more, but I find that all the pancakes can be made ahead and stacked, interleaved with waxed *(greaseproof)* paper. Keep the uncooked pancakes covered while you fry.

INGREDIENTS

2 cups *(¾ pound)* of all-purpose
    (plain) flour
¾ cup *(6 fluid ounces)* of boiling
    water
2 tablespoons *(1 ⅔ tablespoons)* of
    sesame oil or peanut oil

METHOD

1. Place the flour in a mixing bowl, make a well in the center and pour in the boiling water. Mix with a fork or wooden spoon until a soft dough is formed. If using a food processor, fit the metal blade into the bowl, add the flour, turn on the motor and pour the boiling water down the feed tube. Stop as soon as the mixture forms a ball.

2. Lightly flour a pastry board, transfer the dough and knead it for about 10 minutes or until the dough is smooth. Cover with a damp cloth and let the dough rest at room temperature for 30 minutes.

3. Roll and pull the dough into a 12-inch-long cylinder and cut it into 12 equal pieces. Cover the dough with plastic film while you continue.

4. Take a piece of dough and cut it in half. Roll each half into a ball and flatten it with the palm of your hand into a disk about ¼ inch thick. Brush the tops of the disks with sesame oil and then press them together, oiled surfaces touching. (This will ensure that the pancakes will separate after cooking.) Dust the outside surfaces with flour.

5. Working from the center outward, roll the double round into a thin pancake, 7 to 8 inches in diameter. Turn the pancake as you roll to help you form a circular shape.

6. Repeat steps 4 and 5 until you have rolled out all the pancake pairs. Stack the pancakes with a piece of waxed *(greaseproof)* paper between each pair and keep both the unrolled pieces and the stack covered as you work so they do not dry out.

7. Heat an ungreased frying pan over medium-low heat. Add a pancake pair and cook for about 1 minute on each side. The cooked surface should be the color of parchment and lightly speckled with gold. When both surfaces are dry but not brittle, the pancake is cooked.

8. Remove from the pan and carefully pull the pancakes apart. Stack them and cover with a damp cloth until they are all made and you are ready to serve.

9. Fold the pancakes into quarters, place them on a plate or in a shallow basket and serve with Peking Duck (page 318).

ADVANCE PREPARATION AND STORAGE NOTES

The pancakes may be made in advance, interleaved with waxed (greaseproof) paper, wrapped in plastic film or foil and refrigerated or frozen. If refrigerated, they may be steamed for 5 minutes to reheat. If frozen, they may be steamed, unthawed, for 10 minutes. In either case, line the steamer tray with a damp towel, place the unwrapped pancakes inside (leave the pieces of waxed (greaseproof) paper in place) and fold in the towel over the top of them before covering the steamer.

You may also like to serve the pancakes filled with the Spicy Szechwan Chicken with Cashew Nuts (page 287).

❧ Fried Onion Flakes

Many Indian and Southeast Asian recipes call for a garnish of slivered or minced onions, fried until they are crisp and brown. To execute this perfectly is a tedious chore, as the pan must be watched constantly and the onions stirred continuously —otherwise they will blacken and burn.

I have discovered that a crisp and crunchy onion topping can be made from the dried onion flakes which can be found in or near the spice section in the supermarket. The jars of dried onion are generally labeled "minced" or "chopped," according to the size of the pieces. Either will do.

Preparation time: 1 minute   Yield: 1 cup *(4 ½ ounces)*
Cooking time: 2 to 3 minutes

SHOPPING AND TECHNIQUE TIPS

Because the flakes are completely free of moisture, they brown rapidly. Watch them carefully while frying and remove them from the heat *before* they are completely browned as they will continue to brown in the residual heat.

INGREDIENTS
1 *(¾)* tablespoon of peanut oil
1 cup *(4 ½ ounces)* of dried onion
    flakes

METHOD

1. Heat the oil in a frying pan over medium heat. Pour in the onion flakes and stir and toss them continuously until they turn a golden brown. This will happen quickly. Some pieces will brown more rapidly than others, but do not wait until every fragment is toasted, otherwise the darker flakes will overcook and turn bitter in flavor. The oil will be quickly absorbed. Do not add more. It will eventually permeate all the flakes.

2. When you are satisfied that most of the flakes are golden brown, turn them out onto a paper plate lined with the paper towels, and let them drain.

3. When cool, pour them into a jar and cap tightly.

ADVANCE PREPARATION AND
STORAGE NOTES

The Fried Onion Flakes will keep well on a shelf for up to 3 months. Shake out or measure as much as you want for a garnish and then recap the jar tightly.

✿ Egg Strip Garnish

This garnish is used almost universally throughout the Far East. There are many ways in which to prepare it, but I think this works the best.

Preparation time: 1 minute   Garnish for 1 dish
Cooking time: 4 to 5 minutes

SHOPPING AND TECHNIQUE TIPS

I find that adding a little water makes the beaten eggs lighter. Cook the omelet over very low heat. It should set but not brown on the underside. It does not need turning.

INGREDIENTS
2 eggs
1 (¾ teaspoon) teaspoon of water
¼ teaspoon (a pinch) of salt
Vegetable oil

METHOD

1. Break the eggs into a bowl and beat them very lightly with a fork until they are just evenly mixed. Stir in the water and salt and beat again a few times. There should be no air bubbles.

2. Lightly oil a paper towel and wipe a frying pan, leaving a thin film. Set the pan over low heat and warm it through. Pour in *half* the egg mixture, rotating the pan so that the egg forms a very thin, even layer on the bottom. Let it cook until it is set and just coagulated on the top surface. Remove the pan from the heat and let it cool slightly.

3. Use a spatula to carefully remove the egg layer from the pan. Set it aside and let it cool. Repeat with the remainder of the egg mixture.

4. Taking one egg "pancake," roll it up into a tight tube and then thinly slice it crosswise into strips. Repeat with the other egg pancake. The strips may be prepared ahead of time and refrigerated, covered.

Conversion Tables and Equivalents

General

LIQUID VOLUME

United States	Imperial	International (Metric)
½ teaspoon (tsp.)	⅓ tsp.	2.5 milliliters (ml.)
1 tsp.	¾ tsp.	5 ml.
1 tablespoon (tbsp.) = 3 tsp.	¾ tbsp.	15 ml.
1 ounce (oz.) = 2 tbsp.	1 ounce	29 ml.
1 cup (c.) = 8 oz., 16 tbsp., 48 tsp.	⅘ cup	237 ml. (approx. ¼ l.)
1 pint (pt.) = 2 cups	⅘ pt. = 1⅔ cups	473 ml. (approx. ½ l.)
1 quart (qt.) = 2 pt.	⅘ qt. = 3⅓ cups	946 ml. (approx. 1 l.)
1 gallon (gal.) = 4 qt.	⅘ gal.	3.78 l.

Imperial	United States	International (Metric)
½ tsp.	⅝ tsp.	3 ml.
1 tsp.	1¼ tsp.	6 ml.
1 tbsp. = 3 tsp.	1¼ tbsp.	18 ml.
1 oz.	1 oz. (2 tbsp.)	29 ml.
1 cup = 10 oz., 16 tbsp., 48 tsp.	1¼ cups = 10 oz.	296 ml.
1 pt. = 2 cups	1¼ pt. = 2½ cups, 20 oz.	591 ml.
1 qt. = 2 pt.	2½ pt. = 5 cups, 40 oz.	1.18 l.
1 gal. = 4 qt.	5 pt. = 10 cups	2.36 l.

DRY VOLUME

United States	Imperial	International (Metric)
1 pt.	1 pt.	0.55 l.
1 qt.	1 qt.	1.10 l.
1 peck	1 peck	8.81 l.
1 bushel	1 bushel	35.24 l.

Temperatures

$$Fahrenheit = \frac{Celsius \times 9}{5} + 32 \qquad Celsius = \frac{(Fahrenheit - 32) \times 5}{9}$$

100°F.	= 38°C.(37.8°C.)
120°F.	= 49°C.(48.9°C.)
130°F.	= 54°C.(54.4°C.)
140°F.	= 60°C.(60°C.)
150°F.	= 66°C.(65.6°C.)
160°F.	= 71°C.(71.1°C.)
165°F.	= 74°C.(73.9°C.)
170°F.	= 77°C.(76.7°C.)

Fahrenheit	Celsius	British Gas No. (Regulo)
180°F.	= 82°C. (82.2°C.)	
190°F.	= 88°C. (87.8°C.)	
200°F.	= 95°C. (93.3°C.)	
212°F.	= 100°C. (100°C.)	
225°F.	= 110°C. (107.2°C.)	= ¼
250°F.	= 120°C. (121.1°C.)	= ½
275°F.	= 135°C. (135°C.)	= 1
300°F.	= 150°C. (148.9°C.)	= 2
320°F.	= 160°C. (160°C.)	
325°F.	= 163°C. (162.8°C.)	= 3
330°F.	= 165°C. (165.5°C.)	
340°F.	= 170°C. (171.1°C.)	
350°F.	= 175°C. (176.7°C.)	= 4
360°F.	= 180°C. (182.2°C.)	
365°F.	= 185°C. (185°C.)	
370°F.	= 188°C. (187.7°C.)	
375°F.	= 190°C. (190.6°C.)	= 5
380°F.	= 193°C. (193.3°C.)	
400°F.	= 205°C. (204.4°C.)	= 6
425°F.	= 220°C. (218.3°C.)	= 7
450°F.	= 230°C. (232.2°C.)	= 8
475°F.	= 245°C. (246.1°C.)	= 8
500°F.	= 260°C. (260°C.)	= 9

WEIGHT (AVOIRDUPOIS)

For quick conversions use: 30 grams = 1 ounce; 450 grams = 1 pound; 2¼ pounds = 1 kilogram. Below, are some exact equivalents.

1 ounce	= 28.34953 grams
1 pound	= 453.59237 grams
2.20462 pounds	= 1 kilogram
1000 grams	= 1 kilogram

LINEAR

For exact conversion use: 2.540005 × number of inches = centimeters

⅛ inch	= ³⁄₁₀ centimeter
¼ inch	= ⅗ centimeter
1 inch	= 2½ centimeters
2 inches	= 5 centimeters
5 inches	= 13 centimeters
6 inches	= 15 centimeters
10 inches	= 25 centimeters
12 inches	= 30 centimeters

Specific

PAN SIZES (LINEAR AND VOLUME)

8-inch square	= 20-centimeter square (baking pan)
9 × 13 × 1½-inch	= 23 × 33 × 4 centimeters
7½ × 12 × 1½-inch	= 18 × 30 × 4 centimeters (baking pans, dishes)
9 × 5 × 3-inch	= 23 × 13 × 8 centimeters (loaf pan)
10-inch	= 25 centimeter (skillet)
12-inch	= 30 centimeter
14-inch	= 35 centimeter (wok)
1-quart	= 1 liter (baking dishes)
5- to 6-cup	= 1.5 liters (ring mold)

UNITED STATES LIQUID AND DRY VOLUME TO IMPERIAL AND METRIC WEIGHT

1 cup of sliced, diced or ground (*minced*) meat (beef, lamb, pork or chicken)	= 7¾ ounces	= 220 grams
1 generous cup of raw, medium-size shrimp	= 6⅓ ounces	= 180 grams
1 generous cup of cooked baby shrimp	= 5⅔ ounces	= 160 grams
1 cup of cooked, shredded crabmeat	= 7½ ounces	= 210 grams
1 cup of raw fish fillets	= 6⅓ ounces	= 180 grams
1 cup of soft curd cheese	= 4⅔ ounces	= 130 grams
1 cup of large, dried beans	= 6¼ ounces	= 175 grams
1 cup of dried lentils	= 7⅔ ounces	= 215 grams
1 cup of canned (*tinned*) beans, drained	= 6¼ ounces	= 175 grams
1 cup of re-fried beans (*cooked, mashed beans*)	= 9 ounces	= 255 grams
1 cup of *miso* (Japanese soybean paste)	= 9¼ ounces	= 260 grams
1 cup of bean curd, drained	= 4¼ ounces	= 120 grams
1 cup of cooked lentils	= 9 ounces	= 255 grams
1 cup of roasted sesame seeds	= 5⅔ ounces	= 160 grams
1 cup of roasted peanuts	= 5⅓ ounces	= 150 grams
1 cup of roasted, pounded peanuts	= 6⅓ ounces	= 180 grams
1 cup of raw cashew nuts	= 5 ounces	= 145 grams
1 cup of whole almonds, blanched	= 4¾ ounces	= 135 grams
1 cup of slivered almonds	= 4⅓ ounces	= 125 grams
1 cup of ground almonds	= 3¾ ounces	= 105 grams
1 cup of pistachio nuts	= 4⅓ ounces	= 125 grams
1 cup of long-grain or glutinous rice	= 7¾ ounces	= 220 grams
1 cup of cooked, long-grain rice	= 4⅓ ounces	= 125 grams
1 cup of puffed rice cereal	= ¾ ounce	= 25 grams
1 cup of all-purpose flour or rice flour	= 6 ounces	= 170 grams
1 cup of wholewheat flour	= 6 ounces	= 170 grams
1 cup of cornstarch (*cornflour*)	= 6 ounces	= 170 grams
1 cup of black peppercorns	= 3½ ounces	= 100 grams
1 cup of coriander seeds	= 3½ ounces	= 100 grams
1 cup of cumin seeds	= 3⅓ ounces	= 95 grams
1 cup of ground cumin	= 4¼ ounces	= 120 grams
1 cup of freshly-ground, red chilli pepper	= 3½ ounces	= 100 grams
1 cup of salt	= 6¼ ounces	= 175 grams
1 cup of vegetable shortening	= 7 ounces	= 200 grams
1 cup of butter	= 8 ounces	= 230 grams

1 cup of fried, dried onion flakes = 4⅔ ounces = 130 grams
1 cup of canned *(tinned)* pimiento, drained = ½ pound = 230 grams
1 cup of water chestnuts, drained = 6½ ounces = 185 grams
1 cup of bamboo shoots, drained and sliced = 6 ounces = 170 grams
1 cup of whole, canned *(tinned)* tomatoes = 6⅓ ounces = 180 grams
1 cup of bean sprouts = 2¾ ounces = 80 grams
1 cup of fresh green beans, chopped = 4 ounces = 115 grams
1 cup of cabbage, shredded, firmly packed = 3¾ ounces = 110 grams
1 cup of fresh broccoli, sliced = 3½ ounces = 100 grams
1 cup of cauliflower, flowerets = 4⅓ ounces = 125 grams
1 cup of Chinese snow peas = 3½ ounces = 100 grams
1 cup of corn kernels = 4⅓ ounces = 125 grams
1 cup of unsweetened flaked coconut = 2⅓ ounces = 65 grams
1 cup of sweetened flaked coconut = 2⅔ ounces = 75 grams
1 cup of granulated sugar = 7¾ ounces = 220 grams
1 cup of coarse dark-brown sugar = 5⅔ ounces = 160 grams
1 cup of raisins or golden raisins *(sultanas)* = 5⅔ ounces = 160 grams ·
1 cup of pitted dates, firmly packed = 8½ ounces = 245 grams
1 cup of plum jam = 11½ ounces = 330 grams
1 cup of canned *(tinned)* plums, pitted, drained = 8½ ounces = 240 grams
1 cup of canned *(tinned)* pineapple chunks, drained = 6 ounces = 170 grams
1 cup of canned *(tinned)* apricot halves, drained = 8½ ounces = 240 grams

CAN SIZES, APPROXIMATE WEIGHT AND APPROXIMATE CONTENT IN CUPS

8-ounce can	= 8 ounces	= 1 cup
Picnic	= 10½ to 12 ounces	= 1¼ cups
12-ounce can	= 12 ounces	= 1½ cups
No. 300 can	= 14 to 16 ounces	= 1¾ cups
No. 303 can	= 16 to 17 ounces	= 2 cups
No. 2 can	= 1 pound, 4 ounces, or 20 ounces	= 2½ cups
No. 2½ can	= 1 pound, 13 ounces, or 29 ounces	= 3½ cups
No. 3 can	= 2 pounds, 14 ounces, or 1 quart, 14 fluid ounces	= 5¾ cups

SOUPED UP

❁ ❁ ❁

Light and Easy—
The Asian Way with Potage

Soup is indispensable to Asian tables—at least throughout the far Orient (China, Japan and Korea) and Southeast Asia. A classic breakfast for a Chinese, a Thai or a Malay is a large bowl of steaming-hot chicken-based rice soup. Substantial noodle-filled broths, brimming with vegetables and all kinds of meat, are the quick, lunch-to-go mainstays, eaten in noodle shops or off food carts, from Bangkok to Singapore, Canton to Jakarta and Rangoon to Hong Kong. Soup signals the end of a formal Chinese banquet and is also standard fare for old folk and young children. In fact, the Chinese, in common with a large part of the Western world, believe that chicken soup has recuperative and almost magical powers; they feed it to the sick and to pregnant women.

Of the two dominant cultures to color the eating habits of the Orient, China and India, China donated the soups. The Indians are not basically a nation of soup eaters, although the Tamil-initiated mulligatawny soup (from the Tamil language, *molagu,* pepper, and *tunni,* water) has become the arch-typical Indian soup.

Reputed to have originated with the Brahmin yogis of the south of India, who were strict vegetarians, the "pepper water" was adopted by the poor, who added small salty dried fish to it to make a more substantial dish. It is said that the Anglo-Indians (the half-castes with one British parent—and there were a great many of them) then took the soup for their own and further changed it by adding meat, to the horror of the vegetarians. Whatever the real story, this hot yellow curry soup has become standard fare on British tables and in restaurants, and is probably as far removed from the classic Indian dish as the Westernized chop suey is from its origins. There are as many versions of mulligatawny as there are people who enjoy it.

Some of the many Indian *dhal* recipes (a group of spiced vegetarian side dishes made from lentils or split peas) are very souplike in consistency, rather like a thick pea soup *(peas pottage)* and, indeed, are offered in many Indian restaurants in the West as a soup course. The Indians also make a deliciously creamy curried yogurt which, although traditionally served with a *pilau* or other fried rice dish, is virtually a soup. But these three Indian "soups" are almost delicious accidents in a cuisine which really does not recognize the category.

The art of soup-making is essentially Chinese, from the basic rules and instructions, which have been handed down historically, to the incredibly varied range of finished creations. In Chinese society, cooking has always been regarded as a combination of a creative art and an exact science. Accordingly, soup has been extolled in literature and legend.

A Ming dynasty author wrote in the twelfth century about a woman who cooked in a famous restaurant in the northern capital of K'ai-feng and who had fled from invaders, along with the government, to Hangchow, where she cooked in one of a hundred food houses on the shore of West Lake. She was known for the creation of a superb fish soup, and the emperor, remembering it from the former capital, visited the restaurant and sampled it. He voted it delicious and, in doing so, brought her fame and wealth. The Ming author wrote a poem about it, and here is a translation by Frederick W. Mote:

"A bowl of fish soup isn't worth more than a few cents;
Yet, made as in the days of the former capital, it brings smiles to the imperial face.
So people come in droves to buy it at twice the price;
In part, they are buying the imperial gesture, and in part they buy the soup."

The emperor was a forerunner of those powerful gods of the present-day food media, the restaurant critics, who praise a restaurant and everyone runs to try it.

The Chinese word for a meat soup or stew was *keng,* a word used today in the Thai language. It means the art of mixing flavors. This emphasis on the balanced blending of ingredients is just as important in present-day Chinese food. In an ancient treatise on rules of dining, a scholar, Li Chi, wrote, "If a guest adds condiments, the host will apologize for not having had the soup prepared better." The host still feels that way today in China and Japan, where it is an insult to the cook to add soy sauce to a dish after it reaches the table.

In a Chinese meal of several courses, soup is always included but, where as the meal may include two vegetable dishes, only one soup is served, and it should be a light one: heavy, substantial broths are reserved for one-dish meals, such as light lunches or breakfasts.

These rules, together with the techniques of making soup, spread out from China to Japan, Korea and Southeast Asia. Of course, as the soups traveled along with the groups and tribes who migrated to other countries, they gradually took on a local character of their own, depending on what ingredients were available for their preparation. This is particularly noticeable in Japan, an island with a wealth of fish in its coastal waters and a predilection for the soybean, which is found in as many forms of preparation in Japanese cuisine as it is in the parent cuisine of China.

The basic Japanese soup stock, without which no Japanese soup would be truly authentic, is *dashi,* a clear, mild-tasting consommé prepared from seaweed and dried fish. The soybean shows up in Japanese soups as *miso,* this flavorful paste, made from fermented soybeans, gives a robust element to a whole range of soups. *Dashi* and *miso* are available only in specialty food shops, so I have devised substitutes: for *dashi,* see page 170, for *miso,* page 131.

The Southeast Asians also, while retaining the essential character and techniques of the Chinese soups, have adapted them to the ingredients available to them.

Since the heart of an Asian soup is the stock, let us take a look at basic techniques of making it. A stock is a liquid in which bones, meat or fish, and vegetables have been slowly simmered for a long period in order to transfer their essence to the water. The gelatinous substance from the bones jells the stock when it is cooled. Stock may also be made from vegetables only, but it will not jell. Not only is it a foundation of soup but it is also a sauce base for stir-fried and braised dishes.

Chinese stocks, unlike the French, are unspiced. Bay leaves and condiments are never added during their preparation, as the Chinese believe that a stock must only add the pure, unadulterated flavor of its main component to a dish. Additional flavorings belonging to the individual recipe are added later on.

Their stocks are even graded first or second class, according to the quality of the ingredients. A top-rated chicken stock will be made from the whole bird —an old, stewing fowl, preferably a hen. Chinese tradition has it that the meat of a rooster, once it is old enough to crow, is bad for the health! A second-class chicken stock will be prepared from the carcass of a bird, previously uncooked, which will not yield such a rich and flavorful liquid.

Similarly, a pork-based stock must be made from a good quantity of meat, together with the bones. Pig's tail is a favored soup base, together with the feet. Beef is considered to produce too dominant a flavor for a dish and is never used in stock (except by the Koreans). Vegetables are added to basic stocks or they may be used alone to produce their own, as mentioned earlier. Fish soups may be based on either a seafood stock or a chicken stock.

If you are in a hurry and have no time to go through the stock-making process, which is rather lengthy, there are several effective substitutes. Canned *(tinned)* chicken stocks, diluted, work very well, but check the salt content and modify the salt or soy and fish sauce in the recipe you are making. Not quite as good, but still acceptable, are the chicken bouillon crystals or powder; the cubes are not as satisfactory. Clam juice makes an reasonable substitute for fish stock. If using any of these, I still suggest that you simmer vegetables with the substitute to create a fuller-flavored base.

Rules of thumb about most Oriental soups: as already stated, the light and rather delicate soups accompany meals. The heavier hearty soups are better for lunch or supper. The light soups are quick to prepare, the carefully chosen and cut solid ingredients being added to the simmering stock base toward the end of the cooking. Heavy and more substantial broths have a greater proportion of solid ingredients and everything is placed in the pot at the onset of cooking. Slow cooking is the secret of success for both categories of soup. A light stock will cloud if the solid additions are boiled rapidly. A heavy soup will benefit from the gradual mingling of flavors achieved by simmering for a long period.

The vegetables and other ingredients added to a light soup are cut to a size relative to the length of time they take to cook; they are added according to how long they take to cook as well. That way their color and texture are preserved. For instance, carrots are slivered and added to a soup before bean sprouts or lettuce. Dried ingredients, such as mushrooms or fish, are soaked to make them pliable before they go into the soup.

Seasonings such as soy sauce should be added sparingly during the cooking to avoid their dominating the other flavors. A light-colored soup demands the use of a light-colored soy sauce. The heavier and darker soys should be reserved for darker, heavier soups. Cornstarch *(cornflour)*, to thicken some soups, is added toward the end of the cooking, as it is in sauces. Soup garnishes are added just before serving.

✿ Basic Chicken Stock

(CHINESE)

Preparation time: 15 minutes   Makes 7 pints *(5 ½)*
Cooking time: 2 hours

SHOPPING AND TECHNIQUE TIPS
By all means buy a stewing bird: it is cheaper and produces a better-flavored stock. Precut chicken parts will do, but make sure they include the back. Use all parts of the bird except the liver. The volume of water is approximate. Line a strainer with a double layer of extra-strength paper towels to help clarify the stock.

INGREDIENTS
3+ pound stewing fowl, or
    equivalent in chicken parts
4 quarts *(130 fluid ounces)* of cold
    water
2 cups *(¾ pound)* of mixed
    vegetables (carrots, onions,
    celery, turnips, green *(spring)*
    onions)
1-inch piece of fresh ginger root
2 *(1⅔)* teaspoons of soy sauce

PREPARATION
Cut the whole bird into quarters

Peeled and cut into large pieces

Peeled and cut into 2 slices

METHOD
1. Place the chicken and cold water in a stock pot. Bring to a boil and immediately start to skim the surface as the fat rises. Reduce the heat and simmer, covered, for 1½ hours. Remove the chicken.

2. Add the vegetables and ginger to the stock, cover again and simmer for a further 15 minutes.

3. Add the soy sauce, simmer for 5 more minutes, then strain off the solids. Refrigerate the stock and then remove all fat that has risen and solidified.

ADVANCE PREPARATION AND
STORAGE NOTES
You may wish to further reduce the stock and store it in 1-cup or 2-cup measures in sealed plastic bags or containers in your freezer. Do not forget to reconstitute it with the appropriate amount of water when you wish to use it for soup. The stock will keep for 6 months in your freezer.

Southeast Asian Variation

Follow the directions for Chinese chicken stock but omit the ginger and substitute Southeast Asian fish sauce (see Glossary, page 503) for the soy sauce.

❧ Basic Pork Stock (CHINESE)

Preparation time: 10 minutes   Makes 5 *(4)* pints
Cooking time: 2 hours

SHOPPING AND TECHNIQUE TIPS
I suggest you use spareribs because of their relative inexpensiveness and general availability, but a pound of lean pork chops or a mixture of pork and chicken pieces may be substituted. Lining a strainer with a double layer of extra-strength paper towels provides an efficient filter and makes the stock relatively clear.

INGREDIENTS	PREPARATION
3 quarts *(100 fluid ounces)* of cold water	
1 rack (about 2+ pounds) of pork spareribs	Separate into individual ribs
3 leeks	Wash well and remove outer leaves and roots. Cut into 2-inch pieces
8 peppercorns	
1-inch piece of fresh ginger root	Peeled and cut in half
2 *(1⅔)* teaspoons of soy sauce	

METHOD
1. Bring the water to a boil, then add the pork and leeks. Reduce the heat to a bare simmer, cover and cook for 1¾ hours. Skim off the fat.

2. Add the peppercorns, ginger and soy sauce and continue to simmer for 15 minutes. Remove all the solid ingredients and skim off any remaining fat.

3. Strain the stock through a sieve lined with a muslin towel or paper towels and let it cool.

ADVANCE PREPARATION AND
STORAGE NOTES
The same as for Chicken Stock.

Southeast Asian Variation

Omit ginger, add 1 teaspoon of brown sugar, and substitute Southeast Asian fish sauce for soy sauce.

✿ Basic Fish Stock (JAPANESE)

The base for most Japanese soups and many noodle dishes is a stock made from dried seaweed and dried bonita. Both these items are not readily available in supermarkets, although if you live in a city with a sizable Japanese population you may be able to find packets of the instant *dashi* soup powder called *dashi-no-moto*. I have found that bottled clam juice, together with a little chicken, provides a reasonable substitute. Many people do not like a pronounced tang of the sea in a stock, and the chicken dilutes the "fishy" flavor.

Preparation time: 5 minutes   Makes about 4½ pints *(just under 80*
Cooking time: 35 minutes   *fluid ounces)*

SHOPPING AND TECHNIQUE TIPS
Use chicken thighs or breasts (on the bone) for this stock, but make sure that you remove all the skin and snip off every trace of fat with kitchen scissors. As in the other stock recipes, line a strainer with paper towels to filter the stock. If the stock is cooled before straining, any remaining semisolid particles of fat will be trapped in the towels.

INGREDIENTS   PREPARATION
1 pound chicken pieces, bone in   Skin and cut off all fat
2 quarts *(just under 67 fluid ounces)*
   of cold water
2 *(1⅔)* teaspoons of white vinegar
2 green *(spring)* onions   Snip off any brown or tattered ends
2 cups *(16 fluid ounces)* of clam juice

METHOD

1. Place all the ingredients except the clam juice in a saucepan and bring to a boil. Immediately reduce the heat, cover and simmer gently for 30 minutes.

2. Remove the chicken and onions and pour in the clam juice. Bring back to a boil. Reduce the heat and simmer for 5 more minutes.

3. Let the stock cool and then strain it through a sieve, lined with paper towels.

ADVANCE PREPARATION AND
STORAGE NOTES

Follow the directions for the preceding stocks.

& Hot and Sour Meat Soup
(CHINESE)

Probably because I spent so much of my life under the influence of the more spicy of the Asian cuisines, I must confess a great partiality to this rather sharp and tangy soup. Originating in the province of Szechwan, where many of the dishes are satisfyingly spiced, it is an arousing contrast to the blander Chinese soups.

Preparation time: 25 minutes   Serves 4 to 6 people
Cooking time: 15 minutes

SHOPPING AND TECHNIQUE TIPS

The original and authentic soup calls for shredded dried squid, seaweed and dried cloud ear or wood supreme fungus. These can all be omitted without changing the character of the soup; however, bamboo shoots (generally available, canned, in the imported-foods section of markets) are a good addition for body. Fresh mushrooms can be substituted for the dried Chinese mushrooms if the latter are not available in the Oriental-food section of your supermarket. All solid ingredients in the soup should be shredded or thinly sliced into narrow strips. Assemble and prepare all ingredients before you start.

INGREDIENTS

PREPARATION

4 cups *(32 fluid ounces)* of Basic
   Chicken Stock (page 168)

4 dried Chinese mushrooms

Soaked in hot water for 10 minutes,
   stems removed and caps thinly
   sliced

½ cup *(4 ounces)* of lean pork (you
   may use the meat from a pork
   chop)

Thinly sliced, then cut into
   matchstick shreds

¼ cup *(1½ ounces)* of canned
   (tinned) bamboo shoots

Rinsed in cold water, then cut into
   julienne strips

1 *(¾)* tablespoon of soy sauce

1 square of bean curd

Cut into thin strips, ¼-inch thick

1 slice of ham, ¼-inch thick

Cut into julienne strips

½ *(⅓)* teaspoon ground black
   pepper

½ *(⅓)* teaspoon salt

1 *(¾)* teaspoon of granulated sugar

3 *(2⅓)* tablespoons of white vinegar

2 *(1⅔)* tablespoons of cornstarch
   (cornflour)

Stirred into 4 tablespoons of cold
   water

1 egg

Beaten

1-inch piece of fresh ginger root

Peeled, sliced, then cut into very thin
   shreds

1 green *(spring)* onion

Cut into 1-inch pieces and then into
   fine slivers, lengthwise

10 coriander leaves

Chopped

1 *(¾)* teaspoon of sesame oil

METHOD

1. Bring the stock to a boil, together with the mushrooms, pork, bamboo
shoots and soy sauce.

2. Reduce the heat and simmer for 3 minutes. Uncover; add the bean curd
and ham. Then stir in the pepper, salt, sugar and vinegar and simmer for
1½ minutes.

3. Stir the cornstarch *(cornflour)* and water to recombine them, then stir
them slowly into the soup and continue to stir until it thickens.

4. Turn off the heat and pour in the beaten egg in a thin stream, stirring
constantly.

5. Pour into a serving bowl and stir in the ginger, green *(spring)* onion,
coriander leaves and, finally, for the unmistakeable signature of the soup, the
sesame oil.

Serve immediately.

ADVANCE PREPARATION AND STORAGE NOTES

This is a last-minute soup and cannot be made ahead; however, the preparation of the ingredients can be done in advance. If you have a portable cooking ring, you may even like to prepare this soup at the table for your guests, laying out all the ingredients in small attractive Oriental bowls.

Korean Version

Use ¾ cup *(approximately 6 ounces)* of beef (top round), shredded, instead of the pork and ham. Cook the egg into a thin omelet and cut it into shreds for garnish instead of introducing it raw. Omit steps 3 and 4 of the recipe. Add 1 clove of garlic, minced, with the other ingredients in step 5.

✿ Hot and Sour Seafood Soup (THAI)

There is a seafood restaurant at one end of Bangsaen Beach, east of Bangkok on the Gulf of Thailand, which specializes in this soup. You can sit out on the patio, shaded by large trees and tropical plants, while the waiters bring large tureens, brimming with the fragrant, lemony broth and generously packed with all manner of seafood.

The soup has not only survived its long, historical journey from its far-off origins in Szechwan, but has taken on a new dimension of excellence in its transition to a seafood dish by the coastal Thai peoples.

Preparation time: 45 minutes
Cooking time: 40 minutes

Serves 8 to 10 people (depending on the size of the soup bowls)

SHOPPING AND TECHNIQUE TIPS

Lemon grass and citrus leaves are used in the original version to give the lemony flavor. I have substituted the thin parings of outer peel from lemons and limes without losing much of the authenticity. You can substitute other seafoods for those given in the recipe. It is, after all, a Southeast Asian version of the classic seafood soups and stews. Frozen or fresh crabmeat can be used; just remember not to overcook the seafood. Prepare everything before you start to cook.

INGREDIENTS

PREPARATION

1 (¾) tablespoon of vegetable oil

½ pound of fresh, medium (30
   count) shrimp

Shelled (shells reserved), cleaned and
deveined

8 cups (64 fluid ounces) of Basic
   Chicken Stock (page 168)

1 (¾) teaspoon of salt

The outer, yellow peel (zest) of 2
   lemons

Cut into strips

The peel from ½ a lime

Cut into slivers

2 green Serrano chillies or 1 Jalapeño
   chilli

Seeded and cut into slivers

½ pound of firm, white fish fillets

Cut into strips about 2" long

5 dried Chinese mushrooms (fresh
   mushrooms may be substituted,
   in which case no soaking is
   required)

Soaked in hot water until soft, stems
discarded, caps cut into strips

¼ pound cooked crabmeat

Cut into chunks

2 to 3 (approximately 2) tablespoons
   of Southeast Asian fish sauce

Juice of 3 limes

1 fresh red Serrano chilli or

Seeded and slivered

   1 small dried red chilli

Seeded, soaked in hot water until
pliable, then cut into strips

2 green (spring) onions

Coarsely chopped

20 coriander leaves

METHOD

1. Heat the oil in a large saucepan over a medium-high setting and fry
the shrimp shells until they turn pink. Add the chicken stock, salt, lemon and
lime peel and green chillies or the Jalapeño chilli. Bring to a boil, cover, reduce
the heat and simmer for 15 minutes.

2. Strain the contents of the saucepan through a sieve, discarding the
solids, and return the stock to the pan. Bring it to a boil again.

3. Add the fish pieces and the mushrooms and cook for 1 minute. Add
the shrimp and let the soup boil for 2 minutes more. Stir in the crabmeat and
season with the fish sauce. Immediately remove the pan from the heat.

4. Stir in the lime juice, then transfer the contents of the pan to a soup
tureen. Sprinkle with the red chilli slivers, green (spring) onions and coriander
and serve at once.

ADVANCE PREPARATION AND
STORAGE NOTES

The ingredients can be prepared in advance and the recipe taken through step 2. The fish must be added at the last minute so that it does not overcook. If you are using frozen, shelled shrimp, and have no shells, substitute 1 cup *(8 fluid ounces)* of clam juice for one of the cups of chicken stock.

Spinach Soup with Eggs
(JAPAN)

Spinach is a lovely, healthy vegetable that lends itself to all kinds of light soups. This Japanese spinach soup is the first of three variations on a theme, all of them individual in flavor from country to country and all of them depending on a quick and easy soup technique.

Preparation time: 5 minutes   Serves 4 to 6 people depending on
Cooking time: 12 minutes   the size of the soup bowls

SHOPPING AND TECHNIQUE TIPS
Keep the soup on a simmer—not a vigorous boil—so that the spinach remains intact and does not become ragged and mushy.

INGREDIENTS	PREPARATION
4 cups *(32 fluid ounces)* of Basic Fish Stock (page 170)	
8 spinach leaves	Washed and cut across into 1-inch sections
2 eggs	Beaten
1 (¾) teaspoon of soy sauce	
8 to 12 oyster crackers (or Japanese miniature rice crackers *(arare)*)	

METHOD

1. Bring the stock to a boil in a saucepan and add the spinach. Immediately reduce the heat to a simmer and cook the spinach for 3 minutes.

2. Begin to stir the soup and gently pour in the beaten eggs, stirring until they form shreds. Season with the soy sauce and remove the pan from the heat.

3. Pour the soup into individual soup bowls and float two oyster crackers on each.

❧ Spinach and Corn Soup
(INDONESIAN)

Preparation time: 10 minutes   Serves 4 to 6 people, depending on
Cooking time: 20 minutes   the size of the bowls

SHOPPING AND TECHNIQUE TIPS
I have made this soup using both fresh and frozen corn kernels and find that it
works very well with the frozen. The spinach, however, *must* be fresh, as the
frozen variety is very mushy. Anchovy paste is the substitute for the rather
pungent fermented shrimp paste *(trassi)* and is available in tubes in supermarkets.
Powdered ginger substitutes for the more fragrant but hard-to-find *laos,* which
is a Southeast Asian cousin of the same family.

INGREDIENTS   PREPARATION
1 (¾) tablespoon of peanut oil
½ (⅓) teaspoon of anchovy paste
2 cloves of garlic   Peeled and minced
½ a large onion   Sliced into fine slivers
1 (¾) teaspoon of powdered
   turmeric
½ (⅓) teaspoon of powdered ginger
1 green Serrano chilli (or any other   Chopped (the seeds may be removed
   fresh, hot chilli)   if less heat is desired)
4 cups (32 fluid ounces) of Basic
   Chicken Stock (page 168)
½ cup (2¼ ounces) of fresh or   If frozen are used, do not defrost
   frozen corn kernels   them
8 spinach leaves   Washed and roughly chopped
½ (⅓) teaspoon of salt

METHOD
1. Heat the peanut oil over medium heat in a large saucepan and fry the
anchovy paste and garlic, stirring continuously, until the garlic softens and
turns gold.
2. Stir in the onion and turmeric and continue to fry for 2 more minutes.
Then add the ginger, chilli and stock. Bring to a boil, reduce the heat and
simmer for 5 minutes.
3. Return the heat to high. Add the corn kernels and spinach, bring to
a boil and cook, stirring for 5 minutes. Season and pour into a soup tureen or
into individual bowls. Serve immediately.

ADVANCE PREPARATION AND
STORAGE NOTES
Again, this is a quick and simple soup, but steps 1 and 2 could be done in advance and the soup completed about 8 minutes before serving time.

❧ Spinach and Bamboo Soup

(CHINESE)

Preparation time: 5 minutes
Cooking time: 15 minutes

Serves 4 to 6 people, depending on
the size of the soup bowls

SHOPPING AND TECHNIQUE TIPS
Because fresh bamboo shoots are not available in the West, we always substitute the canned variety. Fortunately these do not need to be cooked for nearly as long. This soup is also delicious if it is made with mustard greens instead of spinach.

INGREDIENTS	PREPARATION
4 cups *(32 fluid ounces)* of Basic Chicken Stock (page 168)	
8 spinach leaves	Washed and cut across into 1-inch sections
¼ cup *(1 ½ ounces)* of canned *(tinned)* bamboo shoots	Washed, drained and thinly sliced
1 slice of ham, ¼-inch thick	Cut into ¼-inch dice
4 small fresh mushrooms	Washed, patted dry, stems removed and caps thinly sliced
½ *(⅓)* teaspoon of salt	
½ *(⅓)* teaspoon of sesame oil	

METHOD
1. Bring the stock to a boil in a saucepan and add the spinach and bamboo shoots. Immediately reduce the heat and simmer for 3 minutes.

2. Stir in the ham and mushrooms and continue to simmer for 5 more minutes.

3. Remove from the heat, stir in the salt and sesame oil. Transfer to a soup tureen and serve.

ADVANCE PREPARATION AND
STORAGE NOTES
The ingredients may be prepared ahead of time, but the soup should be cooked just before serving.

THE UNIVERSAL CHICKEN SOUP

No cookbook, Asian or otherwise, would be complete without the inclusion of at least one recipe for that basic soup which shows up in just about every cuisine of the world. The Orient is no exception, and it is amazing how something so rudimentary can be transformed from cuisine to cuisine into a variety of different, delicious soups. We will start with simple light soups from Korea and Japan, and then progress to some of the more hearty, spiced soups of Southeast Asia, ending up with a chicken-based mulligatawny soup from India. In all cases, they start with a good, concentrated chicken stock, the exception being that of the Japanese, who use their fish stock even for a chicken soup (you may, if you wish, substitute plain chicken stock without seasonings).

⊗ Korean Chicken Soup

Preparation time: 8 minutes (not including preparing soup stock)

Cooking time: 15 minutes
Serves 6 to 8 people

SHOPPING AND PREPARATION TIPS
You may buy a whole chicken, bone it, reserving the meat, and make a stock from the bones, or you may use the Chinese Basic Chicken Stock (page 168) and buy boned breasts and thighs (you need dark as well as light meat). While the stock is coming to the boil, make the Egg Strip Garnish (page 157).

INGREDIENTS	PREPARATION
8 cups *(64 fluid ounces)* of Basic Chicken Stock or 8 cups of plain chicken stock	
½ pound of boned chicken meat (thigh and breast)	Cut into 1-inch pieces
1 clove of garlic	Peeled and minced
2 green *(spring)* onions	Chopped
1 *(¾)* tablespoon of soy sauce	
¼ teaspoon *(a pinch)* of freshly ground black pepper	
½ *(⅓)* teaspoon of salt	

INGREDIENTS	PREPARATION
1 *(¾)* tablespoon of sesame seeds	Toasted until golden
1 egg	Made into Egg Strip Garnish

METHOD

1. Bring the chicken stock to a boil over high heat in a large saucepan. Add the chicken pieces and garlic and reduce the heat to medium. Cook until chicken is tender.

2. While stock is coming to the boil, prepare the Egg Strip Garnish and set aside.

3. Now, turn your attention back to the soup and, when the chicken is nicely cooked but still a little tender, add the green onions and stir. Season with the soy sauce, pepper and salt and, just before serving, sprinkle in the sesame seeds.

4. Pour the soup into individual soup bowls, spooning a little chicken into each. Garnish each soup bowl with a few egg strips and serve.

ADVANCE PREPARATION AND
STORAGE NOTES

The stock can be made ahead of time and frozen or refrigerated. The ingredients can also be prepared in advance. You may make the soup a little ahead of time and keep it warm, but do not add the sesame seeds or garnish until just before you are ready to serve.

Japanese Version

Serves 4 people

In the Japanese variation, the chicken pieces are sprinkled with *sake* (or sherry) and a little cornstarch *(cornflour)* before dropping them in the soup. This soup is made with the Japanese Basic Fish Stock (page 170), although you may use chicken stock if you wish. Otherwise it is very similar to the Korean soup.

INGREDIENTS	PREPARATION
½ a boned chicken breast	Skinned and cut across diagonally into 8 strips
1 *(¾)* teaspoon of *sake* (or pale, dry sherry)
1 *(¾)* teaspoon of cornstarch
4 cups *(32 fluid ounces)* of Basic Fish Stock

INGREDIENTS

1 *(¾)* teaspoon of Japanese soy
  sauce
2 large fresh mushroom caps

1 green *(spring)* onion

½ *(⅓)* teaspoon of salt
1 egg

PREPARATION

Brushed clean and thinly sliced into
  strips
Cut on a long diagonal into thin
  slices

Made into Egg Strip Garnish (page
  157)

METHOD

1. Combine the chicken strips, *sake* and cornstarch *(cornflour)* in a small bowl, mixing until the strips are coated.

2. As in step 1 of the Korean recipe, using the fish stock instead of the chicken.

3. As in step 2 of the previous recipe, but roll the egg pancake really tight and do not cut it until just before you garnish.

4. Season the soup with the soy sauce and add the mushroom strips. Let them cook for 1 minute, then add the green *(spring)* onion and salt. Turn off the heat.

5. Immediately slice the egg roll thinly into little coils and place 1 or 2 at the bottom of each soup bowl. Pour the soup over, carefully portioning out the chicken and green *(spring)* onion so that there are 2 strips of each to a bowl. Serve immediately.

ADVANCE PREPARATION AND
STORAGE NOTES

As in the previous recipe. If you are beginning to make the soup a little in advance, take it up to the end cf step 3, and complete it just before you serve.

Vietnamese Version (CHICKEN AND SQUASH SOUP)

Serves 6 to 8 people

Make the soup as in the Korean style, using the Southeast Asian variation (page 169) of the chicken stock. Do not make the egg garnish. Use the same amount of boned chicken as the Korean version and add 2 minced shallots and 1 inch of peeled fresh ginger root cut into paper-thin slices. Season with fish sauce instead of soy, adding the black pepper. Add 2 cups *(8 ounces)* of thinly sliced summer squash or zucchini *(courgette)* and let them simmer for 8 to 10 minutes, or until they are tender, but not mushy. Garnish with a green *(spring)* onion, thinly sliced into fine rings and sprinkled over the top of each bowl before serving.

❈ Hearty Chicken Soup from the Philippines

This robust Filipino soup has many more solid ingredients than the preceding soups and does not contain the spice pastes of the other Southeast Asian soups in this section. It is a toe-warming soup for a cold day and a great lunch dish.

Preparation time: 15 minutes
Cooking time: 45 minutes

Serves 6 as a main course, 8 people as part of a meal

S H O P P I N G   A N D   T E C H N I Q U E   T I P S

As this soup demands a plain chicken broth, you may like to buy a whole chicken and steam it. Then skin the chicken and cut the meat from the bones. The chicken essence will be in the liquid below, which you will use for stock. Steam the chicken for 30 minutes or a little more, depending on the weight and size. The finished soup has a deliciously sour taste, which is produced, in the original, by tamarind juice. We use lime juice and molasses *(treacle)* as a substitute.

INGREDIENTS	PREPARATION
1 3-pound chicken	Steamed, skinned, boned, flesh cut into 1-inch pieces, (let the bird cool in the steamer before boning)
8 cups *(64 fluid ounces)* of the steamed chicken liquid (add additional water if necessary)	
3 medium tomatoes	Skinned and cut into slices
2 medium onions	Peeled and finely chopped
1 large sweet potato	Peeled and cut into 1-inch cubes
6 red radishes, or	Topped and tailed and cut into quarters
Half an Oriental long white radish *(daikon)*	Peeled and cut into ½-inch cubes
2 cups *(7 ounces)* of spinach leaves (firmly packed)	Well washed, drained and torn into pieces
The meat from the chicken	
1 *(¾)* tablespoon of molasses *(treacle)* dissolved in 4 tablespoons of lime juice	

INGREDIENTS

1 *(¾)* tablespoon of Southeast Asian
    fish sauce
1 *(¾)* teaspoon of salt
½ *(⅓)* teaspoon of freshly ground
    black pepper

METHOD

1. Cut the meat off the cooked chicken into 1-inch pieces and set them aside. Measure out 8 cups *(64 fluid ounces)* of the broth from the steaming (you may use additional water if you want a generous amount of liquid with the solid ingredients) and pour it into a large saucepan or stock pot. Add the tomatoes, onions and sweet potato and bring it to a boil over high heat. Reduce the heat to medium and let it cook for 15 minutes.

2. Now add the radishes and let them cook for 8 minutes.

3. Add the spinach and chicken pieces and let them simmer until the spinach is very tender, but not shredding apart. Season with the molasses *(treacle)*/lime juice mixture, the fish sauce and the salt and pepper. Stir and let the soup cook for 1 more minute.

4. Pour into a soup tureen and serve.

ADVANCE PREPARATION AND
STORAGE NOTES

Because of the type of vegetables used, this soup does not keep well. However, it may be prepared up to and including step 2. Then cover the soup and turn off the heat. It may be left for 2 or 3 hours, then reheated and completed before serving.

☙ Spiced Indonesian and Malaysian Chicken Soup

This soup will serve as part of both an Indonesian or Malaysian menu. It is one of the examples of a cuisine partially shared by two nations because of their common roots. Even the name, *soto ayam,* is the same in both languages.

Preparation time: 20 minutes (not
    including the time spent making
    the stock)
Cooking time: 30 minutes

Serves 6 to 8 people (depending on
    whether it is to be a one-dish meal
    or a course)

SHOPPING AND TECHNIQUE TIPS

I like the doubled richness of simmering raw chicken pieces in the prepared chicken stock. If you have made the stock in advance (and perhaps frozen it) it is also quicker. Or you may purchase a whole 3-pound chicken and make a traditional stock from it, afterwards removing the cooked meat from the bones, straining the stock and then making the soup. This soup is garnished from the bottom up—that is to say, the garnishes are placed in the bottom of the soup tureen and the hot soup poured over them. Or you may place a portion of each garnish in individual soup bowls and then pour in the hot liquid.

INGREDIENTS	PREPARATION
Soup	
3 cloves of garlic	Peeled and chopped
5 macadamia nuts or blanched almonds	Chopped
½-inch piece of fresh ginger root	Peeled and minced
½ (⅓) teaspoon of anchovy paste	
3 (2⅓) tablespoons of peanut oil	
1 large onion	Peeled and chopped
1½ (1¼) teaspoons of ground coriander	
1 (¾) teaspoon of ground turmeric	
½ (⅓) teaspoon of ground cumin	
1 (¾) teaspoon of ground black pepper	
8 cups (64 fluid ounces) of Southeast Asian Chicken Stock (page 169)	
1 pound of boned chicken meat (breast and thighs)	Skinned and cut into 1-inch pieces
2 bay leaves	
1 (¾) teaspoon of molasses (treacle), dissolved in 2 (1⅔) tablespoons of lime juice	
1 hank (2 ounces) of rice-stick noodles (also called rice vermicelli)	Soaked in hot water for 10 minutes, drained
½ (⅓) teaspoon of salt	
½ a lemon	
1 (¾) tablespoon of Southeast Asian fish sauce	

INGREDIENTS   PREPARATION
Garnish

6 green *(spring)* onions   Thinly sliced into rounds
1 large boiled potato   Cooled, peeled and sliced into thin
                                        rounds
2 hard-cooked *(hard-boiled)* eggs   Peeled and quartered
The leaves of 2 stalks of celery   Chopped
2 *(1⅔)* tablespoons of Fried Onion
   Flakes (page 156)

METHOD

1. Place the garlic, nuts and ginger in a mortar and pound to a paste. Add the anchovy paste and pound until it is well mixed in.

2. Heat the oil in a saucepan over medium heat and fry the onion until it is pale gold. Add the paste from the mortar and fry, stirring, for 2 minutes, until the pungency has mellowed. Now add the coriander, turmeric, cumin and pepper and stir. Fry the whole mixture for 3 minutes, stirring constantly, until the odor is less sharp.

3. Increase the heat to high and, pouring in the chicken stock, bring it to a boil. Reduce the heat to medium low and add the chicken pieces and the bay leaves.

4. Let the chicken pieces simmer in the stock for 15 minutes, then stir in the molasses *(treacle)* /lime juice mixture. Add the drained noodles and season with salt. Stir and let the soup continue to cook for 5 more minutes.

5. During that time, place all the garnishes, except the onion flakes, in the bottom of a large soup tureen.

6. Remove the soup from the heat, squeeze the lemon half over the top, then pour the entire contents over the garnishes in the tureen. Sprinkle with the onion flakes and bring to the table with a flourish.

ADVANCE PREPARATION AND
STORAGE NOTES

The garnishes may be prepared in advance. The soup preparation may be taken up to and including the addition of the chicken in step 4. Let the chicken cook, then turn off the heat and cover the pan, setting it aside, or refrigerating the contents until you are ready to resume cooking. Begin again by reheating the soup and then adding the molasses *(treacle)* /lime juice mixture. From then on, complete the soup and serve.

❧ Indian Curry Soup
(MULLIGATAWNY)

This rich and hearty soup is actually Anglo-Indian rather than a genuine Indian creation. It originated, as I mentioned before, with the Tamils of southern India, as a thin soup, referred to as "pepper water"—and it was indeed fiery. On its long journey toward Anglicization, it became thicker, with more ingredients. Sometimes—horror of horrors—it even included meat, anathema to the vegetarians of southern India. In its final transformation, it is the perfect, filling soup to be served either by itself for a light supper or as a light lunch dish. Please note: There is *no* flour or curry powder in it, nor should there be. It relies on the inclusion of carefully fried, ground spices for its rich flavor and thick texture.

I give the recipe in its "creamed" version, with a chicken stock base. This style of soup will comfortably accompany a light meal. It may be further enlivened with the addition of small pieces of chicken and a little rice. A vegetarian version is made by substituting water for chicken stock and adding a little thick coconut milk and cream. A more hearty one-dish meal may be made by leaving the vegetables whole and serving it with or without meat. We often cook it that way in our family for a satisfying supper.

Preparation time: 15 minutes (not   Cooking time: 50 minutes
   including the preparation of stock) Serves 6 people

SHOPPING AND TECHNIQUE TIPS
The basic technique is similar to that of the previous Spiced Indonesian and Malaysian Chicken soup and the "currying" technique is probably the ancestor to both. It involves the creation of a spice paste, the frying of onions and then of the paste, followed by the introduction of vegetables and/or meat, followed by the stock. This particular version of Mulligatawny calls for the ingredients to then be pureed in a blender before being returned to the pan and garnished. If meat has been added, it will be removed before the pureeing process, to be returned to the pan as a garnish. Cream, yogurt or coconut milk is added toward the end, and the soup is sometimes given an extra fillip by the addition of onions, fried until golden in Indian Clarified Butter. A squeeze of lemon gives the soup a final tart note which balances the richness of the milk products. In the south of India, the lemon is often replaced by tamarind juice (we would substitute molasses *(treacle)* and lime juice).

INGREDIENTS

Paste

2 cloves of garlic — Peeled and minced

1-inch piece of fresh ginger root — Peeled and minced

½ to 1 *(⅓ +)* teaspoon of ground
    red pepper (Cayenne)

1 *(¾)* teaspoon of ground turmeric

1 *(¾)* tablespoon of ground
    coriander

1 *(¾)* teaspoon of ground cumin

½ *(⅓)* teaspoon of Indian Sweet
    Spice Mix (page 118)

1 bay leaf — Broken into small fragments

1 *(¾)* tablespoon of vegetable oil

Soup

1 *(¾)* tablespoon of Indian Clarified
    Butter (page 139)

1 large onion — Peeled and chopped

1 *(¾)* teaspoon of salt

1 *(¾)* tablespoon of tomato paste

8 cups *(64 fluid ounces)* of Basic
    Chicken Stock (page 168)

1 large carrot — Peeled and cut into small dice

1 large potato — Peeled and cut into small dice

2 stalks of celery — Cut crosswise into thin slices

1 cup *(8 fluid ounces)* of yogurt

Garnish

1 *(¾)* tablespoon of Indian Clarified
    Butter

1 medium onion — Peeled and cut into slivers

½ a lemon

A few fresh coriander (Chinese
    parsley, *cilantro*) leaves
    (optional)

PREPARATION

METHOD

1. Place all the paste ingredients in a blender and blend into a paste. (Add a little more oil if the blades do not turn smoothly.)

2. In a large saucepan, over medium-high heat, heat the Clarified Butter and fry the onion, stirring, until it becomes soft and limp. Add the paste from

the blender and continue to fry, stirring and scraping the pan continually, to keep the contents moving and ensure that the paste does not stick. Fry everything together for 3 to 4 minutes, until the paste darkens and mixes in with the onions, and the odors of the spices blend together.

3. Now stir in the salt and tomato paste. Mix well, then pour in the chicken stock. Increase the heat to high and bring to a boil. Add the vegetables, let the liquid come back to a boil then reduce the heat so that the soup is at a simmer. Cover and let the soup simmer for 20 to 30 minutes, or until the vegetables are soft enough to squash against the sides of the pan with the back of the wooden spoon.

4. Remove the pan from the heat and let the contents cool slightly. (Running them through a blender and straining them can be a messy business and you do not want to burn yourself with splashes.) Now take a ladle and ladle the soup in batches into the blender, processing each batch to a puree. Suspend the strainer over a large bowl and pour each batch through, mashing any solid fragments with the back of the wooden spoon. When all the soup has been pureed, pour it back into the saucepan and set it over medium heat. Stir in the yogurt.

5. While the soup is reheating, heat the clarified butter for the garnish in a frying pan over medium-high heat and fry the sliced onion until it turns a rich gold. Pour it, together with the butter, into the soup and stir.

6. Pour the contents of the saucepan into a soup tureen and squeeze the lemon over the top. Garnish with the coriander leaves if you are using them and serve.

ADVANCE PREPARATION AND STORAGE NOTES

The soup can be prepared all the way through the pureeing in step 4. It can then be cooled and refrigerated, covered, for a day, or it can be poured into freezer bags or containers and frozen. Thaw and reheat in a saucepan, adding a little extra stock to thin it back to its previous consistency. Add the yogurt and continue with the rest of the steps.

Meat Variations

The soup can be made with either lamb stock or beef stock. If meat is desired in the soup, it can be cut into small pieces and added with the salt and tomato paste in step 3. Cooked meat should be added after the pureeing process. ½ to 1 cup *(4 to 6 tablespoons)* of cooked long-grain rice can be added at the same time for a more substantial soup.

Southern Indian Vegetarian Version

Substitute 8 cups of water for chicken stock in step 3. Stir in 1 *(¾)* teaspoon of molasses *(treacle)* and the juice of 2 limes when you add the vegetables. Substitute 1 cup *(8 fluid ounces)* of thick coconut milk and its cream (or 1 cup of half-and-half) *(8 fluid ounces half milk-half cream)* into which you have stirred ½ *(⅓)* teaspoon of coconut extract) for the yogurt. At the end, after pureeing, you may add rice (½ to 1 cup, cooked) to make the soup more substantial. You may also like to increase the amount of fresh coriander leaves to about 20.

Chunky Variation

Cut the vegetables into ½-inch pieces instead of small dice and cook them in the stock until they are tender but still firm. Meat (chicken, lamb or beef) may be added to the stock 5 to 10 minutes before the vegetable. Cooked meat should be added at the end, before the garnish. You may wish to leave out the yogurt in this version, but the coconut milk is a rather nice addition. You may still include the rice for a really substantial one-dish meal.

THE KNACK OF SNACKING

❧ ❧ ❧

Hors d'Oeuvres and Appetizers—
Sometimes Entrees

The Asian peoples eat little and often, as many as eight times a day
—an eating pattern in which finger foods and snacks flourish. From
the sunbaked countries bordering the eastern Mediterranean, through barren
Asia Minor, kaleidoscopic India, tropical Southeast Asia and onward to the
extreme Orient of China, Korea and Japan, small amounts of food are consumed at frequent intervals: at home, at work, in the streets; but primarily they
are purchased, ready-prepared, from food shops, stalls, markets or off stands
of itinerant food vendors.

Therefore the majority of Asian snacks are prepared in advance, which
qualifies them perfectly for our busy Western schedules. A few must be served
straight from the fire, but many can be eaten at room temperature—another
convenience that endears them to our lifestyles.

Because they are eaten on the run or transported ready-made from place
of purchase to be eaten later, they are mostly solid in form, requiring no plastic
or Styrofoam containers and no utensils other than fingers. To facilitate eating

without mess, the more soft and sticky mixtures are wrapped, either in some version of a dough, such as pancakes, filled buns, unleavened breads, rice paper, etc., or, in warmer climates, in large and pliable leaves such as banana, ti and grape leaves. Such leaf wrappings have the added advantage of being freely available and available free. Broiled or grilled foods that may soil the fingers, such as meats and fish, are cut into small pieces and stacked on wooden skewers or long slivers of bamboo, as in the large family of *kebabs* and *satays*. Foods that are somewhat dry are served with an enormous variety of dips and sauces, fresh chutneys and spicy pastes. You will find recipes for these in the section Basic Recipes (page 104), and also in the chapter on relishes and chutneys beginning on page 450.

Although these snacks and hors d'oeuvres utilize different techniques in their preparation, I have grouped them in this chapter under the various styles of composition, rather than spreading them throughout the book under the appropriate technique headings. In this way, you will be able to quickly locate your favorite recipe when you need an appetizer or hors d'oeuvre.

Many of these snacks can be made ahead of time and frozen or re-frigerated and I have indicated this wherever the possibility occurs. It is so nice, when unexpected guests arrive, to be able to go to your freezer and pull out a packet of Spring Rolls stuffed with succulent morsels of shrimp and chicken, pop them into the microwave or regular oven, and serve them with a flourish. Or to set your steamer on the stove and, again from the freezer, remove a bag of pork and gravy-filled Chinese Dough Buns and steam them back to fluffy perfection in a few minutes.

Sauces and dips are mostly freezable as well. I generally spoon or pour them into heavy-duty plastic bags, label them with name, amount and date and then stack them in the freezer. It is the work of a few minutes to defrost them, stir and pour them into attractive little serving bowls.

Snacks as delicious as these have a tendency to disappear very quickly, and many of the wrapped and pastry-covered delicacies are rather fiddling to prepare (great for a rainy day when you have nothing else to do), so I suggest that when you are making them you double or treble the quantity. In this way you will always have an emergency supply in your freezer. I have illustrated and given the instructions for the basic wrapping of spring and egg rolls, packages, and rice rolls and pancakes in the section on basic recipes beginning on page 104. Once you have mastered these few simple movements, your buffet and snack tables will be the envy of everyone.

One last note: These foods do not have to stay in the category of hors d'oeuvres and appetizers. Some of the nicest foods in a restaurant on the menu as starters can easily be eaten as a main dish. If you wish to serve one as an entree, merely increase the amount of the individual portions, and, if it is a particular favorite, increase again! Similarly, many of the recipes will make great, light lunch dishes or star happily at a family supper.

CURRY PUFFS AND TURNOVERS

Nothing seems to be more popular as a snack at cocktail parties, buffets or picnics than a piping-hot baked or deep-fried pastry envelope stuffed with a savory filling. Everyone likes them and there are never enough to go round.

There is reason to believe that this delightful tidbit originated in the Middle East or in India. Even the Chinese version is made with curry powder! In India, these are called *samosas* and are filled with a freshly made stuffing of spiced meat or potatoes and other vegetables. When we lived in India, we always referred to them as "curry puffs" and, although the filling should be made fresh, for the frugally minded they are a practical and delicious way of using up leftover curry. With variations in the pastry, shape and filling, these little turnovers have spread to nearly every country in Asia.

❧ Indian Stuffed Pastry Envelopes

Preparation time: 1½ hours   Makes 24 envelopes
Cooking time: 45 minutes

SHOPPING AND TECHNIQUE TIPS
Pastry making is a simple art. The pastries of the Orient call for the universal techniques of pastry making. The rules for success are the same: cool hands; cool dough; a "resting period" to allow the overworked glutens in the flour to recover; and, above all, a light, delicate and understanding touch (pastry hates to be tortured). Instead of the pastry recipe below, you may substitute the Turnover Pastry on page 149, which is of Philippine origin. Ground beef will work just as well in the filling as ground lamb, or cooked, firm potatoes may be used instead for a satisfying vegetarian filling (in which case, you would add the potatoes together with the spices and cut their frying time down to 5 minutes).

INGREDIENTS
Pastry
1½ cups *(9 ounces)* of whole-wheat
    flour
½ cup *(3 ounces)* of all-purpose
    (plain) flour
½ *(⅓)* teaspoon of salt
4 *(3¼)* tablespoons *(2 ounces)* of
    Indian Clarified Butter (page
    139)
1 *(¾)* tablespoon of plain yogurt
7 *(5⅔)* tablespoons of cold water
    (approximately)

METHOD
1. Sift both the flours and the salt into a bowl. With your hands, lightly
work the clarified butter into the flour, using a light, rubbing motion of your
thumbs against your fingers. When the butter is completely rubbed in, the
mixture should be light and airy and resemble fine breadcrumbs.

2. Make a hole in the center and pour in the yogurt and 2 tablespoons
of the water. Start to mix the liquids into the flour mixture, adding the water
1 tablespoon at a time, until the mixture becomes a smooth and pliable (but
not sticky) dough.

3. On a lightly floured surface, knead the dough by folding it end to end
and pressing down and away from you with the heels of your hands. Repeat
folding and kneading until the dough is soft, elastic and shiny, with no cracks.

4. Gather the dough into a ball, return it to the bowl and cover it with
a dampened cloth to keep it moist. Let the ball rest for about 30 minutes while
preparing the filling.

INGREDIENTS	PREPARATION
Filling	
2 tablespoons *(1 ounce)* of Indian Clarified Butter	
1 large onion	Peeled and minced
1-inch piece of fresh ginger root	Peeled and minced
4 cloves of garlic	Peeled and minced
1 pound of lean ground *(minced)* lamb	
2 green Serrano chillies, or 1 green Jalapeño chilli	Seeds and membranes removed, chillies minced
1 medium tomato	Skin and seeds removed, flesh diced

INGREDIENTS	PREPARATION
6 to 8 mint leaves	Chopped
½ (⅓) teaspoon of ground turmeric	
½ (⅓) teaspoon of ground red pepper (Cayenne)	
1 (¾) teaspoon of salt	
14 coriander (Chinese parsley, cilantro) leaves	Chopped
½ (⅓) teaspoon of Indian Sweet Spice Mix (page 118)	

METHOD

1. In a wok, heat the Clarified Butter over medium-high heat and fry the onion, ginger and garlic, stirring, until the onion becomes soft and translucent.

2. Add the lamb and chillies and cook, stirring well, until the lamb begins to change color. Now add the tomato, mint, turmeric, red pepper and salt and continue frying for 3 more minutes.

3. Reduce the heat to low and continue to cook, uncovered, stirring occasionally, for 10 minutes or until all the moisture has evaporated. Pour off all but 1 tablespoon of the accumulated fat.

4. Remove from the heat, stir in the coriander leaves and Indian Sweet Spice Mix. Transfer to a bowl to cool. Wash and dry the wok.

INGREDIENTS

Stuffed Envelopes
Pastry from above
Filling from above
A little water
Additional flour
4 cups of vegetable oil

METHOD

1. After resting the dough, divide the pastry ball into 24 equal pieces. Flour a pastry board and a rolling pin. Shape the pieces into balls and roll into thin (less than ⅛-inch thick) disks, about 3½ inches in diameter.

2. Cut each circle in half. Taking up one semicircle, moisten the straight edge with a finger dipped in water. Shape the semicircle into a cone, pressing the straight edge together to make a seam. Unless your pastry rolling has been perfect, the top edge of the cone will be a little uneven. Trim it with the scissors.

3. Fill the cone with about 1½ teaspoons of the filling. (The envelopes should only be about ¾ full so that they do not burst open in the frying.) Moisten the top (rounded) edge and press it firmly together to seal the cone.

CREATING SAMOSAS

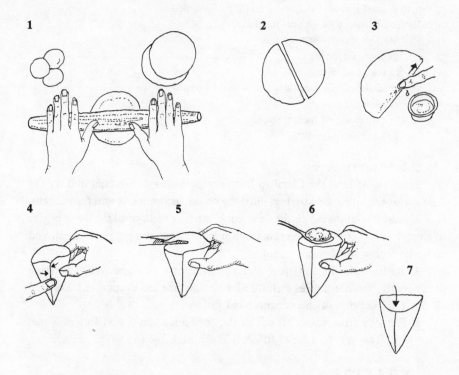

4. Pause here and preheat your oven to a low setting (140°F.). Pour the vegetable oil into a wok, setting a thermometer in it and heating it over a high setting until it reaches 375°F. *(190°C.).*

5. Now continue to fill all the pastry envelopes until (hopefully) filling and pastry circles are all used up.

6. Deep-fry the envelopes, 3 or 4 at a time, for 2 to 3 minutes, or until they are golden-brown on all sides. Remove with a slotted spoon and drain on paper towels. Continue until all are fried, then transfer them to a platter and keep them warm in the oven until ready to serve.

ADVANCE PREPARATION AND STORAGE NOTES

Like most deep-fried pastries, these are very amenable to advance preparation. The filling can be made ahead and stored in a jar in the refrigerator for a day or 2. The pastries can be made and filled (through step 3, Method) and then tightly covered and refrigerated for several hours before frying. The pastries can also be frozen, before or after frying. If you freeze before frying, allow them to thaw at room temperature *to* room temperature before frying. If you have already fried them, defrost at room temperature and then heat them in a 350°F. *(gas mark 4)* oven for 10 minutes to crisp them again before serving. These pastries may be eaten hot or cold.

✸ Philippine Fried Meat Turnovers

The Spanish influence shows both in the rather European ingredients in the filling of these turnovers and also in the rich pastry (in the chapter on Basics). The pastry could also be used for the Indian Stuffed Pastry Envelopes in the preceding recipe, but in that case they should be shaped like a turnover. You may like to try the Philippine Pastry Dough with your own favorite fillings as well.

Preparation time: 15 minutes for the   Cooking time: 30 minutes
   filling; 45 minutes for the pastry   Makes 24 turnovers

SHOPPING AND TECHNIQUE TIPS
Buy lean ground *(minced)* beef, as there is enough fat in the ground *(minced)* pork. You may wish to ask the butcher to grind *(mince)* the chicken meat for you, in which case you will not need to mince it. Ground *(minced)* veal could be substituted for the pork.

Pastry: See Basics, Basic Recipes, Pastry for Turnovers, page 149.

INGREDIENTS	PREPARATION
Filling	
1 *(¾)* tablespoon of vegetable oil	
3 cloves of garlic	Peeled, crushed and chopped
1 large onion	Peeled and finely chopped
1 cup *(8 ounces)* of lean ground *(minced)* beef	
1 cup *(8 ounces)* of ground *(minced)* pork	
1 cup *(8 ounces)* of boned chicken breast	Finely minced
1 *(¾)* teaspoon of salt	
½ *(⅓)* teaspoon of ground black pepper	

METHOD

1. Heat the oil in a medium saucepan over high heat. Fry the garlic and onions, stirring, until onions are limp.

2. Add the meats, salt and pepper, and fry, stirring, until the meats are well cooked. Pour off any accumulated fat and set the pan aside for the contents to cool.

INGREDIENTS	PREPARATION
Turnovers	
Pastry from Pastry for Turnovers, page 149	
Filling from above	
4 hard-cooked *(hard-boiled)* eggs	Peeled, each egg sliced into 6 rounds
4 sweet pickles *(gherkins)*	Drained, each pickle sliced into 6 rounds
4 cups *(32 fluid ounces)* of vegetable oil	

METHOD

1. Place a tablespoon of the filling in the center of each pastry circle. Add a slice of egg and a piece of pickle.

2. Brush ½ the circumference of the pastry circle with water and fold the circle over the filling. Press and crimp the edges to provide a firm seal.

3. Fill a wok with the frying oil and position a thermometer. Set it over high heat to come to a deep-frying temperature of 375°F. *(190°C.)*.

4. Continue to fill and shape the turnovers until all the pastry circles are used.

5. Fry the turnovers, 2 or 3 at a time, until they are golden brown. Drain on paper towels and transfer to a serving platter Serve hot or cold.

ADVANCE PREPARATION AND
STORAGE NOTES
As for the preceding recipe.

❧ Chinese Egg Rolls

Although Egg Rolls are probably one of the most universal snacks in Asia, occurring in some shape or form in almost every country, they originated in China. There are almost endless combinations of ingredients that can be used for the filling, and almost as many recipes for making wrappers. The Chinese Egg

Roll is normally wrapped in a large, circular, pancake-like wrapper made with eggs, hence the name. The more delicate wrapper for Spring Rolls is made from flour and water only. Egg Rolls are traditionally deep-fried and each cut into 3 sections before serving.

Preparation time: 6 minutes   Serves 6
Cooking time: 40 minutes

SHOPPING AND TECHNIQUE TIPS
The easiest way to buy a small quantity of pork loin is to buy a few pork loin chops and bone the meat from them. The combination of techniques used to make these Egg Rolls are stir-frying and then deep-frying.

INGREDIENTS	PREPARATION
1 (¾) tablespoon of dry sherry	
1 (¾) teaspoon of cornstarch (cornflour)	
¼ teaspoon (a pinch) of salt	
1 cup (8 ounces) of boned pork from 3 loin chops	Shredded or cut into matchstick-sized slivers
2 (1 ⅔) tablespoons of vegetable oil	
6 small dried Chinese mushrooms	Soaked in hot water for 10 minutes, stems cut off, caps cut into slivers
2 cups (just under 6 ounces) of bean sprouts	Tails removed, washed and drained
1 medium carrot	Peeled and grated into large shreds
4 green (spring) onions	Finely chopped
1 (¾) teaspoon of salt	
2 (1⅔) teaspoons of granulated sugar	
½ (⅓) teaspoon of freshly ground black pepper	
1 (¾) teaspoon of sesame oil (page 139)	
12 Egg Roll Wrappers (page 148)	
1 (¾) tablespoon of all-purpose (plain) flour	
1 (¾) tablespoon of water	
Vegetable oil for deep frying (about 4 cups (50 fluid ounces))	

METHOD
1. Place the sherry, cornstarch (cornflour) and ¼ teaspoon of salt in a mixing bowl and stir. Add the pork and stir again until the pork is coated.

2. In a wok or large frying pan, heat 2 tablespoons of vegetable oil over high heat and add the pork. Stir-fry rapidly until the pork loses its pink color, then add the mushrooms, bean sprouts, carrot and green *(spring)* onions. Season with the teaspoon of salt, sugar, black pepper and sesame oil and fry briefly for 1 minute, then transfer to a bowl to cool slightly. Wash and dry the wok, replace it on the stove, positioning a thermometer, and pour in the oil for deep-frying. Over medium-low heat, start to let the oil reach deep-frying temperature while you make the egg rolls.

3. Mix the flour and water together in a small bowl. Set an egg roll wrapper before you and moisten the far edge of the circle in a ½-inch band with the flour-water mixture. Place approximately 2 tablespoons of the filling slightly below the center of the circle and fold the flap near you up, away and over the filling. Roll the wrapper tightly over and away from you, tucking in each side as you go.

4. Fold the remaining flap over the roll. The flour-water mixture should seal it tightly. Place the roll seam side down and cover with a dampened towel.

5. Repeat with the remaining wrappers until all the egg rolls are made. Cover them all with the towel so that they do not dry out before frying.

6. Turn the heat up under the wok. The oil should reach a temperature of 360°F. *(180°C.)* before you start frying. Fry the egg rolls, 2 at a time, until the wrappers are golden brown and crisp. Remove with a slotted spoon and drain on paper towels. Keep them in a warm oven until you are ready to serve.

ADVANCE PREPARATION AND STORAGE NOTES

If you wish to prepare the Egg Rolls ahead and freeze them, follow all the steps, but fry them briefly for 1 minute. Let them drain and cool completely, then wrap them individually and tightly in plastic wrap before sealing them in a large freezer-weight, plastic bag. Thaw and then refry in deep fat for 2 minutes before serving. Completely cooked Egg Rolls may be refrigerated for up to 2 days. Warm in a low oven for about 10 to 15 minutes before serving or, for a more crisp coating, deep-fry again for 1 minute each before serving.

Korean Version (BEEF AND VEGETABLE ROLLS)

These rolls are made by each diner at the table, with the filling ingredients placed in individual bowls around a central stack of pancakes.

INGREDIENTS

Pancakes

1 cup *(6 ounces)* of all-purpose
   (plain) flour
1 cup *(8 fluid ounces)* of water
¼ teaspoon *(a pinch)* of salt

Beef Bowl

1 cup *(7¾ ounces)* of lean top round
1 green *(spring)* onion
2 peeled cloves of garlic
1 *(¾)* tablespoon vegetable oil
½ *(⅓)* teaspoon each of Sesame Oil
   (page 139), granulated sugar,
   and soy sauce

Carrot Bowl

1 large carrot, peeled and grated
½ *(⅓)* teaspoon each of chopped
   garlic, chopped onion, sesame
   seeds and Sesame Oil
2 *(1⅔)* teaspoons of soy sauce

Bean Sprout Bowl

1½ cups *(4¼ ounces)* of bean
   sprouts, roots cut off
Remaining ingredients as for the
   Carrot Bowl

Spinach Bowl

1 bunch of spinach leaves, washed
   and chopped
Remaining ingredients as for the
   Carrot Bowl

PREPARATION

Make a batter and fry into thin,
small pancakes, 4 inches in
diameter, in a lightly greased
skillet. Stack until ready to serve.

Chop the beef, green *(spring)* onions
and garlic fine and fry in 1
tablespoon of vegetable oil in a
skillet, seasoning with the
remaining ingredients.

Place the carrot shreds in a strainer
and submerge in boiling water for
2 minutes. Drain, then mix with
the remaining ingredients.

Treat in the same way as the carrots

Treat in the same way as the carrots

Malaysian Version (STRAITS CHINESE SPRING ROLLS)

These may be made with the same Egg Roll Wrapper recipe as the Chinese Egg Rolls. Alternatively, you may wish to make them by frying a series of very thin, pancake-like omelets made with 8 eggs, beaten with 2 tablespoons of cold water.

Preparation and cooking times are
approximately the same as the first
and principal recipe

INGREDIENTS	PREPARATION
2 *(1⅔)* tablespoons of peanut oil	
¼ pound of small, raw shrimp	Shelled, cleaned and chopped
½ a boned chicken breast	Skinned and minced
3 shallots	Peeled and minced
1 clove of garlic	Peeled and minced
½-inch piece of fresh ginger root	Peeled and minced
1 stalk of celery	Finely chopped
1 red or green Serrano chilli pepper	Seeded and minced
2 green *(spring)* onions	Minced
1 small carrot	Peeled and grated
1 *(¾)* teaspoon of soy sauce	
1 *(¾)* teaspoon of cornstarch *(cornflour)*	
½ *(⅓)* teaspoon of salt	

METHOD

1. Heat the oil in a wok and fry the shrimp and chicken until they become opaque. Now follow the directions for Chinese Egg Rolls, substituting the ingredients for this recipe, i.e. add the shallots, garlic, ginger, celery, chilli, green *(spring)* onions and carrot to the chicken and shrimp, then season the mixture with the soy sauce and thicken it with cornstarch *(cornflour)*. Add the salt to taste. If you are making the Large Egg Wrappers, follow the directions in the chapter on Basics, page 148. Alternatively you may make the omelet wrappers mentioned in the introduction to this recipe, using a flour and water paste to seal them. Follow the filling and rolling instructions in steps 3 to 5 in Chinese Egg Rolls (page 198), The rolls may then be deep-fried, as in step 6 for the Chinese Egg Rolls, or steamed for 5 minutes.

Vietnamese Version (VIETNAMESE SPRING ROLLS)

These rolls should be made with the Vietnamese rice paper, those pearly, butterfly-wing brittle sheets that make the crispest and finest rolls in Asia. Unfortunately, they are only available from Vietnamese speciality shops. I have found that you can make quite a credible substitute by using sheets of *filo (phyllo)* dough, brushed with peanut oil to soften them, instead of melted butter. These can be found in packages in the frozen-food sections of better supermarkets.

Preparation and cooking times are approximately the same as the first and principal recipe

Makes 12 rolls

INGREDIENTS

1 *(¾)* tablespoon of vegetable oil
1 clove of garlic
3 green *(spring)* onions
½ pound of pork loin or butt
½ pound of cooked crabmeat
2 *(1⅔)* teaspoons of Southeast Asian fish sauce
1 *(¾)* teaspoon of granulated sugar
¼ teaspoon *(a pinch)* of freshly ground black pepper
12 *filo* leaves
4 tablespoons of peanut oil, warmed
30 mint leaves
30 basil leaves (optional)
12 lettuce leaves
Extra Southeast Asian fish sauce for dipping, or Vietnamese Table Sauce (page 473)

PREPARATION

Peeled and chopped
Chopped fine
Chopped fine (use 2 cleavers)
Flaked

METHOD

1. Follow the directions for the Chinese Egg Roll recipe (page 196), first frying the garlic and onion and then the meat and crabmeat. Season with fish sauce, sugar and pepper.

2. Make the *filo* leaves pliable by painting them with slightly warm oil. Roll up the filling as for the Chinese Egg Rolls. Brush with a little additional oil.

3. Bake the rolls in a 375°F. *(gas mark 5)* oven for 15 to 20 minutes,

turning the rolls over halfway through. Let them cool slightly before serving.

4. Serve accompanied by a platter of lettuce leaves, mint and basil (if latter is available), arranged in separate heaps, and a small bowl of Vietnamese Table Sauce. Each diner takes a roll, places it in a lettuce leaf together with 1 or 2 mint and basil leaves, rolls it up and dips it in the sauce before eating. Delicious!

❧ Cooked Shrimp Sushi
(JAPAN)

Unless you are lucky enough to live near a seaport with an active fishing industry and a cooperative fishermen's market for freshly caught fish, it is extremely difficult to serve *sushi* in your home. The rash of newly popular *sushi* bars that have opened in the major cities have their own sources for beautifully fresh seafood and are able to serve raw fish of the highest quality, and it is through them that many Americans have begun to realize how delicious this style of eating can be.

There are some items of *sushi* which are traditionally served cooked, among them, shrimp *(prawns)*. These, when served raw, are considered a great delicacy by the Japanese, but it is difficult to find them freshly caught; and frozen, thawed shrimp *(prawns)* are not suitable for serving uncooked. So frozen shrimp can be lightly boiled before placing them on the little pads of vinegared rice. This style of presentation is called *nigirizushi,* and you will find it makes a succulent hors d'oeuvre or appetizer.

Preparation time: 30 minutes   Makes 8 appetizers
Cooking time: 8 minutes

SHOPPING AND TECHNIQUE TIPS
First try to find fresh shrimp *(prawns)* in your supermarket or fish market. Inspect the shrimp *(prawns)*. They should be firm and the shells should fit tightly. If you are not satisfied with their quality, buy frozen raw shrimp *(prawns)* in their shells. Choose medium-large shrimp *(prawns)*, about 15 to 20 count to the pound. If your supermarket has an Oriental section, you may be able to locate *wasabi,* the Japanese horseradish that is sold as a green powder, in tins. If you cannot find it, use powdered English or hot mustard to provide the necessary bite. The rice must be short-grain; you can substitute the Italian *risotto* rice, if you cannot find the Japanese short-grain rice.

INGREDIENTS   PREPARATION

2 *(1⅔)* tablespoons of rice vinegar or
    white vinegar
½ *(⅓)* teaspoon of salt
8 medium large shrimp *(prawns)*
1 *(¾)* tablespoon of *wasabi* or hot
    English mustard
2 cups *(8¾ ounces)* of Vinegar-   Cooled
    Dressed Rice (page 110)
3-inch piece of Oriental long white   Peeled
    radish
1 *(⅔) teaspoon of wasabi* or hot
    English mustard
3 tablespoons of Japanese soy sauce

METHOD

1. Fill a small saucepan with cold water and add 1 teaspoon of vinegar and the salt. Bring to a rolling boil. Insert a toothpick along the length of each shrimp *(prawn)* to prevent them from curling when they are cooked. Place them in a small strainer, and, when the water comes to a boil, immerse them in the water for 3 minutes. Drain and set aside to cool.

2. Meanwhile, pour the remainder of the vinegar into a small bowl and add ½ cup *(4 fluid ounces)* of cold water. Divide the rice into 8 equal portions. Moisten your fingers with the vinegared water, to prevent the rice from sticking and take up 1 portion of the rice. Holding it in one hand, press it with the fingers of the other hand and mold it into an oval shape. The oval should be elongated and almost 1 inch thick. Lay it down and continue until you have molded 8 portions of rice, dipping your fingers in the vinegared water as necessary.

3. Remove the shells from the shrimp *(prawns)*, leaving the tail shell intact. Devein them and then make a deep incision along the under or ventral side, cutting them so that they open into a butterfly.

4. Mix the mustard and 2 *(1⅔)* teaspoons of water into a smooth paste in another small bowl.

5. Take a pad of rice in your hand and spread a thin streak of mustard along the top surface. Holding a shrimp *(prawn)* between your thumb and forefinger, lay it along the top, over the mustard. Press the top and sides with the fingers of your other hand, so that the shrimp *(prawn)* is pressed firmly into and over the rice pad, covering it completely.

6. Repeat with the remaining shrimp *(prawns)*. Chill until ready to serve.

SUSHI MOLDING

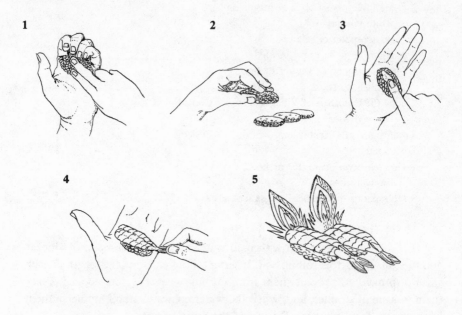

7. Serve with a small pile of grated Oriental long white radish (grate it into long shreds). Stir a little ready-made *wasabi* or hot English mustard into some Japanese soy sauce. Serve in small bowls for dipping.

ADVANCE PREPARATION AND STORAGE NOTES

The Vinegar-Dressed Rice should be made no more than 2 to 3 hours before you make the *sushi*. The *sushi* should be served quite soon after they are made, but can be refrigerated for up to 1 or 2 hours.

Sushi Suggestions and Variations

Another authentic cooked *sushi* is *tamago,* which is a slightly sweetened omelet served in tidy rectangles on top of the rice. It is made by combining beaten eggs with a very small amount of sugar—no more than ½ (⅓) a teaspoon to 4 eggs. The Japanese *sushi* chef makes the omelet in a series of very thin layers in a square omelet pan, stacking them to a thickness of about ½ inch before cutting them into rectangles. I suggest you make a thick omelet and cut that. The rectangles are longer than the rice pad and drape over both ends. They are bound in the center with a strip of seaweed, for which you could substitute a strand of green *(spring)* onion. Steam the strand over a little boiling water to make it limp, so that it will cling to the *sushi*. Although they are not authentic, you may like to try draping some tidily cut slices of smoked salmon over rice pads, and after you have pressed them down, decorate each with half a thin-cut slice of lemon. Another variation might be some slices of smoked eel from the delicatessen, or any similar smoked fish. Make sure the slices are cut to show the grain of the fish to its best advantage. Do not use mustard with smoked fish.

❦ Chinese Fried Dumplings

Although the Chinese call these "dumplings," they are, in fact, turnovers. The Chinese dumplings are usually made with ground pork and curry powder, but as the filling is then a pale imitation of an Indian snack, I have used the filling for another "dumpling" which is more traditional. Both varieties are normally served in the Chinese teahouses as part of a *dim sum* meal.

I have eaten in *dim sum* restaurants throughout Asia, with the good fortune in having one or another of my Chinese friends as a host and guide. On the initial encounter with this delightful style of eating, it really helps to have a knowledgeable person decipher the contents of the innumerable trays of food which are brought to the table. Failing the advantage of having a Chinese host, you will find that the waiters and waitresses, or even surrounding diners, are unfailingly polite and informative in helping you plan your meal choices.

Preparation time: 55 minutes   Makes 24 dumplings
Cooking time: 30 minutes

SHOPPING AND TECHNIQUE TIPS
The Chinese normally use rice wine in the filling; you may substitute the Japanese *sake* or *mirin,* if you can locate them, or pale, dry sherry. I have indicated the pastry and filling instructions together, as you can make the filling while the dough is "resting" to save time.

INGREDIENTS	PREPARATION
Dough and Filling	
2 *(12 ounces)* cups of all-purpose *(plain)* flour	Sifted
⅔ cup *(5 ⅓ fluid ounces)* of boiling water	
2 *(1 ⅔)* tablespoons of vegetable oil	
½ cup *(3 ¾ ounces)* of ground *(minced)* pork	
½ cup *(3 ¼ ounces)* of raw shrimp	Shelled, cleaned, deveined and minced

INGREDIENTS

¼ teaspoon *(a pinch)* of salt

1 *(¾)* teaspoon of rice wine or sherry

2 *(1⅔)* additional tablespoons of vegetable oil

2 dried Chinese mushrooms

1 green *(spring)* onion

1½ *(1¼)* teaspoons of soy sauce

½ *(⅓)* teaspoon of salt

½ *(⅓)* teaspoon of granulated sugar

1 *(¾)* teaspoon of Sesame Oil (page 139)

½ *(⅓)* teaspoon of ground black pepper

1 *(¾)* teaspoon of cornstarch *(cornflour)*

2 *(1⅔)* tablespoons of water

PREPARATION

Soaked in hot water for 10 minutes, stems removed, caps cut into shreds

Finely chopped

METHOD

1. In a large bowl, mix the flour with the boiling water to a soft dough. (Adjust the amounts of water or flour, if necessary.) Let it cool until the mixture can be handled, then knead vigorously until the dough is smooth and satiny. Cover the bowl with a damp cloth and let the dough rest for 15 minutes.

2. While dough is resting, heat 2 tablespoons of vegetable oil in a wok over high heat and add the pork and shrimp. Sprinkle with the salt and the wine and stir-fry until pork has lost its pink and the shrimp is no longer translucent. Remove the mixture to a paper plate.

3. Add the remaining 2 *(1⅔)* tablespoons of oil to the wok and stir-fry the mushrooms and green *(spring)* onion for 1 minute.

4. Mix all the remaining ingredients together in a bowl and add them to the wok. Stir together and then reintroduce the pork and shrimp. Stir-fry for 1 more minute, then remove to a bowl and let the mixture cool. Wash and dry the wok.

5. Form the dough into a long roll. Cut it into 24 equal pieces.

6. Roll each piece into a circle, 3 inches in diameter, flouring a board and rolling pin lightly as needed.

INGREDIENTS
Dumplings
Pastry from above
Filling from above
4 cups of vegetable oil for
    deep-frying

METHOD
1. Place 1½ teaspoons of filling into the middle of the pastry circle and fold it in half over the filling. Starting at one end of the edge, using the thumb and index finger, fold over the edge to the depth of ¼ inch and pinch a pleat. Continue around the circumference of the half circle, folding and pleating until the filling is completely encased. Continue to fill and seal the circles until all the dumplings are completed.

2. Meanwhile, pour the oil into the wok and position a frying thermometer. Set the wok over high heat and bring the oil up to 375°F. *(190°C.).*

3. Fry the dumplings, 2 or 3 at a time, until they are golden brown on the outside.

4. Drain on paper towels then transfer to a serving dish. Serve hot or cold.

CHINESE DUMPLINGS

1

2

3

ADVANCE PREPARATION AND
STORAGE NOTES
Let the dumplings cool completely, then seal them in a large, freezer-weight, plastic bag. Refrigerate for up to 2 days or freeze. Bring them back to room temperature then warm in a low oven for about 10 to 15 minutes before serving or, for a more crisp coating, deep-fry again for 1 minute each before serving.

✾ Malaysian Curry Puffs

This Malay version of curry puffs shows the Chinese influence in the pastry, but the filling is a combination of Malay and Indian.

Preparation time: 55 minutes　　　　　Makes 36 2½-inch crescents
Cooking time: 30 minutes

SHOPPING AND TECHNIQUE TIPS
If you wish to reduce the bite in these little crescents, substitute a milder, larger green chilli pepper for the Serrano, or cut down the amount by half and add a tablespoon of minced green bell pepper *(capsicum).* You will find the dried, unsweetened flaked coconut in the health-food area of the supermarket or in a health-food store.

INGREDIENTS	PREPARATION
Dough and Filling	
Pastry from the Chinese Fried Dumpling recipe (page 205)	
6 fresh green Serrano chilli peppers	Seeded and chopped
1-inch piece of fresh ginger root	Peeled and chopped
4 cloves of garlic	Peeled and chopped
2 *(1⅔)* tablespoons of butter or Indian Clarified Butter (page 139)	
½ a small onion	Peeled and finely chopped
1 cup *(½ pound)* of ground *(minced)* beef (not the leanest)	
½ *(⅓)* teaspoon of ground turmeric	
½ *(⅓)* teaspoon of ground cumin	
½ *(⅓)* teaspoon of ground coriander	
½ *(⅓)* teaspoon of salt	
2 *(1⅔)* tablespoons of dried, unsweetened flaked coconut	
2 *(1⅔)* tablespoons of freshly squeezed lime juice	

METHOD
1. As in step 1 of the Chinese Fried Dumpling recipe.
2. In a food processor, process the chilli peppers, ginger and garlic to a fine paste, stopping between turns to scrape down the sides of the bowl with a spatula.

3. In a wok, heat the butter and fry the onion over high heat until it is limp. Stir in the paste from the processor and stir-fry for 2 minutes. Add the ground *(minced)* beef, mashing and stirring it to break up the lumps.

4. When the meat is brown, add the ground spices, salt, coconut and lime juice. Remove the wok from the heat and stir the contents thoroughly. Transfer everything to a bowl to cool. Wash and dry the wok.

5. Form and roll the dough. As in steps 5 and 6 of the Chinese Fried Dumpling recipe prepare the pastry, but cut the roll into 36 segments and roll each to a diameter of only 2½ inches.

INGREDIENTS
Curry Puffs
Pastry from above
Filling from above
4 cups of vegetable oil for
     deep-frying

METHOD
As for the Chinese Fried Dumpling recipe, page 205.

ADVANCE PREPARATION AND
STORAGE NOTES
As in the Chinese Fried Dumpling recipe, page 205.

⊗ Straits Chinese Chicken Packets (MALAYSIA)

These packets of chicken, fried in their paper wrapping, are an old Chinese recipe. This Malaysian version, which comes from that unique cross of Chinese and Malay cuisines, also known as *Nonya* cooking, have a subtly piquant flavor. The paper packets are unusual and are fun for your guests to open, making a change from the usual hors d'oeuvres.

Preparation time: 45 minutes   Serves 10 to 12 (as hors d'oeuvres)
Cooking time: 40 to 50 minutes

SHOPPING AND TECHNIQUE TIPS
Cooking parchment is used for wrapping these packets in most of the original recipes. However, it is sometimes difficult to find outside of gourmet shops. I have experimented and found that wax *(greaseproof)* paper works just as well. If you

have not made any Oyster Sauce (see recipe, page 146), I suggest you substitute 1 *(¾)* tablespoon of the Chinese All-Purpose Sauce (page 145) or, alternatively, you may like to substitute 2 *(1⅔)* tablespoons of the Indonesian Dark Sweet Soy Sauce (page 142) and leave out the soy sauce in the ingredients list. The Chinese Barbecue Marinade (page 135) also is good (omit the soy sauce and sherry in the ingredients list). The wrapping is merely a matter of folding up flat paper packets, but be sure to tuck the last flap in, otherwise they may come undone in the frying. Note that although you are deep-frying, the heat merely steams the contents and the oil really does not penetrate. (As the oil collects no flavors or bits of burned food in this frying, it is eminently reusable).

INGREDIENTS

1 pound of boned chicken breasts
2 *(1⅔)* tablespoons of Chinese
  Oyster Sauce (page 146)
1 *(¾)* tablespoon of Sesame Oil
  (page 139)
1 *(¾)* tablespoon of pale, dry sherry
1-inch piece of fresh ginger root
¼ teaspoon *(a pinch)* of freshly
  ground black pepper
1 *(¾)* tablespoon of soy sauce
8 dried Oriental mushrooms

4 green *(spring)* onions
4 cups *(32 fluid ounces)* of oil for
  deep-frying

PREPARATION

Skinned and thinly sliced into strips

Peeled and shredded

Soaked until pliable in hot water,
  stems discarded, caps cut into thin
  strips
Chopped

METHOD

1. In a medium bowl, mix the chicken together with the next 6 seasoning ingredients and let it marinate anywhere from 5 minutes to overnight, depending on your time frame and the degree of flavor intensity you want.

2. Cut the wax *(greaseproof)* paper into 20 to 30 6-inch squares and, placing one before you with a corner toward you, place a piece of chicken near that corner. Add several mushroom strips and a few pieces of green *(spring)* onion. Fold the corner away from you over the filling, making a firm crease. Fold first the left and then the right corners over to the middle and continue to fold the package up and over, away from you, tucking in the last flap. (The finished package should be about 3 inches by 2 inches.) Cut more squares of wax paper as you need them.

3. Begin to heat the oil in a wok to a temperature of between 360°F. and 375°F. *(between 180° and 190°C.)* on a frying thermometer. Continue to make packages until all the chicken mixture is wrapped.

4. Fry the packets for 10 minutes, 2 or 3 at a time, pushing them down under the surface of the oil occasionally with the stirrer or the slotted spoon. Turn them once or twice. Transfer them to a paper plate lined with paper towels, first holding them over the wok to drain off the oil. When you have accumulated a plateful, transfer them to a heated serving dish.

5. Continue until you have fried and drained all the packets and keep them hot in the serving dish. Serve, letting your guests unwrap their own packets. Remember to put out a receptacle for the wrappings.

ADVANCE PREPARATION AND STORAGE NOTES

The chicken mixture may be covered and placed in the refrigerator overnight. The chicken packets may also be made in advance and refrigerated until you wish to cook them. Let them come back to room temperature before you start to fry them.

❧ Steamed Pork Dumplings
(SHOU MAI, CHINA)

These tidbits are traditionally served as part of a *dim sum* or Chinese teahouse meal. They are very quick and easy to make. You may like to substitute chopped shrimp, cooked or raw, for the pork; alternatively, if you find a can *(tin)* of little quail eggs in the gourmet section of the supermarket you may use those. Beside the traditional square wonton wrappers, packets of circular "pot-sticker" wrappers, called *kuo teh,* can be found in the same section. They require no trimming.

Preparation time: 55 minutes   Serves 10 to 12 (30 dumplings)
Cooking time: 8 minutes

SHOPPING AND TECHNIQUE TIPS

Although it is easier to use ground *(minced)* pork than buy a piece of pork and dice it fine or mince it, the ground *(minced)* pork tends to lump together in a compact ball after it is steamed. Finely diced pork has a far better texture. Use either wonton wrappers or the round *kuo teh* wrappers.

INGREDIENTS

1¼ cups (9¾ ounces, or less than
     ¾ pound) of meat from pork
     chops (fat and lean)
4 dried Oriental mushrooms

2 green (spring) onions
1 canned (tinned) bamboo shoot or 5
     canned (tinned) water chestnuts
1 egg white
¼ teaspoon (a pinch) of freshly
     ground black pepper
1 (¾) teaspoon of salt
½ (⅓) teaspoon of granulated sugar
½ (⅓) teaspoon of Sesame Oil (page
     139)
1 (¾) teaspoon of pale, dry sherry
1 (¾) tablespoon of cornstarch
     (cornflour)
30 wonton wrappers
1 small carrot
30 fresh coriander leaves (Chinese
     parsley, cilantro)

PREPARATION

Finely chopped or minced

Soaked in hot water for 10 minutes
     until pliable, stems removed, caps
     cut into shreds
Finely chopped
Drained and finely chopped

Trimmed into circles
Peeled, then pared into shavings

METHOD

1. Mix all the ingredients, except the wrappers, carrot and coriander, in a large mixing bowl. Stir thoroughly until everything is well blended.

2. Pour the water into a steamer and bring it up to heat. Cut 30 squares of wax (greaseproof) paper and set them aside.

3. Take a wonton wrapper and place between ½ and 1 teaspoon of the filling in the middle of the circle you have trimmed. Coax the sides up and around the filling, pinching them over the top to make a "waist" with a little frill above it. The filling should not be completely encased but should show in the center.

4. Repeat with all the dumplings. Now take a carrot shaving and a coriander leaf and press them down into the center of each dumpling to decorate it.

5. Set each dumpling on a little square of wax paper and then arrange them in the steamer tray so that there is ½ inch of space between each (so the steam can circulate).

6. The dumplings will fill both trays. Set the trays on the steamer, cover,

CHINESE PORK DUMPLINGS

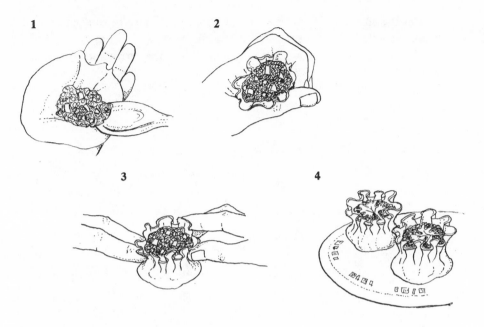

and steam for 8 minutes. Keep warm until ready to serve. You may serve with any of the dipping sauces. For a Southeast Asian version, use Southeast Asian Sweet and Hot Chilli Sauce (page 465), or the Indonesian Satay Sauce (page 469).

ADVANCE PREPARATION AND STORAGE NOTES

The dumplings may be made slightly ahead of time and left in the steamer, off the heat, to keep warm. Do not take them out of the steamer or refrigerate them or the dough will harden. You may make them and let them cool in the steamer, and then wrap them and freeze them. They should then be thawed and warmed in the steamer—not in dry heat.

Shrimp Variation

Merely substitute an equal amount of finely diced raw shelled shrimp for the pork. You may like to add a tablespoon *(¾)* of soy sauce to the filling and omit the salt. Alternatively, you may add 1 inch of fresh ginger root, finely minced.

Quail Egg Variation

Cut the amount of pork down to half. Place a drained quail egg in each wrapper together with ½ teaspoon of the filling. Wrap them as before, but place them crimped side down in the steamer. Omit the carrot and coriander leaf.

DRESSED TO FILL

ॐ ॐ ॐ

The Salads of the Orient

S alads play many different roles in Asian meals in addition to being served as a course or an accompaniment to a main dish. A small salad may be used to clear the palate or cool the mouth; perhaps to mitigate the stinging heat of chilli peppers in heavily spiced stews or curries or to act as foil to a series of bland dishes.

Again, with an emphasis on contrasts in texture, a salad may provide the necessary crunch and crispness to counterpoint the softness of noodles or fried rice. The spartan regime of carefully cut, chilled greens may counterbalance the oil content of a rich gravied dish.

The Orientals also prepare more substantial salads. These are really cold platters, collations of chilled, cooked vegetables and meats, fish, or noodles, which may be sauced or dressed while still hot or combined with a dressing and tossed when cool.

There is almost no limit to the varieties and combinations of vegetables used in the salads of the East. The following are the most common: beans, bean sprouts, broccoli, cabbage (in all its varieties), carrots, cauliflower, celery, cucumber, lettuce, onions, peppers, radishes, snow peas *(mange-tout)*, tomatoes and turnips. Raw asparagus and zucchini *(courgettes)* make their appearance, as do fresh or dried, reconstituted mushrooms.

Such fruits as melon, bananas, mango, papayas and raisins *(sultanas)* play a supporting role in Indian and Indonesian salads. The Thai and Malaysians prefer their fruits semiripe or green, using them as vegetables. Their salads often include crisp, unripe mangoes and papayas. We can substitute tart, green apples or even the hard semiripe peaches found in supermarkets at the beginning of their season.

Dressings and sauces for Asian salads can be either thick or thin, and there is no rule of thumb as to whether they are to be used with side-dish or main-dish salads. The chief requirement is that they enhance the solid ingredients.

Thin dressings are sharpened with lemon juice, lime juice or light and dark vinegars (malt, wine or apple vinegars are never used). The salt-substitute flavorings are soy or fish sauces or, as in Japan, fish stock. Alcohol, such as sweet or dry rice wine or sherry, also contributes to the overall flavor. Bearing in mind the Asian balance of sour, salt and sweet, sugar or honey is mixed into the dressing to mellow the tang of the sharper ingredients.

Where oil is included, it is always peanut and/or sesame oil. Other salad oils can be used, but please, *never* olive oil, which is foreign to Asia.

The Indians thicken their dressings with yogurt, the Indonesians, Malaysians and Thai with thick coconut milk or ground peanuts. The northern Asians, the Japanese, Chinese and Koreans use egg, cornstarch *(cornflour)* or even soybean curd and soybean paste as thickening agents, especially in cooked dressings and sauces.

At first sight, the most noticeable thing about Asian salads is their attractive presentation. A tossed melange of vegetables in a bowl is rare. Salads are presented on platters like carefully composed pictures. Fruits and vegetables are frequently carved to represent flowers, and the component parts of a salad are arranged according to shape and color. Please turn to Basic Techniques (page 86) for instructions on simple but effective fruit and vegetable carving.

The final touch to many Asian salads is the garnish. As many as 5 or 6 different ingredients may be chopped or pounded and sprinkled or carefully arranged over the top. Among the more common garnishes are crushed peanuts, crumbled dried red peppers, chopped hard-cooked egg and sprigs, leaves or fragments of parsley, mint, basil or coriander *(cilantro)*. Serrated cucumber slices, tasseled green *(spring)* onions, cherry tomato and radish flowers, red or white onion rings and carved slices of carrot, turnip or celery will frequently ring a salad platter.

Many of the salad ingredients can be prepared in advance: vegetables and garnishes cut and dropped into iced water; meats, fish and seafood cooked ahead, sliced and refrigerated; dressings mixed and kept in a jar in the refrigerator. Remember to chill the salad platter as well. Taking advantage of the make-ahead method, an impressive salad can be assembled, garnished and dressed 5 minutes before serving time.

❀ Basic Chinese Salad Dressing

In China, this dressing is used for cooked meats and seafood as well as raw vegetables, and for cooked, chilled combinations of vegetables, dried ingredients and meats or seafood.

Preparation time: 3 minutes   Yield: 4 (3 ¼) tablespoons

SHOPPING AND TECHNIQUE TIPS
Try to find the Chinese soy sauce if possible. The flavor is different from the Japanese and will give the proper ethnic quality to the dressing.

INGREDIENTS
1 (¾) tablespoon of Chinese soy
    sauce
1 (¾) tablespoon of rice vinegar, or
    2 (1 ⅔) teaspoons of white
    vinegar and 1 (¾) teaspoon of
    water
1 (¾) tablespoon of granulated sugar
1 (¾) tablespoon of Sesame Oil
    (page 139)

METHOD
Combine all the ingredients in a bowl, stirring until the sugar dissolves.

ADVANCE PREPARATION AND STORAGE NOTES
This dressing can be mixed ahead of time and will keep, tightly capped, in the refrigerator for several days.

Variations on the Basic Chinese Salad Dressing

1. Szechwan-Style Salad Dressing

Omit the soy sauce and sugar. Add ¼ *(less than)* teaspoon of Hot Pepper Paste (page 128), ½ *(⅓)* teaspoon of Chinese Salt and Pepper Dip (page 120) and 1 *(¾)* tablespoon of pale, dry sherry.

2. Chinese Ginger Salad Dressing

Add 1 *(¾)* teaspoon of freshly grated ginger root to the original ingredients.

✿ Chinese Spiced Salad Dressing

This dressing is a slight variation on the classic dressing used for the Crispy Chicken Noodle Salad (page 231). *Hoisin* sauce is the authentic addition, but the Chinese All-Purpose Sauce in this recipe makes a reasonable substitute (page 145).

Preparation time: 2 minutes   Yield: about 7 *(5 ½)* tablespoons

SHOPPING AND TECHNIQUE TIPS
Check that you have some All-Purpose Sauce already made up in your refrigerator. If you have not, then use the opportunity to make a quantity and store it.

INGREDIENTS
2 *(1 ⅔)* tablespoons of rice vinegar,
    or 6 *(4 ¾)* teaspoons of white
    vinegar and 2 *(1 ⅔)* teaspoons of
    water
1 *(¾)* teaspoon of granulated sugar
2 *(1 ⅔)* tablespoons of All-Purpose
    Sauce (page 145)
¼ teaspoon *(a pinch)* of salt
2 *(1 ⅔)* tablespoons of vegetable oil
1 *(¾)* tablespoon of Sesame Oil
    (page 139)

METHOD

1. Pour the vinegar into the bowl and stir in the sugar until it has dissolved.

2. Stir in the remaining ingredients and blend everything well.

ADVANCE PREPARATION AND
STORAGE NOTES

This sauce keeps well, refrigerated, and can be made up 2 or 3 days ahead of time.

❦ Japanese Dressing for Salad I

This dressing echoes the eternal Oriental theme of the balance of flavor qualities: sweet, sour and salt.

Preparation time: 3 minutes   Yield: ¾ cup *(6 fluid ounces)*

SHOPPING AND TECHNIQUE TIPS

Look on the shelves of the Oriental section of the supermarket for *mirin,* the Japanese sweet rice wine. If you cannot find it, substitute sweet sherry, using ¾ of the amount of *mirin.* Use Japanese soy sauce for Japanese dishes; the flavor of the Chinese is different.

INGREDIENTS

4 *(3 ¼)* tablespoons of Japanese soy sauce
4 *(3 ¼)* tablespoons of rice or white vinegar
2 *(1 ⅔)* tablespoons of *mirin* (rice wine)
2 *(1 ⅔)* tablespoons of granulated sugar
¾ *(just over ½)* teaspoon of salt
2 *(1 ⅔)* tablespoons of toasted sesame seeds (optional)

METHOD

1. Combine all the ingredients except the sesame seeds in a small bowl and stir until the sugar has dissolved. Add the sesame seeds if desired.

2. Use to dress simple vegetable salads such as cucumber, carrot, long, white Oriental radish *(daikon),* and seafood salads such as shrimp, crab, scallops, etc. Chill the salads after dressing.

ADVANCE PREPARATION AND
STORAGE NOTES
This dressing can be made well ahead of time and refrigerated, covered.
Do not add the sesame seeds until just before you dress the salad.

❧ Japanese Dressing for Salad II

This sesame oil/vinegar dressing is a perfect partner for crisp, raw vegetables.

Preparation time: 3 minutes   Yield: 5½ *(4⅓)* tablespoons

SHOPPING AND TECHNIQUE TIPS
If you cannot locate sesame oil in your supermarket, use the Sesame Oil recipe
on page 139.

INGREDIENTS
3 *(2⅓)* tablespoons of rice vinegar,
    or 2 *(1⅔)* tablespoons of white
    vinegar and 1 *(¾)* tablespoon of
    water
1 *(¾)* tablespoon of *mirin* (rice
    wine), or 2 *(1⅔)* teaspoons of
    sweet sherry
2 *(1⅔)* teaspoons of granulated sugar
¼ teaspoon *(a pinch)* of salt
2 *(1⅔)* teaspoons of vegetable oil
1 *(¾)* teaspoon of sesame oil

METHOD
Pour the vinegar and *mirin* into a bowl and stir in the sugar until it has
dissolved; then stir in the remaining ingredients.

ADVANCE PREPARATION AND
STORAGE NOTES
This dressing can be made ahead of time and refrigerated.

Variations on Japanese Dressing for Salad

1. To Dressing I, substitute finely chopped peanuts or walnuts for the
sesame seeds.

2. To Dressing I, use only 2 *(1⅔)* tablespoons of soy sauce, substitute lemon juice for the vinegar and honey for the sugar. Stir in ¼ teaspoon *(a pinch)* of red pepper (Cayenne).

3. To Dressing II, add ¼ *(less than ¼)* teaspoon of finely grated lemon rind *(peel)* and omit the oils.

❀ Japanese Miso Dressing for Salad I

In Japan, this dressing would be made with sweet white *miso* (fermented soybean paste) and, if you can find it in your supermarket, by all means use it. If you cannot locate it, then try using the Japanese Soybean Paste Substitute (page 131). Either way, it is quite delicious and complements a number of cooked or raw vegetables and mixtures of both.

Preparation time: 2 minutes   Yields ⅞ cup *(7 fluid ounces)*

SHOPPING AND TECHNIQUE TIPS
Try to buy *mirin,* the Japanese sweet rice wine. Failing that, substitute sweet sherry or dry white wine, using ¾ of the given amount of *mirin.* Japanese Basic Fish Stock (page 170) or water may be added to thin the dressing.

INGREDIENTS
6 *(4¾)* tablespoons of Japanese
    Soybean Paste Substitute (page
    131)
2 *(1⅔)* tablespoons of honey
¼ cup *(2 fluid ounces)* of Japanese
    Basic Fish Stock (page 170)
2 *(1⅔)* tablespoons of *mirin*

METHOD
1. Combine the Soybean Paste and the honey in a bowl, then gradually add the stock and *mirin* (or other wine), blending into a smooth dressing.

ADVANCE PREPARATION AND
STORAGE NOTES
This dressing can be made ahead and refrigerated, covered, but do not keep it for more than 24 hours.

✸ Japanese Miso Dressing for Salad II

This dressing is sharpened by the addition of vinegar, and tangy with a touch of mustard. It is also thicker than the preceding dressing and a little goes far.

Preparation time: 2 minutes   Yield: just over 7 *(5⅔)* tablespoons

SHOPPING AND TECHNIQUE TIPS
Look for rice vinegar in the Oriental section of a good supermarket. If you cannot find it, use white vinegar diluted with water in the proportion of ⅔ vinegar to ⅓ water. Lemon juice is also a good substitute.

INGREDIENTS
4 *(3¼)* tablespoons of Japanese
    Soybean Paste Substitute (page 131)
¼ teaspoon *(a pinch)* of hot mustard
    powder
1 *(¾)* teaspoon of honey
2 *(1⅔)* tablespoons of rice vinegar,
    or 4 *(3¼)* teaspoons of white
    vinegar and 2 *(1⅔)* teaspoons of
    water
1 *(¾)* tablespoon of *mirin* (rice
    wine) or 2 *(1⅔)* teaspoons of
    sweet sherry

METHOD
Combine the Soybean Paste, mustard and honey, then gradually add the liquids, stirring until the mixture becomes smooth.

ADVANCE PREPARATION AND STORAGE NOTES
As in Miso Dressing I.

Variations on Miso Dressings

1. To Dressing I, add 2 *(1⅔)* tablespoons of ground sesame seeds or 1 *(¾)* tablespoon of sesame butter (health-food section of supermarket).

2. To Dressing I, add 1 *(¾)* tablespoon of grated fresh ginger root and use only half of the given amount of Basic Fish Stock.

3. To Dressing II, add 2 mashed, hard-cooked *(hard-boiled)* egg yolks and 2 *(1⅔)* tablespoons of water.

4. To Dressing II, add 1 *(¾)* tablespoon of peanut butter and 1 *(¾)* tablespoon of water, and omit the mustard.

❧ Korean Thin Salad Dressing

Preparation time: 8 minutes   Yield: about ¾ cup *(6 fluid ounces)*

SHOPPING AND TECHNIQUE TIPS
Toast the sesame seeds in a small frying pan over medium heat until they brown and start to jump around. Remove them immediately (don't let them burn) to a mortar or electric spice grinder and pound or grind to a powder.

INGREDIENTS	PREPARATION
1 clove of garlic	Peeled and minced
1 green *(spring)* onion	Finely chopped
2 *(1⅔)* teaspoons of sesame seeds	Roasted and ground
2 *(1⅔)* tablespoons of soy sauce	
1½ *(1¼)* teaspoons of granulated sugar	
1½ *(1¼)* tablespoons of white vinegar	
¼ teaspoon *(a pinch)* of ground red pepper (Cayenne)	
½-inch piece of fresh ginger root (optional)	Peeled and minced
1½ *(1¼)* tablespoons of Sesame Oil (page 139)	

METHOD
Combine all the ingredients in a bowl and stir until the sugar has dissolved.

ADVANCE PREPARATION AND STORAGE NOTES
This dressing can be made up to 1 day ahead and stored, covered, in the refrigerator. If made in advance, the green *(spring)* onion should be added when the dressing has been brought back to room temperature, just before serving.

Southeast Asian Salad Dressings

The Southeast Asian nations share many basics in their salads and dressings, and the ingredients are often interchangeable among their cuisines. The dressings are invariably spicy-hot with chilli peppers, either fresh and minced, or dried, as in ground red pepper or pepper flakes. The sweetness is provided by palm sugar, brown sugar or granulated white sugar. Necessary tart and sour notes of lime juice, lemon juice or tamarind liquid sharpen the dressings, while fish sauce provides the salt accent.

This major quartet of flavors is often augmented by a hint of fish in the form of shrimp paste or dried, whole or powdered shrimp, and often by a touch of ginger or one of its relatives. In Thai dressings, citrus accents of lime rind, lemon grass or citrus leaves are often added.

Thin dressings are used with raw vegetable salads, which are sometimes made more substantial by the addition of small amounts of shrimp or pork, while thick dressings, enriched with coconut milk or ground peanuts, are mostly reserved for the more sturdy collations of cooked vegetables, meats and eggs or fish. These latter salads become one-dish meals.

In the following recipes I have indicated the country with which they are most associated. However, with a very minor change, or even none, you can easily use the formula to dress the salad of another Southeast Asian country, where it will be equally authentic. After some practice, as your palate becomes accustomed to the fine balance of flavors, you will be able to mix a dressing from memory and taste and play your own variations on the eternal themes.

❦ Thick, Creamy Peanut Dressing (INDONESIA)

In this dressing, the garlic needs to be cooked. Sometimes this is done by frying it, together with the chilli peppers and shallots or small onions, or often by merely boiling it with the other ingredients. I prefer the flavor of the former method.

Preparation time: 10 minutes
Cooking time: 10 minutes

Yield: 2¼ cups *(18 fluid ounces)*

SHOPPING AND TECHNIQUE TIPS

Authentically, roasted peanuts are pounded to a powdery paste for this dressing. I have found that the natural peanut butter, without preservatives, works very well. The chunky style produces a texture close to the original. Anchovy paste substitutes nicely for the rather pungent fermented shrimp paste, with the added advantage that it does not need to be roasted or fried before adding it to the dressing. If you do not like the hint of fish, you may happily leave it out altogether.

INGREDIENTS	PREPARATION
1 clove of garlic	Peeled and chopped
2 shallots	Peeled and chopped
½-inch piece of fresh ginger root	Peeled and minced
½ (⅓) teaspoon of salt	
¼ teaspoon (a pinch) of ground red pepper (Cayenne)	
1 (¾) tablespoon of vegetable oil	
4 (3¼) tablespoons of chunky peanut butter	
½ (⅓) teaspoon of anchovy paste (optional)	
1 cup (8 fluid ounces) of water	
1 (¾) tablespoon of brown sugar	
The juice of 1 lime or ½ a lemon	
1 (¾) tablespoon of Southeast Asian fish sauce	

METHOD

1. Pound the garlic, shallots, ginger root, salt and red pepper to a fine paste in a mortar.

2. Heat the oil in a wok or saucepan over medium heat and fry the paste, stirring, until the sharp tang of the garlic mellows (about 1 minute).

3. Stir in the peanut butter and anchovy paste and blend well. Gradually pour in the water, stirring until the mixture is well blended.

4. Add the sugar, increase the heat to medium-high and bring the mixture to a boil, stirring continuously.

5. Remove the wok or saucepan from the heat and pour the dressing into the bowl. Stir in the lime juice and fish sauce and let it cool.

ADVANCE PREPARATION AND STORAGE NOTES

This dressing can be made ahead of time and refrigerated.

Malaysian Variation

Exactly the same as the above except for the addition of ¼ *(just under)* teaspoon of ground turmeric to the ingredients to be pounded to a paste in the mortar.

✌ Thick Coconut Salad Dressing (MALAYSIA)

Another thick dressing which is delicious over lightly cooked vegetables.

Preparation time: 20 minutes   Yield: 1 ¼ cups *(half a pint)*

SHOPPING AND TECHNIQUE TIPS
Coconut Cream is the cream that rises to the top of thick (first pressing) coconut milk after overnight refrigeration. You may substitute whipping cream, flavored with coconut extract.

INGREDIENTS	PREPARATION
4 shallots	Peeled
5 cloves of garlic	Peeled
1 or 2 green Serrano chilli peppers or ½ Jalapeño pepper	Seeded, membranes removed, chopped
¼ teaspoon *(a pinch)* of salt	
½ cup *(4 fluid ounces)* of Coconut Cream (page 114), or ½ cup *(4 fluid ounces)* of whipping cream, flavored with ¼ *(just under)* teaspoon of coconut extract	
1 *(¾)* teaspoon of molasses *(treacle)*, dissolved in 1 *(¾)* tablespoon of lime juice and 1 *(¾)* tablespoon of hot water	
2 *(1⅔)* teaspoons of brown sugar	
2 *(1⅔)* tablespoons of Southeast Asian fish sauce	

METHOD
1. Place a wok over high heat and put in the shallots and garlic. Stir them and shake the wok until they become brown-speckled and blistered. Remove them from the wok and chop them fine. Clean the wok.

2. In a mortar, pound the chilli pepper and the salt until the pepper is pulverized. Add the shallots and garlic and pound into a smooth paste.

3. In the wok, over medium heat, boil the Coconut Cream (or the flavored whipping cream), stirring until it becomes oily and reduces to half its volume. Remove the wok from the heat and stir in the paste from the mortar and add the rest of the ingredients.

4. Return the wok to the heat and bring the dressing to a boil, stirring. Cook for 2 minutes, then set aside to cool.

ADVANCE PREPARATION AND
STORAGE NOTES

This dressing may be made ahead and refrigerated. Before using, thin with a little milk or lime juice, according to taste.

Thai Variation

Same as the above dressing, but add ¼ cup *(7 ounces)* of any smoked, boned, flaked fish to the paste in the mortar and pound, together with the other ingredients, until it reaches a smooth consistency. You may like to add 2 *(1⅔)* more tablespoons of cream or lime juice to thin the dressing further.

Indonesian Variation

Yield: just over 1½ cups *(12 fluid ounces)*

INGREDIENTS
1 clove of garlic
½ *(⅓)* teaspoon of anchovy paste
¼ to ½ *(just under ⅓)* teaspoon of
    ground red pepper (Cayenne)
½ *(⅓)* teaspoon of salt
1 *(¾)* teaspoon of granulated sugar
½ cup *(1¼ ounces)* of dried,
    unsweetened, flaked coconut
1 cup *(8 fluid ounces)* of water

PREPARATION
Peeled and minced

METHOD
1. Pound the garlic and anchovy paste in a mortar, then place in a wok. Add the remaining ingredients and stir well. Turn the heat to high and bring to a boil, stirring.

2. Remove the wok from the heat and pour the contents into a small bowl. Set aside to cool.

☙ Thin Salad Dressing
(THAILAND)

This dressing, with slight variations, is universal throughout the Southeast Asian cuisines. It is used to dress salads of fresh ingredients, often accompanied by cooked meats and fish. Adjust the amount of hot peppers to your taste.

Preparation time: 6 minutes   Yield: about ½ cup *(4 fluid ounces)*

SHOPPING AND TECHNIQUE TIPS
You may substitute ground red pepper for the fresh chilli peppers. This dressing can be made in its entirety in a large mortar.

INGREDIENTS	PREPARATION
3 cloves of garlic	Peeled and minced
2 fresh red or green Serrano chilli peppers, or 1½ *(1 ¼)* teaspoons of ground red pepper (Cayenne) (or less, to taste)	Seeded (optional) and minced
2 *(1⅔)* tablespoons of Southeast Asian fish sauce	
Juice of 3 limes	
2 *(1⅔)* tablespoons of granulated sugar	

METHOD
1. Pound the garlic and chilli peppers or the Cayenne in a mortar until they turn into a juicy paste.
2. Add the remaining ingredients and stir until the sugar has dissolved.

ADVANCE PREPARATION AND STORAGE NOTES
This dressing may be made ahead and refrigerated, covered, for 1 or 2 days.

Variation I (THAILAND)

In step 1 of the method, add the grated zest *(peel)* of half a lime. Add ½ *(⅓)* teaspoon of freshly ground black pepper with the remaining ingredients.

Variation II (PHILIPPINES)

Substitute ½ (⅓) teaspoon of freshly ground black pepper for the chilli peppers, substitute 6 to 8 *(about 5½)* tablespoons of white vinegar for the lime juice.

Variation III (VIETNAM)

When squeezing the limes, include the pulp as well. This then becomes the famous *Nuoc Cham,* which is also used as a table or dipping sauce (page 473).

✿ Indian Spiced Yogurt Dressing

The Indian "salad" is really a selection of vegetables, cooked or raw, or fruit, marinated and chilled in a thick, creamy, spiced yogurt dressing. The spicing may simply be the addition of salt and pepper, or it may be an interesting combination of up to 5 dried, ground spices.

Indian yogurt is generally made from buffalo milk and is sweeter and creamier than our plain yogurts; it has the texture of a thick, creamy blancmange. Homemade yogurt, once a rather delicate and tedious process, is now extremely simple to concoct with the aid of electric yogurt makers. If you prefer to use commercial yogurt, make sure it is the plain, unsweetened variety. I have found a kosher variety and also a Bulgarian yogurt, both of which are a close substitute for homemade. To approach the texture and flavor of Indian yogurt, a little fresh cream should be added to enrich them. If I am making my own, I use whole *(full-fat)* milk, made satiny with the addition of half-and-half, to a proportion of ⅔ milk to ⅓ half-and-half *(half milk, half cream).*

Preparation time: 8 minutes   Yield: just over 2½ cups *(1 pint)*

SHOPPING AND TECHNIQUE TIPS
As I have advised above, look for the kosher or Bulgarian yogurt in the dairy section. At any rate, the yogurt must be plain and unsweetened. When combining the yogurt with the salad ingredients, make sure it is at room temperature. After that, the entire dish should be chilled.

INGREDIENTS

½ *(⅓)* teaspoon of ground cumin

2 cups *(16 fluid ounces)* of plain,
    unsweetened yogurt

½ cup *(8 ounces)* of whipping cream

¼ teaspoon *(a pinch)* of ground
    cardamom

¼ to ½ *(just under ⅓)* teaspoon of
    salt

¼ teaspoon *(a pinch)* of ground
    white pepper

¼ teaspoon *(a pinch)* of ground red
    pepper (Cayenne)

METHOD

1. Briefly heat the ground cumin on either a baking tray in an oven or
in a small frying pan, over medium heat, until it just begins to darken and gives
out a warm, rather nutty aroma. Immediately pour it into the mixing bowl and
let it cool.

2. Combine the yogurt and cream with the cumin, then stir in the remaining ingredients. Blend everything well.

ADVANCE PREPARATION AND
STORAGE NOTES

The dressing can be made up to 2 hours before using, but no longer. Bring
back to room temperature after refrigerating it and combine it with the salad
ingredients immediately. The salad may then be chilled for up to 2 hours (but
no longer) before serving.

Variation I

Omit all the spices except the salt and pepper. This variation is usually
served with the addition of chopped mint leaves as well as salad ingredients.

Variation II

Add 2 *(1⅔)* teaspoons of granulated sugar and stir until the sugar has
dissolved before adding the salad ingredients. This variation is normally served
with fruits such as banana or apple.

❀ Chinese Crispy Chicken Noodle Salad

A well-known and classic salad, this is very popular with Westerners. The emphasis is on texture as well as flavor, and the crunch of crisp-fried noodles and fresh bean sprouts contrasts with the softness of the chicken and lettuce.

Preparation time: 15 minutes
(assuming chicken is already
cooked)

Cooking time (for noodles): 15
minutes
Serves 6

SHOPPING AND TECHNIQUE TIPS
You will need about 3 cups *(1½ pounds)* of cooked chicken meat, and I suggest you purchase a whole chicken and steam it ahead of time. In this way you will have the beginning of a good soup as well. Let the chicken cool, then pull the skin off and shred the meat with your fingers. The long, thin white rice stick noodles *(mee-fun)* are the correct variety to use, and should be deep-fried until crisp, straight from the packet. You can find them in Oriental food shops or in the Oriental section of the supermarket. If you cannot locate them, substitute wonton or spring roll wrappers and cut them into thin strips before deep-frying them until crisp.

INGREDIENTS	PREPARATION
3 cups *(1½ pounds)* of boned, cooked chicken	Shredded
4 *(3¼)* tablespoons of Chinese Spiced Salad Dressing (page 218)	
3 cups *(24 fluid ounces)* of vegetable oil	
1 hank (4 ounces) of rice stick noodles, or	Gently separated (do not break them up)
8 wonton wrappers	Cut into thin (¼-inch) strips
2 green *(spring)* onions	Chopped
1 small carrot	Peeled, then pared into shavings with a potato peeler, soaked in iced water, drained
1 cup *(2¾ ounces or less than ¼ pound)* of bean sprouts	Roots removed, soaked in iced water, drained
1 stalk of celery	Trimmed, cut diagonally into pieces ½-inch thick, soaked in iced water, drained

INGREDIENTS | PREPARATION

1 *(¾)* tablespoon of Sesame Oil
   (page 139)

6 lettuce leaves (romaine, Boston,   Finely shredded
   etc.)

METHOD

1. Place the chicken in a large bowl and combine it with the Spiced Salad Dressing.

2. Heat the oil in a wok to 350°F. *(175°C.)* on a frying thermometer and fry the noodles until they are crisp and pale brown. (You may test the heat with a single noodle or wonton strip. It should sink to the bottom, then immediately rise to the surface.) Remove noodles with a slotted spoon and drain on paper towels.

3. Add the green *(spring)* onions, carrot shavings, bean sprouts and celery to the chicken and toss everything together lightly. Sprinkle with the sesame oil.

4. Arrange the shredded lettuce to form a bed on a large platter. Spoon the chicken mixture on top. Scatter the fried noodles over the salad and serve.

ADVANCE PREPARATION AND
STORAGE NOTES

The chicken can be cooked ahead and shredded. Refrigerate covered. The vegetables may be prepared and left soaking in the iced water in the refrigerator. The noodles may be fried ahead of time and then placed in a plastic bag and tightly sealed. Do not combine the salad ingredients until the last moment. You may toss the noodles in with the salad if you like, but this must also be done immediately before serving; otherwise the noodles will soften in the dressing.

Malaysian Variation

This identical salad also appears as part of a Malaysian (or Singapore) meal, because of the many Chinese in that area.

Vietnamese Variation

Use the Vietnamese version of the Thin Salad Dressing (page 229) and omit the sesame oil. Toss 2 *(1 ⅔)* tablespoons of chopped mint leaves in with the chicken and vegetables. Serve on whole lettuce leaves and garnish with sprigs of mint.

Thai Variation

Instead of the chicken use 2 cups *(1 pound)* of cooked pork, cut into julienne strips, and 1 cup *(just over ⅓ pound)* of cooked, peeled baby shrimp. Use 6 *(4¾)* tablespoons of the Thai Thin Salad Dressing (page 228) and omit the sesame oil. Garnish with 2 *(1⅔)* tablespoons of chopped coriander (Chinese parsley, *cilantro*) leaves.

❀ Chinese Radish and Carrot Curl Salad

This is a cool and refreshing "small" salad. It may also be served as a side dish or garnish to complement cold meats, or as a contrast to a whole, crisp-fried fish.

Preparation time: 2 hours (including   Serves 4
   marination)

SHOPPING AND TECHNIQUE TIPS
You may substitute young turnips if you cannot find the long white Oriental radish in your supermarket. The salt marination removes much of the bite from the turnip. The ingredients of this salad should be as cold and as crisp as possible.

INGREDIENTS	PREPARATION
4-inch piece of Oriental radish, or equal amount of turnip	Peeled
2 *(1⅔)* teaspoons of salt	
2 medium carrots	Tops and tails removed, peeled
Ice water	
2 *(1⅔)* tablespoons of Basic Chinese Salad Dressing (page 217), omitting the soy sauce	

METHOD
1. Using a shredder or sharp knife, shred the radish as fine as possible, making the strips as long and thin as you can. Place the shreds in a bowl and sprinkle with 1 *(¾)* teaspoon of the salt, tossing lightly but thoroughly. Refrigerate for 1½ hours.

2. Fill a second bowl with ice water and stir in the remaining teaspoon of salt. Cut the carrots in half lengthwise then, starting at right angles to the

MAKING CARROT CURLS

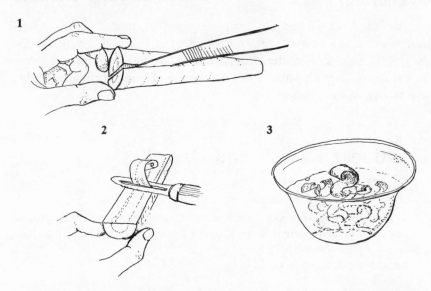

cut surface, pare down the length of each carrot half. Make the parings as thin as you can. The thinner they are, the better they will curl. Drop the parings in the salted ice water and refrigerate for 1½ hours.

3. Remove the radish shreds from their bowl and wash them under cold, running water to remove the salt. Gently squeeze them dry, rinse out their bowl and replace the shreds in it. Sprinkle them with 1 *(¾)* tablespoon of the dressing and toss gently.

4. Drain the carrot curls and empty the water. Replace them in the bowl and sprinkle with the remainder of the dressing. Toss gently.

5. Mound the shredded radish in the center of a plate and surround them with carefully arranged carrot curls, all facing the same way. Chill until ready to serve.

ADVANCE PREPARATION AND STORAGE NOTES

This salad will keep, covered, for up to 3 days, in the refrigerator.

Korean Variation (PEAR SALAD)

Substitute a large, firm, crisp pear for the radish and add the flesh of a peeled and seeded cucumber, shredded or cut into julienne strips. A few green *(spring)* onion slivers may also be included. Dress the salad with 4 tablespoons of Korean Thin Salad Dressing (page 223).

Vietnamese Variation (CARROT SALAD)

Use carrots alone and cut them into julienne strips. Dress them with the Vietnamese Variation (III) of the Thin Salad Dressing (Thailand) (page 228) and serve on lettuce leaves.

✿ Japanese Turnip Chrysanthemum and Carrot Salad

This Japanese salad has the same character as the preceding salad from China, but the style of presentation is very different.

Preparation time: 2 hours   Serves 4

SHOPPING AND TECHNIQUE TIPS

Look for young white turnips that are nice and firm. The technique of carving them decoratively would normally be included in the section on fruit and vegetable carving, but it is such an integral part of this recipe that I have incorporated it in the instructions here. Make sure that you have a well-sharpened knife before commencing the cutting.

INGREDIENTS	PREPARATION
2 medium carrots	Tops and tails removed, peeled
1 (¾) teaspoon of salt	
Ice water	
2 young white turnips	Peeled
1 recipe of Japanese Dressing for Salad II (page 220)	
2 or 3 sprigs of parsley or any other green to suggest chrysanthemum leaves	

METHOD

1. Using a shredder or sharp knife, shred the carrots as fine as possible, making the strips as long and as thin as you can. Place the shreds in a bowl and sprinkle with 1 (¾) teaspoon of salt. Fill the bowl ¾ full of ice water.

2. Cut the tops off the turnips, then turn them over and stand them on the cut surfaces. Bracket the first turnip between two parallel wooden chopsticks so that they touch the turnip on either side. Using a very sharp knife, make a series of parallel cuts across the entire top of the turnip. They should

TURNIP CRYSANTHEMUMS

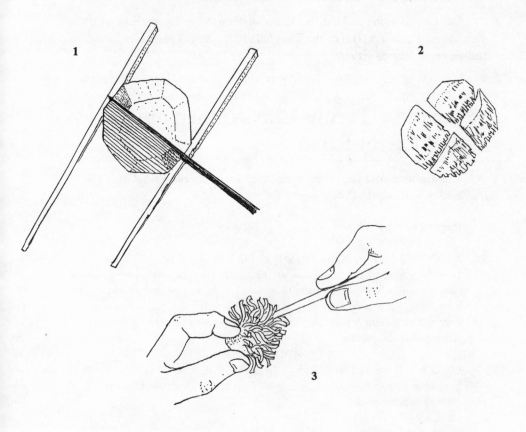

be as close together as possible and should reach to within ⅛-inch to ¼-inch of the bottom. The chopsticks should block the downward thrust of the knife in exactly the right place every time.

3. Give the turnip a quarter-turn and again bracket it with the chopsticks. Once more, make a second series of deep, close, parallel cuts, crosshatching the first set. Carefully slice the cut turnip downward into quarters and place the pieces on top of the carrot shreds in the bowl. Repeat the cutting with the second turnip. Cover the bowl and refrigerate it for 1½ hours.

4. Completely drain the water from the bowl and gently squeeze each turnip quarter to remove the surplus moisture, taking care not to break the delicate tendrils you have created. Set them aside.

5. Gently squeeze the carrot shreds and replace them in the bowl. Place

the turnip quarters on top. Sprinkle them with the dressing and let them marinate for a minimum of 10 minutes.

6. Sometime before serving, remove and drain the turnip segments. Using a chopstick, lightly fluff out and arrange the tendrils to resemble chrysanthemum petals. Gently squeeze the carrot shreds and arrange them in a shallow mound on a decorative platter or small tray. Place the turnip chrysanthemums off center, slightly to one side. Tuck in the parsley or pieces of green so that they resemble leaves. Chill until ready to serve.

ADVANCE PREPARATION AND STORAGE NOTES

This salad can be made through to the end of Step 4 up to 3 days in advance. Cover tightly and refrigerate.

❧ Sweet and Sour Fresh Cucumber Salad (THAILAND)

This is the fresh salad traditionally served as an accompaniment to satays of all kinds. It also goes very well with cold meats and a number of other dishes. It is appropriate in any of the Southeast Asian cuisines.

Preparation time: 12 minutes   Serves 6 people
Cooking time: 5 minutes

SHOPPING AND TECHNIQUE TIPS

The Southeast Asian cucumber is small and has many seeds. The closest variety to it is our pickling cucumbers; however, you may use the traditional cucumber, or the long, hothouse European variety. For aesthetics, the seeds should be removed. In the younger cucumbers, the seeds are not so tough and can be left in.

INGREDIENTS	PREPARATION
1 large cucumber, or its equivalent in small pickling cucumbers	Peeled, halved lengthwise, seeds removed
½ a small red onion, or 2 shallots	Peeled, halved and cut into paper-thin slices
2 fresh red or green Serrano chillies or 1 Jalapeño chilli pepper	Cut into very thin rounds. The seeds may be removed if less heat is desired

INGREDIENTS   PREPARATION

1 cup *(8 fluid ounces)* of rice vinegar
   or white vinegar
½ cup *(4 fluid ounces)* of water
4 *(3 ¼)* tablespoons of granulated
   sugar
¼ teaspoon *(a pinch)* of ground
   turmeric
1 clove of garlic   Crushed, peeled and minced
½ *(⅓)* teaspoon of salt

METHOD

1. Cut the cucumber crosswise into paper-thin slices and place in a bowl. Cover with the onion and chilli pepper slices.

2. In a small saucepan, combine the remaining ingredients and bring to a boil over medium heat, stirring to dissolve the sugar.

3. Pour over the vegetables in the bowl and let cool. Refrigerate, covered.

ADVANCE PREPARATION AND
STORAGE NOTES

This salad can be refrigerated for up to 2 weeks, if tightly covered. In fact, it has more flavor if eaten the day after it is made. The cucumbers become more pliable as they soak in the liquid. In Thailand, where imported food products are expensive, we treated it as a relish and ate it with most meals.

Chinese Variation

Leave out the turmeric and fresh chilli peppers. Add 1 *(¾)* teaspoon of Indonesian Hot Pepper Paste (page 128) and 1 *(¾)* teaspoon of Sesame Oil (page 139). Let all the ingredients blend and marinate the cucumber, without cooking, for at least 6 hours.

Indian Variation

Use the cucumber, red onion and chilli peppers, but marinate them in the Indian Spiced Yogurt Dressing (page 229) for at least 2 hours, in the refrigerator. This salad will not keep as long as the others, but may be made a day ahead and refrigerated, covered.

❧ Cooked Mixed Vegetables in Thick Dressing (INDONESIA)

This salad appears in many forms throughout the Asian cuisines. Variations occur in the dressings which are mostly thick, and range from peanut, through coconut, to a hearty sauce flavored with smoked fish and made tangy with tamarind.

The salad ingredients may be made more substantial with the addition of cooked meats, in which case the salad plays the role of a main dish.

Preparation time: 15 minutes
 (excluding the dressing)

Cooking time: 30 minutes
Serves 6

SHOPPING AND TECHNIQUE TIPS
You may like to vary the ingredients, according to what is available and at the peak of perfection in the market. Sweet potatoes may be used instead of white potatoes; spinach, cabbage, celery, cauliflower, broccoli or Chinese snow peas *(mange-tout)* may be added or substituted. The vegetables should be cooked ahead by blanching them briefly in boiling water or by steaming them. They are then cooled to room temperature before being dressed.

INGREDIENTS	PREPARATION
1 large potato	Peeled and cut into small dice
10 green beans	Tops and tails removed, cut on the diagonal into 2-inch lengths
2 medium carrots	Peeled and cut into julienne strips
1 head of leaf lettuce	Separated into leaves, washed and drained
4 hard-cooked *(hard-boiled)* eggs	Peeled and quartered
1¼ cups *(½ pint)* of Thick, Creamy Peanut Dressing (page 224)	
1 *(¾)* tablespoon of Fried Onion Flakes (page 156)	

METHOD
1. Fill a saucepan with enough water so that when a strainer is suspended over it the contents will be immersed. Bring the water to a rolling boil over high heat.

2. In the strainer, blanch the potato for 8 minutes. Drain well over the saucepan, then place on a paper plate. Bring the water back to a full boil and blanch the green beans for 5 minutes. (If the quantity of any of the vegetables is too large to be completely immersed in water, blanch in 2 batches.) Blanch the carrots for 5 minutes. Let all the vegetables cool to room temperature.

3. Line a large platter with a fan of lettuce leaves. Arrange the vegetables decoratively in groups or in circles, adding the hard-cooked *(boiled)* egg quarters. Pour the dressing carefully over the entire arrangement. Sprinkle the fried onion flakes over the top and serve.

ADVANCE PREPARATION AND STORAGE NOTES

The vegetables may be blanched in advance and refrigerated, covered, for several hours. The entire presentation may also be covered and refrigerated but in that case do not garnish with the fried onion flakes until you are ready to serve; otherwise they will lose their crispness.

Malaysian Variation (STRAITS CHINESE)

Substitute spinach (briefly blanched) and cabbage (also blanched) for the carrots and potato. Add bean-curd cubes, pressed to remove the water and then deep-fried until crisp and golden. Dress with the Malaysian version of the thick, creamy peanut dressing.

Thai Variation

Substitute spinach for the carrots, add zucchini *(courgette),* cut into slices or julienne strips, and 1 cup *(6 ounces)* of canned *(tinned)* bamboo shoots, rinsed and drained, then cut into slices or strips. Mix all the vegetables together in a bowl after blanching and dress with 1 recipe of Thick Coconut Salad Dressing (Thai Variation, page 227). Garnish with ¼ teaspoon *(a pinch)* of dried red chilli pepper flakes, 1 *(¾)* tablespoon of toasted sesame seeds and 1 *(¾)* teaspoon of dried, powdered shrimp. (The dried, powdered shrimp are available in the Latin American sections of supermarkets.) Cooked, sliced roast beef may also be added to this variation.

Japanese Variation

Use a combination of blanched and cooled broccoli flowerets and strips of cooked white turnip and ham slices, cut into diamonds. Dress with the Japanese Miso Dressing for Salad II (page 222), arrange decoratively on a platter, then chill.

❷ Mixed Vegetable and Seafood Salad with Thin Dressing (PHILIPPINES)

This salad sets a pattern for many others from various Asian countries. Sometimes the salad will include fish or meat instead of seafood.

Preparation time: 15 minutes   Serves 4 to 6
Cooking time: 5 minutes

SHOPPING AND TECHNIQUE TIPS
The vegetable selection given must act as a suggestion only. Your choice of vegetables will be dictated by what is really fresh and in season in the produce section of your market. In the Philippines, several vegetables are used that are unavailable to us, such as swamp cabbage, horseradish tree leaves, etc. Even the vegetable, referred to by the Chinese as yam beans (also known as yams or mountain yams, sometimes as "long potatoes") are difficult to find outside Latin markets. The last vegetable, grated and served raw, is an excellent digestive. We can substitute cooked sweet potatoes.

INGREDIENTS	PREPARATION
1 cup *(6⅓ ounces)* of small shrimp	Shelled and cleaned
1 sweet potato	Peeled and thinly sliced
6 leaves of Chinese *(celery or Napa)* cabbage, or an equal amount of white cabbage	Washed, drained and cut into strips about 1½ inches wide
8 spinach leaves	Washed, drained and torn into pieces
2 large tomatoes	Sliced into rounds
2 sweet red or green peppers	Cored, seeded and cut into strips
1 recipe of Thin Salad Dressing, Variation II (Philippines) (page 229)	

METHOD
1. Fill a steamer with water and set it to boil over high heat. When it boils, place the shrimp inside, lower the heat and steam for 3 minutes. Set shrimp aside to cool.

2. Arrange the sweet potato slices in a layer on the steamer tray and let them steam for 8 minutes, or until they are cooked but still firm. Remove and set aside to cool.

3. Arrange the cabbage to form a layer on a platter. Set the spinach in

the center, forming a shallow mound. Surround it with tomato slices. Cut the sweet potato slices into julienne strips and alternate groups of these with the sweet pepper strips in a ring outside the tomato slices. Arrange the shrimp over the spinach mound. Pour the dressing over the entire salad and chill, covered, for at least 5 minutes.

ADVANCE PREPARATION AND STORAGE NOTES

The ingredients can be prepared ahead of time and refrigerated. Alternatively, the entire salad can be made ahead, covered with plastic and chilled. The Filipinos sometimes dress this salad with French dressing, showing the European influence.

Chinese Variation

Use Chinese cabbage as a base, but include pressed, deep-fried bean-curd cubes, sliced cucumber, bean sprouts, sliced green *(spring)* onions and finely shredded carrot together with the shrimp, instead of the vegetables in the preceding recipe. Arrange them decoratively on a platter and dress with Basic Chinese Salad Dressing (page 217).

Indonesian and Thai Variations

The same as the Chinese, but toss the vegetables in a bowl together with the Thai Thin Salad Dressing (page 228). Serve on lettuce leaves, instead of cabbage, and sprinkle chopped peanuts and dried red pepper flakes over the top. If serving it as a Thai salad, include about 16 chopped coriander (Chinese parsley, *cilantro*) leaves in the salad and garnish with coriander sprigs.

Vietnamese Variation

Use the above variation, including mint and/or basil leaves in the salad and the garnish, and omitting the peanuts and red pepper flakes. Dress with the Thin Salad Dressing, Vietnamese Variation (also known as *Nuoc Cham* sauce) (page 229).

❧ Indian Yogurt Salad

As stated before, these small, yogurt-dressed salads are used as side dishes to cool and clear the palate in between the highly spiced hot Indian dishes. There are many varieties and combinations; here is a basic recipe, together with variations.

Preparation time: 5 minutes   Serves 4 as a side dish

SHOPPING AND TECHNIQUE TIPS
This salad may also be made with plain, rather than spiced, yogurt. If it is dressed in that style, then ½ (⅓) teaspoon of salt should be added.

INGREDIENTS	PREPARATION
12 or more pistachio nuts or blanched almonds	Hulled
1 large, crisp apple	Peeled, cored and quartered
1 recipe of Indian Spiced Yogurt Dressing II (page 230)	
Sprig of mint leaves for garnish	

METHOD
1. In a food processor, grind the nuts to a coarse powder. Add the apple and give the processor a few turns until the contents are reduced to a rough puree. Do not grind too fine.

2. Transfer the contents of the processor to a mixing bowl and stir in the yogurt dressing. Mix thoroughly, then transfer to a serving bowl or to individual bowls. Chill until ready to serve, then garnish with mint.

ADVANCE PREPARATION AND
STORAGE NOTES
All forms of this salad are suitable for advance preparation. Do not refrigerate for more than a few hours.

Banana and Coconut Variation

Instead of the apple and nuts, use 2 firm, ripe bananas, thinly sliced, 10 mint leaves, chopped, and ½ cup *(1¼ ounces)* of dried, unsweetened flaked coconut. (In a pinch the sweetened coconut could be used; in that case, balance the sweetness with ½ *(⅓)* teaspoon of salt.)

Onion, Mint and Chilli Pepper Variation

Substitute a large onion, peeled and cut into slivers, 2 small, fresh green chilli peppers, seeded and cut into slivers, and 10 mint leaves, chopped, for the fruit. Dress with the basic Indian Spiced Yogurt Dressing (page 229).

⊗ Indian Potato Salad with Yogurt Dressing

When you are tired of the usual potato salads, you may like to make up this Indian version—it is delicious.

Preparation time: 10 minutes

Cooking time: 25 or more minutes, depending on the size of the potatoes
Serves 4 to 6

SHOPPING AND TECHNIQUE TIPS
Look for the firmest and freshest potatoes you can find. The new season's potatoes will do fine. Scrub the potatoes and cook them in their skins. This retains more vitamins and flavor, both of which are concentrated close to the surface. Skin them when they are just cool enough to handle.

INGREDIENTS	PREPARATION
1 pound of potatoes	Scrubbed clean
½ (⅓) teaspoon of salt	
2 (1⅔) tablespoons of Indian Clarified Butter (page 139), or vegetable oil	
½-inch of fresh ginger root	Peeled and minced
2 green Serrano chilli peppers	Seeded and minced
2 (1⅔) teaspoons of ground cumin	
½ (⅓) teaspoon of salt	
¼ teaspoon (a pinch) of Indian Sweet Spice Mix (page 118)	
2 cups (16 fluid ounces) of plain yogurt	
½ cup (4 fluid ounces) of sour cream	
2 (1⅔) tablespoons of onion	Finely minced
8 to 10 coriander leaves (cilantro, Chinese parsley)	Chopped

METHOD

1. Fill a medium saucepan with cold water. Add ½ (⅓) teaspoon of salt and the potatoes and bring to a rapid boil. Immediately reduce the heat to low and simmer for 20 minutes or more, depending on the size and variety of potato. They should be tender, but still waxy and firm. Drain off the water and shake the pot until any excess moisture evaporates. Turn potatoes out onto a plate until they are just cool enough to handle; then, using the point of a knife, strip off the skins and cut the potatoes into small dice. Let them cool at room temperature.

2. In a wok or large, heavy skillet, heat the clarified butter or oil over medium heat and fry the ginger and chilli peppers, stirring, for 1 minute. Add the potatoes and stir them for about 30 seconds. Sprinkle with the cumin, salt and Indian Sweet Spice Mix. Toss the potatoes for about a minute, until they are covered with the spice mixture, then turn off the heat.

3. Pour the yogurt and sour cream into a mixing bowl and beat well with a wooden spoon. Add the potato mixture from the wok and stir until everything is well blended.

4. Now stir in the onion and coriander leaves and turn the potatoes over and over until they are well distributed. Transfer to a serving dish and chill until ready to serve.

ADVANCE PREPARATION AND
STORAGE NOTES

This potato salad can be made well ahead, covered and refrigerated. I think it is even better when it has been made the day before and the flavors have had enough time to blend together.

FULL STEAM AHEAD

❧ ❧ ❧

Steaming Techniques—
a Bonus in Nutrition

T his easy, almost magical, technique, is one of the finest, simplest and fastest ways to cook food. It preserves almost all the vitamins, minerals and flavor, adds no extra fat, and cooks almost everything in less than an hour.

A whole meal can be cooked in one multi-tiered container and over one source of heat, which conserves energy, and because the food is surrounded by steam, the cooking utensils can be cleaned without scrubbing or scouring.

Cooking with convection steam is rapidly gaining favor with diet- and health-conscious Westerners who are experimenting with a cooking technique that has been known and practiced for centuries by the peoples of Asia and the South Pacific.

The Chinese have steam-cooked since the dawn of their civilization, originally using steam baskets constructed from bamboo. Nowadays, layered metal tray steamers are widely used.

The islanders of Polynesia, Micronesia and Melanesia, from Hawaii to

Tahiti and Guam to Fiji, dig earth ovens or pits in which meat, fish and vegetables wrapped in ti, taro or palm leaves are placed between layers of hot stones to steam in the moisture from the leaves. In the same way, any package of food that you wrap in foil and place in your oven is actually steam-cooked, not baked.

In India, curries and other dishes are often steamed at the last stage of their preparation. Large pots with flat lids, called *dekshis,* are placed on a charcoal stove and more hot coals are heaped on their lids, steaming the contents. The Indian name for this type of steam cooking is called *dum.* It proceeds very slowly because the heat is gentle, and the coals on the lid prevent almost any condensation from forming so that the contents are not diluted by any further moisture.

Variations aside, there are two basic methods of steaming: wet and dry. Asians usually cook by the former method, which is also known as convection steaming. Wet steaming allows the steam to surround and come in contact with the food. This steam occurs at temperatures above 212°F. *(100°C.)* and, under pressure, such as in pressure cookers, temperatures of up to 400°F. *(205°C.)* can be reached.

Dry (conductive) or indirect steaming utilizes a double boiler, in which food in the upper receptacle is sealed off from, and merely receives the heat from the steam created below it. This is a more gentle heat, about 212°F. You use this steaming technique when you make custard in a double boiler on your range top.

Steamed foods are most attractive in appearance and taste; the colors remain vivid, the textures firm, and the flavor locked in the food.

Chinese (wet) steaming is done either by using a rack or a bowl to hold the food container above the water. Either utensil must be placed in a covered pot containing the boiling water. "Rack" steaming means that some sort of perforated tray is set about 2 to 3 inches above the water and a shallow heatproof dish containing the food is placed on the tray or rack. The "bowl" method consists of setting a bowl on the bottom of the pot, surrounded two-thirds of the way up with water. With the heat, this results in part convection, part conduction.

The Japanese and Southeast Asians also use the multi-tiered steamers mentioned earlier. These are made either of bamboo or aluminum. The bamboo racks sit in the wok, into which is poured enough water for at least half an hour's steaming. Bamboo steamers are best suited for foods such as *dim sum,* the dough-wrapped delicacies eaten as snacks in China. The bamboo absorbs some of the condensation so that the dumpling buns remain fluffy and not soggy. The bamboo racks have a finite life as they tend to mildew and come apart after a while. They do look decorative on kitchen walls, however. The aluminum multi-tiered steamers, which I prefer, conduct the heat better, do not retain the odors from steaming food, and last longer. (For details and buying tips, as well as care and maintenance, read the chapter "Kitchen Equipment" beginning on page 6.)

The main advantage of multi-tiered steamers is that you can cook a different food on each steamer tray; the uppermost tier and high-domed lid will accommodate a whole 3-pound chicken.

If the foods you are steaming (wet) are wrapped with dough or leaves, you may place them directly on the rack. Meat, vegetables, fish and poultry should be placed on plates or in casseroles when steaming, otherwise their juices will drain into the water below. (This may also be turned to your advantage, however, because if steaming a combination of, say, chicken and vegetables on the tiers, the juices draining into the water below will flavor it and make a stock suitable for a marvelous soup base.)

Sticky foods, such as some cakes and puddings, fish cakes and crabmeat patties, may be set on muslin, cheesecloth or wax-paper squares in the steamer. If wax paper is used, care must be taken that sufficient holes in the steamer tray are left uncovered so that the steam can circulate. If a large piece of paper is used and too many holes are blocked, make perforations in the paper.

The best kind of food containers for steaming are made from either metal or heatproof glass. Ovenproof pottery and ceramics may also be used. Whichever large container you use, make sure there is at least 1 inch of clearance between the perimeter of the food container and the interior wall of the steamer tray to allow the steam to rise and circulate.

If you do not already own a steamer and do not intend to buy one immediately, with a little imagination you may fashion a "steamer" from a variety of implements that probably already live in your kitchen. For instance, a canning ring or metal ashtray or shallow can with both ends removed may be used as a trivet inside a large pot with a well-fitting lid. You merely set a plate or dish with its contents to be steamed upon the homemade trivet, fill the pot with water to an inch or less under the bottom of the dish and place the lid on the whole arrangement. A dish towel placed under the lid and across the top of the pot will absorb the condensation on the lid and prevent the moisture from dripping on the food. An electric frying pan or skillet makes an excellent substitute for a steamer with the same improvisations of a trivet. Open the steam vents to help prevent condensation.

Even if you do not own a bamboo rack, your wok may still be used for steaming. Some woks can be bought with accompanying steam racks—either circular, perforated metal trays or two pieces of wood, notched and crossed in an X, upon which a dish can be set.

A pressure cooker, of course, is the ultimate quick steamer because, at 15 pounds of pressure (p.s.i.) it racks up 252°F. *(120°C.)* steam heat and, using the accompanying trivet, a whole chicken or duck will cook in ¼ the time a standard steamer would require. A word of caution, however: it is very easy to overcook foods in a pressure cooker so, for safety, I recommend that you reserve it for foods that would normally take a long time to steam tender. Leafy vegetables, fish and small delicacies such as dough buns are better left to a regular steamer.

SOME TIPS ON STEAMING

Aluminum multi-tiered steamers cook faster than bamboo because of their better conductivity. Foods in the lower trays, closer to the water, are subject to greater steam pressure and cook faster. Faster still are foods set in a dish on a trivet directly above the water, as in a covered wok or saucepan. To give an example: crab, which normally takes 20 minutes of cooking time on the bottom tray of an aluminum steamer, will take 25 minutes on the top tray, 25 on the bottom tray of a bamboo steamer and 28 minutes on the top bamboo tray. If that same crab were placed on a trivet in a wok or saucepan, it would take only 15 minutes to cook.

Keep these variables in mind and check by pressing or probing the item of food for doneness. When you look inside to check or test while steaming is progressing, remember that lifting the lid loses steam and you should then add about another minute to the cooking time for every time you open the lid.

The water in a steamer should be brought to a full, rolling boil before the food is placed inside, and the cooking time will commence from the moment that the lid is closed. After the initial rolling boil, the heat may be reduced, but should still be enough to ensure that a steady bubbling is maintained.

Here is a general guide to wet-steaming times for some foods that you will commonly prepare. The times are based on placing these on the bottom tray of an aluminum steamer, as are the times given in the recipes that follow; I use this for all my steaming because of its utility and ease of cooking. The timing given for vegetables is valid only if they are diced, sliced or chopped, generally into 1-inch or chopstick or bite-sized pieces.

A final tip and word of warning about steam cooking: steam burns are painful. I suggest you protect your hands and wrists with oven gloves whenever you are handling a hot steamer. If you must take the lid off to peek inside or to remove a tray, tip the steamer away from you and keep your face averted from the steam until it has subsided. Food should always be loaded or removed from trays away from the heat; when removing a tray from the steamer, set it on a heatproof surface, do whatever you need to do, and then replace the tray on the steamer, remembering to replace the lid in the meanwhile so that

Steaming Time	Food
50 minutes to 1 hour	whole (2½ to 3-pound) chicken or small duckling
40 minutes	half a pound of squash, yams, potatoes, sweet potatoes, etc.
30 minutes	large chicken pieces, whole corn on the cob, okra, eggplant (aubergines)
20 minutes	crab, oysters, white fish (pieces), bananas, mushrooms
15 minutes	mustard greens, Chinese cabbage, collards, kale
10 minutes	large shrimp or prawns, broccoli, carrots
5 minutes	cauliflower flowerets, bok choy (Swiss chard), snow peas (mange-tout), zucchini (courgette), small shrimp, leftover rice and general re-heating*

*Steaming is by far the best technique to use for reheating leftovers. Leftover rice, which may become hard and dry when refrigerated, becomes fluffy and moist again. Other already-cooked dishes that dry out when refrigerated perk up again and do not need the addition of more water or other liquid. If they were originally served in ovenproof dishes, they may also be steamed in the same containers—an additional benefit.

a minimum of steam is lost during the procedure. If you should burn your hand, immediately plunge it into ice water and keep it immersed until the pain subsides. Or place ice cubes, wrapped in cloth, in contact with the burn. If the burn is severe, call your doctor immediately. Generally speaking, you stand in far more danger of burns from frying than from handling a steamer. Care and common sense when cooking will go far to prevent accidents.

Full steam ahead!

❀ Korean Stuffed Steamed Squid with Dipping Sauce

Squid is plentiful in the markets nowadays but few people try it, put off either by its appearance or by the fact that they have eaten it somewhere and found it rubbery and tough. Again, many people do not know how to clean and prepare squid, so they pass it up.

When properly cooked, squid is beautifully tender. Like a prime steak it becomes tough and rubbery only when it is overcooked. When it toughens, only long cooking will bring it round to tenderness again, and when that stage is reached, the squid will have a slightly pastelike, almost velvety consistency.

In the Basic Techniques section you will find a step-by-step guide to cleaning and preparing squid, together with illustrations (page 79). This Korean recipe, like the Thai one following, shows how delicious this sea creature can be when it is stuffed with meat and then briefly steamed.

Preparation time: 25 minutes
Cooking time: 25 minutes (including the filling)
Serves 6 with rice, or 8 with one other dish

SHOPPING AND TECHNIQUE TIPS

Buy the small squid, if possible. The smaller they are, the more tender they will be and the less time they will take to cook. Only small squid should be stuffed. The larger ones are more suitable for stir-frying, in which the body is first cut into small pieces. The stuffing can be varied, but any ingredients that take longer to cook than the squid should be precooked, either by blanching or frying or both.

INGREDIENTS	PREPARATION
12 small squid (2 inches to 4 inches in body length)	Cleaned and prepared (page 79)
2 dried Chinese mushrooms,	Soaked in hot water for 10 minutes
or 2 fresh mushrooms	Wiped clean
2 outer leaves of cabbage	Washed and finely chopped
½ cup *(1½ ounces)* of bean sprouts	Washed, heads and roots removed
½ cup *(¼ pound)* of lean ground *(minced)* beef	
4 green *(spring)* onions	Washed, trimmed, roots removed, finely chopped
2 cloves of garlic	Peeled and finely chopped
1 *(¾)* tablespoon of sesame seeds	Ground in the mortar
1 *(¾)* tablespoon of soy sauce	
½ *(⅓)* teaspoon of salt	
1 *(¾)* tablespoon of Sesame Oil (page 139)	
½ *(⅓)* teaspoon of granulated sugar	
¼ teaspoon *(a pinch)* of ground white pepper	
1 *(¾)* tablespoon of vegetable oil	

METHOD

1. Wash the squid in water and pull away any remaining skin. Cut the tentacles off where they join the head and chop them finely. The bodies of the squid will now look like little pointed pockets with side flaps.

2. Remove the dried mushrooms from the water and squeeze them dry. Remove the stems and discard. Cut the caps into thin slivers. (If using fresh mushrooms, separate the caps from the stems. Cut off the discolored bases of

the stems and discard; slice the caps and stems.) Place in a mixing bowl.

3. Fill a saucepan with water and bring to a rolling boil over high heat. Place the cabbage in a sieve and immerse it in the boiling water for 3 minutes. Remove, drain and place in a mixing bowl. Fill the sieve with bean sprouts and blanch them for 1 minute. Drain and add to the mixing bowl.

4. Place all the remaining ingredients, except the vegetable oil, in the bowl and mix thoroughly.

5. Place a frying pan over medium-high heat, pour in the oil and heat it. Add the contents of the mixing bowl and fry, stirring, until the beef almost loses its pink color (about 2 minutes).

6. Set aside to cool.

7. Fill a steamer with water and remove the tray. Cover it and bring the water to a boil.

8. Fill the squid with the stuffing, using a spoon to fill and tamp it down. Do not overfill. Secure the top flaps together with toothpicks. As each squid is filled, place it on a heatproof plate.

9. Place the plate on the steamer tray and replace it in the steamer. Steam for 5 minutes. Immediately remove the tray to prevent any further cooking.

10. Let the squid cool slightly, then cut into thick slices. Remove the toothpicks and serve with Korean Dipping Sauce (page 478).

ADVANCE PREPARATION AND
STORAGE NOTES

Steps 1 through 8 can be done in advance, and the squid steamed just before serving. Do not cook squid ahead and reheat or the squid will toughen.

❦ Thai Stuffed Baby Squid in Soup

The technique for cleaning, preparing, stuffing and steaming the squid is the same as in the preceding Korean dish, although the Thai traditionally serve theirs as part of a delicious soup. Because of the aesthetic appearance, baby squid are used; the larger ones would be too clumsy. The Thai also like to float the tentacles separately in a ring. When they are cooked, they curl up and look like little curly-petaled daisies. The stuffing is the same one that is used for many Thai fillings. The mixture of garlic, black pepper and coriander provides that unique Thai flavor.

Preparation time: 30 minutes   Serves 6 to 8
Cooking time: 12 minutes

SHOPPING AND TECHNIQUE TIPS

This dish demands the smallest possible squid. If you must use slightly larger ones, cut them carefully into slices, after steaming and cooling, using a very sharp knife. Instead of serving the soup from a serving bowl, place several slices of squid in each soup bowl and pour the soup over. In this way, the stuffing will not fall out.

INGREDIENTS	PREPARATION
8 to 10 baby squid (2 inches to 3 inches in body length)	Cleaned and prepared (page 79)
3 cloves of garlic	Smashed, peeled and minced
½ (⅓) teaspoon of ground black pepper	
1 (¾) teaspoon of coriander roots or stems	Washed, dried and minced
½ cup (¼ pound) of ground (minced) pork	
½ (⅓) teaspoon of salt	
6 cups (48 fluid ounces) of Basic Chicken Stock (page 168)	
2 cups (16 fluid ounces) of bottled clam juice (if the squid is steamed directly on the tray, 2 cups (16 fluid ounces) of the steaming liquid may be substituted)	
4 dried Chinese mushrooms,	Soaked in hot water for 10 minutes
or 4 fresh mushrooms	Wiped clean
2 (1⅔) tablespoons of vegetable oil	
8 more cloves of garlic	Peeled and thinly sliced
½ (⅓) teaspoon of freshly ground black pepper	
12 to 16 coriander leaves	Separated from the stems

METHOD

1. Wash the squid as in the previous recipe. Cut off the tentacles ¼ inch behind the point where they are attached to the head, so that they remain in a ring. The bodies of the squid will now form little pockets.

2. In a mortar, pound together the garlic, black pepper and coriander roots into a paste. Add the pork and mix everything together well. Stuff this mixture loosely into the squid, securing the open ends with toothpicks. Place on a plate.

3. Fill a steamer with water and remove the tray. Cover the steamer and bring the water to a boil.

4. While the steamer is coming to a boil, pour the vegetable oil into a small frying pan over medium-high heat and fry the garlic until it is golden brown and crisp (do not overfry). Remove with a slotted spatula and drain on paper towels.

5. When the steamer is up to a boil, place the plate containing the squid on the steamer tray and replace it in the steamer. Steam for 5 minutes.

6. While squid is steaming, pour the chicken stock and clam juice into a large saucepan and bring to a boil. Add the mushrooms and squid tentacles and cook for 3 minutes.

7. Watch the timing on both the steamer and the saucepan so nothing overcooks. Remove the tray containing the baby squid. Unfasten the toothpicks and discard them. Add the squid to the saucepan and immediately remove the soup from the heat. Transfer the soup to a serving bowl and sprinkle with the fried garlic flakes, black pepper and coriander leaves. Serve at once.

ADVANCE PREPARATION AND STORAGE NOTES

The soup stock and mushrooms may be prepared ahead. The squid may be stuffed in advance. Do not add the tentacles to the soup or steam the squid until just before serving, or they will be overcooked. Do not plan to cook the squid ahead and reheat; if you do, it will toughen.

Vietnamese Variation of Stuffed Squid

Prepare the baby squid as for the preceding Thai recipe, but substitute 1 finely chopped green *(spring)* onion for the coriander roots and add it after pounding the garlic and pepper, together with the pork.

Steam the squid but, instead of putting into soup, serve them as an appetizer on a bed of lettuce and mint leaves. Serve with Southeast Asian fish sauce.

If you prefer the squid with a more golden look, steam for 3 minutes only, then stir-fry in 2 *(1⅔)* tablespoons of vegetable oil until the outsides are pale gold.

❦ Korean Beef and Egg Savory Custards

In Korea this dish is eaten as part of a main meal or for breakfast. It would make a delicious light lunch dish, accompanied perhaps by a small salad.

Preparation time: 20 minutes   Serves 4
Cooking time: 30 to 35 minutes

SHOPPING AND TECHNIQUE TIPS
Dried shrimp are to be found in the Latin American sections of supermarkets. If you cannot locate them, or if you do not like their rather pronounced flavor, you may substitute ready-cooked frozen baby shrimp. Remember, when dealing with a steamer, always to load and unload the trays off the heat. When removing trays from the steamer, recover the steamer, keeping it on the boil.

INGREDIENTS

½ cup *(¼ pound)* of lean ground *(minced)* beef

2 green *(spring)* onions — Minced

1½ *(1¼)* teaspoons of sesame seeds — Toasted until light brown, then ground to a powder

1 *(¾)* teaspoon of soy sauce

1 *(¾)* teaspoon of Sesame Oil (page 139)

¼ teaspoon *(a pinch)* of freshly ground black pepper

6 eggs

6 tablespoons *(3 fluid ounces)* of water

¼ teaspoon *(a pinch)* of salt

2 *(1⅔)* tablespoons of dried shrimp, — Soaked in hot water for 10 minutes, drained

or 2 *(1⅔)* tablespoons of cooked baby shrimp — Squeezed dry in paper towels

¼ teaspoon *(a pinch)* of ground red pepper (Cayenne)

METHOD

1. Place the beef in a mixing bowl. Add half the minced green *(spring)* onions (reserving the remainder for garnish), ground sesame seeds, soy sauce, sesame oil and black pepper. Mix and knead well to blend the ingredients.

2. Roll into meatballs the size of small marbles and set aside.

3. Set aside a steamer tray. Fill a steamer, cover it and start to bring it to a boil.

4. Beat the eggs, water and salt until the eggs are well blended. Stir in the shrimp and mix well.

5. Place 4 ovenproof bowls on the steamer tray and divide the meatballs among them. Pour the egg mixture over them and replace the tray on the steamer. Place a tea towel over the tray, replace the lid and wrap the ends of the towel up and over the lid. (This will absorb the condensation and prevent moisture from falling into the custards. Steam the custards for 5 minutes.

6. Uncover and scatter the remainder of the green *(spring)* onion and a dusting of red pepper over the surface of each. Re-cover and steam for 20 minutes more, or until the custards are set and firm. Remove and serve immediately.

ADVANCE PREPARATION AND STORAGE NOTES

The ingredients may be prepared in advance and refrigerated; the meatballs may also be made ahead and chilled. Bring them back to room temperature before continuing with the dish. If the custards are made slightly before serving time they may be left in the steamer with the heat turned off for about 10 minutes—they will stay warm and moist in the residual heat.

Thai Variation

Substitute an equal amount of ground *(minced)* pork for the beef and stir it into the egg mixture. Leave out the sesame seeds and oil, but replace them with 1 teaspoon of Thai Curry Spice Paste (page 124), blended well into the egg mixture. Substitute Southeast Asian fish sauce for the soy sauce. Pour the whole mixture into a greased ovenproof dish and steam for 30 minutes, or until the custard is set and firm.

Chinese Variation

Omit the meat entirely. Beat the eggs together with the water, 1 *(¾)* teaspoon of pale, dry sherry, 1 *(¾)* tablespoon of soy sauce, the shrimp and all the green *(spring)* onions. Cook as for the Thai Variation above.

❧ Philippine Whole, Boned, Stuffed Chicken

A whole, boned chicken is a culinary *tour de force,* and will make your reputation as a cook. It takes a while to prepare, but everything can be done ahead. It is a most impressive dish to take center stage at a dinner party or a buffet. It may be served hot or cold.

Preparation time: 1½ to 2 hours   Serves 8 (or 12 as part of a buffet)
Cooking time: 2½ hours

SHOPPING AND TECHNIQUE TIPS

Shop for a roasting chicken of approximately 5 pounds. If it is larger, you will need a little more stuffing. The boning technique is explained step by step in the Basic Techniques section (page 72). You may vary the ground *(minced)* meats in the stuffing as long as you keep to the total amount. Equal quantities of ground *(minced)* pork and ground *(minced)* lean beef will work very well, or you may wish to substitute ground *(minced)* chicken and veal. If you cannot locate the Portuguese *chorizo de Bilbao,* use the Mexican *chorizos.* The Italian sausage will work in a pinch, although the flavor of the stuffing will not be so authentic. Try to find the Mexican hard, crumbly curd cheese. The Greek *feta* cheese is also suitable.

The Filipinos cook this chicken in a variety of ways. In the cities, where more people possess ovens, it is roasted. If you wish to treat it this way, roast it at 350°F. *(gas mark 4)* for about 1½ hours, basting it with melted butter about every 15 minutes. Let it stand for 10 minutes to make carving easier. Remember to remove both thread and trussing string before serving. A note of caution: The chicken skin becomes extremely fragile during the steaming and will split open unless you encase the bird in cheesecloth. I find that dipping the cheesecloth in vegetable oil before wrapping the bird eases the task of pulling it off without tearing the skin.

INGREDIENTS   PREPARATION
1 roasting chicken (about 5 pounds)   Boned (page 72)

Marinade
5 tablespoons *(2½ fluid ounces)* of
    soy sauce
The juice of 1 lemon
1 *(¾)* tablespoon of granulated sugar

INGREDIENTS   PREPARATION

Stuffing

1½ pounds of ground *(minced)* pork
1 medium onion   Peeled and minced
The meat from 2 *chorizo* sausages
4 ounces of hard curd cheese   Crumbled into large
                                  breadcrumb-sized pieces

¼ cup *(1 ½ ounces)* of dark raisins
2 sweet cucumber pickles   Drained and minced
1 large tomato   Finely chopped
3 eggs   Beaten
1 *(¾)* teaspoon of ground black
   pepper
6 ounces of sliced ham   Cut into long, thin strips
2 hard-cooked eggs   Peeled

Frying

6 tablespoons *(3 ounces)* of butter
6 tablespoons *(3 fluid ounces)* of
   vegetable oil

Gravy

2 *(1 ⅔)* tablespoons of the oil from
   above
3 cloves of garlic   Peeled, mashed
The liver of the chicken   Mashed
1 *(¾)* tablespoon of all-purpose flour
1½ cups *(12 fluid ounces)* of the
   chicken liquid from the steamer
1 *(¾)* tablespoon of soy sauce
¼ teaspoon *(a pinch)* of ground
   black pepper

METHOD

1. Bone the chicken according to the instructions on page 72, placing the discarded wing tips, bones and carcass in the bottom of a steamer, together with the necessary water for steaming.

2. In a medium mixing bowl, stir the soy sauce, lemon juice and sugar together until the sugar has dissolved. Place the boned chicken into this and turn it several times until it is thoroughly coated with the marinade. Let it sit at room temperature while you prepare the stuffing. (You may break off at this point and let the skin and flesh marinate for up to 3 hours, or overnight if refrigerated.)

3. Place all the stuffing ingredients, except the ham and hard-cooked eggs, in a large mixing bowl and combine thoroughly. (Your hands are more suitable for this than a spoon.)

4. Drain the chicken from the marinade and set it in front of you. Pour the remaining marinade into the steamer water. If the bird has a split from the tail opening, take needle and thread and sew this together before working on the closing. Run the needle in a basting stitch through the flesh and skin all around the tail opening. Hold both ends of the thread in your hands and draw it together like a drawstring. Knot to fasten. Now take a length of thread and wind it around both of the leg ends, about 1 inch up from the end of the skin. Draw it tight and knot it, leaving a lump of frill. (You will need leg frills later.) Do not tie the legs to each other.

5. Place the chicken breast side up with the neck opening toward you. Start to insert a 1-inch layer of stuffing into the bird, pushing stuffing into the leg cavities with your fingertips. (Do not stuff them too full, or they will burst in the cooking.) Push a little into the wing shapes, but not too much, as the ends are open.

6. Now place the hard-cooked eggs end to end on the bed of stuffing so that they bulge in the center where the breast ridge would be. Carefully lay a small bundle of ham strips lengthwise on either side and cover the eggs with more ham strips, end to end so that they form a long core along the length of the bird. Pack in more stuffing over and around the central core, taking care not to disturb it. Gradually fill the bird. (You may find you will not need to use all the stuffing if the bird looks full to bursting—you do not want it to split under pressure when cooking.)

STUFFING THE WHOLE CHICKEN

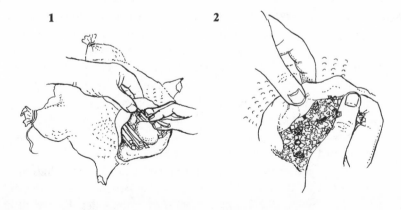

1   2

SHAPING THE CHICKEN

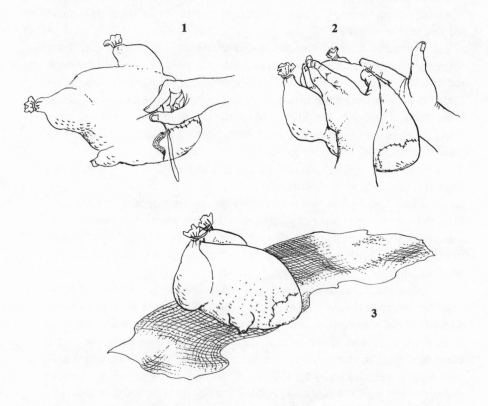

7. Ease the stuffing back into the bird, away from the aperture so that you have a flap of skin and flesh to sew up. Take the needle and doubled thread and again employ a drawstring technique to sew up the neck opening. Now shape the bird with your hands, remembering that you need a division between the legs and body. Don't worry if it looks rather like a shapeless sausage. When the legs are tied and the bird is wound and trussed, it will take more form.

8. Take a short length of trussing string and wind it round one of the leg frills. Attach it to the other leg frill and draw them together across the chicken. Knot securely. Lay the chicken across the length of the cheesecloth and wind the cheesecloth firmly around the bird. Take a long length of trussing string and fasten it around one end of the bird. Wind it around and around the bird and then several times along the length as well. Secure it firmly. (You may refrigerate the bird at this stage for up to 12 hours.)

9. Bring the liquid in the steamer up to a boil and place the chicken in the top section so that the domed lid will accommodate its bulk. Cover and steam for 1½ to 2 hours. If steaming for less than 2 hours, let the bird sit in

the steamer, covered and off the heat, until it is cool. Remove the bird from the steamer and dry it. (You can speed this process by using a hair dryer!) Cut away the trussing string and carefully unwind the bird from the cheesecloth. Pat it dry thoroughly with paper towels. You may freeze the chicken at this point.

10. In a large wok, heat the butter and oil until a haze forms on top. Using 2 spatulas, carefully fry the bird, browning it on all sides, 10 minutes a side. (Or, you may place the bird on a rack over a roasting pan and brown it in a 350°F. *(gas mark 4)* oven, basting it with a little melted butter. Roast for 15 minutes a side, ending breast up.)

11. Remove the bird to a heated platter and keep it warm in a low oven while you make the gravy. (At this point, you may break off and refrigerate or freeze the bird—see Advance Preparation.) Pour off all but 2 *(1⅔)* tablespoons of oil from the wok. Remove the bones from the steamer and discard them. Place the liver in a small bowl and mash it. Reserve the giblets if you wish. Measure out 1½ cups *(12 fluid ounces)* of the stock and place it close to the stove. Keep the rest of the stock for soup.

12. Heat the oil in the wok and fry the garlic until light gold. Stir in the mashed liver, mixing it in with the back of the spatula until the mixture becomes smooth and oily. Stir in the flour and continue to cook, stirring, until you have a smooth paste. Now add the stock, little by little, stirring until the gravy thickens and there are no lumps. Season with the soy sauce and pepper and pour it into a gravy boat.

PRESENTATION

You may serve the whole bird, bringing it to the table and then cutting it, passing the gravy around to the guests, or you may slice it, hot or cold, and pour the gravy over or pass it separately. If you are serving it cold, like a terrine, you may wish to omit the gravy.

ADVANCE PREPARATION AND STORAGE NOTES

As you have seen, there are many pausing points in the recipe. If you refrigerate the chicken before steaming, allow an extra 15 minutes of steaming time to compensate for the temperature of the bird. If you freeze the steamed bird, defrost it in the refrigerator overnight, then leave it for 1 hour at room temperature before frying or roasting. (Remove the cheesecloth before wrapping the bird for freezing.) If you freeze the chicken after frying or roasting, bring it back to room temperature, then cover with foil and place it in a low (250°F. to 300°F.) *(gas mark ½ to 2)* oven for 1 to 1½ hours, then continue the recipe.

ℰ Whole, Steamed Fish with Spiced Ginger Sauce
(CHINA)

Fish is served complete with the head in China. This is to show that the fish is fresh, and also to honor a guest (who may even be offered the fish eye as a great delicacy!). While you do not have to go that far in search of authenticity, this is a way to feature a brace of fresh trout, or, indeed, any catch of the fisherman or fisherwoman in your family. For those of you without access to a fresh catch, carefully check your fish market or the fresh fish section of your supermarket. Living in Los Angeles, as I used to, I often drove down to the fish shops at Redondo Beach by the pier, or visited Chinatown to see what fresh whole fish are available. A small (2½-to-3-pound) red snapper is superb, but you do need a large steamer. Of course a perforated fish poacher would be perfect, but you can improvise with a perforated trivet and your wok.

Preparation time: 45 minutes
Cooking time: Depends on the size of
   the fish (see the table below).

Serves 4 to 6 (allow ½ pound of fish
   per person)

SHOPPING AND TECHNIQUE TIPS

Select a fish, whatever the variety, with bright eyes—there should be no dull film over them. Inspect the gill flaps. They should be a nice bright red. There should be no fishy odor and the scales should be shiny. Poke at the side of the fish with your finger. The flesh should be firm and bounce back, leaving no imprint. If you are buying the fish, have the counterman clean it and scale it for you, but remember to tell him to leave the head on or he will probably cut it off. When you get the fish home, rinse it thoroughly in cold running water and then pat it dry, inside and out, with paper towels. Rub it with salt (you may like to use rock or sea salt) inside and out and leave it in a cool place. If you are going to keep it until the next day, wrap it in foil or plastic wrap, sealing it completely, and place it in the coldest part of your refrigerator. When handling a large, whole fish, remember that, after cooking, it will break easily. I find that laying the fish on a cradle of cheesecloth in the steamer tray works very well when I have to move it afterward. I merely pick up the ends and move it in its sling. Lift up a portion of the fish at a time with a spatula to slide the cheesecloth out from under, after you have placed it on the serving platter.

Below are the steaming times for fish. Remember, if you leave the fish in the steamer to keep warm, it will continue to cook, even if you have turned off the heat, so take this into account.

1½-pound fish	20 minutes	3-pound fish	30–35 minutes
2-pound fish	25 minutes	Thick fish fillets	15 minutes
2⅓-pound fish	25 minutes	Flat fish or thinly sliced fish	5 to 10 minutes

INGREDIENTS	PREPARATION
Fish:	
2 *(1⅔)* tablespoons of soy sauce	
1 *(¾)* tablespoon of pale, dry sherry	
1-inch piece of fresh ginger root	Peeled and minced
1 green *(spring)* onion	Minced
1 whole 2-to-2½-pound fish, or 2 smaller fish	Cleaned and scaled and rubbed with salt, inside and out
Rock or sea salt for rubbing	
3 *(2⅓)* tablespoons of peanut oil (optional)	
Sauce:	
1 *(¾)* tablespoon of peanut oil	
2 green *(spring)* onions	Minced
2-inch piece of fresh ginger root	Peeled and minced
½ cup *(4 fluid ounces)* of the fish stock from the bottom of the steamer	
¼ cup *(2 fluid ounces)* of white vinegar	
2 *(1⅔)* tablespoons of granulated sugar	
1 *(¾)* tablespoon of cornstarch *(cornflour)*	
1 *(¾)* tablespoon of soy sauce	
1 *(¾)* tablespoon of pale, dry sherry	
2 green *(spring)* onions, cut into brushes, for garnish	
8 to 10 fresh coriander (Chinese parsley, *cilantro*) leaves, for garnish	

METHOD

1. Heat the water in a steamer. Place a length of cheesecloth across the tray with the ends hanging over the sides. Place the fish in the tray and lay the ends back inside, on either side of the fish.

2. Mix together the soy sauce, sherry, ginger and onion and, placing the tray on the steamer, pour the mixture carefully over the fish. Place the lid on top and steam the fish, timing it according to its weight (see table on page 263).

3. Pour the peanut oil into a small frying pan, if you are going to use it. (The heated oil will be poured over the steamed fish, giving it a shiny and slightly fried appearance. It is not a necessary step, but I find it adds to the appearance and flavor.) Place it on the stove or close to it, but do not heat it yet.

4. While the fish is cooking, start to prepare the sauce. Place all the sauce ingredients near the stove and prepare the garnishes.

5. Lift the fish from the steamer, using the cheesecloth cradle, and place it on a warmed platter. Remove the cheesecloth. If you are using it, heat the 3 *(2 ⅓)* tablespoons of peanut oil in the frying pan over high heat until a haze forms over the top, then immediately pour it over the entire fish. Place the fish in a warm oven while you are preparing the sauce.

6. In a wok or saucepan, heat the tablespoon of oil over medium-high heat and fry the onions and ginger, stirring, for 1 minute. Pour in ½ cup *(8 fluid ounces)* of the stock from the bottom of the steamer and add the vinegar and sugar. Stir and bring to a boil.

7. Combine the cornstarch *(cornflour)*, soy sauce and sherry in a small bowl, stirring until the cornstarch *(cornflour)* is thoroughly mixed. Reduce the heat under the wok and stir in the cornstarch *(cornflour)* mixture. Continue to stir until the sauce thickens, then remove it from the heat and pour it over the fish.

8. Garnish with the green *(spring)* onion brushes or tassels and sprinkle with coriander leaves.

ADVANCE PREPARATION AND
STORAGE NOTES

The preparation of all the ingredients can be done in advance except for the fish; that should be steamed, sauced and garnished just before serving.

Korean Version (WHOLE STEAMED FISH

WITH VEGETABLE SAUCE)

Ginger is omitted in this Korean version, but vinegar is used, both on the fish before steaming and in the sauce, which has vegetables in it.

The peanut oil step is omitted. The fish is topped with the sauce given below:

INGREDIENTS

Sauce

1½ cups *(12 fluid ounces)* of the fish
    stock from steaming
1 *(¾)* tablespoon of white vinegar
2 *(1⅔)* tablespoons of soy sauce
4 *(3¼)* tablespoons of granulated
    sugar
2 Oriental dried mushrooms

1 small carrot

¼ cup *(1½ ounces)* of canned
    (tinned) bamboo shoots
2 green *(spring)* onions
2 *(1⅔)* tablespoons of cornstarch
    (cornflour), stirred into 2 *(1⅔)*
    tablespoons of cold water

PREPARATION

Soaked in hot water for 10 minutes
    until pliable. Stems discarded, caps
    sliced thinly
Peeled, thinly sliced lengthwise into
    strips, each strip cut into small
    diamond shapes
Drained, rinsed and cut into thin
    slices
Thinly sliced into rounds

METHOD

1. Pour the fish stock, vinegar, soy sauce and sugar into a saucepan and stir over medium-high heat until the sugar has dissolved.

2. Add the carrot, bring to a boil, and cook for 5 minutes, stirring, until the carrot pieces are tender. Add the bamboo shoots and green *(spring)* onion and cook for another 2 minutes.

3. Pour in the cornstarch *(cornflour)* mixture and lower the heat to medium-low. Stir until the sauce thickens. Pour over the fish. The brightly colored vegetables act as a garnish.

Vietnamese Version (WHOLE STEAMED FISH

WITH FENNEL SAUCE)

This version is much like the Chinese, except that 1 *(¾)* teaspoon of granulated sugar, ¼ teaspoon *(a pinch)* of freshly ground black pepper and 1½ *(1¼)* tablespoons of Southeast Asian fish sauce are sprinkled over the fish before steaming. You may also lightly slash the sides of the fish 3 or 4 times to let the seasoning permeate further. The fish is served with the following sauce poured over it.

INGREDIENTS

Sauce

2 *(1⅔)* tablespoons of vegetable oil

3 green *(spring)* onions

3 cloves of garlic

1 *(¾)* teaspoon of fennel seeds

¼ teaspoon *(a pinch)* of ground red
　pepper (Cayenne)

½ cup *(4 fluid ounces)* of the fish
　stock from the steamer

Juice of 1 lime

2 *(1⅔)* teaspoons of Southeast Asian
　fish sauce

2 *(1⅔)* teaspoons of granulated
　sugar

Sprigs of mint leaves

PREPARATION

Chopped

Peeled and finely chopped

Crushed

METHOD

1. Heat the vegetable oil in a wok or saucepan over medium heat. Fry the onions and garlic, stirring, for 1 minute, until the onions are soft and the garlic is light brown. Add the fennel and red pepper and stir until the fennel seeds release their aroma.

2. Now increase the heat to high and pour in the fish stock. Stir for 1 more minute, then add the lime juice, fish sauce and sugar. Stir until the sugar has dissolved. Remove the sauce from the heat and pour over the fish. Garnish with the mint sprigs and serve.

Malaysian Version (WHOLE, STEAMED FISH

WITH CHILLI SAUCE)

The Malay version is also very like the Chinese and the sauce is thickened with cornstarch *(cornflour)*. However, merely sprinkle 2 tablespoons of Southeast Asian fish sauce over the fish before steaming. You may add the peanut oil to the fish, if you wish, before saucing. The sauce is made in the same way, with the following variations: In step 6 of the Chinese recipe (page 264) (the first step in the sauce), cut the vinegar down to 1 *(¾)* tablespoon. In step 7, add ½ *(⅓)* teaspoon of ground red pepper (Cayenne) and 1 minced Serrano chilli pepper before adding the cornstarch *(cornflour)* mixture. Garnish in the same way.

Philippine Version (WHOLE, STEAMED FISH

WITH TOMATO AND GREEN PEPPER SAUCE)

Omit the Chinese toppings and sprinkle the fish with salt and pepper (1 (⅔) teaspoon) before steaming. Sauce it with the following:

INGREDIENTS	PREPARATION
Sauce	
3 *(2⅓)* tablespoons of vegetable oil	
1 medium onion	Peeled and finely chopped
2 cloves of garlic	Peeled and thinly sliced
1-inch piece of fresh ginger root	Peeled and thinly sliced
1 Serrano chilli pepper	Seeded and cut into thin strips
1½ cups *(12 fluid ounces)* of the fish stock from the steamer	
2 *(1⅔)* tablespoons of white vinegar	
1 *(¾)* tablespoon of soy sauce	
1 cup *(6⅓ ounces)* of canned *(tinned)* whole tomatoes	Drained and chopped
½ a sweet green pepper	Seeds and membranes removed, finely chopped
1 *(¾)* teaspoon of granulated sugar	
½ *(⅓)* teaspoon of freshly ground black pepper	
2 green *(spring)* onions	Finely chopped

METHOD

1. Heat the oil in a wok or saucepan over high heat. Fry the onion, garlic, ginger and chilli pepper, stirring until onions are limp and light gold.

2. Pour in the fish stock, vinegar, soy sauce and tomatoes and stir in the green pepper. Bring to a boil, reduce the heat to medium-low and simmer, stirring occasionally, for 5 minutes. Season with the sugar and black pepper. Stir and pour over the fish.

3. Sprinkle with the chopped green *(spring)* onion and serve.

ADVANCE PREPARATION AND
STORAGE NOTES

The same instructions for the Chinese recipe apply to all the other recipes. NOTE: You may try all these versions substituting firm, white fish fillets—or even shark or snapper—for the whole fish.

❧ Chinese Steamed Lemon Chicken

This method of cooking chicken is simple and delicious, preserving both the moisture and the flavor.

Preparation time: 50 minutes   Serves 6
Cooking time: 30 minutes

SHOPPING AND TECHNIQUE TIPS
The chicken benefits in flavor from the marination time, although you may shorten the time if you are in a hurry. You can substitute fresh mushrooms for the Chinese mushrooms if the latter are unavailable. Sliced green *(spring)* onions would make an interesting substitute or variation.

INGREDIENTS	PREPARATION
3 whole chicken breasts	Skinned, boned and cut into 1-inch pieces
4 dried Chinese mushrooms	Soaked in hot water for 10 minutes, stems removed, caps cut into thin strips
1 *(¾)* tablespoon of soy sauce	
1 *(¾)* tablespoon of Oyster Sauce (page 146)	
1 *(¾)* teaspoon of salt	
1 *(¾)* tablespoon of salad oil	
1-inch piece of fresh ginger root	Peeled and cut into shreds
1 lemon	Cut into thin rounds
1 *(¾)* tablespoon of cornstarch *(cornflour)*	
½ cup *(4 fluid ounces)* (approximately) of the steaming liquid	
2 *(1⅔)* tablespoons of lemon juice	
1 *(¾)* tablespoon of granulated sugar	
¼ teaspoon *(a pinch)* of salt	

METHOD
1. Place the chicken pieces and mushrooms in a casserole and pour the soy and oyster sauces over. Allow the chicken to marinate for 30 minutes.

2. Meanwhile, fill the base of a steamer with water and let it come to a boil.

3. Sprinkle the chicken with salt and pour the salad oil over the surface.

Scatter the ginger shreds over the chicken and arrange the lemon slices on top. Place the casserole in the top tray of the steamer, close the lid firmly and let the dish steam for 20 minutes.

4. Place the cornstarch *(cornflour)* in a measuring jug. Remove the casserole from the steamer and set it to one side. Use a bulb baster to draw off any accumulated liquid from the casserole and stir it into the cornstarch *(cornflour)*. Add enough of the liquid from the bottom of the steamer to make ½ cup *(4 fluid ounces)*.

5. Pour the cornstarch *(cornflour)* liquid into a small saucepan and stir in the lemon juice, sugar and salt. Heat it over a medium setting, stirring constantly until the sugar is dissolved and the sauce thickens.

6. Pour the sauce over the chicken and serve.

ADVANCE PREPARATION AND
STORAGE NOTES
The chicken can be marinated and steamed in advance. Rewarm in the steamer for 4 to 5 minutes, and make the sauce just before serving.

Southeast Asian Variation (STEAMED CHICKEN

WITH TOMATOES)

INGREDIENTS	PREPARATION
3 whole chicken breasts	Skinned, boned and cut into 1-inch pieces
3 medium tomatoes	Cut into wedges
3 green *(spring)* onions	Thinly sliced into rounds
1-inch piece of fresh ginger root	Peeled and cut into shreds
2 *(1 ⅔)* tablespoons of Southeast Asian fish sauce	
½ *(⅓)* teaspoon of salt	
1 *(¾)* teaspoon of granulated sugar	
½ *(⅓)* teaspoon of ground black pepper	
8 to 10 coriander (Chinese parsley, *cilantro*) leaves	Chopped

METHOD
Place the chicken, tomatoes and green *(spring)* onions in a casserole and sprinkle with the ginger. Mix and pour the fish sauce and seasonings over the top. Omit the marinating process in the preceding recipe. Steam for 20 minutes. Sprinkle with the coriander leaves just before serving.

❧ Indonesian Beef Packets

In Indonesia these flavorful mouthfuls are wrapped in banana leaves and secured with a splinter of bamboo. Fresh corn husks will make a good substitute for banana leaves, or you may like to use cabbage leaves, blanched to make them pliable. (In the latter case, the wrapping can also be eaten.) Of course there is always kitchen foil, but leaves are far more authentic. Secure the packets with sharp toothpicks.

Preparation time: 30 minutes   Serves 4
Cooking time: 30 minutes

SHOPPING AND TECHNIQUE TIPS

Choose medium-lean ground *(minced)* beef for this dish—you do not want too much fat. One large corn husk or one fairly large cabbage leaf will wrap each packet adequately. Using a V incision, remove the tough, wide portion of the cabbage leaf rib before wrapping. If you use foil, cut it into 7-inch squares. Serve 3 to 4 packets to each diner.

INGREDIENTS	PREPARATION
1 pound of ground *(minced)* beef	
1 small onion	Peeled and minced
3 cloves of garlic	Crushed, peeled and minced
4 macadamia nuts	Pounded or crushed finely
2 *(1⅔)* teaspoons of ground coriander	
1 *(¾)* teaspoon of ground cumin	
½ *(⅓)* teaspoon (or less, to taste) of ground red pepper (Cayenne)	
2 *(1⅔)* teaspoons of salt	
The outer peel (zest) of ½ lemon	Grated
½ inch of fresh ginger root	Peeled and grated
1 *(¾)* tablespoon of molasses *(treacle)*, dissolved in 2 *(1⅔)* tablespoons of lime juice	
3 *(2⅓)* tablespoons of vegetable oil	
1 cup *(8 fluid ounces)* of thick Coconut Milk (page 114), or 1 cup *(8 fluid ounces)* of milk, flavored with ½ *(⅓)* teaspoon of coconut extract	

INGREDIENTS	PREPARATION
3 eggs	Hard-cooked *(boiled)*, peeled and sliced. Discard the portions without yolk
16 large corn husks or medium cabbage leaves	If using cabbage leaves, blanch them first to make them pliable, then cut out the lower part of the rib.

METHOD

1. Place the beef, onion and garlic in a mixing bowl. Add the nuts and all the seasonings, up to and including the molasses *(treacle)* and lime juice, and stir until the mixture is well blended.

2. Heat the oil in a wok or frying pan over medium-high heat and fry the mixture, stirring for 5 minutes, or until the spices have mellowed and the meat and onions are well cooked. Pour in the coconut milk and continue to cook, stirring from time to time, until the liquid has evaporated. Set aside to cool.

3. Fill the base of a steamer with water and bring it to a boil.

4. Place a slice of hard-cooked *(boiled)* egg in the center of each husk or leaf. Cover it with a generous tablespoon of the meat mixture, then wrap the husk or leaf around the mixture as if wrapping a package. Secure the last flap firmly with a toothpick. Continue until all the wrappers are used up and you have prepared 16 packets.

5. Place the packets on the steamer trays and steam for 30 minutes.

6. Remove the toothpicks and serve with rice, a Southeast Asian sauce of your choice, and a vegetable side dish.

ADVANCE PREPARATION AND STORAGE NOTES

These packets can be prepared ahead of time and refrigerated, then steamed before serving. They may also be steamed in advance, cooled, and then reheated in the steamer for 4 to 5 minutes before serving.

Variations

Minced shrimp or fish may be used instead of the beef. Minced chicken or veal could also be substituted. These packets may also be served as part of a Malaysian meal. By substituting 1 to 2 *(¾ to 1⅔)* tablespoons of the Thai Curry Spice Paste (page 124) for the seasonings, the packets become a Thai dish or snack.

STIRRINGLY
FRIED

🐦 🐦 🐦

*High-Speed Cooking
with the Universal Wok*

Stir-frying, sometimes called flash-frying or agitate-frying, is the fastest and most fuel-economizing way of cooking. It is an ancient cooking technique which probably evolved in the sparsely forested regions of southern China, where charcoal was at a premium, and has been practiced steadily and refined ever since.

Its economic and time-saving qualities have made stir-frying so popular that the technique has spread throughout Asia. These same attributes have made it a natural choice in restaurant cooking.

The prevalence of stir-fry cooking in restaurants also has a historical background. The southern Chinese, particularly those from the Canton area, tended to emigrate in great numbers to escape from overcrowding, famines, crop failures, droughts, floods and other adversities, and, on reaching other parts of Asia and the West, many of them opened restaurants, perpetuating the cooking technique so prevalent in their homeland.

Traditionally, the stir-fry method of cooking was executed over earthenware "fire pots," funnel-shaped charcoal stoves with a circular opening in the top above the coals. Similar stoves are widely used throughout Southeast Asia and India. Because of the shape of the stove, a cooking vessel evolved shaped like a wide-mouthed, shallow cone, with a curved base that sat snugly inside the opening of the stove. In China, this is called a *ts'ai kuo*—and we know it as a wok. Generally made of iron, which retains a steady, intense heat, the wok usually has two looped handles, although some have a single long handle like a frying pan. It also has a tight-fitting, raised or domed lid, which fits inside the flared rim of the wok. On the other side of Asia, the Indians also cook with a similar, bowl-shaped utensil with two handles, called a *karhi;* however, after the initial fast frying, the Indians tend to braise or simmer their dishes.

Stir-frying is the technique of sautéing small pieces of meats, fish and vegetables in a little oil over a fierce heat while stirring and tossing the ingredients continuously to cook them evenly on all sides. The average stir-fry dish takes between 3 to 5 minutes of cooking time.

Gas is the best heat source for stir-frying as it produces an intense heat that can be varied instantly. If electricity is used, the ring should be turned to the hottest setting and the wok lifted from the source of heat when a lower temperature is needed.

If you do not own a wok, a heavy iron skillet with curved, flared sides or an electric frying pan makes a good substitute; the former is particularly suited to cooking over an electric ring as the flat, heavy base comes into total contact with the source of heat.

A wok is much more fun, however, and once the technique of using it is learned, it is the perfect cooking utensil. If I were stranded on a desert island and could have only one piece of cooking equipment with me, I would choose my wok above everything else in my kitchen.

See page 7 in the chapter "Kitchen Equipment" for complete descriptions of the varieties of woks, the materials from which they are made, what to look for in buying one and how to season it and take care of it. It is a sneaky utensil —once you become accustomed to using it, you will find that it gradually supplants the other pots and pans in the kitchen. Beside producing a perfect stir-fry, it adapts easily to deep-frying, steaming, braising and simmering. I have even made preserves in mine.

Returning to the first use of the wok—stir-frying. Once the simple steps for the technique are followed, you will be able to produce a multitude of dishes with ease and speed.

1. Pre-prepare.

Before you begin to stir-fry, assemble all your ingredients. Each meat or vegetable should be precut, preseasoned, precooked or premarinated according to the dictates of the recipe. Because the cooking takes such a short period of time, ingredients which usually demand longer cooking, such as meat or root vegetables, are either marinated to tenderize them or precooked (blanched), and are cut into small, thin pieces or strips so that the maximum surface is exposed to the heat, to reduce the cooking time. Root vegetables such as carrots are put into the wok before vegetables that require a mere kiss of heat, such as bean sprouts. A good habit, and one you can apply to all your cooking, is to premeasure all ingredients, including the spices and liquid seasonings, and set them out close to the stove in the order in which they will be added to the wok. In this way the cooking can progress quickly and without interruption. Having laid out all the ingredients in marching order, we can now start the steps of the stir-fry.

2. Heat the dry, clean wok.

This ensures that the oil will quickly reach cooking temperature and that the ingredients will cook with exposure to the sides of the wok as well as the bottom. The curved base ensures that the heat convects evenly up the sides.

3. Add the oil.

One to 3 tablespoons of oil—usually vegetable (polyunsaturated is fine) or peanut oil—is sufficient—another instance of economy in using a wok. The oil is introduced by pouring or dribbling it around the sides of the wok, ensuring that it is warm before it reaches the bottom and that the sides are coated. During a stir-fry, if more oil is needed, it should be introduced in the same way. Or push the food away from the bottom and up the sides of the wok, leaving a hole in the middle; pour the oil into this and let it heat before moving the food back. Both these techniques ensure that the food will not become saturated with cold oil.

4. Hold the wok.

You cannot execute a stir-fry unless you are in complete control of the movement of the wok. Firmly clasp the handle with one hand, leaving the other free to wield a spatula to stir, scrape or toss the ingredients. Now you will be able to tilt the wok to scrape or to maneuver the solids or sauce, or lift it from the heat source if the cooking is proceeding too quickly. (Use a pot holder, oven glove or hot pad if the wok has a metal handle.)

5. Add the flavoring agents to the oil.

These are usually onion, ginger and garlic, or combinations of the three. When stir-fried in the oil, they will flavor it so that subsequent ingredients will take on the essence. When the flavoring agents are lightly cooked to a golden color, they may either be removed and discarded (as in the case of garlic, if a more subtle flavor is desired), or left in to fry with the remainder of the ingredients.

6. Introduce the meat.

The meat must be well dried and may even be dusted with cornstarch *(cornflour)*. This is particularly necessary if the meat was previously frozen. Meat is normally stir-fried by itself in very hot, almost smoking oil. This ensures that the surfaces are seared and that the juices do not leach out. Never put more than 1 cup of meat at a time into the wok. If you have a larger quantity, stir-fry it in 2 batches. After the meat is introduced, toss it and stir continually with an under-and-over motion of the spatula. This ensures that the meat cooks evenly and that any moisture evaporates.

Beef is cooked when it turns light brown. Pork, chicken and fish are cooked when they lose their translucency and turn opaque white. Shrimp, lobster and crab will turn pink or red if cooked in their shells, and the flesh will become white. When the meat is cooked, it may either be removed and set aside, to be reintroduced later, or left in the wok to be combined with the vegetables.

7. Add any dried, reconstituted ingredients.

Ingredients such as dried mushrooms, dried lily buds or dried ginger that have been reconstituted by soaking in hot water are drained or squeezed dry before going into the wok. They will generally need a longer period of cooking than the vegetables, and will lend their stronger flavors to the subsequent ingredients.

8. Put in the vegetables, a handful at a time.

The vegetables, which have been precut in large or small pieces according to the length of cooking time, are now added, again in cooking sequence: tougher vegetables first; green-leafed and/or fragile vegetables later. They are tossed and turned until thoroughly coated with the cooking oil and lightly cooked through. Stir-fried vegetables should always be tender-crisp. *Never* overcook. Even if they are still undercooked at the end of the cooking period, they will continue to cook in residual heat. Some Chinese cooks add salt at this time as it helps to preserve the fresh color of green vegetables.

9. Add the water, stock or other liquid and dry seasonings.

These are generally added separately, the ingredients in the wok being stirred between each addition so that the individual flavors permeate the mixture. Liquid seasonings and condiments such as soy and fish sauces, or sherry or other wine, should be added sparingly and, like the oil, poured down the sides of the wok to warm first.

10. Add the thickening agent.

Cornstarch *(cornflour)*, moistened to a paste with water, and sometimes with additional seasonings, is added now to thicken the sauce and enable it to coat the solid ingredients. The wok should be stirred steadily to distribute the

STIR-FRYING STEPS

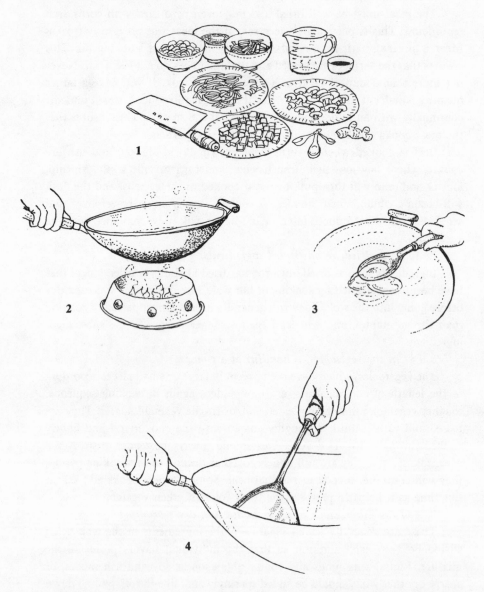

cornstarch *(cornflour)* evenly, and the finished sauce should be small in quantity (do not swamp the ingredients in gravy) and of a smooth, velvety texture. Although Chinese restaurants invariably use cornstarch *(cornflour)*, many Chinese home cooks do not; neither do the Southeast Asians, preferring their stir-fried dishes unthickened.

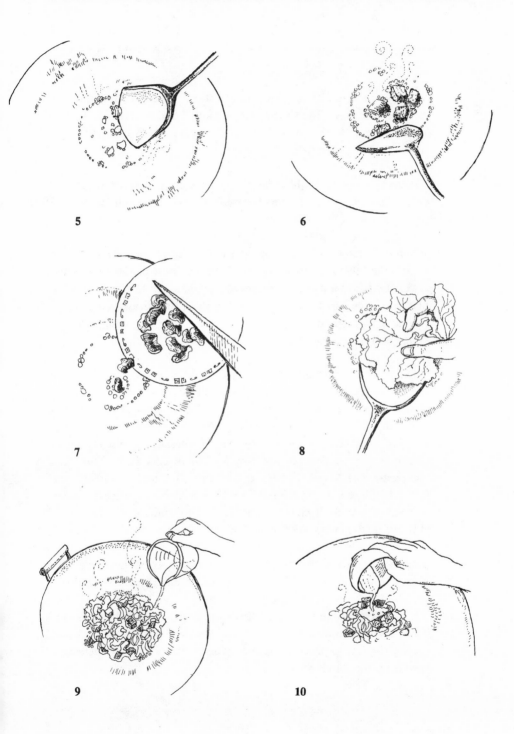

5

6

7

8

9

10

As in every well-tried cooking technique, there are always little tricks of the trade, shortcuts or tips that produce better results and make the cooking process easier. Here are a few ideas:

- When you are blanching vegetables to shorten their stir-fry time, the moment you have lifted them with a slotted spoon from the boiling water, plunge them into cold water. This puts an abrupt stop to any further cooking and keeps the colors bright.

- Similarly, vegetables which have first been soaked in ice water and quickly patted dry or drained before frying will be much crisper and will retain their flavor better.

- When blanching small amounts of 3 or 4 different vegetables, or even meat, place them, one variety after another, in a handled sieve and lower them into a pot of boiling water or stock. In this way, you can blanch a large variety of vegetables in a short time, leaving the pot on the stove throughout the process, and even have the beginnings of a good soup in the pot at the end.

- When soft bean curd is to be fried, it should first be pressed to remove surplus water before cutting into cubes. Place the cakes in a colander over a plate to catch the moisture, and place a small plate on top of the bean curd. Place a small weight, such as a coffee mug, on top of the plate at first (a heavy weight to start off will split the curd) and then gradually add to it or replace it by heavier objects as the bean curd compacts. The longer you leave the bean curd under pressure, the firmer it will become. If soft bean curd is specified in a recipe, it should be fried separately from the other ingredients and without too much stirring, as the cubes are fragile and split easily.

- Firm bean curd can be cut into cubes and deep-fried until crisp and brown several hours in advance of its appearance in a stir-fry.

- Always have all the solid ingredients for a stir-fry as dry as possible. This prevents moisture from splattering the oil, eliminates excess liquid during the frying process (we are frying, not boiling) and generally speeds up the whole stir-fry.

- Vegetables in a stir-fry can be made to glisten attractively by the addition of a sprinkling of vegetable or sesame seed oil at the conclusion of the cooking. (This is an old trick of food photographers.) The sesame oil gives a delicate and subtle, nutty flavor, but do not use it in every dish or there will be a sameness to your food. Incidentally, sesame oil is never used as a cooking medium, merely as a flavoring.

- One last hint: check, check and recheck that you have completed all the advance preparation *before* you start to stir-fry.

❀ Chinese Stir-Fried Squid with Vegetables

This recipe features the very decorative Chinese technique of scoring the rectangles of squid before cooking. The pieces curl with the heat and the scored segments spread out, resembling pine cones. Both the squid and the vegetables are blanched in boiling water before stir-frying. In formal versions of the dish, they can be briefly deep-fried instead of blanched, then drained and used in the stir-fry. However, because this necessitates the one-time use of an extravagant amount of oil, the blanching technique is much more practical.

Preparation time: 30 minutes   Serves 6 people
Cooking time: 20 minutes

SHOPPING AND TECHNIQUE TIPS
Larger squid may be used for this dish. The mantle is thicker and more suited to scoring (which also increases the amount of cooking surface and reduces the cooking time). The tentacles are not used.

INGREDIENTS	PREPARATION
1 pound of squid	Cleaned and prepared (page 79)
½ cup *(1¾ ounces)* of snow peas *(mange-tout)*	Topped and tailed and halved crosswise
1 carrot	Cut into thin slices, lengthwise, then into 1½-inch-long rectangles
3 *(2⅓)* tablespoons of vegetable oil	
1-inch piece of fresh ginger root	Peeled, cut lengthwise into thin slices and then into julienne strips
1 clove of garlic	Peeled, crushed and minced

INGREDIENTS	PREPARATION
2 green *(spring)* onions	Washed, trimmed, roots removed, cut into 1-inch sections
1 sweet green pepper	Seeded, cored and flesh cut into 1-inch diamonds
1 *(¾)* teaspoon of salt	
½ *(⅓)* teaspoon of granulated sugar	
¼ teaspoon *(a pinch)* of ground black pepper	
1 *(¾)* teaspoon of cornstarch *(cornflour)*	Stirred together
1 *(¾)* tablespoon of water	
½ *(⅓)* teaspoon of Sesame Oil (page 139)	

METHOD

1. Remove the tentacles from the squid and use for some other dish or discard. Cut the body of the squid open so it lies flat and wash thoroughly, pulling off any membrane remaining. Cut it lengthwise into 3 strips. With the

SCORING THE SQUID

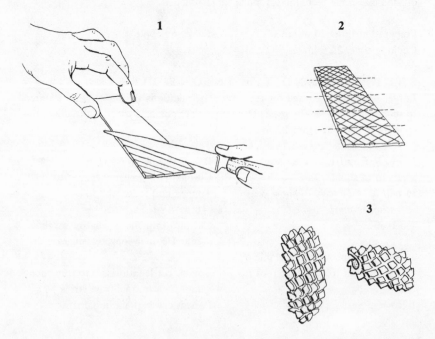

point of sharp knife, score the squid lengthwise and then crosswise, forming a lattice pattern. Take care not to cut all the way through. Cut the meat into rectangles, approximately 1 by 2 inches.

2. Fill a large saucepan with water and bring to a rolling boil over high heat. Place the squid in a strainer and submerge it in the water, blanching it for 30 seconds. Remove and place the meat on a paper plate.

3. Now fill the strainer with the snow peas and submerge them for 1 minute. Place them on a paper plate. Repeat with the carrot rectangles, but blanch these for 3 minutes. Use paper towels to mop the squid and vegetables dry.

4. Place a wok over high heat and pour in the oil. When hot, stir-fry the ginger, garlic and onions until garlic is light gold. Add the green pepper and stir-fry for 2 more minutes. Add the snow peas *(mange-tout)* and carrot and stir-fry for another minute.

5. Add the squid and immediately season with the salt, sugar and pepper. Stir in the cornstarch *(cornflour)* liquid and toss everything until it thickens. Sprinkle with the sesame oil, stir, and remove everything to a serving dish. Serve at once.

ADVANCE PREPARATION AND
STORAGE NOTES

The squid and vegetables can be prepared and blanched in advance, but the dish, like most stir-fry dishes, cannot be cooked until just before serving or it will overcook and the squid will toughen.

❀ Indonesian Stir-Fried Squid

A simple Indonesian recipe from Borneo (Kalimantan), the squid is served without vegetables. It is first marinated for flavor and then stir-fried briefly. In the original recipe, tamarind is used.

Preparation time: 30 minutes   Serves 4 with rice
Cooking time: 5 minutes

SHOPPING AND TECHNIQUE TIPS
The same as Chinese Stir-Fried Squid in the preceding recipe.

INGREDIENTS

1 pound of squid

1 (¾) teaspoon of salt

1 (¾) tablespoon of Tamarind
  Substitute (page 137)

2 (1⅔) tablespoons of peanut oil or
  butter

2 (1⅔) tablespoons of Dark Sweet
  Soy Sauce (page 142)

PREPARATION

Cleaned and prepared (page 79)

METHOD

1. Follow steps 1 and 2 of the preceding Chinese recipe, but place the blanched squid in a mixing bowl.

2. Rub the pieces of squid with the salt and Tamarind Substitute and let them marinate for 20 minutes.

3. Heat the peanut oil in a wok over medium-high heat. Put the squid into the wok and stir-fry for 1 minute. Sprinkle with the Dark Sweet Soy Sauce and stir-fry for another minute. Remove to a serving dish. Serve with plain rice.

ADVANCE PREPARATION AND
STORAGE NOTES

The squid can be blanched and marinated in advance. Stir-fry before serving.

STIR-FRIED CHICKEN

Here is a trio of chicken dishes from Vietnam, Malaysia and the Philippines. Each starts off as a simple stir-fried dish; each has chicken as the main ingredient; and each uses vinegar as a souring agent. However, after the initial stir-frying, the techniques diverge slightly and the end results are 3 completely different dishes, each with a flavor unique to its country.

Characteristically, the Malay dish uses a complex spice paste to marinate the chicken before the frying. The Vietnamese chicken is also marinated, but in a simpler mixture. The Philippine dish relies on the simmering liquid during braising to give it flavor. In each dish the chicken is cut in a slightly different way.

& Vietnamese Stir-Fried Chicken with Vinegar

In this dish, as in other recipes in this book, the grated zest *(peel)* of a lemon is used as a substitute for fresh lemon grass. I do not find that pieces of dried lemon grass which are available in some supermarkets have enough flavor compared to the juicy, fresh stalk, and I prefer to use the lemon.

Preparation time: 25 minutes
Cooking time: 20 minutes

Serves 4 to 6 (with 1 other dish)

SHOPPING AND TECHNIQUE TIPS
You should use both dark and white chicken meat for this recipe. Boned thigh meat, as well as boned chicken breasts, is now available in many meat departments, although it is far cheaper to bone your own.

INGREDIENTS	PREPARATION
2 cups *(1 pound)* of chicken meat	Boned, skinned and cut into bite-sized pieces
2 green *(spring)* onions	Finely chopped
The peel *(zest)* of 1 lemon	Grated
½ *(⅓)* teaspoon of salt	
½ *(⅓)* teaspoon of freshly ground black pepper	
3-inch piece of fresh ginger root	Peeled and grated or minced
4 tablespoons *(2 fluid ounces)* of white vinegar	
2 *(1⅔)* tablespoons of vegetable oil	
5 cloves of garlic	Peeled and chopped
1 small onion	Peeled and finely chopped
½ cup *(4 fluid ounces)* of water	
2 *(1⅔)* tablespoons of Southeast Asian fish sauce	
1 *(¾)* teaspoon of granulated sugar	
15 to 20 mint leaves	Chopped

METHOD
1. Place the chicken meat, green onions, lemon zest, salt and pepper in a medium mixing bowl. Mix well and let marinate for 20 minutes.

2. Place the grated ginger in a small bowl and pour the vinegar over.

3. Heat the oil in a wok over medium-high heat and stir-fry the garlic and

onion until the onion is soft but not golden. Add the chicken mixture from the bowl, turn the heat to high, and fry, stirring and tossing continually, until the chicken turns white and becomes firm (about 5 minutes).

4. Now add the ginger-vinegar mixture and the water and cover. Reduce the heat to medium-low and let the chicken simmer for 5 minutes.

5. Uncover, season with the fish sauce and sugar and stir well. Let it simmer for 5 more minutes, stirring occasionally, then sprinkle with the mint leaves and stir one more time.

6. Transfer to a serving bowl and accompany with plain, boiled rice.

ADVANCE PREPARATION AND STORAGE NOTES

This dish can be made a little ahead of time and transfered to a casserole, covered and left in a low oven. Do not stir in the mint leaves until 5 minutes before serving time if you are keeping it in the oven.

❧ Malaysian Spiced Chicken

Preparation time: 25 minutes   Serves 6
Cooking time: 45 minutes

SHOPPING AND TECHNIQUE TIPS

The traditional way to prepare the spice mix for this dish is to brown the whole spices and then grind them to a powder in a spice grinder, or pound them in a mortar. While the flavor thus produced is more pungent and fresh than using powdered spices, I have found that the powdered spices work quite well, as the heating revitalizes them. Cutting a chicken bone in means chopping through the bone with a heavy cleaver. If you do not feel confident about doing this, or if your cleaver is not heavy enough, you may leave the chicken in joints. If you do this, be sure to increase the cooking time slightly so that the chicken will be properly cooked.

INGREDIENTS

1½ (1¼) teaspoons of ground
     nutmeg
2 (1⅔) teaspoons of ground red
     pepper (Cayenne)
2 (1⅔) teaspoons of ground turmeric
1 (¾) tablespoon of ground cumin
1 (¾) teaspoon of ground cinnamon
2 (1⅔) tablespoons of ground
     coriander

INGREDIENTS

1 *(¾)* teaspoon of ground cloves
1½ *(1¼)* teaspoons of ground
    cardamom
3 pounds of chicken parts

4 tablespoons *(2 fluid ounces)* of
    peanut oil
2 medium onions

5 cloves of garlic

2-inch piece of fresh ginger root
The peel *(zest)* of ½ lemon
1 cup *(8 fluid ounces)* of water
5 tablespoons *(2½ fluid ounces)* of
    white vinegar
3 *(2⅓)* tablespoons of granulated
    sugar
1½ *(1¼)* teaspoons of salt
2 *(1⅔)* tablespoons of roasted
    peanuts

PREPARATION

Skinned and cut through the bone
    into smaller pieces (thigh cut in 2,
    half-breast into 3, etc.)

Peeled, finely chopped, then squeezed
    in paper towels to remove the
    moisture
Crushed with a cleaver, peeled and
    then minced
Peeled and minced
Grated

Coarsely chopped

METHOD

1. Place all the ground spices in a heavy iron frying pan over medium heat and shake the pan, stirring until the spices release their aroma and become slightly toasted. Do not let them burn on the bottom. Remove from the heat and scrape them into a large bowl.

2. Add the chicken to the spices and stir until the pieces are well coated with the spice mix. Leave them to marinate for 20 minutes, or longer if you desire.

3. Heat the oil in a wok over high heat and add the onions, garlic, ginger and lemon zest. Stir-fry until all the moisture has evaporated and the mixture turns a light brown (about 6 minutes, depending on the amount of moisture left in the onions).

4. Add the chicken and scrape in all the spices. Fry, stirring and tossing continually until the chicken is well coated with the mixture in the wok. Continue to stir-fry for 5 minutes, scraping the pan to make sure that the spices do not stick.

5. Pour in the water, stir and let it come to a boil. Reduce the heat to low, cover the wok and let the mixture simmer for 10 minutes.

6. Uncover, increase the heat to medium-high, and stir in the vinegar, sugar and salt. Cook, stirring, until the gravy thickens and reduces by half. Stir in the peanuts.

7. Transfer everything to a serving bowl and accompany with plain rice.

ADVANCE PREPARATION AND
STORAGE NOTES

The chicken may be marinated in spices well ahead of time. Cover the bowl and refrigerate for up to 4 or 5 hours. The dish may also be made ahead and refrigerated, covered, or frozen. If you have frozen it, thaw gradually and then reheat it in a wok or saucepan, adding enough water or chicken stock to reconstitute the gravy to its original consistency.

❧ Philippine Chicken and Pineapple Adobo

In its original version, the chicken is not stir-fried but is simmered directly in the liquid. I find that the stir-frying adds more color and flavor to the chicken, although it is not a technique which is typical in the Philippines.

Preparation time: 10 minutes   Serves 6
Cooking time: 50 minutes

SHOPPING AND TECHNIQUE TIPS

You may use either a wok or a large, heavy saucepan for this dish. I find that the wok works better as the greater width exposes more of the gravy to the air and cuts down on the time necessary to reduce the liquid.

INGREDIENTS	PREPARATION
3 *(2⅓)* tablespoons of butter, or Indian Clarified Butter (page 139)	
A 3-pound chicken	Cut into joints, skinned and patted dry
or 3 pounds of mixed chicken parts	Skinned and patted dry
1 *(¾)* teaspoon of salt	
½ *(⅓)* teaspoon of freshly ground black pepper	
2 cloves of garlic	Peeled and minced
½ cup *(4 fluid ounces)* of white vinegar	

INGREDIENTS
1½ cups *(12 fluid ounces)* of water
1 bay leaf
1 cup *(6 ounces)* of pineapple chunks
    (canned *(tinned)* or fresh)
2 medium tomatoes

PREPARATION

If using canned *(tinned)* pineapple,
    drain off the juice
Peeled and cut into quarters

METHOD

1. Heat the butter in a wok or saucepan over medium-high heat. Add the chicken and the salt, pepper and garlic and fry, stirring and tossing, until the chicken pieces begin to brown slightly. Do not let them become too dark.

2. Pour in the vinegar and water and add the bay leaf. Bring to a boil, cover, reduce the heat to low and let the chicken simmer for 20 minutes.

3. Uncover, stir, then transfer the chicken pieces to a plate, first using a slotted spoon to drain them over the wok.

4. Increase the heat to high and let the liquid boil until it has reduced to half the original quantity.

5. Return the chicken to the wok and stir in the pineapple and tomatoes. Bring to a boil, then reduce the heat, cover and simmer for 10 minutes.

6. Uncover, stir and transfer to a serving bowl.

ADVANCE PREPARATION AND
STORAGE NOTES

This dish can be made ahead and left, covered, in a low oven for up to 1 hour until you are ready to serve. If made in advance, it can also be refrigerated, covered and reheated in the oven to serve. It does not freeze well.

❷ Spicy Szechwan Chicken with Cashew Nuts

This dish, known as *Kung Pao* chicken in restaurants, can be made as spicy as you wish merely by increasing the amount of Hot Pepper Paste. It is a great favorite of most of my students, whose tolerance and appetite for spicy foods has been increased by cooking and eating so much Southeast Asian food. In fact, many of them aver that the only Chinese food they really like now is Szechwan, as they find the other cuisines of China too bland. A pity, but that's the way it goes.

Preparation time: 45 minutes   Serves 4 to 6
Cooking time: 6 to 8 minutes

SHOPPING AND TECHNIQUE TIPS
Buy the raw cashew nuts. Some people prefer to marinate the chicken in a number
of seasonings before frying. I prefer to marinate it in the egg white and cornstarch
alone before frying and to add the seasonings later, as I like the chicken to be
slightly crisp. The cashew nuts do not take long to fry, so watch them carefully.
You may like to substitute raw pinenuts for the cashews as a change. Treat them
the same way.

INGREDIENTS

PREPARATION

3 whole chicken breasts — Skinned, boned and cut crosswise into strips, ½ inch in width, each strip cut again into ½-inch pieces

1 (¾) tablespoon of cornstarch (cornflour)

The white of 1 large egg — Beaten until slightly foamy

3 (2⅓) tablespoons of peanut oil

1 cup (just over 5 ounces) of raw cashew nuts

1-inch piece of fresh ginger root — Peeled and minced

2 green (spring) onions — Chopped

½ to 1 (⅓ to ¾) teaspoon of Indonesian Hot Pepper Paste (page 128)

2 (1⅔) teaspoons of Chinese All-Purpose Sauce (page 145)

1 (¾) tablespoon of pale dry sherry

½ (⅓) teaspoon of salt

1 (¾) teaspoon of Sesame Oil (page 139)

1 (¾) teaspoon of granulated sugar

METHOD
1. Place the chicken pieces and cornstarch (cornflour) in a bag and,
holding the top of the bag shut tightly, shake it well until the pieces are
thoroughly coated. Beat the egg white in a bowl and add the chicken pieces.
Stir. Refrigerate them for 30 minutes.

2. Meanwhile, heat the oil in a wok over medium heat and, when it
develops a slight haze over the top (do not let it smoke), fry the cashew nuts
until they are a light golden brown. Drain them over the wok and set them
aside on a paper plate.

3. When the chicken has finished chilling, reheat the oil, if necessary, over
a medium-high setting, and stir-fry the chicken pieces until they are firm and

light golden. Drain them over the wok with a slotted spoon and set aside on paper plates.

4. In the same oil, fry the ginger and green *(spring)* onions for 1 minute, stirring and tossing constantly. Stir in all the seasonings except the sesame oil and the sugar. Add the chicken pieces to the wok again and stir-fry for 1 minute. Add the sesame oil and sugar and stir in the cashew nuts.

5. Immediately transfer to a platter and serve.

ADVANCE PREPARATION AND STORAGE NOTES

This dish may be taken up to and including Step 3. You may wait an hour and complete it just before serving. In a pinch you may finish making it and keep it warm in a low oven, if it must wait. If you do this, however, you should not refry the cashew nuts, but should stir them into the dish in the oven, or sprinkle them over the top, allowing just enough oven time to let them warm through.

Thai Variation (SPICY STIR-FRIED CHICKEN WITH PEANUTS)

The technique and most of the ingredients are the same as in the preceding recipe. Dried red chilli peppers are substituted for the Hot Pepper Paste, peanuts for cashew nuts, and fish sauce and garlic provide the key flavors, together with coriander leaves (Chinese parsley, *cilantro*).

INGREDIENTS	PREPARATION
3 whole chicken breasts	Skinned, boned and cut crosswise into strips, ½ inch in width, each strip cut again into ½ inch pieces
1 *(¾)* tablespoon of cornstarch *(cornflour)*	
The white of 1 large egg	Beaten until foamy
3 *(2⅓)* tablespoons of peanut oil	
1 cup *(about 5⅓ ounces)* of raw peanuts	Shelled and skinned
5 to 8 dried red chilli peppers	
5 cloves of garlic	Peeled and minced
1-inch piece of fresh ginger root	Peeled and minced
2 green *(spring)* onions	Chopped
About 35 coriander (Chinese parsley, *cilantro*) leaves	Chopped
2 *(1⅔)* tablespoons of Southeast Asian fish sauce	

INGREDIENTS

2 *(1⅔)* teaspoons of granulated
   sugar
1 *(¾)* teaspoon of white vinegar
1 *(¾)* teaspoon of Sesame Oil (page
   139)

METHOD

1. Follow steps 1 and 2 of the preceding Chinese recipe, substituting peanuts for the cashews.

2. Reheat the oil and fry the chilli peppers until they turn dark brown (this is a very quick affair, so do not burn them). Set them aside on paper towels. Now fry the chicken pieces and set them aside also.

3. Continue as in step 4, frying the garlic and ginger, then the green *(spring)* onions and coriander leaves. Reintroduce the chicken, then the chilli peppers. Season with fish sauce, sugar and vinegar. Stir until the sugar is dissolved, then stir in the sesame oil and return the nuts to the wok. Serve immediately.

ADVANCE PREPARATION AND
STORAGE NOTES

As in the preceding recipe.

❧ Japanese Quick Teriyaki Chicken

Teriyaki restaurants are rapidly the most prevalent and popular eating venues in the cities of Japan. The wave of teriyaki preparations is spreading to other countries that have a large Japanese population or entertain Japanese tourists.

On Guam, in the Northern Marianas, a popular holiday area for Japanese tourists and honeymooners, eating out Japanese-style is often a toss-up between noodle houses or teriyaki restaurants. Even the local Chamorro fiestas now often include teriyaki chicken among the indigenous dishes on the buffet tables.

Preparation time: 20 minutes   Serves 4
Cooking time: 8 to 9 minutes

SHOPPING AND TECHNIQUE TIPS

See if you can locate the Japanese *mirin* or *sake* rice wine. If you cannot, then substitute pale, dry sherry. I prefer to use the long, sweet-skinned hothouse or English cucumbers for this recipe as the skin is not bitter.

INGREDIENTS

½ an imported, or hothouse
  cucumber
2 (1⅔) tablespoons of rice vinegar,
  or 1 (¾) tablespoon of white
  vinegar and 1 (¾) tablespoon of
  water
1 (¾) teaspoon of Japanese soy
  sauce
½ (⅓) teaspoon of granulated sugar
4 half chicken breasts

½ cup (4 fluid ounces) of Japanese
  Teriyaki Sauce (page 474)
2 (1⅔) tablespoons of vegetable oil

PREPARATION

Skinned, patted dry, each lightly
  scored in parallel lines along its
  top surface

METHOD

1. Cut the pointed end off the cucumber and discard. Score the skin of the cucumber lengthwise with the tines of a fork so that it is marked with parallel lines. Cut the cucumber in half lengthwise and scoop the seeds out of each portion. Cut the halves crosswise into thin slices. Combine the vinegar, soy sauce and sugar in a nonmetallic bowl and marinate the cucumber slices for about 20 minutes.

2. Pour the teriyaki sauce into another bowl and add the half-breasts of chicken. Move them around gently until they have been coated with the sauce. Marinate them for 10 minutes, then remove them, reserving the sauce, and pat them dry with paper towels.

3. Heat the oil in a wok over medium-high heat, and stir-fry the chicken breasts for about 5 minutes, turning them frequently so that they brown lightly on both sides. Remove them to a plate lined with paper towels and blot them to remove any surplus oil.

4. Pour the oil from the wok and wipe it with paper towels. Replace it on the heat and immediately reintroduce the chicken breasts while the wok is still fairly cool. Pour the reserved marinade over the chicken and cook the breasts for 2 minutes, turning them 2 or 3 times. Remove the wok from the heat.

5. Set out 4 platters, 1 for each diner. Remove the cucumber slices from the marinade and arrange 3 or 4 slices carefully at one side of each plate. Lift the chicken breasts from the sauce, draining them over the wok, and place them on the plates, ½ to each. Serve, accompanied by plain Japanese short-grain rice.

ADVANCE PREPARATION AND
STORAGE NOTES

The chicken and the cucumber may be marinated for up to 1 hour ahead,
but otherwise the dish should be made and served immediately.

Korean Version (STIR-FRIED CHICKEN BREASTS

WITH VEGETABLES)

The technique of marinating and frying the chicken is the same, but in
this Korean version, the marinade is different and vegetables are added to the
chicken while it is cooking. Typically, the dish should be garnished with egg
strips.

INGREDIENTS	PREPARATION
4 half chicken breasts	Skinned, patted dry, then lightly scored in parallel lines along the top surface of each
2 (1⅔) tablespoons of soy sauce	
1 (¾) tablespoon of granulated sugar	
1 green (spring) onion	Minced
½-inch slice of fresh ginger root	Peeled and minced
1 (¾) teaspoon of sesame seeds	Toasted until pale brown in a dry frying pan
1 (¾) tablespoon of Sesame Oil (page 139)	
2 (1⅔) tablespoons of vegetable oil	
3 dried Chinese mushrooms	Soaked in hot water until pliable, stems cut out and discarded, caps cut into strips
1 small, young carrot	Scraped, top and bottom cut off, thinly sliced and then blanched in boiling water for 5 minutes, drained and patted dry
1 sweet green pepper	Cored, seeded and the flesh cut into thin strips
1 recipe of Egg Strip Garnish (page 157)	

METHOD

1. Follow step 2 of the preceding Japanese recipe, substituting the marinade ingredients, down to and including the sesame oil.

2. Follow step 3 for frying the chicken breasts but do not remove the oil

from the wok. Leaving the oil on the heat, stir-fry the mushrooms and carrot for 2 minutes, then add the green pepper and stir-fry for 1 more minute. Add the chicken breasts again to the wok and pour in the reserved marinade.

3. Stir and cook everything together for 1 minute after the marinade has come to a boil. Transfer to a serving dish and garnish with egg strips. Serve at once.

ADVANCE PREPARATION AND
STORAGE NOTES
As for the preceding Japanese recipe. The Egg Strips may also be prepared in advance.

✌ Balinese Coconut Pork
(INDONESIA)

Bali, one of the few areas in Indonesia which is not mainly Muslim, is known for its pork dishes. The spices in this recipe hint at its Hindu origins.

Preparation time: 15 minutes   Serves 6
Cooking time: 45 minutes

SHOPPING AND TECHNIQUE TIPS
Pick the leanest pork loin or butt that you can find (shoulder is too fatty). If the meat is on the bone, allow extra weight for it and, to make sure you have enough, when you ask the butcher to bone it for you, stipulate that you want 2 pounds of meat *after* boning. Although the dish tastes better if you make your own coconut milk from dried, unsweetened coconut, you may use coconut extract to flavor a mixture of whole milk and half-and-half.

INGREDIENTS   PREPARATION
2 *(1⅔)* tablespoons of peanut oil
1 large onion   Peeled and finely chopped, squeezed
                                          in paper towels
6 cloves of garlic   Peeled and minced
3 Serrano chilli peppers, or 2 small   Minced (the seeds may be removed if
   Jalapeño chilli peppers   less heat is wanted)
1 *(¾)* tablespoon of ground
   coriander
1½ *(1¼)* teaspoons of ground
   turmeric

INGREDIENTS

½ (⅓) teaspoon of powdered ginger

1 (¾) teaspoon of salt

2 pounds of lean pork

2 cups (16 fluid ounces) of thick
    coconut milk (first pressing)
    (page 114), or 1 cup (8 fluid
    ounces) of milk and 1 cup (8
    fluid ounces) of half-and-half
    (half cream, half milk), flavored
    with 1 (¾) teaspoon of coconut
    extract

2 bay leaves

PREPARATION

Thinly sliced, then cut into strips, ½
    inch wide by 2 inches long,
    squeezed in paper towels

METHOD

1. In a wok, over high heat, heat the oil and fry the onion and garlic until onion is golden.

2. Add the chilli peppers, spices and salt and continue to fry, stirring and scraping continually to prevent the spices from sticking, for 3 more minutes.

3. Add the pork, a handful at a time, stir-frying and tossing the mixture until the pork is coated with the spices and is cooked through.

4. Pour in the coconut milk and add the bay leaves. Bring to a boil. Reduce the heat to low and simmer, stirring occasionally, until pork is tender (about 25 to 30 minutes).

5. Transfer to a serving bowl and accompany with plain rice.

ADVANCE PREPARATION AND
STORAGE NOTES

This dish may be made the day before and refrigerated, covered. Reheat in a saucepan, adding a little fresh milk, if necessary, to reconstitute the gravy to its previous consistency. It may also be frozen. Again, after thawing, heat in a saucepan and add milk if necessary.

Thai Version (GARLIC PORK)

Serves 4

This dish from Thailand, although following the same technique, is not gravied and no liquid is added other than the fish sauce seasoning. Canned water chestnuts are added for a crunchy texture. Although the amount of garlic used may seem large, it mellows in flavor because it is cooked slowly.

INGREDIENTS

2 *(1⅔)* tablespoons of vegetable oil

8 cloves of garlic

4 whole dried red chilli peppers

1 pound of lean pork (loin or butt)

1 cup *(6 to 7 ounces)* of canned
    water chestnuts

½ *(⅓)* teaspoon of freshly ground
    black pepper

1 *(¾)* teaspoon of granulated sugar

3 *(2⅓)* tablespoons of Southeast
    Asian fish sauce

2 green *(spring)* onions

PREPARATION

Crushed, peeled and chopped

Cut into thin (⅛-inch) slices, then
    into strips, ¼ inch wide by 1½
    inches long, squeezed in paper
    towels

Drained and thinly sliced

Chopped

METHOD

1. As in step 1 of the previous recipe, but the chilli peppers are used instead of the onion, and the spices should be fried over medium-low heat, stirring, until the garlic becomes golden brown and the chillies darken.

2. As in step 3 of the previous recipe. Increase the heat to high before adding the pork. It should be well cooked. Stir-fry for about 5 minutes.

3. The water chestnuts are now added and fried for about 30 seconds. Follow them immediately with the seasonings of pepper, sugar and fish sauce. Stir until the sugar granules have dissolved, then stir in the green *(spring)* onions and fry them for about 30 seconds. Transfer to a dish and serve.

ADVANCE PREPARATION AND
STORAGE NOTES

The ingredients can be cut and prepared ahead, but this is a real stir-fry and should be made just before serving. (If you have an electric wok, you might like to stir-fry it at the table in front of your guests.)

Malay Version (STRAITS CHINESE SEASONED, SHREDDED PORK)

Serves 4

In this Malay variation, which is *Nonya,* or Chinese-Malay, the pork is first mixed with the cornstarch and then with the seasonings before frying.

INGREDIENTS	PREPARATION
1 pound of lean pork (loin or butt)	Cut into thin slices (⅛-inch thick), then into thin shreds, the size of book matches.
1 *(¾)* tablespoon of peanut oil	
2 *(1⅔)* tablespoons of cornstarch *(cornflour)*	
1 *(¾)* tablespoon of soy sauce	
2 *(1⅔)* teaspoons of granulated sugar	
½ *(⅓)* teaspoon of freshly ground black pepper	
2 *(1⅔)* tablespoons of vegetable oil	
1 medium onion	Peeled and sliced into rings
2 cloves of garlic	Peeled and crushed, then minced
1-inch piece of fresh ginger root	Peeled, then cut into paper-thin slices
3 *(2⅓)* tablespoons of water	

METHOD

1. In a paper or plastic bag, toss together the pork and cornstarch *(cornflour)* until the pork is thoroughly coated. Place the pork in a large bowl and stir in the peanut oil, soy sauce, sugar and black pepper. Mix thoroughly.

2. As in step 1 of the Balinese recipe, but include the ginger with the onions and garlic.

3. Now stir in the pork and stir-fry over high heat for 5 minutes, moving the pork continuously, until it is well cooked and golden brown.

4. Add the water, and cook, stirring, for 2 minutes, until a little gravy is formed. Transfer to a serving dish.

ADVANCE PREPARATION AND
STORAGE NOTES

The pork may be mixed with the cornstarch *(cornflour)* ahead of time, but the seasonings should not be introduced until you are ready to fry; otherwise the mixture will coagulate and stick together. The dish may be made in advance and kept in a low oven for a short time. It may also be refrigerated, covered. In that case, warm through in a wok or saucepan, stirring and moistening with a tablespoon of water while you reheat it.

☯ Szechwan Stir-Fried Cabbage with Hot Peppers (CHINA)

This quick and adaptable stir-fry is the kind of last-minute dish that you can put together when you discover that you have an extra guest. The peppers are seeded before frying, so the dish will not be quite as hot.

Preparation time: 10 minutes

Serves 6 to 8 (with 2 other dishes)

Cooking time: 5 minutes

SHOPPING AND TECHNIQUE TIPS

You may use any variety of cabbage for this dish: American, Chinese, Napa celery cabbage, curly leaf cabbage, etc. The stir-fry should be done over the highest heat possible. Do not forget to preheat the wok before adding the oil. Line up all the ingredients before starting.

INGREDIENTS	PREPARATION
6 tablespoons *(3 fluid ounces)* of vegetable oil	
8 dried red chilli peppers	Seeded and cut into quarters
1-inch piece of fresh ginger root	Peeled and minced or shredded
1 medium head of cabbage (any variety)	Washed, drained and chopped into 2-inch pieces
½ *(⅓)* teaspoon of cornstarch *(cornflour)*	
1 *(¾)* tablespoon of soy sauce	
1 *(¾)* teaspoon of pale, dry sherry	
1 *(¾)* teaspoon of granulated sugar	
1 *(¾)* teaspoon of white vinegar	
1 *(¾)* teaspoon of Sesame Oil (page 139)	

METHOD

1. Heat 4 tablespoons *(2 fluid ounces)* of oil in a wok over high heat. Stir in the peppers and fry, stirring, for 1 minute, or until peppers turn a dark red-brown. Immediately empty the oil and peppers into a small bowl and set aside.

2. Pour the last 2 tablespoons *(1 fluid ounce)* of oil into the wok and, still over high heat, fry the ginger for a few seconds. Immediately add the cabbage and stir well. Fry, stirring, for 1 minute, then stir the cornstarch *(cornflour)*, soy sauce and sherry together, and add to the wok.

3. Stir the mixture until the cornstarch *(cornflour)* cooks and begins to glisten and thicken, then season with the sugar and vinegar. Sprinkle with the sesame oil and pour in the red peppers and their oil. Stir again, then transfer to a serving bowl or platter.

ADVANCE PREPARATION AND STORAGE NOTES

This classic stir-fry cannot be made ahead, but you can prepare all the ingredients ahead of time and set them out. The peppers in oil can be fried ahead and set aside, but the other steps must be done just before serving.

Indonesian Version (SPICED CABBAGE WITH COCONUT MILK)

This version is basically the same in technique, but coconut milk is added instead of the other liquids and there is no thickening used.

INGREDIENTS
1 *(¾)* tablespoon of peanut oil
1 medium onion
2 dried red chilli peppers
½ *(⅓)* teaspoon of anchovy paste
1 *(¾)* teaspoon of brown sugar
½ *(⅓)* teaspoon of powdered ginger
1 medium head of cabbage (any
   variety)
½ cup *(2¾ to 3 ounces)* of cooked,
   shelled small shrimp
¼ cup *(2 fluid ounces)* of thick
   Coconut Milk (page 139), or ¼
   cup *(2 fluid ounces)* of
   half-and-half *(half cream, half
   milk),* flavored with 4 drops of
   coconut extract

PREPARATION

Peeled and thinly sliced
Chopped

Washed, drained and chopped into
   2-inch pieces

METHOD
1. Heat the oil and fry the onion until it turns gold. Add the peppers, anchovy paste, brown sugar and ginger and fry, stirring, for 1 minute.
2. As in step 2 of the previous recipe. Fry the cabbage for 1 minute, then add the shrimp and coconut milk. Reduce the heat to medium low, cover the wok and let the mixture simmer, stirring occasionally, until the cabbage is crisp-tender. Then transfer to a serving bowl.

FRIED TO A CRISP

❀ ❀ ❀

Deep-Fried Delicacies

T he technique of immersing foods in hot fat and frying them until their exterior is crisp has long been practiced in Oriental cooking. From the morsels of meat, fish or vegetables coated in feather-light batter that make the traditional Japanese *tempura* to the hundreds of little deep-fried snacks, mostly vegetarian, that are so popular in Indian cuisine, deep-frying is a universal cooking technique throughout Asia.

The deep-frying method is frequently used in combination with other cooking techniques as well. For instance, cubes of bean curd, which have been previously deep-fried until crisp and golden, are often combined with vegetables in stir-fried dishes. The Chinese version of sweet and sour pork requires that the pieces of meat be dipped in a light batter and deep-fried before being reheated in a velvety sweet and sour sauce.

In a different cooking sequence, many dishes require that the ingredients be steamed before being deep-fried. This is the combination of techniques used in the Thai fried crab cakes, or in the whole crispy duck or chicken as prepared in China. When deep-frying a whole bird, the fowl is first steamed to reduce the fat, dried well, and then immersed in hot oil and fried until the outside is crisp.

The Chinese also employ a double-stage technique when deep-fat frying in order to make the finished food crisper. The first time the food is immersed in the hot oil it is fried only until it turns a light gold. It is then removed and drained while the oil is reheated. The food is then again immersed in the oil and fried until it is completely crisp. (Some Chinese chefs even repeat this process a third time, swearing that it brings the food to the ultimate state of crispness.) When this technique is used, at no time is the food overcooked. Each frying is only taken to a certain point, rather like dividing the single process into three equal parts with a rest in between each.

In order to deep-fry successfully, you do not need a battery of special equipment. You will require a large, heavy and stable saucepan, preferably about 4 to 6 quarts in capacity; a long-handled sieve or strainer; a large slotted spoon or perforated ladle; and a deep-frying or candy thermometer. The last piece of equipment is most important and is the key to success.

An electric deep-fat fryer is nice to have as it is generally thermostatically controlled, keeping the oil at the right temperature—which is mandatory for perfect frying. If you own a wok, use it for deep-frying. The wide surface allows more pieces of food to be cooked at one time. A long pair of cooking tongs are also useful for removing individual pieces of food that may be ready before the rest.

There are a few rules which, if faithfully followed, lead to successful results. I have listed these, together with an outline of the technique itself. Although the steps look long, they are not. I have merely broken down each stage and requirement and given the reasons for their employment. When you have read it through once or twice, you will be able to turn out a perfect deep-fry every time.

1. As a general rule, a food absorbs more fat the longer it is fried and the greater the surface exposed to the oil.

2. Use enough oil to allow the food to move around freely. In addition, the larger the amount of oil, the better it will maintain the required temperature.

3. Fill the vessel in which you are frying to half its capacity only. This will allow room for the bubbling up of the oil when food is introduced and will also guard you if the fat begins to spit.

4. Cut all the food to be fried into uniform-sized pieces, when possible.

5. The food to be fried should be at room temperature. If it comes directly

from the refrigerator it will cause the temperature of the oil to drop drastically. Blot or squeeze the food with paper towels to remove excess moisture.

6. When foods are dipped in batter, the coating, plus the high heat of the oil, seals the juices inside. The less rich the batter, the less oil it will absorb. The more shortening or sugar in a batter, the more oil it will attract during the frying.

7. For safety, keep a lid for the pot close by. If the oil should catch fire, clapping the lid on it will cut off the oxygen and extinguish the flames. Salt will also work. *Do not use water:* it will only spread the flames. Safety is also the reason, as I specified earlier, that the vessel used should be stable and heavy, so that it cannot easily be knocked over.

8. Maintenance of a constant, correct temperature while deep-frying is most important. If food is fried at too high a temperature, it will overcook on the outside and be undercooked on the inside. Frying food at too low a temperature makes it greasy because it absorbs the oil. For these reasons, the use of a thermometer is important.

9. Position the thermometer before you begin to heat the oil to prevent the glass from breaking. If you have forgotten to do this and the oil is already heated, run hot water over the thermometer and dry it before putting it into the oil.

10. The correct temperature for most deep-fat frying is 375°F. *(190°C.).* This temperature is for frying at sea level. The higher the altitude, the lower the boiling point of liquids. A useful rule of thumb is: Reduce the frying temperature by 5 to 10 percent for altitudes of 1,000 to 5,000 feet above sea level, and 10 to 15 percent for altitudes over 5,000 feet.

11. If you are temporarily without a thermometer, a 1-inch cube of bread may be used to test the temperature of the oil. Time to see how long it takes to turn golden brown. If it takes 20 seconds, the oil is at 385°F. *(196°C.)* and too hot. If it takes 40 seconds, the oil is at the correct temperature—375°F. *(190°C.).* If it takes 60 seconds to brown, the oil is too cool—about 350°F. *(176°C.).* The age-old Chinese test is to take an unused wooden cooking chopstick and plunge it straight down in the middle of the oil in the wok. If, immediately after immersion, bubbles start to rush up the sides of the chopstick to the surface, then the oil is at correct temperature. This will not work if the chopstick had been previously used as a cooking utensil or for testing, as the wood will already be impregnated with oil. I have frequently used the reverse end of a long wooden barbecue match for this test. The last way to check is visually. When deep-frying oil is reaching the correct temperature, it begins to squirm and move in long, undulating rivulets across the bottom of the pan. At the same time, a slight haze will form above the surface of the oil.

TESTING THE OIL FOR READINESS
WITH CHOPSTICKS

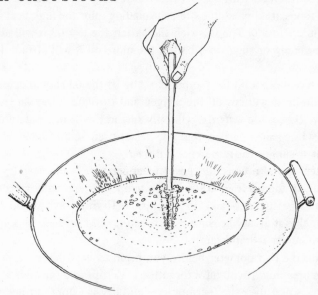

(Be sure that it is a haze, and not smoke, which would indicate that the oil is already too hot.) The visual test is easier to make in a wok than in a deep-fryer.

12. Do not let the oil smoke at any time during the deep-frying process. Smoke means that the oil is beginning to deteriorate and take on an unpleasant odor and flavor. If this does happen, and the oil is badly discolored, turn off the heat, pour the oil carefully into another receptacle to cool before you discard it, refil the pot and start again.

13. When you are ready to fry, first dip the utensils that you will use for transferring the food into the hot oil. This will help to prevent the food from sticking to them.

14. Place a small tray or spoon rest by the side of the fryer to hold the greasy frying utensils between use.

15. Fry a small amount of food at a time. The introduction of too great a quantity causes the temperature of the oil to drop drastically. The oil may also bubble violently and rise to the rim of the frying container.

16. Let the oil come back up to correct temperature between each frying.

17. Skim or strain all leftover particles after each frying. If you leave them in the pan, they will burn and flavor the oil.

18. Drain foods well, on dishes or paper plates lined with paper towels. Crumpling the towels increases the area which will absorb excess grease.

19. If you wish to deep-fry ahead of time, underfry the food and then drain it and keep it warm in a low oven. Refry it briefly to crisp it again before serving.

20. Cooking oil may be reused under certain conditions: if it does not retain too much flavor and odor from dominant foods; if it has not been overheated during the frying process; and if it is strained thoroughly before storing. A certain amount of odor and flavor may be removed by frying pieces of raw potato in the oil. Fragments of burned food may be removed by pouring the cooled oil through a funnel lined with muslin or paper towels. However, oil should not be overutilized. Certain studies have shown that oil that has been repeatly used for frying contains a high proportion of carcinogens.

FRITTERS

These crisp deep-fried morsels appear in some form throughout the cuisines of Asia. Although they are sometimes eaten as snacks, it is more usual to find them served as a side dish or a course in a meal. Their crisp texture provides a perfect foil to gravied dishes, and, as you have read earlier, the Asians balance textures as well as flavors when composing a meal.

There are two basic types of fritters: the variety in which meats, fish, or vegetables (sometimes fruit) are cut into small pieces, then individually dipped in batter and fried, and the variety in which small fragments of any of the above ingredients, as well as finely chopped herbs and spices, are beaten or stirred into a batter all at once before the fritters are dropped by spoonfuls into the hot oil.

The batters may be made from wheat or rice flour. Some of the batters of India are made from the legume family (mainly chickpeas) and the dried peas or beans are ground into fine flours that bring a special flavor of their own to the batters.

Batters must be thick enough to stick to the food that is dipped into them. This is made easier by patting the pieces with paper towels before dipping. A batter is generally thick enough to coat food successfully if it drops from a raised spoon in long, triangular sheets. If it spills down in a continuous ribbon, it is too thin. When you are satisfied with the consistency, beat the batter well until it is smooth and then let it rest, refrigerated, for at least an hour, unless recipe directions state otherwise.

As a rule, uncooked foods that are dipped in batter should be fried at a lower temperature and for a longer period than precooked foods. The cooking time and temperature also vary with the size of the fritter. Large fritters and those containing raw ingredients should be fried for about 6 to 7 minutes at temperatures ranging from 350°F. to 360°F. *(175°C. to 180°C.)*. Precooked food in smaller pieces should be fried for about 2 to 3 minutes at the standard, deep-frying temperature of 375°F *(190°C.)*.

There is one other category of batter-coated foods that is considered a kind of fritter. These foods are not coated with a standard beaten batter, but are dipped first in flour and then in egg. Surprisingly enough, where as we in the West would ordinarily dip an ingredient first in egg and then in flour, the Asians often reverse the process, producing a wonderfully light and crisp coating. Dipping an object in flour first also ensures that any residual surface moisture is absorbed before the food is finally sealed off from the hot oil by the coating of beaten egg.

❦ Indonesian Peanut Fritters

In Indonesia, these fritters are often served as part of the *Rijsttafel,* or Rice Table —a long meal of many courses that accompanies a central dish of rice.

Preparation time: 20 minutes   Serves 6 to 8 as a side dish
Cooking time: 25 minutes

SHOPPING AND TECHNIQUE TIPS
The small round red-skinned Spanish peanuts are the variety closest to those used in Indonesia. Soak the raw peanuts in warm water for ½ hour, then remove the skins. Dry them well before incorporating them in the batter. The longer peanuts, raw, may also be used.

INGREDIENTS	PREPARATION
1 cup *(6 ounces)* of all-purpose *(plain)* flour	Sifted
1 *(¾)* teaspoon of baking powder	Sifted
1 *(¾)* teaspoon of salt	
1 *(¾)* tablespoon of ground coriander	
1 *(¾)* teaspoon of ground caraway	
¼ teaspoon *(a pinch)* of ground black pepper	

INGREDIENTS	PREPARATION

INGREDIENTS	PREPARATION
1 cup *(8 fluid ounces)* of thick Coconut Milk (page 114)	
1 large egg	Beaten
2 *(1⅔)* tablespoons of onion	Minced, then squeezed dry with paper towels
¾ cup *(about ¼ pound)* of Spanish peanuts	Soaked, skins removed, dried
4 or more cups *(32 fluid ounces)* of peanut oil	

METHOD

1. Pour the oil into a wok or deep-fryer and set a thermometer in place. Begin to heat the oil.

2. Sift the flour, baking powder and salt into a large mixing bowl, stir in the spices and seasonings and then add the coconut milk and the egg. Beat until everything is thoroughly mixed into a smooth batter. Stir in the onion and peanuts and let the batter rest for 10 minutes.

3. When the oil has reached 375°F. *(190°C.)*, drop a tablespoon of the batter into it and fry for 2 to 3 minutes, or until the fritter is golden and crisp. Turn the fritter from time to time to ensure that it is evenly cooked. Remove and drain on paper towels. (You may wish to let the first fritter cool and taste it to check that the texture and seasoning are to your liking, before proceeding with the rest.)

4. Now fry the remaining fritters, 3 or 4 at a time. Do not overcrowd the wok and be sure to allow time between batches to let the temperature of the oil return to 375°F. *(190°C.)*. Drain fritters on fresh paper towels and continue until all the batter is used. Place on a warmed dish and serve hot or at room temperature.

ADVANCE PREPARATION AND
STORAGE NOTES

These fritters can be fried up to 1 hour ahead of time. To ensure maximum crispness, they should be refried briefly (1 minute each) before you wish to eat, then placed in a warm oven after draining. If you do not wish to double-fry them, you may place them in a hot oven for 10 minutes before serving. If you wish to keep them on hand for a longer period, after warming at high heat turn the oven to low and keep them warm. Do not cover the dish.

✿ Indonesian Twice-Fried Spicy Peanut Fritters

This peanut fritter is cooked by shallow-frying and then by deep-frying. The flavor and texture are different from the first, as well as the technique.

This fritter is also eaten as a snack in Thailand, although there it is generally made commercially rather than in the home kitchen. We frequently bought the Thai version of these fritters from the street vendors and, on taking them home, broke them into large fragments to be served as an inexpensive local substitute for crackers with dips.

Preparation time: 15 minutes   Serves 6
Cooking time: 30 minutes

SHOPPING AND TECHNIQUE TIPS
The traditional Indonesian recipe contains candlenuts *(kemiri)* among the ingredients. I find that macadamia nuts or Brazil nuts make a good substitute. One Brazil nut equals 3 macadamia nuts. This recipe also uses rice flour instead of wheat flour. You will find rice flour in the Oriental section of your supermarket.

INGREDIENTS	PREPARATION
3 macadamia nuts, or 1 large Brazil nut	Chopped Blanched and chopped
3 cloves of garlic	Peeled and chopped
1 *(¾)* teaspoon of salt	
2 *(1⅔)* teaspoons of ground coriander	
½ *(⅓)* teaspoon (or less) of ground red pepper (Cayenne)	
½ *(⅓)* teaspoon of ground cumin	
¾ cup *(4½ ounces)* of rice flour	
1 cup *(9 fluid ounces)* and 2 tablespoons of water	
½ cup *(just over 3 ounces)* of Spanish peanuts	Soaked, drained, skins removed, dried
4 or more *(32 fluid ounces)* cups of vegetable oil for deep-frying	
Vegetable oil for shallow-frying	

METHOD
1. In a mortar, pound the macadamia or Brazil nuts and garlic to a paste, then transfer them to a mixing bowl. Stir in the salt, spices and rice flour.

2. Add the water, a little at a time, stirring and beating thoroughly until a thick batter is formed—it should still be of pouring consistency. Stir in the peanuts.

3. Position a thermometer in a wok, turn on the heat and pour the oil into the wok for deep-frying. Start to bring it to 375°F. *(190°C.)*.

4. Put 2 tablespoons of oil in a frying pan and have it ready over medium-high heat.

5. Pour about 2 *(1 ⅔)* tablespoons of batter, together with 4 or 5 peanuts, into the frying pan to make a flat fritter. Pour in enough batter to make 2 more fritters. Fry the fritters for about 30 seconds, or until they are set but not cooked through.

6. Transfer the first 3 fritters to the wok and deep-fry them until they are crisp throughout and golden brown (about 1 to 2 minutes). Drain on paper towels.

7. Repeat until all the batter is used up, alternating the cooking between the frying pan and the wok and adding more oil to the frying pan as necessary. Let the fritters cool before serving.

ADVANCE PREPARATION AND
STORAGE NOTES

These fritters should be really crisp. They make great snacks to serve with cocktails. They may be stored in an airtight container, lined with paper towels, when completely cool, and they will stay fresh for up to 2 weeks.

✿ Indonesian Shrimp Fritters

Preparation time: 25 minutes   Serves 4 as a side dish
Cooking time: 15 to 20 minutes

SHOPPING AND TECHNIQUE TIPS

You may use the precooked, peeled and frozen baby shrimp for this recipe. Thaw and wash well, drain thoroughly and then pat them dry.

INGREDIENTS	PREPARATION
½ cup *(2¾ ounces)* of cooked, peeled small shrimp	Minced and squeezed dry in paper towels
1 cup *(2¾ ounces)* of bean sprouts	Roots removed and discarded, chopped
4 green *(spring)* onions	Minced

INGREDIENTS	PREPARATION
2 shallots	Peeled and minced
2 cloves of garlic	Peeled and minced
1 *(¾)* tablespoon of unsweetened, dried, flaked coconut	
2 eggs	Beaten
½ cup *(3 ounces)* of all-purpose *(plain)* flour	
½ *(⅓)* teaspoon of baking soda *(bicarbonate of soda)*	
½ *(⅓)* teaspoon of salt	
¼ teaspoon *(a pinch)* of ground black pepper	
¼ teaspoon *(a pinch)* of ground ginger	
1 *(¾)* teaspoon of ground coriander	
½ *(⅓)* teaspoon of ground red pepper (Cayenne)	
2 *(1⅔)* tablespoons *(1 fluid ounce)* of water	
4 cups *(32 fluid ounces)* of vegetable oil	

METHOD

1. In a mixing bowl, combine the shrimp, bean sprouts, green *(spring)* onions, shallots, garlic, coconut and eggs.

2. Stir in the flour, baking soda, salt, pepper and spices. Add the water and stir until all the ingredients are well blended.

3. Heat the oil in a wok or deep-fryer to 375°F. *(190°C.)* on a frying thermometer.

4. When the oil has reached 375°F. *(190°C.)*, drop tablespoons of the mixture, 2 or 3 at a time (1 tablespoon to a fritter) into the oil and fry until the fritters are crisp and golden brown.

5. Remove with a spatula and drain on paper towels. Transfer to a serving dish and keep warm until all the fritters are fried.

ADVANCE PREPARATION AND
STORAGE NOTES

The ingredients and the batter may be made ahead of time, but the fritters should not be fried until shortly before you are ready to serve.

Indian Variation (VEGETABLE AND SHRIMP FRITTERS)

This Indian version contains different ingredients from the preceding Indonesian recipe (without the shrimp it is purely vegetarian) and different flour and spices, but the technique is similar.

Preparation time: 30 minutes   Serves 6 to 8 people
Cooking time: 30 minutes

SHOPPING AND TECHNIQUE TIPS

You may use whatever vegetables are fresh and in season in the supermarket. If you cannot find chick-pea flour, you may grind your own from dried chick peas (a food processor works well) or you may substitute all-purpose flour, which will produce a different flavor, color and texture, but which makes a good alternative. Should you happen to have a good selection of leftover cooked vegetables in your refrigerator, you can substitute them for fresh vegetables, but, because they are already cooked, you must fry the fritters for only 2 to 3 minutes.

INGREDIENTS	PREPARATION
1½ cups *(9 ounces)* of chick-pea flour or all purpose *(plain)* flour	
½ *(⅓)* teaspoon of baking soda *(bicarbonate of soda)*	
1 *(¾)* teaspoon of Indian Sweet Spice Mix (page 118)	
2 *(1⅔)* teaspoons of salt	
½ *(⅓)* teaspoon of ground red pepper (Cayenne)	
½ *(⅓)* teaspoon of ground cumin	
1 cup *(8 fluid ounces)* of water	
1 clove of garlic	Peeled, crushed and chopped
30 or more coriander (Chinese parsley, *cilantro*) leaves	Chopped
3½ cups *(¾ to 1 pound)* of mixed vegetables (suggestions: potatoes, onions, cauliflower, eggplant *(aubergine)*, zucchini *(courgette)*, chilli peppers, broccoli, etc.)	Finely chopped
½ cup *(2¾ ounces)* of raw, small shrimp (optional)	Peeled, cleaned and chopped
4 to 5 cups *(up to 40 fluid ounces)* of vegetable oil	

METHOD

1. Sift the flour, baking soda *(bicarbonate of soda)*, Sweet Spice Mix, salt, red pepper and cumin into a large mixing bowl. Add the water gradually, stirring well to form a stiff batter. Stir in the garlic and coriander and beat well. Let the batter rest for 15 minutes, covered and refrigerated.

2. Beat the batter again and fold in the vegetables and shrimp.

Follow the preceding recipe for the remaining steps. Serve the fritters hot, accompanied by Indian Mint and Fruit Chutney (page 454).

❧ Indian Potato Fritters

These fritters are actually little balls of mashed potato which are flavored with spices and herbs before being dipped in batter and deep-fried. They are a speciality of southern India.

Preparation time: 1 hour and 10 minutes (including refrigeration time)

Cooking time: 15 to 20 minutes
Serves 4 as a side dish

SHOPPING AND TECHNIQUE TIPS

If you have leftover mashed potatoes, this is an ideal and delicious way of using them up. The potato mixture must be chilled to a consistency that will allow you to mold them into balls.

INGREDIENTS	PREPARATION
Filling	
2 tablespoons *(1 fluid ounce)* of vegetable oil	
1-inch piece of ginger root	Peeled and minced
4 green Serrano chilli peppers, or 2 Jalapeño peppers	Seeded and minced
¼ teaspoon *(a pinch)* of ground turmeric	
2 cups *(¾ pound)* of potatoes	Cooked and mashed
Juice of 1 lime	
½ *(⅓)* teaspoon of salt	
1 *(¾)* teaspoon of granulated sugar	
30 or more coriander (Chinese parsley, *cilantro*) leaves	Chopped

INGREDIENTS   PREPARATION
Batter
1 cup *(6 ounces)* of chick-pea or
    all-purpose *(plain)* flour
½ *(⅓)* teaspoon of baking soda
    (bicarbonate of soda)
½ *(⅓)* teaspoon of ground coriander
¼ teaspoon *(a pinch)* of ground red
    pepper (Cayenne)
½ *(⅓)* teaspoon of salt
¼ cup *(2 fluid ounces)* of plain   Stirred
    yogurt
6 tablespoons *(3 fluid ounces)*
    (approximately) of cold water
4 cups *(32 fluid ounces)* of vegetable
    oil

METHOD
1. Set a wok over medium-high heat and add the 2 tablespoons of vegetable oil. When the oil is hot, fry the ginger and chilli peppers for 1 minute, stirring. (Do not put your face near the wok, as the vapor is pungent.)

2. Stir in the turmeric and let it darken slightly. Now stir in the mashed potatoes, mix together and remove the wok from the heat.

3. Stir in the remaining filling ingredients, mix until they are evenly distributed and turn the contents of the wok into a small bowl. Cover and refrigerate for 1 hour. Wash and dry the wok and set it near the stove.

4. Meanwhile, prepare the batter. Place the dry ingredients in a mixing bowl and stir in the yogurt. Now add the water gradually, beating the mixture as you add it. Beat thoroughly until the batter is smooth and of a consistency that will coat the back of a spoon. Set the batter aside.

5. Pour the oil for deep-frying in the wok, set the thermometer in place and start to bring the oil up to a temperature of 375°F. *(190°C.)*.

6. Remove the chilled potato mixture from the refrigerator and roll it into small balls the size of a walnut.

7. Dip the balls, 2 or 3 at a time, into the batter and then deep-fry them for 2 to 3 minutes, until the coating is crisp and golden brown. Drain on paper towels. Keep the fritters on a dish in a warm oven until you have completed the frying.

ADVANCE PREPARATION AND
STORAGE NOTES

The potato filling may be made the day before and left to refrigerate, covered, overnight. Or, if you wish to cut down on the cooling time, you may place the completed potato filling in the freezer for 15 minutes instead of in the refrigerator. (Set a timer.) The completed fritters should be eaten shortly after they are fried, as they will become soggy if left too long.

Vegetable Variation

The same batter and technique may be used to make Vegetable Fritters (known in India as *pakhoras*). A selection of mixed vegetables such as cauliflower flowerets, broccoli flowerets, carrot pieces, potato pieces, zucchini *(courgette)* slices and green bean segments may be used. I suggest you blanch them briefly (1 to 2 minutes) in boiling water and drain them well before dipping them in the batter. This ensures that the frying time is not too long and that the vegetables are properly cooked.

Lentil Variation

Any cold, leftover lentils that you have cooked in Indian style (page 370) may also be rolled into balls and dipped into the same batter. Lentils coagulate during refrigeration and, provided you have not made the lentil dish too liquid, will roll easily into balls. Alternatively, you may like to pat them into small, round cakes before dipping them.

All these fritters should be served accompanied by a fresh or cooked Indian chutney.

❀ Japanese Vegetable and Shrimp Fritters (TEMPURA)

There is a marked difference between Japanese fritters—those feather-light, batter-dipped morsels of vegetables and shrimp—and most of those in other Asian countries. The eternal question among newcomers to Japanese food is always "How do they make the batter so light?"

The following recipe will show you the easy tips and techniques with which to achieve that hallmark of a good *tempura*.

Preparation time: 25 minutes   Serves 4
Cooking time: 35 to 40 minutes,
   depending on the number of items

SHOPPING AND TECHNIQUE TIPS

Look for the freshest possible vegetables and shrimp and make sure you select only those in perfect condition. Beside the ingredients listed below in the recipe, many different seasonal vegetables and fish can be included. Choose from: squid, the mantle cut into squares, then scored; whole, small fresh fish like grunion or smelt; white fish fillets, cut into bite-sized pieces; onions, halved then cut crosswise into half-moon rings; Japanese eggplant *(aubergine)*, sliced into thin rounds; zucchini *(courgette),* sliced; large green beans cut into 1½-inch pieces; strips of sweet green pepper; cauliflower or broccoli flowerets; celery cut into 1-inch lengths.

The batter should be freshly made *just* before frying; in fact, if you are frying a large amount, divide the batter, making it in 2 batches. Do not prepare the second batch until you have used up the first. The batter must be cold and lumpy. Use ice water and fold the ingredients together with chopsticks or a fork. *Do not beat the batter.*

INGREDIENTS

INGREDIENTS	PREPARATION
12 Chinese snow peas *(mange-tout)*	Tops and tails removed
4 medium to large white mushrooms	Caps wiped clean, halved
1 medium carrot	Peeled, then cut into matchstick pieces
4 thin, young asparagus stalks	Tough bases removed, cut into 2-inch pieces
1 small sweet potato	Peeled and cut into thin slices
8 medium shrimp	Shelled, leaving tails attached, cleaned and deveined

Batter coating
2¼ cups *(15 ounces)* of all-purpose *(plain)* flour
½ *(⅓)* teaspoon of baking soda *(bicarbonate of soda)*
2 egg yolks
2 cups *(16 fluid ounces)* of iced water (a little more if a thinner batter is desired)
4 cups *(32 fluid ounces)* of vegetable oil for deep-fat frying

METHOD

1. Prepare the vegetables and set them aside. Cut several slits crosswise on the underside (where you removed the legs) of the shrimp to prevent them from curling during the frying. Pat all the ingredients with paper towels to remove any moisture and set them on paper plates near the stove.

2. Pour the oil into a wok, set the thermometer in place and start to bring

the oil to the frying temperature of 350°F. *(175°C.).* (*Tempura* is fried at a somewhat lower temperature than the preceding dishes.) Pour ¼ cup of flour onto a paper plate.

3. Just before the oil reaches the desired temperature, sift 1 cup of flour and half the baking soda into the small bowl. Stir 1 egg yolk in a medium bowl and pour in 1 cup of ice water. Mix the egg and water together in 5 or 6 strokes. Pour in all of the cup of flour at once, stirring with a few strokes of the chopsticks or fork until the mixture becomes a barely combined, lumpy batter. Set the batter near the stove, together with the paper plate containing the ¼ cup of flour.

4. Fry the vegetables first. Dip 1 piece into the flour, and then into the batter, shake it lightly to drain off the surplus, then drop it gently into the oil. It should sink, then rise immediately to the surface, surrounded by a ring of bubbles. Fry it for a total of 2 to 3 minutes, then remove and drain on the paper towels. Repeat with all the pieces of vegetable in turn, then transfer them to a heated plate and place in a warm oven.

5. Let the oil increase to a temperature of 360°F. *(180°C.)* and then repeat the process with the shrimp, again frying them for 2 to 3 minutes. As the batter runs out, interrupt the process to make more and then continue.

6. Place the cooked *tempura* in baskets or bowls lined with white absorbent paper and bring to the table immediately. Serve with a Japanese Dipping Sauce (page 477).

ADVANCE PREPARATION AND
STORAGE NOTES

You really cannot make these fritters ahead, but vegetables may be prepared in advance.

ᘓ Philippine Deep-Fried Stuffed Crabs

The traditional recipe for these stuffed crabs calls for whole, fresh crabs to be cooked, legs and claws removed, the top of the shell (apron) taken off and all the meat and roe removed from the shell. Then, when ready for deep-frying, the crab meat is returned to its shell, coated and fried. No less authentic, but certainly more convenient, because of the regional and seasonal unavailability of whole, fresh crabs, frozen crab meat and scallop shells are used here.

Preparation time: 20 minutes   Cooking time: 25 minutes
                                        Serves 4 to 5 people

SHOPPING AND TECHNIQUE TIPS
You can find bay or sea scallop shells in packages in the gourmet section of the
supermarket or in specialty food shops. After careful washing, they are reusable.

INGREDIENTS	PREPARATION
3 tablespoons *(1 ½ fluid ounces)* of vegetable oil	
2 green *(spring)* onions	Finely chopped
2 cloves of garlic	Peeled and finely chopped
1 small tomato	Coarsely chopped
1 pound of fresh, frozen or canned crab meat	Washed and drained
1¼ *(1)* teaspoons of salt	
Freshly ground black pepper	
2 eggs	Separated
1 head of leaf lettuce (romaine, Bibb, etc. *(cos or any common variety of lettuce)*)	Washed, drained and separated
3 cups *(24 fluid ounces)* of vegetable oil	
1 medium tomato	Cut lengthwise into 6 wedges
2 lemons	Each cut lengthwise into 6 wedges

METHOD

1. Heat the 3 tablespoons of oil in a medium frying pan over medium heat.
Drop in the green *(spring)* onions and garlic and quickly stir-fry. When the
onions and garlic are soft and light gold, add the chopped tomato and continue
cooking and stirring for about 5 more minutes, or until most of the liquid has
evaporated.

2. Reduce the heat to low and add the crab meat, 1 *(¾)* teaspoon of the
salt and a few grindings of the pepper. Stir constantly to mix the ingredients
and keep the crab from browning. When everything is heated through, remove
the pan from the heat and set aside.

3. Beat the egg whites in a deep bowl with the remaining salt until they
form stiff peaks. In a separate bowl, with the same beater, beat the yolks until
they are foamy and thick. With a rubber spatula, fold the yolks into the whites
to form a smooth, uniform mixture.

4. Spoon the crab meat mixture into the shells, mounding the meat
slightly in the center. With the rubber spatula, spread the beaten eggs over the
crab mixture to a thickness of about 1 inch.

5. Line a platter with lettuce leaves.

6. Pour the oil into a large, heavy frying pan or wok. Heat the oil to
375°F. *(190°C.)* on the frying thermometer. Carefully put in the stuffed shells,

shell side down in the oil, (2 or 3 at a time if using the small shells). Cook each filled shell for about 1 minute, spooning the hot oil over the eggs so they puff up and turn pale gold. As each stuffed crab is cooked, remove it with the tongs and set aside to drain and cool.

7. When all the stuffed crabs are cooked, arrange them decoratively, together with the tomato and lemon slices, on the platter and serve immediately.

ADVANCE PREPARATION AND STORAGE NOTES

The crab-meat filling can be made in advance. The crabs can be fried and placed in a warm oven until ready to serve. If this is done, place them on another dish and do not transfer to the lettuce-lined platter until just before you are ready to serve.

Malaysian Variation (CURRIED DEEP-FRIED CRAB)

The technique and most of the ingredients are the same, except that the following spice paste and ingredients are fried with the crab meat before it is replaced in the shells:

INGREDIENTS	PREPARATION
4 macadamia nuts or blanched almonds	Chopped
1 green Serrano chilli pepper	Minced (remove the seeds if less heat is desired)
1 small onion, or ½ medium onion	Peeled and chopped
The peel *(zest)* of ½ a lemon	Grated
½ *(⅓)* teaspoon of anchovy paste	
3 tablespoons *(1½ fluid ounces)* of vegetable oil	
¼ teaspoon *(a pinch)* of ground turmeric	
¼ cup *(2 fluid ounces)* of thick Coconut Milk (page 114)	
The last 8 ingredients from the previous Philippine crab recipe including the crab. Substitute 2 limes for the lemons.	

METHOD

1. Place the nuts and chilli pepper in a mortar and pound to a paste.

Transfer the paste to a processor or blender and add the onion, lemon rind and anchovy paste. Process to a paste. Heat the oil in a wok and fry the paste for 3 minutes, stirring.

2. Stir in the turmeric and coconut milk. Continue to cook until the liquid has almost evaporated, stirring to prevent the mixture sticking.

3. Reduce the heat to low and add the crab meat, 1 (¾) teaspoon of the salt and a few grindings of the pepper. Stir constantly to mix the ingredients and keep the crab from browning. When everything is heated through, remove the pan from the heat and set aside.

4. Beat the egg whites in a deep bowl with the remaining salt until they form stiff peaks. In a separate bowl, with the same beater, beat the yolks until they are foamy and thick. With a rubber spatula, fold the yolks into the whites to form a smooth, uniform mixture.

5. Spoon the crab meat mixture into the shells, mounding the meat slightly in the center. With the rubber spatula, spread the beaten eggs over the crab mixture to a thickness of about 1 inch.

6. Line a platter with lettuce leaves.

7. Pour the oil into a large, heavy frying pan or wok. Heat the oil to 375°F. (190°C.) on the frying thermometer. Carefully put in the stuffed shells, shell side down in the oil (2 or 3 at a time if using the small shells). Cook each filled shell for about 1 minute, spooning the hot oil over the eggs so they puff up and turn pale gold. As each stuffed crab is cooked, remove it with the tongs and set aside to drain and cool.

8. When all the stuffed crabs are cooked, arrange them decoratively, together with the tomato and lime slices, on the platter and serve immediately.

ADVANCE PREPARATION AND
STORAGE NOTES
As in the previous Philippine crab recipe.

Thai Version (CURRIED CRAB OR CRAB CAKES)

This is also basically the same as the above versions, except that in step 1 of the Philippine method 1 (¾) teaspoon of Thai Curry Paste (page 124) is added to the mixture instead of the tomato. It is fried with the onion and garlic. You may substitute 3 or 4 minced shallots for the green (spring) onion for further authenticity. This Thai version can also be made without the crab shells by dropping tablespoons of the mixture directly into the oil. The cakes may also be shallow-fried.

❦ Peking Duck (CHINA)

You may be surprised to see this classic dish in a section on deep-frying, but I have found that deep-frying the bird works better than roasting it. Although traditional Chinese cooks use a bicycle pump to separate the skin of the duck from the flesh so that it becomes nice and crisp, with proper air-drying you can achieve good results without one. I do suggest that you use an electric hair dryer (if you have one) to air-dry the duck. An electric fan also works well.

Preparation time: Approximately 2½   Cooking time: A total of 1 hour
   hours   (including frying the pancakes)
                                               Serves 6

SHOPPING AND TECHNIQUE TIPS

Order a small (between 3½ and 4½ pounds) duck, fresh if possible. If you have to use a frozen bird, make sure it is well defrosted and quite dry before you begin. In order for the skin to attain the right degree of crispness, it must first be immersed in boiling water, then coated with a marinade and air-dried completely. This is where I have found a hair dryer useful for reducing the drying time. The crisp, cooked skin is removed from the duck and cut into squares. The meat is removed and cut into small, uniform pieces. Both are served with small lengths of green *(spring)* onions and are wrapped in thin, circular pancakes (called "mandarin pancakes," page 154) before being dipped by each diner in individual dishes of plum sauce. You will find that you can utilize the recipe for Large Egg Roll Wrappers (page 148) for the pancakes, and dilute the Chinese Plum Sauce (page 466) with white vinegar to provide a dipping sauce.

INGREDIENTS	PREPARATION
1 small, plump duck (about 3½ to 4 ½ pounds)	Cleaned
1 *(¾)* teaspoon of Five-Plus-One Spice Powder (page 119)	
2 *(1⅔)* teaspoons of salt	
¼ cup *(3¼ tablespoons)* of honey	
2-inch piece of fresh ginger root	Peeled and thinly sliced
½ cup *(4 fluid ounces)* of water	
1 *(¾)* tablespoon of white vinegar	
2 *(1⅔)* teaspoons of pale, dry sherry	
8 green *(spring)* onions	
1 cucumber	
1 recipe Mandarin Pancakes (page 154)	

INGREDIENTS

¼ cup *(2 fluid ounces)* of Chinese
    Plum Sauce (page 466)
2 *(1 ⅔)* tablespoons of white vinegar
6 cups *(48 fluid ounces)* of vegetable
    oil

METHOD

1. Wash the duck thoroughly and dry it with paper towels, inside and out. Cut off the wing tips. Securely tie a 3-foot length of string round the neck of the bird and fasten the ends into a loop.

2. Bring at least 6 quarts (enough to cover the bird) of water to a rolling boil in a large stock pot and immerse the bird for 30 seconds. Hang the bird up and dry it off with an electric hairdryer. Repeat this procedure 3 times. After the last time, let the bird dry and cool slightly, then rub the inside cavity with the 5-Plus-One Spice Powder and the salt.

PEKING DUCK

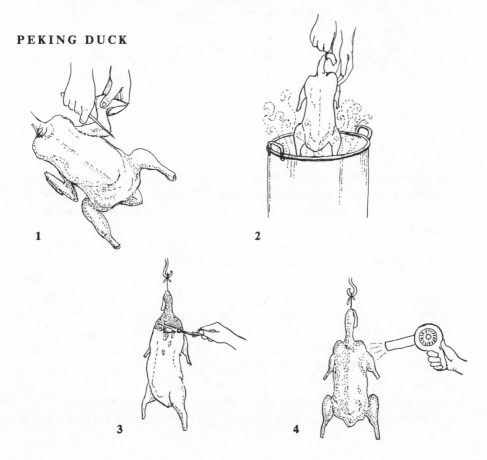

1

2

3

4

PEKING DUCK

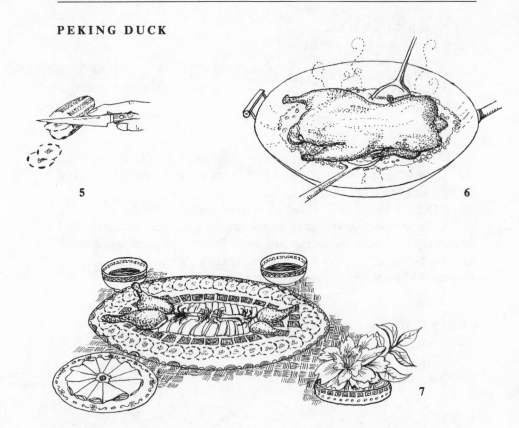

5

6

7

3. In a small saucepan, bring the honey, ginger root, water, vinegar and sherry to a boil, then let it cool slightly. While the bird is hanging, paint the exterior skin completely and thoroughly with this syrup. (Set a basin underneath to catch the drips.)

4. Use an electric hair dryer to dry the duck completely. This will take about 30 minutes. Leave the duck hanging up while you prepare the pancakes and stack them. Cut the green *(spring)* onions into 3-inch lengths. Score both ends of the onion pieces deeply and repeatedly so that the cut slivers curl outwards and each length forms a two-ended "brush." Drop the onion brushes into a bowl of ice water to help them curl and keep them crisp.

5. Score the skin of the cucumber lengthwise with the tines of a fork, then cut into paper-thin slices. Mix the Chinese Plum Sauce with the vinegar and pour it into small bowls or saucers, one for each diner.

6. Set a thermometer inside a wok and pour in 6 cups of vegetable oil. Bring to 375°F. *(190°C.)* over high heat. Then when the oil is up to tempera-

ture, take the duck down and lower it carefully into the oil. Fry the duck for 25 to 30 minutes, or until the skin is beautifully brown and crisp. Turn the duck with the spatulas as you fry it. Remove the duck and let it drain on paper towels.

7. Remove the skin carefully from the duck and cut it into small (2-inch) squares and pieces. Lay these decoratively on a large platter. Carve the meat from the duck and cut it into bite-sized pieces. Arrange these alongside the skin. Ring the platter with the cucumber slices and lay the green *(spring)* onion on top. Arrange the pancakes on a plate and bring everything to the table with the bowls of dipping sauce. Each diner takes pieces of skin and meat and places them on a pancake, together with a length of green *(spring)* onion and a piece of cucumber as they wish. The pancake is then folded around the duck pieces and dipped into the sauce before being eaten.

ADVANCE PREPARATION AND STORAGE NOTES

The duck may be taken to the final dry stage and then left hanging for an hour or two before being fried. The duck may be carved and the skin and meat put on separate plates and placed in the oven. The meat should be covered, but the skin should be left uncovered so that it remains crisp. The pancakes, sauce and vegetables may all be prepared ahead of time.

❀ Crisp-Fried Catfish
(THAILAND)

There are well over 100 varieties of catfish in Thailand and they appear frequently in the cuisine. This dish is unusual among fish dishes as the fish are fried until they become crunchy throughout, providing a welcome change of texture to gravied dishes and wet curries.

Preparation time: 15 minutes   Serves 6
Cooking time: 30 minutes

SHOPPING AND TECHNIQUE TIPS

Now that catfish are becoming more plentiful in supermarkets and fish markets, it is relatively easy to find them. You may find whole sections of catfish or catfish steaks. The latter are easier to debone as you merely remove the central portion of backbone and adjoining bones, leaving the fish in 3 or 4 conveniently sized pieces. Fry the fish far longer than you instinctively feel that you should. It should be crisp throughout. The accompanying tangy fruit relish is a lovely contrast of texture and flavor. In Thailand the flesh of an unripe green mango would be used, but unripe mangoes are rarely found in our markets. I suggest you look for hard, semiripe peaches, which are available at the beginning of the peach season. If you wish to make this dish at another time of the year, try thin slices of tart, crisp apples.

INGREDIENTS	PREPARATION
2 pounds of catfish (see Shopping and Technique Tips above)	Washed and dried
4 cups *(32 fluid ounces)* of vegetable oil
8 cloves of garlic	Peeled and thinly sliced
3-inch piece of fresh ginger root	Peeled and minced or finely shredded
1 hard, semiripe peach	Peeled, halved, pit removed and the flesh shredded
The juice of 2 limes
2 *(1⅔)* tablespoons of granulated sugar
2 *(1⅔)* tablespoons of Southeast Asian fish sauce
2 red or green Serrano chilli peppers or a Jalapeño pepper	Seeded and cut into slivers
15 to 20 coriander (Chinese parsley, *cilantro*) leaves

METHOD

1. Place water in a steamer and bring it to a boil. Steam the fish for 8 to 10 minutes (depending on the size of the fillets), then set aside to cool.

2. Pat the fish dry, then carefully remove all the bones, if necessary, and cut the flesh into bite-sized pieces. Reserve 1 *(¾)* tablespoon of the oil and pour the rest into a wok. Set a thermometer in the wok and bring the oil to 350°F. *(175°C.)* over high heat.

3. Fry the fish pieces, a few at a time, until they are completely crisp and well browned. Drain on paper towels. Set a small frying pan on the heat and fry the garlic in the remaining 1 *(¾)* tablespoon of oil until it is crisp and light brown. Drain on paper towels.

4. In a small bowl, combine the garlic, ginger and peach shreds and mound in the center of a serving platter. Surround the mound with the fried catfish pieces.

5. In another small bowl, combine the lime juice, granulated sugar and

fish sauce, stirring until the sugar has dissolved. Sprinkle most of this sauce over the ginger-peach mound and scatter the remainder over the catfish pieces.

6. Garnish with the chilli pepper slivers and coriander leaves and serve immediately. This makes a good first course for a meal.

ADVANCE PREPARATION AND
STORAGE NOTES
The fish may be fried ahead of time and kept in a warm oven. The fruit may be prepared and dressed with the sauce. Combine everything and arrange at the last moment before serving.

❀ Vietnamese Fried Fish Toasts

Perfect fare for picnics, a light lunch or as hors d'oeuvres, these Fried Fish Toasts have a delicate flavor and an interesting texture.

Preparation time: 15 minutes   Serves 8
Cooking time: 25 minutes

SHOPPING AND TECHNIQUE TIPS
Any kind of white fish fillets are suitable for this recipe. Make sure that all bones still remaining are removed before you start to process them.

INGREDIENTS

¾ pound of white fish fillets

¼ pound of small, cooked shrimp
2 (1⅔) tablespoons (or 1 fluid ounce) of Southeast Asian fish sauce
1 (¾) teaspoon of cornstarch (cornflour)
¼ teaspoon (a pinch) of salt
¼ teaspoon (a pinch) of freshly ground black pepper
¼ teaspoon (a pinch) of ground cinnamon
1 (¾) tablespoon of water
1 egg white

PREPARATION

Picked over for bones, cut into 1-inch pieces
Thawed, if frozen, shelled

INGREDIENTS   PREPARATION

2 *(1⅔)* tablespoons of vegetable oil

2 green *(spring)* onions   Finely chopped

8 slices of day-old white bread   Crusts removed

4 cups *(32 fluid ounces)* of vegetable
    oil

1 head of leaf lettuce (butter, Boston,   Washed, drained, leaves separated
    Bibb)

¼ cup *(1 ounce)* of mint leaves

10 sweet basil leaves (if available)

¼ cup *(1 ounce)* of coriander
    (Chinese parsley, *cilantro*) leaves

Vietnamese Dipping Sauce (page 473)

METHOD

1. Place the fish, shrimp, fish sauce, cornstarch *(cornflour)*, salt, pepper, cinnamon, water, egg white, vegetable oil and green *(spring)* onions in a food processor or blender and process to a smooth paste (process in 3 batches). Mix the processed paste together in a bowl.

2. Spread the bread slices evenly with the paste and cut each slice diagonally to make 4 triangles.

3. Place the thermometer in the wok and pour in the oil. Heat to a temperature of 375°F. *(190°C.),* then fry the toasts, 2 or 3 at a time, until each is golden brown. Drain on paper towels, then place on a platter and keep warm in a low oven until ready to serve.

4. Arrange the lettuce leaves and the herbs in separate piles on another platter and pour the Vietnamese Dipping Sauce into individual bowls, one for each diner. Each person takes a fish toast and rolls it up in a lettuce leaf, together with a few of the herbs, before dipping it in the sauce.

ADVANCE PREPARATION AND
STORAGE NOTES

The triangles may be made ahead of time and refrigerated until you are ready to fry. Alternatively, the toasts may be fried and left in a low oven until serving time.

Chinese Crab Toasts

These may be served as hot appetizers. Substitute 2 cups *(½ pound)* of cooked crab, squeezed dry in paper towels, for the fish and shrimp. Replace the fish sauce with 1 *(¾)* tablespoon of pale, dry sherry, and the cinnamon with 1 *(¾)* teaspoon of minced ginger. Omit the herbs and lettuce for wrapping, but add a *(¾)* tablespoon of coriander (Chinese parsely, *cilantro*) leaves to the paste, folding them in for a couple of turns of the processor at the end.

Thai Pork and Shrimp Toasts

Substitute ¾ cup *(just over ⅓ pound)* of ground fresh pork for the fish, increase the black pepper to 1 *(¾)* teaspoon. Replace the cinnamon with 3 minced cloves of garlic, and use a whole egg. Again, as in the Chinese version, serve the Pork Toasts hot and by themselves. Omit the lettuce. You may like to garnish them with springs of coriander.

CURRYING FAVOR

❀ ❀ ❀

*Curry as a Method—
Not a Ready-Made Powder*

India does not have sole and exclusive rights to the art of curry making: curries in delicious shapes and flavors are to be found throughout Pakistan, Sri Lanka (Ceylon), Malaysia, Thailand, Burma, Indonesia and Kampuchea (Cambodia).

Before the advent of refrigeration, it was discovered (probably by trial and error) that if meats and other perishables were cooked with generous amounts of certain spices it would delay their deterioration for some days. If not cooked immediately, fresh meat, bought in the market in the cool of the early morning, will start to spoil before the hot, tropical sun has crossed the noon sky. Even then, if not refrigerated, it is barely edible after twelve hours. So, out of necessity, the process of curry-making evolved.

To many people, the term "curry" denotes a stew flavored with curry powder. If you ask them what curry powder is, they will venture an opinion that it is a single dried spice in powdered from. Sadly, the commercial curry powders to be found on the supermarket shelves do little to change this viewpoint except to inform the shopper by their labels that a mixture of spices goes into their composition.

Curry powder is merely a ready-mixed amalgam of ground spices in convenient form to be used in the spicing of Indian or other Asian savory foods. Legend has it that a British *sahib* with an addiction to Indian food, upon leaving India, asked his servant to mix up the spices and place them in a jar so that on his arrival in England, he would be able to enjoy his favorite dishes. Whether true or not, unfortunately this ready-made spice mix has continued to be used in the worst imitations of curries that deter many people from eating Indian food.

The true Indian term for a spice mix or for the spicing that goes into a dish is *masala.* This spice mix is always freshly prepared from a combination of ground dry spices and "wet" ingredients, such as garlic, onions, ginger and fresh herbs. The ingredients of each curry will dictate the blend of spices or *masala* to be used. If, for convenience, the spice mix is ground in advance, it must be stored in a tightly sealed jar, either in a cool, dry and dark cupboard (for dry spices) or, in the case of wet curry pastes, in a refrigerator.

As a generalization, in the north of India, dry spices, usually powdered, are used to make a curry mix. In southern India and in Southeast Asia, a combination of fresh or green spices and other ingredients is ground with water, lime juice, vinegar or coconut milk to make wet *masalas* or pastes.

Curries are foods for health. Every spice used in their preparation is a preservative, and most have antiseptic and digestive values. (For more information on spices, their history and nutritional values, turn to the Glossary, page 499.)

The "Big Four"—the cornerstones of most spice mixes—are: hot chilli peppers (either fresh, such as Serrano, Jalapeño, or any other of the small, hot varieties, or dried, as powdered Cayenne); cumin seeds (the *cominos* of Mexican cuisine); coriander *(cilantro)* seeds; and turmeric (a root, native to Asia and similar to ginger in appearance but available in the West, dried and ground to a brilliant yellow powder). Three out of four of these are generally present in most curry powder or paste mixes, together with various other spices.

Of the secondary spices used in *masalas,* the most common is fenugreek. This is the flavor that dominates so many commercial curry powders. Other spice mixes may include black pepper, asafetida, and any number of the "mellow" spices such as allspice, cardamom, cinnamon, nutmeg, etc.

These sweet or mellow spices also form the base of an aromatic Indian spice blend called a *garam masala,* which is often added to a dish after the main cooking is done, or sprinkled over the finished preparation. *Garam masala* is seldom used for fish or vegetable dishes or in any preparation with a delicate flavor as its pervasive aroma would overpower the main ingredients.

So, as you see, the Asian art of spicing in cooking can be complex and individualistic. Over twenty different spices are used in varying combinations for currying. It's quite possible that in 200 dishes, the same exact spice mix will not be duplicated! So much for the "single" spice mix theory of commercial curry powder.

However, there are simple and common-sense rules of thumb in mixing your own curry powders and pastes. The first is that strong-flavored ingredients in a dish need the balance of pungent spices. In the same way that a French beef stew demands the presence of bay leaves, black peppercorns and a robust Burgundy wine, so an Indian beef curry calls for a *masala* based on ground chilli peppers, coriander, cumin and turmeric with the added punch of a *garam masala,* a combination of mellow spices to be added at a later stage in the preparation.

Secondly, the strong and pungent spices such as turmeric, cumin and pepper need slow cooking and a certain amount of time before the sharp and somewhat acrid qualities are mellowed. For this reason, they are part of the spice paste that is cooked at the beginning of curry preparation. Turmeric, in particular, is very bitter and must be cooked for a long time before the flavor mellows.

The *garam masala,* or mellow spice mix, needs only a brief baptism of heat to bring out the qualities of its sweet spices. It is therefore added toward the end of the cooking period, or even sprinkled on top and stirred in just before serving.

In the "Basics" chapter, I have included simple recipes for Indian spice mixes, both powdered and in paste form, which you can make ahead and store until you wish to use them. I have also indicated the curries in which they should be used. You will find them infinitely superior in flavor to the store-bought varieties and your curries will have variety and the full spectrum of taste. Together with them, you will see a recipe for Indian Sweet Spice Mix, or *garam masala* (page 118). The inclusion of this in your dishes will add a touch of authenticity guaranteed to please a Maharajah.

There are other spice pastes in the same section. These all name the country in whose cuisine they should be used. You will find them all fascinatingly different, and in time you will instantly recognize the particular hallmark of flavors that unerringly places the dish in a specific country.

There are two basic types of curries: wet and dry. In the wet curries, after the spice mix has been fried, together with garlic and/or onions, and after the main ingredients (meat, fish or vegetable) have been slowly cooked in the mixture until they are permeated with the flavors, liquid is added and blends with the juices from the meat. This forms a stewlike gravy which is thickened naturally by the ground spices and the puree consistency of the cooked onions and other ingredients.

Dry curries demand that at some stage, usually after a period of simmering to tenderize the main ingredients and even after the introduction of some liquid, the dish is cooked uncovered until the moisture evaporates, leaving a rich, delicious coating of spices on the solid ingredients.

To generalize, the drier dishes are most frequently served in the north of India while the wet curries are found in the south and throughout Southeast Asia. Logically enough, the dry curries are accompanied by unleavened breads, which are used as utensils to scoop up the meats, while the wet curries are served over rice, which absorbs the flavor of the gravy and extends the rather smaller servings of solid ingredients—a very economical way to eat.

In northern India and Pakistan, among the few areas of Asia using dairy products, the people add yogurt or milk curds to produce gravy in a dish. Coconut milk is a universal source of gravy throughout all the southern countries.

Two main techniques are used in the preparation of curries, and both center around the timing of the introduction of the spices.

In one technique, the spices are fried and then the meat is sautéed in the mixture. (The onions and "wet" flavor agents may be fried before or after the spice paste, or may even be ground up as part of it.) Following this period of browning, the liquid is then added.

In the second technique, the meat is cooked in the liquid (preferably coconut milk) and the spices are then added, to cook in the long, simmering period before the completion of the curry. This latter technique is frequently used in Southeast Asia.

Generally, about two to four tablespoons of spice mix or paste are used for a curry. The dry powdered spices are mixed with sufficient water or vinegar (sometimes oil) to make a soft paste: the ready-made paste can, of course, be fried directly.

Vegetable oil, vegetable shortening or *ghee* (clarified butter), are used in India and Pakistan—the last in the north. The Southeast Asian countries, Sri Lanka and southern India, tend to fry in coconut oil or reduced coconut cream, peanut and other vegetable oils.

This frying period is extremely important. It is done over a low flame and the paste must be stirred constantly to prevent sticking or burning. The slow-frying darkens the color, mellows the odor, and the spices loose their acute pungency, blending their flavors so no one specific flavor becomes dominant and discernible. Many good curries have been ruined because the spices are still raw and harsh through insufficient or improper cooking.

To add a completely different flavor to a curry preparation, the whole spices may be dry-roasted before grinding and then incorporated into a paste. If you are using ready-ground, powdered spices, they will still benefit from being shaken in a heavy iron frying pan over a low flame until they darken and the aroma emerges. (This is also an excellent way to revitalize powdered spices which have stayed overlong on the shelf.)

Because of the long simmering period in curry making, cheaper cuts of meat may be used. As you would for a stew, you may also use your crock pot for making the curry, after you have done the initial frying in a pan. Because this extended period of cooking is so necessary to bring out the full flavors of a curry, if you find that your meat, fish or fowl is becoming overcooked, remove it and set it aside, reduce the gravy for the required time and then put the meat back in the pot. Curries also benefit from a resting period after cooking. You may also accomplish this by transferring the curry to a fireproof casserole dish and leaving it in a slow oven until it is time to serve.

Curries are wonderfully accommodating and forgiving. They can be made well ahead and indeed will frequently benefit from an extra day in which the flavors can intensify. Similarly, curries, unless they contain certain vegetables that do not freeze well, can be happily stowed away in the freezer until needed.

While the art of making curries originated in India, the Indian traders who set sail for the tropic shores of the Spice Islands in search of their prized curry ingredients brought their culture and their cuisine with them. This cuisine was further popularized in Southeast Asia by subsequent waves of missionaries, monks and merchants. So the curry spread far beyond the original shores that had given it birth. The Southeast Asian stepchild, however, became curiously and delightfully changed as the local spices and herbs were introduced to the spice pastes. Other ingredients, such as nuts, also crept into the mixture, and the Southeast Asia curries, such as the Indonesian, Malaysian and Thai curries of today, have a full complement of interesting additional ingredients.

While I place the main emphasis on the curries of the Indian subcontinent, there are also some intriguing curries from Southeast Asia for you to try. They are worth experimenting with, not only for their characteristic flavors, but also because they demonstrate just how wide, wonderful and varied a dish a curry can be.

❧ Indian Beef Curry from Madras

This is the most basic and traditional curry. The same ingredients and technique may be used when substituting other meats, seafood or vegetables.

Preparation time: 15 minutes
Cooking time: 45 minutes to 1 hour

Serves 4 to 6, depending on the
accompanying dishes

S H O P P I N G   A N D   T E C H N I Q U E   T I P S

Cuts of meat such as lean chuck or round *(rump or topside)* are suitable for curries because of the lengthy simmering time, which will tenderize them. Trim off any fat and sinew.

INGREDIENTS	PREPARATION
2 to 3 *(about 2)* tablespoons of Indian Curry Spice Mix (the increased amount gives a stronger-flavored curry) (page 116)	
3 tablespoons *(1 ½ fluid ounces)* of white vinegar	
4 tablespoons *(2 ounces)* of Indian Clarified Butter (page 139)	
2 large onions	Peeled and chopped, patted dry
2 cloves of garlic	Peeled and finely chopped
2 pounds of lean beef	Cut into 1-inch cubes, patted dry
1 *(¾)* teaspoon of salt	
3 *(tinned)* canned tomatoes	Drained and chopped
½ cup *(4 fluid ounces)* of Coconut Milk (page 114) or water	
¼ to ½ *(up to ⅓)* teaspoon of Indian Sweet Spice Mix (page 118)	

M E T H O D

1. In a small bowl, mix the Curry Spice Mix and the vinegar into a paste. Set aside.

2. Heat the Clarified Butter in a saucepan over medium heat until it has melted and a slight haze forms on top. Add the onions and garlic and fry them, stirring, until the onions are a deep gold. Add the paste from step 1 and fry

it, stirring continuously, until the paste changes color and the sharp odors mellow (about 3 minutes).

3. Increase the heat to high and add the beef cubes. Stir and mix them in the paste and onion mixture until they are coated and look brown. Scrape the bottom of the pan with the wooden spoon while you are doing this so that the paste does not stick and burn. Sprinkle the meat with salt and reduce the heat to low. Cover the pan and simmer, uncovering to stir occasionally, for up to 30 minutes. During this time a thick gravy will form.

4. Add the tomatoes, re-cover and simmer for 5 more minutes. Now uncover and pour in the Coconut Milk or water. Increase the heat to medium-high and bring the liquid to a boil. Immediately reduce the heat to low again, add the Indian Sweet Spice Mix, and simmer, uncovered, stirring from time to time, for another 10 minutes, or until the beef is tender and the gravy has thickened again to a consistency of thin custard. Curry is very forgiving, and if you should cook the dish longer, you will merely have more tender meat and a thicker, more concentrated gravy.

5. Pour the curry into a serving bowl and leave in a warm oven until you are ready to serve. Accompany with plain or *pilau* rice, a lentil dish and perhaps a vegetable dish and a chutney, if you are making it an occasion for entertaining. A rice accompaniment and a chutney or *raita,* or perhaps a deep-fried snack, are sufficient for a family meal.

ADVANCE PREPARATION AND
STORAGE NOTES

An all-meat curry, like this one, freezes beautifully. You may make it at your leisure and freeze it in a freezer bag. Defrost and warm in the oven in a covered baking dish or on top of the stove in a saucepan. You may need to add a little more water or coconut milk to reconstitute the gravy. The curry is better eaten the next day; the flavor is better balanced (rather like a *chile con carne*). It can be refrigerated, covered, for up to 24 hours.

Beef and Vegetable Variation

Add 2 or 3 medium potatoes, cut into 2-inch pieces, with the tomatoes in step 4. One-half cup *(2¼ ounces)* of fresh or frozen peas should be added about 5 minutes before the end of the cooking. The curry will be more substantial with these vegetables and will serve 1 or 2 extra people. It may be refrigerated, but may not be frozen because the potatoes will become mushy.

✿ Muslim Beef Curry from Thailand

This hybrid curry of mixed Indian and Thai ancestry makes a satisfying meal. Its flavor and aroma improve with keeping.

Preparation time: 15 minutes   Serves 6 to 8, with rice
Cooking time: 45 to 50 minutes

SHOPPING AND TECHNIQUE TIPS

Again, choose an inexpensive cut of beef. You may use ordinary roasted peanuts or the dry-roasted variety. Whole cardamom pods can be found in jars in better spice departments. This is a "wet" curry and the spice paste is added halfway through.

INGREDIENTS

2½ pound of beef (chuck, round, *(rump, topside)* or other inexpensive cut)

4 cups *(32 fluid ounces)* of thick Coconut Milk (page 114), or 4 cups *(32 fluid ounces)* of half-and-half *(half cream, half milk)* flavored with 2 *(1⅔)* teaspoons of coconut extract

½ cup *(2⅔ ounces)* of roasted peanuts

3 tablespoons *(1½ ounces)* of Southeast Asian fish sauce

2 medium potatoes (optional)

6 *(4¾)* tablespoons of Thai Muslim Curry Spice Paste (page 125)

2-inch stick of cinnamon

8 whole cardamom pods

1 *(¾)* teaspoon of molasses *(treacle)*

Juice of 2 limes

2 *(1⅔)* tablespoons of moist dark-brown sugar

PREPARATION

Trimmed of most fat and cut into ½-inch cubes

Peeled and cut into 2-inch pieces

METHOD

1. Place the beef, Coconut Milk (or flavored half-and-half), peanuts and

fish sauce in a wok or large saucepan. Bring to a boil over medium-high heat. Reduce the heat to low and simmer, stirring occasionally, for 20 minutes. Add the potatoes (if you are using them) and continue to cook until the potatoes are tender but still firm. (If not, simply continue to cook until the beef is tender.)

2. Remove the meat, potatoes and peanuts to a bowl with a slotted spoon, then increase the heat to high and boil the sauce until it is reduced to half its volume. Now stir in the Curry Spice Paste until the gravy becomes smooth and thickens considerably. Return the removed ingredients to the pan and add the cinnamon stick and cardamoms.

3. Reduce the heat to low again and simmer for 5 minutes. Stir in the molasses *(treacle),* lime juice and sugar. Remove the curry from the heat and transfer the contents to a serving bowl. Remove the cinnamon stick. The curry should be accompanied by plain rice.

ADVANCE PREPARATION AND STORAGE NOTES

This curry can be refrigerated overnight, covered, and is more aromatic on the second day. If you omit the potatoes, it freezes very well. It should be thawed at room temperature and then transferred to a saucepan to be reheated. You will need to add ½ cup *(4 fluid ounces)* of coconut milk or plain milk to reconstitute the gravy to its former consistency.

❧ Indonesian Lamb Curry from Sumatra

The Indonesian name for this curry is *Gule Kambing;* it is of Indian and Arabic origin. In the fifteenth century, traders brought such dishes with them to the Spice Islands (Indonesia), and recipes vary from island to island. This recipe is from the north of the large island of Sumatra and is similar to some of the Malay curries.

Preparation time: 20 minutes   Serves 6
Cooking time: 25 minutes

SHOPPING AND TECHNIQUE TIPS

Leg of lamb is the most suitable for this dish. Either buy it boned or remove the meat from the bone yourself. Remember that the bone is heavy and that you must allow about an additional 1½ pounds for it in the total weight. Blanch the tomato briefly in boiling water until the skin splits, then let it cool slightly and peel it.

INGREDIENTS

4 tablespoons *(2 fluid ounces)* of peanut oil

½ cup *(6⅓ tablespoons)* of Indonesian Curry Spice Paste (page 127)

2 pounds of lean lamb (without bone)

1 large tomato

2½ cups *(1 pint)* of thick Coconut Milk (page 114), or 2½ cups *(1 pint)* of milk flavored with 2 *(1⅔)* teaspoons of coconut extract

The outer yellow peel (zest) from ½ a lemon

1 *(¾)* teaspoon of salt

Juice of 1 lime

PREPARATION

Cut into ¾-inch cubes

Peeled and coarsely chopped

Peeled in 1 or 2 strips

METHOD

1. Heat the oil in a wok over medium-high heat and add the Curry Spice Paste. Stirring continuously, fry the paste for 3 minutes until it darkens and the odor mellows. Scrape the bottom of the pan while you are frying to make sure that the paste does not catch and burn.

2. Now add the cubes of lamb and stir-fry them, turning them over until brown on all sides and completely coated with the paste.

3. Add the tomato pieces, pour in the Coconut Milk and add the lemon peel and salt. Bring the mixture to a boil, cover, reduce the heat to low and simmer for 10 minutes. Uncover, pick out the lemon peel, turn off the heat and stir in the lime juice. Transfer the curry to a serving bowl and accompany with plain rice.

ADVANCE PREPARATION AND STORAGE NOTES

This curry may be made ahead of time and refrigerated overnight. It may also be frozen, but after defrosting, ½ cup *(4 fluid ounces)* of additional Coconut Milk should be stirred in while you are reheating it, to bring the gravy back to the proper consistency.

Beef Curry Variation

This is a dry curry without gravy. Substitute 2 pounds of chuck, *(rump, topside)* or beef round for the lamb and cut into ½-inch cubes. Follow the method for the previous curry, but in step 3, after simmering it for 10 minutes, continue to cook the curry until the gravy has completely evaporated. At this stage you will need to stir continuously once again to make sure that the dish does not burn. Add another 2 *(1⅔)* tablespoons of peanut oil and continue to stir-fry the coated meat for another 5 minutes. The meat will now be fragrant, heavily coated and dry, with a little residual oil. Transfer to a serving dish and serve with a gravied vegetable dish.

❦ Indian Pork Curry

Whenever you find pork used in an Indian dish, you know that dish originated in the central or southern part of India. The reason is religious, not geographical. This spicy curry is a standard among Hindus, who may eat pork, but not beef— and the Hindus generally populate the southern areas of the subcontinent.

This curry is called a *vindaloo* and the Indian Sharp Spice Paste complements the richness of the pork. In hot and humid southern India, the meat is marinated in vinegar before it is cooked in the spices. Not only does this technique help to cut the oiliness of the pork, but it also helps to preserve it.

This delicious dish is one of the most requested of the Indian curries that I cook and I often include it in curry lunch buffets.

Preparation time: 15 minutes   Serves 6 (or 8, if other dishes are
Cooking time: 40 minutes   added)

SHOPPING AND TECHNIQUE TIPS
Shoulder butt, picnic shoulder or loin are suitable cuts for this dish. The pork should be marbled with fat. Cut off any large pieces of fat when cubing the meat. If you find too much oil at the conclusion of cooking, merely skim it off. Malt, cider or white vinegar may be used for the marinade.

INGREDIENTS
3 pounds of pork
½ cup *(4 fluid ounces)* of vinegar
3 *(2⅓)* tablespoons of Indian
     Clarified Butter (page 139), or
     vegetable oil

PREPARATION
Cut into ½-inch cubes

INGREDIENTS	PREPARATION
2 large onions	Peeled and finely chopped
3 cloves of garlic	Peeled and finely chopped
3 *(2 ⅓)* tablespoons of Indian Sharp Spice Paste (page 121) (add another tablespoon if a stronger curry is wanted)	
½ cup *(4 fluid ounces)* of water (if necessary)	
1 *(¾)* teaspoon of salt	

METHOD

1. Place the pork in a large bowl and pour the vinegar over. Let it marinate for 10 minutes, stirring from time to time to ensure that all the pork comes in contact with the vinegar.

2. Heat the Clarified Butter over medium heat and fry the onions, stirring for 3 minutes. Add the garlic and continue to stir and fry until the onions are translucent.

3. Add the Sharp Spice Paste and reduce the heat to low. Fry the mixture for 3 minutes, stirring continually to prevent it from sticking to the pan. During this time the sharpness of the spice paste will mellow.

4. Drain the pork and add it to the pan. Increase the heat to medium and cook for 5 minutes, stirring until the pork is thoroughly coated with the paste.

5. Cover, reduce the heat to low, and cook for 20 minutes. Check from time to time, stirring and adding a little water if the pork appears too dry. Toward the end of the cooking time there should be enough liquid to form a small amount of rich, thick gravy.

6. Add the salt, transfer to a serving dish and serve with plain rice.

ADVANCE PREPARATION AND
STORAGE NOTES

This curry can be cooked a day ahead and refrigerated. In fact, the flavor is better on the second day. Reheat over a gentle flame and add ¼ to ½ cup *(2 to 4 fluid ounces)* of additional water. The curry freezes well. Cool after cooking and freeze in freezer container with a tight lid, or a large freezer-weight plastic lock-top bag.

Thaw at room temperature and warm in a saucepan or in a heatproof dish in a low oven. Whether simply refrigerated or frozen, add ¼ to ½ cup *(2 to 4 fluid ounces)* of water when reheating. A dish of bland lentils is the ideal accompaniment.

❧ Malaysian Pork Curry

This dish from Malacca is often referred to as "devil's curry," probably because of the heat and spiciness of the ingredients. I first ate it in Singapore, which is the culinary melting pot of the Malay, Chinese and Indian cuisines. It was so delicious that I couldn't wait until I had re-created it in my own kitchen. As you can see, the technique is similar to the previous southern Indian Pork Curry, and the Indian influence on the dish is plain. The Malaysian Spice Paste ingredients make it totally different, however, and you will find no resemblance to the traditional flavor associated with "curry."

Preparation time: 40 minutes   Serves 4 (6 with 1 other dish)
Cooking time: 60 minutes

SHOPPING AND TECHNIQUE TIPS
As in the preceding Indian Pork Curry recipe, but use white vinegar, not malt or cider, for the marinade. Use the Indonesian Dark Sweet Soy Sauce (page 142) instead of regular soy sauce.

INGREDIENTS   PREPARATION
1½ pounds of pork   Cut into ½-inch cubes
3 tablespoons *(1½ fluid ounces)* of
    white vinegar
2 *(1⅔)* tablespoons of Indonesian
    Dark Sweet Soy Sauce (page 142)
2 *(1⅔)* tablespoons of vegetable oil
1 large red onion   Peeled and chopped
4 cloves of garlic   Peeled and chopped
1-inch piece of fresh ginger root   Peeled and thinly sliced
4 *(3⅓)* tablespoons of Malaysian
    Curry Spice Paste (page 130)
1½ cups *(12 fluid ounces)* of Basic
    Pork Stock (Southeast Asian
    variation) (page 170)
½ *(⅓)* teaspoon of salt
½ *(⅓)* teaspoon of ground black
    pepper

METHOD
1. Place the pork in a large bowl and pour the vinegar and Dark Sweet Soy Sauce over. Let it marinate for 30 minutes.
2. Heat the vegetable oil over medium heat and fry the onion, garlic and ginger, stirring for 3 minutes, or until the onions are translucent.

3. Add the Malaysian Curry Spice Paste and reduce the heat to low. Fry the mixture for 3 minutes, stirring continually to prevent it from sticking to the wok.

4. Drain the pork and add it to the wok. Increase the heat to medium and continue to cook and stir for 5 more minutes.

5. Add the Pork Stock and season with salt and pepper. Increase the heat to high and bring to a boil. Reduce the heat to low, cover and simmer for 20 minutes. Do *not* open the lid during this period, but shake the wok from time to time to prevent the contents from sticking.

6. Remove the lid, increase the heat to medium and cook, stirring from time to time, until the liquid is absorbed. Towards the end of this period, stir more frequently as the liquid evaporates, to prevent the pork from sticking.

7. Transfer to a serving bowl and accompany with plain rice.

ADVANCE PREPARATION AND
STORAGE NOTES

As in the Indian Pork Curry. However, when reheating, add only 2 to 3 (1⅔ to 2 ⅓) tablespoons of water, just to help the process along, but not to provide a gravy, as this curry should be dry.

❧ Thai Pork Curry, Country Style

This curry is more robust than most Thai curries, as it includes a variety of vegetables with the pork. It is also economical, requiring a smaller amount of meat than the previous curries. Country style refers to the above attributes and also to the fact that it does not contain coconut milk, unlike most Thai curries, and can therefore be made in a short period of time.

Preparation time: 20 minutes   Cooking time: 20 minutes
                                      Serves 6

SHOPPING AND TECHNIQUE TIPS

Leaner pork, such as loin, is preferable for this Thai curry. Alternatively, you may buy pork chops and remove the meat from the bones. In the latter case, the meat should weigh 1 pound after boning, so allow for the weight of the bones when selecting the pork chops. This dish is essentially a stir-fry followed by braising in a little liquid. The vegetables are soaked in ice water before adding to the wok so that they retain their crispness and color. Vary the vegetables according to what is in season and in prime quality.

INGREDIENTS

4 *(2 fluid ounces)* tablespoons of
   vegetable oil
3 *(2⅓)* tablespoons of Thai Curry
   Spice Paste (page 124)
1 pound of lean pork

2 *(1⅔)* tablespoons of Southeast
   Asian fish sauce
1 cup *(¼ pound)* of green beans

2 zucchini *(courgettes)*

4-inch-segment of long white Oriental
   radish
1 cup *(¼ pound)* of cabbage (any
   variety)
2 red or green fresh Serrano chilli
   peppers, or 1 Jalapeño chilli
   pepper
2 *(1⅔)* tablespoons of Tamarind
   Substitute (page 137)
30+ mint or basil leaves

PREPARATION

Cut into thin slices and then into
   strips, about 2 inches long by ½
   inch wide

Topped and tailed, cut diagonally
   into 2-inch lengths, soaked in ice
   water
Stem ends removed, quartered
   lengthwise, cut into 1-inch pieces,
   soaked in ice water
Cut into 1-inch cubes, soaked in ice
   water
Coarsely shredded, soaked in ice
   water
Halved, seeds and membranes
   removed, cut into thin slivers

Chopped

METHOD

1. Heat the oil in a wok over high heat. Add the Thai Curry Spice Paste
and stir-fry, for 3 minutes, until the color darkens and the odor mellows,
scraping the wok so the paste does not stick.

2. Add the pork and stir-fry for 5 minutes, working it with a spatula so
that it is completely coated with the paste. Season with the fish sauce.

3. Drain the vegetables well and add them to the wok. Stir-fry them for
5 minutes, then add the chilli pepper strips and Tamarind Substitute. Reduce
the heat to low, cover the wok and let the curry simmer for 3 minutes.

4. Uncover, stir, transfer to a serving bowl and sprinkle with the mint or
basil leaves. Serve with plain rice.

ADVANCE PREPARATION AND
STORAGE NOTES

The preparation of the meat and vegetables can be done ahead and they
can be refrigerated until cooking time. The curry should be cooked just before

serving as the vegetables will lose their crispness with reheating. This dish does not freeze well.

THE BALL CURRIES
OF INDIA

In India, food is molded into balls which are called *koftas.* These are found throughout every regional cuisine in the country and can be made from meat, poultry, fish or vegetables. Sometimes the ingredients are formed into small balls or sausage shapes and fried, to be served as snacks; sometimes the balls are served in thick, spiced sauces as curries.

In the north, from Kashmir to the Punjab and what is now Pakistan, meatballs are most frequently formed from ground lamb and spices, sometimes served alone, or slowly simmered in a rich cream gravy. An even more elaborate version, made with either ground lamb or beef, calls for the spiced mixture to be wrapped around hardcooked eggs before frying and saucing. These are called *nargisi* or *nargesi kofta* because, when they are cut open, the yellow-and-white centers remind people of the *nargis* or narcissus flowers found in the hills in springtime. These "narcissus meatballs" are generally served on special occasions and were featured frequently in the lavish banquets of the Moghul emperors.

Beef meatballs are common throughout central India and the Deccan and some of the more classic versions come from around the city of Madras. Fish, seafood and vegetable balls are found along the southern sea coasts and in vegetarian southern India. Vegetable ball curries are made from a surprising variety of ingredients including lentils, coconut, pumpkin, spinach, potatoes, lotus roots and even green bananas and papayas. Most of the vegetable *koftas* are thickened and held together with *besan,* or split-pea flour.

Let's take a look at a classic ground-beef meatball curry and then follow it through some variations. After cooking several of these, you will be able to make up your own versions, both meat and vegetable. They are all delicious and inexpensive; they can be made ahead and generally freeze easily. No wonder they are so popular.

☙ Indian Meatball Curry from Madras

Preparation time: 35 minutes
Cooking time: 1 hour

Makes 24 1-inch to 1½-inch
  meatballs
Serves 4

SHOPPING AND TECHNIQUE TIPS

Purchase lean ground beef and ask the butcher to put the meat through the grinder twice, as it must be finely ground. Alternatively, if you have a food processor or meat grinder, process or grind it yourself a second time. (An advantage of possessing your own grinder is that you can choose your cuts of meat and control the lean-fat ratio.)

Some people extend and bind the meat with split-pea flour but I do not; however, I think that the making of meatballs, whether Indian or Western, is as individualistic as making a meat loaf or any other ground meat dish: everybody has a favorite or traditional family method. Sometimes the meatballs are coated with beaten egg before being fried; other recipes call for the egg to be mixed with the ingredients. When you are frying the meatballs, rotate the pan rapidly. This allows the balls to roll around and helps them retain their shape. Meatballs also benefit from being made ahead and allowed to "sit" after frying. When they have cooled and firmed, they are far less likely to break up in the curry sauce.

INGREDIENTS
Meatballs

INGREDIENTS	PREPARATION
1 small onion	Peeled and finely chopped
1 small sweet green pepper	Seeded, cored and finely chopped
15 coriander (Chinese parsley, cilantro) leaves, or parsley	Chopped
2 cloves of garlic	Crushed, peeled and chopped
1 pound of lean, finely ground (minced) beef	Twice ground
2 (1⅔) teaspoons of salt (or to taste)	
1 (¾) teaspoon of Indian Sweet Spice Mix (page 118)	
½ (⅓) teaspoon of ground red pepper (Cayenne)	
½ (⅓) teaspoon of ground cumin	
1 egg	Beaten with 2 tablespoons of water
¼ cup (4 ounces) Indian Clarified Butter (page 139), or vegetable oil, if shallow-frying, or 3 cups of vegetable oil for deep-fat frying	

METHOD

1. In a food processor or blender (or a large mortar if you have neither), coarsely grind the onion, pepper, coriander and garlic.

2. Place the ground *(minced)* beef in a large mixing bowl and combine it with the mixture from the processor. Add the salt, Indian Sweet Spice Mix, red pepper and cumin. Knead until it becomes a smooth, uniform mixture.

3. If using a deep-fryer, begin to heat the oil. It should reach 350°F. *(175°C.)*.

4. Form the mixture into balls, 1 inch in diameter (about the size of large marbles). If the mixture is sticky, chill it for 10 minutes before rolling the balls. Roll the balls lightly but thoroughly between the palms of the hands. Many meatballs break open in frying because they are not rolled long enough. There should be no cracks in the meat mixture.

5. If using a skillet or wok and Indian Clarified Butter or oil for shallow-frying, heat the fat until a slight haze forms over the surface.

6. Dip each meatball in the beaten egg mixture and fry, 4 or 5 at a time, until the outsides are crusty and brown. (If you are not going to cook the meatballs in a curry sauce, fry them for 3 to 4 minutes. If you are cooking them further, merely brown the outsides.)

7. Drain the meatballs on paper towels and leave to cool. (In this state, they can be served either hot or cold as hors d'oeuvres, accompanied by a fresh chutney dip.)

Curry Sauce

You may either want to serve them in the Quick All-Purpose Indian Curry Sauce (page 143) or in the Curry Sauce below.

INGREDIENTS	PREPARATION
¼ cup *(4 ounces)* of Indian Clarified Butter (page 139)	
3 large onions	Peeled and chopped
2" piece of fresh ginger root	Peeled and minced
8 cloves of garlic	Crushed, peeled and chopped
1 cup *(8 fluid ounces)* of plain yogurt	
1 *(¾)* tablespoon of Indian Sweet Spice Mix (page 118)	
1 *(¾)* teaspoon of ground turmeric	
½ *(⅓)* teaspoon of ground red pepper (Cayenne)	
1 *(¾)* teaspoon of salt	
3 canned, peeled tomatoes and their juice (making 1 cup in all)	Chopped

INGREDIENTS   PREPARATION
1½ cups *(12 fluid ounces)* of water
¼ cup *(1 ounce)* of coriander   Chopped
    (Chinese parsley, *cilantro*) leaves

METHOD

1. Heat the Clarified Butter in a saucepan over medium heat. Add the onions and fry, stirring continually, until the onions are light gold and translucent.

2. Using a slotted spoon, drain them over the saucepan and transfer to the bowl of a processor or blender. Turn off the heat under the saucepan.

3. Add the ginger, garlic and yogurt to the processor and process to a smooth puree, stopping the machine from time to time to scrape down the sides with a spatula.

4. Heat the saucepan again over medium heat until the clarified butter is back to heat, then fry the puree, stirring, for 6 minutes, until the odors have blended and mellowed.

5. Add the Indian Sweet Spice Mix, turmeric, red pepper and salt. Stir and cook for 5 more minutes until the spices have blended in. Now stir in the tomatoes and water. Increase the heat to high and bring to a boil. Reduce the heat to medium-low and simmer, stirring from time to time, for 10 minutes.

6. Add the meatballs, stir gently to coat them with the sauce, then cover the pan and let them heat through for 10 minutes.

7. Transfer the meatballs to a serving bowl with a spoon and pour the sauce over the top. Sprinkle with the coriander leaves and serve, accompanied by plain rice. (For special occasions, you could serve it with an Indian sautéed rice dish, *pilau,* pages 108, 372–79).

ADVANCE PREPARATION AND
STORAGE NOTES

This is the perfect do-ahead dish. The meatballs can be made and fried and then refrigerated or frozen until they are wanted. The curry sauce can also be made ahead of time and refrigerated or frozen. The dish can be made and combined a day ahead (in which case, the meatballs are even more fragrant as they absorb the spices from the sauce). The entire dish can be made ahead and, when carefully wrapped, frozen for up to 2 months. Thaw at room temperature and reheat, stirring in 4 to 6 tablespoons of plain yogurt to make the sauce creamy again.

Meat-Wrapped Egg Variation

These are the "narcissus meatballs" or *nargisi kofta* mentioned in the general discussion of ball curries, page 341. The Western dish closest to them is Scotch eggs. The British took the idea back from India but, somewhere along the way, this delicious dish lost out in its translation to hard-boiled eggs wrapped in sausage meat and breadcrumbs—beloved fare of the railway station buffets in England! This original is far nicer.

When I recently appeared as a guest cook on a national television show, I prepared these meatballs. Being thoroughly immersed in demonstrating the technique of coaxing the ground *(minced)* meat up and around the eggs, I was oblivious to the host's intent gaze until he remarked that I was obviously enjoying a sensual experience. Well, I was. Preparing food is very satisfying to the senses, and forming these balls is as tactile as modeling in clay. To change a well-known saying, "If you don't like to handle food, stay out of the kitchen!"

Preparation time: 40 minutes   Serves 8 to 10
Cooking time: 1 hour

SHOPPING AND TECHNIQUE TIPS

Use the smallest eggs you can find for the centers of the meatballs—otherwise they become gargantuan. If you wish to serve them for hors d'oeuvres, why not look for fresh or canned quail eggs and make miniature *koftas*?

The secret in making these is to coax the ground meat around the eggs. Do not stretch it or, as the meat contracts in the frying, it will pull away and your eggs will have bald patches. The chick-pea flour helps bind the meat so that it stays in place. Roll the coating firmly but gently and inspect the finished egg balls before frying to make sure there are no hairline cracks in the coating.

Meat-Wrapped Eggs

INGREDIENTS	PREPARATION
2 pounds of lean beef or lamb, finely ground *(minced)*	Twice ground
2 eggs	Beaten
10 small eggs	Hard-cooked, peeled
¼ cup *(1 ounce)* of coriander (Chinese parsley, *cilantro*) leaves, or parsley	Chopped
⅓ cup *(2 ounces)* of chick-pea flour	
1¼ *(1)* teaspoons of salt	
½ *(⅓)* teaspoon of ground cumin	

INGREDIENTS

½ (⅓) teaspoon of Indian Sweet
    Spice Mix (page 118)
½ (⅓) teaspoon of ground red
    pepper (Cayenne) (optional)
3 cups (24 fluid ounces) of vegetable
    oil for deep-fat frying

METHOD

1. In a large mixing bowl, combine the meat, beaten eggs, coriander, flour, salt and spices and knead vigorously until the mixture binds and becomes smooth.

2. Divide the meat mixture into portions equivalent to the number of hard-cooked eggs—10 in this case.

3. Shape each meat portion into a patty about 4 inches in diameter. Center an egg on each patty and gently coax and shape the meat mixture around it. Carefully press the meat around the egg, making sure that there are no seams or irregularities and that the surface is smooth. Gently roll the meat into a sphere. Continue until all the eggs are properly covered, then set them aside.

4. Heat the oil in a wok or deep-fryer to 350°F. (175°C.) and deepfry the koftas, 2 or 3 at a time, until they are a rich, dark brown. Drain on paper towels and leave to cool. (In this state, they can be served either hot or cold, halved or whole, as hors d'oeuvres, accompanied by a fresh chutney dip.)

COAXING MEAT AROUND EGGS

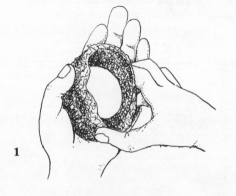

1

2

Curry Sauce

Make the Curry Sauce from the Curry Sauce recipe on page 343 and cook the egg balls in the same way as the meatballs are cooked in the Indian Meatball Curry on page 342. The same instructions and tips apply to their advance preparation and storage.

❧ Shrimp Ball Curry

This seafood-ball curry comes from southern India. The same amount of lobster or crab meat substituted for the shrimp will make a party version if you are feeling extravagant.

Preparation time: 40 minutes   Serves 6 to 8
Cooking time: 45 minutes

SHOPPING AND TECHNIQUE TIPS

Since the shrimp are to be finely chopped, the smallest shrimp you can find are satisfactory. Sometimes raw shrimp are available already shelled and cleaned in the frozen-food section of the supermarket. They certainly save a great deal of preparation time, but be sure that they are properly defrosted, washed and blotted dry in paper towels before you proceed further.

On one occasion, when I was in a hurry, I used cooked and peeled baby shrimp. The finished shrimp balls were not as flavorful and juicy, but it made a reasonable shortcut.

INGREDIENTS	PREPARATION
Shrimp Balls	
2 cups *(12½ ounces)* of shrimp	Shelled, cleaned, deveined and measured after removing shells
1 small onion	Peeled, chopped and squeezed dry in paper towels
2 cloves of garlic	Peeled and minced
½ inch of fresh ginger root	Peeled and minced
1 fresh green Serrano chilli pepper	Seeded and minced
½ *(⅓)* teaspoon of ground coriander seeds	
¼ teaspoon *(a pinch)* of ground turmeric	
½ *(⅓)* teaspoon of ground cumin	
1 egg	Beaten

INGREDIENTS

¼ cup *(1 ½ ounces)* of all-purpose
  (plain) flour
3 cups *(24 fluid ounces)* of vegetable
  oil for deep-frying

METHOD

1. Place all the ingredients, except the egg, flour and oil, into a food processor or blender and process to a smooth paste, scraping down the sides with a spatula.

2. Transfer to a large bowl, stir in the beaten egg and mix well. Add enough of the ¼ cup of flour to make a thick, uniform mass.

3. Flour your hands with the remaining flour and using your hands, separate the mass into lumps about the size of a walnut. Lightly roll them into balls and set aside.

4. Heat the oil in the wok or deep-fryer to 375°F. *(190°C.)* on a frying thermometer. Quickly fry the shrimp balls, 3 or 4 at a time, until they are golden brown and crisp on the outside. Drain them on paper towels. (At this stage they may also be served, warm, as appetizers.)

INGREDIENTS	PREPARATION
Curry Sauce	
2 *(1 ⅔)* tablespoons of Indian Clarified Butter (page 139)	
1 large onion	Peeled and sliced, top to bottom, into slivers
2 cloves of garlic	Peeled and thinly sliced
2 *(1 ⅔)* tablespoons of Indian Curry Spice Mix (page 116)	
2 cups *(16 fluid ounces)* of thick Coconut Milk (method 1 or 2, page 114)	
1 *(¾)* teaspoon of salt	
¼ teaspoon *(a generous pinch)* of Indian Sweet Spice Mix (page 118)	
1 *(¾)* tablespoon of freshly squeezed lemon juice	

METHOD

1. Heat the Clarified Butter in a saucepan over medium-high heat and fry the onion and garlic, stirring, until onion becomes soft but not brown.

2. Sprinkle in the Indian Curry Spice Mix and continue to fry, stirring constantly, for 3 minutes, until the spices mellow.

3. Pour in the thick Coconut Milk and bring to a boil, stirring. Immediately lower the heat until the mixture achieves a simmer. Simmer for 15 minutes, stirring occasionally, until the sauce is slightly thicker and somewhat creamy.

4. Add the salt and Indian Sweet Spice Mix and stir in the shrimp balls gently so as not to break them up. Warm the balls in the sauce.

5. Turn off the heat, stir in the lemon juice and transfer to a serving bowl. Serve with plain rice.

ADVANCE PREPARATION AND
STORAGE NOTES

As in the Indian Meatball Curry, page 342, but Coconut Milk should be added instead of yogurt to reconstitute the gravy after thawing or refrigeration.

❀ Coconut Ball Curry

A great curry for vegetarians, and even the most adamant meat eaters will enjoy it. This curry also originates in the south of India, from around the town of Hyderabad. The same technique of first making the balls and frying them, then concocting a sauce and lightly cooking the *koftas* in the sauce, applies to this recipe, although the ingredients of the balls and the sauce are different.

Preparation time: 20 minutes   Serves 6
Cooking time: 35 minutes

SHOPPING AND TECHNIQUE TIPS

You will find the dried, unsweetened, flaked coconut in either the health-food section of a good supermarket or in health-food stores. If fresh coconuts are in season, you may substitute 1 cup *(2 ¾ ounces)* of freshly grated coconut for the dried coconut and the water used to reconstitute it. Vary the amounts of fresh green Serrano or Jalapeño chilli peppers to suit your taste and that of your guests. If you really cannot stand the bite of chillies, substitute an equal quantity of green *(sweet)* pepper, but remember that the flavor is not exactly the same.

INGREDIENTS

Coconut Balls

1 cup *(2 ⅓ ounces)* of dried,
    unsweetened, flaked coconut
¼ cup *(2 fluid ounces)* of water
4 *(3 ¼)* tablespoons of chick-pea
    flour
4 green Serrano chilli peppers, or 2
    Jalapeño chilli peppers (or equal
    amount of chopped green bell
    pepper)
4 *(3 ¼)* tablespoons of Indian Green
    Herb and Spice Paste (page 122)
1 small onion
6 cloves of garlic
1″ piece of fresh ginger root
¼ teaspoon *(a pinch)* of ground red
    pepper (Cayenne)
1 *(¾)* teaspoon of Indian Sweet
    Spice Mix (page 118)
3 cups *(24 fluid ounces)* of vegetable
    oil for deep frying

PREPARATION

Reconstitute with the water in a
    small mixing bowl

Seeded and minced

Peeled and minced
Peeled and minced
Peeled and minced

METHOD

1. Place all the *kofta* ingredients, except the oil, in a large bowl and mix
to a stiff paste, adding a little more water if necessary. Roll into small balls,
1 inch in diameter (about the size of large marbles).

2. In a wok or deep-fryer, heat the oil to a temperature of 350°F.
(175°C.) on a frying thermometer and fry the *koftas,* a few at a time, until light
brown and crisp on the outside. Remove with a slotted spoon and drain on
paper towels.

INGREDIENTS

Curry Sauce

1 teaspoon of poppy seeds
4 whole cloves
½ *(⅓)* teaspoon of cardamom seeds
1 *(¾)* teaspoon of cumin seeds
1 inch piece of cinnamon stick
1 *(¾)* tablespoon of dried,
    unsweetened, flaked coconut
1 large onion

PREPARATION

Hulled from the pods

Broken into fragments

Peeled and chopped

INGREDIENTS	PREPARATION
4 cloves of garlic	Peeled and chopped
1-inch piece of fresh ginger root	Peeled and chopped
3 *(2⅓)* tablespoons of vegetable oil
1 *(¾)* teaspoon of ground turmeric
1 *(¾)* teaspoon (or less) of ground red pepper (Cayenne)
1 *(¾)* teaspoon of salt (or to taste)
2 *(6⅓ ounces)* cups of canned *(tinned)* tomatoes, or 2 cups of tomato puree	Finely chopped
1 cup *(8 fluid ounces)* of water
1 *(¾)* teaspoon of Indian Clarified Butter (page 139)
10 to 12 raw cashew nuts
15 or more coriander (Chinese parsley, *cilantro*) leaves	Chopped

METHOD

1. Place the first 6 ingredients, including the coconut, in a spice grinder and grind to a powder. (If you choose to use ready-ground ingredients, omit this step.)

2. Place the onion, garlic and ginger in a food processor and grind to a paste. Add the powder from the grinder and give the blades a few more turns.

3. Heat the 3 *(2⅓)* tablespoons of vegetable oil in a saucepan over medium-high heat and add the paste from the processor. Fry, stirring, until the paste darkens and mellows (about 3 to 5 minutes). Add the turmeric, red pepper and salt and fry, stirring, for 2 more minutes.

4. Pour in the tomatoes, or the tomato puree, and water, stir, increase the heat to high and bring to a boil. Reduce the heat to medium-low and continue to simmer fairly rapidly for 5 minutes.

5. Add the Coconut Balls and cook for a further 5 minutes.

6. While the balls are cooking, heat the Clarified Butter in a frying pan over medium heat and fry the cashew nuts until they turn a golden brown. Set aside.

7. Turn the curry into a serving bowl and pour the cashew nuts with the butter on top. Sprinkle with coriander leaves and serve.

ADVANCE PREPARATION AND STORAGE NOTES

Both the balls and the sauce can be made up to a day ahead of time and refrigerated, either separately or together. This curry does not freeze well.

Other vegetarian ball curries can be made from this recipe, such as:

Spinach Ball Curry

Substitute 1 *(⅘)* cup of cooked, drained and chopped spinach for the coconut and water.

Potato Ball Curry

Substitute 1 *(⅘)* cup of cooked, mashed potatoes for the coconut and water. Add ½ *(⅓)* teaspoon of salt.

Zucchini (Courgette) **Ball Curry**

Substitute 1 *(⅘)* cup of cooked, peeled and mashed zucchini *(courgette)* for the coconut and water.

Lentil or Split-Pea Ball Curry

Substitute 1 *(⅘)* cup of cooked, drained and mashed lentils or split-peas for the coconut and water. Add ½ *(⅓)* teaspoon of salt.

❀ Thai Meatball Curry

This Thai version shows the Indian influence in the technique, but most of the ingredients are uniquely Thai.

Preparation time: 35 minutes
Cooking time: 30 minutes

Makes 24 1-inch-to-1½-inch
   meatballs
Serves 4 to 6

SHOPPING AND TECHNIQUE TIPS
This recipe calls for medium-lean ground beef and the meat does not need to be ground twice. The egg is mixed into the meat mixture and the balls are coated with flour before being fried.

INGREDIENTS
Meatballs

PREPARATION

4 cloves of garlic	Peeled and chopped
5 to 6 coriander (Chinese parsley, *cilantro*) stems and leaves	Chopped
1 *(¾)* teaspoon of ground black pepper	
2 shallots	Peeled and chopped
½ *(⅓)* teaspoon of ground cumin	
1 *(¾)* teaspoon of salt	
1 pound of medium-lean ground *(minced)* beef	
1 egg	Beaten
½ cup *(3 ounces)* of all-purpose *(plain)* flour	
1 cup *(8 fluid ounces)* of vegetable oil	

METHOD

1. Place all the ingredients up to (but not including) the ground *(minced)* beef into a food processor and process into a paste.

2. Place the ground *(minced)* beef in a large mixing bowl and combine it with the mixture from the processor. Add the egg and mix well.

3. As in step 3 of the Indian Meatball Curry recipe.

4. As in step 4 of the Indian Meatball Curry, but the balls should be lightly rolled in flour after forming.

5. Fry the meatballs, 4 or 5 at a time, until the outsides are crusty and brown. Drain them on paper towels and leave to cool. (In this state, they can be served either hot or cold as an hors d'oeuvre, accompanied by a Thai dipping sauce.)

INGREDIENTS
Curry Sauce

PREPARATION

2 *(1⅔)* tablespoons of oil left in the wok	
4 cloves of garlic	Peeled and minced
2 *(1⅔)* tablespoons of Thai Curry Spice Paste (page 124)	
2 cups *(16 fluid ounces)* of thick Coconut Milk (page 114)	

INGREDIENTS	PREPARATION
2 *(1⅔)* tablespoons of chunky peanut butter, or 14 to 16 of roasted peanuts	Coarsely ground
1½ *(1¼)* tablespoons of granulated sugar	
2 *(1⅔)* tablespoons of Southeast Asian fish sauce	
10 to 15 of mint or sweet basil leaves	Chopped

METHOD

1. Empty all the oil but 2 *(1⅔)* tablespoons from the wok and set it back over medium-high heat. Fry the garlic briefly, stirring, until golden. (Do not overcook.)

2. Stir in the Curry Spice Paste and fry, stirring, until the odor has mellowed (about 3 minutes).

3. Pour in the thick Coconut Milk and stir in the peanut butter. Continue stirring and simmering until the sauce has a smooth, uniform consistency. Season with the sugar and fish sauce.

4. Return the meatballs to the wok, stirring for 5 minutes, until the balls are heated through.

5. Transfer the meatballs and sauce to a serving bowl. Sprinkle with the mint or sweet basil leaves and serve, accompanied by plain rice.

ADVANCE PREPARATION AND
STORAGE NOTES

As in the Indian Meatball Curry. However, when the curry has been frozen and thawed, reconstitute with ½ cup *(4 fluid ounces)* of coconut milk instead of the yogurt.

SLOW AND TENDER

❧ ❧ ❧

Simmering—
The Oriental Crock Pot

This technique concerns the slow-simmering of meat in a flavored liquid over a low heat for a long period of time. The dishes thus produced fall into two basic categories.

The first is the cooking of a single variety of meat in liquid with spices —much the same as we in the West will boil a ham. The second is the simmering of a mixture of meat and vegetables to produce a stewlike dish. In technique, the curries in the preceding chapter would actually come under the latter category, but their spicing is so unique and their variety so wide that they deserve a chapter of their own.

These slow-simmered dishes are basically Chinese in origin, for the earliest culinary reference to their practice occurred in ancient China during the twelfth century B.C. at the commencement of the Chou period. The Chou Chinese boiled and simmered much of their food. The most widely known dish was a *keng,* a kind of meat soup or stew. In Southeast Asia today, the term *keng (gaeng)* is still used to describe a whole range of gravied dishes.

A *keng* might contain vegetables, grains and mixed meats; another version, called a *ta-keng,* or grand stew, was made with a single meat: ox, pig, sheep, deer, chicken, duck, pheasant, etc. Traditionally these stews were cooked in heavy metal caldrons set on tripods.

Much later on, at the time of the Mongol invasion, thirteenth- and fourteenth-century travelers described meals shared with the "barbarians" that consisted of a whole, boiled sheep which was cut up in front of the guests. Today, mutton is still characteristic fare in northern China.

The northern cuisine contains many dishes which are slow-simmered, and pot dishes and "red-cooked" foods are common. Slow-cooking is the appropriate technique for large cuts of meat and whole birds, and for ingredients that need prolonged simmering to make them tender. These dishes are cooked in a heavy pot or a container similar to a Dutch oven.

"Red-cooked" dishes are meats stewed in water and soy sauce, producing a ruddy color in the finished food. Dark soy sauce is used for its color, although light soy is sometimes added for additional flavor. The meat is generally braised rather than stewed. It is first browned rapidly in oil, and the liquid is then added together with seasonings such as ginger and sherry. The dish is then covered and simmered over a low heat until tender, the meat being turned from time to time so that it colors evenly. This style of cooking typically produces a rich, red-brown gravy which is served either with the meat or reserved as a separate sauce for noodles or rice.

When the gravy is reserved for another and subsequent use it is referred to as a "master sauce." This sauce will consist of the gravy and additional water and seasonings. It is used as a cooking medium for other meats and poultry dishes, after which it is again retained for further use. Each time it is cooked, it takes on additional flavor from the new ingredients, becoming progressively richer and more complex in character. The master sauce is refrigerated between uses and is boiled at least once a week, the soy sauce and sherry being replenished from time to time.

Master sauces keep almost indefinitely. It is common for them to last throughout a generation, and there are records of some that are almost 100 years old!

Red-cooked foods can be prepared well in advance and will keep for a week under refrigeration, being rewarmed before eating. If vegetables are to be included, they are cooked only in sufficient quantity for that particular meal —leftover vegetables are not saved with the meat. Root vegetables are added during the last half-hour of cooking; young, tender vegetables are stir-fried separately and added to the sauce at the last minute to warm through. Red-cooked meats are also served cold, and the accompanying gravy becomes an aspic-like jelly. Vegetables are not included in cold dishes as they tend to become saturated with the gravy and somewhat spongy and unappetizing.

In Southeast Asia, the soy sauce used in red-cooking by the Chinese is replaced with fish sauce, and sugar is often added to balance the salt content. This is a common method of cooking whole cuts of pork.

Another variation in slow-cooking is clear-simmering (sometimes referred to as white-stewing), where meat and vegetables are cooked in water or stock only, the soy sauce being omitted. White meats such as chicken or fish are used, and the dishes are more delicate in flavor. The resultant liquid is often strained off to become a basis for clear soup. Meats to be clear-simmered are often scalded in boiling water first to seal in the juices.

In the cuisine of India, many dishes are simmered in pots called *dekshis,* including the whole range of curries. There is a category of dishes, however, that corresponds roughly to the slow-cooking technique of the far Orient— these are known as *kormas.*

In a *korma,* the meat is braised in water, stock, yogurt or cream, or a mixture of all of the above. The braising is traditionally carried out over a slow fire, and additional coals or lumps of charcoal are placed on the lid of the container, the heat being applied above and below the dish. The same effect can be obtained by starting the dish on top of the stove and then transfering the contents to a casserole and cooking it in the oven. The whole process works quite well on top of the stove, although the dish has to be watched to ensure that the contents do not catch fire and burn.

The meat is first marinated in a spiced liquid and then drained and browned in butter or oil. The marinade is combined with a spice paste and added gradually to the meat during the frying process. Each time liquid is added, the meat is cooked until the moisture evaporates. During the cooking period, additional liquid is added several times. The final dish may be served with its liquid, or it may be cooked until the liquid has evaporated and produced a glaze on the meat. The finished appearance is dictated by the individual recipe.

Now, a look at the basic technique of simmering meat. Simmering takes place at about 200°F. *(93.3°C.).* At this temperature the collagen in the connective tissues breaks down and turns into water-soluble gelatin. The fibers of the meat separate and it becomes tender. If the meat boils vigorously at a higher temperature, the fibers toughen and the texture becomes stringy and rubbery.

You can check a simmer by watching the surface of the liquid. Bubbles should rise to the surface slowly and lazily, breaking and popping intermittently. The liquid should be barely moving.

The use of acids in the gravy or stock, such as sherry or other wine, vinegar or citrus juices, softens the connective tissues in the meat, thereby shortening the cooking time needed for it to become tender. These are introduced at the beginning of the simmer for maximum effect. If wines are added at the end, they have no time to tenderize the meat, and are merely used for flavor.

A heavy pan with a tight-fitting lid is the most suitable container for slow-cooked foods. If the meat is to be browned first, the thick base of a heavy pan will withstand the degree of heat necessary for the frying process without warping and buckling. A solid and well-seasoned cast-iron casserole is most appropriate.

The chief difference between braising and stewing is that braised meats are usually cooked in one piece, and stewed foods are cooked in a greater quantity of liquid and the meat is generally cut into pieces beforehand. In stewing, the vegetables are served with the meat, whereas in braising, they may be used for flavoring only and removed before serving.

Braised meat is always well done. The nearest equivalent that we have to the Oriental technique of slow-simmering and braising meat is our pot roast, the difference being in the type of seasonings used.

❧ Philippine Braised, Stuffed Rolled Steak

In Asian cooking, this dish stands alone because the technique and ingredients show a very strong Spanish influence; however, it is such a delicious and spectacular party dish that I had to include it for you.

Preparation time: 50 minutes   Serves 8
Cooking time: 2 hours and 15
    minutes

SHOPPING AND TECHNIQUE TIPS

This dish requires a 3-pound flank *(brisket)* steak. You may ask your butcher to butterfly it for you, but it can easily be accomplished at home with a thin, long, sharp knife. Holding one hand on top of the *chilled* piece of steak, bisection it along its length, leaving about ¾ inch uncut at the far end. Open up the steak into a long strip and pound down the joining seam, then pound it along the entire length until it is flattened and the fibers are slightly broken. The filling ingredients for the roll vary from recipe to recipe, but it traditionally contains hard-cooked *(boiled)* eggs, pickles and one or two other varieties of meat. Choose the ingredients for their color as well as texture and flavor.

INGREDIENTS

3 pounds of flank *(brisket)* steak

2 *(1⅔)* tablespoons of soy sauce
2 *(1⅔)* tablespoons of lemon juice
3 cloves of garlic
2 small carrots

2 thick slices of ham
6 ounces of Mexican, Vienna or
    Portuguese sausage

2 eggs

2 long dill pickles *(large gherkins)*
2 *(1⅔)* tablespoons of seedless
    raisins
3 tablespoons *(1½ fluid ounces)* of
    lard, or oil
2 cups *(16 fluid ounces)* of water
¾ cup *(4¾ ounces)* of canned
    (tinned) tomatoes, with their
    juice
¼ cup *(2 fluid ounces)* of white
    vinegar
1 bay leaf
1 *(¾)* teaspoon of salt
½ *(⅓)* teaspoon of ground black
    pepper

PREPARATION

Butterflied, pounded and trimmed of
    excess fat

Crushed, peeled and minced
Scraped, each sliced lengthwise into 6
    strips
Cut into julienne strips
Precooked and sliced lengthwise into
    strips
Hard-cooked *(boiled)* and shelled,
    quartered lengthwise
Each sliced lengthwise into 6 strips

METHOD

1. Place the butterflied steak, cut side uppermost, in a large, shallow baking dish. Rub the exposed surface of the meat with the soy sauce, lemon juice and garlic. Let the meat stand and marinate at room temperature for at least 30 minutes.

2. Starting at the smaller end of the rectangle, arrange the carrots across and perpendicular to the grain of the meat in parallel rows, evenly spaced along the length of the steak. In similar fashion, intersperse them with evenly spaced ham, sausage, eggs and dill pickles. Sprinkle the raisins evenly along the surface. Leave an uncovered flap (about 2 inches wide) at the far end.

3. Carefully and tightly roll the steak over the filling, jelly-roll fashion, into a long, thick cylinder. As you roll, the ingredients will tend to shift outward and toward the far end, taking up the flap space which you have left. Carefully push them back into place as you roll.

PHILIPPINE STUFFED ROLLED STEAK

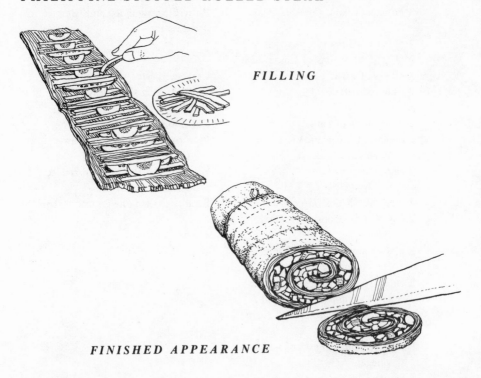

FILLING

FINISHED APPEARANCE

4. With kitchen string, secure one end of the roll with a loop and a knot. This loop should be placed about 1 inch from the end of the cylinder. With some tension on the cord, spiral the remaining length around the entire beef roll. Again, secure the string at the end, leaving about 1 inch of roll remaining.

5. Place the lard in a large, heavy saucepan and, when the fat is sputteringly hot, carefully place the roll in it. Brown the meat on all sides by turning it frequently with tongs or a fork. Regulate the temperature and turn frequently to prevent it from burning. Transfer the roll to a plate, remove the saucepan from the stove and carefully pour off all but a thin film of fat. Replace the pot on the stove.

6. Pour in the water and increase the heat to high. Vigorously scrape the browned bits at the sides and bottom of the casserole into the water. Add the remaining ingredients and bring to a boil. Reduce the heat to medium-low and return the beef roll to the pot. When the liquid returns to a boil, cover, reduce the heat to low and simmer the meat for 1½ hours, or until the meat is tender, uncovering occasionally to turn it.

7. When the meat is cooked, remove it from the pan and let it stand for

a few minutes. When it is cool enough to handle, remove the string and slice meat across into ¾-inch-wide sections, arranging them on a heat-proof platter. Place in a low oven to keep warm.

8. Drain the contents of the saucepan into a food processor or blender and whirl on high speed for a few seconds to make a sauce. Check the seasoning and intensity of flavoring. If it is not concentrated enough, you may return it to the pan and reduce it further. Strain the sauce through a sieve into a bowl and either pour it over the meat slices, or into a gravy boat to accompany the dish. I prefer the latter, as the slices are such a lovely and attractive combination of colors and patterns that it is a pity to mask them with a sauce.

ADVANCE PREPARATION AND STORAGE NOTES

This is the perfect buffet dish and can be made well ahead and left in the oven, uncut. It may also be refrigerated in its own sauce, uncut, and then cut when serving the next day. Reheat, covered with foil, in a slow oven.

✿ Chinese Beef Braised in Soy Sauce

In Chinese style, the beef in this dish is blanched briefly in boiling water to remove surplus fat before being cooked further.

Preparation time: 15 minutes   Serves 6, with rice
Cooking time: 1 hour and 45 minutes

SHOPPING AND TECHNIQUE TIPS

Unlike the less refined country stews of other cuisines, which are essentially one-pot dishes, the separate ingredients, in a technique reminiscent of the French, are brought to the stage of perfectly cooked readiness and are then combined and the sauce thickened. Use a cut of beef with plenty of connective tissue, such as brisket, blade, etc. Turnips, yams or sweet potatoes may be used instead of the Chinese radish; merely ensure that they are cooked to the right consistency before introducing them to the dish.

INGREDIENTS	PREPARATION
8-inch segment Oriental large white radish	Peeled and cut into 1-inch cubes or pieces
2 pounds of stewing beef	Trimmed of surplus fat, then cut into 1-inch cubes

INGREDIENTS

PREPARATION

½ cup *(4 fluid ounces)* of soy sauce

2 *(1⅔)* teaspoons of granulated
    sugar

1-inch piece of fresh ginger root   Peeled and cut into quarters

3 whole green *(spring)* onions

2 *(1⅔)* tablespoons of pale dry
    sherry

2 cups *(16 fluid ounces)* of water

2 *(1⅔)* teaspoons of cornstarch
    (cornflour)

1 *(¾)* tablespoon of water

1 *(¾)* teaspoon of Chinese
    All-Purpose Sauce (page 145)

METHOD

1. Fill a large saucepan (not the one you will use for the braising) with
water and suspend a sieve in it, to ensure that the bottom curve of the sieve
is well under the surface of the water. Remove the sieve and bring the water
to a rolling boil over high heat.

2. Place the radish in the sieve and immerse it in the boiling water for 5
minutes. Remove the sieve, draining it over the water, and place the radish on
a plate.

3. Now divide the beef cubes into 3 portions and blanch the meat, ⅓ at
a time, until the cubes become pale brown and the surface of the water collects
the scum and surplus fat from the meat. Drain the meat and set it aside on
another plate. Empty the pan, rinse it out and set aside.

4. Place the soy sauce, sugar, ginger, green *(spring)* onions and sherry in
a stewing pan or wok and add the beef. Bring to a boil over medium high heat,
stirring occasionally so that all sides of the beef are in contact with the flavor
mixture.

5. Now pour in the 2 cups *(16 fluid ounces)* of water, cover and bring to
a boil again. Immediately reduce the heat to low and let the meat cook for 1
hour (or until the beef is tender).

6. Using the original saucepan and sieve, pour the stock through the sieve.
Pick out and discard the green *(spring)* onions and ginger and replace the beef
in the stew pot.

7. Measure ⅔ cup *(5⅓ fluid ounces)* of the stock and add it to the beef.
Mix the cornstarch *(cornflour)*, water and All-Purpose Sauce to a smooth
consistency and stir it into the beef. Add the cooked radish and set the pot over

medium heat. Stir until the ingredients are heated through and the sauce has thickened. Transfer to a serving dish and serve, accompanied by plain rice.

ADVANCE PREPARATION AND STORAGE NOTES
Both the beef and radish can be cooked ahead of time and refrigerated. Be sure to let them come to room temperature before commencing the rest of the cooking. Retain the stock for a soup base, or reduce it further and keep for the beginning of a master stock.

❀ Vietnamese Beef Stew

My Vietnamese cook used to prepare this filling dish for us at least once a week. The children especially loved it and would request it often.

Preparation time: 15 minutes   Serves 5
Cooking time: 2½ hours

SHOPPING AND TECHNIQUE TIPS
Choose a cheaper cut of beef with quite an amount of connective tissue. The long, slow simmering will soften and allow the tissue to become glutinous, adding to the texture. You may like to substitute canned bamboo shoots for the turnips. Slice them into pieces about ½-inch thick and add them during the last 5 minutes of cooking.

INGREDIENTS	PREPARATION
1 (¾) tablespoon of vegetable oil	
2 pounds of stew beef (blade pot roast, bottom round, chuck, etc.)	Cut into 1-inch cubes (no larger), patted dry with paper towels
1-inch piece of fresh ginger root	Peeled and cut into paper-thin slices
The outer peel (zest) of 2 lemons	Grated
4 shallots	Peeled and chopped
2 cloves of garlic	Peeled and minced
½ (⅓) teaspoon of salt	
¼ teaspoon (a pinch) of freshly ground black pepper	
1 (⅓) teaspoon of granulated sugar	
8 cups (64 fluid ounces) of cold water	
One 4-inch stick of cinnamon	
2 bay leaves	

INGREDIENTS

2 *(1 ⅔)* tablespoons of Southeast
   Asian fish sauce
2 *(1 ⅔)* teaspoons of tomato paste
2 young white turnips
1 medium carrot

PREPARATION

Peeled and cut into 1-inch cubes
Scraped and roll-cut into 6 pieces

METHOD

1. Heat the oil in a pot over high heat and, when a slight haze forms over the top, brown half the beef. Remove with a slotted spoon, allow any moisture to evaporate and then brown the remainder.

2. Reintroduce the first batch and add the ginger, lemon peel, shallots and garlic, stirring after each addition. Continue to stir for 1 more minute and then season with the salt, pepper and sugar.

3. Stir again and add the water, cinnamon stick, bay leaves, fish sauce and tomato paste. Stir to blend the ingredients and then cover the pot. Bring to a boil, then reduce the heat to low and let the stew simmer for 2 hours, or until the meat is tender.

4. Remove the lid and add the turnips and carrot. Increase the heat to medium and let the stew cook, uncovered, until the vegetables are tender (about 10 minutes, depending on the age of the vegetables). Remove the cinnamon stick and bay leaves.

5. Transfer the stew to a serving bowl and serve accompanied by plain rice or rice-stick noodles.

ADVANCE PREPARATION AND
STORAGE NOTES

The stew may be cooked through step 3 and then frozen in a tightly lidded freezer container or lock-top plastic bag. Defrost, then bring back to a boil and add the vegetables. Do not freeze the stew with the vegetables as they tend to become soft and mushy.

❧ Philippine Braised Beef with Vegetables

In this braised beef dish, the beef is left whole and floured before being fried, creating a thicker gravy. In typical Philippine fashion, the sauce is a little sharp and tangy, using vinegar and tomatoes to achieve this. In Manila, this dish is called *Estofado*.

Preparation time: 15 minutes   Serves 6
Cooking time: 2½ hours

SHOPPING AND TECHNIQUE TIPS
A good-looking piece of pot-roast beef is perfect for this dish, as the meat, as in pot roast, is cooked for a long time. You may also ring in changes with the vegetables, but tomatoes should always be included for flavor and color. Fresh or canned, elongated Italian tomatoes work well.

INGREDIENTS	PREPARATION
2 pounds of pot roast beef	Lightly patted dry with paper towels
1½ tablespoons *(a rounded tablespoon)* of all-purpose *(plain)* flour	
½ *(⅓)* teaspoon of salt	
½ *(⅓)* teaspoon of freshly ground black pepper	
3 *(2⅓)* tablespoons of vegetable oil	
3 cloves of garlic	Peeled and minced
2 large onions	Peeled and finely chopped
2 large Italian tomatoes	Finely chopped
½ cup *(4 fluid ounces)* of white vinegar	
2 cups of water *(16 fluid ounces)*	
8 small white boiling onions	Peeled
1 cup *(¼ pound)* of green beans	Cut into 2-inch lengths
2 small carrots	Scraped and cut on the diagonal into 1-inch pieces

METHOD
1. Place the beef, flour, salt and pepper in a paper or plastic bag and, holding the top closed, shake gently until the beef is evenly coated with the seasoned flour. Place the beef on a plate and dust off the surplus flour.

2. Heat the oil in a large, heavy pot over medium-high heat and brown the beef until it is evenly colored on all sides. Set the beef aside on a plate.

3. In the oil remaining in the pot, fry the garlic, the large, chopped onions and the tomatoes until garlic is brown, then reduce the heat to medium-low, cover the pot and let mixture simmer for 3 minutes.

4. Uncover and add the beef, pour in the vinegar and water and increase the heat, bringing the liquid to a boil. At once cover the pot and reduce the heat to low. Let the meat simmer for about 2 hours, or until it is tender but not falling apart.

5. Add the small onions, beans and carrots and stir. Cook until the vegetables are tender but still crisp.

6. Remove the beef and set it in the center of a heated serving dish. Lift the vegetables out with a slotted spoon and use them to surround and garnish the beef. Place the serving dish in a very low oven to keep warm.

7. Increase the heat to high under the pot and reduce the liquid down, stirring, until it forms a fairly thick and smooth sauce. Pour this sauce over the beef and serve.

ADVANCE PREPARATION AND STORAGE NOTES

This is a good make-ahead dish. It can be refrigerated, covered, for a day. It will freeze fairly well, but be prepared to have rather soft vegetables when you thaw it. You may also slice any leftover beef and freeze it in the gravy.

& Indian Whole Chicken with Spices, Moghul Style

The palace cooks of the Moghul emperors, probably contending with scrawny and tough yard-raised chickens, devised this heavenly dish, slow-simmering the whole bird in "sweet" spices and yogurt until it became tender and fragrant. Although our supermarket birds are tender fryers, the principle remains the same, and the flavor of the cooked bird is indescribably delicious. This dish will become a star in your culinary repertoire. At the same time, it is not complicated and does not demand your continuous presence at the stove.

Preparation time: 1 hour (including marination)

Cooking time: 1 hour and 10 minutes
Serves 6

SHOPPING AND TECHNIQUE TIPS

You may use either a frying or a roasting chicken for this dish—and even a stewing fowl. If, however, you decide to use the stewing fowl, you must increase the simmering time to 2 to 3 hours, depending on the weight and age of the bird. The chicken is first marinated in yogurt and spices before being browned in the saucepan. It is then simmered to perfection in the spiced yogurt gravy. If you cannot find the saffron threads, use the powdered saffron. Do not use cheap, inferior substitutes; the flavor will suffer.

INGREDIENTS

4 *(3 ¼)* tablespoons of plain yogurt

¼ teaspoon *(a pinch)* of saffron
   threads (or powdered saffron)

½ *(⅓)* teaspoon each of:
   ground black pepper
   ground turmeric
   ground cumin
   ground red pepper (Cayenne)

¼ teaspoon *(a pinch)* each of:
   ground cardamom
   ground cloves
   ground cinnamon
   ground nutmeg
   ground mace

2 cloves of garlic

1-inch piece of fresh ginger root

1 *(¾)* teaspoon of salt

3½-pound chicken

3 tablespoons *(1½ ounces)* of Indian
   Clarified Butter (page 139)

2 large onions

1¼ cups *(10 fluid ounces)* of chicken
   stock

PREPARATION

Soaked in 1 tablespoon of hot water
for 5 minutes

Peeled and chopped

Peeled and minced

Washed, skinned and thoroughly
   patted dry with paper towels

Peeled and cut into thin slivers

METHOD

1. Mix the yogurt and the saffron, with its water, together in a large bowl. Add all the ground spices and mix thoroughly. Pound the garlic, ginger and salt together in a mortar and then stir the paste into the yogurt mixture.

2. Rub 1 tablespoon of the yogurt mixture into the cavity of the chicken, and coat the outside of the bird with the remainder. Let it marinate at room temperature for at least 45 minutes (1 hour or longer, if refrigerated.)

3. Heat the Indian Clarified Butter in a large saucepan over a medium-high setting and fry the onions until they are golden. Using a slotted spoon, remove the onions to a plate. Place the chicken in the remaining Clarified Butter and brown on all sides, turning frequently. Return the onions to the pan, together with any remaining marinade from the chicken. Pour in the chicken stock. Bring to a boil. Reduce the heat to low, cover the saucepan and simmer the chicken for 45 minutes, or until the chicken is tender, but not falling off the bones. (Turn the chicken from time to time so it cooks on all sides, but during the last 10 minutes the bird should cook breast side down.)

Much of the liquid will evaporate, leaving a thick gravy.

4. Transfer the chicken carefully to a serving dish and pour the gravy over.

ADVANCE PREPARATION AND STORAGE NOTES

This dish can be made at least 2 hours ahead of time and kept warm in a covered casserole in a warm oven. It may be made the day before and refrigerated. Upon reheating in a saucepan, add another 3 to 4 *(2½ to 3)* tablespoons of yogurt and turn the chicken every 2 minutes so that the yogurt combines with the spices and moistens the bird. It may also be frozen, but thaw gently. When reheating, also add a few tablespoons of yogurt.

Thai Variation (WHOLE SPICED CHICKEN IN COCONUT MILK)

In this Thai-style chicken, the basic principle is the same as in the above recipe. The spices are different, however, and must be well cooked. Thick Coconut Milk is used instead of the yogurt. Because Coconut Milk tends to separate and curdle when covered and boiled with juices from any kind of meat, the gravy must be reconstituted toward the end of the cooking with a little Coconut Cream or even whipping cream. The ingredients are given below, together with indications where the technique differs from the preceding recipe.

INGREDIENTS	PREPARATION
10 dried red chilli peppers	Seeded, soaked in hot water until pliable, then minced
1 *(¾)* teaspoon each of: ground black pepper ground cumin ground coriander	
½ *(⅓)* teaspoon of ground ginger	
The outer, yellow peel *(zest)* of 1 lemon	Grated
½ small red onion	Peeled and minced
5 cloves of garlic	Peeled and chopped
½ *(⅓)* teaspoon of anchovy paste	
1 *(¾)* tablespoon of peanut butter	
1 *(¾)* tablespoon of vegetable oil	
1 *(¾)* teaspoon of salt	
3½ pound chicken	Washed, skinned and thoroughly patted dry with paper towels

INGREDIENTS

2 cups *(16 fluid ounces)* of thick
    Coconut Milk, or 2 cups *(16
    fluid ounces)* of half-and-half
    (half cream, half milk), flavored
    with 1 *(¾)* teaspoon of coconut
    extract (page 114)
2 *(1⅔)* tablespoons of Southeast
    Asian fish sauce
1 *(¾)* teaspoon of granulated sugar
The grated peel *(zest)* from ½ lime
3 dried red chilli peppers (whole)
½ cup *(4 fluid ounces)* of Coconut
    Cream (page 226), or ½ *(4 fluid
    ounces)* cup of whipping cream
4 sprigs of coriander (Chinese
    parsley, *cilantro*) leaves

METHOD

1. In a food processor or a large mortar, process to a paste all ingredients listed *before* the chicken. Place the paste in a bowl.

2. Follow step 2 of the previous recipe, using the paste instead of the yogurt marinade.

3. Pour the thick Coconut Milk into a saucepan and add the chicken. Turn the chicken in the mixture and stir in any remaining paste. Add the fish sauce, sugar and lime rind *(peel)* and bring to a boil. Reduce the heat to low, cover the saucepan and simmer the chicken for 45 minutes, or until the chicken is tender but not falling off the bones. (Turn the chicken from time to time so it cooks on all sides, but during the last 10 minutes the bird should cook breast side down.) Much of the liquid will evaporate, leaving a thick gravy.

4. When the chicken is cooked, add the whole dried peppers and pour in the Coconut Cream or whipping cream. Stir and cook for 3 more minutes, scraping the bottom of the pan to combine any bits of paste and chicken with the gravy. Turn the chicken so that it is well coated with sauce. Transfer it to a serving dish and pour the sauce over. Decorate with the coriander sprigs.

ADVANCE PREPARATION AND
STORAGE NOTES

The same as the previous recipe.

✸ Family Spiced Lentils
(INDIA)

This is a family recipe, handed down from my grandmother to my aunts. In my family, who are all good cooks, everyone always assumes that quantities of ingredients are a matter of prior knowledge, so, when I came upon this recipe, there were no measurements whatsoever (probably the cause of variations in quality that I have noticed when eating at family dinner tables throughout the years). This recipe now seems to pass muster. However, it is not as good as my grandmother's; but again, nothing ever is!

Preparation time: 15 to 40 minutes   Cooking time: 55 minutes
   (depending how clean the lentils   Serves 6
   are)

SHOPPING AND TECHNIQUE TIPS
You may use either lentils or split peas for this recipe; the turmeric will turn them both the typical yellow color associated with Indian lentil dishes *(dhals)*. Spread the lentils out on a plate before starting and pick them over to ensure that there are no small stones or other foreign matter hidden among them. (The lentils which are imported from India are notoriously adulterated with stones, and you can break a tooth if they have not been cleaned properly prior to cooking.) Tamarind water is traditionally used in this recipe. We will use the usual molasses-lime juice substitute (Basics, page 137).

INGREDIENTS

2 cups *(15 ounces)* of lentils (any
   variety)

2 *(1⅔)* tablespoons of Indian
   Clarified Butter (page 139), or
   vegetable oil
1 medium onion
2 cloves of garlic
1-inch piece of fresh ginger root
1 *(¾)* teaspoon of ground turmeric
1 *(¾)* teaspoon of salt (or more to
   taste)
4 cups *(32 fluid ounces)* of hot water
1 *(¾)* teaspoon of molasses *(treacle)*
   stirred into 2 *(1⅔)* tablespoons
   of lime juice
2 *(1⅔)* tablespoons of vegetable oil

PREPARATION

Picked clean of foreign matter and
   washed well in several changes of
   water (discard those that float)

Peeled and chopped
Peeled and sliced
Peeled and minced

INGREDIENTS	PREPARATION
½ a medium onion	Peeled and cut into thin slivers
2 more cloves of garlic	Peeled and minced
2 green Serrano chilli peppers, or 1 Jalapeño pepper	Seeded and minced
1 (¾) teaspoon of cumin seeds (optional)	

METHOD

1. Drain the lentils well and set them aside.

2. In a saucepan over medium-high heat, heat the Clarified Butter and fry the onion, 2 cloves of garlic and ginger, stirring, until the onion is limp and golden.

3. Add the lentils and stir until they are mixed in. Sprinkle with the turmeric and salt and continue to fry them for 3 minutes. Increase the heat to high and pour in the hot water. Bring to a boil, reduce the heat to low, cover the pan, and simmer the dish for 25 to 35 minutes, or until the lentils are soft but not mushy, and still whole. Stir in the molasses *(treacle)* /lime juice mixture and re-cover the pan. Let it remain on the heat for 5 more minutes.

4. Meanwhile heat the oil in a frying pan over medium heat and add the onion slivers, garlic, minced chilli peppers and cumin seeds (if using these). Fry, stirring, until the onion is a rich brown. Immediately uncover the saucepan and pour in the contents of the frying pan, including the oil. Stir again and keep the saucepan covered and warm until ready to serve. (The lentils should have the consistency of porridge and should not be too disintegrated.)

ADVANCE PREPARATION AND
STORAGE NOTES

Lentils can easily be made one day, refrigerated, and eaten the next. However, they solidify when refrigerated (which is great for their use in cutlets and other dishes, but is not the consistency you now want). Reheat them in a saucepan, adding up to a cup of water or stock, a little at a time, until they regain their original texture.

Lentil Soup Variation

Serves 6 to 8 (as part of a dinner)

Lentil dishes, as served in many Indian restaurants, have a thin, souplike consistency, but this is a regional preference. It is very easy to turn the dish into a delicious soup. Increase the cooking water by a cup. Bring the lentils through step 3 in the previous recipe, at which time take the pan off the heat and, reserving about a cup of lentils, run the rest through the blender in several batches. Return it to the pan and add the reserved lentils. Check the consistency. You may wish to thin the soup further by adding a little chicken stock. Continue with step 4, but when everything is combined in the soup pot, squeeze ½ a lemon over the soup. Transfer it to a serving bowl and scatter a few coriander leaves on top before serving.

❧ Simmered Chicken and Raisin Rice with Lentils
(INDIA)

This dish is essentially a *pilau* rice dish and a one-pot meal. The rice is simmered and then steamed in the residual heat and moisture from the cooking. It is a fragrant, delicious meal in itself, but it can be served with one of the Indian chutneys and, perhaps, the Mulligatawny Soup (page 185). You could equally well make it with cubed lamb instead of the chicken. Alternatively, by substituting vegetable stock or water for the liquid and omitting the meat, you will have a dish that a vegetarian will consider magnificent.

Preparation time: 45 minutes   Serves 6 to 8 people
Cooking time: 45 to 50 minutes

SHOPPING AND TECHNIQUE TIPS
If you cannot find whole cumin seed, you may substitute ½ (⅓) teaspoon of caraway seed, and then add ½ (⅓) teaspoon of ground cumin after you have fried the onion. This dish is a good example of the combination of techniques used in India to produce their *pilaus*. The order is always the same. The whole spices and onions are fried first; then the rice (with or without lentils) is added and fried for a few minutes. If meat is to be added, it is generally combined with the rice. The liquid is then introduced and the rice mixture is simmered in the liquid over a very low heat. After the simmering, it is left to steam. Any garnish ingredients are fried separately and then stirred in or sprinkled over the top. Sometimes they are even buried in the middle of the rice as a surprise. The spicing is always sweet and fragrant, never hot.

INGREDIENTS
1 (¾) tablespoon of vegetable oil
3-inch stick of cinnamon

INGREDIENTS

1 (¾) teaspoon of whole cumin seed,
   or ½ (⅓) teaspoon of caraway
   seed and ½ (⅓) teaspoon of
   ground cumin
5 cloves
4 whole cardamom pods
6 tablespoons (3 ounces) of Indian
   Clarified Butter (page 139)
1 large onion
2 boned chicken breasts
3 cups (1½ pounds) of long-grain
   rice
½ cup (just under ¼ pound) of
   lentils
6 cups (48 fluid ounces) of chicken
   stock
1 (¾) teaspoon of ground turmeric
1½ (1¼) teaspoons of salt
¾ (⅔) teaspoon of ground black
   pepper
1 cup (5½ ounces) of golden raisins
   (sultanas)
½ cup (2¼ ounces) of blanched,
   slivered almonds
½ cup (2½ ounces) of raw cashew
   nuts
30 or more coriander (Chinese
   parsley, cilantro) leaves

PREPARATION

Peeled and cut into slivers
Skinned and cut into dice
Washed in 5 changes of water,
   drained
Cleaned, washed well and then
   drained

Chopped

METHOD

1. In a large, heavy saucepan, heat the oil over medium-high heat and fry the whole spices, stirring, for 2 minutes. (If substituting caraway seed, add now, reserving the ground cumin for step 2.)

2. Add 4 tablespoons of Clarified Butter and let it melt. Fry the onion, stirring, until it becomes limp and deep gold. Add the ground cumin, if you are using it. Stir in the chicken pieces and continue to stir until they become white and opaque.

3. Pour in the rice and lentils and stir for another 5 minutes, until the rice becomes opaque and slightly golden.

4. Increase the heat to high, pour in the stock and add the turmeric, salt,

pepper and raisins *(sultanas)*. Bring to a boil, cover, reduce the heat to low and simmer for 10 minutes.

5. While the rice is cooking, heat the remaining 2 *(1 ⅔)* tablespoons of clarified butter in a small frying pan and fry the almonds and cashews until they are a light gold. Do not overcook them. Uncover the saucepan and stir in the nuts. Re-cover the pan and let all cook for 10 minutes more. Turn off the heat and let the pan sit, covered, for an additional 5 minutes (do not remove the lid during this time).

6. Uncover the pan. You will find that the cinnamon stick and the cloves are stranded on top. Pick out all you can. Transfer the whole mixture to a large platter. Sprinkle with the coriander and serve.

ADVANCE PREPARATION AND
STORAGE NOTES
The *pilau* may be prepared ahead of time and transferred to the platter. Cover it with a well-dampened cloth and leave it in a warm oven until you are ready to serve. Left over rice may be refrigerated and then re-warmed. Either place in a microwave oven, covered with plastic wrap, or put on a shallow serving dish and into a steamer. Steam for 2 to 3 minutes. At a pinch, it may be rewarmed in a saucepan, but you will need to warm it over extremely low heat and add a couple of tablespoons of water or stock to create some steam. It may also be placed on a platter, sprinkled with water, covered with a damp cloth and warmed up in the oven.

Vegetarian Version with Peas

Omit the meat. Substitute vegetable stock or water for the chicken stock. Add ⅔ cup *(3 ounces)* of green peas at the same time that you stir the fried nuts into the rice mixture. You may also like to garnish the dish with segments of hard-boiled eggs for added protein.

❦ Rice of the Emperor's Nine Gems (INDIA)

This *pilau* rice dish has a heritage directly from the Moghul emperors and has been passed down from generation to generation. It is named after the Nine Gems (said to be the nine courtiers) of the Emperor Akbah, the mightiest of all the Moghuls. While complex, this dish (also called *Navrattan Pilau*) is a superb centerpiece for any buffet or dinner party.

Preparation time: 1 hour   Serves 8 to 10
Cooking time: 35 minutes

SHOPPING AND TECHNIQUE TIPS
This recipe uses four recipes from the Basic Techniques section: Indian Clarified
Butter (page 139), Indian Curd Cheese (page 141), Indian Sweet Spice Mix (page
118) and Crisp Fried Onion Flakes (page 156). Look up the recipes, and make
sure you have all these products at hand before you start to cook. You may
substitute feta cheese for the Indian Curd Cheese, but feta is quite a bit saltier.
The raw cashews are available in health food stores or in the health food section
of the supermarket. Basically, the technique employed is that used in making the
simmered rice, in the preceding Simmered Chicken and Raisin Rice recipe. The
rice is divided into 3 parts, each flavored with different ingredients. The 3 parts
are also differently colored—green, red and white. The garnish is prepared and
is buried in the middle of the dish like a core of buried treasure, and is covered
with the 3 layers of rice. Serve this in a heatproof glass dish so your guests can
get the full effect of the layering.

INGREDIENTS
Basic Rice Mix

2½ cups *(1 ¼ pounds)* of long-grain
    rice

4 tablespoons *(2 ounces)* of Indian
    Clarified Butter (page 139)

1 medium onion

6 cloves of garlic

12 whole black peppercorns

1½-inch piece of fresh ginger root

6 whole cloves

6 whole cardamoms

3-inch stick of cinnamon

2 green Serrano chilli peppers, or 1
    Jalapeño pepper

1 *(¾)* teaspoon of salt

½ *(⅓)* teaspoon of ground cumin

For Green Layer

1 cup *(just over ¼ pound)* of cooked
    green peas

¼ teaspoon *(a pinch)* of salt

¼ teaspoon *(a pinch)* of ground
    white pepper

PREPARATION

Washed until the water runs clear
    and then left to soak for 30
    minutes in the last water

Peeled and finely sliced

Peeled and minced

Peeled and minced

Seeded and minced

INGREDIENTS	PREPARATION
15 to 20 coriander leaves (Chinese parsley, *cilantro*)	Finely chopped
6 drops of green food coloring mixed with 1 *(¾)* tablespoon of water	

For Red Layer

1 large tomato	Skinned, seeded and diced
½ *(⅓)* teaspoon of ground red pepper (Cayenne)	
¼ teaspoon *(a pinch)* of salt	
½ *(⅓)* teaspoon of Indian Sweet Spice Mix (page 118)	
6 drops of red food coloring, mixed with 1 *(¾)* tablespoon of water	

For White Layer

2 tablespoons *(1 ounce)* of Indian Clarified Butter (page 139)	
½ cup *(2⅓ ounces)* of Indian Curd Cheese (page 141)	Cut into dice
1 *(¾)* tablespoon of white sesame seeds	
¼ teaspoon *(a pinch)* of salt	
¼ teaspoon *(a pinch)* of ground white pepper	

Core

4 tablespoons *(2 ounces)* of Indian Clarified Butter (page 139)	
¼ cup *(just over 1 ounce)* of blanched, slivered almonds	
¼ cup *(just over 1⅓ ounces)* of raw cashew nuts	
¼ cup *(1 ounce)* of shelled pistachio nuts	
½ cup *(2¾ ounces)* of golden raisins *(sultanas)*	
2 green Serrano chilli peppers, or 1 Jalapeño pepper	Seeded and slivered
1-inch piece of fresh ginger root	Peeled and thinly sliced
¼ cup *(a generous ounce)* of Fried Onion Flakes (page 156)	

INGREDIENTS   PREPARATION
¼ teaspoon *(a pinch)* of salt
¼ teaspoon *(a pinch)* of ground red
   pepper (Cayenne)
2 hard-boiled eggs   Peeled and chopped

METHOD
Basic Rice Mix

1. Drain the rice well, reserving the water. Turn oven to the lowest setting.

2. Heat the Clarified Butter in a large, heavy saucepan over medium-high heat, and fry the onion and garlic until the onion becomes transparent and limp. Add all the spices and the remaining ingredients for the Basic Rice and fry, stirring, for 1 minute. Now add the rice and fry it, stirring, for 3 minutes.

3. Measure out 3½ cups *(28 fluid ounces)* of the water in which the rice was soaked and pour it into the saucepan. Increase the heat to high and bring it to a boil. Cover, reduce the heat to low, and let the rice simmer for 12 minutes. Turn off the heat and let the pan sit for 5 minutes. Do *not* uncover.

4. Now uncover the rice and stir it to let the steam escape and break up any lumps. Divide the rice into 3 equal parts, placing each in a mixing bowl.

Green Layer

5. Stir in the peas, salt and pepper, coriander leaves and diluted green food coloring. Mix well, cover the bowl with foil and place in the oven.

Red Layer

6. Stir in the tomato and the rest of the ingredients for the red layer into the next bowl of rice. Mix it well to distribute the red food coloring. Cover with foil and place in the oven.

White Layer

7. Wash out the saucepan and set it over medium heat. Add the 2 tablespoons *(1 ounce)* of clarified butter and let it melt. Stir in the cheese cubes and sprinkle with the sesame seeds. Just as the cheese begins to soften, empty the contents of the saucepan into the last rice bowl. Stir, then add the salt and pepper and stir again. Cover the bowl with foil and place it with the other 2 in the oven.

Core

8. Wash the saucepan again and replace it on the stove, adding the 4 tablespoons *(2 ounces)* of clarified butter. Heat over medium-high heat and

ASSEMBLING AND LAYERING
NINE GEMS RICE

then add the nuts, golden raisins *(sultanas)*, chilli peppers and ginger. Fry, stirring, until the raisins start to swell and the nuts begin to turn gold.

9. Now add the onion flakes, reduce the heat to low and stir in the remaining ingredients. Stir until the eggs are just warmed through, then take off the stove.

Assembling the Nine Gems
Now for the fun part.

10. Place the core ingredients in a shallow mound in the middle of a large, ovenproof glass dish. Remove the 3 bowls containing the rice from the oven and uncover them.

11. Decide in which order you would like to layer the colored rice and then carefully spread it, one layer at a time, over the mound, gradually filling in the hollows around it, so that the last layer is even.

12. Although I have not included garnish with the ingredients, you may like to garnish the dish with a sprinkling of chopped coriander leaves or with more fried onion flakes. The surface could be spiked with almond slivers set in neat rows. This would be the kind of dish that the Moghuls would have decorated with silver leaf, so, if you are ever near an Indian store, splurge and buy some. Apply 2 or 3 sheets, like a transfer, to the surface.

ADVANCE PREPARATION AND
STORAGE NOTES

This dish may be made ahead of time, covered with a dampened cloth and placed in a warm oven for up to 1 hour. Garnish after you bring it from the oven.

❀ Japanese Beef and Vegetable Fondue

For this dish, which is cooked at the table by the diners, you will need either a fondue pot or an electric frying pan. If you have neither, then you will need a single electric ring and a heavy saucepan. The beef is cut into small, thin strips and the vegetables are cut into bite-sized pieces; both are then cooked in the simmering stock in the pan. The morsels are dipped in individual bowls of sauce before being eaten. The Japanese call this dish *Shabu-Shabu,* and the name is supposed to represent the sound of the ingredients being dipped in the liquid.

Preparation time: 45 minutes   Serves 6
Cooking time: 5 minutes

SHOPPING AND TECHNIQUE TIPS

Choose really good-quality steak and place it in the freezer until it is very firm —almost frozen. You will then easily be able to slice it to the necessary thinness. All the vegetables should be cut into small, bite-sized pieces so that they will be easy to pick up and will cook quickly. You will find the recipes for the accompanying dipping sauces in the chapter on sauces and chutneys (page 450).

INGREDIENTS	PREPARATION
1½ to 2 pounds of top sirloin or fillet of beef	Partly frozen, then thinly sliced and cut into strips, 1 inch by 2 inches
8 leaves of Chinese or celery cabbage	Washed, drained and cut into 2-inch strips
12 leaves of spinach	Washed, drained and cut into 2-inch strips
8 green *(spring)* onions	Cut on the diagonal into 2-inch pieces
10 to 12 fresh, white mushrooms	Wiped clean, stems trimmed
2 rectangles of bean curd	Drained and cut into 1-inch cubes
1 or 2 pieces of canned *(tinned)* bamboo shoots	Thinly sliced, then cut into strips
1 recipe of Japanese Dipping Sauce for Meat Fondue (page 477)	

INGREDIENTS

Lemon-Soy Dipping Sauce: ½ cup *(4
      fluid ounces)* soy sauce mixed
      with ½ cup *(4 fluid ounces)*
      lemon juice, and diluted with ½
      cup *(4 fluid ounces)* of chicken
      stock
4 cups *(32 fluid ounces)* of Japanese
      Basic Fish Stock (page 170)

METHOD

1. Prepare the first 7 ingredients and arrange them attractively on a large platter.

2. Prepare both the dipping sauces and pour each into individual bowls, 2 for each diner.

3. Pour the stock into a skillet and bring it to a boil. Reduce the heat so that it continues to simmer throughout the meal. If you are using a fondue pot, bring the stock to a boil in a saucepan, before pouring it into the fondue pot.

4. Each diner spears pieces of beef and vegetables with chopsticks or fondue forks and cooks them in the stock before dipping them into sauce and eating them. At the conclusion of the meal, a little of the sauce, or soy sauce, can be poured into the remaining liquid to enhance the flavor. It is then poured into soup bowls and drunk as soup.

ADVANCE PREPARATION AND
STORAGE NOTES

The ingredients may be prepared as in steps 1 and 2 and covered with plastic wrap and refrigerated until you are ready to eat. Prepare the stock just before you serve.

Korean Version

This is somewhat similar to the above, except that the meat is first marinated for 30 minutes in the marinade given below. It is then seared in a dry pan before the stock (a similar quantity of plain beef stock) is added. The vegetables are then placed in the skillet or fondue or fire pot, and everything is simmered together before the diners retrieve the pieces. Dipping sauces are not served. For vegetables, use 3 medium onions cut into slivers; 6 stalks of celery, cut into 1-inch pieces; 2 carrots, peeled and cut diagonally into very thin slices; also the mushrooms, bean curd and cabbage indicated in the preceding recipe. Omit the bamboo shoots and spinach. An egg for each diner may be broken into the pan, just as everything else is cooked, and the cover put on to let them steam until firm.

INGREDIENTS	PREPARATION
Marinade for Beef	
¼ cup *(2 ounces)* of granulated sugar	
½ cup *(4 fluid ounces)* of soy sauce	
2 *(1⅔)* tablespoons of vegetable oil	
2 cloves of garlic	Peeled and crushed
1 *(¾)* tablespoon of sesame seeds	Toasted to pale brown, then ground
1 green Serrano chilli pepper	Finely chopped

CHARBECUING

෨ ෨ ෨

Barbecuing, Grilling—
Satays, Kabobs, and Spitted Meats

G rilled foods go back to the dawn of history and the origin of fire.
Legend has it that a clumsy caveman probably dropped a piece of
raw meat he was eating into the fire that he had kindled to keep himself warm.
The delicious aroma of roasting meat filled the cave and, after a successful
attempt to retrieve the meat with a twig, he must have decided to eat it in
whatever state it was in. It was love at first taste, and cooking was born.

Aristotle, the Greek philosopher, observed that in ancient times men
roasted everything. It is a sweeping statement, but there is no doubt that
roasting is associated with the beginnings of civilization. The primitive peoples
regarded roasting as the man's preserve. When they hunted, they roasted meat
over open fires. Gradually the process became associated with royalty and
nobility, as roasting wasted the juices from the meat, thereby representing an
extravagance that was the preserve of the aristocracy and a sign of wealth.
Conversely, boiling food was thought of as a sign of home and regarded as a
woman's task, although a sign of cultural progress in that it required the

manufacture of a pot. Maybe the remnants of this philosophy exist today in the masculine belief that the backyard barbecue is the man's preserve while the women prepare the accompanying foods in the kitchen.

In times of war and conquest, meat was spitted upon long swords and roasted over campfires. The kabobs (kebabs) and satays *(sates)* of the Middle East, India and Southeast Asia—chunks of meat speared in serried ranks on metal or wooden skewers and grilled to perfection over charcoal—are probably the direct and peaceful descendants of this wartime cooking practice. In some luxury restaurants, the grilled meats are presented on flaming swords, a piece of showmanship which may have originated with the Russian *shashlik,* or kabob. In fact, the Mongols, or Tartars, cooked over open fires and brought this tradition to Russia. They also introduced to the north of China the custom of roasting whole sheep over flaming coals.

The Koreans feature many Mongol-originated barbecued dishes in their cuisine, and the Japanese, from possibly the same source, have a whole class of dishes called *yakimono,* meaning "grilled foods." The most well-known dish in that category is *yakitori,* chicken grilled on skewers and brushed with sauce.

It may well be that the entire practice of skewering whole chunks or small pieces of meat or impaling them upon a spit originated with the Mongol tribes.

The Muslims were also responsible for the propagation of roasted meat. The cuisines of Pakistan, the Punjab and much of northern India are based on a wide range of grilled kebabs and spitted meats, either cooked over open fires or baked in circular earthen ovens called *tandoor.*

The lechon de leche of the Philippines, where a whole suckling pig is skewered on a spit and turned over an open fire until the flesh is tender and succulent and the skin becomes brittle and crisp, is quite independent of the cultural origins of the north. It shares a common history, spread over the vast Pacific, with the roast pig of Micronesia, Melanesia and Hawaii and Tahiti in Polynesia.

The Han dynasty in China, which existed for a period of two hundred years before and after the birth of Christ, featured rectangular four-legged iron stoves in the kitchen, which were used for grilling meat. They were similar to the modern Japanese *hibachi.* In China today, in the northern capital of Peking (or Beijjin, as it is now known), there are Mongolian-beef restaurants in which the diner cooks his own beef with two-foot-long chopsticks over a large charcoal burner set on the table. However, most roasting in China is done in restaurants or by speciality merchants as the average household does not have the necessary kitchen equipment.

This cooking of roast meats outside the home kitchen has spread to

Southeast Asia, where in every city one can see food stands selling roasted and smoked meat and poultry. Rows of glistening brown cuts of barbecued pork, soy-sauce chicken and camphor-smoked duck decorate the windows of meat shops from Hong Kong to Singapore. These meats are prepared daily by the merchants, and customers may buy any quantity or variety they desire, from a chicken leg to a whole piglet. The rich brown color and high glaze of these meats is obtained by using two different techniques. In one, the meat is first marinated in soy sauce and spices, then air-dried before it is rubbed with oil and roasted. To increase the prized crispness of the skin, it may then be cooked further by deep-frying in oil. In the other technique, the skin of the pig or duck can first be rubbed with sesame oil or lard, then the meat seared briefly in an oven or over an open fire. After the searing, the roasting proceeds at a slower pace, during which the meat is basted frequently with either soy sauce or another marinade. Roasting always takes place with the meat elevated upon a rack, or hanging from a hook, with a pan of water beneath to catch the dripping fat and marinade. This is probably a refinement of the ancient practice of cooking meat on a spit or suspending it from a hook over an open fire. While the Chinese techniques of roasting may vary, the finished result is always the same. The meat is crisp and brown on the outside and tender and juicy within.

Other Chinese dishes featuring meat which is marinated and then grilled may well involve a combination of techniques. Flesh that has a high percentage of fat, such as that of pork or duck, may first be steamed or braised in liquid, during which the fat content is reduced. After the meat is tender, it is then brought to the finished state by barbecuing over glowing coals, together with repeated applications of the highly flavored marinade.

"One can become a cook, but one has to be born a roaster of meat," pronounced Brillat-Savarin, the renowned French food philospher. I disagree with that statement. Roasting, grilling and all forms of cooking over or under a direct flame need only an understanding of the techniques involved, a correct choice of the quality of meat, poultry or fish, and attention to temperature in order to produce outstanding results consistently.

The choice of meat for grilling follows a simple rule: The higher the quality and the more tender the cut, the fiercer the heat and the quicker the cooking time. Grilling itself will not tenderize meat: marinating will help to do that. Grilling merely melts the fat and chars the outside surface, turning it brown, making it appear attractive to the eye and appealing to the palate. In an oven, quick roasting on a spit is similar to cooking on a rotisserie under a grill. The same timing and temperatures apply, and the meats should be top quality.

Less choice cuts or meat that has been defrosted should be pan-roasted at a lower temperature in order to produce a tender result. To prevent the surface from drying out, the meat can be tented with foil until the last 15 or 20 minutes of cooking, when any covering should be removed in order to brown the outside. This process is properly termed roasting, as opposed to grilling.

Although the Asians rarely use ovens, we do, and it frequently saves valuable time to adapt an Oriental recipe to the oven, where it needs little attention, rather than to adhere rigidly to their traditional methods, which require the vigilant eye and continued presence of the cook. For this reason I have included an explanation of the techniques of roasting, as well as grilling, meat.

Let us take a look at the basic sequence of steps involved in the techniques of both grilling (also called broiling) and roasting (sometimes referred to as baking, in that it also involves the application of dry heat in some kind of enclosure, such as an oven).

First, the marinade. From the Middle East, through India, Southeast Asia and on to the Far East (China, Korea and Japan), immersing foods in a seasoned liquid or rubbing them with a dry mixture of flavoring agents is common practice. Marinades fulfill several functions. Depending on their composition, they can be used to tenderize meat, to flavor it, or to color it to make it appear more attractive—or for a combination of any or all of the above. The longer a food is immersed in a marinade, the more flavorful it will become. Meat for an evening meal can be left in a marinade in the morning and refrigerated throughout the day. Meat to be eaten at midday can be prepared the day before by marinating it overnight. If a marinade contains a tenderizer, such as papaya juice, tougher cuts of meat will become tender.

When choosing cuts of meat to be grilled, look for those which are marbled, or streaked with fat. These will be tender after cooking and will require few or no additional applications of fat or oil during cooking. The thicker cuts of meat (1½ inches to 2 inches) will be juicier when cooked than thinner slices. If a steak has a wide border of fat, trim off most of it and then score the remaining fat in several places to avoid curling up of the meat under the heat.

Preheat your broiler or grill. Grilling demands temperatures of between 350°F. *(gas mark 4)* and 400°F. *(gas mark 6),* and the grill must be at the right temperature *before* the meat is put on it. The meat should be at room temperature before grilling, so take it out of the refrigerator at least an hour before. Line the broiler pan with aluminum foil to cut down on cleaning time afterward and place the meat on a greased rack inside the pan.

The placement of the rack in relation to the source of heat is also very important. Gas and electric broilers *(grills)* give off different types of heat. Food can burn if placed too close to the flames from a gas broiler *(grill),* while under an electric broiler *(grill)* it can be placed nearer the coils. Thinner cuts of meat should be placed about 2 inches to 3 inches away from the source of heat, while thicker cuts of meat can be placed up to 5 inches away. If the meat is wanted rare on the inside and charred on the outside, it should be placed closer to the heat. The greater the distance from the heat, the more uniform the cooking will be and the less the smoke and spattering. If you leave the door of an electric broiler *(grill)* slightly ajar, it will prevent the thermostat from turning off the current when the desired heat setting has been reached, and the coils will continue to glow red.

Different recipes dictate different positions for grilling. A recipe may require that meat be placed close to the heat initially to seal in the juices and then removed to a greater distance. Some techniques, such as *tandoori* cooking (the exception to the Asian practice of stovetop cooking), demand that the meat be given a final application of marinade and butter and then replaced close to the heat to form a glistening, flavorful crust.

Cooking times will vary with the thickness of the cuts of meat and the desired degree of doneness. One and one-half minutes on the first side and a minute on the other is enough for thin cuts to be served rare or for minute steaks. Thicker cuts and medium or well-done meat should be first seared close to the heat for 1½ minutes on either side and then placed farther away from the coils or flame for the remainder of the cooking time. When turning meat, use tongs or two metal spatulas. Do not use forks, because piercing the meat will break the seal and allow the juices to escape. You can, however, use a fork to probe the meat at the end of the cooking time when you are testing it for doneness. A convenient guide to the cooking period for a cut of meat 1 inch thick is to allow 6 minutes total grilling time for a rare steak, 8 minutes for a medium and 10 minutes for well-done meat. For every ½ inch of additional depth, add an extra 5 minutes.

Use a meat thermometer for testing the meat: it should register 125°F. *(51°C.)* internal temperature for rare meat, 140°F.*(60°C.)* for medium done and 170°F.*(76°C.)* for well done. If you do not have a meat thermometer (I do suggest you buy one), pierce the meat with a fork or knife and examine the inside when you think it is done. The color should tip you off as to its state. If rare, it will be quite red. A strong pink will indicate that it is medium done, and a pale pink will signify that it is well done. Remember that the meat will continue to cook for a short time after you remove it from the heat.

Roasting on a spit is much the same as grilling. If the spit is close to the source of heat, the process is exactly the same except that the rotation of the spit means that you do not need to turn the meat over: it will brown evenly on all sides automatically. Many spits have several placement slots so that the spit can be raised or lowered at will. If the spit is in the center of your oven and not close to the broiler *(grill)*, the methods will be similar to roasting in a pan, except the use of the spit means the meat is self-basting.

The usual roasting is done in an open pan in the oven. If the pan is covered, either with a lid or completely sealed with foil, the meat will braise or steam. Closed-pan cooking is appropriate for tough cuts of meat and is akin to pot-roasting, but it cannot properly be called roast. Roasting ensures that dry heat envelops the meat and seals the surface, browning it and allowing a crust to form. Closed-pan roasting keeps the surface of the meat open, allowing the steam from the escaping juices to penetrate the meat and make it tender. The resultant appearance of the meat will be grayish rather than brown.

In roasting, as in grilling, variations in heat will give different results. Cooking meat at a lower temperature means that it will take longer, produce more gravy and will not shrink as much as meat that has been cooked in a fierce heat. Slow roasting takes place at temperatures between 300°F. *(gas mark 2)* and 325°F. *(gas mark 3)*, roasting at a medium temperature, 375°F. *(gas mark 5)*, produces meat which is juicer internally but with fewer pan drippings. The most popular method of roasting is to sear the meat initially in a 500°F. *(gas mark 9)* oven and then reduce the cooking temperature to about 325°F. *(gas mark 3)* for the remainder of the cooking period.

A convenient rule of thumb for oven-roasted meats is to allow them a certain specified amount of time per pound of weight and 15 to 20 minutes of resting time (during which the inside will continue to cook) after they have been removed from the oven. Approximate cooking times are on page 388.

All the grilling and roasting techniques can be applied to barbecuing over charcoal. The great advantage of all Oriental grilled recipes is that they are well suited to outdoor barbecuing and therefore make ideal dishes for summer entertaining. There are several points to remember, not the least important of which is the construction of the charcoal fire so that it will provide the most efficient vehicle for cooking the food. (Ask any Boy Scout.)

Pile the charcoal pieces into a pyramid, light them and let them burn for 30 to 45 minutes, until the flames have died down and the coals are thinly coated with a chalky layer of ash, through which you should be able to see glowing red embers. The fire is then ready. Now, with a metal rod or poker, before you place the grill on top, push the coals into a ring. This enables you to place a drip pan (it should be heavy) under the meat to catch the juices, unless you wish them to fall on the coals to create smoke to add to the flavor. This ring formation also helps to prevent flames from flaring up, and it centers

Meat	Oven Temperature	Cooking Time (not including resting time)
Beef	350°F. *(gas mark 4/177°C.)*	25 minutes per pound and 25 extra (rare) 30 minutes per pound and 30 extra (medium) 35 minutes per pound and 35 extra (well-done)
Lamb	375°F. *(gas mark 5/190°C.)*	13 to 15 minutes per pound (rare) 16 to 18 minutes per pound (medium) 18 to 20 minutes per pound (well-done)
Pork	325°F. *(gas mark 3/163°C.)*	30 minutes per pound for bone in 35 to 40 minutes per pound for boneless
Chicken (roaster)	375°F. *(gas mark 5/190°C.)*	30 to 35 minutes per pound
Duck	325°F. *(gas mark 3/163°C.)*	30 to 35 minutes per pound

the heat evenly. This means that you can place the grill close to the source of heat without the meat catching fire. A little charring and a smoky flavor can be part of the character of barbecued meats, but the burnt offerings I have been handed at some barbecues tasted bitter, added unwanted carbons to my system and did nothing for the reputation of the chef.

At grill level, the temperature should be between 350°F. *(gas mark 4)* and 400°F. *(gas mark 6)*. Use a barbecue thermometer or, if you do not have one, you can make a rough test by placing your hand just above the grill (not on it, please!). If you can bear to hold your hand there for three seconds, the temperature is correct. If you can hold it there longer, the coals are too cool. Rake away some of the ash and add some more coals to the edges of the fire (never to the center) to raise the heat. Use a water gun or spray for hot spots.

If your barbecue is a deluxe model with a rotating spit, you can roast large pieces of meat and whole birds. Spit-roasting temperatures are lower than those of the barbecue grid—being between 225°F. *(gas mark ¼)* and 350°F. *(gas mark 4),* and the meat will take longer to cook. Fish should be cooked at the lowest end of this temperature range, lamb, pork and poultry in the middle, and beef at the highest temperature.

When barbecuing, use long-handled implements and stout, insulated, fireproof gloves. Keep a fire extinguisher handy for flareups. If you are cooking kabobs make sure that you have extra-long metal skewers and pack the meats close to the top end, leaving a long expanse of handle to project over the edge of the barbecue. This makes for easier and cooler handling when you rotate the skewers. Wooden satay sticks should be soaked in water until the last minute before threading to discourage the wood from charring and breaking (put them in a tall vase of water). Both kabobs and satays will cook much more quickly than the larger pieces of meat.

BARBECUED SPARERIBS

One of the most universal barbecued items, ribs play as important a part of eating in the Orient as they do in the West. There are a few variations, however. Some countries veer toward pork chops and others, such as India, prefer to barbecue chicken—halved, whole, or in pieces.

Cooking techniques also vary. Some groups grill over charcoal, others barbecue in an oven. All marinate their meat, and it is in the marinades that the ethnic and gastronomic flavor of the specific country can be found.

❀ Chinese Barbecued Spareribs

The parent of this recipe comes from Shanghai, in the northern part of the coastal region of China. This is an oven barbecue and once was probably prepared in the specialized barbecue shops of the city rather than in individual homes.

Preparation time: 3¼ hours   Serves 6 to 8
Cooking time: 1 hour

SHOPPING AND TECHNIQUE TIPS

Look for a whole rack of pork spareribs (approximately 3½ pounds) and trim off the surplus fat. Use a cleaver to cut away any part of the breast bone, if it has been left attached, or ask the butcher to do it for you. If you have any S-shaped hooks, such as curtain hooks, or parts of wire coat hangers, or even bent wire, you can suspend the ribs from the top rack of your oven by attaching the hooks at both ends of the ribs and slinging them, like a hammock, underneath the top oven rack. This is the authentic Chinese style of barbecuing. You then place a baking pan filled with water on the bottom rack to keep the ribs moist and to catch the drips from the marinade and the melting fat. If you do not wish to use this technique, merely place the ribs on a rack over a pan of water.

INGREDIENTS	PREPARATION
Marinade	
2 ʹʹ ⅔) tablespoons of peanut oil	
6 *(4¾)* tablespoons of honey	Bring to room temperature
6 *(4¾ or 3 fluid ounces)* tablespoons of soy sauce	
4 *(3¼)* tablespoons of pale dry sherry	
2 cloves of garlic	Peeled, crushed and minced
2 *(1⅔)* tablespoons Chinese All-Purpose Sauce (page 145)	
½ *(⅓)* teaspoon of ground black pepper	
1 *(¾)* teaspoon of Chinese Five-Plus-One Spice Mix (page 119)	

METHOD

Mix all the ingredients together thoroughly in a small bowl. Alternately, you may wish to use the Chinese Barbecue Marinade (page 135).

INGREDIENTS	PREPARATION
Ribs	
1 rack (approximately 3½ pounds) of pork spareribs	Trimmed of fat
Marinade from above	

METHOD

1. Place the rack of ribs in a large, shallow dish and pour the marinade over the entire surface of the rack. Because of its unwieldy size you may wish

to use an alternative that I have found works very well: place the ribs in a medium-size plastic bag and pour in the marinade. Press the air from the bag and close it securely with a fastener. Shake the ribs in the bag occasionally to ensure that they are well covered with the marinade.

2. Marinate the ribs at room temperature for 3 hours, basting from time to time. If you have bagged the ribs, merely squeeze the rack of ribs now and then to redistribute the marinade.

3. Preheat the oven to 375°F. *(gas mark 5)*.

4. Place a baking pan filled with water on the lower rack of the oven.

5. Remove the ribs from the marinade and suspend them from the upper oven rack—or place them on a grid over the baking pan. Reserve the marinade and use it for basting.

6. Roast the ribs for 45 minutes, basting them twice with the reserved marinade.

7. If they are on a grid, turn them over after 30 minutes.

8. Increase the oven temperature to 450°F. *(gas mark 8)* and sear the ribs for 7½ minutes on each side, until the exterior is crisp and a rich, deep brown.

9. Remove the rack of ribs to a cutting board and use a cleaver to separate it into individual ribs. Place them on a platter and serve, accompanied by Chinese Plum Sauce (page 466) for dipping.

ADVANCE PREPARATION AND
STORAGE NOTES

The marinade may be prepared up to 3 days ahead and refrigerated in a tightly capped jar. The ribs may be marinated overnight. The barbecuing should be done within 2 hours of serving and the ribs kept warm in a low oven. These ribs can also be cooked over an open-air barbecue (see page 387 for technique tips).

❧ Malaysian Barbecued Spareribs

This Malaysian recipe probably originates with the Straits Chinese, as the Muslim Malays do not eat pork. The technique closely follows that used in Chinese Barbecued Spareribs, except that the ribs are marinated in a thicker marinade and should frequently be basted with the marinade while cooking (a procedure rather like the Indian *tandoori* barbecue).

Preparation time: 3¼ hours   Serves 6 to 8
Cooking time: 1 hour

SHOPPING AND TECHNIQUE TIPS

Because the ribs will be basted frequently and therefore will not dry out, omit filling the baking tray with water; use it to hold the marinade that drips from the ribs and baste them with it.

INGREDIENTS	PREPARATION
Marinade	
1 *(¾)* tablespoon of fennel seeds	
8 macadamia nuts, or 4 Brazil nuts	
The outer yellow peel *(zest)* of 1 lemon	Finely minced
3 large onions	Peeled and finely chopped
3 cloves of garlic	Peeled and chopped
1 *(¾)* teaspoon of anchovy paste	
½ *(⅓)* teaspoon of ground red pepper (Cayenne)	
1 *(¾)* tablespoon of ground coriander	
1½ *(1¼)* teaspoons of salt	
1 *(¾)* tablespoon of granulated sugar	
1 cup *(8 fluid ounces)* of half-and-half *(half cream-half milk)* flavored with ½ *(⅓)* teaspoon of coconut extract	
2 *(1⅔ or 1 fluid ounce)* tablespoons of peanut oil	

METHOD

1. In a mortar, pound the fennel seeds to a powder and then add the nuts, pounding until the mixture becomes a dry paste. Transfer this to the processor.

2. Add the remaining ingredients and process to a saucelike marinade. You may need to do this in 2 batches. It does not matter in which order the ingredients are processed as long as they are thoroughly combined in a bowl at the conclusion.

3. As batches are processed, transfer the marinade to the bowl.

INGREDIENTS	PREPARATION
Ribs	
1 rack (approximately 3½ pounds) of pork spareribs	Trimmed of fat
Marinade from above	

INGREDIENTS
1 cucumber

PREPARATION
Skin scored along the length with the tines of a fork, thinly sliced into rounds

METHOD
Follow steps 1 through 3 of the preceding Chinese recipe.

4. Place a baking pan on the lower rack of the oven.

5. As in the Chinese recipe.

6. Roast the ribs for 45 minutes, basting them 4 times with the reserved marinade.

7. As in the Chinese recipe.

8. As in the Chinese recipe, but baste them one more time before increasing the heat.

9. As in the Chinese recipe, but after placing the ribs on the platter, ring them with the cucumber slices. Serve accompanied by plain rice. Southeast Asian Sweet and Hot Chilli Sauce (page 465) may be poured into a small bowl as an accompaniment.

ADVANCE PREPARATION AND STORAGE NOTES

The marinade and ribs may be prepared ahead and marinated overnight. Barbecueing should be done within 2 hours of serving; the ribs may be kept warm in a low oven. These ribs can also be cooked over an open-air barbecue (see page 387 for technique tips).

✿ Thai Barbecued Spareribs

Follow the Malaysian Barbecued Spareribs recipe for barbecuing technique. The marinade, which is different, is given below.

INGREDIENTS
Marinade
2 *(1⅔)* tablespoons of coriander (Chinese parsley, *cilantro*) stems
4 cloves of garlic
1 *(¾)* teaspoon of whole black peppercorns, or 1 *(¾)* teaspoon of ground black pepper

PREPARATION

Minced

Peeled and chopped

INGREDIENTS

The outer, green peel *(zest)* of 1 lime
1 *(¾)* tablespoon of Thai Curry
        Spice Paste (page 124)
2 *(1⅔)* tablespoons of Southeast
        Asian fish sauce
1 *(¾)* tablespoon of granulated sugar
1 cup *(8 fluid ounces)* of
        half-and-half *(half cream-half
        milk)* flavored with ½ *(⅓)*
        teaspoon of coconut extract

PREPARATION

Minced finely

METHOD

1. In a mortar, pound the coriander stems, garlic, peppercorns and lime rind to a juicy paste.

2. Transfer the paste to a food processor and proceed as for Malaysian Barbecued Spareribs.

❧ Korean Barbecued Beef Short Ribs

The Korean ribs are marinated in a sauce containing the flavors typical of Korean cooking: minced green *(spring)* onion, garlic, ginger, sesame seeds and soy sauce. Pork spareribs may be used as an alternative to beef, but the latter are more authentic.

Preparation time: 3 hours   Serves 6 to 8
Cooking time: 30 minutes

SHOPPING AND TECHNIQUE TIPS

As well as short ribs, beef spareribs may also be used for this dish. Have the butcher cut the ribs into 3-inch lengths, or, if you have a very heavy, sharp cleaver, you may do it yourself. Then crisscross the meat and bone with light blows of the cleaver, first marking it diagonally in one direction and then crossing those cuts by making light incisions the other way. This will reduce the cooking time and ensure that the ribs are permeated by the marinade.

INGREDIENTS

Marinade

2 *(1⅔)* tablespoons of sesame seeds

PREPARATION

Dry-fried until golden brown in a
    small frying pan (shake the pan
    and watch for burning)

3 cloves of garlic — Peeled and crushed

4 green *(spring)* onions — Finely chopped

1-inch piece of fresh ginger root — Peeled and minced

4 tablespoons *(2 fluid ounces)* of
    sake, mirin, dry sherry or dry
    vermouth

4 *(1⅔ or 2 fluid ounces)* tablespoons
    of soy sauce

2 *(1⅔)* tablespoons of Sesame Oil
    (page 139)

METHOD

1. Place the toasted sesame seeds in an electric spice grinder or in a mortar
and grind or pound them to a powder. Place this powder in a bowl.

2. Add the remaining marinade ingredients to the bowl and stir well.

INGREDIENTS

Ribs

3 to 4 pounds of beef short ribs

Marinade from above

2 *(1⅔)* tablespoons of vegetable oil

2 *(1⅔)* additional teaspoons of
    toasted sesame seeds (optional)

PREPARATION

Cut as described above

METHOD

1. Place the prepared ribs in a large, shallow dish or a plastic bag and add
the marinade. Marinate for a minimum of 2½ hours, refrigerated. (The ribs
also may be marinated overnight.)

2. Preheat the oven to 375°F. *(gas mark 5).*

3. Half an hour before serving time, remove the ribs from the marinade,
retaining it for basting. Brush the ribs lightly on both sides with the vegetable
oil.

4. Place them on a rack (if using the oven grill) or over a barbecue grill
and grill the ribs for 15 minutes on each side, brushing with the marinade, or
spooning it over, every 5 minutes. Grill until the ribs are a rich golden brown.

5. Sprinkle the ribs with the sesame seeds (if using them) and place on a serving platter.

ADVANCE PREPARATION AND
STORAGE NOTES
The same as the preceding barbecue recipes.

❀ Japanese Barbecued Meats

The Japanese are given to refinement in eating, and spareribs would be considered somewhat clumsy and barbaric, except in outlying areas. Pieces of chicken, small birds and duck are cut into small pieces, impaled on skewers and grilled over charcoal. This style of cooking is called *yakitori* (see Japan under Backgrounds on the Countries, page 39). Steaks are grilled on flat metal plates or on domed grills of perforated metal. This style is known as *teppanyaki. Tonkatsu* (pork cutlets) are marinated and then grilled. Sometimes they are lightly breaded and then fried.

This recipe is adapted to the outdoor barbecue or to the oven grill.

Preparation time: 1¼ hours   Serves 6
Cooking time: 3 to 8 minutes

SHOPPING AND TECHNIQUE TIPS
High-quality beef or pork is essential. If you are using beefsteaks, shop for fillet (tenderloin), boneless top sirloin or sirloin tip. If choosing pork, any of the cuts from the pork loin, such as loin chops, sirloin chops, butterfly chops and top loin. The bones should be removed and the steaks or pork meat should be cut no thicker than ½ inch.

INGREDIENTS   PREPARATION
6 beefsteaks steaks or pork fillets   Patted dry
Japanese Marinade for Grilled Meats
     (page 136)
1 *(¾)* tablespoon of Sesame Oil
     (page 139, optional)

METHOD
1. Trim and slice the steaks or pork carefully. The slices should look picture-perfect in the Japanese style. Gently pat them dry with paper towels.
2. Place them in a shallow baking tray or in a large plastic bag. Pour marinade over and make sure that the meat is completely covered. Refrigerate

and marinate for 1 hour. At room temperature, the meat may be marinated for as little as 45 minutes.

3. Read the instructions at the beginning of this chapter for barbecuing or grilling, estimate the cooking time needed for the thickness of the meat (see instructions, page 386) and preheat the barbecue or grill.

4. Remove the meat from the marinade and lightly pat it with paper towels to remove surplus moisture. Barbecue or grill, following the appropriate timing and temperature for the quality and thickness of the meat. Remember that pork must be completely cooked through. Do not overcook, but test the interior with the tip of a knife or skewer to be sure no pink remains.

5. Serve immediately, accompanied by lightly fried vegetables such as broccoli tops, bean sprouts, Chinese white cabbage (shredded Western cabbage may be used), asparagus tips, sweet green peppers or mushrooms. Also set out small bowls of Japanese Dipping Sauce (pages 474–78).

ADVANCE PREPARATION AND
STORAGE NOTES

The marinade may be prepared well ahead of time (see page 385), and the meats may be marinated for up to 3 or 4 hours. The barbecuing or grilling should be done immediately before eating. If you have a small *hibachi* grill, why not do it beside or on the table so that your guests can watch?

✿ Indian "Steamrollered" Barbecued Chicken

This recipe comes from the Punjab, near Peshawar, in what is now Pakistan. Unlike the *tandoori* recipes, the marinade is drier—closer to a paste—and is rubbed on the chicken. It is called "steamroller" because the flattened chicken halves look as if they have been run over! You may also use this marinade for barbecuing lamb chops. Pork would not be used in the north of India as it is predominantly Muslim. For lesser appetites and smaller servings, I suggest you use halves of Cornish game hens for each serving. This barbecued chicken may be served cold and is ideal for picnics.

Preparation time: 2½ hours   4 enormous servings, or 4 smaller
Cooking time: 35 minutes   ones if game hens are used

SHOPPING AND TECHNIQUE TIPS
Look for tender young frying chickens with plenty of meat. If your cleaver

techniques are not yet up to the task of cutting the chickens exactly in half, ask the butcher to do it for you. They should be halved lengthwise, so that each half has a leg and a wing. To "steamroller" them, place them on a dry towel, cover them with a second towel, and whack them repeatedly with the flat of a heavy cleaver blade or with a rolling pin, until they flatten. There is nothing delicate about this lusty dish, but the fierce hill tribesmen of the northwest frontier are not delicate either!

INGREDIENTS	PREPARATION
Marinade	
1 medium onion	Peeled and coarsely chopped
1-inch piece of fresh ginger root	Peeled and chopped
3 *(1½ ounces)* tablespoons of Indian Clarified Butter (page 139)	
1 *(¾)* tablespoon of ground coriander	
1½ *(1¼)* teaspoons of ground cumin	
1 *(¾)* teaspoon of ground turmeric	
½ *(⅓)* teaspoon of ground red pepper (Cayenne)	
1 *(¾)* teaspoon of Indian Sweet Spice Mix (page 118)	
3 *(2⅓)* tablespoons of white vinegar	
2 *(1⅔)* teaspoons of salt	
30 or more of mint leaves	Finely chopped

METHOD

1. Place the onion and ginger in a processor and process for 45 seconds, stopping from time to time to scrape down the sides of the container with a spatula.

2. Add the remaining marinade ingredients and process for approximately 15 seconds or until a fine paste is formed.

INGREDIENTS	PREPARATION
Chicken	
2 small (2½-pound) frying chickens	Halved and flattened (see above)
The marinade from above	
¼ cup *(2 fluid ounces)* of Indian Clarified Butter (page 139)	Melted
3 limes	Cut into wedges or slices

METHOD

1. Place the flat chicken halves on a large board and, using your hands, rub them with about half the marinade.

2. Place them in pans or a plastic bag and spoon over the remainder of the marinade, making sure they are well covered. Marinate for a minimum of 2 hours, or even overnight.

3. Preheat broiler *(grill)* or barbecue and set the rack about 4 inches to 6 inches away from the source of the heat.

4. Remove the chicken from the marinade, scraping off the surplus. Reserve the marinade. Place the chickens over or under the source of heat and cook for 20 minutes on the first side, and 15 on the second (if using the barbecue). If using the fiercer enclosed heat of the oven grill, cook for 10 minutes on the first side and 8 minutes on the second side.

5. Baste the chicken with the marinade after the first 5 minutes, allow the marinade to dry on the surface and then baste again.

6. Test the chicken for doneness by piercing the thickest part, under the leg, with a fork. The juices should run clear and at this point the flesh should be white, barely tinged with pink.

7. Remove chicken from the grill and baste all surfaces with the Clarified Butter. Move the grilling racks up as close as possible to the heat and sear the chicken on the top side until it is golden brown and crusty.

9. Place the chicken on a platter and garnish with lime slices. The chicken should be properly accompanied by the Indian oven bread *(naan)* and by a fresh mint chutney. Eat with the fingers, Punjabi style, and enjoy.

ADVANCE PREPARATION AND
STORAGE NOTES

The marinade may be made a day in advance. The chicken may be marinated overnight. After cooking, it may be cooled and served at room temperature, or, wrapped in foil, it may be taken to a picnic. For less hearty appetites, cut chickens in quarters for each serving—or, as stated above, use Cornish game hens.

✿ Indian Oven-Barbecued Chicken (TANDOORI)

The Indian *tandoori* technique for preparing oven-roasted meat has recently become very popular in the West. You will find a full description of the culinary process in the section on India and its food under Backgrounds on the Countries, page 22. It is nice to know that you do not have to own an authentic *tandoor* oven to produce *tandoori* dishes; your own rotisserie or oven grill will perform splendidly as long as you pay heed to a few simple rules. The main point to note is the appearance and texture of the ideally cooked *tandoori* meats. They should be crisply coated on the outside but perfectly cooked and juicy inside. This is achieved by searing them initially in high heat to seal in the juices. 425°F. *(gas mark 7)* to 450°F. *(gas mark 8)* will seal the surface of the meat (generally chicken is used) if it is placed to the heat source. After searing, the meat is then cooked at a gentler 375°F. *(gas mark 5)* for the remainder of the time. The meat is not basted with fat and the marinade contains only a little; therefore the meat must be basted frequently and the surface just allowed to dry before the next application of marinade. If the meat is insufficiently basted—which is too often the case in restaurant *tandoori*—it becomes sawdust-dry. Conversely, too much basting produces excess moisture and spoils the texture of the exterior crust.

Preparation time: 2 to 10 hours   Serves 4 to 6
Cooking time: 45 minutes

SHOPPING AND TECHNIQUE TIPS
The Indians usually tenderize their older and tougher birds with ground papaya. If you buy young, plump frying chickens, there is no need for this step—marination is enough. Sometimes, the *tandoori* chickens are cooked whole on a spit. I prefer the convenience of chicken pieces. To ensure a final crisp coat, after the last application of marinade has dried the pieces are basted with melted Clarified Butter and then grilled under fierce heat.

INGREDIENTS   PREPARATION
Chicken
3 pounds of chicken parts   Skinned
Juice of 2 lemons
1 *(¾)* teaspoon of paprika
¼ teaspoon *(a pinch)* of ground red
    pepper (Cayenne)
1 *(¾)* teaspoon of salt

METHOD
1. Wash and thoroughly dry the chicken parts. With the point of a sharp knife, score several deep, parallel incisions through the fleshy parts of the chicken pieces and place them in a large mixing bowl.

2. Mix together the lemon juice, paprika, red pepper and salt and rub it well into the chicken pieces. (Use rubber gloves if your hands are sensitive.)

3. Let the chicken pieces sit at room temperature for 1 hour. Meanwhile prepare the marinade and basting sauce.

INGREDIENTS	PREPARATION
Marinade	
1 small onion	Peeled and chopped
4 shallots	Peeled and chopped
2-inch piece of ginger root	Peeled and chopped
6 cloves of garlic	Peeled and chopped
3 green Serrano chilli peppers, or 1 Jalapeño chilli	Chopped
1½ cups *(12 fluid ounces)* of plain yogurt	
4 *(3 ¼)* tablespoons of Indian Clarified Butter (page 139)	Melted
1 *(¾)* tablespoon of Indian Sweet Spice Mix (page 118)	
1 *(¾)* teaspoon of ground cumin	
½ *(⅓)* teaspoon salt	
A few drops each of red and yellow food coloring	

METHOD

1. Place the onion, shallots, ginger, garlic and chilli peppers in a food processor and process to a juicy paste, stopping the motor from time to time to scrape down the sides of the jar with a spatula.

2. Add yogurt, melted Clarified Butter, Sweet Spice Mix, cumin and salt and process to a smooth sauce.

3. Gradually add the red and yellow food coloring alternately, a drop at a time, while the motor is still running, until the mixture becomes a bright orange-yellow. Do not worry if the color seems garish—it will tone down under the grill.

4. Using a spatula to scrape the bowl, pour the mixture from the processor over the chicken pieces and rub it well into and on every piece. Set the chicken aside to marinate at room temperature for 2 hours. The chicken may also be covered and marinated in the refrigerator for up to 10 hours.

INGREDIENTS	PREPARATION
Cooking and Presentation	
Chicken and marinade from above	
½ cup *(4 ounces)* of Indian Clarified Butter (page 139)	Melted
1 small red onion	Peeled and thinly sliced into rings
2 limes	Thinly sliced into rounds

METHOD

1. Preheat the oven to 450°F. *(gas mark 8)*. (If using a charcoal barbecue, make sure the coals are glowing; if using a rotisserie, that it is at a higher temperature.)

2. Thoroughly drain the chicken from the marinade and let it dry. An electric blow-dryer at a cool setting will speed the process considerably.) Reserve the marinade.

3. Place the chicken pieces on a raised rack or on an oven spit with a roasting pan set below to catch the basting marinade. (If using a barbecue, set the chicken directly on the grid, but raise it to about 2 inches above the coals. On a rotisserie, spit the chicken and set the spit at a similar distance from the source of heat.

4. Sear the chicken on all sides, turning with tongs to avoid piercing the seal being built up. Immediately lower the heat to 375°F. *(gas mark 5)* or place the chicken pieces farther away from the source of heat.

5. Immediately baste with the marinade and cook for 5 minutes. Baste again if the surface has dried, and cook for another 5 minutes.

6. Turn the pieces over carefully with the tongs and baste the reverse sides with the marinade. Keep turning as necessary, basting when the surface looks dry, for a total of 40 minutes.

7. Now increase the heat to 450°F. *(gas mark 8)* and brush the chicken pieces with a complete coating of melted Clarified Butter. Replace them under the grill so that the coating and butter fuse to a crisp, hard crust.

8. Remove the chicken pieces with tongs and set them on a platter. Ring the platter with alternating red onion rings and lime rounds and serve immediately.

ADVANCE PREPARATION AND
STORAGE NOTES

The marinade can be made 24 hours in advance and the chicken marinated overnight. Barbecuing or baking *must* be done just before eating or the chicken dries out and the flesh takes on an unwelcome sawdust texture. With that in mind, please remember that Indian *tandoori* chicken does not make a good cold snack.

❧ Chinese Roast Pork

In Chinese meat stores in Hong Kong and Chinatowns throughout Southeast Asia, you can walk down the streets of food and meat shops and see rows of dark pink and red pork loins hanging from hooks; the Asian counterpart to the sausages of the *charcuterie.* In the same manner as European housewives buy sausage, the Chinese women request that a particular loin be taken down and enough for her needs sliced off and packaged for her next dinner dish.

Pork roasted in this manner can be thinly sliced and served as part of a platter of cold meats or cut into small pieces as a filling for Roast Pork Buns (page 446).

Preparation time: 3 hours and 20   Cooking time: 1 hour and 15 minutes
   minutes   Serves 6 to 8

SHOPPING AND TECHNIQUE TIPS
Try to find pork sirloin end, boned, or blade end, and have the butcher bone it. Both cuts are more tender and desirable than the shoulder (butt). Boned leg is also ideal, but it is difficult to find outside Oriental butcher shops; in the West it is mostly reserved for ham. The long marination makes for a strongly flavored roast. Basting it with honey while roasting seals in the juices and also produces a high glaze.

INGREDIENTS   PREPARATION
3 pounds of pork sirloin (see above)
2 *(1⅔)* tablespoons of pale dry
      sherry
2 *(1⅔)* tablespoons of granulated
      sugar
¼ cup *(2 fluid ounces)* of soy sauce
3 *(2⅓)* tablespoons of Chinese
      All-Purpose Sauce (page 145)
¼ teaspoon *(6 drops)* of red food
      coloring
½ cup *(6½ tablespoons)* of honey   Warmed

METHOD
   1. Cut the pork into strips about 2 inches in width and thickness. These strips should run along the grain of the meat. Place them in a plastic bag.
   2. Mix together all the remaining ingredients, except the honey, and pour them into the bag with the pork. Seal the bag and move the contents around to distribute the marinade evenly. Let the pork marinate at room temperature

for 3 hours. If you wish to refrigerate it, it should then marinate for about 4 or 5 hours.

3. While the pork is marinating, fashion S-shaped hooks from wire coat hangers, 1 hook for each pork strip. These will hang from the highest rack in your oven. (If your oven is not equipped to accommodate hangers, you can roast the pork strips directly on the grid inside the baking pan.)

4. Toward the end of the marination period, preheat the oven to 325°F. *(gas mark 3)*. Set a small bowl containing the honey inside, so that the honey liquefies.

5. Remove the pork strips from the bag and attach them to the hooks. Lay them across the grid and paint them on both sides with the honey, then attach them to the top rack of the oven with the baking pan underneath. Roast the pork for 1 hour, brushing the strips with honey 3 times during that period.

6. Remove the pork and let it stand for 20 minutes before carving into thin pieces.

Note: If you wish to roast the pork in one piece, you may. Allow 30 minutes plus 15 minutes per pound roasting time, and then an extra 20 minutes for setting up at room temperature. Example: A 3-pound roast will take 1¼ hours in a 325°F. *(gas mark 3)* oven, and then an extra 20 minutes outside.

ADVANCE PREPARATION AND
STORAGE NOTES

Since pork cooked this way is normally served cold, or used as a filling, or as an addition to stir-fried dishes or noodles and soups, it can be prepared whenever you wish. It will keep, covered, in the refrigerator, for a week. It can also be frozen and thawed in a microwave, or at room temperature, before using.

Korean Variation

Marinate the pork in the following marinade:

INGREDIENTS	PREPARATION
6 *(4¾)* tablespoons of soy sauce	
1 *(¾)* tablespoon of granulated sugar	
2 green *(spring)* onions	Minced
2 cloves of garlic	Smashed, peeled and minced
1 *(¾)* tablespoon of sesame seeds	Dry-toasted until light brown, then pounded to a powder in a mortar
2 or 3 pieces of candied or crystallized ginger	Minced

INGREDIENTS
1 (¾) tablespoon of Sesame Oil
    (page 139)
¼ teaspoon *(a pinch)* of ground
    black pepper

METHOD
Follow the Chinese Roast Pork recipe, but baste with the remaining marinade instead of honey. Serve hot or cold, sliced.

Vietnamese Variation

Substitute the following marinade:

INGREDIENTS	PREPARATION
3 cloves of garlic	Peeled and chopped
3 shallots	Peeled and chopped
1 (¾) tablespoon of granulated sugar	
¼ teaspoon *(a pinch)* of ground black pepper	
3 (2⅓) tablespoons of Southeast Asian fish sauce	

METHOD
Pound the garlic, shallots and sugar together in a mortar. Stir in the remaining ingredients and marinate the pork in the mixture. Follow the Chinese Roast Pork recipe for roasting, but brush on any remaining marinade. Serve sliced, accompanied by separate bowls of noodles and vinegared raw vegetables. Sprinkle the pork with crushed roasted peanuts.

SATAY, THE KEBAB OF SOUTHEAST ASIA

Satay, *sate,* as it is correctly spelled in Southeast Asia, is one of the universal snacks of the area. Although both Thailand and Malaysia claim it as their own, its Southeast Asian origin was in Java, Indonesia. There satay was developed from the Indian kebab brought by the Muslim traders. Even India cannot claim its origin, for there it was a legacy of Middle Eastern influence.

While the kebab is composed of large chunks of meat, often interspersed with vegetables, the satay is smaller and consists solely of bite-sized strips or ribbons of meat or fish threaded on bamboo skewers or sticks fashioned from the tough central spine of the banana leaf. The meat can be beef, pork, chicken or even lamb.

In the coastal villages of Indonesia, turtle and shrimp are threaded on satay sticks. Water buffalo, or *carabao sate,* is found in Makasar, in southern Sulawesi. Pork satay is eaten mainly by the Chinese and the Buddhists, as the many Muslims in Indonesia and the rest of Southeast Asia are forbidden by their religion to eat pork. In Thailand the most popular satay is chicken.

The loaded satay skewers are marinated in varying concoctions of dark soy sauce mixed with lime juice, garlic, sugar, salt, pepper and other spices. The marinade varies with the local area. There are endless varieties of satay. Every little village and town seems to have its own recipe, every chef his favorite.

After several hours of soaking in the marinade, when the meat or fish is saturated with sauce and spices, the threaded sticks are then grilled over glowing charcoal.

The most common accompaniment to satay, and the one best known in the West, is the thick peanut-based sauce which is served as a dip. In Indonesia, however, a soy-based sauce is often substituted. Sometimes the sauce is "curry" flavored, with the addition of turmeric and other spices thinned with coconut milk.

Cooking satay is part of the fun of eating it. For guest participation in cooking it it rivals the fondue. Set up 3 or 4 of the inexpensive charcoal *hibachis* on your patio or in your garden. Load trays with prethreaded and marinated bamboo skewers of chicken, pork and beef. Let the charcoal settle to an even, glowing crimson before your guests start to barbecue. Have side bowls of various satay sauces set out, and fresh relishes of finely sliced vegetables such as cucumber and onion, tomatoes and sweet green peppers, all marinated in a balanced mixture of sugar and white vinegar (see Philippine Variation II, page 229). Prepare a large amount of steaming white rice, then pile it on a platter. Let your guests select and grill their own satays and choose the accompaniments. Allow 4 to 6 sticks per person.

Finish off the al fresco meal with a large platter of fresh fruit. Include as many tropical fruits as you can find: mangoes, papayas, bananas and pineapple. Then sit back and receive compliments.

❀ Indonesian Beef Satay

Preparation time: 1 hour
Cooking time: 5 minutes

Serves 6 to 8

SHOPPING AND TECHNIQUE TIPS
Look for lean, boneless rib, loin or top round. Place the meat in the freezer for about 20 minutes until it is just beginning to freeze and is very firm. In this state you will be able to slice it to the necessary thinness. The wooden *sate* sticks are available in packages in most supermarkets or in Oriental shops. Before you begin the *sate,* soak sticks in cold water for several hours. This will prevent them from burning through and breaking into pieces on or under the grill. The sticks are available in 2 sizes—the larger size for hungrier people.

INGREDIENTS	PREPARATION
Marinade	
3 *(2⅓)* tablespoons of peanut oil	
1 small onion	Peeled and finely chopped
4 macadamia nuts, or 2 Brazil nuts	Crushed or pounded to a powder
¼ teaspoon *(a pinch)* of ground ginger	
1 *(¾)* teaspoon of ground coriander	
1 *(¾)* teaspoon of Indonesian Hot Pepper Paste (page 128)	
1 *(¾)* teaspoon of molasses *(treacle)* dissolved in 2 *(1⅔)* tablespoons of lime juice	
3 *(2⅓)* tablespoons of hot water	
½ *(⅓)* teaspoon of salt	

METHOD
1. Heat the oil over medium heat in a frying pan and fry the onions until they turn a pale gold. Set the pan aside.
2. In a small bowl, mix together the remaining marinade ingredients thoroughly, then pour them into the pan containing the onions and stir well.

INGREDIENTS	PREPARATION
Satay	
Satay sticks	Soaked in cold water
1 pound of lean, boneless steak	Cut into thin (⅛-inch) slices, then into ribbons 1 inch wide by 2 to 3 inches long
Marinade from above	

THREADING
SATAY STICKS

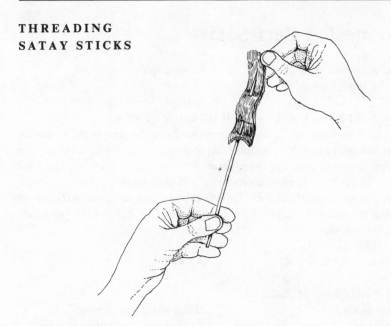

METHOD

1. Thread the point of the satay stick through the smaller end of each piece of meat as you would a needle along a length of ribbon. Leave about 4 inches of bare stick at the blunt end as a handle to turn the beef, and leave some space between the individual strips of meat so they will cook uniformly. Continue threading until all the meat is used. (The number of sticks you will require will depend on how densely you thread each stick with the beef.)

2. Lay the threaded sticks in a row on a large, shallow cookie sheet and pour the onion marinade from the pan over them.

3. Let the satays marinate at room temperature for at least 30 minutes.

4. Meanwhile heat the barbecue or oven broiler to about 400°F. *(gas mark 6).*

5. Grill the satays over or under intense heat for about 1½ to 2½ minutes per side.

6. Serve at once, accompanied by any of the satay sauces from the chapter on chutneys and sauces (page 450) and a fresh, vinegared vegetable relish from the same chapter.

ADVANCE PREPARATION AND
STORAGE NOTES

The meat may be cut and refrigerated, covered with plastic wrap, for up to 3 or 4 hours beforehand. The marinade may be made up to half a day in advance. Do not barbecue the meat until just before serving.

❧ Malaysian Pork Satay

This recipe differs from other satay recipes in that the meat is precooked in spices, which act as the marinade and then become the sauce served with the dish.

Preparation time: 10 minutes   Serves 8
Cooking time: 35 minutes

SHOPPING AND TECHNIQUE TIPS
Choose loin or pork butt, as the shoulder has too much fat. Alternatively, you may wish to buy thick (¾-inch) pork chops and remove the meat from the bone before cubing it. For the satay sticks *see* Shopping and Technique Tips in the recipe for Indonesian Beef Satay, page 407.

INGREDIENTS
2 pounds of lean pork
1 small onion
1 *(¾)* teaspoon of ground turmeric
1 *(¾)* teaspoon of salt
½ *(⅓)* teaspoon of freshly ground
    black pepper
½ *(⅓)* teaspoon ground red pepper
    (Cayenne)
1 *(¾)* teaspoon of ground coriander
2 cups *(16 fluid ounces)* of whole
    milk, flavored with 1 *(¾)*
    teaspoon of coconut extract
1 *(¾)* teaspoon of granulated sugar

PREPARATION
Boned and cut into ¾-inch cubes
Peeled and minced

METHOD
1. Wash and drain the pork and place it in a large saucepan together with the remaining ingredients. Bring the mixture to a boil over medium-high heat. Immediately when it reaches a boil, reduce the heat to low and simmer for 10 minutes.

2. With a slotted spoon, remove the pork to a dish, draining it well over the saucepan. Increase the heat under the sauce and continue to cook on a moderate boil until the mixture is reduced by half.

3. Preheat the barbecue or oven grill—450°F. *(gas mark 8)*. While the sauce is reducing, place the pork on the presoaked sticks, 5 or 6 cubes on each. When arranging the cubes, remember to leave a 4-inch space at the blunt end to act as a handle when turning the satays.

4. When the sauce has been sufficiently reduced, begin grilling the satays over or under intense heat, turning frequently, for about 5 minutes.

5. Place all the sticks on a platter, pour the sauce over them or serve it separately in a small bowl. Serve immediately, accompanied by a fresh vegetable relish and plain rice.

ADVANCE PREPARATION AND STORAGE NOTES

The sauce and pork may be cooked ahead and cooled. Remove the pork cubes from the sauce about 10 minutes before broiling, to allow them to dry sufficiently. While the satays are broiling, reheat the sauce.

❧ Thai Chicken Satay

The street vendors in Thailand sell this satay speared on ribs stripped from banana leaves. The ribs look rather like arrows with their pointed leaf segments (like the feathered tips of darts). Street style, the chicken is left in 1 whole strip on the short stick.

Preparation time: 2 hours   Serves 6 to 8
Cooking time 3 minutes

SHOPPING AND TECHNIQUE TIPS

Buy chicken breasts already boned, or bone your own. Freezing the breasts for 15 minutes before you slice them will facilitate cutting them into neat strips. The marinade is in the form of a paste and should be rubbed on the chicken.

INGREDIENTS	PREPARATION
1-inch piece of fresh ginger root	Peeled and minced
3 cloves of garlic	Peeled and chopped
1 (¾) tablespoon of Thai Curry Spice Paste (page 124)	
1 (¾) teaspoon of ground turmeric	
2 (1⅔) tablespoons of whipping cream flavored with 4 drops of coconut extract	
2 pounds of chicken breasts	Skinned, boned, slightly frozen, then cut on the diagonal into slices ¼-inch thick
½ cup (4 fluid ounces) of whole milk flavored with ¼ teaspoon (6 drops) of coconut extract	

METHOD

1. In a mortar, pound the ginger and garlic into a juicy paste. Add the Curry Spice Paste, turmeric and whipping cream, stirring with the pestle until a liquid paste results.

2. Place the chicken slices on a plate and, scraping the paste from the mortar, rub it thoroughly into the chicken. Cover the plate with plastic wrap and leave it to marinate at room temperature for 2 hours.

3. Preheat the barbecue or oven grill to between 400°F. and 450°F. *(between gas mark 6 and 8).*

4. At the end of the marination time, thread each chicken slice on a satay stick, inserting the stick through the thickness of the slice so that it does not show on either surface. Leave enough room at the blunt end so that the loaded sticks can be easily handled.

5. Grill them over or under fierce heat for 1½ minutes on each side, sprinkling the chicken with a little coconut milk so that it does not dry out while cooking. (The chicken should be cooked very close to the heat so that there are characteristic dark brown flecks on the cooked satays.)

6. Remove the satays and arrange them on a platter. Serve immediately, accompanied by Thai Peanut Sauce (page 470) and the Fresh Cucumber Salad (page 237).

ADVANCE PREPARATION AND STORAGE NOTES

The paste for marinating can be made up to 1 day in advance. The chicken can be cut and refrigerated, covered. The chicken can also be marinated up to half a day ahead.

NOODLING

❧ ❧ ❧

The Pasta of Asia

The old story has it that Marco Polo discovered noodles in China and brought them back to Italy, thereby introducing them to Europe. The Italians disagree, claiming the invention of pasta in addition to that of ice cream. Either country may well be right, because the origin of the noodle is lost in the mists of history. Dumplings and various fillings wrapped in flour-and-water pastes were eaten all over central Europe and Asia, from Poland to Afghanistan, and noodles could have been a natural and logical descendant from these hearty, peasant origins. Mills for the large-scale grinding of flour were in operation in China during the Han Dynasty, around the time of the birth of Christ, but Chinese historians indicate that the technique for the preparation of noodles came from the West.

Whatever their origin, noodles have been the mainstay of the laboring people for centuries. They were always regarded as peasant food, although in second-century China the emperor ate them. Noodle shops were widespread in China in those days, much as they are today throughout Asia. They were known as "laborers' shops" and regarded as lower than the taverns because they did not serve wine. These shops did not provide full meals, but customers had a choice of noodles with vegetables or noodles with meat, which they ate as snacks during breaks in the working day.

Today, noodles in some shape or form are eaten all over Asia. Even India, which does not traditionally include them in its cuisine, has a form of noodle, called *sevia*, which is made from lentil four and made in a machine rather like our pasta machines, to be deep-fried in oil until crisp and eaten as a snack. Burma, bridging the gap between India and Chinese-influenced Southeast Asia, serves its curries with noodles. Throughout the rest of the Orient, festoons of noodles can be seen drying in the sun much as they are dried in Italy, to find their way into thousands of soup bowls daily.

Noodles are available in many shapes, forms and substances. Although the majority are made from some mixture of wheat flour, they are also made from rice, mung-bean flour, even seaweed and yams. Rice noodles are popular, naturally, in the south of China and throughout Southeast Asia. Rice-stick noodles, also known as long rice (in Hawaii) and as rice vermicelli, are white, brittle, thin dried noodles and are soaked before use in stir-fried dishes or in soups. They can also be deep-fried straight from the package—they then puff up into a delicious tangle of crisp, crunchy texture. In this form, they are used in the Thai fried-noodle dish *Mee Krob,* and also in the Chinese chicken salad with crisp noodles. Both dishes are a marvelous counterpoint of textures and flavors.

Dried rice noodles are also to be found in thicker strands, while fresh rice noodles, usually available in packages, are made in both noodle shapes and large, flat sheets, which are then folded before packaging. The latter noodles are made from glutinous rice flour and are already partly cooked by steaming, so they need little further cooking after purchase. The folded layers are merely cut to whatever width is needed and the noodles briefly immersed in stock or water.

Bean-thread noodles look rather like the rice-stick noodles, but they are slightly thinner and somewhat translucent, while the rice noodles are opaque. They are made from extruded strands of mung-bean starch, which are then dried over lines in the sun. They are packaged under many names, variously referred to as mung-bean noodles, cellophane noodles, shining noodles, silver threads or jelly noodles. They are very tough in their dried form, and indeed, if you try to break the hanks apart with your hands, you may cut yourself. After they are soaked, they become soft, gelatinous and transparent and can be easily broken. Mung-bean noodles have no particular flavor of their own, but when they are cooked in a soup they absorb a great amount of liquid, and

Noodle	Description	Comments
Rice Stick Noodles Chinese: *(py)-mee-fun, ngunsi-fun, lai-fun* Thai: *sen-mee* Indonesian: *bee-hun* Vietnamese: *banh-pho* Malay: *chee-cheong-fun*	Thin, white, opaque, brittle, dried noodle. Sold in hanks, packaged in 8-ounce or 1-pound bundles.	Soak in cold water for 20 minutes. Cut into 3-inch lengths. Cook for 2 to 3 minutes. Use in soups and stir-fried dishes. Can also be crisp-fried directly from the package and used in salads or as a crunchy topping for cooked vegetables. Substitute: vermicelli
Fresh Soft Rice Noodles Chinese: *look-fun* Thai: *gwaytio*	Sheets or strips of soft, wet dough, lightly cooked. Made from sweet, glutinous rice. Packaged in plastic. In refrigerated section of markets.	Cut into pieces and cook for 1 to 2 minutes. The noodles are delicate and overcook very easily. Use in soups and stir-fried vegetable dishes. Substitute: homemade rice-noodle dough
Dried Rice Noodles Chinese: *ho-fun*	Wider than rice sticks. Often flat. Many different varieties.	Soak for 20 to 60 minutes, depending on type. Cut into 3-inch pieces and drop into boiling water for 6 to 10 minutes. Drain and rinse in cold water. Use in soups and stir-fried dishes. Substitute: linguini

Noodle	Description	Comments
Bean Thread, Cellophane Noodles Chinese: *fun-see, fen szu, sai fun* (falling rain) Japanese: *harusame* (spring rain) Thai: *wun-sen* Indonesian: *so-un, lak-sa*	Tough, thin, wiry, translucent dried noodle, made from mung-bean starch. The Japanese variety is wider and ribbonlike. Packaged in hanks.	Cut the amount needed with scissors. Do not try to break them by hand. Soak in warm water for 20 minutes to soften, then cut into 3-inch lengths. Three minutes is sufficient cooking time. Use in soups and gravied stir-fry dishes. Can also be deep-fried directly from the package. Chinese seaweed noodles are somewhat similar but are longer, thinner and more gelatinous. Substitute: vermicelli
Egg Noodles Chinese: *dan-min* (Cantonese), *Hokkien mee* Thai: *ba-mee* Malaysian: *mee* Indonesian: *ba-mee*	Available in wide ribbons, loose in packages or as thin noodles in hanks, 7 to 8 bundles to a pack. Yellow and shiny-surfaced. Drawn out or pulled from wheat flour-and-egg dough.	Soak in hot water for 10 minutes to soften and separate noodles. Drop in boiling water with a teaspoon of oil to prevent boiling over. Cook thin noodles for 2 to 3 minutes; wide noodles for 4 to 5 minutes. Rinse in cold water. For crisp-fried noodles, cook first, drain and dry on a tray, then deep-fry. Substitute: Linguini, egg noodles, fettuccini, or #8 or 9 spaghetti, spaghettini
Wheat Flour Noodles Chinese: *lo-mein* Japanese: See Japanese Wheat Noodles, below	Pulled-dough noodles. Some varieties look like spaghetti. Longer and whiter than egg noodles. Available fresh and dried.	Parboil before adding to soups. Cook in boiling water: 2 to 3 minutes for fresh noodles, 7 to 10 for dried. For soups and fried noodle dishes. Substitute: wonton skins cut into strips, spaghetti or any similar pasta

Noodle	Description	Comments
Japanese Wheat Noodles		
Soba (nearness)	Dried noodle, made from finely ground buckwheat flour in straight flat sticks, 7 to 10 inches long. Some varieties are flavored with tea. Available in packages or boxes. Served hot or cold.	Cook in boiling water for 7 minutes. Drain, rinse in cold water. Noodles to be served hot are placed in individual bowls and soup poured over them. To serve cold: chill in cold water, drain and place on plates to be topped with garnishes and served with a chilled sauce. Substitute: whole-wheat noodles
Udon	Thick white noodle. Fresh are called *nama udon*. The dried variety look like long, flat sticks and are sold in boxes or packages.	Traditionally served hot in the winter in Japan. The fresh noodles are cooked in boiling water for 3 minutes, dried noodles for 10 minutes. Rinse in cold, running water and drain. Alternatively, dried noodles are put in boiling water and ½ cup of cold water added. They are brought back to a boil and this process is repeated adding another ½ cup of cold water. Repeat 3 times all told, and then cook for 10 minutes, rinse and drain. To reheat: pour boiling water over the noodles, let them stand for 1 minute, then drain and serve. Substitute: any ribbon pasta
Kishimen	Broad, flat noodle.	Cook in the same manner as dried *udon*.

Noodle	Description	Comments
Somen	White, very thin round noodle. Sold in bundles or packages. Mostly served iced in summer dishes or salads.	Cook for 4 minutes in boiling water, drain, rinse in cold water and drain again. Or cook in boiling water, adding ½ cup (4 ounces) of cold water, and repeat (2 times in all). Boil for 3 minutes, drain and chill. Serve over ice cubes in individual bowls and accompany with a dipping sauce. Substitute: vermicelli, spaghettini, *ramen*, *sai-min*
Hiyamugi	Thin, dried wheat-flour noodles.	Cook in the same manner as *somen*.
Shirataki (white waterfall)	Translucent noodle made from tubers of devil's tongue or snake-palm plant *(kon-nyaku)*, a yam of the arum family. Available water-packed in cans or vacuum-packet plastic packages.	Cook in the same manner as bean thread noodles.
Instant Noodles Japanese: *ramen, yaki-soba, chuka soba* Hawaiian: *sai-min*	Many varieties and shapes. They are available in hanks or as tangled cakes, in packages. Precooked and dried, they are mainly made from wheat flour.	Because these are precooked, they need no soaking. Cook in liquid, soup or gravy for 3 minutes. Widely available in the soup or Oriental sections of supermarkets.

with it the flavor of the soup. They are used predominantly in soups, but also in stir-fried dishes as well.

Wheat-flour noodles, with or without the inclusion of eggs, are the most common noodle throughout China, Japan and Korea. Their varieties are almost endless; a chart listing and describing them under their Asian names follows, together with instructions for their preparation. Increasingly they are making an appearance on the shelves of our supermarkets, but without a guide it is difficult to recognize them or to know their particular use. The nice thing about the Asian noodles is that they are mostly interchangeable in dishes. With a few exceptions, the choice of noodle is left to the cook, in the same manner as pasta. When the Asian noodle is not available, the nearest shape and size of pasta can be easily substituted without losing authenticity, and I have indicated possible substitutions.

✿ Pork and Shrimp Rice Noodles in Broth (CHINA)

This is a "one bowl" snack dish, suitable for a light lunch or a supper. It is a "wet" noodle dish, close to a soup, but more substantial. It is served in a bowl.

Preparation time: 45 minutes   Serves 6
Cooking time: 25 minutes

SHOPPING AND TECHNIQUE TIPS
Pork loin is traditionally used for this dish, but since only a small quantity is needed, center loin pork chops are more feasible. I buy the chops and remove the meat from the bone. Use dried Oriental mushrooms if you can find them; their flavor really enhances the dish. If you cannot, however, substitute fresh mushrooms. The Chinese Tientsin (celery) cabbage is the correct variety to use, but you may substitute white cabbage if you can't get the Chinese.

INGREDIENTS
½ pound (after boning) of pork-chop
   meat
1 (¾) tablespoon of soy sauce
1 (¾) teaspoon of Chinese
   All-Purpose Sauce (page 145)
2 (1⅔) teaspoons of cornstarch
   (cornflour)

PREPARATION
Thinly sliced into narrow (¼-inch)
   strips

INGREDIENTS

3 *(2⅓)* tablespoons of water
1 cup *(5½ ounces)* of small shrimp
4 *(3¼)* tablespoons of vegetable oil
4 dried Oriental mushrooms, or 6
    fresh mushrooms

3 green *(spring)* onions

6 leaves of Chinese Tientsin (celery)
    cabbage, or white cabbage

8 cups *(48 fluid ounces)* of Basic
    Chicken Stock (page 168)
½ pound of rice-stick noodles (you
    may substitute egg noodles or
    vermicelli)
1 *(¾)* teaspoon of salt
¼ teaspoon *(a pinch)* of ground
    black pepper

PREPARATION

Soaked in hot water for 10 minutes,
    stems removed, caps sliced into
    strips (the fresh mushrooms should
    merely be sliced)
Cut into 2-inch lengths, then into
    slivers
Stacked, cut across into strips 2
    inches wide, each strip cut across
    the width into slivers 2 inches in
    length

METHOD

1. Place the pork strips in a bowl, together with the soy sauce, All-Purpose Sauce, water and cornstarch *(cornflour)* and mix well until the pork is thoroughly coated. Let it marinate for 20 minutes.

2. While the pork is marinating, shell, clean and devein the shrimp.

3. Heat the oil in a wok over high heat and stir-fry the pork for 3 minutes. Using a slotted spoon, drain it over the wok and remove to a paper plate.

4. Bring the oil back up to high heat and stir-fry the mushrooms and green *(spring)* onions for 2 minutes. Add the shredded cabbage and shrimp and fry until the shrimp becomes pink and the cabbage turns limp.

5. Pour in the stock and bring it to a boil. Add the rice noodles and boil for 1 minute. Return the pork to the wok to reheat and season with the salt and pepper. Pour into a large bowl or into individual bowls to serve.

ADVANCE PREPARATION AND
STORAGE NOTES

The pork may be marinated, the vegetables and mushrooms prepared and the shrimp cleaned in advance. They may then be refrigerated. However, the dish cannot be cooked until just before serving.

Thai and Malaysian Variation

Do not marinate the pork. Fry 4 minced cloves of garlic and 4 minced shallots as in step 4 of the recipe above before adding the mushrooms and green *(spring)* onions. In step 5, season with 2 *(1⅔)* tablespoons of Southeast Asian fish sauce instead of the salt, and increase the black pepper to ½ *(⅓)* teaspoon. Stir in 1 *(¾)* tablespoon of chopped coriander (Chinese parsley, *cilantro*) leaves, or sprinkle them on top of the soup after it is transferred to the serving bowl.

Vietnamese Variation

Omit the marination of the pork. Fry the green *(spring)* onions together with the pork and omit the mushrooms. Substitute 3 large tomatoes, each cut into 6 segments, for the cabbage. Serve the soup in individual bowls, first placing a lettuce leaf torn into a few pieces, a few bean sprouts, 4 or 5 narrow strips of cucumber, 3 mint leaves and a scattering of chopped coriander leaves in the bottom of each bowl before pouring the soup in. Garnish with a sprinkling of crushed peanuts. This Vietnamese dish may also be made with chicken instead of pork.

❧ Beef and Shrimp Noodles in Broth (INDONESIA)

This noodle dish is somewhat different from those preceding it as it requires a spice paste, in its preparation; in addition, the noodles are cooked separately. It is called *Bahmee Godog*. It can also be made without the stock, as a "dry" noodle dish, in which case it is known as *Bahmee Goreng*.

Preparation time: 20 minutes   Serves 6
Cooking time: 25 minutes

SHOPPING AND TECHNIQUE TIPS

You may use the Oriental wheat-and-egg noodles for this dish, or even Western egg noodles. Linguine or fettuccine are also suitable. The Chinese immigrants to Indonesia originally made the dish with pork or chicken, but the Muslim Javanese changed the meat to beef. You may make it with any of these. If using beef, good cuts are top loin or sirloin tip.

INGREDIENTS

½ (⅓) teaspoon of salt

½ pound of egg noodles

4 cloves of garlic

4 macadamia nuts, or 2 skinned
    Brazil nuts

2 (1⅔) tablespoons of vegetable oil

6 shallots

½ pound of beef (see Shopping and
    Technique Tips)

2 carrots

2 leaves of white cabbage

4 cups (32 fluid ounces) of Basic
    Chicken Stock (page 168)

½ cup (3¼ ounces) of canned
    (tinned) tomatoes

¼ teaspoon (a pinch) of ground
    cinnamon

2 (1⅔) tablespoons of soy sauce

½ cup (3¼ ounces) (after shelling)
    of small shrimp

½ cup (1⅓ ounces) of bean sprouts

2 green (spring) onions

¼ teaspoon (a pinch) of ground
    black pepper

1 stalk of celery

2 (1⅔) tablespoons of Fried Onion
    Flakes (page 156)

1 or 2 fresh Serrano chillies

PREPARATION

Peeled and chopped

Chopped

Peeled and thinly sliced crosswise

Thinly sliced and then cut into strips
    2 inches long by ½-inch wide

Peeled and thinly sliced diagonally

Shredded

Chopped

Shelled, cleaned and deveined

Washed, drained, roots removed

Chopped

Finely chopped

Seeded and cut into slivers

METHOD

1. Fill a large saucepan with water and add the salt. Bring to a rolling boil over high heat and add the noodles, stirring. Boil them for 5 minutes, or follow the directions on the package. When the noodles are cooked, place them in a colander and immediately run cold water over them to stop any further cooking and to prevent them from sticking together. Wash the noodles well and leave them to drain.

2. Place the garlic and nuts in a mortar and pound to a smooth paste.

3. Measure the oil into a wok and set it over medium-high heat. Add the shallots and stir-fry them for 1 minute. Stir in the paste from the mortar and fry for 30 seconds. Add the beef and stir-fry until beef is brown. Now add the carrots and cabbage and stir-fry for about 4 minutes, or until both are almost tender.

4. Pour in the stock and add the tomatoes, cinnamon and soy sauce. Bring the liquid to a boil and reduce the heat to a simmer. Simmer for 4 minutes, then stir in the shrimp, bean sprouts and green *(spring)* onions. Season with the black pepper and stir in the noodles. Increase the heat to medium-high and cook until the noodles are hot.

5. Pour into a serving bowl or individual bowls and garnish with the celery, Onion Flakes and chilli pepper slivers.

ADVANCE PREPARATION AND
STORAGE NOTES
The noodles can be cooked, the vegetables cleaned and cut and all the preparatory work done ahead. The dish should be cooked just before serving.

✿ White Flour Noodles and Chicken in Broth (JAPAN)

This dish is made with either the fresh or dried white flour Japanese noodles. The buckwheat flour noodles may also be used. The noodles are cooked separately and the stock poured over them. The dish is cooked in flameproof casseroles, but if you do not have them, use ovenproof casseroles and cook the dish in the oven.

Preparation time: 25 minutes
Cooking time: 25 to 35 minutes,
    depending on the type of noodle
    and the method of cooking in the
    casseroles.

Serves 4 to 6, depending on the size of the casseroles and people's appetites.

SHOPPING AND TECHNIQUE TIPS
Look in the Oriental section of a good supermarket for Japanese noodles. If you cannot find them, you may either make your own (page 152) or substitute any ribbon pasta. You may also be able to use the instant noodles from the packages of noodles combined with dried stock which are now widely available in supermarkets. Among the other ingredients in the original Japanese dish are: the Japanese compressed fish cake called *kamaboko*, dried Japanese mushrooms, chicken, green *(spring)* onions, spinach and edible chrysanthemum leaves. The fish cake and chrysanthemum leaves can be omitted without loss of authenticity —this comes with the technique and presentation.

INGREDIENTS

1 pound of noodles (see Shopping
   and Technique Tips)
10 leaves of young spinach
½ chicken breast

2 dried Japanese mushrooms, if
   available, or
4 small fresh mushrooms

4 to 6 cups *(32 fluid ounces to 48
   fluid ounces)* of Japanese Basic
   Fish Stock (page 170)
4 to 6 medium shrimp
4 to 6 eggs (optional)

PREPARATION

Washed and drained
Boned, skinned and cut crosswise
   into strips about ¼-inch wide

Soaked in hot water for 10 minutes,
   stems removed, caps cut into strips
Sliced thinly into cross sections,
   including stems

Shelled and deveined, tails left intact

METHOD

1. Fill a large saucepan with water and cook the noodles according to the directions for the type of noodle (see chart on pages 414–417). Lift the noodles from the saucepan (leaving the water in the pot), put them in a colander, run cold water over them to stop any further cooking and set them aside.

2. Set the saucepan back on the heat and bring back to a boil. Put the spinach leaves in a strainer, immerse it in the water and cook for 1 minute. Drain the spinach and let it cool. Stack it into a bundle with all the leaves facing the same way. Squeeze out the moisture gently, then cut the compressed bundle into 2-inch lengths.

3. Place the chicken pieces in a strainer and immerse them in the boiling water for 2 minutes. Drain and remove.

4. Pour the stock (1 cup per person) into a medium saucepan and bring to a boil. Reduce to a simmer.

5. Divide the noodles equally among the casseroles. Divide the chicken pieces, mushroom strips and green *(spring)* onions equally among the casseroles and place them on top of the noodles. Put a shrimp and a spinach bundle into each casserole.

6. Pour the simmering stock very gently over everything to avoid disturbing the arrangement of ingredients. If using flameproof casseroles cover and place each casserole over a burner and bring to a boil (about 4 to 5 minutes). If using ovenproof casseroles, place them in a preheated 350°F. *(gas mark 4)* oven for 15 minutes.

7. At the end of the cooking time, if you wish to add eggs, break an egg carefully into each casserole, cover again, turn off the heat and let the eggs cook

in the residual heat until the whites are solid and the yolks are still fairly liquid.
Serve immediately.

ADVANCE PREPARATION AND STORAGE NOTES

The ingredients may be prepared ahead, but the dish should be cooked
just before serving. You may, if you wish, make it in 1 large casserole. The
effect is a little different, but the presentation is unmistakably Japanese.

❧ Philippine Egg Noodles with Meats and Vegetables

This dish is one version of the famous Philippine *pancit,* or fried noodle dish.
There are other versions, some of which call for a "red" sauce, thickened with
flour and colored with the water from steeped annatto seeds. These seeds from
a tropical South or Central American tree are also called *achiote* or *achuete* and
are available from the Latin American grocery stores and Latin American sections
of supermarkets. This *pancit* is easier to make than some because it does not call
for unusual ingredients.

Preparation time: 25 minutes   Serves 6
Cooking time: 35 to 45 minutes

SHOPPING AND TECHNIQUE TIPS

This dish requires that most of the ingredients be cooked first by dipping them
in boiling water before they are fried. You may make substitutions in the ingredients and use leftover cooked pork and chicken, provided it was previously cooked
rather simply.

INGREDIENTS	PREPARATION
1 pound of egg noodles (flat or round)	
½ chicken breast	Skinned and boned
½ cup *(3 ¼ ounces)* of medium shrimp	Shelled, cleaned and deveined
The meat from 2 center-cut *(the center of a pork loin chop)* pork chops	Bone removed, otherwise left whole
¼ cup *(2 fluid ounces)* of vegetable oil or shortening	

INGREDIENTS

6 cloves of garlic

1 large onion

½ cup (¼ pound) of lean ham

2 (1⅔) tablespoons of soy sauce

1 cup (¼ pound) of white cabbage

½ (⅓) teaspoon of salt

¼ teaspoon (a pinch) of ground
    black pepper

3 lemons, cut into quarters

PREPARATION

Peeled and sliced

Peeled, sliced and squeezed dry in
    paper towels

Cut into thin strips

Shredded

METHOD

1. Fill a large saucepan with water and bring it to a rapid boil over high heat. Place the noodles in a strainer and immerse them in the boiling water for 3 minutes, or for the length of time stated on the package. Remove noodles from the strainer, leaving the water on the boil, and rinse them in a colander under running cold water. Set them aside.

2. Put the chicken in the strainer and immerse it in the boiling water for 5 minutes. Remove chicken and let it cool.

3. Put the shrimp in the strainer and immerse them in the boiling water for 1 minute, or until they turn pink. Remove and set aside to cool. Repeat with the pork, immersing it for 4 minutes.

4. Turn the heat off under the saucepan and measure out ½ cup (4 fluid ounces) of the liquid. Retain the rest for soup, if you wish.

5. Cut the chicken and pork into julienne strips and set aside. Cut the shrimp into halves lengthwise, and then into long strips.

6. Heat the oil in a wok over medium-high heat and fry separately, and in order, the garlic, onion, shrimps, pork, chicken and ham, frying the first 2 ingredients until they are golden and setting them aside separately on paper plates. Fry the rest of the ingredients briefly and also set them aside in individual heaps on paper plates.

7. Leaving a small portion of each ingredient on the plates for garnish later, return the rest to the wok and mix them together.

8. Season the mixture with soy sauce and pour in the reserved ½ cup (4 fluid ounces) of cooking liquid. Now add the cabbage and cook, stirring, until all the ingredients are well mixed and the liquid has almost evaporated.

9. Stir in the noodles and toss until they are thoroughly mixed with the other ingredients. Season with salt and pepper, stir, and transfer the mixture to a large platter.

10. Garnish the platter with the reserved garnish ingredients and ring with the lemon slices. Serve immediately.

ADVANCE PREPARATION AND
STORAGE NOTES
You can prepare the ingredients and take this dish up through step 5.
Refrigerate all the ingredients, covered, until you wish to finish the cooking.
This must be done directly before serving.

❧ Indonesian Fried Noodles

This is an easier dish to make than the preceding one, as only the noodles have
to be precooked before adding them to the wok.

Preparation time: 25 minutes   Serves 6
Cooking time: 16 minutes

SHOPPING AND TECHNIQUE TIPS
Use Italian vermicelli for this dish. As you become more familiar with it, you may
wish to vary the ingredients to suit your own tastes.

INGREDIENTS	PREPARATION
4 (3 ¼) tablespoons of peanut or any vegetable oil	
1 medium onion	Peeled and finely chopped
3 cloves of garlic	Peeled and minced
½ chicken breast	Boned, skinned and cut into thin strips, 1 inch long by ¼-inch wide
The meat from a center-cut pork (loin) chop	Sliced thinly, then cut into strips
2 carrots	Peeled and sliced into paper-thin rounds
2 leaves of white cabbage	Shredded
2 stalks of celery	Stalks thinly sliced crosswise, leaves reserved for garnish
½ cup (2 ¾ ounces) of small cooked shrimp	Shelled and cleaned
½ pound of fine egg noodles (vermicelli)	Cooked al dente for 3 minutes in boiling water, drained and rinsed in cold water
½ cup (1 ⅓ ounce) of bean sprouts	Roots removed, washed and drained
½ (⅓) teaspoon of freshly ground black pepper	
3 (2 ⅓) tablespoons of soy sauce	

INGREDIENTS

1 (¾) teaspoon of brown sugar
2 canned (tinned) tomatoes
4 green (spring) onions
½ cup (2¼ ounces) of Fried Onion
    Flakes (page 156)

PREPARATION

Drained and chopped
Cut crosswise into thin rounds

METHOD

1. In a wok, heat the oil over medium-high heat and fry the onion and garlic until the garlic is light brown.

2. Stir in the chicken and pork and fry, stirring, for 2 minutes; then add the carrots, cabbage and celery. Stir-fry for 4 minutes more.

3. Add the shrimp, noodles and bean sprouts and fry, tossing and turning until everything is thoroughly mixed and heated through.

4. Season with the pepper, soy sauce and brown sugar and stir in the tomatoes and green (spring) onions. Stir for another minute and then turn out onto a large serving platter. Garnish with the reserved celery leaves and a topping of Fried Onion Flakes. Serve immediately.

ADVANCE PREPARATION AND
STORAGE NOTES

Prepare all the ingredients ahead but do not start the frying until just before serving.

Malaysian Version (SINGAPORE)

This variation is much more directly in touch with its Chinese ancestry than the preceding recipe and indeed may be considered a Chinese dish. In step 1, fry a 2-inch piece of ginger, sliced, instead of the garlic. In step 2, add presoaked, dried Oriental mushroom caps, cut into strips. In step 3, substitute ¼ pound of presoaked bean-thread noodles (if you can get them) for the vermicelli. If you cannot find them, use the vermicelli. Also in this step, add ¼ cup (1½ ounces) of canned (tinned), sliced bamboo shoots. In step 4, instead of the soy sauce, brown sugar and tomatoes, stir in ½ (⅓) teaspoon of cornstarch mixed with 2 (1⅔) teaspoons of pale dry sherry, 1 (¾) tablespoon of soy sauce and ½ (⅓) teaspoon each of salt and black pepper. Add the green (spring) onions and stir in 1½ (1¼) teaspoons of Sesame Oil (page 139) just before turning onto the platter.

❧ Thai Soft-Fried Rice Noodles and Chicken

This recipe, like the Beef and Shrimp Noodles in Broth on page 420, includes the use of a spice paste. While many noodle dishes are bland, this one is slightly spicy and will appeal to those who like the bite of chilli peppers.

Preparation time: 45 minutes   Serves 6
Cooking time: 20 minutes

SHOPPING AND TECHNIQUE TIPS
If you can't find shallots, rice-stick noodles, dried Oriental mushrooms and fresh basil, substitute the white part of green *(spring)* onions, Italian vermicelli, fresh mushrooms and mint, respectively.

INGREDIENTS	PREPARATION
Noodles	
2 whole chicken breasts	Boned, skinned and thinly sliced crosswise
2 *(1⅔)* tablespoons of pale dry sherry	
3 *(2⅓)* tablespoons of vegetable oil	
8 cloves of garlic	Peeled and thinly sliced
6 shallots	Peeled and cut into slivers lengthwise
¾ pound (3 hanks) of rice-stick noodles or vermicelli	Boiled in water for 2 minutes, drained
4 fresh red Serrano chilli peppers, or 4 dried red chilli peppers	Seeded and chopped
1 *(¾)* teaspoon of anchovy paste	
½ *(⅓)* teaspoon of salt	
1 *(¾)* additional tablespoon of vegetable oil	
6 dried Oriental mushrooms	Soaked in hot water until soft, stems discarded and caps sliced
6 ounces of cooked baby shrimp	Shelled and patted dry in paper towels
3 *(2⅓)* tablespoons of tomato paste	
2 *(1⅔)* tablespoons of granulated sugar	
1 *(¾)* tablespoon of Southeast Asian fish sauce	
½ cup *(1⅓ ounces)* of bean sprouts	Washed and roots removed
¼ cup *(1 ounce)* of fresh basil leaves	

INGREDIENTS	PREPARATION
Garnish	
2 *(1⅔)* tablespoons of roasted peanuts	Coarsely pounded
¼ cup *(1 ounce)* more of basil leaves	Fried until crisp in 2 tablespoons of vegetable oil, and drained on paper towels
½ *(⅓)* teaspoon of dried red pepper flakes	
4 cherry tomatoes	Cut ¾ of the way through into 8 segments to resemble flowers

METHOD

1. In a small bowl, marinate the chicken in the sherry for at least 30 minutes.

2. Place a small frying pan over medium heat and slowly fry the garlic and shallots in 3 tablespoons of vegetable oil until crisp. Drain the oil into a large mixing bowl and reserve the garlic and shallots.

3. Add the cooked noodles to the bowl and gently toss in the oil.

4. In a mortar, pound together the chilli peppers, anchovy paste and salt until smooth.

5. In a wok, over high heat, heat the tablespoon of vegetable oil, add the paste from the mortar and fry for 1 minute, stirring, until the odor mellows. Add the chicken and its marinade and the mushroom slices and stir-fry for 3 minutes.

5. Add the shrimp and heat through, then stir in the tomato paste, sugar and fish sauce. Add the bean sprouts and basil and continue to stir for 2 more minutes. Tip in the noodles from the bowl and gently toss the mixture, turning the noodles until they are thoroughly coated and heated through.

6. Transfer to a serving platter and sprinkle with the reserved garlic and shallots and the garnishes: the peanuts, fried basil, pepper flakes and the tomato flowers. Serve immediately.

ADVANCE PREPARATION AND STORAGE NOTES

Do all the advance preparation and marinate the chicken. The dish itself should not be cooked until just before serving.

BAKER'S DOZEN

ঽ ঽ ঽ

Thirteen Leavened and Unleavened Breads

Because grain starches are one of the most basic food groups, every country in the world prepares and eats them. The climatic zones determine which grains will flourish in which location and that, in turn, dictates the style and form of their finished appearance. Naturally, the peoples of the cold northern countries grow wheat and are bread eaters, while those living in countries nearer the Equator favor rice.

Asia conforms to this natural division. In the north of both China and India, grains are fashioned into some sort of bread, while in the southern portions of those countries, and in Southeast Asia, the term for rice is often the same as that meaning food. Japan and Korea, northern countries both, are the exceptions, tending to prefer rice, noodles and dumplings to breads. However, modern mechanized methods of food preparation, distribution and transportation have somewhat blurred the picture.

A baker on a cook's tour of Asia, both north and south, would find Western-style loaves of leavened bread in every city and in most small towns.

This spongy, fragile and rather inferior baking product is, unfortunately, generally made from bleached, refined white flour. The exception to this soft white loaf was, until the 1970s, the bread of Indochina, where the culinary legacy of the French was delightfully noticeable in the lightest, crustiest and most delicious bread east of Paris. Traveling through Laos, or living in Vietnam, one of my joys was to breakfast in little restaurants on hot, strong coffee, crusty French bread and feather-light, flaky croissants.

These loaf breads are one of the most visible signs of European contact with the Orient. As the early Portuguese and Spanish colonialists established toeholds in Asia, followed by the British and Dutch, they claimed whole countries in the names of their monarchs, and after settling, they taught legions of local cooks to prepare the foods of their homelands, including breads. Until the arrival of the Europeans, the Asians, with few exceptions, did not bake. Although grain flours were widely used, stovetop cooking dictated that breads and buns were steamed or fried; ovens were the preserve of eating houses.

This does not mean that bread took a subsidiary role. The Chinese put food into two categories: *fan,* which covers all food prepared from grains, and *t'sai,* meaning all other dishes that accompany the *fan.* The only time this emphasis is reversed is during feasts and festivals, such as Chinese New Year, when the *t'sai* dishes play the dominant role, as they are expensive and therefore demonstrate the extravagance that should rightly belong to a festival.

The *fan* of the north is bread and bread-dough products. *Man t'ou,* a steamed or baked wheat bread, is given the respect of its own bowl—one for each diner. Sometimes the bread will be in the form of a flat pancake made with onion, salt and lard in addition to wheat.

In southern China and in Southeast Asia, rice is the *fan,* demonstrating its importance in the scheme of things by being the centerpiece of the table, with all the accompanying dishes relegated to the role of flavoring the rice. In Indonesia, this translates into the *rijstaffel,* or Rice Table.

In ancient China, flour mills originated around the first century B.C. The Chinese invented noodles and cakelike buns, but the methods of cooking them were influenced by other countries, principally India, which traditionally fried breads. The following anecdote illustrates the importance of bread to the early Chinese. The founder of the Ming Dynasty, Emperor Chu Yuan-chang, who came from peasant stock and who, until he educated himself, was an illiterate ruffian, compensated for his lowly birth by insisting that elaborate, ritualistic food offerings be made to his ancestors. Records from the Imperial household in Nanking in the 1370s noted that the Empress and the consorts prepared and offered all kinds of breads, cakes and buns at the Imperial shrine. The substance and shape of each offering was properly determined by the correct day of the lunar month. That is how we know that steamed rolls with stewed mutton were offered every sixth day; oven-baked breads, called *shao-ping*, placated the Imperial ancestors on the eleventh; and scalded-dough breads that were then baked kept the spirits happy on the twenty-third day. Today there is something a little incongruous in reading these carefully kept records of so long ago, when we, with our busy and hectic lives, cannot even remember what we baked last week.

In modern China, restaurants and tea shops still prepare most of the breads and buns. Steamed buns, colored scarlet for good luck and prosperity, are a constant favorite. In Hong Kong an annual Buddhist festival on Cheung Chau Island is referred to as the Bun Festival. Three towers of scarlet buns are erected. In the old days they were constructed solely from buns, but nowadays the buns are glued to a framework of paper and wood. At the conclusion of the festival young men climb the towers and vie with each other to see who can snatch the most and highest buns, to the delight of the spectators.

> *Nini, baba, nini!*
> *Roti, muckan, chini.*
> *Roti muckan hogya,*
> *Hamara baba sogya.*

So go the words of an ancient Indian lullaby that I remember as a child in India. It means: "Sleep, baby, sleep! / Bread, butter and sugar / Bread and butter's finished / My baby's gone to sleep." And I, too, was given bread and butter spread with sugar.

Indian breads have no Western counterpart; while some bear a cousinly likeness to *pita* bread, having been influenced by the Persian conquests and the Arabs, others resemble *tortillas*. The breads are mostly unleavened, although some are rich, flaky-textured wonders of buttery leavened dough.

As rice is to southern India, so bread is to the north and to Pakistan. Meat dishes tend to be drier in the cuisines of the northern regions and food is commonly eaten with the fingers, with bread used as an utensil to scoop up the food.

Wheat is the principal flour in breadmaking. The main grades are: *atta*, a whole-meal flour; *mydah*, a very fine, white pastry *(plain)* flour; *soojee*, a kind of wheat semolina. Besides wheat, *channa* or Gram flour, called *besan* and made from chick peas, is also used for certain crisp breads and dumplings.

The most popular bread in northern India is called a *chapati*. These are flat discs of whole-meal flour and water, rolled thin and baked on a curved griddle or *tawa.* The *tawa* varies from the size of a saucer to that of a dinner plate. To make *chapati* flour, or *atta,* from scratch, as is commonly done in most Indian homes, a small mill called a *chakki* is used. This consists of two large, heavy stone discs, the uppermost of which has a handle set into the rim and two holes on top, into which handfuls of grain are poured. The rotation of the top stone on the lower performs the grinding. If you think your cooking chores are awesome, consider doing this milling daily and the fact that it requires two people—one to pour and one to grind!

Parathas are also a whole-meal bread. The dough is rolled out and spread with clarified butter *(ghee),* then folded and rerolled several times. After they have been rolled out into thin, circular wafers, the *parathas* are fried on a lightly greased griddle until they puff slightly and turn a pale gold. *Puris* are another whole-meal fried dough preparation—these are deep-fat fried. They start out as saucer-sized pancakes, which puff up like miniature balloons when cooked.

In the northern plains of the Punjab, the most popular breads are those baked in a *tandoor* oven. The *tandoor* breads include *tandoori roti, tandoori-*baked *chapatis,* and *naan.* The *tandoor* oven is shaped like a large Ali Baba jar, usually made from clay and buried up to the neck in the ground. A small air hole at the bottom, curved side of the oven is vented with a trench. This hole may be opened or closed, depending on the kind of cooking desired. Sometimes portable *tandoors,* which are smaller, cylindrical drums made of metal, are used. The heat is not retained as effectively as in the larger, ground-insulated ovens and they also tend to smoke a lot. *Tandoori rotis* and *chapatis* are merely plain whole-meal breads baked in the *tandoor* rather than on a griddle or *tawa. Naan,* a leavened bread that has become popular in the West, is made from a rich dough of wheat flour, curds, eggs, *ghee,* salt and sugar. The dough is kneaded vigorously and allowed to stand overnight to enable the curds to ferment and cause the dough to rise. It then becomes very smooth and elastic in consistency. The bread is then shaped into an oval or heart shape and partly stuck to the curved side of the hot *tandoor.* A large, unattached mass of dough hangs downward over the heat and stretches into a teardrop during baking. *Naan* is typically thicker around the rim than the middle and should be spongy in texture at the sides, more brittle in the center. It can also be baked over a direct fire or grill although the results are not as authentic.

There are many other Indian breads, but these are some of the most common. They are easy to bake at home, and, should you encounter them in an Indian restaurant, you will know what to order and what to expect.

When preparing Asian breads, buns and cakes, you do not need special equipment. Your own oven can substitute for the Indian *tandoor,* a heavy iron frying pan for the *tawa,* or handled griddle, and a steamer, whether bought or makeshift, will handle most Chinese steamed breads and buns. The Oriental techniques for making leavened dough with yeast or baking powder follow the same rules as ours; and anyone who makes pies and pastries can soon get the knack of making the various Indian unleavened breads. Regional variations throughout most of the Southeast Asian countries follow the principles of either Indian or Chinese bread-making.

✿ Unleavened Whole-Wheat Bread (INDIA)

As a small child in India, I remember my grandmother in the kitchen, making these breads, or *chapatis,* for breakfast. The warm, delicious smell of toasting dough filled the room, and I looked forward with anticipation to eating them thickly spread with my grandmother's home-churned, creamy, white buffalo-milk butter. Later, when I was seven, I learned to make them myself. These are the basic breads of India and are made from a whole-wheat flour called *atta.* I find the best approximation is a mixture of whole-wheat and all-purpose *(plain)* flours.

Preparation time: 1 hour and 45   Cooking time: 24 minutes
   minutes (including resting time for   Yields 10 to 12 breads
   the dough)

SHOPPING AND TECHNIQUE TIPS
You will find very good whole-wheat flour in the health-food section of your supermarket. As in most Indian breads, these flat, round discs demand a great deal of kneading and working the dough. It should then be left to rest for a minimum of 30 minutes, even overnight, covered with a damp cloth. This resting period makes the bread more pliable and digestible.

INGREDIENTS
1½ cups *(9 ounces)* of whole-wheat
   flour
¾ *(4½ ounces)* of all-purpose *(plain)*
   flour
¼ *teaspoon (a pinch)* of salt
1 cup *(8 fluid ounces)* (or a little
   more) of lukewarm water
Indian Clarified Butter (page 139) for
   spreading

METHOD

1. Sift the flours and salt into a mixing bowl and make a well in the middle. Add the water, 1 tablespoon at a time, until the dough comes together in a ball without crumbling. The dough should be soft but not sticky.

2. Knead the dough in the bowl until all the flour is gathered up and sides of the bowl are clean. Transfer it to a lightly floured pastry board. Using the heels of your hands and pushing the dough down and away from you, knead the dough, then fold it back on itself and knead again. The longer you knead, the lighter and more supple the dough will be. Between 5 and 10 minutes is the usual time range.

3. After kneading the dough, gather it back into a ball and place it in the bowl, covering it with a damp cloth. Let the dough rest at room temperature for at least 30 minutes.

4. After resting the dough, take it out and work it once or twice to make it pliable again, then divide it into 10 to 12 pieces, depending on the preferred size of your finished *chapatis*. They will range from 5 inches to 7 inches in diameter.

5. Lightly flouring the board and a rolling pin, roll out the first piece of dough into an even circle. Use long, steady strokes, away from you, and turn the dough slightly after each stroke. (The more you change the direction of the stroke, and the more narrow the turning radius between each stroke, the more symmetrical the circle will be.)

6. Stack the completed *chapatis* as you finish them. Cover them with a dampened cloth, as they should not dry out before cooking.

7. Set a heavy griddle or frying pan over high heat. When a drop of water bounces off the surface, it is ready for the first *chapati*. Place one in the frying pan and, when air bubbles rise to the surface of the dough, turn it over. The first side should be speckled brown, and this stage will normally be reached in just under 1 minute. Fry the other side for about 30 seconds, then, pushing the frying pan to one side, lift the *chapati* with a slotted spatula and hold it over the heat until it puffs up. (Hold it close to the ring if you are using electricity, farther away if you have a gas flame.)

8. You may like to quickly butter it before placing it on a warm platter. Repeat with the rest of the breads.

ADVANCE PREPARATION AND
STORAGE NOTES

The dough may be refrigerated overnight covered with a damp cloth. Bring back to room temperature and knead once or twice before rolling. The *chapatis* may be made slightly in advance. Line a basket with a dry cloth and keep the stack covered. To serve, warm them for 10 minutes in a moderate oven, sealed in foil.

Fried Balloon Bread Variation

Using the same dough and the same method, it may be rolled out into smaller breads of up to 5 inches in diameter. These are deep-fried in a wok or frying pan in vegetable oil (about 3 cups) at a temperature of 250°F. *(120°C.).* Press each one down with the back of a spatula until it puffs up into a little balloon. Fry each bread for about 15 seconds on each side. As it begins to puff up, release it, or the expanding air will break through the side. Remove immediately and drain on paper towels. These breads, which are called *puris,* are delicious slit open and stuffed with a little leftover curry.

Potato Balloon Bread Variation

These potato puffs are known as *alu,* or potato, *puris.* They are usually left unfilled and are eaten immediately as hot snacks. The method of kneading and rolling out is the same as in the Unleavened Whole-Wheat Bread *(chapati)* recipe; the frying is identical to that in the variation above. The potato puffs are rolled to a diameter of 4 inches. The recipe for the dough follows.

INGREDIENTS	PREPARATION
1 cup *(9 ounces)* of mashed potato	
1 cup *(6 ounces)* of all-purpose *(plain)* flour	Sifted
1 cup *(6 ounces)* of whole-wheat flour	Sifted
2 *(1⅔)* teaspoons of salt	Sifted
¼ to ½ cup *(2 to 4 fluid ounces)* of warm water (sufficient to form a soft, pliable dough)	
1¾ cups *(14 fluid ounces)* of vegetable oil and ½ cup *(4 ounces)* of Indian Clarified Butter (page 139) for frying	

METHOD

Mix the potato thoroughly with the sifted flours and salt. Add the water, a little at a time, to make a soft, pliable dough. Proceed as in the Fried Balloon Bread variation, but use the mixture of vegetable oil and Clarified Butter to make a more flavorful frying medium.

✿ Flaky, Buttery Unleavened Bread (INDIA)

These breads, like most of the Indian unleavened breads, require patience, a good rolling surface (preferably marble) a rolling pin and a light, even touch. The results are rewarding; the breads easily surpass many of those you encounter in restaurants. This particular bread is called a *paratha* and is a layered and lighter version of *chapati,* the basic tortilla-like Indian bread.

Preparation time: 1 hour and 25
   minutes

Cooking time: 28 minutes
Yields 4 breads

SHOPPING AND TECHNIQUE TIPS
Parathas may be made with either whole-wheat flour or pastry (plain) flour—I rather like this combination of both. The dough demands a long period of kneading until it becomes satiny in texture and elastic. After the kneading it should rest in order to allow the glutens time to relax.

INGREDIENTS
½ cup *(3 ounces)* of whole-wheat flour

½ cup *(3 ounces)* of pastry *(plain)* flour (plus a little extra for rolling out)

¼ teaspoon *(a pinch)* of salt

1 *(¾)* tablespoon of Indian Clarified Butter (page 139)

5 *(4)* more tablespoons of Indian Clarified Butter

Up to ¾ cup *(6 fluid ounces)* of cold water

PREPARATION

Chilled

Melted over low heat

METHOD
1. Sift the flours and salt into a mixing bowl and add the tablespoon of chilled butter. Rub the flour and butter together with your fingertips until the mixture takes on the appearance and consistency of coarse meal. Gradually pour in ¼ cup *(2 fluid ounces)* of cold water, kneading and gathering up the dough until it holds into a compact ball. If the dough crumbles, add up to ½ cup *(4 fluid ounces)* more water, a tablespoon at a time, until the particles adhere to form a uniform mass.

2. Lightly flour a pastry board, place the dough on it and knead by folding it end to end (as in a letter), then pressing it down and pushing it away from

you with the heels of your hands. Continue folding and kneading for 7 to 8 minutes, or until the dough feels velvety smooth and becomes elastic. Gather the dough into a ball again, place it in the bowl and cover it with a dampened cloth. Let it rest in a warm place for at least 30 minutes.

3. After resting, divide the dough into quarters. Shape the first quarter into a ball with the palms of your hands. Flour it lightly and roll the ball into a thin disc of about 7 inches in diameter. Turn the dough as you roll, so that it becomes an even circle.

4. Brush the entire surface of the circle with a very light coating of melted butter. Fold the disc in half and brush the top surface of the semicircle lightly with butter. Fold the semicircle in half so that you have a quarter section of a circle, 4 thicknesses deep. Roll this rough triangle lightly until it becomes half as thick and proportionately larger in area. Set aside and repeat step 4 with the remaining quarters of dough. You now have your 4 *parathas*.

5. Heat a frying pan until it is so hot that a drop of water sputters instantly on the surface. Brush the pan with a little butter. Place one of the *parathas* in the pan and, pressing it down lightly with a spatula, fry it until the bottom is lightly speckled with brown. Paint the top surface with butter and, turning it over, fry it on the other side for 2 minutes. Press the surface lightly again with the spatula and lightly brush it again with butter. Turn it once more and fry for another 30 seconds. Transfer it to a heated platter.

6. Repeat until all the breads are cooked. Serve warm to accompany an Indian meal.

ROLLING PARATHAS

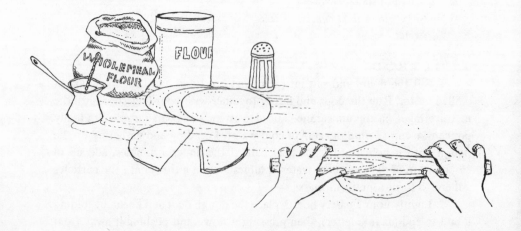

ADVANCE PREPARATION AND
STORAGE NOTES

At the end of step 4, you may cover the *parathas* with a damp cloth and keep them at room temperature for 3 to 4 hours before frying. They may also be made an hour or so ahead. They should then be reheated by frying for 1 minute on each side in an ungreased frying pan.

❧ Buttery Unleavened Bread with Cauliflower Filling
(INDIA)

These breads are a little more elaborate than the preceding ones. Filled and fried, they make great snacks, or they can be served, broken into pieces, as appetizers. One of the Indian yogurt "salads" (pages 243–44), such as the cucumber, could be served as a dip, as could any of the chutneys.

Preparation time: 2 hours   Yields 16 small, filled breads
Cooking time: 35 minutes

SHOPPING AND TECHNIQUE TIPS

These breads are not as flaky as the plain *parathas,* because they are not layered. The dough is made and then divided into little patties. A small quantity of the filling is placed in the center of each and the dough then coaxed up and around the filling. The edges are pinched together at the top and the filled ball is then patted flat and rolled out gently before being fried. The fillings may be varied; some suggestions are at the end of this recipe.

INGREDIENTS   PREPARATION
Pastry
2 cups *(12 ounces)* of all-purpose
    (plain) or whole-wheat flour
    (plus a little extra for rolling
    out)
½ *(⅓)* teaspoon of salt
3 to 4 *(2⅓ to 3¼)* tablespoons of   Chill 1 *(¾)* tablespoon of the butter
    Indian Clarified Butter (page
    139)
⅔ cup *(5⅓ fluid ounces)* of warm
    water

INGREDIENTS   PREPARATION
Filling
2 *(1 ⅔)* tablespoons of onion   Chopped
1-inch piece of fresh ginger root   Peeled and chopped
1 cup *(4 ½ ounces)* of cauliflower   Coarsely chopped
    flowerets
1 *(¾)* tablespoon of Indian Clarified
    Butter
1 *(¾)* teaspoon of Indian Sweet
    Spice Mix (page 118)
½ *(⅓)* teaspoon of ground red
    pepper (Cayenne)

METHOD

1. As in step 1 of the preceding recipe Flaky, Buttery Unleavened Bread, but use warm water as in the above measurement.

2. As in step 2 of the preceding recipe.

3. While the dough is resting, start to make the filling. Process the onion and ginger in a processor until they are finely chopped. Remove and squeeze out surplus moisture in paper towels. Set them aside.

4. Process the cauliflower to the consistency of fine breadcrumbs. Remove and gently squeeze out the surplus moisture in paper towels. Set aside.

5. Place the tablespoon of Clarified Butter in a frying pan and heat over medium heat. Fry the onion and ginger, stirring and turning until the onion turns a light gold. Add the cauliflower and fry for 2 more minutes.

6. Stir in the seasonings and mix well. Cook for 1 more minute, then turn out the mixture into a small mixing bowl and set it aside to cool. Clean the frying pan.

7. Bring the dough back to the working surface and divide it in 16 equal portions. Taking 1 portion, form it into a ball and then gently pat it into a thick circle, the shape of a hamburger patty. With your thumb, make a depression in the middle and place ½ *(⅓)* teaspoon or more of the filling into it. Carefully coax and draw up the edges of the dough over the filling. Pinch them together at the top with your fingertips. Turn the filled ball over and place it, sealed edges down, on the board. Gently roll it out to a disc, about 3½ inches in diameter. Take care not to press too heavily so the filling does not burst through.

8. Repeat with the remaining dough until you have 16 filled *parathas* on the board. Cover them with a damp towel to prevent them from drying out.

9. Place the remaining 2 to 3 *(1 ⅔ to 2⅓)* tablespoons of Clarified Butter from the pastry ingredients in a small saucepan and melt over low heat. Set it to one side of the stove. Place the clean frying pan back on the heat and

increase it to medium-high. Brush the surface with melted butter.

10. Place one of the filled breads in the frying pan and fry it for 2 minutes, or until the bottom surface is speckled with brown. Brush the top surface with a thin coating of melted butter and turn it over. Fry on the other side for 2 minutes, pressing it down with a spatula so that the bread puffs up a little. Brush the surface again with a little melted butter and turn it over for a brief 15 seconds. Press it with the spatula and remove it to a platter.

11. Repeat the procedure until all the breads are fried. Serve them warm.

ADVANCE PREPARATION AND STORAGE NOTES

The dough can be made a day ahead and refrigerated, tightly wrapped and sealed. It should be brought back to a pliable consistency at room temperature for about ½ hour before you start rolling. The filled and rolled breads can be kept for about an hour at room temperature before frying, if they are covered with a damp cloth. They should not be stacked, however, or they will stick together. The breads can also be fried several hours ahead of time. Covered loosely with a sheet of foil, they should then be reheated in a moderate oven before serving.

Potato-Filled Bread

The pastry remains the same as in the Cauliflower Filling recipe. The breads are stuffed with the following filling before frying.

INGREDIENTS	PREPARATION
1 (¾) tablespoon of Indian Clarified Butter (page 139)	
2 (1⅔) tablespoons of onion	Minced
1 clove of garlic	Peeled and minced
½-inch piece of fresh ginger root	Peeled and minced
2 medium potatoes	Boiled, peeled and mashed (there should be about 1 cup of mashed potato)
¼ teaspoon (a generous pinch) of ground turmeric	
¼ teaspoon (a generous pinch) of Indian Sweet Spice Mix (page 118)	
1 fresh green Serrano chilli pepper	Seeded and minced
15 coriander (Chinese parsley, cilantro) leaves (or substitute parsley)	Chopped
½ (⅓) teaspoon of salt	

METHOD

1. Heat the Clarified Butter in a frying pan and fry the onions, ginger and garlic for 2 minutes, stirring until the ingredients turn golden. Empty into a mixing bowl.

2. Add all the remaining ingredients to the mixing bowl and mix everything together well. Set aside or refrigerate, covered, until you are ready to fill the breads.

Variation with Peas

As in the Potato-Filled Breads above, substituting fresh or frozen peas, cooked, drained and mashed, for the potatoes. There should be 1 cup of peas. Omit the coriander or the parsley.

✿ Indian Oven Bread

Along with the growing popularity of Indian *tandoori* (oven-barbecued) dishes in the West, this bread, which is commonly served with them, is also becoming a familiar item. Known as *naan,* it is one of the few leavened and oven-baked breads in the Indian subcontinent.

Preparation time: 3 hours and 30   Cooking time: 7 to 8 minutes
   minutes   Yields 6 breads

SHOPPING AND TECHNIQUE TIPS

You will need 2 to 3 hours, depending on the room temperature (the warmer, the less time), to allow the leavening agent to work on the dough. This bread is traditionally stuck to the side walls of the funnel-shaped *tandoor* oven, while other foods are cooking inside. The breads will become teardrop in shape because of the downward pull of the weight of the dough. In this version, which is baked flat, you will have to shape the dough into the teardrop or leaf form.

INGREDIENTS

2 cups *(12 ounces)* of all-purpose
   flour *(plain),* plus a little more
   for working the dough
1½ *(1¼)* teaspoons of baking
   powder
1½ *(1¼)* teaspoons of granulated
   sugar

INGREDIENTS	PREPARATION
½ (⅓) teaspoon of salt	
1 egg	Beaten
2 (1⅔) tablespoons of plain yogurt	Stirred until smooth
⅔ cup (5⅓ fluid ounces) of milk	
2 to 3 (1⅔ to 2⅓) tablespoons of Indian Clarified Butter (page 139)	
2 (1⅔) teaspoons of poppy seeds	

METHOD

1. Sift the flour, baking powder, sugar and salt into a large mixing bowl. Add the egg and yogurt and stir them in.

2. Gradually add the milk, pouring it slowly in a thin stream.

3. Rub a teaspoon of Clarified Butter on your hands and begin to move the mixture together, gathering it up and working it into a soft dough.

4. Place the dough on a board or slab and begin to knead it, pressing it down and away from you with the heels of your hands. Fold it back on itself and knead it again. Continue for up to 10 minutes, or until the dough is soft, smooth and velvety. Cover the bowl with a damp cloth and set aside in a warm place for up to 3 hours.

5. Toward the end of that period, preheat the oven to 450°F. (gas mark 8) and place the baking trays inside.

6. Knead the dough again twice, then divide it equally into 6 balls. Cover them with a damp cloth so they will not dry out. Grease your hands with a little Clarified Butter and, taking one portion, flatten and mold it into a teardrop or leaf shape about 6 inches long and up to 3½ inches wide—it should be no more than ¼ inch thick.

7. Mold the remaining portions, greasing your hands as you work with each one. Use any remaining Clarified Butter to brush the top surfaces of the leaf shapes, then sprinkle each with poppy seeds.

8. Arrange the breads on the baking trays and bake in the middle of the oven for 6 minutes. Switch the broiler on and lightly brown the top surfaces. Serve the *naan* bread hot or warm.

ADVANCE PREPARATION AND
STORAGE NOTES

These breads are best served directly after they are made. If necessary, however, you can make them in advance and warm them again, covered with a damp cloth, in a moderate oven for 2 to 3 minutes.

❧ Chinese Silver Loaves

Preparation time: 3 hours and 30
  minutes

Yields 6 loaves
Cooking time: 15 minutes

SHOPPING AND TECHNIQUE TIPS

This particular technique uses baking powder as the leavening agent. You may substitute 1 tablespoon of yeast, mixing it into the sugar and warm water and letting it stand for 12 minutes before adding it to the flour and shortening. Remember that if you do use yeast, you must let the dough stand for at least 3 hours, or until it has more than doubled in bulk, before you start making the loaves.

INGREDIENTS

1¾ cups (14 fluid ounces) of hot
  water
3 (2⅓) tablespoons of granulated
  sugar
2 (1⅔) tablespoons of vegetable
  shortening or oil
6 cups (2¼ pounds) of all-purpose
  (plain) flour, plus a little extra
  for rolling out
2 (1⅔) tablespoons of baking
  powder
½ (⅓) teaspoon of salt
6 tablespoons (3 ounces or 4¾
  tablespoons) of margarine or
  Sesame Oil (page 139)

PREPARATION

Melted

METHOD

1. Add the sugar and shortening to the hot water and stir until the sugar is dissolved. Let the mixture cool down several degrees until it is barely warm.

2. Sift the flour, baking powder and salt into a large mixing bowl and gradually stir in the warm mixture. Mix well, then gradually draw the dough together with your hands. It should be soft, but not sticky.

3. Place the dough on a board and start to knead it, pressing it down and away from you with the heels of your hands, then folding it back on itself before kneading again. Knead for about 5 to 8 minutes, until the dough is smooth and elastic. Place it back in the bowl, cover with a damp cloth and let it rest for at least 1 hour.

4. Lightly flour the surface of the pastry board and place the dough on

it. Knead again for about 5 minutes and then divide into 6 portions. Place the damp cloth over the portions that you are not working on.

5. Take 1 portion and divide it in half. Roll out each half into a 6-inch square. (Trim the edges with the knife to even them.)

6. Take 1 square and roll it into a rectangle about 8 inches long. (The sides will shrink in to about 4 inches as you roll, which is fine.)

7. Brush the surface of the rectangle lightly with melted margarine, then fold it in half. Brush the top surface with shortening and then fold in half again. (Your dough is now in 4 layers and should measure about 2 inches by 4 inches.) Cut this rectangle into julienne strips 2 inches in length.

8. Take up the bundle of these strips and pull them slightly, elongating them another inch. Place a square of waxed paper in front of you and position the first (uncut) square of rolled dough on it. Arrange the bundle of strips at one end so that the edges of the strips protrude evenly about ½ inch over each side of the square.

9. Using the wax (greaseproof) paper to help you, roll up into a wrapped bundle. Set it aside, seam down, and repeat with the 5 remaining portions.

10. When you have 6 loaves completed, fill a steamer with water and bring it to a boil. Cut 6 squares of wax (greaseproof) paper, the size of the rolls, and setting a roll on each, arrange them on the steamer trays. Leave a 2-inch space between each "loaf" to allow for expansion during the cooking.

11. Steam the loaves for 15 minutes. Remove and let them cool. Slice each loaf into portions before serving.

ARRANGING CHINESE SILVER LOAVES

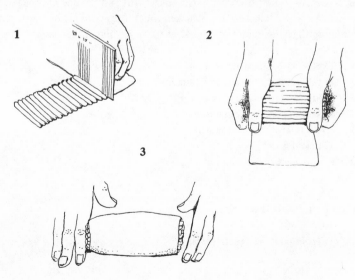

ADVANCE PREPARATION AND
STORAGE NOTES

The loaves can be prepared ahead of time and left at room temperature, covered with a damp cloth, before steaming. Or they may be completed and cooled, then reheated in the steamer for 2 minutes to refresh them.

Chinese Golden Loaves

These are made in exactly the same way as the Silver Loaves, but they are then deep-fried in oil for 2 minutes, until they are golden brown on the outside. Drain them on paper towels, slice and serve.

❧ Steamed Buns with Roast Pork Filling (CHINA)

These savory buns are great for picnics and lunch snacks. In China they are served as part of a *dim sum* meal.

Preparation time: 50 minutes   Makes 24 buns
Cooking time: 18 minutes

SHOPPING AND TECHNIQUE TIPS

This recipe combines several previous recipes. The dough for the buns is the same dough used for the Silver Loaves (page 444). The Roast Pork is on page 403. The pork is seasoned with Oyster Sauce (page 146) and Sesame Oil (page 139), and is cooked with Chinese Basic Chicken Stock (page 168). For the technique on steaming the buns, refer to page 247 at the beginning of the chapter on steaming.

INGREDIENTS

1 (¾) tablespoon of granulated sugar
1½ (1¼) tablespoons of soy sauce
1 (¾) tablespoon of Oyster Sauce
½ cup (4 *fluid ounces*) of Basic
   Chicken Stock
1 (¾) teaspoon of Sesame Oil
¼ teaspoon (*a pinch*) of ground
   black pepper
1 drop of red food coloring
   (optional)
1 (¾) tablespoon of vegetable oil

INGREDIENTS | PREPARATION
¾ pound of Roast Pork — Sliced and then diced
½-inch piece of fresh ginger root — Peeled and minced
1 large green *(spring)* onion or 2 small ones — Chopped (including the green tops)
1 *(¾)* tablespoon of cornstarch *(cornflour)*
2 *(1⅔)* tablespoons of water
1 recipe of Silver Loaves dough

METHOD

1. Mix together the sugar, soy sauce, Oyster Sauce, Chicken Stock, Sesame Oil, pepper and red food coloring in a bowl and set aside.

2. Heat the oil in a wok over medium-high heat and stir-fry the pork, ginger and green *(spring)* onion for 2 minutes. Pour in the seasoning mixture and stir for another minute. Stir the cornstarch *(cornflour)* into the water and pour into the wok. Continue to cook, stirring, until the sauce is like thick custard. Set the wok aside.

3. Knead the dough for 3 minutes. Cover it with a dampened cloth and let it sit for 10 minutes. Divide it into 24 pieces and cover them again with the cloth.

4. Pat 1 piece into a circle about 4 inches in diameter. Place a teaspoon of the filling in the center and start to pleat the edges of the circle all the way around. Bring the edges up and over the filling as you pleat, finally pinching them firmly together at the center top with a twist of the thumb and fingers. Set the bun aside and repeat the technique with all the remaining pieces of dough until you have 24 buns. Let the buns sit for 10 minutes.

5. Fill a steamer with water, remove the trays, set the steamer over high heat and bring it to a boil. Cut 24 3-inch squares of wax *(greaseproof)* paper and, placing a bun on each, set them on the steamer trays with ½ inch of space between each. Set the trays in the steamer and steam the buns for 12 minutes. During the steaming, the tops of the buns should split open (this is characteristic of the dish). Do not open the steamer during the cooking process or this splitting will not take place. Serve the buns hot.

ADVANCE PREPARATION AND
STORAGE NOTES

Both the dough and the filling can be made ahead and refrigerated, covered, for several hours or overnight. Bring both back to room temperature before beginning to form the buns. The finished buns can be kept warm in the steamer, off the heat, for 10 to 15 minutes.

Vegetable Filling Variation

The buns may be made with the filling below:

INGREDIENTS	PREPARATION
1 *(¾)* tablespoon of vegetable oil	
2 cloves of garlic	Peeled and minced
1 green *(spring)* onion	Finely chopped
¾ pound of Chinese or white cabbage	Chopped, blanched in boiling water for 1 minute, drained and squeezed dry in paper towels
¼ cup *(1½ ounces)* of cooked baby shrimp	Minced
1 *(¾)* teaspoon of granulated sugar	
1 *(¾)* teaspoon of soy sauce	
½ *(⅓)* teaspoon of ground black pepper	
1 *(¾)* teaspoon of Sesame Oil (page 139)	
1 *(¾)* teaspoon of cornstarch *(cornflour)*	
1 *(¾)* tablespoon of water	

METHOD

Heat the oil in a wok over medium-high heat and fry the garlic and green onion until the garlic is a light gold. Immediately stir in the cabbage and shrimp and stir-fry for 1 minute. Add the sugar, soy sauce, black pepper and sesame oil, stir, then add the cornstarch mixed with water. Stir again. The mixture should immediately thicken slightly. Set aside until ready to fill the buns.

Curry Variation

Use the first 5 ingredients of the Vegetable Filling recipe, but then stir in ¼ cup *(2 fluid ounces)* of Indian Quick All-Purpose Curry Sauce (page 143), into which you have stirred 1 *(¾)* teaspoon of cornstarch. Substitute this sauce for the remaining flavoring ingredients. Alternatively, you may reduce the amount of cabbage by ¼ and substitute 1 cup *(8 ounces)* of diced, cooked chicken or pork for the shrimp.

Sweet Red Bean Paste Filling Variation

Use the same technique as for the first recipe but fill the buns with 1 recipe of Chinese Sweet Red Bean Paste (page 132). Pinch the buns tightly together and then set them upside down on the wax-paper squares. Sweet buns are marked with red coloring on the top to denote that the filling is sweet and not savory. Using a sharp knife or a razor-blade knife, make an incision 1 to 2 inches deep in the square end of a chopstick. Make another incision at right angles to the first, quartering the surface. Open the first incision with a knife blade and insert an toothpick as far up the crevice as you can. It should lie in the slit with both ends protruding. Repeat with the cross incision. The end of the chopstick will now be split into four quarters with a dividing space between each. Dip this end in a little red food coloring and, using it as a design stamp, stamp the center of each bun, after it has been steamed, with the decorative design.

MARKING CHINESE SWEET RED BEAN PASTE BUNS

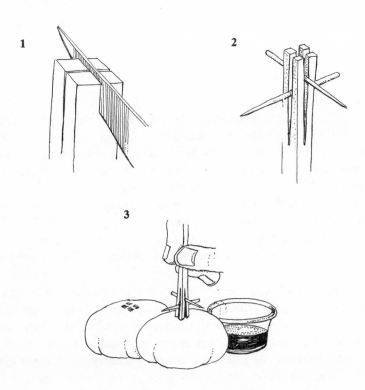

PICKLED AND
WELL
PRESERVED

֍ ֍ ֍

*Chutneys, Relishes, Pickles,
and Sauces*

Chutneys, a complete category of condiments in themselves, originated in India; the very name comes from an Indian word for a
relish, *chatni*. However, many people labor under the misapprehension that
there is only one chutney—mango—and that it is the sole preserve of a
mysterious British Army officer named Major Grey.

Nothing could be further from the truth. There are a host of delicious,
tangy chutneys, both fresh and cooked, and Major Grey was probably one of
the many British in India, both civil and military, who went home to England
clutching precious recipes for these delectable mixtures of fruit, vegetables,
spices, sugar and vinegar.

Mrs. Beeton, the famous British housewife and cookbook writer of the
mid-nineteenth century, includes a "Bengal Recipe for Making Mango Chet-
ney" in her 1861 tome of household management in which she says, "This
recipe was given by a native to an English lady, who had long been a resident
in India, and who, since her return to her native country, has become quite
celebrated among her friends for the excellence of this Eastern relish."

The recipe goes on to make a mango chutney with thirty unripe apples! Because of lack of rapid transportation in the nineteenth century, mangoes were altogether unavailable, so apples were quite a sensible substitute. Nowadays we are usually able to find mangoes, in season, in supermarkets and fruit and vegetable markets. If not, firm, slightly unripe peaches are, I find, a better substitute than unripe apples.

The Indians refer to their chutneys and relishes as "tongue touchers" and eat them with main dishes or as separate courses to sharpen and clear the palate. Most of their chutneys are prepared daily from fresh, uncooked mixtures of ingredients. Only a few, including mango, are cooked and canned or bottled for future use. These chutneys, both fresh and preserved, are generally sweet as well as tangy, and some are fiery with chilli peppers.

Chutneys have spread from India to the cuisines of Southeast Asia, particularly to those of Indonesia and Malaysia, where they are called *sambals* and are a freshly concocted mixture of vegetables, fruits and spices, soured with vinegar, citrus juice or tamarind and occasionally fired with small chilli peppers. This fresh form shows its direct connection with the Indian fresh chutneys or relishes.

Indian pickles are sharper than their chutneys, with the bite of vinegar and mustard oil in the northern varieties, while those of the south tend to substitute the milder sesame oil. Most pickles are cooked, although those containing citrus fruits are preserved in salt or brine. Some pickles are even processed by being placed in the sun for 5 or 6 days, much in the same way that we brew "sun tea."

Pickles seem to have originated independently in both India and China. However, the Chinese pickle is rarely as hot as the Indian and includes vegetables, vinegar, salt and ginger in its makeup, with, occasionally, a dusting of Cayenne pepper. From China the pickle spread to Korea, home of the famous (or infamous) mixture of pickled vegetables, fermented in jars, called *kimchee,* which is a staple of Korean households.

Japan has a whole category of pickled foods called *tsukemono,* which appear on the table at the end of the meal, together with the rice. Traditionally, the art of pickling was a point of pride among Japanese housewives, and every household would have a large cask of salted rice bran into which vegetables were placed and then pressed under a heavy stone while they fermented. Today the most common method is salt pickling *(shiozuke),* although soybean paste *(miso)* and vinegar are still used for some pickles.

Throughout Asia, both chutneys and pickles are made from a wide variety of vegetables and fruits. Common ingredients of fresh chutneys or relishes are mint, coriander (Chinese parsley or *cilantro*), onions, tomatoes, ginger, raisins, radishes, cucumbers, pineapple, coconut and tomatoes. The cooked chutneys include mangoes, apples, pears, tomatoes, garlic, onions, limes and lemons. Indian pickles feature limes, lemons, chilli peppers and even shrimp and chicken. The Chinese and Koreans tend to center their pickles around cabbage, carrots, radishes and turnips, while the Japanese also love pickled plums, ginger and eggplant *(aubergine)*.

The main requirement for the preparation of fresh chutneys or relishes and *sambals* is that the ingredients be finely chopped and well blended. With our food processors and blenders, a fresh chutney can be produced in a few minutes, or even seconds—a fact that would be the envy of most Asians.

Cooked chutneys are prepared from fruits and vegetables which are chopped, seasoned and then cooked to a thick consistency before being put in jars and sterilized.

Fruits and vegetables used for pickling must be as firm and fresh as possible. The salt used should not be iodized, as the iodization tends to darken the pickles. When vinegar is included, it should be the white distilled variety, which preserves the light, clear color of the fruits and vegetables.

All cooked chutneys and pickles should be heated in enameled, teflon or oven-proof glass saucepans. Uncoated metals interact with the acids and salts in the mixtures and produce changes in color and flavor. For fermenting or brining, glass, pottery or stone jars should be used, again for the same reason. A heavy plate or lid, together with a weight, should be used to keep the ingredients pressed down in the solution. All pickled ingredients must be totally immersed in liquid.

Glass jars for canning or bottling should have the proper sealers and caps. The jars and lids should be sterilized beforehand by total immersion in a boiling-water bath for about 15 minutes. They should then be drained on a clean tray and kept warm until filling. After sterilization, the insides and rims of the jars should not be handled at all. There are special tongs for grasping a hot jar firmly, which are perfect for handling these.

After filling, the tops of the jars should be wiped with a clean cloth so that no particle or drop of mixture interferes with a clean, complete seal. Lids should be screwed down tight and then given a slight turn (about ¼ inch) back before sterilizing. After sterilization, the lids should be tightened immediately.

The final canning or bottling sterilization process merely means totally immersing the closed jars in continuously boiling water. The length of time will depend on the type of pickle or chutney and will be anywhere from 5 to 20 minutes. Without this final sterilization, the filled jars must be stored in the refrigerator. When jars are properly sterilized they may be stored without refrigeration.

Jars should be cooled for 12 to 24 hours after sterilization, after which time, the metal caps should be removed and the disk checked for a complete seal. If the disk has a slight dip in the center and stays down when pressed, the seal is good. If there is no leakage when the jar is turned upside down without the cap, this, too indicates that the seal is successful.

Do not forget to label and date the jars. Store them in a dark, cool cupboard, but not where there is danger of their freezing during the winter— freezing can cause the seals to break or the jars to crack. Exposure to light may cause the contents to change in color or to deteriorate in flavor.

These rules apply in much the same way to the bottled Asian sauces, the recipes for some of which are included in this section. Most of the sauces, however, contain large amounts of chillies and garlic, both of which are natural preservatives.

If you are giving bottled chutneys, pickles and sauces as gifts (and they make welcome gifts), do not forget to tell the recipient whether to store in the refrigerator or in the cool, dark cupboard, and make sure that you have put the canning *(bottling)* date on the label.

❀ Indian Fresh Coriander Chutney

A tangy chutney for those who like the flavor of this pungent herb.

Preparation time: 7 minutes   Yields about 1¼ cups

SHOPPING AND TECHNIQUE TIPS
Make this chutney when coriander (Chinese parsley, *cilantro*) is in peak condition (it does vary).

INGREDIENTS	PREPARATION
1 cup *(3 ½ ounces)* of tightly packed coriander leaves and stems	Chopped
1″ piece of fresh ginger root	Peeled and minced
2 green Serrano chillies, or 1 Jalapeño chilli	Chopped (remove the seeds if less heat is desired)
1 *(¾)* tablespoon of molasses *(treacle)*	
2 *(1⅔)* tablespoons of lime juice	
½ *(⅓)* teaspoon of salt	
1 *(¾)* teaspoon of brown sugar	

METHOD

Place all the ingredients in a blender or processor and process to a smooth puree, stopping the machine and poking the mixture down with a spatula if the blades do not immediately engage the ingredients. (This may occur when the blender is filled with dry ingredients.)

ADVANCE PREPARATION AND
STORAGE NOTES

This chutney may be made up to several hours ahead and then refrigerated, covered. It will not keep well for more than one day, as the coriander will discolor.

❧ Indian Mint and Fruit Chutney

This is a delicious fresh chutney. I made it on the television show "Hour Magazine," much to the appreciation of the host, Gary Collins. It is tangy and full of the essence of mint and makes a perfect accompaniment to meatball dishes and curries.

Preparation time: 12 to 15 minutes   Enough for 6 to 8

SHOPPING AND TECHNIQUE TIPS

Make this chutney only when you can find mint in the peak of condition. You may find that the blender will not turn at first when loaded with the ingredients. If this is the case, stop the motor and poke at the ingredients with the spatula. Do not do what we did, in the heat of excitement and urgency on the television show—we poked at it while the blades were whirling, and I have one mutilated spatula as a remembrance of the event.

INGREDIENTS	PREPARATION
½ cup *(2 ounces)* of mint leaves (well packed)	
4 *(3 ¼)* tablespoons of lemon or lime juice	
2 green Serrano chilli peppers, or 1 Jalapeño pepper	Seeded and chopped
1 medium-sized tart apple	Peeled, cored and diced just before blending
1 orange	Peeled, seeded and cubed
1 *(¾)* teaspoon of salt	

METHOD

Combine all the ingredients in the container of a blender or processor and blend on high speed until you have a smooth, even paste or puree.

ADVANCE PREPARATION AND
STORAGE NOTES

This chutney can be made up to 3 hours beforehand and then refrigerated. Do not try to keep it longer as the mint will darken and discolor.

❦ Indian Fresh Tomato Chutney

All of the Indian fresh chutneys are best made and eaten on the same day. It is a shame, because they are so delicious that it is natural to want to keep them. This Tomato Chutney is a good accompaniment to curries and lentil dishes, and also to Indian snacks and deep-fried tidbits.

Preparation time: 8 to 10 minutes   Enough to accompany a meal for 8

SHOPPING AND TECHNIQUE TIPS

You may use the canned Italian plum tomatoes, drained of juice, but the chutney is really far nicer when it is made with fresh tomatoes. Immerse the tomatoes in boiling water until the skins start to split (plunge each tomato in the water separately, using a slotted spoon). Let the tomatoes cool until you can handle them, then peel off the skins. If basil leaves are out of season, substitute mint leaves in an equal quantity.

INGREDIENTS	PREPARATION
1 pound of tomatoes	Skins removed, roughly chopped
Green, outer peel *(zest)* of 1 lime	Finely chopped
1 *(¾)* teaspoon of freshly ground black pepper	
2-inch piece of fresh ginger root	Peeled and finely chopped
1 medium onion	Peeled and chopped
12 to 15 basil leaves	Chopped
½ *(⅓)* teaspoon of ground paprika	
¼ to ½ *(⅓)* teaspoon of ground red pepper (Cayenne)	
¼ teaspoon *(a pinch)* of ground turmeric	

METHOD
1. Place all the ingredients in a food processor or blender and process to a rough puree. (You may want to do this in 2 batches, depending on the capacity of your machine.)
2. Transfer to serving bowls and refrigerate until ready to serve.

ADVANCE PREPARATION AND
STORAGE NOTES
Should be made the same day it will be eaten.

ℰ Lady MacFarquhar's Tomato Chutney (INDIA)

This is a charming family recipe acquired by my aunt, Lady MacFarquhar, during her many years in India. The units for quantities in the original recipe are interesting (hence the charm), for instance, *seers,* an Indian unit of measurement equal to 2⅔ pounds, are indicated for the solids and "... a little less than a whisky bottle" for some of the liquids. As you can see, this is a canning *(bottling)* recipe. Properly stored, this marvelous all-purpose chutney will remain in good shape for more than several months.

Preparation time: 1½ hours   Yields about 5 quarts
Cooking time: 1 hour

SHOPPING AND TECHNIQUE TIPS
There is a great deal of time involved in peeling the large quantity of garlic and ginger called for in this recipe, so I suggest that you either set aside a free afternoon or persuade some friends or relatives to help you in the kitchen. The results well justify your hard work and patience.

INGREDIENTS	PREPARATION
1½ pounds of granulated sugar	
3 cups *(24 fluid ounces)* of white vinegar	
½ pound of garlic	Separated into cloves, peeled, and roughly chopped
1½ pounds of fresh ginger root	Peeled and coarsely chopped
5½ pounds of firm tomatoes	Blanched, skins removed, quartered
1½ pounds of raisins	
6 ounces of golden raisins *(sultanas)*	

INGREDIENTS
10 dried red peppers
Salt to taste

PREPARATION
Seed if you wish to lessen the heat

METHOD
1. In a large saucepan, bring the sugar and vinegar to a boil over medium heat. Stir and scrape the sides to wash down the sugar crystals and continue to boil until the sugar is dissolved and a thin syrup is formed.

2. Stir in the garlic and ginger. When the mixture returns to a boil, add the tomatoes, both varieties of raisins and chilli peppers. Bring to a boil once more, stirring, then reduce the heat to low and simmer until the mixture thickens and the solids (tomatoes, ginger, garlic, etc.) start to soften and become mushy. Stir from time to time.

3. Remove from the heat and, when cool enough to handle, salt to taste. Pour into sterilized *(bottling)* canning jars and seal tightly. If you wish to sterilize further, immerse the jars in a boiling-water bath for 20 minutes.

ADVANCE PREPARATION AND
STORAGE NOTES
This is such a delicious chutney, I suggest you double the quantities and make some for gifts.

❦ Indian Sweet Lime Chutney

An aromatic, piquant, thick chutney which goes well with cold meats and many dishes in need of a little livening up, as well as with the classic range of Indian foods.

If you are unable to find limes, you may like to substitute lemons. The flavor of the completed chutney is less tangy, more on the mellow side, but the resultant preserve is still delightful.

Preparation time: 40 minutes
Cooking time: 40 minutes

Yields between 9 and 11 cups,
depending on the size of the limes

SHOPPING AND PREPARATION TIPS
The price of limes in the supermarkets varies markedly. Choose to make the chutney when there is a good supply and the price is low.

INGREDIENTS
24 limes
3 *(2⅓)* tablespoons of salt
1 cup *(5⅔ ounces)* of golden raisins
    (sultanas)
½ cup *(4½ ounces)* of dates
1 *(¾)* tablespoon of hot powdered
    mustard
1 cup *(8 fluid ounces)* of white
    vinegar
4-inch piece of fresh ginger root
8 cloves of garlic
5 dried red chilli peppers
1 cup *(5⅔ ounces)* of brown sugar

PREPARATION
Quartered and seeded

Pitted and chopped

Peeled and chopped
Peeled and chopped
Seeded and chopped

METHOD

1. Rub the cut surfaces of the limes with salt and place them on a cookie tray. Heat them in a 140°F. *(low)* oven until the surfaces are fairly dry. Remove limes and chop roughly.

2. In a large mixing bowl, combine the remaining ingredients and add the limes. Feed the mixture, a small batch at a time, into a blender or food processor and blend until the mixture is finely chopped. Accumulate the batches in a large saucepan.

3. Set the saucepan over moderate heat and bring the mixture to a boil, stirring steadily. Reduce the heat to low and simmer the chutney for 30 minutes, stirring occasionally to prevent the mixture from sticking to the bottom of the pan.

4. Let the mixture cool slightly, then fill into canning jars. If you wish the chutney to have a long (unrefrigerated) shelf life, sterilize the jars in a boiling-water bath for 15 minutes (see canning instructions at the beginning of this chapter, pages 452–53).

ADVANCE PREPARATION AND
STORAGE NOTES

Unsterilized, this chutney will keep in the refrigerator for 3 months.

❧ Indonesian Fish Relish

In Indonesia, this piquant side dish, or *sambal,* is most commonly prepared with eel or small, dried anchovies, but it is delicious when made with good-quality canned tuna. You may serve it as an accompaniment to a main dish, or as one of the many components of a full, buffet rice table *(Rijsttafel).* I have also eaten it as part of a sandwich filling.

Preparation time: 8 minutes
Cooking time: 8 minutes

Serves 6 to 8 (in small amounts because it is pepper hot)

SHOPPING AND TECHNIQUE TIPS

Select a good tuna in water. You may also experiment with substituting canned mackerel or sardines. Smoked oysters would be interesting too. This *sambal,* like most, is supposed to be spicy hot and have a concentrated flavor. However, you may wish to reduce the amount of ground red pepper at first and in time work up to the full amount. Try half the Cayenne initially.

INGREDIENTS	PREPARATION
4 cloves of garlic	Peeled and chopped
4 shallots	Peeled and chopped
4 macadamia nuts, or 2 Brazil nuts, skin removed	Chopped
2 *(1 ⅔)* teaspoons of ground red pepper (Cayenne) (or less, to taste)	
2 *(1 ⅔)* tablespoons of peanut or vegetable oil	
1 cup *(7 to 8 ounces)* of firm canned *(tinned)* water-packed tuna *(7 to 8 ounces/tinned waterpacked)*	Drained
1 *(¾)* tablespoon of canned *(tinned)* tomato puree or paste	
1 *(¾)* tablespoon of brown sugar	
1 *(¾)* tablespoon of fresh lemon juice	
½ *(⅓)* teaspoon of salt	

METHOD

1. In a mortar or food processor, pound or grind the garlic, shallots, nuts and red pepper to a rough paste. (You may need to add a *(¾)* teaspoon of oil if you use a processor, in which case reduce the oil for frying correspondingly.)

2. Heat the oil in a wok or large frying pan over medium-high heat, and fry the paste stirring and scraping continually so that it does not burn. Fry for approximately 1 minute, or until the odor mellows.

3. Add the tuna and all the remaining ingredients and continue to fry, stirring, until the mixture becomes thick and most of the moisture has evaporated. Do not worry when the fish breaks up into uneven pieces—it is meant to.

4. Transfer to a serving dish and serve hot or cold.

ADVANCE PREPARATION AND
STORAGE NOTES
Because of the spices, this relish keeps well. It can be made several days ahead of time and refrigerated in a covered container. Bring back to room temperature before serving, or heat gently in a pan on top of the stove or in the oven.

✿ Indonesian Green Pepper Relish

This side dish or *sambal* is made with a mixture of sweet, mild and hot peppers. You may cut down on the amount of hot peppers if you wish, or replace them with larger, slightly milder peppers. The relish should, however, be slightly hot to the palate.

Preparation time: 10 minutes   Serves 6 (small portions)
Cooking time: 10 minutes

SHOPPING AND TECHNIQUE TIPS
This pepper relish is traditionally green, but if there are plenty of sweet red peppers in season, you may like to make a red version, using ripened hot red peppers as well, if you can find them. You may even like to combine colors and make a red-and-green relish, which would be very festive.

INGREDIENTS	PREPARATION
1 (¾) tablespoon of peanut or vegetable oil	
2 medium sweet green peppers	Seeded, cored and the membranes removed, flesh cut into dice
2 green Serrano chilli peppers, or 1 Jalapeño pepper (or equivalent)	Minced (seeding is optional)

INGREDIENTS	PREPARATION
1 medium onion	Peeled and sliced into slivers
4 cloves of garlic	Peeled and cut into paper-thin slices
1 (¾) tablespoon of granulated sugar	
2 (1⅔) tablespoons of lime juice	
1 (¾) tablespoon of Southeast Asian fish sauce	
¼ to ½ (⅓) teaspoon of salt	

METHOD

1. Heat the oil over medium-high heat and fry the peppers, onion and garlic for 3 minutes, stirring continually.

2. Add the remaining ingredients and lower the heat. Simmer the mixture, stirring occasionally, for 5 or 6 minutes, until the solid ingredients are soft and everything is well mixed to a relish-like consistency. Transfer to a bowl and serve.

ADVANCE PREPARATION AND
STORAGE NOTES

This relish may be made ahead and refrigerated in a covered container for up to 3 or 4 days. If more hot peppers are added, it will keep even longer. Bring it back to room temperature before serving.

❧ Indonesian Peanut and Coconut Sambal

This lovely spiced mixture is sprinkled over the top of Indonesian curries. It is served as a side dish at a buffet, or you may offer it as an accompaniment to a stir-fried melange. It would also be suitable to offer with a Malay dish, as it is eaten in that country as well.

Preparation time: 5 minutes   Serves 6 to 8 (small portions)
Cooking time: 5 minutes

SHOPPING AND TECHNIQUE TIPS

You may buy the dry-roasted peanuts or the usual variety. Look for the unsweetened flaked coconut in the health-food section of your supermarket or in a health-food store. Tamarind water is used in the original recipe. You may substitute a mixture of molasses (treacle) and lime juice.

INGREDIENTS

PREPARATION

1½ cups *(just over 3 ⅓ ounces)* of
    dried, unsweetened, flaked
    coconut
1½ *(1 ¼)* teaspoons of ground cumin
½ *(⅓)* teaspoon of ground red
    pepper (Cayenne)
½ *(⅓)* teaspoon of salt
1 *(¾)* tablespoon of brown sugar
1 small onion

Peeled and minced

2 cloves of garlic

Peeled and smashed, minced

½-inch piece of fresh ginger root

Peeled and minced

1 *(¾)* teaspoon of molasses *(treacle)*
    dissolved in 3 tablespoons of
    lime juice
¾ cup *(4 ¾ ounces)* of roasted,
    salted peanuts

Roughly chopped

METHOD

1. Place all the ingredients, except the peanuts, in a large bowl and mix together until they are thoroughly combined.

2. Grease or spray a frying pan or wok and place it over medium-low heat. Add the contents from the bowl and fry, turning constantly and stirring until the mixture turns a golden-brown. Remove from the heat and let it cool.

3. Stir in the peanuts and transfer to a serving bowl.

ADVANCE PREPARATION AND
STORAGE NOTES

This mixture can be made a day or two ahead of time and refrigerated in a covered container. Bring to room temperature before serving.

❦ Korean Cabbage Pickle

This is the famous *kimchee,* a rather pungent, pickled and slightly fermented mixed cabbage and vegetable pickle. Freshly made, it is quite mild. However, the Koreans also like it fermented until it is pungent in odor and flavor.

Preparation time: 30 minutes, plus 3
    days and 3 hours of marinating
    and pickling time

Makes about 6 pounds

SHOPPING AND TECHNIQUE TIPS

Look for the Chinese cabbage (Tientsin), sometimes called celery cabbage. You may use the ordinary white cabbage if you cannot find the Chinese. Ordinary turnips may be substituted for the large, long, white Oriental radish.

INGREDIENTS	PREPARATION
2 heads of Chinese (or white) cabbage	Outer leaves removed, heads cut lengthwise into quarters
½ cup *(3 ounces)* of salt	
1½ pounds of long, white Oriental radish (or equivalent amount of turnips)	Peeled and cut into thin strips
6 green *(spring)* onions	Cut into 1½-inch lengths, shredded lengthwise into slivers
4 cloves of garlic	Peeled and chopped
1½ inches of fresh ginger root	Peeled and minced
1 stalk of celery	Cut into 1-inch lengths, thinly shredded lengthwise
1 hard, semiripe pear	Peeled, cored and sliced, then cut into thin strips
4 *(3¼)* tablespoons of ground red pepper (Cayenne)	
1 *(¾)* tablespoon of granulated sugar	

METHOD

1. Place the quartered cabbage heads and the outside leaves in a large bowl and sprinkle with the salt. Let them stand for 3 hours, turning occasionally.

2. Meanwhile, place the radish strips and green *(spring)* onion slivers in another bowl and mix together.

3. In a smaller bowl, mix together the remaining ingredients well, then add them to the radish mixture and stir.

4. Remove the outer leaves from the brine and set them aside. Take a quarter of the cabbage head and rinse it off under running water. Pack some of the radish mixture down between the leaves and set it in the bottom of the crock (or other container). Repeat with the remaining quarters and place any remaining radish mixture in a layer over the cabbage quarters. Press it down.

5. Place the outer leaves in a layer over the top and press down. Set a small plate over the top and cover the container. Leave for 3 days before using. If a stronger, more pungent pickle is wanted, increase the standing time—up to as much as 1 month. The pickle should be kept in a cool (60°F.) place.

ADVANCE PREPARATION AND
STORAGE NOTES

Obviously, as you can see from step 5, the pickling and fermentation period depends on your individual taste. After that, you may want to pack it into individual glass canning jars.

Japanese Variation

Use only the cabbage and salt. Pack down the quartered heads, sprinkling the layers with salt. Allow to ferment for up to 1 month. Rinse off the cabbage and press moisture out before serving. It may be sprinkled with a little lemon juice and grated ginger after it is put in the serving dish.

❀ Chinese Mixed Pickles

This is not a long-keeping pickle and should be refrigerated. These pickles may be served as part of an appetizer tray.

Preparation time: 12 hours   Yields 3-plus cups
Cooking time: 5 minutes

SHOPPING AND TECHNIQUE TIPS

You may use any selection of vegetables. Suggestions are: green beans, carrots, sweet red or green peppers, long, white radish, celery, zucchini *(courgette)*, cauliflower, Chinese cabbage, etc.

INGREDIENTS	PREPARATION
1 pound (total weight) of mixed vegetables	Cleaned, peeled (if necessary) and cut into bite-size pieces (celery into 1-inch lengths, cabbage into 1-inch squares, etc.)
2-inch piece of fresh ginger root	Peeled and cut into shreds
2 *(1⅔)* tablespoons of salt	
2 *(1⅔)* tablespoons of granulated sugar	
½ *(⅓)* teaspoon of ground red pepper (Cayenne)	
1 cup *(8 fluid ounces)* of water	
½ cup *(4 fluid ounces)* of white vinegar	
¼ teaspoon *(a large pinch)* of Chinese Five-Plus-One Spice Powder (page 119)	

METHOD

1. Layer the vegetables and ginger in a bowl, sprinkling salt between each layer. Refrigerate for about 8 hours or overnight.

2. Remove the vegetables from the bowl and pack into jars. Place the remaining ingredients in a saucepan and heat, stirring, until the sugar has dissolved. Let the liquid cool, then pour over the vegetables, making sure that they are totally immersed. Cover and refrigerate for 3 days.

3. To serve, remove the vegetables with a slotted spoon and place on a tray or in a small bowl.

ADVANCE PREPARATION AND
STORAGE NOTES
This pickle keeps in the refrigerator for about 1 week after maturity.

Pickled Ginger Variation (CHINESE AND SOUTHEAST ASIAN)

Use 1 pound of fresh ginger root, peeled and cut into paper-thin slices crosswise. Omit the red pepper and Five-Plus-One Spice Powder from the pickling solution, but add a few drops of red food coloring. Keeps for up to 3 weeks, refrigerated.

✿ Southeast Asian Sweet and Hot Chilli Sauce

This sauce can travel happily from cuisine to cuisine in Southeast Asia. It is a delicious dipping sauce for hors d'oeuvres and snacks and will provide a perfect counterpoint to such deep-fried foods as Stuffed Chicken Wings, Shrimp Toasts and all manner of barbecued meats. If you find it too pepper hot, you may reduce the amount of ground red pepper and pepper flakes or dilute it with tomato ketchup. When mixed with the latter, it makes an excellent marinade for barbecued poultry and meats. If I could only have one sauce on my table, it would probably be this one.

Preparation time: 10 minutes   Yield: approximately 8½ cups
Cooking time: 20 minutes

SHOPPING AND TECHNIQUE TIPS
Have your sterilized jars and lids ready and covered by a clean cloth. You may want to keep them on a tray in a warm oven so that they do not crack when you pour in the hot sauce.

INGREDIENTS

½ cup *(1¾ ounces)* of ground red
     chilli powder (Cayenne)
3 cups *(1 pound, 7½ ounces)* of
     granulated sugar
3¼ cups *(26 fluid ounces)* of white
     vinegar
1½ cups *(8½ ounces)* of seedless
     golden raisins *(sultanas)*
12 cloves of garlic
3 *(2⅓)* teaspoons of salt
2 *(1⅔)* teaspoons of dried red chilli
     pepper flakes
3-inch piece of fresh ginger root

PREPARATION

Peeled and minced

Peeled and minced

METHOD

1. Place all the ingredients in a saucepan and bring to a boil over high heat.

2. Reduce the temperature and simmer the mixture about 20 minutes, until the raisins are soft and almost pulpy.

3. Pour the mixture, 1 cup at a time, into a blender or food processor and blend into a smooth puree.

4. Using a funnel, pour the sauce into sterilized bottles or jars, cap or seal tightly and refrigerate. If a longer storage period is wanted, sterilize the filled bottles or jars once more.

❧ Chinese Plum Sauce

Preparation time: 10 minutes
Cooking time: 30 minutes

Yields: Approximately 4 cups

SHOPPING AND TECHNIQUE TIPS
The plum jam in the ingredients list is the smooth variety in which the plums have been mashed down and there are no pits. It is best to sterilize the jars or bottles before filling them.

INGREDIENTS

1 cup *(8½ ounces)* of canned
     (tinned) red plums
1 cup *(8½ ounces)* of canned
     (tinned) apricot halves

PREPARATION

Drained and pits removed

Drained

INGREDIENTS

½ cup *(4 ounces)* of canned *(tinned)*
   pimiento
1 cup *(7¾ ounces)* of granulated
   sugar
½ cup *(5¾ ounces)* of plum jam
½ cup *(4 fluid ounces)* of white
   vinegar

PREPARATION

Drained and chopped

METHOD

1. Place all the ingredients into a blender and blend to a smooth puree.

2. Pour and scrape the contents of the blender into a saucepan and bring to a boil, stirring, over medium-high heat. Cover, reduce the heat to low and simmer for 20 minutes, uncovering occasionally to stir.

3. Turn off the heat and let the mixture cool slightly. Using the funnel, fill the jars or bottles. Cap tightly.

ADVANCE PREPARATION AND
STORAGE NOTES

If a long storage life is wanted, sterilize the filled jars (see the instructions at the beginning of this chapter, pages 452–53). This Plum Sauce should be allowed to mellow for 2 weeks before using. If the jars are not sterilized again, keep refrigerated. Use as a table sauce with duck, pork or chicken, or as a dip for egg rolls and snacks.

❀ Southeast Asian Peanut Sauce for Satay

This recipe produces the standard Southeast Asian peanut sauce, that usually accompanies a satay, together with the mandatory side dish of thinly sliced cucumbers in a sweet-sour dressing.

Preparation time: 5 minutes   Yields approximately 1½ cups
Cooking time: 15 minutes

SHOPPING AND TECHNIQUE TIPS

While many Asians traditionally grind or pound roasted peanuts to make this sauce, many in the big cities have found the easy alternative of using commercial peanut butter. The natural, chunky variety containing no preservatives is the closest approximation of the original.

INGREDIENTS

2 *(1⅔)* teaspoons of peanut oil
2 *(1⅔)* teaspoons of butter or
    margarine
1 medium onion
3 cloves of garlic
3 heaped *(3)* tablespoons of chunky
    (crunchy) peanut butter
¼ teaspoon *(just under ¼ teaspoon)*
    of anchovy paste (optional)
1 *(¾)* teaspoon of molasses *(treacle),*
    dissolved in 4 tablespoons *(2*
    fluid ounces) of hot water
4 tablespoons *(2 fluid ounces)* of lime
    juice
2 *(1⅔)* teaspoons of Hot Pepper
    Paste (page 128)
½ *(⅓)* teaspoon of salt
1 *(¾)* teaspoon of dark brown sugar
1 *(¾)* tablespoon of Dark Sweet Soy
    Sauce (page 142)

PREPARATION

Peeled and finely sliced into slivers
Peeled and minced

METHOD

1. Heat the peanut oil and butter in a wok or saucepan over a medium-high setting. Stir-fry the onions and garlic until the onion is golden brown. Remove the onion and garlic with a slotted spoon, draining them over the pan, and place them on paper towels.

2. Leave the wok on the heat and add the peanut butter, anchovy paste, molasses *(treacle)* liquid and lime juice. Bring the mixture to a boil, stirring, then immediately remove from the heat.

3. Stir in the remaining ingredients and mix thoroughly. Return the onions and garlic to the sauce and stir again.

4. Transfer to serving bowls and serve warm or at room temperature with satay.

ADVANCE PREPARATION AND
STORAGE NOTES

The sauce may be made ahead and refrigerated, covered. Let it come back to room temperature and stir before serving. After removing from the refrigerator, you may need to add a tablespoon of water as the mixture tends to thicken at colder temperatures.

❦ Indonesian Satay Sauce

Although many of the Indonesian satay sauces are variations of a peanut sauce, this one is based on their Dark Sweet Soy Sauce *(Ketjap Manis).*

Preparation time: 2 minutes   Yields 1 cup

SHOPPING AND TECHNIQUE TIPS

This recipe incorporates 3 other basic recipes for make-ahead staples for your Oriental-foods cupboard. The Indonesian Dark Sweet Soy Sauce and the Indonesian Hot Pepper Paste are both homemade substitutes for commercial preparations ordinarily available in Oriental stores. The Fried Onion Flakes are a quick shortcut for the normally tedious process of frying onions until they are crisp.

INGREDIENTS

½ a stick *(2 ounces)* of butter (¼
     cup)
½ cup *(4 fluid ounces)* of Dark
     Sweet Soy Sauce (page 142)
Juice of 2 limes
¼ teaspoon *(a pinch)* of ground
     black pepper
1 *(¾)* tablespoon (or less if a milder
     sauce is wanted) of Hot Pepper
     Paste (page 128)
½ cup *(2 ¼ ounces)* of Fried Onion
     Flakes (page 156)

METHOD

1. In a small saucepan, melt the butter over medium heat until it is frothy but not brown.

2. Add all the ingredients except the Fried Onion Flakes. Bring to a boil, reduce heat and simmer the mixture, stirring constantly, for 2 minutes. Pour into serving bowls, sprinkle with the Onion Flakes and serve warm with satay.

ADVANCE PREPARATION AND STORAGE NOTES

The sauce may be made ahead and refrigerated, covered. The Fried Onion Flakes should not be added until sauce has been reheated.

✿ Thai Sauce for Satay

Although the Southeast Asian Peanut Sauce can accompany Thai satays happily, this slightly spicier sauce is a delicious accent. You may also wish to treat it as a dip or accompaniment for other hors d'oeuvres.

Preparation time: 3 minutes
Cooking time: 10 minutes

Yields approximately 1¾ cups

SHOPPING AND TECHNIQUE TIPS

This sauce is smoother than the Southeast Asian Peanut Sauce, so use the smooth natural peanut butter.

INGREDIENTS

1 cup *(8 fluid ounces)* of Coconut
    Milk made with 1 cup of whole
    milk and ½ cup *(4 fluid ounces)*
    of half-and-half *(half cream-half
    milk)* flavored with 1 *(¾)*
    teaspoon of coconut extract
1 heaped *(1)* tablespoon of Thai
    Curry Spice Paste (page 124)
3 *(2⅓)* tablespoons of smooth
    peanut butter
1 *(¾)* teaspoon of salt
1 *(¾)* tablespoon of granulated sugar
1 *(¾)* tablespoon of Southeast Asian
    fish sauce
¼ *(just under ¼)* teaspoon of
    anchovy paste
1 *(¾)* tablespoon of lime juice

METHOD

1. Heat the coconut milk in a wok over medium-high heat and bring to a bubbling boil. Stir in the Thai Curry Spice Paste and cook, stirring, for 3 minutes.

2. Stir in the remaining ingredients and cook, stirring, for 4 more minutes.

3. Pour the sauce into individual bowls for dipping the satay.

ADVANCE PREPARATION AND STORAGE NOTES

This sauce may be made up to 3 or 4 days ahead and refrigerated in a covered container. It may also be placed in a freezer container or self-locking freezer bag and frozen for up to 3 months. In both cases, bring to room temperature and stir in 1 or 2 tablespoons of coconut milk to reconstitute before serving.

❧ Thai Chilli and Garlic Fish Sauce

This is a real country sauce. You will not find its counterpart in Thai restaurants —not even those in Thailand. When he was very small, my son, Adam, used to haunt the "outside" kitchen, which was in the servants' territory. He knew the kitchen was always a source of all manner of interesting snacks and dishes. The cook, Cham Raat, would make this sauce to accompany plain rice and the small roasted fish of which the Thai are so fond. When we returned to the United States, and as my son grew older, he experimented in the kitchen until he duplicated the sauce perfectly. His recipe is the one given below.

This pungent and spicy sauce is for true *aficionados* of Thai food. A little goes a long way over plain rice or to accompany the blander dishes. It is also rich in nutrients. I have modified this recipe for palates unused to the full strength of Thai sauces.

Preparation time: 12 to 15 minutes   Yields approximately ¾ cup

SHOPPING AND TECHNIQUE TIPS
The dried, powdered shrimp can be found in the Latin (Mexican) sections of supermarkets in the Southwest United States. A satisfactory substitute is a table-spoon of any smoked fish, flaked and pounded. It will not produce the same effect but will change the sauce slightly into an equally authentic version. This sauce is best made in a large mortar—a processor does not handle the pulverizing necessary to the texture. Add the drier solids first and pound them to a paste before blending with the liquid, or the sauce will splash right back at you. For those pursuing absolute authenticity, I have departed from my usual practice and given the original ingredients and amounts in parenthesis after the modified ingredients.

INGREDIENTS	PREPARATION
4 cloves of garlic (6)	Peeled and minced
3 green Serrano chilli peppers (6)	Chopped and seeded (do not seed for the original)
1 (¾) teaspoon of anchovy paste (1 (¾) tablespoon of Thai shrimp paste—*kapi*)	

INGREDIENTS

4 tablespoons *(2 fluid ounces)* of
   Southeast Asian fish sauce
1 *(¾)* tablespoon of molasses
   (treacle), dissolved in 4
   tablespoons *(2 fluid ounces)* of
   lime juice (1 *(¾)* tablespoon of
   tamarind concentrate, dissolved
   in 4 *(2 fluid ounces)* tablespoons
   of hot water)
1 *(¾)* tablespoon of smoked, flaked
   fish (1 *(¾)* tablespoon of dried,
   powdered shrimp)
2 dried red chilli peppers (1 *(¾)*
   tablespoon of dried red pepper
   flakes)
1½ *(1¼)* teaspoons of dark brown
   sugar
1 *(¾)* teaspoon of peanut oil (1 *(¾)*
   tablespoon of garlic-flavored oil)

PREPARATION

Seeded and finely minced

METHOD

1. In a large mortar, pound the garlic and chilli peppers into a juicy paste.

2. Add the anchovy paste and continue to pound into a homogenous mixture.

3. Gradually pour in the fish sauce and molasses *(treacle)*/lime juice mixture, stirring with the pestle until the paste is diluted into a smooth sauce. Now stir in the remaining ingredients and continue to stir until the sugar has dissolved.

4. Pour into a jar and cap *tightly* until ready to use.

ADVANCE PREPARATION AND
STORAGE NOTES   .

You may make this sauce whenever you have time to spend. The sauce will keep refrigerated for up to 3 months.

❧ Vietnamese Dipping and Table Sauce

Known as *Nuoc Cham* in Vietnamese, this sauce is ever present at their meals and goes well with almost every Vietnamese dish. It is sometimes used as a salad dressing (see page 229).

Preparation time: 6 minutes   Yields about ½ cup

SHOPPING AND TECHNIQUE TIPS
This sauce may be made entirely in the mortar.

INGREDIENTS	PREPARATION
2 cloves of garlic	Peeled and minced
2 dried red chilli peppers	Seeded and finely chopped
1 heaped *(1)* tablespoon of granulated sugar	
Juice and pulp of 2 limes	
3 tablespoons *(1½ fluid ounces)* of Southeast Asian fish sauce	
2 tablespoons *(1 fluid ounce)* (or more) of water	

METHOD
1. Pound the garlic, peppers and sugar together in a mortar, until garlic is paste-like and sugar has become a powder.

2. Stir in the remaining ingredients and pour into small bowls.

ADVANCE PREPARATION AND STORAGE NOTES
This sauce may be made up to 2 days in advance and then refrigerated in a tightly covered jar. It is possible to keep it longer, but if you do, the lime juice loses its fresh taste and much of its Vitamin C.

A QUARTET OF JAPANESE DIPPING SAUCES—THEME WITH VARIATIONS

There are a multitude of freshly made sauces in Japan—not to mention the marinades—that are served with broiled foods, steamed foods, *sashimi* and the meats from one-pot cooking. Here are 4 recipes with variations and suggestions for their use.

❀ Teriyaki Sauce for Broiled Meats and Poultry

Preparation time: 2 minutes   Yields 1¼ cups
Cooking time: 3 minutes

SHOPPING AND TECHNIQUE TIPS
Look on the shelves of a liquor store or the Oriental section of the supermarket for *mirin,* the Japanese sweet rice wine. If you cannot find it, substitute ¾ of the given amount of sweet sherry. Use Japanese soy sauce—not Chinese—for Japanese dishes. The flavor is different.

INGREDIENTS
¼ cup *(2 fluid ounces) mirin* or 3 *(2
    ⅓)* tablespoons of sweet sherry
½ cup *(4 fluid ounces)* of Basic Fish
    Stock
½ cup *(4 fluid ounces)* of soy sauce
1 *(¾)* tablespoon of granulated sugar

METHOD
1. Warm the wine in a small saucepan. Stir in the remaining ingredients, bring to a boil and set aside to cool.
2. Pour into bowls and serve to accompany *teriyaki* beef or chicken.

ADVANCE PREPARATION AND
STORAGE NOTES

This sauce may be made in larger quantities and stored in a tightly closed jar in the refrigerator for up to a month. Before reusing, bring to a boil again and skim any residue from the surface. The sauce may be incorporated in a *teriyaki* basting sauce.

❧ Teriyaki Basting Sauce

Preparation time: 2 minutes   Cooking time: 10 minutes

SHOPPING AND TECHNIQUE TIPS
As above.

INGREDIENTS   PREPARATION
½ cup *(4 fluid ounces)* of the
    Teriyaki Sauce above
2 *(1 ⅔)* tablespoons of granulated
    sugar
1-inch piece of fresh ginger root   Peeled and grated or finely minced

METHOD

1. Place all the ingredients in a small saucepan over medium heat and bring to a boil, stirring. Lower the heat and simmer until the sauce becomes slightly sticky and syrupy (about 6 minutes).

2. Pour into a bowl and use for basting *teriyaki*-grilled foods.

ADVANCE PREPARATION AND
STORAGE NOTES

This basting sauce or glaze can also be prepared ahead and refrigerated in a tightly covered jar for up to a month. Bring to room temperature before using. You may also need to add an additional tablespoon of the Teriyaki Sauce to thin it—or soy sauce (1 tablespoon) may be added for the same purpose.

❧ Japanese Ginger Sauce for Grilled Meats

Preparation time: 5 minutes · · · · · Yields just over 1 cup

SHOPPING AND TECHNIQUE TIPS
As for Teriyaki Sauce for Broiled Meats

INGREDIENTS	PREPARATION
2-inch piece of fresh ginger root	Peeled and finely grated
½ cup *(4 fluid ounces)* of Basic Fish Stock (page 170)	
4 tablespoons *(2 fluid ounces)* of soy sauce	
2 *(1⅔)* tablespoons of *mirin* (rice wine) or 1½ *(1¼)* tablespoons of sweet sherry	

METHOD
Combine all the ingredients in a small bowl. Mix well and transfer to serving bowls.

ADVANCE PREPARATION AND STORAGE NOTES
This sauce will keep for a week if tightly covered and refrigerated.

Japanese Sesame Sauce Variation

Preparation time: 7 minutes · · · · · Yields just over 1½ cups

SHOPPING AND TECHNIQUE TIPS
You may like to toast (dry-fry) a large amount of sesame seeds in advance and keep them in a tightly capped jar. Grind as needed.

INGREDIENTS	PREPARATION
As for Japanese Ginger Sauce, but substituting ½ cup *(just over 2¾ ounces)* of white sesame seeds for the ginger	Toasted until golden, ground to a powder in an electric spice grinder or pounded to a powder in a mortar.
½ *(⅓)* tablespoon of Japanese Soybean Paste Substitute (page 131)	

METHOD
As for Japanese Ginger Sauce.

ADVANCE PREPARATION AND
STORAGE NOTES
As for Japanese Ginger Sauce.

❧ Japanese Dipping Sauce for Beef and Vegetable Fondue
(SHABU-SHABU)

In this recipe soy, soup stock and *mirin*—rice vinegar or white vinegar is added to the basic trio of ingredients.

Preparation time: 2 minutes   Yields 1¼ cups

SHOPPING AND TECHNIQUE TIPS
As for Teriyaki Sauce for Broiled Meats

INGREDIENTS
1 cup *(8 fluid ounces)* of Basic Fish
     Stock (page 170)
2 *(1⅔)* tablespoons of soy sauce
1 *(¾)* tablespoon of *mirin* (rice
     wine) or 2 *(1⅔)* teaspoons of
     sweet sherry
1 *(¾)* tablespoon of rice vinegar or
     white vinegar

METHOD
As for Japanese Ginger Sauce.

ADVANCE PREPARATION AND
STORAGE NOTES
As for Japanese Ginger Sauce.

Before we finish with the dipping sauces, here are two simple suggestions for alternative dips:
    1. Mix together equal quantities of soy sauce and lemon juice.

2. Mix together ½ cup *(4 fluid ounces)* of soy sauce and 3 tablespoons *(1 ½ fluid ounces)* of Japanese *sake* (rice wine), or 2 *(1 ⅔)* tablespoons of dry vermouth.

❦ Korean Dipping Sauce I

This sauce is mainly for fried foods.

Preparation time: 2 minutes   Enough for 4

INGREDIENTS	PREPARATION
½ cup *(4 fluid ounces)* of soy sauce	
½ cup *(4 fluid ounces)* of white vinegar	
3 *(2 ⅓)* tablespoons of granulated sugar	
2 *(1 ⅔)* tablespoons of pine nuts	Chopped

METHOD
1. Combine the soy sauce, vinegar and sugar in a bowl, stirring until the sugar has dissolved.
2. Transfer to individual bowls and sprinkle with the pine nuts.

ADVANCE PREPARATION AND
STORAGE NOTES
The sauce may be mixed several hours in advance, but do not top with the pine nuts until just before you set it on the table.

❦ Korean Dipping Sauce II

This can act as a general table sauce. Servings are the same as for the previous sauce. Preparation takes a few minutes longer.

INGREDIENTS	PREPARATION
½ cup *(4 fluid ounces)* of soy sauce	
3 *(2 ⅓)* tablespoons of granulated sugar	
1 green *(spring)* onion	Minced

INGREDIENTS

2 *(1⅔)* tablespoons of sesame seeds
1 *(¾)* tablespoon of Sesame Oil
    (page 139)

PREPARATION

Toasted a pale brown, then ground

METHOD

Combine all the ingredients together in a bowl, stirring until the sugar has dissolved.

ADVANCE PREPARATION AND STORAGE NOTES

The same as Korean Dipping Sauce I.

SWEET AND DESSERTED

ঙ ঙ ঙ

Puddings, Cakes, and Confections

The role of candies, cakes and puddings is a difficult one to define in the eating patterns of the Orient. Unlike most Western meals, which conclude with a dessert, the everyday Asian meal eaten at home will end with a platter of fresh fruit, peeled and prepared, or presented in its natural beauty.

So when do Asians eat confections, cakes and desserts?

Candylike confections are often professionally made and are bought from the markets as we stop to purchase a bar of chocolate or a pound of fudge. In Asia, during the day, such sweets make an appearance at snack time or teatime or are served when guests pay an informal visit. Cakes and cookies are also mostly store-bought, are served on similar occasions.

Festivals and feasts are also celebrated with cookies and confections, and, as there are so many during the year in every country, they become the perfect excuse for indulgence. The rich, sesame paste-filled pastries called "moon cakes," are eaten during the Chinese Moon Festival. Confections of all kinds are packaged in beautiful boxes and presented as gifts by the Japanese at the

New Year. Weddings throughout Asia are also the occasion for consumption of innumerable cakes and candies.

Formal meals and banquets are occasions for puddings and other desserts. In China, and within the sphere of its culinary influence, these sweet dishes sometimes appear at the end of the multicourse meal, but they will often be served in the middle of the meal as a change of pace and flavor. They may take the shape of pastries and "dry" confections, such as sweets made from glutinous rice and other ingredients, or they may be liquid desserts such as fruit soups, or chilled pieces of fruit or rice shapes in coconut milk, and even steamed puddings ornamented with preserved fruits.

There is also the tea snack, because Asians love their tea. While in China a savory snack is preferred, such as pork-filled buns, wontons or egg rolls, in countries which have had a long relationship with Europeans these savories are replaced by cakes and cookies.

The Philippines, because of their lengthy association with the Spanish, boast a wide repertoire of cakes, cookies and doughnut-type buns, with Western-style ingredients and methods of preparation. Some are served at breakfast and some for the *merienda,* or snack break after siesta, which corresponds to the British tea. The Dutch-influenced Indonesians also mark the cooling of the afternoon with a light meal, at which cakes and such delicacies as coconut-coated fried bananas are eaten.

India, one of the few countries in Asia to eat milk products, has a strong culinary tradition of delicious and rich confections and desserts, many of which are made by reducing cream to a solid form and combining it with cooked wheat semolina or rice and sugar. This dessert tradition was fostered and strengthened by the centuries of British influence. Most formal meals end in desserts. Tea (the beverage) was introduced to India by the British in the early 1900s, and the English teatime still exists with its accompanying array of sweetmeats and cakes.

The more complex Indian confections are professionally made and certain shops concentrate wholly on sweetmeats. There is no lack of customers, for the Indians have a pronounced sweet tooth and will snack on sweets and various confections throughout the day, purchasing them from shops or street vendors.

The techniques of making Asian sweets and desserts are as many and varied as the range of confections and cakes themselves. Some, like the Chinese buns and puddings, are steamed; some, like ginger and plum delicacies, are preserved in syrup or crystalized; others are "jelled" with agar-agar, a seaweed extract which is used instead of gelatin in hot countries, because it does not melt in the heat.

The most unfamiliar technique is the basis for most Indian sweets, involving the reduction by slow simmering of whole milk to a thick cream. This is a lengthy process: the milk is kept just under a boil and necessitates stirring every few minutes. I have worked with shortcuts and substitutions and have found that some sweets work quite well if made with a paste of powdered milk, while the reduction process can be speeded up by the use of canned evaporated milk, which is already somewhat reduced. (The thick cream made by the traditional reduction method tastes very much like commercial evaporated milk, anyway.)

To make most Indian sweets, you need a source of heat that can be turned to a steady low setting, heavy, enameled or Teflon saucepans and an inexhaustible supply of patience. I have found it helps to start making them at the beginning of preparation for a full meal, and to let them simmer away and reduce while I am busy at the stove with the other courses. One nice thing about Indian desserts and sweets is that they can be made well in advance. Some can be refrigerated, others store well in canisters, depending on their particular storage requirement. They also make interesting and different gifts during the holidays.

An Indian tradition is the use of small squares of silver or gold leaf, beaten to the thinness of a butterfly's wing, to decorate their puddings and sweets for special occasions. These sheets are quite dramatic in effect, and the uninitiated sometimes wonder if they are edible. In fact, they merely add, in the most minute way, to the trace elements of many metals and minerals that we already carry in our bodies. Old traditions in Europe centered around the consumption of trace quantities of gold for medicinal purposes, and dental work with gold and silver still contributes to those metals entering our systems. These sheets, carefully separated by tissue paper, are available only from Indian food shops. They are quite tricky to work with, as they tend to adhere to fingers and everything but the surfaces they are supposed to decorate. They are also so flimsy and fragile that one has to hold one's breath while applying them—one sneeze can scatter the whole package to the elements. A final word of caution to those who would like to use a substitute to reproduce the effect: No! Aluminum foil is NOT suitable!

❧ Eight Precious Treasure Rice Pudding (CHINA)

This classic Chinese dessert is far removed from our rice puddings. The traditional version contains a number of "treasures" in the form of rather exotic candied and preserved fruits and nuts such as preserved red dates, candied *(crystallized)* kumquats, candied *(crystallized)* papaya and lotus seeds. These are not available to us outside of Chinese specialty stores. However, there are many substitutes in harmony with the spirit of the dessert. The finished, molded rice pudding should have a stained-glass pattern of fruits and nuts in contrasting colors and flavors—so choose your ingredients accordingly.

Preparation time: 2½ hours (including soaking time for the rice)

Cooking time: 1 hour and 15 minutes
Serves 8

SHOPPING AND TECHNIQUE TIPS
After the rice is cooked, the pudding is steamed. Please refer to the chapter Steaming Techniques (pages 246–50) before you begin.

This pudding adds a festive note during the holiday season; also, supermarkets then stock the best selection of candied *(crystallized)* and preserved fruits and nuts. Here are some suggestions from which you can choose seven of the "Eight Treasures" (the eighth is the Chinese Sweet Red Bean Paste (page 132): red and green maraschino cherries; raisins; golden raisins; *(sultanas);* candied *(crystallized)* citron; pitted dates; candied *(crystallized)* pineapple; angelica; candied *(crystallized)* apricots; raw cashew nuts; blanched almonds; canned *(tinned)* litchi nuts; cooked chestnuts. Only one variety of nut is traditionally used, the other 6 ingredients being fruit.

The largest proportion of preparation time involves soaking the glutinous rice (also known as "sweet rice" in the Oriental markets or Oriental sections of supermarkets). If you cannot obtain it, use the Italian *risotto* rice, which also has a sticky consistency when cooked. If using the latter, soak it for only an hour, and use 1¾ cups *(14 fluid ounces)* of water to each cup. For either variety, follow the directions given in the basic recipe for rice (page 112).

INGREDIENTS	PREPARATION
2 cups *(15½ ounces)* of glutinous rice (sweet rice)	Washed, then soaked in cold water
or Italian *risotto* rice	Washed, then soaked in cold water
1 *(¾)* tablespoon of vegetable shortening	
6 raw cashew nuts or blanched almonds, or 3 cooked chestnuts	Sliced in half

INGREDIENTS

INGREDIENTS	PREPARATION
3 red maraschino cherries	Sliced into rounds
3 green maraschino cherries	Sliced into rounds
3 dates	Pitted and sliced in half
3 small pieces of candied (*crystallized*) pineapple	Sliced in half
1 piece of candied (*crystallized*) lemon (citron)	Sliced into 6 pieces
6 golden raisins (*sultanas*)	Soaked in hot water until they swell
2 (*1⅔*) tablespoons of vegetable shortening or margarine	
3 (*2⅓*) tablespoons of granulated sugar	
⅓ cup (*3 ounces*) of Chinese Sweet Red Bean Paste (page 132)	
3 more (*1⅔*) tablespoons of granulated sugar	
¾ cup (*6 fluid ounces*) of water	
2 (*1⅔*) teaspoons of cornstarch (*cornflour*)	
¼ cup (*2 fluid ounces*) of the red maraschino cherry liquid	

METHOD

1. Cook the rice according to the directions in the basic recipe (page 112).

2. While the rice is cooking, rub the inside of a bowl liberally and thoroughly with shortening. Arrange the "Treasure" ingredients in a pattern, pressing them so they will adhere to the bottom of the bowl; place the nuts in the center and circle them with the red cherry slices. Either arrange the remaining fruit in rings around the center or space them evenly in groups.

3. When the rice is cooked and the moisture evaporated, take the pan off the heat and stir in 2 tablespoons of shortening or margarine and 3 tablespoons of sugar. Mix thoroughly.

4. Carefully spoon half the rice into the bowl. Try to avoid disturbing the fruit arrangement. Gently compress it into an even and compact layer.

5. Using the back of a tablespoon, make a shallow indentation in the center. Place the Red Bean Paste in this and cover it with the remaining rice, pressing it down gently.

6. Remove a tray from a steamer and place the bowl on it, covering the pudding with a cloth. Bring the steamer up to a boil and place the tray in it. Steam the pudding for 1 hour.

7. Toward the end of the steaming time, place the last 3 tablespoons of

SETTING FRUIT AND NUTS IN THE BOWL FOR EIGHT PRECIOUS RICE PUDDING

FINISHED PUDDING

sugar in a small saucepan, together with the water. Stir the cornstarch *(cornflour)* and the cherry liquid together in a bowl. Bring the sugar water to a boil, stirring until the sugar is dissolved. Pour in the cornstarch *(cornflour)* mixture and stir until the sauce thickens. Remove it from the heat.

8. Remove the pudding from the steamer and gently slide a knife blade around the edge to loosen it. Place a serving plate upside down over the top and invert the pudding, unmolding it onto the plate (the melted shortening lining the bowl should help it slide out easily).

9. Pour the sauce over the entire pudding and serve.

Note: It is not traditional, but I like to flavor the sauce with the addition of 2 or 3 slices of fresh ginger root, removing them before pouring the sauce over the pudding.

ADVANCE PREPARATION AND STORAGE NOTES

The pudding can be made ahead through step 6. Do not unmold. Reheat it by steaming it for 5–10 minutes. Then make the sauce and finish the recipe.

Korean Variation (RICE PUDDING WITH

FRUIT, NUTS AND HONEY)

This delicious Korean version rather resembles a rice Christmas pudding and is more spiced than the Chinese. The rice is cooked first and the flavorings and other ingredients are stirred into it. In step 3, instead of the shortening and sugar, stir in 1 cup *(⅓ pound)* of dark-brown sugar, 2 *(1⅔)* tablespoons of soy sauce, 1½ *(1¼)* tablespoons of Sesame Oil (page 139), ½ *(⅓)* teaspoon of ground cinnamon and ¼ teaspoon *(one pinch)* of ground allspice. Mix thoroughly into the hot rice and then stir in ⅓ cup *(1¾ ounces)* of raisins, 8 pitted and chopped dates and ½ pound of cooked, peeled and chopped chestnuts. Follow the directions for steaming, but open the steamer from time to time and drizzle a *(¾)* tablespoon of honey over the pudding each time, for a total of 3 *(2⅓)* tablespoons. Just before the pudding is finished, sprinkle the top with 1 *(¾)* tablespoon of pine nuts. Add an extra 20 minutes to the steaming time to compensate for the loss of heat when you open the steamer. This pudding is served without a sauce. You may wish to reserve some of the fruit and nuts to sprinkle in the bottom of the bowl before putting in the pudding. In this way, when you unmold, you will have a decorative topping. This variation is equally delicious served hot or cold. When cold, it is so firm that you can slice it like a cake.

✿ Rice Cream with Almonds and Cardamom (INDIA)

Throughout India there are many variations of this dessert and many names for them. The dish ranges from the lavish Moghul sweet *pilaus,* which came from the Persians, to rice fried in butter with cardamoms and cloves, steamed and then enriched with raisins, almonds, cashew nuts and hazelnuts, to the creamed rice and coconut purees of the extreme south. Most of these desserts are extremely rich and are meant to be eaten in small quantities. The sweet *pilaus* were served at the start of a meal to sweeten the mouth, but the cream desserts were additionally chilled and served at the conclusion. They are served as desserts today.

Preparation time: 2 hours (including   Cooking time: 2 hours
  soaking the rice)   Serves 6

SHOPPING AND TECHNIQUE TIPS

Although the rice is cooked until it disintegrates, long-grain rice is the correct variety to choose. The short-grain "rice pudding" rice is too sticky. See if you can locate rose water to flavor the cream; it makes such a difference. If you cannot, then substitute a few drops of rose essence, which you may find in the better specialty spice and flavoring lines. If you can find neither, add a few drops of vanilla extract, but be sure it is the real thing, not a synthetic. In any event, the cardamom will provide the dominant flavor note.

INGREDIENTS	PREPARATION
⅓ cup *(2 ½ ounces)* of long-grain rice	Washed well, then soaked in cold water to cover for 2 hours
1 cup *(8 fluid ounces)* of whole milk	
¼ teaspoon *(a pinch)* of salt	
5 cups *(40 fluid ounces)* of half-and-half *(half cream-half milk)*	
1 cup *(7¾ ounces)* of granulated sugar	
2 *(1⅔)* tablespoons of golden raisins *(sultanas)*	Soaked in hot water for 10 minutes until they swell, well drained
2 *(1⅔)* tablespoons of blanched and slivered almonds	Coarsely chopped
2 *(1⅔)* tablespoons of hulled pistachios	Coarsely chopped
½ *(⅓)* teaspoon of ground cardamom	
1 *(¾)* tablespoon of rose water, or a few drops of rose essence or vanilla extract	

METHOD

1. Drain the rice and leave it in the saucepan. Pour in the milk and bring to a boil over medium heat, stirring. Reduce the heat to low and cover. Simmer for 5 minutes, uncovering to stir from time to time.

2. Uncover, add the salt and pour in the half-and-half *(half cream-half milk)*. Increase the heat to medium and bring slowly to just under a boil, stirring occasionally. Continue to cook, uncovered, stirring from time to time until the mixture thickens. (This will take about an hour or more, so be prepared to be doing something else in the kitchen at the same time.)

3. Stir in the sugar and continue to cook, stirring fairly steadily until the mixture becomes the consistency of thick custard and will drop slowly from

a spoon. (At this stage the rice will have almost completely disintegrated.)

4. Now stir in the raisins, almonds, pistachios and cardamom. Blend everything well and take the pan off the heat. Stir in the rose water and spoon the pudding into a serving dish. (This is where you would delicately press a few gossamer leaves of silver on top if you were in India). Refrigerate until ready to serve.

ADVANCE PREPARATION AND STORAGE NOTES

Because of the length of time involved, it is fortunate that you can make this dessert at your leisure. The rice can be soaked overnight, if need be. The dessert can be made the day before and covered with plastic wrap before being stored in the refrigerator. You may want to reserve a few slivered almonds with which to decorate the top just before you are ready to serve. I have also eaten it with heavy cream poured over—rich but delicious.

Rice Cream with Cashew Nuts and Coconut Variation

This is the southern India version. You merely substitute thin and thick Coconut Milk (page 114) for the milk and half-and-half *(half cream-half milk)*, and replace the white sugar with the moister brown sugar. Fry 3 *(2⅓)* tablespoons of raw cashew nuts and 3 *(2⅓)* tablespoons of dark raisins in 1 *(¾)* tablespoon of Indian Clarified Butter (page 139) until the raisins puff and the nuts turn golden; then stir them into the mixture as in step 4 of the preceding recipe instead of the golden raisins, almonds and pistachios. Increase the cardamom to 1 *(¾)* teaspoon and omit the rose water. You may reserve some of the fried nuts and raisins for garnish. This version may be served hot or cold.

❧ Fried Batter Spirals in Syrup (INDIA)

These are saucer-sized coils of crisply fried batter with a rose-flavored syrup inside each coil. It seems like a magical culinary trick to get the syrup inside the batter, where it oozes out deliciously with every crisp bite, but in fact it is quite easy. These delectable sweets are called *jalebis* in Hindustani. They are served cold, but *must* be eaten fresh. The traditional phrase of all-inclusive contempt for an inept Indian housewife is: "She runs the kind of house where you expect to be served stale *jalebis!*"

Preparation time: 12 hours
   (yeast-rising time)
Cooking time: 45 minutes to 1 hour

Serves 6 to 8 (depending on how
   greedy they are!)

SHOPPING AND TECHNIQUE TIPS

Do your very best to get hold of some rose water, or at least some essential oil of rose or, failing that, some rose extract—it makes such a difference in the flavor. The usual techniques in syrup making apply to this recipe. Be sure that you set out the bowl of syrup alongside the wok, together with a pair of tongs and the platter on which you will accumulate the finished coils. Assembly-line techniques work very well, so you may even like to get a friend or relative to assist you. It is fun; watch how many *jalebis* disappear before they get to the table.

INGREDIENTS

Batter

3 cups *(1 pound, 2 ounces)* of
   all-purpose *(plain)* flour
¼ cup *(1 ½ ounces)* of rice flour
¼ teaspoon *(a pinch)* of baking
   powder
¼ teaspoon *(a pinch)* of saffron
   strands
2½ cups *(1 pint)* of lukewarm water
¼ teaspoon *(a pinch)* of dried yeast

Syrup

4 cups *(2 pounds)* of granulated
   sugar
3 cups *(24 fluid ounces)* of cold
   water
⅛ teaspoon *(a small pinch)* of cream
   of tartar
2 *(1⅔)* teaspoons of yellow food
   coloring
⅛ teaspoon *(7 to 8 drops)* of red
   food coloring
1 *(¾)* teaspoon of rose water, or a
   drop of essential oil of rose, or 2
   or 3 drops of rose extract
The seeds from 6 cardamom pods
4 cups *(32 fluid ounces)* of vegetable
   oil for deep-frying.

PREPARATION

Soaked in 1 *(¾)* tablespoon of
boiling water

Slightly crushed

METHOD

1. In a bowl, combine the batter ingredients, beating until the batter is very smooth and the consistency of thick cream. Let it stand, uncovered, in a warm place for 11 to 12 hours.

2. Pour the oil into a wok, set a thermometer inside, and begin to bring it gradually up to 350°F. *(175°C.).* You can do this while you are making the syrup.

3. In a saucepan, combine the sugar, water and cream of tartar. Stir over moderate heat until the sugar has dissolved. Increase the heat to high and, timing when the syrup boils, boil briskly for 5 minutes (until sugar mixture reaches 220°F.) *(110°C.).* Remove from the heat, stir in the colorings, rose water and cardamom seeds. Set aside near the stove.

4. Fill a pastry bag or funnel with batter and pour the batter in a steady stream in a circular motion over the oil in the wok, making circles or figures of eight. Do not try to make more than 4 coils in the oil at one time. Keep your finger near the tip of the funnel so that you can quickly stop the flow when you have enough batter.

POURING BATTER SPIRALS

5. Fry the coils, turning once, until they are crisp and golden on both sides. Lift them out of the oil with tongs or a slotted spoon, drain them over the wok, then drop them immediately into the syrup and leave them for 1 minute. (It is during this time that the hot batter will absorb the syrup into itself without losing crispness.)

6. Lift the spirals from the syrup, draining them over the saucepan, and place them on a platter to cool. Try to accomplish the frying and syrup-dunking processes as quickly as possible, before the syrup begins to cool and thicken. You may slow this by placing the syrup pan in another one of boiling water.

7. When all the *jalebis* are completed, transfer them to a clean platter and serve.

ADVANCE PREPARATION AND
STORAGE NOTES
The *jalebis* may be made up to 3 or 4 hours ahead, but be sure that they are kept in a tightly sealed container, lined with paper towels, otherwise they will soften and lose their crispness.

✿ Indian Carrot Fudge Pudding

This delicious dessert, a cross between carrot cake and fudge, is a good example of the Indian technique of simmering milk and cream until they become semisolid. The carrots are also cooked until almost pulpy. A little of this dessert goes a long way, as it is concentrated and rich, as well as being extremely nutritious.

Preparation time: 5 to 10 minutes   Cooking time: about 1 hour and 15
                                                   minutes
                                          Serves 8 to 10

SHOPPING AND TECHNIQUE TIPS
If you have a food processor and an electric spice grinder, you will find that the time spent in grating the carrots and grinding the almonds will be considerably reduced.

INGREDIENTS	PREPARATION
1½ pounds of carrots	Tops and tips removed, peeled and finely grated
4 cups *(32 fluid ounces)* of whole milk	

INGREDIENTS

2 cups *(16 fluid ounces)* of whipping
   cream
1 cup *(5⅔ ounces)* of moist
   dark-brown sugar
½ cup *(3¾ ounces)* of granulated
   sugar
1 cup *(4¾ ounces)* of blanched
   almonds
¼ cup *(2 ounces)* of Indian Clarified
   Butter (page 139)
¼ teaspoon *(just under ¼ teaspoon)*
   of hulled cardamom seeds or ⅓
   (¼) teaspoon of ground
   cardamom
¼ cup *(1 generous ounce)* of slivered
   almonds
1½ *(1¼)* teaspoons of rose water

PREPARATION

Peeled and ground to a powder

METHOD

1. Combine the carrots, milk and cream in a saucepan and bring to a boil, stirring constantly to prevent sticking. Reduce the heat to medium and cook, stirring occasionally, until the mixture has reduced in volume by about half and is thick enough to coat the spoon. This will take at least 30 minutes or more.

2. Add the brown and white sugars and stir. Continue to cook and stir for 10 minutes.

3. Reduce the heat to low and add the almond powder and the Clarified Butter. Stir and cook for 10 minutes more, or until the mixture is thick enough to draw away from the sides and bottom of the pan in a solid mass.

4. Remove from the heat and stir in the cardamom, half the slivered almonds and the rose water.

5. Spread the dessert into a decorative glass dish and spike the top surface with a pattern of slivered almonds. Serve the carrot pudding warm or at room temperature. It is also good if thoroughly chilled and then cut into squares. It loses some of its fragrance with the chilling but makes a delicious snack.

ADVANCE PREPARATION AND
STORAGE NOTES

As stated above, the dessert may be made in advance and chilled. I once experimented and froze some. It was rather like eating a semifrozen carrot cake and was very good, although quite different in texture and temperature from the classic dish.

❧ Coconut Bananas in Batter
(THAILAND)

This dessert has to be one of the more delicious you will ever put into your mouth —sinfully good, in fact. We have made these bananas several times in my cooking classes and they have managed to tempt and convert even the most hardened dessert hater. The original recipe, which I found in Thailand, called for crisp rice cakes to be used. These are the hardened layers left in the pan after boiling rice, and they are baked until crisp. However, this means that a whole recipe has to be made before starting the dessert, and I have found that any crisp puffed-rice cereal works equally well. This is one of the few times that an Asian recipe actually demands sweetened flaked coconut. This dessert may be served with other Southeast Asian meals.

Preparation time: 20 minutes   Serves 8 to 12
Cooking time: 55 minutes

SHOPPING AND TECHNIQUE TIPS
Look for firm bananas. They will soften and almost dissolve in the frying. Try to locate the smaller coconut shreds. Some of the varieties are very large and will not make an efficient coating.

INGREDIENTS

PREPARATION

1 cup (2⅔ ounces) sweetened
    coconut flakes
½ cup (2¾ ounces) of moist
    dark-brown sugar
¼ cup (2 fluid ounces) of water
2 cups (1¾ ounces) of any   Coarsely crushed
    puffed-rice cereal (unsweetened)
6 large, firm bananas   Peeled and cut diagonally into
                              quarters

½ cup of all-purpose (plain) flour
1 (¾) teaspoon of baking soda
    (bicarbonate of soda)
2 (1⅔) teaspoons of granulated
    sugar
½ cup (4 fluid ounces) of water

INGREDIENTS   PREPARATION
1 (¾) tablespoon of vegetable oil
6 cups (48 fluid ounces) of oil for
     deep-fat frying
2 limes   Cut into slices for garnish

METHOD

1. Place the coconut, brown sugar and water in a small saucepan and stir over medium-low heat until the mixture becomes thick and sticky. Remove the pan from the heat and stir in the crushed cereal. Set aside until cool enough to handle.

2. Start to heat the 6 cups of oil in a wok or a deep-fryer to a temperature of 375°F. (190°C.).

3. Greasing your hands with a little oil, mold a small amount of the coconut mixture around each piece of banana, enclosing it completely. Pat it as you are coaxing the coating around it so that it spreads smoothly over the surface, leaving no bald spots.

4. Combine the flour, baking powder, sugar, water and the tablespoon of oil in a mixing bowl and stir (do not beat) into a batter.

5. Dip each piece of banana in the batter and deep-fry, 2 or 3 at a time, until the batter coating is crisp and golden brown. Drain on paper towels and keep warm until all the bananas are fried. Either place the dish in a warm oven until you are ready to serve or serve immediately. Garnish with slices of lime.

ADVANCE PREPARATION AND
STORAGE NOTES

As noted above, this dessert may be made ahead and kept warm in a low oven for up to 1 hour.

❀ Chinese Almond Cookies

Preparation time: 25 minutes   Makes 20 cookies
Cooking time: 15 minutes

SHOPPING AND TECHNIQUE TIPS

These light cookies are very easy to make. You may like to vary them by decorating the tops with pine nuts instead of almonds.

INGREDIENTS

PREPARATION

½ cup *(4 ounces)* of butter

1 cup *(7¾ ounces)* of granulated
   sugar

1 egg   At room temperature

3 drops of almond extract

2¼ cups *(13½ ounces)* of
   all-purpose *(plain)* flour

1½ *(1¼)* teaspoons of baking
   powder

20 blanched almonds

1 egg yolk   Beaten

METHOD

1. Preheat the oven to 350°F. *(gas mark 4).*

2. In a large mixing bowl, cream the butter and sugar together until the mixture is smooth and the color is very pale. Stir in the egg and the almond extract and beat until everything is well blended and almost homogenized.

3. Place the flour and baking powder in a sifter and gradually sift and stir it into the mixture until it has the consistency of a soft dough.

4. Separate the dough into 20 pieces and roll each one lightly into a soft ball. Flatten each ball into a cookie and arrange them on a cookie sheet. Press an almond into the center of each and brush the top of each cookie with a little beaten egg yolk.

5. Bake for 15 minutes, or until the cookies are a light golden brown. Remove and cool.

ADVANCE PREPARATION AND
STORAGE NOTES

Store the cookies in an airtight cake tin or cookie jar.

Sesame Variation

Instead of the almond decoration, brush cookies with beaten egg yolk and then press the top of each into sesame seeds until it is evenly covered. Bake as directed above.

❧ Philippine Coconut and Cheese Cakes

These delicious cakes can take the place of coffeecakes for a mid-morning snack or at teatime.

Preparation time: 15 minutes
Cooking time: 25 minutes

Serves 6 people

SHOPPING AND TECHNIQUE TIPS
Look for the white soft crumbly farmer's or curd cheese, which is similar to the country cheese of the Philippines. If beating the cake by hand, I suggest 100 to 150 strokes. If you are using an electric mixer, 2 minutes at medium speed should be enough. Do not overbeat.

INGREDIENTS	PREPARATION
¾ cup *(5¾ ounces)* of granulated sugar	
1¼ cups *(½ pint)* of Coconut Milk (page 114)	
3 eggs	Beaten until light and creamy
2 cups *(12 ounces)* of all-purpose *(plain)* flour	
4 *(3¼)* teaspoons of baking powder	
½ cup *(4 ounces)* of butter	Melted
⅓ cup *(1½ ounces)* of soft farmer's cheese	Broken into small crumbs
2 *(1⅔)* tablespoons additional of granulated sugar	
2 *(1⅔)* tablespoons of sweetened coconut flakes	

METHOD
1. Preheat the oven to 350°F. *(gas mark 4)* and lightly grease two cake pans.

2. Place the sugar and half the Coconut Milk in a large mixing bowl and stir until the sugar has dissolved.

3. Measure the flour and baking powder into a sifter and gradually sift half of it into the sugared Coconut Milk, stirring a few times while sifting. Add the remainder of the Coconut Milk gradually, together with the remainder of

the sifted flour and baking powder. When you have added it all, beat the mixture well. (If using an electric mixer, carry out this complete step in the mixer bowl.)

4. Now stir in the beaten eggs and all of the melted butter, except 1 *(¾)* tablespoon. Stir the batter until it is well blended, then pour into the 2 cake pans, spreading it evenly.

5. Bake for 20 minutes.

6. Turn on the broiler *(grill)*. Remove the cakes and brush the tops with the remaining melted butter. Sprinkle them with the cheese crumbs and sugar, then with the coconut. Place them briefly under the broiler *(grill)* and broil until the topping is melted and light brown. Serve while still warm.

ADVANCE PREPARATION AND STORAGE NOTES

These cakes are best eaten immediately after they are made. You can eat them when they are cooled, but they do not keep too well.

✿ Indonesian Steamed Nut Cake

In Indonesia, *kemiri* nuts, or candlenuts, are used for this cake. In most recipes, macadamia or Brazil nuts can be substituted, but for this one, which demands that the nuts be ground to a flour, they are too oily and almonds, first blanched, should be substituted.

Preparation time: 20 minutes   Serves 4 to 6
Cooking time: 30 minutes

SHOPPING AND TECHNIQUE TIPS

Look for whole or sliced blanched almonds. This cake is similar to a steamed sponge cake; it is light, delicate and relatively fat-free. Grind the nuts to as fine a flour as possible. You may use an electric mixer, or beat the eggs and the mixture by hand.

INGREDIENTS

6 eggs
6 *(4¾)* tablespoons *(or 2 ounces)* of
     moist dark-brown sugar
1 *(¾)* teaspoon of shortening or oil

PREPARATION

Separated

INGREDIENTS	PREPARATION
2 *(1⅔)* tablespoons of dried, unsweetened, small-flake coconut	
½ cup *(just over 1¾ ounces)* of blanched almonds (after grinding)	Ground into a fine flour
2 *(1⅔)* tablespoons of sweetened coconut flakes (optional)	

METHOD

1. Fill a steamer with water and let it come to a boil over high heat.

2. Meanwhile, place the yolks in a large mixing bowl and beat until light yellow and creamy. Add the sugar and continue beating until the mixture is thick and drops slowly from a spoon. Lightly grease a cake pan.

3. In another bowl, beat the whites until they stand up in stiff peaks.

4. Fold the coconut and almond flour into the egg-sugar mixture until it is thoroughly combined. Do not beat. Now carefully fold in the egg whites and pour the mixture into the cake pan.

5. Set the pan carefully in a steamer tray and steam the mixture for 30 minutes or until the cake is set and firm. Invert the pan over a plate and tap the cake gently to unmold it. Sprinkle the sweetened coconut on top if desired.

ADVANCE PREPARATION AND STORAGE NOTES

This cake may be served warm or cold. Store like any other sponge cake.

Glossary

Agar-agar *(Gelidium and Gracilaria)*

A gelatinous seaweed product, sold in powder form or in long strips or bricks. It dissolves in boiling water and can absorb up to 20 times its own weight. Used in Asia instead of gelatin, it is, in fact, superior because dishes made with it do not need refrigeration to remain firm and set.

SUBSTITUTE: Gelatin.

Annato *(Bixa orellana)*

(Called *achuete* or *achiote* in Spanish)

The small, hard, reddish seeds of the annato tree. Used in Latin American, Philippine and Pacific cuisines for coloring. When soaked in hot water for 30 minutes, the seeds produce a reddish-orange-yellow liquid with a trace of flavor.

SUBSTITUTE: A mixture of turmeric and paprika, stirred into water.

Asafetida (Asafoetida) *(Ferula asafoetida)*

(Called *hing* in Hindustani)

The dried resin of a plant akin to the fennel. When powdered, it has a very acrid flavor, but when it is fried it has a taste reminiscent of onions. It is used in India as a substitute for onion flavor by those whose religious beliefs forbid them to eat that vegetable. It has medicinal properties, including that of an antiflatulant.

SUBSTITUTE: Onion powder.

Bamboo Shoots *(Bambuseae)*

The young shoots of a large bamboo. They must be cooked, as they contain a poison when raw. Available in the West canned *(tinned),* either in chunks or in slices. Rinse and drain before using. (They are already cooked before being canned *(tinned).*) Use in stir-fried dishes, soups, and with poultry or fish.

SUBSTITUTE: Slices of the core of white cabbage.

Basil, Sweet *(Ocimum basilicum)*

Our Western sweet basil, an annual herb, indigenous to India and parts of the Middle East. A number of varieties are used in Southeast Asian cuisines, some of which have flavors closer to mint, others, to eau de cologne or to anise. Two other commonly used varieties are: *Ocimum canum,* referred to as lemon basil, and *Ocimum sanctum,* or holy basil, which has narrow, slightly purplish leaves.

SUBSTITUTE: Mint; or sweet basil leaves can substitute for all other basil varieties.

Bay, Indian *(Cinnamomum cassia)*

(Called *taj patta* in Hindustani)

Not our bay leaf *(Laurus nobilis);* these are the leaves of the cassia tree, whose bark is used as a kind of cinnamon. Indian bay leaves are dried before use. They are smaller than Western bay and are thin, dull-surfaced and brittle and easily crumbled for spice mixes. Milder in taste than our variety, they are used to flavor meat dishes and *pilaus*.

SUBSTITUTE: Our Western bay leaf. Use in half the amount indicated for the Indian bay.

Bean Curd

(*tofu,* Japanese; *tao foo,* Chinese; *tahu,* Indonesian and Thai; *tokwa,* Philippines)

A curdled, soft, cheeselike preparation made from soybean milk. Used as a source of protein in Asian cooking. Available loose or in packages in supermarkets or Oriental markets.

Bean Paste, Red Sweet

A sweet puree of Chinese red beans, used as a filling in buns, pastries and puddings.

SUBSTITUTE: Chinese Sweet Red Bean Paste (page 132).

Bean Paste, Yellow

A salty, pungent soybean paste, used as a flavoring in many Chinese dishes.

SUBSTITUTE: Japanese red and Japanese white *miso* (half of each), or Japanese Soybean Paste Substitute (page 131).

Beans, Black Salted Fermented

(Called *dow see* in Chinese)

These are very salty soybeans, sold in cans in Chinese markets. Used with garlic as a flavoring for fish and pork dishes.

SUBSTITUTE: Soybeans, cooked until soft and seasoned with plenty of soy sauce.

Bean Sprouts

Usually the sprouts of mung beans, although alfalfa and soybean sprouts are also used. Widely available in the produce sections of supermarkets. Look for crisp, fresh sprouts with very pale roots and light-green heads. The stalks should be white, snap-fresh and plump. Store in the refrigerator in a plastic bag. Remove the roots and any casings on the sprout heads before using. Bean sprouts have a slight protein content and also contain small quantities of iron and Vitamin C. Use in salads and stir-fry dishes to provide texture.

Bombay Duck

A small, dried, salted fish, sold in packages. In India it is fried and cut into pieces and used as an accompaniment to curry dishes.

SUBSTITUTE: Any small, dried fish from the Oriental or Latin American shops or sections of supermarkets. Fry them in a little oil until very crisp, drain on paper towels and cut into pieces, if necessary.

Candlenut *(Aleurites moluccana)*

(Called *kemiri* in Indonesian, *buah keras* in Malay)

Smallish, white-fleshed nut, shaped like a hazelnut, candlenuts are used in both these cuisines as a component of spice pastes. They are waxlike and rich in oil and are threaded on palm slivers and burned as candles by primitive tribes.

SUBSTITUTE: Macadamia or Brazil nuts.

Cardamom *(Elettaria cardamomum)*
(Called *illaichi* in Hindustani)
> The seed pods of a member of the ginger family. There are two varieties: green and brown. The former is also available with the pods bleached white. The multiple seeds inside the pods are small, black and very fragrant. The brown (or black) cardamom is larger, about 1 inch in size, and has a thick skin and a rather nutlike aroma. Cardamom is available in the pod or seeds only, or ground. Ground cardamom is not as strongly flavored as the seeds as it is adulterated with the ground pods. This fragrant spice is a component of the Indian Sweet Spice Mix (page 118), or *garam masala,* and is also used in northern Indian and Moghul dishes including sweetmeats and desserts. Available from spice departments in supermarkets and specialty food shops. No substitute.

Cashew Nut *(Anacardium occidentale)*
> The nut of a tropical and subtropical shrub or tree native to Central and South America. The Portuguese brought it to India and to East Africa in the fifteenth century. Cashews are used in a processed, raw state in Indian and Chinese dishes. The processing removes prussic acid, which is present in their raw, newly picked state. No substitute.

Chestnut *(Castanea mollissima*—China; *Castanea crenata*—Japan)
> An ingredient in Oriental and Southeast Asian cooking, both for savory dishes and sweets. They are used, dried, in China and are boiled for 2 hours before skinning. Our own chestnuts *(Castanea sativa)* are perfectly suitable. Do not confuse them with water chestnuts. No substitute.

Chick-Pea Flour
(Called *besan* in Hindustani)
> Used for Indian snacks and breads. Available in Indian stores. You can make your own by lightly roasting chick peas, then grinding them to a flour in a blender. SUBSTITUTE: Pea flour available from the health-food section of supermarkets or health-food stores. Alternatively, you can roast yellow split peas in a dry saucepan for 5 minutes, stirring constantly, then grind them to a flour in the blender or food processor.

Chilli Peppers *(Capsicum)*
> Many varieties are grown all over Asia; ranging from the mild sweet, green pepper, through medium-hot Kashmiri chillies (relatives of the Mexican Serrano and Jalapeño chillies), to the tiny and fiery-hot bird's-eye peppers and the Japanese *santaka* chillies. The larger, hot chilli peppers are dried and powdered to produce Cayenne (now produced from many other varieties beside the Cayenne chilli), and the milder red peppers are ground to produce paprika. Chilli peppers are native to the Americas and were first introduced to Asia by the Portuguese. Immature peppers are green. If they are left on the plant to mature, they will turn yellow or red. Chilli peppers are a rich source of Vitamin C and also contain Vitamin A. The substance that makes them "hot" is called *capsaicin;* it is concentrated in the seeds and membranes. It is a volatile oil; therefore, if your mouth burns from too

much heat, do not drink water. Bread, rice or a similar starch, or beer or yogurt and milk drinks will help to ameliorate the burn.

Chinese Sausage

These are highly flavored sausages filled with chopped lean and fat pork and spices. They are dried and are attached in links. They freeze well and also can be refrigerated for a considerable period. They are used in many stir-fries, fried-rice dishes and Chinese soups. Most of the Chinese sausage available in the United States is produced in Canada.

SUBSTITUTE: Chopped spiced ham and Portuguese sausage.

Cinnamon *(Cinnamomum zeylanicum)*

The dried, rolled bark of the cinnamon tree, native to Sri Lanka (Ceylon). True cinnamon is rolled into thin, hard, fairly solid sticks or quills, unlike the thicker, lighter and looser quills of Cassia bark *(Cinnamomum cassia),* with which it is often confused. Cassia is an evergreen of the laurel family, grown in Vietnam, China and the eastern Himalayas. It has a similar to, but stronger flavor than, the true cinnamon. The two are interchangeable in use.

Cloves *(Syzygium aromaticum)*

The clove tree is a member of the myrtle family. Indigenous to the Moluccas (Spice Islands) in Indonesia, cloves have been in use since at least the third century B.C. The clove itself is the dried, unopened flower bud. Nowadays, Zanzibar, off East Africa, is the world's largest producer of the spice. The oil contains phenol, which is an antiseptic. Cloves are an ingredient in both the Indian Sweet Spice Mix *(garam masala)* and of the Chinese Five-Spice Powder. No substitute.

Coconut *(Cocos nucifera)*

One of the most important ingredients of Southeast Asian and southern Indian cuisines. The meat is used in foods, or grated for the extraction of coconut milk. Coconut milk is the liquid expressed from the meat of the nut after it is steeping in water. The milk and the coconut oil are the two main food products of the nut. The meat of the immature coconut is widely used in Philippine and Southeast Asian cooking. It is available only in jars and cans from Oriental specialty shops.

SUBSTITUTE: Cow's milk, flavored with coconut extract.

Coriander (Chinese parsley, *cilantro*) *(Coriandrum sativum)*

An annual of the parsley family, coriander is one of the oldest flavorings used by man. It is both a herb and a spice. The pungent leaves are used in southern Chinese, Indian and Southeast Asian cuisines (as well as Latin America, particularly Mexican.) The seed, which has a sweeter and different flavor, is a main ingredient of spice-powder blends and pastes. Incidentally, it was one of the first herbs grown in America by the early colonists.

SUBSTITUTE: Parsley for decoration. There is no substitute for flavor.

Cumin *(Cuminum cyminum)*

Another member of the parsley family, cumin originated in the eastern Mediterranean area and the Middle East, from whence it was brought to India and China. The spice was widely used in Europe in the Middle Ages. Nowadays its use in the

Western world has been largely replaced by caraway. In Asia, the ground seed is an important part of curry powders and spice mixes. It is still widely used in India, Southeast Asia and also in Latin America. Caraway may be substituted in a pinch. Use ⅓ of the given amount for cumin.

Curry Leaves *(Murraya koenigii)*

These leaves are used in India, Malaysia and Indonesia in curry dishes. Cassia leaves, which are smaller and thinner, are also used for the same purpose.

SUBSTITUTE: Bay leaves may be used, although the flavor is different.

Daikon (of the *Raphanus sativus* family)

This is referred to as the long, or large, white Oriental or Japanese radish. It can grow up to 2 feet in length. It is a rich source of Vitamin C. It is used widely in both Japanese and Chinese cooking: raw, in salads, pickles and as an accompaniment to *sashimi,* and cooked, in soups and stews. Available in some supermarkets and in Oriental markets, it is crisp, juicy and mild in flavor, slightly reminiscent of turnip.

SUBSTITUTE: Icicle radishes.

Dashi

The Japanese name for a basic stock made from dried bonito shavings and a kelplike seaweed. The stock is prepared fresh, but is also available in powdered form from the Oriental section of some of the better supermarkets, also from Oriental markets. It is a basic of Japanese cooking.

SUBSTITUTE: Japanese Fish Stock (page 170).

Dill *(Anethum graveolens)*

An annual of the parsley family, it is regarded as a digestive and a sedative. The leaves and seeds are widely used in Europe and the United States. It appears in spice pastes in India and Sri Lanka (Ceylon).

Fennel *(Foeniculum vulgare)*

Another member of the large parsley family, fennel has been used since ancient times by the Indians and Chinese for food and medicine. In Asia, the seed and root only are used and are excellent for stomach and intestinal problems. It is also an appetite stimulant. Used in spice mixes in India, Indonesia, Malaysia, Burma and Sri Lanka.

Fenugreek *(Trigonella foenumgraecum)*

A member of the bean family and indigenous to western Asia and the Mediterranean area. The seed is ground and used in spice mixes. It is the flavor most noticeable in commercial curry powders. Fenugreek (called *methi* in Hindustani) is mostly used in Indian vegetarian cooking and in pickling. It is also an important medicine for gastric complaints. The seed has a rather bitter, celerylike flavor. Available, ground, in the better spice departments of supermarkets and specialty food stores. No substitute.

Fish Sauce

A thin, translucent, salty brown liquid, it is an indispensable flavoring in Southeast Asian cooking. Fish sauce is made from salted, fresh shrimp or fish and is rich in protein and the B vitamins. Milder in flavor than soy sauce, it is used to salt dishes.

Fish sauce is particularly necessary to Thai, Vietnamese and Philippine cooking. It is also used in southern China. No substitute.

Five-Spice Powder

An essential flavoring in Chinese cooking, this spice powder is a blend of star anise, fennel, cinnamon, cloves and Szechwan pepper. Because it is rarely available in supermarkets and because star anise and Szechwan pepper are also difficult to obtain, this book contains a substitute recipe.

SUBSTITUTE: Five-Plus-One Spice Mix (page 119).

Galangal *(Alpinia galanga)*

(Called *laos* in Indonesian, *ka* in Thai, *lengkuas* in Malay)

A member of the ginger family, in its fresh state the root is bulbous and yellow, with pink knobs and sprouts. It was used in England and Europe in the Middle Ages as an aphrodisiac but now appears only in Southeast Asian cuisines. The flavor is more aromatic and less pungent than ginger. Galangal is usually available dried, in small pieces or ground to a powder. Unavailable outside Southeast Asian food stores.

SUBSTITUTE: Powdered ginger in half the given amount for Galangal.

Garam Masala

A sweet, mellow mixture of freshly ground spices, used in Indian cooking toward the end of the preparation time (as opposed to a curry *masala* spice mix). There are individual variations in its preparation, many of them regional. See Indian Sweet Spice Mix (page 118).

Garlic *(Allium sativum)*

Vital to southern Indian, Southeast Asian and southern Chinese cooking, garlic is used in Asia both for flavor and medicinal properties. Garlic is rich in Vitamins B, C and D, as well in the trace elements: zinc, copper, aluminum, manganese, sulphur, iron. It contains a powerful antiseptic called crotonic aldehyde and is used as a food preservative. Consumption of garlic has been found to help lower blood pressure as well as to aid in reducing cholesterol levels in the blood.

Ghee

The Indian name for clarified butter, *ghee* is pure butterfat from which all the milk solids have been removed.

Ginger *(Zingiber officinale)*

Fresh ginger root is universally used throughout all the cuisines of Asia. It is an important source of Vitamin C and is used by the Chinese to neutralize the fishy qualities of seafood. When buying fresh ginger root, look for firm, swollen tubers with unwrinkled, shiny skin. When the ginger is young and is the new season's growth, the knobs will be tinged with yellow-green. To store and preserve:

    a. Keep it unpeeled, in any cool, dry place.

    b. If you have a garden, bury it in the ground, digging up as much as you want when you need it.

    c. Freeze it, unpeeled, in a freezer bag or container, cutting off as much as you

need and slicing or grating it without thawing. It may also be peeled, diced
and then frozen.

d. Peel the ginger and cut into 2-inch slices. Place it in a jar and cover with
vodka. Cap and store in the refrigerator. Remove, drain and rinse off before
using. Lasts indefinitely.

e. Peel and chop and gently fry it in peanut or another vegetable oil for about
2 to 3 minutes. Remove, drain and place in a covered container. Refrigerate.
Lasts for about 2 months.

f. Store it, wrapped in paper towels, in a paper bag in the vegetable drawer of
your refrigerator. Lasts for about 3 to 4 weeks.

Dried, ground ginger is suitable for use only in some Indian and Chinese recipes.
Use where indicated but do not substitute for fresh ginger. Pickled, candied
(crystalized) or preserved ginger is used in some Asian recipes. Use where specified.
SUBSTITUTE: Candied *(crystalized)* ginger, washed and well dried. It is not a
perfect substitute but is better than using ground ginger.

Ginkgo Nuts *(Ginkgo biloba)*
The small, white-fleshed nuts of the maidenhair tree, which is regarded as a living
fossil, because the rest of the Paleozoic era plants are extinct, and the tree does
not grow in a wild state. The nuts are used in soups and simmered dishes in both
Chinese and Japanese cooking.
SUBSTITUTE: Blanched almonds.

Hoisin Sauce
A medium-thick, dark reddish-brown spice sauce made from soybeans, garlic,
chilli peppers and various other spices and ingredients. Used in Chinese cooking
in poultry, pork and shellfish recipes and as a table condiment. Also used in
barbecue marinades.
SUBSTITUTE: Chinese All-Purpose Sauce (page 145).

Jaggery; Palm Sugar
A coarse brown sugar, sold in lumps or cakes. It is made from the sap of the
Palmyra palm and is used in Indian and Southeast Asian cuisines as a sweetener.
SUBSTITUTE: Dark-brown, moist, cane sugar.

Ka   *See* Galangal

Kaffir Lime *(Citrus hystrix)*
(Called *makrut* in Thai)
A member of the citrus family and native to Southeast Asia, Kaffir limes look like
knobbly, green golf balls. The rind of the fruit and the double-pinnate leaves of
the tree are highly citrus-scented and aromatic. The Malays use the juice and peel
in medicines and cosmetics. The rind and leaves are used in Thai cooking as one
of the sources for the important citrus flavor in soups and stewlike dishes. The
leaves are finely shredded and sprinkled over soups, curries and salads.
SUBSTITUTE: The peel of fresh limes for the peel and citrus leaves (where available)
for the leaves.

Katsuobushi

The Japanese name for dried bonito, a component of *dashi* soup stock. *See* Dashi.

Kemiri Nuts   *See* Candlenuts

Kombu

The Japanese name for a kelp seaweed, used dried in ribbonlike sheets for *dashi* (*see* Dashi) and to flavor rice for *sushi*.

Laos   *See* Galangal

Lemon Grass *(Cymbopogon citratus)*

(Called *takrai* in Thai, *sereh* in Indonesian)

Tall plant with long, spear-shaped, grasslike leaves (hence the name). It has a strong lemony-citrus flavor. It is used in Southeast Asian cuisines to flavor spice pastes, soups and stew dishes. The leaves and stem are fibrous, but the lower part of the firm stalk has a white, somewhat juicy base. It is related to the citronella. Grown now in India, Australia, Africa, Latin America and in the United States (in Florida and California), but it is not widely available in markets, owing to general unfamiliarity with it. However, the dried, chopped leaves are often found in packages in the Latin American section of supermarkets and in health-food stores for the brewing of lemon grass tea. The dried leaves contribute very little flavor to cooked dishes and are not a good substitute for the fresh plant.

SUBSTITUTE: The outer, yellow peel (zest) of lemon: zest of ½ lemon substitutes for 1 stalk of lemon grass.

Lentils, Split Peas or Beans

(Called *dhals* in Hindustani)

Used widely in Indian vegetarian cooking. There are many varieties, sizes and colors, including:

> Pink lentils—*masoor dhal*
> Yellow lentils—*toor dhal*
> Split, dried mung beans—*moong dhal*
> Gram beans—*urad dhal*
> Yellow split peas—*channa dhal*
> Chick-peas, garbanzos—also *channa dhal*

All of these need picking over and washing well before cooking. The cooking and soaking times vary with the type of legume. Four ounces of uncooked lentils or other legumes provides an adequate serving per person.

SUBSTITUTE: Supermarket lentils or split peas.

Lesser Ginger *(Kaempferia pandurata)*

(*krachai* in Thai, *kencur* in Malay and Indonesian)

This rhizome, related to the gingers, is largely unknown to the Western world and does not have a common name in the English language. It resembles the tuberous roots of Galangal but is yellow on the inside and milder in flavor. The Chinese use the plant for medicine, not for a spice. It is used fresh or dried as a vegetable in Southeast Asia, and to flavor certain dishes. Available only in Oriental stores in dried slivers or powder. It is often merely labelled "rhizome." No substitute.

Lichee (Litchi, Lychee) *(Litchi chinensis)*
A native of south China, this is the fruit of the litchi tree. It is a small, delicately flavored, white-fleshed fruit with a central kernel and a hard, tough, brown skin like a shell. Used in Chinese cuisine in some dishes and eaten fresh, litchis are available here in cans in the canned-fruit sections or Oriental food sections of better supermarkets. It is sometimes found fresh in the produce sections of specialty shops or better markets around June or July.

Lily Buds
Also known as golden needles, lily flowers, or tiger lilies, these are dried lily buds, about 2 inches in length, and look like pale brown strips. They are used in Chinese-influenced dishes and stir-fries and must first be soaked for at least 30 minutes in hot water before draining and using. There is no substitute.

Lime *(Citrus aurantifolia)*
The juice of limes are used throughout Southeast Asia as a souring agent in cooking and for beverages. In India, the lemon is used for the same purpose. The peel of the lime may be substituted for Kaffir lime peel in curry pastes and Southeast Asian dishes. In this book, lime juice is used, together with molasses *(treacle),* as a substitute for tamarind water.

Long Beans
Actually long-podded cowpeas, these beans grow up to 1 yard long. Cut into 2-inch lengths they are used in vegetable dishes and stir-fried dishes throughout China and Southeast Asia.
SUBSTITUTE: String beans.

Long Rice
The Hawaiian-Chinese term for rice-stick noodles.

Longan *(Euphoria longana)*
The fruit of the soapberry tree family. Similar to litchis, but not as fragrant. They are called "dragon's eyes" by the Chinese.

Lotus Root *(Nelumbo nucifera)*
The stem or root of the lotus plant, with a delicate flavor and crisp texture. Roots are highly decorative in cross section because of the hollow spaces that run along their length. Used fresh, dried (they must be soaked in that case) or canned, as a vegetable in stir-fried dishes, soups and stews. Somewhat similar to a potato in texture and flavor.
SUBSTITUTE: There is no substitute for its decorative value, but members of the potato or yam families could be used for texture.

Lotus Seeds
The seeds of the above plant, these are about ½-inch long and are eaten raw or candied *(crystallized)* by the Chinese. They are also used in soups.
SUBSTITUTE: Blanched whole or slivered almonds.

Mace *(Myristica fragrans)*

The outer fibrous wrapping of the nutmeg kernel, with a similar, but more delicate, flavor. The wrapping is dried before use and is usually available in powdered form. It appears in Moghul and Kashmiri dishes and in some chutneys and pickles.

Mango *(Mangifera indica)*

Native to India and Southeast Asia, it is considered one of the world's most luscious fruits. There are well over 100 varieties, ranging in size from a large fist to the oval Rugby ball. Shapes, skin and flesh colors also vary. The unripe mango is also dried and ground to a powder *(amchur* in Hindustani) in India and used as a souring agent. The Southeast Asians are also fond of the sour, unripe fruit, which they eat with salt, sugar and a sprinkling of dried red pepper flakes or powder.

Mint: Peppermint *(Mentha piperita)*; Spearmint *(Mentha spicata)*

These two varieties and others are grown in Asia and used in several cuisines, primarily Indian and Southeast Asian. In India, mint is used in fresh chutneys and *raitas* (yogurt-based salads) and also in Moghul dishes. The Vietnamese include it in their leaf-wrapped items and in salads. In Thai and other cuisines, it is used in stir-fried dishes and as a garnish.

Mirin

Japanese sweet rice wine, used mainly in cooking. Available from well-stocked liquor stores or Oriental or liquor sections of better supermarkets that sell wines. SUBSTITUTE: Sweet sherry.

Miso

A Japanese paste made from cooked, fermented soybeans. SUBSTITUTE: Japanese Soybean Paste Substitute (page 131).

Monosodium Glutamate (MSG)

Used extensively and often excessively as a flavor enhancer in Oriental cuisines. Commercially produced as Vetsin, Aji-No-Moto). It has been found to produce unfortunate side effects such as headaches and dizziness in many people. I feel that good cooking and fresh ingredients need no further help; I do not use it nor do I recommend its use.

Mung Beans

Native to India, they are the smallest of all the bean family. Used for bean sprouts or ground as flour. The latter is made into the mung bean noodles (also called cellophane noodles).

Mushrooms Oriental *(Lentinus edodes)*

Dried Chinese and Japanese mushrooms

Also known as dried black mushrooms or winter mushrooms.

The caps are brownish and the ribs or gills underneath are black. Sizes range from 1½ inches to 2½ inches in diameter. The flavor is intense and fragrant and cannot be duplicated by Western dried mushrooms. The Chinese variety is often smaller and more irregular in size than the Japanese and the caps are often crazed with cracks. The Japanese varieties, known as *shiitaki* and *matsutaki,* are among the finest dried mushrooms in the world. They are packaged without stems. Soak in hot or boiling water for 15 minutes, or until the mushrooms are pliable. Remove and discard the stems (they are tough and inedible). Squeeze the caps and retain the liquid to add to soups or stocks. Thinly slice the caps and cook. Used in Chinese, Japanese, Korean and Southeast Asian dishes.

Cloud Ear Mushrooms or Fungus *(Auricalaria polytricha)*
Also known as wood fungus, tree fungus, wood ears, jelly mushrooms.
Small, dried black pieces of crinkled fungus, looking like burned paper. When reconstituted in hot water, they swell and turn a rich brown, looking rather like pig's ears. They have a delicate flavor and a rather resilient texture, similar to jellyfish. Also used in most Asian cuisines, for soups, stir-fried dishes and stews.

Straw Mushrooms *(Volvariella volvacea)*
Also known as grass or paddy straw mushrooms.
These are thin, tall, leaflike mushrooms, popular in Chinese and Japanese dishes. Also available in cans *(tins)* or jars.

Enokitaki Mushrooms (fresh)
Long, slender-stemmed, small white mushrooms with tiny button caps. Indigenous to Japan, they are now available in the produce sections of better supermarkets. Their name comes from the enoki tree, on which they grow. Used raw in salads, or cooked in soups and one-pot dishes, they have rather a mild flavor and a slightly crisp texture. Cut off the roots and wash the mushrooms before using.

Standard Cultivated Mushrooms (regular size and button)
Look for a partially closed underside with no gills showing, which is a sign of a fresh mushroom. If gills are visible they should be pink or pinkish-brown. If they are dark brown, the mushroom is old. Do not wash, but wipe the caps with a paper towel.

All of the above varieties are used in Asian cooking. The dried Chinese or Japanese mushrooms are available in the Oriental food sections of most supermarkets. Substitute them for the other varieties of dried mushrooms and fungus if the latter are unavailable. At a pinch, substitute fresh mushrooms for all of the others, but be aware that the flavor will not be as pronounced nor will it be the same.

Mustard Oil
An oil extracted from mustard seed with a relatively high smoking point. It is used as a deep-frying oil in the north and northwest of India and for fish dishes in Bengal. It is also a component of many pickles.

Mustard, Powdered Hot
Often referred to as English or Chinese mustard. Made by grinding black mustard seeds. Mix to the desired consistency with water or with vinegar and water. Used for Chinese dipping sauces and as a component of marinades. Substitute it for the Japanese *wasabi* (green horseradish paste) in *sushi* and with *sashimi.*

Mustard Seeds: yellow *(Brassica hirta)*; brown *(Brassica juncea)*; black (Brassica nigra)

The brown and black varieties are native to India and look rather like large poppy seeds. Both are used to make the hot mustard powder. The seeds are used whole in Indian vegetarian dishes and are fried until they pop open, revealing their yellow interiors. They are also incorporated in the pickles of the north, often with mustard oil. Both brown and black varieties are smaller and more pungent than the yellow seeds. Nowadays they are grown mainly in India, China and Africa. The yellow variety is not used in Asian cooking, but is featured in the milder Western pickles and mustards.

Nutmeg *(Myristica fragrans)*
(Also see Mace)

The kernel of the fruit of the nutmeg tree. Nutmegs are around 1 inch to 1¼ inches in length and about ¾ inch in width. They are indigenous to the Moluccas. The Dutch, controlling their production and price, restricted them to the islands of Amboina and Banda, until the French broke the Dutch monopoly by smuggling them to Mauritius. Nutmegs are now grown in Indonesia, the West Indies and Ceylon. There are two basic types of nutmegs: the East Indian and the West Indian. The East Indian nutmeg is stronger in flavor, with a greater oil content. Nutmegs are used medicinally in India as a cure for headaches and intestinal problems. In Indian cooking, they are used as a component of *garam masala,* in Moghul and Kashmiri cooking and in vegetable dishes and some desserts.

Onion *(Allium cepa)*

Many varieties of onion are used in Asia. In India, the brown-skinned globe onion is commonly used for cooking. The Indian variety is about 2 inches to 3 inches in diameter, slightly smaller and less juicy then our onions.
SUBSTITUTE: Spanish onions.

Throughout Southeast Asia, the small (1 inch to 2 inches), red globe onions are common. A cousin to our small white boiling or pearl onions, they are rather similar to shallots. They are strongly flavored, with less moisture than our large onions, making them very suited to stir-frying.
SUBSTITUTE: Shallots or, if you cannot find them, a portion of a large red onion (squeeze dry after chopping to remove the moisture).

In China, green *(spring)* onions or scallions are most commonly used, as well as shallots and sometimes globe or Spanish onions.

In Japan and Korea they use a long onion rather resembling a leek in size and shape, as well as a green *(spring)* onion that is a cousin to ours.
SUBSTITUTE: Leeks or green *(spring)* onions.

Onion Flakes

Many Asian dishes call for crisp-fried onions, chopped or cut, as a garnish. See Fried Onion Flakes (page 156).

Oyster Sauce

A Chinese sauce, made from oysters cooked in soy sauce and brine. Used as a seasoning in stir-fried dishes, and with seafood, poultry, soups and fried rice. Also used as a table sauce.

Palm Sugar   *See* Jaggery

Pandanus or Screw Pine *(Pandanus odoratissimus)*

Used as a flavoring and coloring in India and Southeast Asia, and sometimes, in the Philippines and the Pacific. The long, flat leaves are crushed and cooked, producing a rather warm nutlike flavor and a pale-green color in cakes, desserts and sweets. Available in the West from Oriental stores, in packages or as an extract, bottled.

SUBSTITUTE: Vanilla may be used as an alternative, but flavor and color are dissimilar.

Papads or Pappadams

Dried, commercially-produced large round wafers made from lentil flour. *Papads* are sometimes spiced with cracked cumin and black peppercorns. The dried wafers are shallow-fried in a little oil until they puff up and become crisp and brittle. Delicious in flavor, they accompany Indian meals, and may be eaten whole, like a bread, or crumbled and sprinkled over the food for added texture and flavor. Available in packages from Indian stores.

SUBSTITUTE: There is no real substitute, but you may like to fry tortillas until they are crisp, and serve them as a crisp bread to accompany a curry.

Pepper *(Piper nigrum)*

Black and white peppercorns are the dried berries of the pepper vine. Black peppercorns are picked unripe and then dried until their skins become black and wrinkled. White peppercorns are merely the same berries picked when ripe, without their skins. These have a milder, less pungent taste than the black. Green peppercorns are the soft, immature berries. They are often pickled in brine and sometimes freeze-dried.

Pepper, Long *(Piper longum, Piper officinarum)*

The first variety grows in India and the second in Southeast Asia, in Java. They are not a true pepper. The berries grow in long strings, which could also be described as elongated clusters. They are used in curry pastes and in medicines.

Pepper, Szechwan (Anise Pepper, Flower Pepper, Fagara) *(Xanthoxylum pipesitum)*

These dried berries are not related to the more familiar peppercorns. They are reddish-brown dried flower heads with a slightly bitter, numbing flavor before cooking, very like eau de cologne. Grown in Szechwan, they are used in local duck dishes, pickles, salt-and-pepper dips and are a component of Five-Spice Powder.

SUBSTITUTE: Peppercorns and anise.

Plum Sauce

A sweet, thick, chutney-like Chinese sauce made from dried plums, apricots, vinegar, sugar and spices. Used as a table sauce with barbecued meats and spring rolls.

SUBSTITUTE: See recipe for Chinese Plum Sauce (page 466).

Poppy Seeds *(Papaver somniferum)*

(Called *khus-khus* in Hindustani)

The Indian seeds are small and white with a nutlike flavor. They are ground and used in certain spice mixes and as a thickening agent in gravies. The seeds are sometimes roasted before grinding.

SUBSTITUTE: Use black poppy seeds.

Red Bean Sauce

A strong table sauce made from mashed soybeans. Available in cans from Chinese stores.

SUBSTITUTE: It is not the same, but at a pinch you may use the Japanese Soy Bean Paste Substitute (page 131) and thin it with a little soy sauce and water.

Rice Wine, Chinese

Used in Chinese cooking and also as a beverage. Somewhat similar to the Japanese rice wines. There are two types: yellow and white.

SUBSTITUTE: Pale dry sherry.

Rose Water

A diluted extract of roses originally from Persia and much used in Indian sweets and some desserts. It can be obtained from drugstores as well as Middle Eastern stores.

SUBSTITUTE: You can make your own by steeping rose petals in water or by adding essential oil of rose to water. Some specialty shops carry synthetic substitutes.

Saffron *(Crocus sativus)*

The world's costliest spice, saffron is the dried stigma of crocus flowers. Available as dark orange to reddish-brown threads and also in powdered form. It is used in Indian desserts and in lamb and poultry preparations. Use ¼ teaspoon to each pound of meat or to each cup of raw rice. Because of its expense, turmeric is used as a substitute in many areas of India. There are no bargains in buying saffron. It is expensive, even in Spain and Kashmir, where it is grown. The reason for its price is that the picking and processing is slow and laborious. Beware of anything touted as saffron that is cheap in price. It is either highly adulterated or an inferior substitute. Steep the threads in warm water and add both the threads and their liquid to a dish. Stir the powdered saffron into warm water and, again, use the liquid.

Sambals

Mixtures of chilli peppers and spices, used in Indonesian cooking and as condiments.

Sake

Japanese dry rice wine. Used in cooking, it acts as a tenderizer and helps to remove strong odors. Available in the liquor departments and Oriental sections of supermarkets (if wines are sold there) and in liquor stores with a wide selection. It is sometimes poured into porcelain flasks, which are placed in hot water to heat the contents, before being served with meals.

SUBSTITUTE: Pale dry sherry or dry vermouth.

Scallions   *See* Onions

Semolina

Used for Indian puddings and sweets. This product is known as farina in the United States. In India, the fine grade is most commonly used.

Sesame *(Sesamum indicum)*

The seed of an annual herb. The plant is indigenous to Indonesia and Africa and is cultivated for both seeds and oil. The seeds are often toasted and used whole or ground to a paste in Korea. Chinese and Japanese use them either raw or toasted for candies, cakes, as a garnish for salads, desserts and for many other varieties of dishes. There are two varieties of seeds: black and white. Both varieties are used in China, India and Japan. Sesame oil is used as a flavoring in stir-fried dishes, salad dressings, etc., but not to cook with. The Chinese sesame oil is darker than many other varieties, and with a more pronounced flavor. In its preparation, the seeds are first toasted before the oil is extracted. A recipe for homemade Sesame Oil is on page 139.

Shallots *See* Onions

Shrimp, Dried (whole, powdered, paste)

All three are used extensively in Southeast Asian cuisines and the first two to a greater extent in Chinese cooking. All three products have a strong flavor and odor. Whole dried shrimp and powdered dried shrimp are often to be found in packages in the Latin sections of supermarkets. Before the advent of freezing as a method of preserving food, there was a booming industry in drying shrimp in northern California, owned and worked by Chinese-Americans. The advent of freezing virtually wiped out the industry overnight. There is a shrimp-processing plant on the way down the coast of Baja California, in Mexico, as your nose attests when you pass it on the highway. The strong odor of whole dried shrimp can be somewhat ameliorated if they are first soaked in sherry before using. Shrimp paste is a common flavoring ingredient in the spice pastes of Southeast Asia. It is a fermented shrimp preparation, highly odiferous, but full of vitamins and protein. It is generally a pinkish-gray in color. A liquid version is known as "shrimp sauce" and is much used in the Philippines and in Vietnam, and almost as much in Thailand.

SUBSTITUTE: Fresh shrimp for dried shrimp; anchovy paste or mashed anchovies for shrimp paste.

Shrimp Chips *(Prawn Crackers)*

These are dried wafers of shrimp and tapioca. When deep-fried they puff up to 3 times their original size into delicious, feather-light, crisp chips. Good for snacks or to accompany dishes. Common in China, Southeast Asia and in parts of India. They are available in Oriental stores and the Oriental sections of better super-markets. I have also seen them in the gourmet sections alongside Japanese rice crackers.

Silver and Gold Leaf

The pure metal, beaten into gossamer-thin squares, which are sold in packages and interleaved with tissue paper. They are used in cooking to decorate Indian and Moghul rice dishes and sweets for special occasions. Available only in Indian stores. There is no substitute.

Soy Sauce

Made from soybeans and an indispensable flavoring and salting agent as well as a table sauce in the Orient. Low-salt versions are now becoming available in supermarkets, in both Chinese and Japanese varieties.

Spring Onions, Green Onions   *See* Onions

Star Anise *(Illicium verum)*

This spice is similar in flavor to our anise seed *(Pimpinella anisum)* of the parsley family. But the star anise is no relation. It is an 8-pointed star of segmented sepals, each bearing a shiny brown elongated seed. The tree bearing the seed pods is of the magnolia family. It is used in Chinese cooking, particularly in marinades, and is a component of Five-Spice Powder.

SUBSTITUTE: Anise seed.

Tamarind *(Tamarindus indica)*

The dark-brown, sticky flesh of the seed pod of the tamarind tree, tamarind is used throughout southern India, Southeast Asia and, to a certain extent, Latin America as a souring agent in cooking. It contributes a tang, as well as a brown color, to gravies, soups, stews and curries, as well as dressings, chutneys and sauces. The pods, or just the pulp, are sometimes available in the Latin American sections of supermarkets. The pulp is generally diluted with water and then strained before use. The Indians have recently processed a tamarind concentrate which looks rather like a yeast extract. It is available in jars from Indian markets, and must be diluted with double the amount of water as the original pulp. Tamarind is usually diluted with three parts of water to one of the pulp.

SUBSTITUTE: Use molasses *(treacle)* diluted with lime juice (fresh) in the same proportions.

Tangerine Peel, Dried

Dried tangerine skin, used as a flavoring in many dishes from Western China.

SUBSTITUTE: Fresh mandarin orange peel or tangerine peel. You may dry the peel in a slow oven.

Tapioca *(Manihot esculenta)*

Also known as cassava, it is cultivated in Thailand and other parts of Southeast Asia and also in India. After processing, the cereal is used for desserts and also made into tapioca flour and starch.

Taro *(Colocasia esculenta)*

A starchy tuber the size of a potato, taro has a hairy brown-black skin and firm white flesh. Cooked and eaten widely throughout south China, Japan, Southeast Asia and the Pacific. It is available in the produce sections of supermarkets with an Oriental clientele.

SUBSTITUTE: Potatoes, sweet potatoes or yams.

Tea *(Camellia sinensis)*

Made from the young leaves and buds of a member of the camellia family. The Chinese probably were the first people to cultivate the plants. The tea plant was introduced to Japan in about 800 A.D. Wild tea was found growing in Assam, between India and Burma, in the early eighteenth century, and the British encouraged its cultivation in India.

Turmeric *(Curcuma domestica)*

Turmeric is native to India, but is used in both Indian and Southeast Asian cooking. A close relative of the arrowroot and ginger families, this rhizome is a fingerlike root with brown skin and bright-yellow flesh. It is boiled, dried and ground to a powder, and used widely in curries, lentil dishes and in spice mixes of Indian origin. In the north of India it is used as a cheap substitute for saffron. In Thailand it was formerly used as a dye to color the robes of the Buddhist monks until the advent of chemical dyes.

Vinegar, Rice

In the Orient and Southeast Asia, rice vinegar is used for pickling, preserving and as a souring agent in cooking. It is the mildest of all the vinegars and slightly sweet. It is obtainable in both dark and light vinegars.

SUBSTITUTE: White vinegar, diluted slightly with water (1 part water to 3 of vinegar). A trace of sugar may be added, if not already called for in the recipe.

Wasabi *(Wasabia japonica)*

Indigenous to Japan, *wasabi* is not related to the Western horseradish. The flesh of the root is a delicate green color. It is often bought in dried, powdered form, which is then mixed with water to form a paste, indispensable to the preparation of *sushi* and *sashimi.*

SUBSTITUTE: English or Chinese hot, powdered mustard.

Water Chestnut *(Trapa bicornis)*

Also known as water caltrop, this nut is the bulb of an Asian water plant. The flesh is crisp and white and is used in stir-fried dishes, and as a snack or a sweetmeat. It is available canned *(tinned).* Drain and rinse before using. Confusingly, there is another vegetable, also called a water chestnut *(Eleocharis dulcis)* or horse-hoof. It is stir-fried with meat. Water-chestnut flour is used as a binder and thickener.

SUBSTITUTE: Those living in the Southwestern United States or other areas with a Latin American population can substitute *jicama,* a large, white, turniplike tuber with a mild flavor and a crunchy, juicy texture.

Basic Recipes List

Recipes Listed Under Country, by Category

CHINA

KOREA

MALAYSIA AND SINGAPORE

Salads
Creamy Peanut Dressing 226
Thick Coconut Salad Dressing 226
Crispy Chicken Noodle Salad 232
Straits Chinese Cooked Mixed
    Vegetables in Thick Dressing 240

Stir-Fried Foods
Spiced Chicken 284
Straits Chinese Seasoned, Shredded
    Pork 295

Deep-Fried Foods
Curried Deep-Fried Crab 316

Curries
Pork Curry 338

Barbecued Foods
Barbecued Spareribs 391
Pork Satay 409

Noodles
Pork and Shrimp Rice Noodles in
    Broth 420
Fried Noodles (Singapore) 427

Preserves
Pickled Ginger 465
Southeast Asian Sweet and Hot Chilli
    Sauce 465
Southeast Asian Peanut Sauce for Satay
    467

THE PHILIPPINES

Soups
Hearty Chicken Soup 181

Snacks
Fried Meat Turnovers 195

Salads
Thin Salad Dressing 229
Mixed Vegetable and Seafood Salad 240

Steamed Foods
Whole, Boned, Stuffed Chicken 257
Whole, Steamed Fish with Tomato and
    Green Pepper Sauce 267
Southeast Asian Steamed Chicken with
    Tomatoes 269

Stir-Fried Foods
Chicken and Pineapple Adobo 286

Deep-Fried Foods
Deep-Fried Stuffed Crab 314

Simmered Foods
Braised, Stuffed Rolled Steak 358
Braised Beef with Vegetables 364

Noodles
Egg Noodles with Meats and
    Vegetables 424

Preserves
Pickled Ginger 465
Southeast Asian Sweet and Hot Chilli
    Sauce 465
Southeast Asian Peanut Sauce for Satay
    467

Puddings and Cakes
Coconut and Cheese Cakes 496

THAILAND

Soups
Hot and Sour Seafood Soup 173

Salads
Thick Coconut Salad Dressing 227

VIETNAM

Index

beef, 37–38, 42, 50, 275, 388
  barbecued, Japanese, 396–397
  bowl, 199
  braised, stuffed rolled steak, Philippine, 358–361
  braised in soy sauce, Chinese, 361–363
  curry, Indonesian, 336
  curry from Madras, Indian, 331–332
  curry from Thailand, Muslim, 333
  dietary taboos and, 24
  and egg savory custards, Korean, 255–256
  packets, Indonesian, 270–271
  satay, Indonesian, 407–408
  short ribs, Korean barbecued, 394–396
  shredded, 19
  and shrimp noodles in broth, 420–422
  stew, Vietnamese, 363–364
  turnovers, 195–196
  and vegetable curry, 332
  and vegetable fondue, Japanese, 379–380
  and vegetable fondue, Korean, 380–381
  and vegetable rolls, 51, 198–199
  with vegetables, Philippine braised, 364–366
Beeton, Mrs., 450
bento, 46–47
besan, 432, 501
biryanis, 28, 31
boiling, boiled food, roasting vs., 382–383
Bombay duck, 500
bonito:
  dried, 45, 506
  substitute for, 170
Borneo (Kalimantan), 34, 35–36, 38, 52
Brazil nuts, 130, 497
bread, 17, 430–449
  with cauliflower filling, buttery unleavened, 439–441
  Chinese golden loaves, 446
  Chinese silver loaves, 444–446
  equipment required for, 433–434
  flaky, buttery unleavened, 437–439
  fried balloon, 436
  as implement, 4
  Indian, 25, 31, 431, 432–443
  Indian oven, 442–443
  pea-filled, 442
  potato balloon, 436
  potato-filled, 441–442
  steamed buns with curry filling, 448
  steamed buns with roast pork filling, 446–447

steamed buns with sweet red bean paste filling, 449
steamed buns with vegetable filling, 448
unleavened whole-wheat, 434–436
breakfast, 19, 50, 62, 164
Brillat-Savarin, Jean Anthelme, 384
broiling, broiled food, *see* grilling, grilled food
Buddhism, 18, 24, 34, 41, 49, 100, 432
Bun Festival, 432
Burma, 18, 19, 413
burns, steam, 249–250
butter:
  clarified, 97, 139–141, 504
  unsalted vs. salted, 140

cabbage:
  Japanese pickled, 464
  Korean pickled, 462–464
  leaves, 270
  spiced, with coconut milk, 298
  Szechwan stir-fried, with hot peppers, 297–298
cake:
  Indonesian steamed nut, 497–498
  Philippine coconut and cheese, 496–497
calamansi, 58
candlenuts, 500
  Indonesian steamed nut cake, 497–498
  substitutes for, 130, 497
Canton, Cantonese cuisine, 14–15, 16–17, 98, 99
  emigration from, 14, 272
caraway, 36, 503
cardamom, 327, 501
  rice cream with almonds and, 486–488
carp, 16, 18
carrot:
  bowl, 199
  curl and radish salad, Chinese, 233–234
  flowers, 87
  fudge pudding, Indian, 491–493
  salad, 235
  and turnip chrysanthemum salad, Japanese, 235–237
carving techniques, fruit and vegetable, 63, 88–95, 216
cashew nuts, 501
  rice cream with coconut and, 488
  spicy Szechwan chicken with, 156, 287–289
cassia, 36, 499–500, 503